BOSTON and MAINE RAILROAD
"MINUTE MAN SERVICE"

THE BESSEMER ROUTE

B.A. & P.

CANADIAN NATIONAL RAILWAYS

Chicago GREAT WESTERN

Burlington Route

CHICAGO AND NORTH WESTERN SYSTEM

CENTRAL OF GEORGIA

Rock Island

JERSEY CENTRAL LINES

BANGOR AND AROOSTOOK RAILROAD Serving NORTHERN MAINE

C. & W.

THE SOUTH SHORE

CENTRAL VERMONT RAILWAY

CHICAGO & ILLINOIS MIDLAND

THE ROUTE OF PHOEBE SNOW
Lackawanna

D. & T.S.L.

DELTA ROUTE

DULUTH MISSABE AND IRON RANGE

D T&I

& W.C.

The Land of Opportunity
Georgia Florida South Carolina
G&F

I. U. R.

KANSAS CITY SOUTHERN Lines

GRAND TRUNK RAILWAY SYSTEM

GREEN BAY ROUTE

GREAT NORTHERN RAILWAY

H. & B.T.M.

K&ITRRC
AT THE CROSS ROADS OF THE NATION

K.O. & G.

RAILROAD ILLINOIS TERMINAL COMPANY

ILLINOIS CENTRAL

M·K·T
Missouri-Kansas-Texas Lines

MONONGAHELA

SOO LINE

The New York New Haven and Hartford RAILROAD CO.

MANUFACTURERS

MONON
THE HOOSIER LINE

MINNEAPOLIS & ST. LOUIS RAILWAY
THE PEORIA GATEWAY LINE

MAINE CENTRAL RAILROAD

NORFOLK SOUTHERN

FERROCARRIL MEXICANO

S

N&W RAILWAY

O.C.-A-A

THE SOUTHERN SR SERVES THE SOUTH

N. N.

RUTLAND RAILROAD

W

Quanah ROUTE

RICHMOND WASHINGTON LINE
RICHMOND FREDERICKSBURG AND POTOMAC RAILROAD

RAILWAY EXPRESS AGENCY

T. & N.

THE ST. LOUIS GATEWAY ROUTE

Reading Lines

TERMINAL RAILROAD ASSOCIATION OF ST. LOUIS
TRRA

ON BELT OUTE

SEASHORE P-R LINES

T.H.&B.

THE NASHVILLE ROUTE
TC

T.P.&W.

TAG ROUTE

WESTERN MARYLAND
Fast Freight Line

TEXARKANA SHREVEPORT
THE TEXAS T AND P PACIFIC RAILWAY
EL PASO NEW ORLEANS

W-S SOUTHBOUND RY.

TEX.MEX.

Rochester
N.Y.

A TREASURY OF RAILROAD FOLKLORE

BY B. A. BOTKIN

Party Song (Out of print), 1937

EDITED:

Folk-Say: A Regional Miscellany, 1929 (Out of print), 1930, 1931, 1932 (University of Oklahoma Press)

Lay My Burden Down: A Folk History of Slavery (University of Chicago Press), 1945

A Treasury of American Folklore, 1944

A Treasury of New England Folklore, 1947

A Treasury of Southern Folklore, 1949

The Pocket Treasury of American Folklore, 1950

A Treasury of Western Folklore, 1951

A Treasury of Railroad Folklore, 1953

BOOKS BY A. F. HARLOW

Old Towpaths; the Story of the American Canal Era, 1926

Old Post Bags; the Story of Mail Service, 1928

Clowning Through Life (with Eddie Foy), 1928

A Vagabond Trouper (with Jefferson de Angelis), 1931

Old Bowery Days; the Chronicles of a Famous Street, 1931

Old Waybills; the Romance of the Express Companies, 1934

Old Wires and New Waves; the Story of the Telegraph, Telephone and Wireless, 1936

Schoolhouse in the Foothills, 1936

Murders Not Quite Solved, 1938

Paper Chase; the Amenities of Stamp Collecting, 1940

Schoolmaster of Yesterday (with Millard F. Kennedy), 1940

Weep No More, My Lady; a Book about Kentucky, 1942

Steelways of New England, 1946

The Road of the Century, 1947

The Serene Cincinnatians (Dutton's Society in America series), 1950

A Treasury of Railroad Folklore, 1953

BIOGRAPHIES FOR TEEN-AGE READERS:

Joel Chandler Harris, Plantation Story-Teller, 1941

Bret Harte of the Old West, 1943

Theodore Roosevelt, Strenuous American, 1943

The Ringlings, Wizards of the Circus, 1951

Andrew Carnegie, 1953

A TREASURY OF
RAILROAD FOLKLORE

The Stories, Tall Tales, Traditions, Ballads and Songs of the American Railroad Man

Edited by

B. A. BOTKIN and ALVIN F. HARLOW

The rails go westward in the dark.
Brother, have you seen starlight on the rails?
Have you heard the thunder of the fast express?
—Thomas Wolfe

BONANZA BOOKS · NEW YORK

LIBRARY OF CONGRESS CATALOG CARD NUMBER: 53-9973

PRINTED IN THE UNITED STATES OF AMERICA

This edition is published by Bonanza Books,
a division of Crown Publishers, Inc.
(A)

COPYRIGHT ACKNOWLEDGMENTS

The editors and publishers wish to thank the following authors or their representatives, folklore, historical, and railroad societies, publishers and publications for their kind permission to use material in this book. Full copyright notices are given on the pages on which the material appears:

E. P. Alexander; Thomas Allen, Ltd.; Appleton-Century-Crofts, Inc.; Lucius Beebe and Charles Clegg; Bobbs-Merrill Co., Inc.; Mrs. Anne D. Bromley (for estate of Joseph Bromley); California Folklore Society; Earnest Elmo Calkins; Bennett Cerf; Chesapeake & Ohio Railway Co. (*Tracks* and *Railway Progress*), by Edwin G. Long, Public Relations Dept.; Estate of Irvin S. Cobb; Thomas Y. Crowell Co.; Frank Cunningham, Sequoia University; (Denver) Post Printing & Publishing Co.; Frank J. Donovan, Jr.; Dorrance & Co.; Doubleday & Co., Inc.; Duell, Sloan & Pearce, Inc.; E. P. Dutton & Co., Inc.; Esquire, Inc. (*Coronet*); Farrar, Straus & Young, Inc.; Folkways Records; J. C. Furnas; Harcourt, Brace & Co., Inc.; Harvard University Press; Harry Henderson and Sam Shaw; Stewart H. Holbrook; Freeman H. Hubbard; Kalmbach Publishing Co. (*Trains & Travel*); Alfred Knopf, Inc.; J. B. Lippincott Co., Inc.; Alan Lomax; Mrs. Ruby T. Lomax; The Macmillan Co.; George Milburn; Bob Miller, Inc.; Mrs. Roswell (Carnegie) Miller, Jr.; Victor L. Morse; Naylor Co., by Joe O. Naylor, Pres.; New York Folklore Society; Thomas C. O'Donnell; Pacific Books, by Stanley M. Croonquist, Pres.; C. B. Palmer; Peer International, Inc.; Popular Publications, Inc. (*Railroad Man's Magazine, Railroad Stories* and *Railroad Magazine*); Railway & Locomotive Historical Society, by Charles E. Fisher, Pres.; Random House; RCA Victor; Archie Robertson; Charles Scribner's Sons; Shapiro, Bernstein & Co.; Simmons-Boardman Pub. Corp. (books and *Railway Age*); State Historical Society of Iowa, Wm. J. Peterson, Supt.; University of Kansas Press; University of Pennsylvania Press; *Variety;* Wehman Bros.; Wells, Fargo & Co., by E. R. Jones, Pres.

PICTURE CREDITS: D. Appleton-Century, p. 67; Association of American Railroads, title page, pp. 93, 154, 158, 291, 438; E. P. Dutton, p. 187; *Frank Leslie's Illustrated Newspaper,* p. 4; Library of Congress, p. 221; George Milburn, p. 459; N. Y. Central, p. 1; *N. Y. Illustrated Graphic,* p. 137; N. Y. Public Library, pp. 112, 449; Norfolk & Western, p. 241; Popular Publications, pp. 352, 390, 392; Railroadians of America, p. 405; *Railway Progress,* half-title page; Shapiro, Bernstein, p. 434; Simmons-Boardman, pp. 294, 416, 445, 465, 467; Southern Railway Co., p. 64; *Tracks,* p. 463; University of Pennsylvania Press, p. 19.

An exhaustive effort has been made to locate all persons having any rights or interests in material, and to clear reprint permissions. If any required acknowledgments have been omitted or any rights overlooked, it is by accident and forgiveness is desired.

Contents

II. The Iron Horse Goes to War

III. The Advancing Frontier

IV. Grand Strategy

Part Three: Vanishing Types

I. Boomer and Home Guard

II. Banditti of the Rails

II. It Did Happen Here

III. Told in the Roundhouse

Introduction

The folklore of the railroader, like his personality, is inevitably shaped by his occupation. To mirror the one through the other and to give a picture of railroading as a way of life and of railroad folklore as a way of looking at life is the purpose of this book. The impact of the railroad on the American imagination has been greater than that of any other industry, and for good reason. As a "widespread, accurately timed, intimately subdivided, highly co-ordinated activity," in the words of W. Fred Cottrell, railroading is "perhaps the prototype of modern industrialism." At the same time, like seafaring, it preserves a tradition of individual courage, high emprise, and wanderlust. Like a ship, an engine is called "she," and not merely because she wears apron, collar, yoke, binder, muffler, jacket, cap, bonnet, petticoat, shoes, pumps, hose, sleeve, wrapper, hood, and sash, according to the old wheeze. An engine is a thing of beauty, with a whim of iron, for a man to master or be mastered by. And "her" romance is inseparable from "her" reality.

That last goes for railroading as a whole—"a business for many men," says Robert S. Henry, "a hobby for others, an absorbing passion for some." Every one can become part of its fabulous adventure by riding on trains or by simply watching them. And waving at trains is the time-honored, universal symbol of the non-railroader's participation, if only vicarious, in the vastness and excitement of their drama. It would be hard to conceive of America without trains, both being a place (in Thomas Wolfe's words) "where miracles not only happen, but where they happen all the time." James Norman Hall goes a step further: "I can no more conceive of a world without railroads and trains to run on them than I can imagine wishing to live in such a world."

But not all the fascination of trains lies in what a writer in 1882 called the "fastness of life on the rail . . . the suggestion of change, of constant excitement, of being always on the move and seeing new places, new people, and new things out of the common run." This collection appears at the end of an era in railroad history, so that for a good many Americans brought up in the Age of Steam, a good deal of the charm of trains lies in the nostalgic pleasure of a "slow train to yesterday," when the local flourished and everybody was a neighbor.

This book grew out of a suggestion of Sylvester L. Vigilante, former chief of the American History Room of the New York Public Library, who was also responsible for bringing together as editorial collaborators a railroad historian and a folklorist. Each has brought to his task a special approach and point of view.

The historian has regarded railroadiana as a kind of "lore," in which anecdote, personal narrative of railroad experience and travel, illustrate and illuminate the history of railroad development and the railroader's occupation, especially the quaint ideas and methods of the early days. In his many reminiscent pieces and compilations as well as in the extracts from his other works in the transportation field, he has drawn upon personal experience as well as wide and detailed knowledge. He has been chiefly responsible for the section, "Apprentice Years," the sub-section, "Banditti of the Rails," and the Appendix. He would have liked to see as a motto for the book the words of Don Herold:

> . . . I like trains! The human race has been going to pieces on me pretty fast lately. On the whole, I think we are a sad and sorry sight. But trains are a human institution, and they are pretty nearly perfect, and they restore to some extent my esteem for the mankind who made them. I like the kind of people who run trains. There always seems to be something trustworthy and fatherly in a railroad engineer or the conductor who punches your ticket. Railroads, being regular, seem to attract regular people . . . not crackpots.

The folklorist has regarded railroadiana primarily as a body of traditional or "own" stories (including legends, yarns, tall tales, jests, and ballads) such as railroaders swap or might have swapped, told as nearly as possible in their own idiom, which recreate for the reader the railroader's life and way of looking at life, on and off the job, especially the dramatic, human interest, and humorous stories. He has been chiefly responsible for the sub-sections, "Rail Stiffs," "Tools and Tricks of the Trade," "Told in the Roundhouse," "The Passenger Is Always Right," and the section, "Blues, Ballads, and Work Songs." He would like to have chosen as the book's motto these lines from W. Fred Cottrell's *The Railroader:*

> Around this young giant [in the nineteenth century] there grew a mythology that made a romance of railroading, a romance not yet dead but now grown retrospective. . . . No matter how humble his own role, a railroader long felt himself in some degree superior for being a soldier in so glorious an army.

Designed as a *Treasury,* in the *Folklore Series,* the book makes no attempt to be encyclopedic or historically complete. Otherwise it would have fallen into the error of the correspondent who wrote to the Association of American Railroads: "Please send me the Association of American Railroads." A book of this type resembles a railroad in that it takes things from one place and puts them in another. Something inevitably gets lost or overlooked in the shuffle.

B. A. B.

Croton-on-Hudson, N. Y.
October 31, 1953

Acknowledgments

The editors wish to thank the following individuals and organizations, including libraries and railroad executive, public relations, advertising, and publicity departments, for assistance in suggesting, servicing, loaning, and contributing material and verifying references.

Libraries: Bureau of Railway Economics Library, Washington, D.C., Elizabeth O. Cullen, Helen R. Richardson, Edmond A. Freeman, Harry L. Eddy, John McLeod; Library of Congress: Rae Korson, of the Folklore Section, David J. Haykin, and the Stack and Reader Division; New York Public Library: Sylvester Vigilante, F. Ivor D. Avellino, and Mrs. Maude Cole, of the American History Room, and the staffs of the Local History and Genealogy Room, the Music Room (especially Margaret Kenny), and the Information Desk; *Railway Age* Library: Edith C. Stone, Alice Hope.

Railroads: Atchison, Topeka & Santa Fe: J. P. Reinhold; Atlantic Coast Line: R. G. Hodgkin, Jr.; Baltimore & Ohio: Robert M. Van Sant; Belfast & Moosehead Lake: W. I. Hall; Boston & Maine: George H. Hill; Burlington: L. F. Hauke; Chesapeake & Ohio: Frank Knotts, Edwin G. Long, Ted O'Meara; Chicago, Milwaukee, St. Paul & Pacific: W. A. Dietze; Chicago, St. Paul, Minneapolis & Omaha: Quentin M. Lambert; Delaware & Hudson: F. L. Hanlon; Florida East Coast: J. T. Van Campen; Great Northern: H. R. Wiecking; Gulf, Mobile & Ohio: B. M. Sheridan; Illinois Central: Cliff G. Massoth; Lancaster & Chester: Elliott W. Springs; Louisville & Nashville: Julian L. James; Missouri Pacific: Ray Maxwell; New York Central: Russell T. Walker, Francis A. Grogan, William T. Gaynor, Hugh Colvin, J. C. Connors, D. V. Hyde, Ann Kuss, D. B. Priest, John E. Salter; Nickel Plate Road (New York, Chicago & St. Louis): Harold C. McKinley; Northern Pacific: L. L. Perrin; Pennsylvania: Eugene DuBois, Elva M. Ferguson; Rock Island: William E. Hayes; Seaboard Air Line: C. E. Bell; Southern: B. E. Young; Southern Pacific: K. C. Ingram; Texas & Pacific: D. B. Ohrum; Union Pacific: William R. Moore, David J. Phillips, Edwin C. Schafer; Wabash: L. A. Brown; Washington, Idaho & Montana: Roy Huffman.

Individuals: Ann and Boyd Bennett, Russel Goudey (Radio Music Service), Herbert Haufrecht, Bill Randolph, Charles Seeger, Pete Seeger, Ruth Crawford Seeger, L. Parker ("Pick") Temple, who assisted in recording, transcribing, and checking the music; George Zabriskie, Washington, D.C., who read the galleys for technical errors and contributed the essay on locomotives; Mamie Meredith, University of Nebraska, and Harry Nestle, New York Central conductor, Harmon, N.Y., for unstinting help and encouragement; and the following: H. Bailey Carroll, Texas State Historical Society, Austin, Texas; John F. Carroll, Local Manager, Pullman Co., New York; Frank P. Donovan, Jr., Minneapolis, Minn.; Evan Esar, New York; Lois M. Fawcett, Head of Reference Dept., Minnesota Historical Society; Charles R. Green, Librarian, Jones Library, Amherst, Mass.; A. E. Greco, Assistant to Vice-President, Pullman Co., Chicago; Stewart H. Holbrook, Portland, Ore.; Cyrus Hosmer, Jr., Belmont, Mass.; John S. Kendall, St. Johnsbury, Vt.; Walter Lempke, New York Central engineer, Harmon, N.Y.; Ruben Levin, Editor, *Labor,* Washington, D.C.; Walter A. Lucas, Simmons-Boardman Publishing Corp., New York; Alex MacKenzie, New York Central freight yard foreman, Harmon, N.Y.; John Worcester Merrill, Boston, Mass.; Archie Robertson, Washington, D.C.; Gene Rose, Ossining, N.Y.; Joseph D. Ryan, Postmaster, Willoughby, Ohio; Robert C. Schmid, West Englewood, N.J.; Floyd C. Shoemaker, Secretary, State Historical Society of Missouri, Columbia, Mo.; C. Frank Starbuck, Waltham, Mass.; Caroline S. Toms, Treasurer, South Carolina Historical Society, Charleston, S.C.; Edward L. Ullman, University of Washington, Seattle, Wash.; Thomas R. Waring, Editor, *Charleston News & Courier,* Charleston, S.C.

Special thanks should be given to Charles E. Fisher, Waban, Mass., President of the Railway & Locomotive Historical Society, who not only permitted the use of any of the Society's copyrighted material in its long list of *Bulletins* since 1903 but also wrote many long, informative letters.

Without the all-out, friendly co-operation and help of the Association of American Railroads, Washington, D.C., and its staff, including Robert S. Henry, Vice-President; Albert R. Beatty, Assistant Vice-President; Carlton J. Corliss, Manager, Public Section, T. J. Sinclair, Manager, School and College Service, Harold H. Baetjer, William H. Bunce, and Leonidas I. McDougle, all of whom played hosts to the visiting folklorist for a month, this book could not have been completed.

For assistance in preparing the manuscript and seeing it through the press, the editors are indebted to their wives, Gertrude F. Botkin and Dora S. Harlow, and to Bertha Krantz and the editorial and production departments of Crown Publishers, Inc.

PART ONE

Iron Horses and Iron Men

Introduction

Mrs. Houstoun, an English tourist of the 1850's, remarked, as she rode around on American trains, "I really think there must be some natural affinity between Yankee 'keep-moving' nature and a locomotive engine. . . . Whatever the cause, it is certain that the 'humans' seem to treat the 'ingine,' as they call it, more like a familiar friend than as the dangerous and desperate thing it really is." [1]

Primarily, the American railroad man, both as builder and as operator, was freer than his European counterpart from the rigidity of custom and system. This freedom was part of the American character as developed by the new, heady atmosphere of liberty and by the challenge of the American wilderness and its vast natural resources. Freed from the restrictions of the Old World, American mechanical genius expanded and blossomed, sometimes a little wildly. Railroad lines, tossed hastily into new territory while rule-making lagged behind, threw trainmen on their own responsibility and bred ingenuity in meeting problems—then mostly unexpected ones—as well as a considerable degree of recklessness. "Familiar friend" though the engine might be, in Mrs. Houstoun's words, unknown dangers lurked in its path and called for desperate expedients, in which Yankee genius was as fertile as it was in invention.

But as lines lengthened, equipment improved, became more massive and intricate and consequently higher in danger potentials, the railroad man became steadier, better educated, more deeply impressed with his responsibilities, more capable of coping with problems. Rules, regulations, and mechanical devices have increased enormously in number and in the near infinitude of their effort to cover every situation. Yet even the rule-makers know that there is a realm beyond the rule-books—a region of crises and emergencies, where the railroader's judgment and courage must take over. And it is a matter of record that he has seldom failed to do his best, even at the cost of his own life or limb.

It is to this unpredictable realm beyond the reach of rules as well as of the call of duty that the more fabulous feats of "Iron Horses and Iron Men" belong. Each day in the railroader's routine is a page of casual, unconscious heroism—"All in the Day's Work." The calm mas-

[1] *Hesperos: or, Travels in the West* (London, 1850), Vol. I, p. 99.

tery and direction of the giant forces which science has placed in the hands of men, the risking of great disaster by the slightest mishandling —these are a sort of heroism to which the rest of us, who confidently entrust our lives to their care, seldom give a thought. But when disaster occurs or threatens, the railroad man rises to true greatness. There are numberless instances in which the engineman or brakeman creeps forward on the running board or leaps to the spot as brakeshoes shriek, to snatch a child or bewildered person from death on the rail. A man might easily give his life in one of these gallant, desperate moments, and sometimes does. Nor is heroism limited to the man in the cab. "American railroad men in just about every job classification that can be named," writes Ted O'Meara, "have, at some time, exhibited sacrificial courage; and for many of them, their feats have gone unnoticed and unsung, except for the recognition tendered by their fellow-workers and a line of praise in their service records." [2]

Few occupations evoke and hold such enthusiastic interest, devotion, loyalty, and sense of obligation and responsibility, among both management and labor, as does railroading. A New York Central engineer, in an interview with one of the editors, summed up the railroader's creed of service as follows: "I love my job. It's my livelihood. I try to keep my record clean. I try to be courteous to every one. I try to keep my train on time. I try to be safe."

Try as he will, however, the railroader's luck or judgment, machinery or the human factor, may fail. In some cases, the exigencies of maintaining a schedule, in the days when the equipment was not equal to the pressure, have caused a man to take chances and achieve headlines and/or immortality. In other cases, "acts of God" have increased the "desperate chances" of railroading.

"Headlines and Heroes" runs the gamut of the railroader's courage and ingenuity, from steel nerves and lightning-quick thinking to daredeviltry and the sporting instinct, in grappling with danger and sticking to his post.

A. F. H.

---

[2] "Heroes of the High Iron," *Railway Progress*, Vol. VI (February, 1953), No. 12, p. 13.

I. ALL IN THE DAY'S WORK

"Hold-the-Fort" Ross

From Helena to Pioche, and from Carson to Salt Lake City, the biggest feet attached to any express rider were those that formed the base of Aaron Y. Ross. They were well-known feet. When Ross drove buckboard stage in the Sixties between Helena and Fort Benton, a region infested with inquisitive Flatheads and Sioux, the mere sight of those feet on the dashboard, piling up their imposing silhouette against the sunset, quelled all aboriginal enthusiasm for a quarrel.

And the broad-rooted pine from Maine was proportioned to his feet. When he took them down from the dashboard and stood on them—preferably in his socks—he loomed up to an elevation of six feet four, presenting a bone and muscle massif of some two hundred and fifty pounds. This eighth of a ton of real man was efficiently distributed; there was nothing paunchy about Ross.

Ross's hair was black and his eyes were black, and his cheeks and chin were given over to a rugged stand of beard. Black beard. Add the fact that he was as brave as he was large, and put a shotgun in his hands, and you have a lot of express messenger. Like most big men, however, he was even tempered. Beyond all challenges to strife he preferred riding comfortably in his socks with the wind blowing over his feet. "He is one of those peculiar men," said an admiring journal of his time, "who if struck in the back of the neck with a slungshot would turn upon the assailant and say 'Fun's fun, boys, but don't you tickle me with that straw again. It puts my shirt collar out of kilter.' "

Ross first appeared on the Coast in 1857, digging for gold at Murphy's

---

From *Treasure Express,* Epic Days of the Wells Fargo, by Neill C. Wilson, pp. 289–299. Copyright, 1936, by The Macmillan Company. New York.

Camp in the Mother Lode placers. Four years of that, and he moved on to eastern Oregon. Then for a year or two Idaho's gold fields knew him; then Montana's. In 1867, when the wonderfully rich placers of Montana were beginning to fail, Ross the prospector turned Ross the stage driver. From the driver's seat he slid over, taking his feet with him, to become a Wells Fargo shotgun messenger between Helena, Montana, and Corinne, Utah. When Bodie shipments became heavy he was transferred to the bloody Bodie-Carson run, conveying raw silver up the California-Nevada border to the mint whose output was rocking the monetary balance of two hemispheres. He next carried the sawed-off shotgun for the express company between Pioche and Salt Lake, and on other runs where civil tranquillity was more a legal theory than a local practice.

Several times Ross had encounters and he bore the scars incident to a large target, but he had safely arrived within two months of his forty-seventh birthday and his record on this sharp January morning in 1882 was still one hundred per cent. He had never given up an express box or a box of bullion. It was as messenger in a Wells Fargo express car that Ross was lying on his pallet in the crisp hours preceding sun-up, as No. One Central Pacific Eastbound moved across Nevada toward the Utah border.

Montello lay ahead, all but invisible in murky dawn under a powdering of snow; though even in brightest day it would have been barely visible. For Montello's improvements were but three: a rail siding, a water tank, and a clapboard shack. At the moment, the first was empty; the second was full and frozen; and the third, being a stove-heated Chinese bunkhouse, was crammed full and very sultry.

As dawn came blearily up out of Great Salt Lake Desert, poppied dreams, paper-stuffed window, and bolted door were shattered by a crash of rifle bullets. The salvo was augmented by heavily thrown stones, thump of gunstocks, and white men's yells. The section hands waited not to stop, look, or listen. They sprang straight from tropic blankets into the midwinter outdoors, and kept going on bare toes over crusted snow for Toano, next stop west. Toano had a six-stall roundhouse, some coal sheds, and several shanties. More important, it had twenty-five miles' distance between it and Montello, and twenty-five miles' distance at the moment was just what the celestials craved.

With shots into the air to keep them going, the raiders took possession of the bunkhouse. The eastbound express would soon come puffing up the long straight grade, which reached its summit just west of Montello station. Meanwhile desert dawn was decidedly chill. The five white men stoked up the stove and sat down to review their plans.

Number One was faithfully approaching. Behind its bell-funneled locomotive lurched United States mail car, express car, baggage, and two or three passenger coaches. Three clerks were asleep in the mail car. They said later that they were unarmed, which was curious; they probably counted on attacks, if any, centering on the traditional express. In the baggage car an attendant also slumbered. Wells Fargo's car, rolling along between, chanced to contain little specie or bullion. Ross had sorted his waybills at Toano, found everything in order, and was now likewise snatching an hour of sleep.

He was roused by a rap at his door. He assumed this to be the greeting of the station agent at Tecoma and rose from his pallet. Tecoma was a metropolis of three stores, five saloons, and a stockyard; it usually delivered to him a consignment of silver from the mines of Buel City, Lucin, Silver Islet, Deep Creek, and Delano. Ross moved in stocking feet to the door, opened it slightly against its chain.

What he beheld was not teeming Tecoma but unimportant Montello, lately occupied by the eight Chinese track tampers and now by their five Caucasian successors, one of whom had jammed a rifle barrel through the crack. Its owner announced: "Hop out! We are going through you."

Fourteen years, by stagecoach and steam car, Aaron Ross had been escorting express matter. First and last, his orders had been to take this or that in charge and see that it reached, without deviation, a specific so-and-so. The orders were succinct and had always proved sufficient. Eleven years before, the Montana stage he was defending had been stopped by armed men and contrary directions given. Ross had been at a slight disadvantage: his boots off and his stockinged feet on the dashboard; but when the shooting finished, several Montanans were discoverable on the ground and none was Ross. Those who got away felt that they owed it entirely to the shoeless state of the messenger. Men in that part of the country sometimes wondered what would happen if Ross got into a real battle with his boots on. Well, here they were again.

Ross leaped back, slammed his door, and shot its bolts and chain. Then he turned to his bunk for a few fast preparations.

More pounding, this time on the opposite door. The voices were irritated. "Open up and jump out! We are going to rob this train!"

There was a momentary silence within, followed by a slowly drawled answer:

"Just wait till I get my boots on," the messenger requested.

"Never mind your boots! Hop right out here and we'll get through with you. Then you can pull your boots on."

Ross said no more. He continued drawing on his tremendous footgear. Socks were for comfort and informality, but this looked like official business. Then he drew his kit chest into position and threw his blankets over it. Following which, he caught up his Winchester, looked to its magazine, and waited for the next remark from the opposition.

It came, yelled through whiskers that were stiff with frost and anger. "Open up or we will burn you out and murder you!"

Ross calculated the direction and answered with a lead slug through the side of his car. Silence ensued for a matter of minutes. Then a voice with a little more distance before it bore the pained appeal: "Ain't you going to open the door and come out?"

Ross replaced the spent cartridge.

Footsteps crunched around his car in a wide circle. There was murmured colloquy. Then a last gruff order: "Hop out!"

Ross chose instead to purse his lips in "Young Kate of Kilcummer," favorite and incessant air of Number One's brakeman.

Five shots, from five different angles, rang out in the cold air. They ripped five holes in Ross's citadel. They smashed the swinging lamp, which had been burning wanly; they ricocheted about on the car hardware; three struck the defender. Ross dropped behind his kit box with one wound in hip, another in his hand, a third just to the left of his watch pocket. The hip wound, caused by a spent ball, was more bruising than fateful. The breast shot had staggered him with the weight of its blow, but had been partially turned by a thick paper-crammed wallet.

Prolonged stillness followed. At length the robbers felt satisfied. Their man, it would seem, had been accounted for. They climbed to the rear of the car to cut the train. Ross was waiting for that maneuver. He pushed his rifle across the kit box and sent two shots through the wall in that direction. The climbers hastily got down.

There was another war council held in his hearing: "I thought there was only one in there." "Sure, there's only one!" "Not on your life! I distinctly saw two!"

Ross grinned. Seen hastily through a dark opening, he undoubtedly looked like two.

"Let's get coal and put a fire under them. That'll chase them out."

Ross took firmer grip of his rifle, and ceased grinning.

"No—we need the fuel for the engine. I've got a better idea."

A whistle was heard from the east. It was Number Two, the westbound overland. The raiders ordered Number One backed onto the Montello siding. When the two trains were abreast, westbound Conductor Clement shouted to eastbound Conductor Cassin: "What are you doing here? I want to talk to you." As he spoke, he became aware of the row of guns trained on his chest and forehead and heard peremptory orders to keep going. Westbound Number Two kept going. "That was the coldest shake I got," said Ross later, "hearing that train go by while the fusillade was on."

A few passengers had stepped down from their tarrying eastbound to observe the uncouth West in action. Probably seven out of ten had small pocket pistols, but these were of little avail against riding men's artillery. Show of the latter sent them hurriedly back to their cars. After all, human brotherhood might be human brotherhood, but this wasn't their fight.

The robbers went into another conference. One came out of it to make a leap for the express car's front end. He sought to clamber to its roof. Ross heard his feet on the ladder. He knew the location of those rungs precisely. With his shot through the woodwork a man's body plumped hastily to the platform; the shot had gone between the knees.

More conferring outside. "I tell you I saw two men in there before we shot the light out." "Two or six, they're a plucky bunch of hombres."

The train crew had been impounded under guard of one highwayman up by the water tank. Robbers tramped thither and selected a brakeman. He was ordered, with some prompting from the hot end of a rifle, to uncouple Ross's car from the baggage car following. It was a ticklish assignment for the brakeman, who wanted to be friends with everybody. Ross might fire on him from within. To sustain his courage and prove his identity, he vigorously whistled. It took some doing to maintain the pucker, but he managed it.

> As the rose to the bee,
> As the sunshine to summer,
> So welcome to me
> Is young Kate of Kilcummer—

Ross recognized the whistler and withheld his fire. The wheels of his car began to roll. He wondered if he were to be kidnapped, and with mild interest considered whither. Then the brakes set hard. The defender heard the whistler swing off and run to the forward end, where again there was sound of uncoupling.

Ross's wounds hurt horribly. A crimson handkerchief was twisted around his damaged hand. The bullet had gouged the length of the index finger. For hip and breast he had nothing to staunch the flow, and no free hand with which to manage. Got to keep grip somehow on this rifle. . . .

Again the engine labored forward, but this time Ross's car did not move. So that was it; they had cut his car out, and now it was standing alone.

One last offer to parley, and a banging of coal picks against his door. Was he coming out?

For answer the defender lifted the famous Aaron Ross bootsole and drove it resoundingly against the side of the door.

"Leapin' antelopes!" commented an awe-struck brigand. "What was that?"

"He musta slung the stove."

"Well, boys, I guess we'll throw something back. It'll be plenty."

The next move came fast. The engineer, nudged with a rifle, had pulled off. Now he launched locomotive, tender, and attendant mail car full at the obdurate express. The steam-driven missiles struck the stalled car with a titanic bang. At the impact, both express doors sprang open the length of their chain-fastenings. Ross saw daylight in sudden vertical rectangles. He made a leap for one door, slammed it shut, then reached for the other—good thing now he had that six and a half feet of Herculean arm-reach—and readjusted their bolts. Then back to the rear end of his fort. There, using one hand, he struggled to pile up more boxes.

Engine and mail were drawn off, shot at him again. They sprang as from a catapult. Again the doors burst open. Laying down his rifle and working with his good hand, Ross closed and rechained one door before a firearm could poke through, then turned to the other. A man was at the orifice, swinging a gun on him. And this time the monumental boots, which had awed Flatheads and Sioux with their grandeur and made legend in the intermountain basin, went into action—or one of them did. Ross, minus his rifle, kicked. A body pitched through the air, fell heavily.

"Gawd," said an awe-struck voice again, as the messenger slammed and chained his door. "They heaved the safe."

Ross was bleeding ruinously and found it necessary to lean on his box parapet for a moment before regaining his rifle.

"Now we've *got* to build that fire. We'll holocaust the car."

Silence. The robbers swarmed for the tender. But the siege had lasted long; it was now past ten o'clock in the morning. And from the tender practically all fuel had been extracted to keep up steam. Ross grinned again when he heard a debate over this discovery. The raiders would find timber scarce in the intermountain country.

The familiar voice of the leader challenged him once more, this time a little more wheedlingly.

"Ain't you ever going to hop out."

No, Ross was never going to hop out.

One last slam from the catapulted mail car. But the blow was less stalwart. The up-grade was against it. The force was furnished by steam from a dying boiler.

Over the white desert shut a more lasting silence. It endured some minutes: perhaps the robbers were planning one last devilment. Then, faint at first and steadily nearing, another locomotive was discernible. Had Conductor Clement delivered his story at Toano? The robbers did not wait to learn. When the messenger applied eye to a bullet hole to review the field, he saw five defeated bandits posting swiftly for the horizon, one doubled over his saddle.

Three hours and twenty minutes had the siege endured when conductor, engineer, mail clerks, and brakeman opened to the one-man defender in his triumphant fort. Boots, pants, pockets, and rifle magazine were full of valiant blood. The express money was secure. Loudly the mail clerks lamented that, had they been armed, they could have disposed of the highwaymen with ease. Ross shrugged. Forty bullets had entered his rolling fortress, including one that had pierced the double-walled wooden end, the zinc lining behind the stove, and the stovepipe, and finally had buried itself in the opposite wall.

Official business was over. Seating himself, Ross permitted his rescuers to take off his fighting boots.[1]

The Wells Fargo car had contained but six hundred dollars. But it transpired that the mail car which had been used as a projectile had contained, all unsuspected, nearly half a million dollars in minted silver.

Andrew Carnegie Takes Over the Line

After my return to Pittsburgh it was not long before I made the acquaintance of an extraordinary man, Thomas A. Scott, one to whom the term "genius" in his department may safely be applied. He had come to Pittsburgh as superintendent of that division of the Pennsylvania Railroad. Frequent telegraphic communication was necessary between him and his superior Mr. Lombaert, general superintendent at Altoona. This brought him to the telegraph office at nights, and upon several occasions I happened to be the operator. One day I was surprised by one of his assistants, with whom I was acquainted, telling me that Mr. Scott had asked him whether he thought that I could be obtained as his clerk and telegraph operator, to which this young man told me he had replied: "That is impossible. He is now an operator."

But when I heard this I said at once: "Not so fast. He can have me. I want to get out of a mere office life. Please go and tell him so."

The result was I was engaged February 1, 1853, at a salary of thirty-five dollars a month as Mr. Scott's clerk and operator. A raise in wages from twenty-five to thirty-five dollars per month was the greatest I had ever known. The public telegraph line was temporarily put into Mr. Scott's office at the outer depot and the Pennsylvania Railroad Company was given permission to use the wire at seasons when such use would not interfere with the general public business, until their own line, then being built, was completed.

* * * * *

It was not long after this that the railroad company constructed its own telegraph line. We had to supply it with operators. Most of these were taught in our offices at Pittsburgh. The telegraph business con-

[1] And in the saga of Wells, Fargo and Company, he was to be forever known as "Hold-the-Fort" Ross.—Edward Hungerford, *Wells Fargo, Advancing the American Frontier* (1949), p. 135.

From *Autobiography of Andrew Carnegie,* pp. 63–64, 69–72. Copyright, 1920, by Louise Whitfield Carnegie. Boston and New York: Houghton Mifflin Company.

tinued to increase with startling rapidity. We could scarcely provide facilities fast enough. New telegraph offices were required. My fellow-messenger boy, "Davy" McCargo, I appointed superintendent of the telegraph department, March 11, 1859. I have been told that "Davy" and myself are entitled to the credit of being the first to employ young women as telegraph operators in the United States upon railroads, or perhaps in any branch. At all events, we placed girls in various offices as pupils, taught and then put them in charge of offices as occasion required. Among the first of these was my cousin, Miss Maria Hogan. She was the operator at the freight station in Pittsburgh, and with her were placed successive pupils, her office becoming a school. Our experience was that young women operators were more to be relied upon than young men. Among all the new occupations invaded by women I do not know of any better suited for them than that of telegraph operator.

Mr. Scott was one of the most delightful superiors that anybody could have and I soon became warmly attached to him. He was my great man and all the hero worship that is inherent in youth I showered upon him. I soon began placing him in imagination in the presidency of the great Pennsylvania Railroad—a position which he afterwards attained. Under him I gradually performed duties not strictly belonging to my department and I can attribute my decided advancement in the service to one well-remembered incident.

The railway was a single line. Telegraph orders to trains often became necessary, although it was not then a regular practice to run trains by telegraph. No one but the superintendent himself was permitted to give a train order on any part of the Pennsylvania system, or indeed of any other system, I believe, at that time. It was then a dangerous expedient to give telegraphic orders, for the whole system of railway management was still in its infancy, and men had not yet been trained for it. It was necessary for Mr. Scott to go out night after night to break-downs or wrecks to superintend the clearing of the line. He was necessarily absent from the office on many mornings.

One morning I reached the office and found that a serious accident on the Eastern Division had delayed the express passenger train westward, and that the passenger train eastward was proceeding with a flagman in advance at every curve. The freight trains in both directions were all standing still upon the sidings. Mr. Scott was not to be found. Finally I could not resist the temptation to plunge in, take the responsibility, give "train orders," and set matters going. "Death or Westminster Abbey," flashed across my mind. I knew it was dismissal, disgrace, perhaps criminal punishment for me if I erred. On the other hand, I could bring in the wearied freight-train men who had lain out all night. I could set everything in motion. I knew I could. I had often done it in wiring Mr. Scott's orders. I knew just what to do, and so I began. I gave the orders in his name, started every train, sat at the instrument watching every tick, carried the trains along from station to station, took extra precautions, and had everything running smoothly when Mr. Scott at last reached the office. He had heard of the delay. His first words were: "Well! How are matters?"

He came to my side quickly, grasped his pencil, and began to write his orders. I had then to speak, and timidly said: "Mr. Scott, I could not find you anywhere and I gave these orders in your name early this morning."

"Are they going all right? Where is the Eastern Express?"

I showed him the messages and gave him the position of every train on the line—freights, ballast trains, everything—showed him the answers of the various conductors, the latest reports at the stations where the various trains had passed. All was right. He looked in my face for a second. I scarcely dared look in his. I did not know what was going to happen. He did not say one word, but again looked carefully over all that had taken place. Still he said nothing. After a little he moved away from my desk to his own, and that was the end of it. He was afraid to approve what I had done, yet he had not censured me. If it came out all right, it was all right; if it came out all wrong, the responsibility was mine. So it stood, but I noticed that he came in very regularly and in good time for some mornings after that.

Of course I never spoke to any one about it. None of the trainmen knew that Mr. Scott had not personally given the orders. I had almost made up my mind that if the like occurred again, I would not repeat my proceeding of that morning unless I was authorized to do so. I was feeling rather distressed about what I had done until I heard from Mr. Franciscus, who was then in charge of the freighting department at Pittsburgh, that Mr. Scott, the evening after the memorable morning, had said to him: "Do you know what that little white-haired Scotch devil of mine did?"

"No."

"I'm blamed if he didn't run every train on the division in my name without the slightest authority."

"And did he do it all right?" asked Franciscus.

"Oh, yes, all right."

This satisfied me. Of course I had my cue for the next occasion and went boldly in. From that date it was very seldom that Mr. Scott gave a train order.

A Night on the Edge of Nothing

I was an Adams Express messenger, that spring of 1867, on the Louisville, Cincinnati & Lexington—the Short Line, it was popularly

---

As told by J. Edwin Harlow to Alvin F. Harlow many years ago.

called; it's a part of the main line of the Louisville & Nashville now. It was a night in March, the break-up of winter, you might call it, when a slight thaw, combined with a couple of days of steady downpour, had set the whole country afloat. It still was only a little above freezing, at that. I was jogging down from Cincinnati towards Louisville on a night train, in the car with Bill McFerran, baggageman; he in the front half, I in the rear; no partition between us, you understand. There were two doors on each side of the car, one for each of us. Express or baggage might sometimes overflow into the other man's half of the car, and when one man was swamped with work, the other fellow helped him.

We had a six-car train; a small, locked mail car—no clerk in it, just through mail—next the engine, then ours, with four coaches behind it. We made some stops early in the evening, but at length came to where the agents didn't meet trains that late in the night, and we had few stops scheduled, anyhow. I had checked and written up my "run," had everything shipshape; I put some more coal in our stove and sat down on my safe to read a Cincinnati paper. Bill was dozing on some carpet-bags.

Then we were jarred by a sudden check in speed; we heard the engineer reverse and start hollering for brakes—short, sharp blasts calling for the train crew and even passengers to dash out on the end platforms of the cars and twist the brake-wheels—no air-brakes then, you know. But there were also no vestibuled cars and with rain pouring down, few passengers hankered to go outside and wring brake-wheels, even to save their own necks; they'd rather just trust to luck. Bill and I would have joined in the effort, but we had the end doors of our car blocked with baggage and freight. But we both sprang up, leaped each to his own side door—both on the left side, as it happened—slid them open and looked out. What we saw dimly through the rain wasn't pleasant.

We saw water beneath us and the fireman dropping from his engine, splashing alongside the embankment. We were approaching—we were too darn close, in fact—a bridge, a light timber affair, of course, over a little creek that I'd hardly ever noticed before, but which was now out of its banks, and in fact, no more than four feet below the track, I guessed, though in ordinary times the bridge was forty feet above the stream. As the engineer neared it, he saw by the dim light of his oil headlight through the rain that the track was warped and sagging in one place. He knew what that meant—that it would go down as soon as the weight of his engine rolled onto it.

Because of the flooded country, he had been running cautiously—the fireman guessed afterward that we were doing twenty-five an hour—when he saw the weakening bridge, though by that time it was only a few rods away. He and the fireman yelled to each other and the fireman jumped, into water several feet deep. He was on the upstream side, too, where the embankment sheltered him from the force of the current. But the engineer, true to the best traditions of his profession, was determined to save the train, his passengers and fellow-workers from the torrent, if he could. He stuck to his seat until the last moment, keeping her in reverse, sanding the rails and sounding his cry for help. As the engine went onto the bridge, he may have left it, but it was too late then. He was out where the current was fierce, and he was probably caught in the swirl made by the sinking locomotive. Anyhow, his body was found several miles downstream.

But he had done a lot for us before he gave up; and the men back in the coaches were helping, too; our speed was steadily slowing.

"We better jump, Ed!" Bill yelled at me.

"No! Stick!" I called back. "She won't go off." I meant I hoped she wouldn't. My thoughts were racing wildly—my wife, back in Cincinnati—would I ever see her again?—but of course I would—I'd get out of this, even if the car went overboard—I was a good swimmer—though I dreaded the thought of that icy water—I wasn't going into it unless I had to—

All this in half a dozen seconds, as we went slower and slower—then the front truck of our car dropped off the stone abutment, and our bottom slid, slower and slower, over its edge; no air-brake machinery on its under-belly to impede us; only the slender rod braces, now evidently flattened, which wasn't so good for the car. You see, we hadn't steel rails then; only iron and light-weight at that, very brittle when cold; under the engine's weight, the rails had sheared off right at the edge of the abutment. Slower—slower—with feet planted hard against the floor, I was gripping the hand-hold rod above the door, leaning back away from the brink, straining until sweat ran down my face in the silly, subconscious effort to hold that train back. The edge of the abutment was creeping back towards us. "It's under my door now!" yelled Bill. Then there was a loud clank at the rear end of our car, and it began to rise still more—three or four feet—my safe and two or three other slick-bottomed articles went sliding leisurely towards the front end of the car—then with a clatter and a crash, we stopped. And I mean, we really stopped! We weren't tilting any more and best of all, we weren't moving forward. And then I noticed that Bill was back in my half of the car, clinging to the wall just as I was, with his legs braced against the slope of the floor—twenty degrees, I guess—not as steep as a cottage roof, but like standing on a hillside.

For a moment or two, we were afraid to move, for fear we'd topple our car off the edge. I don't know how about him, but I was wet with perspiration. Finally, we ventured to turn our heads and look at each other.

"Well, we're still here," he said in a shaky voice, and then we both laughed hysterically.

"But how long are we going to be here?" I wondered. Very cautiously I leaned out of my door and looked back, but though the rain had slackened to a drizzle, I couldn't make out in the darkness what the situation was just back of us. Presently I heard Smith, the conductor, call out to ask if we were all right, and in a few minutes he came along on the ends of the ties, clinging to the cars. He couldn't have gone much farther than my door—it was that near the edge.

"My God, Ed!" he said. "You boys better get out of this car. It's liable to go by the board, any moment."

"What's holding us back there?" I asked, and he explained as far as he could, though we didn't get the whole thing figured out until later. It was fantastic. When the mail car went down, our front truck went into the briny, and we slid along until we were nearly half over the edge of the abutment, when the weight of the mail car and of the baggage in the front end of our car (heavier than my express matter) dragged down on that end of the car as we neared a balance until it broke the slender, brittle coupling between us and the coach behind us, and my end of the car rose from the rails. As it did so, the last bit of momentum of the train shoved the platform of that coach under the platform of our car, which slowly rose until it caught under the projecting roof of the coach. Thus, just as the last impetus of the train died, the platforms and roofs of the two cars locked into each other like two sets of gear-teeth, and there we were. Somewhere about this time, the mail-car broke loose from us and relieved us of that strain.

Smith told us that Joe, the fireman, had gotten out and was back there in a coach, but they could neither see nor hear anything of the engineer, and they were afraid he was gone. Smith again urged us to abandon our car.

"I'm not supposed to leave my valuables under any circumstances," I told him. (About $9,000 in cash and some packages of jewelry and bonds, to begin with, I may say.)

"Hell, the express company wouldn't expect you to stay here and get drowned, would they?" he asked.

"Well, that seems to be the general idea," I said.

"But the car's liable to break in two," he argued.

"Bill and I can drag most of the baggage back into my half of the car—" I began.

"Oh, can we?" says Bill, sarcastically.

"--And relieve the strain so she'll hold together."

"Well, if you get drowned," says Smith, "remember I warned you." And he went away, grumbling.

"You mean you're really going to stay here, Ed?" said Bill.

"I've got to," I replied. I was young and hadn't been in the business long, and I was very much impressed by my orders not to leave my car for a moment for any reason whatsoever. I was a little vain about it, too, I guess; made me feel important; and I wanted to show that I wasn't afraid.

"Now I'm going to start moving that baggage," I said. "If you want to help me—"

"You know that end of the car's in the water a little," he reminded me.

Yes, I said I knew that.

"And the current's liable to break it off—"

"Not if we get most of the weight out of it," I said, and I went down the slope to drag my safe back, first thing. I should have said that our two lamps had stayed in their frames, and our stove was still solid as a rock. The baggage-express car stove of those days was a bulbous, cast-iron affair which stood at one side of the car, midway between the side doors. It had large, round iron plates at top and near the bottom. At four places in the rims of those plates, vertical rods passed through holes, their ends being screwed to the floor and ceiling—held the stove firmly in place.

"How you going to keep those trunks from sliding?" Bill asked; he hadn't turned his hand to help me yet. I think he knew as well as I did how I was going to place them; Bill was no fool.

"I'm going to raise the downhill end of the trunk and put an old valise or carpet bag, maybe one of my rolls of leather or bundles of castings under it to hold it nearly level," I said. "And I'll put my safe back of the rods of this stove."

"You can't put too much strain on those rods," Bill objected.

"The safe doesn't weigh more than sixty or seventy pounds," I said. "I may even add a light trunk or two. Now if you're going to help me with those trunks, the owners of 'em and the railroad company will be grateful; they may even give you a gold watch, suitably inscribed; I never heard of a watch awarded by a railroad for a noble deed yet that the newspapers didn't say it was 'suitably inscribed.' The water's come under the end door and half a dozen of those trunks are already partly wet—"

"I s'pose you're playing for one of those suitably inscribed watches, too," jeered Bill, as he started down the slope to help me with a trunk.

"No, we don't get any rewards of merit," I said. "If I get half drowned or plumb drowned, the express company would consider it no more than I was hired for."

It was a tough job, carrying those trunks up that slope, and it cost us a lot of perspiration. We couldn't get all the baggage into the rear half of the car, though I think we did wonders at packing it in. It was shuddery, seeing those few inches of water slopping around in that lower end of the car; we watched it all the time and assured ourselves that it wasn't rising any; in fact, we began to tell each other that we believed it was going down, though maybe that was because taking the weight off that end of the car had let it spring up a little. She was a pretty sturdy little car, I'll say that for her; thirty-five feet long and the braces under her broken, but she still held together.

When we had moved everything we could, I said, "Now, Bill, if you can get out of the door and walk back on the ties like Smith did, go back into a coach and get some sleep."

He glanced towards the front end of the car. "Naw," he growled, "if you're damfool enough to stay here, I'll stay with you." And I couldn't talk him out of it.

I arranged some soft packages and bags so that we could both of us half lie and half sit, back among my freight. Bill attended to the fire, and we lay down, and after a long time I went to sleep.

The brakeman had gone back with a red lantern, of course, as soon as the accident happened, though there wasn't any other train expected during the night hours. His main chore was to walk back—through drizzle and an occasional cold shower—three miles or more, to the nearest station, hunt around until he found the agent's home, rout him out of bed, and get him down to the telegraph office to wire for the wreckers. They didn't come until long after daylight.

I was awakened, late in the night, by Bill poking the fire. He admitted that his sleep had been choppy and beset by dreams. So had mine.

"What's the news?" I asked.

"Water's all gone out of the car," he reported. We slept better after that.

When the wreckers came, they tied long ropes to the rear end of our car on each side, and fastened them to trees before they even dared to hook onto our last coach. A hand's push might have shoved us over the brink.

No, neither Bill nor I ever got any gold watch, suitably inscribed, and didn't expect any. It was all regarded as a part of our regular routine.

Kid Hadlock Gets Jay Gould Through

When Jay Gould was in his prime and all the other railroad magnates were wondering which tree would be the easiest to climb, Gould did most of his traveling, particularly through the West, behind an engineer named Kid Hadlock. Kid Hadlock took Jay Gould around the world, is the way you'd hear it expressed. At any rate, Kid Had-

---

From "Comin' Down the Railroad," by A. W. Somerville, *The Saturday Evening Post,* Vol. 201 (September 15, 1928), No. 11, p. 162. Copyright, 1928, by the Curtis Publishing Company. Philadelphia.

lock had one engine he showed a particular fondness for, numbered 264. If ever there was an engine that held a candle to the famous 999, it was the 264. As a matter of fact, according to Hadlock, the 264 extinguished the 999—made the Gold Medal Engine look like a wash bucket. There was no comparison between the two engines when it came to mechanical perfection. The 264 could leave the 999 back in the bushes on any stretch of double track in creation—absolutely. The 264 was a ten-wheeler, and she'd ride like a wild bronco on the finest stretch of track ever built, but Hadlock swore she rode like a Pullman—and to him she did.

Hadlock is dead now—been dead several years—but in his time he was as fine an engineer and as good a mechanic as could be found anywhere. He was Gould's engineer because he was the best. And this story is told of Hadlock and his engine, and the story is true. I used it not long ago to bolster up a short story and had the pleasure of getting a number of indignant letters from readers asking me to quit telling such awful lies. So it's written again to give some background to my imagination.

Gould was out on an inspection trip on one of his Western lines, and for some reason, on account of the stock market—so the story goes—his presence was required in the city. He was more than 100 miles from this city, and he told Hadlock, upon the receipt of the message calling him back, to get back to town and get there fast. Because Gould was what he was, they literally owned the railroad. They were on a mountain division. All Hadlock had to do was use his head, keep the train from falling off a cliff, and other such small items.

So they lit out. To maintain a speed of between fifty and sixty miles an hour over a mountain range is a little better than remarkable, but that's what Hadlock did. And on the last stretch of the run, while roaring down a mountainside, at sixty or more miles an hour, an engine truck box ran hot.

The engine truck is under the front end of a locomotive, and on some engines the leading boxes of this truck can be reached from above—the waste boxes, oil boxes, that lubricate the journals. This particular type of box was held in place by a slot and a heavy bolt, with a split key—big cotter key—to retain the bolt. It's barely possible to take one of these boxes out from above, but it takes a man with an iron nerve and extraordinary ability to perform such an operation. But Hadlock did it, upside down, on the front end of the 264! He got it out, repacked it, soaked it in oil, and replaced it! And he was going down a mountainside and around dangerous curves at better than sixty miles an hour when he did it! The story further tells that Gould arrived in the city in time to prevent some of his financial playmates from swiping everything but the switch stands off one of Gould's pet railroads.

II. HEADLINES AND HEROES

Nellie Bly

Early in November, 1889, an editor of the *New York World* had an idea. He had been reading the works of M. Jules Verne, French novelist whose heroes were always flying off to the moon on rocket ships or going to the North Pole in submarines. His latest was *Around the World in Eighty Days* and its hero was Phineas Fogg, a melancholy and silent Englishman who made the trip on a bet, seldom speaking during the elapsed time, except to order fresh elephants, bribe black gangs on liners or charter special trains. The *World* man crooked his finger at Miss Nellie Bly, his girl reporter, and said:

"Nellie, how fast can you go around the world?"

"Seventy-five days, Sir!" replied Nellie, who also had been reading M. Verne.

In twelve hours she had drawn expense money, packed a bag, and was off.

She managed to beat Mr. Fogg's record from the start and landed in San Francisco, January 21, 1890, five days ahead of the Fogg schedule, but just even with her promise to her editor. There was only one way to beat that promise—and the Santa Fe provided a special train.

This was a one-Pullman-and-baggage-car affair, and it raced east over some rough track in midwinter, with division superintendents riding with time cards and watches out most of the way. R. M. Bacheller, Assistant General Freight and Passenger Agent at Albuquerque, had charge of the train, aboard which were nine people. Orders were the train had right of way over everything and speed limits were off.

From *Sante Fe,* The Railroad That Built an Empire, by James L. Marshall, pp. 239–241. Copyright, 1945, by Random House, Inc. New York.

Enginemen could let out the Taunton and Schenectady engines all they wanted.

Crews became interested in the race. Engines were changed at Needles in one minute, and the time wired ahead to Seligman, where the boys made the change again in forty-five seconds. Some remarkable change records were made, La Junta claiming forty-two seconds, with an engine ready on the track ahead of a crossover, so that, as the old engine uncoupled and rolled onto the opposite track, the new one backed down and coupled on. There was little time for thorough air testing.

The run was clocked at sixty-nine hours for the 2,577 miles, San Francisco to Chicago, an average of thirty-seven and one-third miles an hour. It was the first race across the country though later the Santa Fe was to become famous for such races against time. The fastest division was from La Junta, Colorado, to Coolidge, on the race track with 86.2 miles in eighty minutes. Winslow to Gallup, an upgrade for 128 miles with a water stop, was run in 127 minutes. T. M. Hamill was the hoghead of this division and at Gallup he ran his Taunton off onto a sidetrack, headed for the roundhouse, when one of the truck wheels rolled off and the engine stopped suddenly. If it had happened a few minutes before, there would have been no record —and maybe no Nellie Bly. Miss Bly, as the train stopped, had darted forward to the engine and handed Mr. Hamill a quart of Mumm's Extra Dry, as a souvenir. After the truck wheel had fallen off, the champagne was found intact and Mr. Hamill was absolved of all responsibility.

Nellie had been feasted and greeted all over the world, and had a drawing room full of gifts from Rajahs and Princes. Among these were a pet monkey and a box of rhinestones—and around a curve in the Glorietas these got mixed up. All but two were recovered and the theory was the monkey ate those. The animal was unwell the rest of the trip.

Out on the prairies, where the hoggers let the engines roll, the speed was recorded by Superintendent H. U. Mudge, who clocked short bursts at eighty, seventy-eight, eighty-five, and one mile at ninety. Mr. Mudge looked up from his watch and told Miss Bly it might be unfortunate if the train left the track, as it might wreck a farmhouse somewhere. Crowds watched the train go by scores of depots, the Santa Fe's public relations department having judiciously sent word ahead of its coming. It arrived at Kansas City five hours ahead of schedule and took it easy into Chicago, having plenty of time to make the connection there.

Miss Bly turned up at the *World* a little over seventy-two days after she'd started out and was asked by the city editor where the heck she'd been all this time. Miss Bly smiled, wrote her story and turned in her expense account, listing Mumm's Extra Dry under "Miscellaneous."

Death Valley Scotty's Special

At one o'clock in the afternoon of Sunday, July 9, 1905, a special [three-car] train, chartered by Mr. Walter Scott, pulled out of La Grande Station of the Santa Fe System at Los Angeles. . . . This was the train which came to be known as the Death Valley Coyote and the Scott Special.

At 11:54 on the forenoon of July 11th, it came to a stop in the Dearborn Street Station, Chicago, having made the run of 2,265 miles in 44 hours and 54 minutes. . . .

* * * * *

A few minutes before noon on Saturday, the eighth of July, a man walked into Mr. John J. Byrne's private office, in the Conservative Life Building, Los Angeles. Mr. Byrne is General Passenger Agent of the Santa Fe lines west of Albuquerque. The stranger wore a cheap serge suit, a blue woolen shirt, high-heeled vaquero boots, a cowboy hat, and a fiery red tie. He pitched the hat into one corner of the office, tossed his coat on a settee, and, dropping into a chair, remarked quietly: "Mister Byrne, I've been thinking some of taking a train over your road to Chicago. I want you to put me in there in forty-six hours. Kin you do it?"

General Passenger Agent Byrne whistled.

"Forty-six hours?" said he. "That's a big contract, Mr. Scott. That is eleven hours and fifty-six minutes faster than the eastbound run has ever been made. Man, do you realize that half the road is over mountain divisions?"

"I ought to," answered Scott. "I've been over the Santa Fe thirty-two times between here and Chicago. I ought to! Here's the money!" And the man in the blue shirt began to shed $1,000 bills. "I'm willing to pay any old figure, but I want to make the *time!* Kin you do it for me, or can't you? Let's talk business!"

Mr. Byrne drew out his pencil, and as he figured he talked. The miner broke in every few minutes with a shrewd remark. The conference lasted a long time, and in the end Mr. Byrne put the $5,500 in his safe. The train had been bought and paid for.

"Young man," said Mr. Byrne, "the Santa Fe will put you into Chicago in forty-six hours, if steam and steel will hold together. We've got the road-bed, the equipment, and the men; don't forget that. But let me tell you that you'll be riding faster than a white man ever rode before!"

"Pardner," said Scott, simply, "I like your talk. It sounds good to me. Line 'em up all along the way and tell 'em we're coming."

From the Santa Fe's official contemporary account, reprinted in *High Iron,* A Book of Trains, by Lucius Beebe, pp. 59–64, 82–84. Copyright, 1938, by D. Appleton-Century Company, Inc. New York and London.

An hour before the time appointed, the Coyote Special was standing in the depot. Thousands of curious sightseers were on hand to see the miner start on his wild ride for a record. As the time drew near, the crowd increased until the train sheds were packed and from every eminence faces looked down.

A big engine slowly backed up and wheezed into place at the head of the train. It was No. 442 in charge of Engineer John Finlay. A big automobile dashed up to the entrance of the station and Walter Scott alighted. He had to fight his way through the crowd to get to the train. Entering the cab, he shook hands with the engineer, greeted the fireman, and, urged by the crowd, made a short speech from the tender.

In the meantime the party who were to accompany him had boarded the train. Mrs. Scott, a comely young woman, altogether without nerves, awaited her husband in the Pullman. C. E. Van Loan, the newspaper representative who was to write the story of the run, busied himself with his typewriter, and the writer hereof completed the quartette.

At last the clock pointed to the hour, old No. 442 gave a warning toot, visitors scrambled off the train, Conductor George Simpson raised a long forefinger, and the Coyote began to move. A great cheer went up from the spectators, Scott waved his slouch hat in response, and inside of fifteen seconds the Coyote disappeared from sight.

The passage through the city was a fleeting ovation, crowds lining every side street to see the train dash along. The little towns outside Los Angeles flitted by like shadows, the cheers of the crowds shrilling an instant and then dropping away from the tail of the racing train.

Thirty-five miles out of Los Angeles, the jar of the air-brakes told that something was wrong. The big engine was slowing down and high on the flank of the mountain of steel, a fireman was clinging.

"Too bad!" said Conductor Simpson. "The tank box has gone hot on us! The fireman's playing the hose on it."

But the trouble was immediately rectified and then the train began to whiz in earnest. John Finlay meant to make up that lost time. And he did. One hour and fifteen minutes had been the railroad schedule to San Bernardino. The Coyote cut ten minutes off this time. Here a helper engine was picked up and in a few minutes the engine-drivers were attacking the heavy grade of the Cajon Pass. Up near Summit, at the crest of the hill, we saw the first bit of what to the amateur railroaders of the party seemed almost miraculous railroading. A mile before we reached Summit the helper engine was uncoupled on the fly, and, while the speed of the train never slackened for an instant, the light engine dashed ahead, ran onto a siding, the switch was thrown back, and the oncoming special whirled over the crest of the hill.

Here it was a different story. We were on our first descending grade. The problem now was not how fast we could run, but how fast we dared run. So we shot down toward Barstow at a mile a minute, turning and twisting in and out, Engineer Finlay's hand always on the air-brake. When we made the mile between mile-posts 44 and 43 in 39 seconds, or at the rate of 96 miles an hour, we began to feel that the great race was fairly on.

We whistled into Barstow 26 minutes ahead of the killing schedule which had been laid out for us. That 26 minutes was the gift of Engineer Finlay and his crew, and any one looking for good railroading may rely on them to repeat it as often as the call comes in.

At Barstow we changed engines for the race across the desert. It was a warm run from Barstow to Needles, but the Coyote took it on the fly, causing the lizards hastily to hunt their holes and making the cacti by the roadside look like a hedge fence.

At 7:13 the Colorado River shimmered in the distance; at 7:17 the Coyote came to a standstill at the head of the Needles yard. In exactly eighty seconds the train was moving again, a fresh engine taking up the work. Thousands lined the track near the depot, but they had no more than a fleeting glimpse of the flying special and she was gone.

Twelve tortuous miles below Needles the Santa Fe crosses the Colorado River on a steel cantilever bridge—a marvel of modern engineering, flung solidly across a wide tawny stream. Engineer Jackson swung over that twisting track at 65 miles an hour and the glasses leaped in the diner. A rush of sound, a creaking of the bridge timbers, and with a dull whirl the Coyote found Arizona soil.

* * * * *

Three hours of hard mountain railroading brought us to Seligman, where we picked up an hour. Division Superintendent Gibson climbed into the Pullman, and his first facetious words were: "What detained you?" Jackson's daredevil run will go down in song and story as the most spectacular dash of the western section.

Then began the real fight of the trip—a war against heavy grades. Clouds of sparks whirled by the windows—the little Arizona towns winked once as the Coyote passed. It was here, they said, that we were to win or lose, for if we could make the schedule up and down the divides which separate Seligman from Albuquerque, win over the famous Glorieta Pass, and hold our own on the Raton Mountains, the record was ours beyond question.

It is impossible, recalling the events of that nerve-racking night, to pick out for special mention the names of the railroad heroes who won for their road a victory over those grim Arizona mountains.

I only know that from time to time crews of stern-visaged men succeeded one another; that engines were changed in record haste, and that Division Superintendent Gibson, heavy-jawed, laconic, and resourceful, rode the train, alert, confident, and conquering. Outside the cool mountain wind swept through the stunted pines and over all twinkled the clear stars of the great Southwest.

There was no sleep on board the Coyote that night. In far-off cities tireless presses were reeling off the story of the flying Coyote, and on board the train "Van" hammered away at his staggering typewriter, clicking off the tale of the run which now belongs to railroad history.

It was not until the first switch at the outer edge of the Albuquerque yards clattered beneath the flying wheels that Superintendent Gibson smiled.

"I've brought you over the Albuquerque Division 34 minutes faster than any train went over it before," said he, as he bade us good-by. He had beaten the time of the Lowe Special by 34 minutes; he expected to beat it by 30.

The two Indian villages between Albuquerque and Lamy have never seen a train dropped down a hill at such a rate of speed. Engineer Ed Sears was at the throttle and every inch of the track is well known to this big engineer. A helper engine swung in at Lamy for the climb to the top of the Glorieta, one of the steepest grades on the entire run, 158 feet to the mile. Back in the Pullman, Trainman Jim Kurn grinned as he greeted Scott.

"Here's where you get a touch of real mountain railroading," said he," and we're going to beat the schedule if we have to sidetrack that dining car. She's got another hot box."

"Sure," said Scott. "If she smokes any more, cut 'er out!"

A few minutes later the Coyote struck the Apache Canyon, a wild bit of mountain country, memorable as the scene of many an Indian fight. At the rate of 40 miles an hour the train climbed the incline; there was a few seconds delay as the helper engine dropped out and then began the "real mountain railroading."

Down the steep grade, Sears drove his engine, the white mile-posts flashing by at the rate of one every minute. The whole train lurched and staggered over the reverse curves, the typewriter carriage banged from side to side, and the passengers, looking at each other, smiled. It seemed that the train must leave the tracks as it took those great curves. . . . It was impossible to stand up in the leaping, swaying Pullman. One man tried it; his shoulder went through the window. After that we were all content to sit still and hang on. Only Jim Kurn was calm. He knew Sears' reputation for careful running, but it seems to me the engineer crowded the limit rather hard that morning. None of us were sorry when the train stopped at Las Vegas.

At Raton, Jim Kurn said good-by.

"You're a long way ahead of that schedule now," he said, "and it won't be our fault if the people east of here don't shoot you into Chicago on time! It's hard work fighting these mountains twenty-three hours out of every twenty-four, but show me a mountain railroad man who wants a job on a plains division! Good luck!"

Two engines took the Coyote at Raton. The time of the change was a trifle over a minute, and we were off again. "Hud" Gardner is another mountain engineer who knows the game. He brought us into La Junta at 5:13, hours ahead of schedule, and the worst part of the journey behind us.

East of La Junta lies the Santa Fe "rack track." It is here that trains are supposed to make time. With a straight track, the Kansas plains lying level as a floor and a good roadbed underneath, the Coyote took up the second part of the journey.

With Engineers Lesher, Simmons, Norton, and Halsey alternating in the cab all the way from La Junta to Newton, the new and mighty balanced compounds whizzed down the Arkansas Valley. "Scotty" rode the engine into Dodge, with the telegraph poles looking like a fine-tooth comb. It was from Dodge he wired President Roosevelt:

> An American cowboy is coming east on a special train faster than any cowpuncher ever rode before; how much shall I break transcontinental record?

All that Monday night the miles flew from under the whirring wheels; in places at the rate of 85 and 90 miles an hour; the average for 300 miles being a mile every 50 seconds. . . .

Josiah Gossard, who has been an engineer on the Santa Fe for twenty-three years, took the train from Emporia to Argentine in the quickest time ever made between those two points—124 miles in 130 minutes, notwithstanding four slow orders and several grade crossings. . . .

It was nearly eight o'clock Tuesday morning when the Coyote crossed the Mississippi. The end was almost in sight now.

We had taken on another engineer at Fort Madison shops just on the western edge of Illinois. He was a German named Losee. As a fine finisher in the stretch you will look a long time for his equal. Stolid, modest, destitute of nerves, he is the direct antithesis of the dare-devil engineer of fiction. With Losee at the throttle and a straightaway stretch to the wire, the Coyote cut loose for the run home across the State of Illinois. They knew all about "Scotty" and his private train in Illinois. And so they made a holiday of that July morning, and every little hamlet along the line from Shopton to Chicago turned out to cheer the Coyote on to the goal.

It was one ovation all through Illinois. And Losee was earning every bit of it. The special had made some splendid miles in Colorado and Kansas. She was to outdo them all in Illinois. Losee ran engine No. 510 from Fort Madison to Chillicothe, 105 miles, in 101 minutes, changing at the latter point to clear track into Chicago, with every switch spiked and the entire operating department standing on its toes "rooting."

"Scotty" rode a part of the distance on the engine with Losee, and helped the fireman feed coal into the furnace.

From the little hamlet of Cameron to the still smaller one of Surrey is 2.8 miles. She made it in one minute and thirty-five seconds, at the rate of 106 miles an hour. The world's record before had been held by the Pennsylvania road, which covered the 2.5 miles between Landover and Anacostia in 102 miles-an-hour time. That was in August, 1895.

We lost five minutes at Chillicothe and four more at South Joliet. Nevertheless we made the run of 239 miles from Shopton to the Dearborn Station in Chicago in 239 minutes.

The record-breaking run was ended!

The Day Express and the Johnstown Flood

The two sections composing this train eastward left Pittsburgh at the usual hour on Friday morning, with a liberal complement of passengers. The swollen Conemaugh, whose banks the main line of the Pennsylvania Railroad follows for forty miles, looked threatening as it bore off numberless saw-logs and masses of driftwood. At Johnstown the streets were submerged and reports of landslides and washouts caused a delay. Proceeding to East Conemaugh, the sections were run on separate tracks, with a freight train between them. Other freights occupied different positions near the depot and the mail train was placed in the rear of the first section of the express. Telegraph wires and poles had fallen and definite information regarding the track could not be obtained by the anxious railway officials. For a time the passengers sought to dispel their uneasiness by reading and chatting. Three weary hours passed. Whispers that the dam at Lake Conemaugh might break blanched the faces of the stoutest. Assistant Superintendent Tromp had gone a couple of miles farther, with an engine and coach, to ascertain the state of affairs. Another locomotive, handled by Engineer John Hess, was stationed a mile east of the express train as a precaution. Rain beat on the cars and the wind moaned distressfully. Each moment seemed a short eternity, nor could the feeling of impending evil be shaken off. Most of the passengers on the mail train were familiar with the country and knew the dangerous situation, should the reservoir burst its bounds. They left the train about noon, but the through passengers stayed in the vestibuled parlor cars of the Day Ex-

---

From *The Pennsylvania Railroad, Pictorial History,* by Edwin P. Alexander, pp. 228–230. Copyright, 1947, by E. P. Alexander. New York: W. W. Norton and Company, Inc.

[In the Johnstown flood of 1889] Conemaugh, about a mile and a half above Johnstown, was the scene of a railroad thriller far more exciting than most fiction. Although most of those involved were saved, about 26 people lost their lives in attempting to escape from the two sections of No. 8, the Day Express. The story as published a few months later follows.—E.P.A.

press. At last the shrieks of a locomotive whistle were heard, sounding like the wailings of a lost soul. The passengers rose from their seats instinctively, realizing that something serious had happened. A conductor or brakeman entered each coach and remarked quietly: "Please step up on the hillside as quickly as possible!"

There was no time for explanation and none was needed. . . . Already the roar of advancing waters filled the air. Those who first reached the platform saw wrecked houses, broken bridges, trees and rocks borne on a tidal wave just turning the bend three hundred yards away. Frantic exertions were made to escape to the protecting hills back of the station. An old mill-race, never filled up, was in the way, with narrow planks for crossings. Some of the terrified passengers jumped or fell into the waters and drowned, the deluge from the reservoir overtaking them as they floundered in the ditch. A few of those who could not leave the train survived with painful bruises, a drenching, and a paralyzing fright, the waters rising half-way to the car-roofs. Several were caught in the deadly swirl as they tried to crawl under the vestibuled coaches of the second section, which lay on the inside track. It was the work of a moment to envelop the trains. The horror-stricken spectators beheld a sight unexampled in the history of railroading. An ominous roar and the round-house and nine heavy engines disappeared. Everything in the line of the flood was displaced or swallowed up. Locomotives were tossed aside and their tenders spirited off. A baggage-car of the mail train broke its couplings and drifted out of view, while the rear car swung around at right angles to the track. A Pullman coach rolled off and was crushed, a resident picking up one of its gas fixtures next day at the lower end of Woodvale. Mere playthings for the whirlpool, engines and cars were hidden beneath timbers, brush, and dirt. Slaked by the water, a cargo of lime on the train between the sections of the express set two Pullman cars blazing. Thus fire and flood combined to lend fresh horrors to the onslaught. The coaches burned to the trucks. By five o'clock the force of the torrent had subsided and an estimate of the carnage was attempted. Hardly a shred was saved from the trains, the passengers having left baggage and garments in their frenzied flight. Many had neither hats nor wraps but this was scarcely thought of in the confusion and excitement. Bitter lamentations for missing ones tempered the joy of the survivors over their own safety.

Upon the first warning of the death-dealing wave Engineer Hess tied the whistle of his locomotive open, put on all steam, and dashed towards East Conemaugh. The whistle screamed and howled as if a tortured fiend possessed it, bringing people to their doors in hot haste and enabling hundreds to flee to high ground ere their houses were engulfed. The brave engineer jumped from the iron steed barely in time to save his life by a hasty race beyond the invading waters. Next instant the flood swept the engine from the track, whirling and rolling it over and over, and embedded it in the dirt. Lying bruised and pummeled and disabled, pitiful was its helplessness compared with its strength as it had stood upon the track in its burnished bravery of steel and brass, ready at the lever's touch to pluck big handfuls of power and fling them in fleecy welcome to the skies. Silent was the whistle that had informed the passengers and citizens of the coming destruction. During the height of the flood the sound of locomotive whistles from the midst of the waters startled and surprised the fugitives huddled on the hill. Two engineers, with the nerve typical of their class, had stuck to their cabs. While awful wreck and devastation environed them, the brazen throats pealed a defiant note at intervals, the last time with exultant vigor as the waters were slowly receding. Locomotive 1309, a fifty-ton eight-wheeler, stood in its place, smoke curling from its stack, steam issuing from the safety-valve, and driftwood heaped up to the top of the headlight, the glass in which, by a queer fantasy of the flood, was not cracked. Not far away, Locomotive 477, its tender tipped over, a mass of refuse surrounding it, headed the train which sustained the least damage. The mighty arms were powerless and the fiery bosom was chilled. Engineer Henry, who escaped to the hills, could not restrain a sigh at the sight of his giant pet, feeble and useless in the midst of a waste that so much needed the assistance of the strong to bring order out of chaos.

The Hinckley Fire

September 1, 1894 marks an epoch in the annals of Minnesota which will long be remembered. Day dawned at Hinckley much as other days had done many times in its existence, with a hazy blue smoke enveloping everything. Forest fires had been raging to the south of them for some time. For nearly three months, at one place and another, the fire would start and run over a mile or two of woodland, and would die down or smolder until another opportunity or another breeze swept it in another direction and gave it a new lease on life. All noticed that the smoke had grown more troublesome than on the preceding day. The entire section could be well compared to a gigantic tinder-box. The season had been almost entirely lacking in moisture, no rain having fallen for nearly three months.

Abridged from *A History of the Great Minnesota Forest Fires,* Sandstone, Mission Creek, Hinckley, Pokegama, Skunk Lake, by Elton T. Brown, pp. 15–16, 23–24, 27–51. Copyright, 1894, by Brown Bros. St. Paul.

Hinckley was an incorporated village of about twelve hundred inhabitants, situated at the junction of the St. Paul & Duluth and Eastern Minnesota Railway, which is a part of the G. N. system, 77 miles from St. Paul and 70 miles from Duluth. Both roads run in a northerly direction, and have Duluth for their destination. They cross each other just south of the town proper.

The depots of the respective roads were situated a short distance north of the junction and about 1,500 feet apart. All the business portion of Hinckley, and in fact, all the town with the exception of a few buildings west of the Duluth tracks, lay between these two roads; while directly north of it, about a quarter-mile distant, ran the Grindstone River. This stream ran directly east and west and was crossed by both railroads and by a wagon bridge, situated about midway between the railroad bridges.

Directly east of the town itself is a gravel pit about three acres in extent, which held from two to three feet of water at the time of the fire. It was the nearest and proved to be the safest possible means of escape from the fury of the flames.

The first intimation to the people of Hinckley that anything unusual was soon to occur was about noon, when the smoke, which had been rather troublesome all morning, seemed to grow more dense, and was accompanied by a heat which, though it was not much, was enough to be quite perceptible. No one thought anything of it or was alarmed about it until an hour later, when, as it still increased, they thought the Fire Department might have something to do before the day was over. The storm cloud itself, which, when it burst, swept everything before it, rose like an almost perpendicular wall of black smoke, surging and roaring, rising into the very heavens as far as the eye could reach.

[Often] in a forest fire, the fire ran over the ground, burned the underbrush and fallen limbs, but did comparatively little damage to the trees for lumbering purposes. Oftimes the pines were killed or died from the effects of the fire, but were not actually burned. In this case, however, while it does not hold true in all parts of the fire-swept district, in certain portions of the Western section, the heat was so intense, it not only burned the pines, roots, trunks and all, but actually consumed the top soil or loam, and where there had been a forest of standing pine and underbrush, there is nothing left but the clay subsoil, and the rocks and stones which happened to be held in the upper deposit.

About 2 o'clock in the afternoon the Fire Department was called to the west side of town to fight a small blaze which had broken out there. Two thousand feet of hose was laid down, and as that was found to be inadequate, a telegram was sent to Rush City for 600 feet more. That telegram was never answered and the hose never arrived—before that was possible, Hinckley, as it had been, was a thing of the past.

Before half an hour had elapsed, half a dozen small buildings in the outskirts were in flames. The big fire was seen to be approaching quite close to the town. The wind was blowing a hurricane from a direction a little west of south. The smoke, which had grown more and more dense, now darkened the sun as it mounted to the zenith, and the heat became, even to the hardiest, almost beyond endurance. Then it was that the terrified populace fully appreciated their peril; then and not until then did the terrible race for life begin.

The gravel pit was large enough to have saved all the people, if only they had sought refuge there, but it was only the cool-headed ones that seemed to think of this as an avenue of escape.

The northbound Limited on the St. Paul & Duluth road had reached Hinckley at 2 P.M., two hours late, and a few of the more timorous and those who felt the danger at that time had escaped on that train. The southbound local freight on the Eastern Minnesota, which has a daily run from Duluth to Hinckley and return, reached Hinckley at 2:40. Engineer Ed Barry had a train of thirty empties and ten loads. Everything was afire at that time, and the heat and smoke were intense, almost to suffocation. The freight was sidetracked until the arrival of passenger train No. 4 from the North at 3:25 with Engineer Best and Conductor Powers in charge. After a short consultation with them, Engineer Barry ran up to the other end of the yard and coupled onto three box cars and the caboose, and backed down on the main track and joined the passenger, making a train of three box cars, a caboose and five passenger coaches, besides the two engines.

All this time the fire had been pushing on, and now it was announced by Captain Craig of the Fire Department to the throng that the whole town would soon be in flames and they must save themselves, for he could do nothing for them. Then began the mad rush for life. Yet with it all was exhibited a spirit of self-sacrifice of the strong in the succor of the weak. Men who saw their families safe on board turned back at the risk of their own lives to carry the helpless children of their friends to places of safety.

After escaping from being burned in their own homes, those who succeeded in boarding this Eastern Minnesota emergency train placed their lives in the hands of a few men upon whose courage and strength of character rested the responsibility of carrying them out of danger. Best and Powers decided how long it was possible to delay the train. It took nerve to stand still with flames leaping towards and around them on the wings of a tornado. After waiting at the depot for three-quarters of an hour, and until men and animals were falling in the streets from the heat, at a quarter past four Best loosed his air brakes, and the train moved out across Grindstone bridge.

After crossing the bridge, the train waited five minutes and took on forty more of the panic-stricken townspeople; then, as the ties under the train were burning, and even the cars themselves blistering and almost blazing, the train pulled out, though in so doing, they were obliged to leave men, women and children to that fiery ordeal. But the heat had become so intense that the very rails were beginning to warp and twist out of shape.

After having taken on all that could be saved by them, the engineers put on all steam and rushed towards safety as fast as wheels could turn. Everything was burning, fire on all sides, and the heat continued to be so intense that, combined with the smoke, it seemed as if those on board would die of suffocation. But seven miles out of Hinckley they found a cool current of air and breathed easier. Though they were by no means out of the fire limits, the heat did not seem so intense, and the smoke was a little less blinding, though through all the run from Hinckley to Duluth the headlight was kept burning, it having been found necessary at Partridge on the down trip of the freight in the morning. [But the leading engine was backing, so there was no headlight.]

When the engineers knew, by their knowledge of the road, that a bridge was close by, Best would put on his brakes—his engine controlled the air brakes of the five passenger coaches which made up the bulk of the train in weight—and slow down to a three- or four-mile gait until they were certain the bridge was there, when they would pass on. Two brakemen rode on the back end of Barry's tender, as they backed up, and as they reached a bridge, would signal Barry whether or not it was all right, and he in turn would whistle off to Best, when they would go on to the next bridge and repeat the operation. Nineteen bridges in fourteen miles of road over which they passed were totally destroyed, and they were all burning more or less furiously when the train passed over them; the brakemen unflinching through all that perilous ride of sixty miles through flame and smoke.

When Sandstone was reached, the train halted and people were begged to get aboard and fly for their lives. Some grasped the opportunity, but more did not, laboring under the impression that although Hinckley was burned, Sandstone was safe; a notion they had cause to regret an hour later. Only a short stop was made at Sandstone, then the heavily loaded train started again. On reaching Kettle River, just out of Sandstone, the bridge was burning and the train slowed up, when a cry from the watchman, "For God's sake, go on, you can cross it now, and it will go down in five minutes," made Barry draw a quick breath and with set teeth throw his throttle wide open and run out on the bridge. They crossed in safety as by a miracle, and five minutes later the bridge fell. [The watchman and his family saved themselves by immersion in the little river.]

By this time the closely-huddled passengers, having been exposed to the heat for so long, were suffering agony for a drink of water. At Partridge it was found necessary to take twenty minutes to get the engines ready to go on, and the time was improved in getting water to the occupants of the cars. Up to this time the train had been running without orders and against the time of a down freight. At Partridge the crew got a message to use their own judgment in running, coupled with the information that the down train No. 23 had been abandoned. Like their Sandstone neighbors, the people of Partridge refused to leave, and the train pulled out again. At Kerrick Engineer Barry found that his eyes had become so affected by smoke and heat that he could scarcely see at all, to say nothing of running an engine with a train-load of people in his care. He thought he would be compelled to give up, but after ten minutes' rest, he plucked up courage and ran her through to West Superior, where he could go no further, as he could see nothing. When he left his engine, he was so exhausted with the heat and smoke and the mental strain he had been under that he could not stand, but was carried to the roundhouse.

The southbound Limited on the St. Paul & Duluth road left Duluth at 2 o'clock on the afternoon of that eventful Saturday. The train was in charge of Conductor Thomas Sullivan, Engineer James Root,[1] Fireman Jack McGowan, Brakeman John Monihan, Baggageman George F. Morris, Porter John W. Blair, News Agent Herrmann Mannhart. The train consisted of one combination car, one coach, two chair cars and Engine 69. The atmosphere was heavy with smoke, even as the train pulled out of Duluth depot, and all the way down to Carlton it grew gradually thicker, until it was found necessary to light the headlight and all the lamps in the train. The passengers began to show signs of uneasiness. Onward swept the ill-fated train with its cargo of humanity, and but for the heroism of two men, it might have been to certain destruction. But James Root and John McGowan were made of sterner stuff than the ordinary mortal, and when the terrible ordeal came, they were not found wanting.

[Root] with many others was under a false impression as to the actual extent and intensity of the fire, and never dreamed that Hinckley would be destroyed in this way. Still the smoke increased, the heat became more intense. It filled all the coaches until it was difficult to breathe, and of course added to the dismay of the already panicky passengers. The trainmen tried to reassure the passengers, but by this time the train had approached near enough so that the flames could be seen to the right of the track, and the roar of the blazing demon could be distinctly heard. [At its height, it could be heard at Pine City, fifteen miles away.]

On rumbled the train, every instant adding terror to the scene, until within a mile and a half of Hinckley. Here came the first information that anything extraordinary had happened or was happening to the town. The smoke was so dense it was impossible to see it. A number of fleeing citizens flagged the train and in a few words told the crew

---

1 For Root's own account, see Brown, pp. 139–147.

their story, then with their party, boarded the train. About 150 or 200 people in all were saved in this way. They boarded the train, a gasping, excited, half-crazed concourse.

The fire was coming with the speed of a locomotive, backed by that horrible wind. Engineer Root's first impulse was to put on all speed and run through the fire, but a second of deliberation caused him to reverse his engine and back away from it. Then came a race which has no parallel. No one can have any conception of the awfulness, the suffering of that terrible ride. At first, Root had no definite destination in mind, and no orders to run on but those of common sense and humanity. Then he thought of a little marsh lake known as Skunk Lake, near the track about four miles from where they had met the refugees and turned back; this he determined to reach at all hazards.

On came the flames, and he saw that they were gaining on him—gaining until they burst over him in a hurricane blast! Flame and smoke were everywhere. They came in through the ventilators at the tops of the cars, through the cracks at the sides of the windows. The rear coach was on fire, and its passengers fled to the other coaches to escape from the immediate danger, but the effort was futile; one after another, all the coaches first blistered with the heat and finally began to blaze. Then ensued a scene horrible beyond description. The roar of the flame, the stifling suffocation and darkness of the smoke—the intense heat, the shrieks and moans of the unfortunate almost baking in the crowded cars, made it a pandemonium. The heat broke the glass in the windows of the cars, and as it did so, one man lost his reason, literally went mad, and with a shriek threw himself through one of the windows and was swallowed up in the seething mass. Another and another followed him, and all were caught and destroyed by the insatiable flames. In the panic that ensued, ten more unfortunates thought death itself preferable to such suspense and torture, and threw themselves from the windows of the doomed train.

While these scenes were being enacted in the coaches, Engineer Root was suffering terrible agony. His hands were blistered as he held the lever, his clothes were afire, as were those of Fireman McGowan. Jack leaped into the manhole of the tank and put out the fire in his own clothes, then grasping a pail, soused Jim with the water from the tank. Still on they flew, Jim holding the lever and Jack dashing water over him. The glass in the cab window at Jim's side burst, and a piece struck him in the neck, cutting a gash which bled profusely. When the window broke, the curtain caught fire, the flames swept into the cab, burning the wooden handles of the steam connections, scorching the seats and melting the cab lamp. Weakened by heat and smoke, the loss of blood and the tension, Root was twice overcome and fell from his seat, and twice was bolstered up by the faithful Jack.

Minutes they were, but they seemed like hours before Skunk Lake was reached, the engineer brought the train to a standstill, and the fireman pointed out to the passengers the direction of the lake. McGowan assisted his engineer to the water and lay down in it himself. Owing to his superior physical strength, he was able to care for Root and others until the arrival of relief trains from Duluth. Mannhart, the news agent, and John Blair, the colored porter, did much to save the women and children. While practically everyone else was prostrate in the shallow water, Blair stood sprinkling the women with a fire extinguisher.

The train had on board from 135 to 150 regular passengers, and took aboard from 150 to 200 refugees from Hinckley. The exact number will never be known. Certain it is that more than 300 people owe their lives to the little water that remained in that lake, which, owing to the continued drought, had been reduced to a mere morass of mud and water. Here they lay for four mortal hours, their faces close to the muddy water, endeavoring to survive the heat and smoke that lay so close to the ground that they were in danger of suffocation. Most of the passengers reached the lake, except some few who became confused and ran wildly in other directions.

The only fatalities occurring on the train itself were two Chinese who seemed dazed or demented, and could not be moved from their seats. They stayed there until overcome by the heat and burned with the train, which was entirely consumed. Then, too, there were those who threw themselves from the train before it reached Skunk Lake, all of whom perished.

Conductor Sullivan, as soon as he saw his passengers safe, started staggering back along the track to the next station to protect his train, as he knew that he was running on the time of a freight train that was following, and feared that the calamity of a collision would be added to what had already occurred. After a terrible ordeal of battling through heat and smoke, he reached Miller Station and sent his message; then having fulfilled his trust, he collapsed.

After the fire had abated somewhat, Root and McGowan went back to see if they could not save the engine and tender. Finding it impossible to extinguish the burning coal in the tender, they uncoupled the engine from it and ran her ahead a short distance; this saved most of the engine. Root had by this time become thoroughly chilled from lying in the water, and he lay down on the floor of his cab, where he was found by the first relief—[which, by the way, consisted of some heroic section men with handcars].

Two more heroic railroad men are yet unmentioned. Tom Dunn, telegraph operator at the St. Paul & Duluth station at Hinckley, stayed at his post to direct the movements of trains until it was too late to save himself. Another was a section hand named Henley who, in the semi-darkness of smoke and heat, with falling embers burning holes in his clothing, stood in a street, directing terrified, fleeing citizens to the safety of the shallow water in the gravel pit. Seventy lives were saved in that pool, including that of brave Henley himself, who sought its refuge only at the last moment.

Here and there, creeping spots of fire continued to burn for five days after the destruction of Hinckley, being finally checked by a rain which began falling on September 6th.

The total number of deaths caused by the fire will never be definitely known. For months afterward, lumbermen and hunters were finding scattered bodies of unfortunates who had been overtaken by the galloping flames and perished, leaving no trace of their identity. These included 22 identified as Indians. So far as known, the total number of lives lost is 476. [Later the estimate was placed at more than 500.]

Kate Shelley

Late in the afternoon of July 6, 1881, heavy black clouds rolled up from the horizon and the gloom presaging a violent storm swept over the Des Moines Valley. Farmers hastened their evening chores while anxious housewives hurried to bring in their washing and see that the chickens had found shelter. As the dense cloud-veil spread over the sky, twilight deepened into the darkness of night, which was made blacker in contrast to the vivid illumination of the lightning flashes. Nearer and nearer came the ominous rumble and crash of the thunder until it made the windows rattle. Then down came the rain in sheets.

In a little cottage up the valley of Honey Creek beside the Chicago & Northwestern Railroad about half a mile from the Des Moines River, the Shelley children watched the appalling storm until "fright took possession" and drove them from the window, "through which the lightning flashed dreadful pictures of destruction." The creek became a raging torrent, and the turbulent waters rose until they threatened the stable halfway down the slope where the stock had taken refuge. Something had to be done. Kate, who was fifteen, the oldest of the children, dashed out into the rain, waded through the water that was pouring down the hillside, let out the horses and cows to take care of themselves, and rescued some little pigs that had climbed on a pile of hay for safety.

The storm continued with unabated violence during the long evening and on into the night. At the Shelley home there was no inclination to retire. While the younger children dozed, Kate and her mother remained alert and vigilant—apprehensive of danger. Honey Creek, filled with fence posts and uprooted trees, was still rising. They feared

---

By J. A. Swisher. From *The Palimpsest,* edited by John Ely Briggs, Vol. VI (February, 1925), No. 2, pp. 45–55.

that the railroad bridge across the creek a quarter of a mile up the track could not withstand the flood, and they knew the long wooden trestle across the Des Moines River must be under a terrific strain.

The spring and early summer had been unusually rainy, so that the river had stood for days at high-water mark. Railroad embankments had been undermined and bridge piling had loosened. M. J. Shelley, an immigrant from Tipperary, Ireland, had been section foreman before he died in 1878, and well his family knew the perils of the railroad on such a night as this. . . .

It must have been after eleven o'clock when Kate and her mother heard the rumble of a train crossing the Des Moines River bridge. It was the "pusher," an engine stationed at Moingona to serve as an auxiliary in pulling heavy trains up the grade on either side of the river. The crew, consisting of Ed Wood, George Olmstead, Adam Agar, and Patrick Donahue, had been ordered to "run to Boone and return to Moingona regardless of all trains." The engine came backing down the track with the brakeman and section foreman standing on the running board behind the tender looking for washouts. Past the Shelley house they went and onto the swaying Honey Creek bridge. Twice Kate heard the engine bell toll distinctly, and "then came the horrible crash and the fierce hissing of steam" as the engine plunged down with her crew into twenty-five feet of rapid, swirling water.

"Oh, Mother," Kate exclaimed, "they have gone down." The storm and all else was forgotten. "It seemed as still as death, as silent as the grave." Kate decided that she must go to help the men and stop the passenger train that would soon be due at Moingona—the midnight express from the west. Many lives were in her hands that night. The remonstrances of her mother were of no avail. She felt she simply had to go. Attired in an old skirt and jacket, she caught up a straw hat, improvised a lantern by hanging a little miner's lamp in an old lantern frame, and started out into the night and the storm to do her duty as she saw it, knowing that Mother and the children were praying God to keep her from harm.

The entire valley was flooded by that time, and the yard of the Shelley home resembled the "inside of a huge oval bowl" filled with water which extended to the railroad track. Unable to go directly to the railroad and thence up the track to the wreck at the bridge, Kate climbed the bluff back of the house, made a semi-circular detour to the southwest until she reached a place where the wagon road came through a cut in the bluffs and crossed the railroad. Once on the track, she ran to the broken bridge.

Upon arriving at the scene of the wreck, she saw by the lightning that two of the men, Wood and Agar, had chanced to clamber upon some convenient trees in the midst of the swelling flood and thus escape drowning for the time being. The other two were lost. One of the men called to her again and again, but in the tumult she could not understand what he said.

Unable to render aid to the ill-fated crew and realizing that the midnight train would soon be due, she turned westward and hastened as fast as she could go toward Moingona in an effort to save the lives of the passengers on board the approaching train. Moingona was only a mile and a quarter away, but the Des Moines River with its long wooden bridge trembling from the incessant rush of the high water lay between her and the little village.

After a temporary lull the storm had burst out anew. The thunder and lightning were frightful, while the rain came in gusts and torrents. The attempt to reach Moingona across the raging Des Moines seemed almost certain death: to hesitate might mean the death of hundreds of passengers on the train speeding to destruction. That was the thought that kept pounding at Kate's consciousness as she ran along the track. If she could only get there on time. What if the train should catch her on the bridge? What if the train should go thundering by in the darkness? She pictured the engine plunging into Honey Creek, the coaches piling up in the water. In imagination she could almost hear the screams of the people. She must hurry—hurry! How hard the wind blew! Sometimes it almost took her off her feet. There seemed to be no strength left in her. But she must go on!

Drenched to the skin, trembling and breathless, she reached the river. Never before had she seen the water so high. It was roaring by almost level with the track. The muddy river was filled with debris—even big trees uprooted by the wind and carried away by the water were sweeping headlong toward Des Moines. Across the seething flood stretched the long bridge that seemed just on the point of joining the general rush down stream.

Pedestrians had never been invited to use the bridge and as a method of discouraging such a practice some of the planking had been removed. The ties were a full pace apart and studded thickly with twisted rusty spikes. There was danger in crossing during fair weather and in daylight, but to attempt the feat in pitch darkness with the wind blowing a gale, rain pouring on the slippery ties, and a raging torrent below was an exploit to daunt the courage of any man.

Unchecked by the timbered bluffs of Honey Creek Valley, the wind swept the river bridge with terrific force. As Kate hesitated a moment to catch her breath and appraise the situation, a gust more violent than usual extinguished the feeble light of her lantern and left her in inky darkness relieved only by the lightning. A feeling of terror seized her, but at the thought of the drowning men back at the broken bridge and the oncoming express, she dropped to her knees and began to crawl slowly, laboriously, across the long wind-swept trestle. Guided by the rails, she felt her way from tie to tie. Again and again her skirt caught on a nail and she all but lost her balance. Now and then a sharp pain shot through her hands and knees as a protruding spike or splinter gouged into her flesh. As each flash of lightning displayed the angry swirling water only a few feet below, she almost fell beneath the ties from dizziness.

Halfway over a piercing flash of lightning revealed an enormous tree rushing down upon the very spot where she was clinging. In the instant of vision she noticed that the earth was still hanging to the roots of the tree. Momentary panic brought her upright on her knees as she clasped her hands in terror and in prayer, for it seemed inevitable that the shock would carry out the bridge. But the monster glided between the piers with a rush, the branches scattering foam and water over the girl as they passed.

Finding herself still unharmed, she resumed her painful progress. It seemed as though she had been on that bridge for hours. She could scarcely remember when she started, while the beginning of the storm and her rescue of the little pigs earlier in the evening seemed years ago. Each minute stretched out interminably and the impression grew upon her that the end of the bridge was constantly receding. At last, however, she felt the solid ground beneath her. Standing erect, she stopped to breathe for a moment and then set out on the run to the station a quarter of a mile away. It was getting late and her strength was failing fast.

How she finally arrived and told her story, Kate Shelley could never remember. She only recalled that some one said, "The girl is crazy." Then one of the railroad men recognized her and the dreadful import of the message was realized. The whistle of an engine in the yards aroused the town. [A red lamp halted the midnight express.] In a few minutes men with ropes and other equipment were ready to go to the rescue of Wood and Agar at the Honey Creek bridge. Kate accompanied the rescue party across the river on the engine, guided them along the bluff to the track above the washout, and thence back to the scene of the disaster on the east bank of the creek, where the survivors of the wreck could be helped. After many efforts a rope was cast to Wood, who made it fast to his tree and then came ashore hand over hand. Agar could not be rescued until the water began to subside when he too was taken from his refuge, completely exhausted from his long exposure.

During the days that followed the sixth of July, rest or relaxation was not to be considered. On Thursday, eager crowds visited the scene of the tragedy and the Shelley house. Newspaper reporters arrived on the second day, burdened with questions and insistent upon exploring the whole neighborhood lest some dramatic detail should be overlooked. Saturday passed in much the same manner, but on Sunday, when Donahue's body was found in a corn field, the excitement subsided. It was then that Kate Shelley's strength gave way. For three months she was confined to her bed, but at last her natural vitality triumphed.

Restored to health, Kate found that the sun shone on a brighter world for her. She was no longer the unknown girl dwelling in a poor little home beside the railroad. News of her heroism had been flashed abroad, and almost instantly she had become one of the famous women of her time. Press comments concerning her bravery were widespread. Poems were composed, dramatic readings produced, and editorials written—all presenting the story of her courage and character.

Probably the best known poem inspired by the daring act of the modest Irish girl was written by Eugene J. Hall. . . .

She was literally showered with letters filled with testimonials of gratitude and praise. Some contained verses in her honor, others eulogized her in prose, while there was no end of hair-raising, heart-throbbing descriptions of the adventure. There were letters of sympathy, letters requesting a photograph, a fragment of her dress, or a splinter from the bridge, and letters offering glowing opportunities for investing her fortune.

Numerous gifts and tokens of esteem were bestowed upon her. The school children of Dubuque gave her a medal. The Chicago *Tribune* raised a fund to help the Shelley family out of debt. As an emblem of appreciation of her "brave and humane action" and in recognition of her "efforts to save the lives of railway passengers and employees during the terrible storm of the night of July 6, 1881," the Nineteenth General Assembly of Iowa passed an act in 1882 authorizing the Senator and Representative of Boone County, together with the Governor of the State, to procure and present her with a gold medal bearing an appropriate inscription. The legislature also appropriated $200 in cash to be given to Miss Shelley. A drinking fountain erected in a Dubuque park was dedicated to her. The employees of the North Western Railroad gave her a gold watch and chain while the company issued her a life pass over the road.

* * * * *

In 1903 [after attending Simpson College in 1883 and 1884], she accepted employment as station agent at Moingona—a position which she held until a short time before her death on January 21, 1912. Twice each day during all these years she went from her home to the little depot, crossing the new iron bridge that had replaced the one over which she crawled on that fateful July night so many years before. Trains always stopped at her little cottage when she was on board. At the time of her funeral the company sent a special train to her home for the convenience of the family and hundreds of friends.

On the main line of the North Western Railroad between Boone and Ogden and about four miles north of the village of Moingona, a fine new bridge now spans the Des Moines River. This structure, one of the longest and highest of its kind, is widely known as the Kate Shelley bridge—a fitting monument to perpetuate the memory of the famous Iowa heroine.

The Saga of Casey Jones

Come, all you rounders, I want you to hear
  The story told of a brave engineer;
Casey Jones was the rounder's name,
  On a high right-wheeler he rode to fame.

Every railroad man who speaks the English language is familiar with the famous ballad of "Casey Jones." The song reached the height of its popularity during the decade preceding the First World War. Millions of copies of the ballad were sold. And there was no end to the unprinted verses and parodies and versions that were sung, not only by railroad men but by sailors at sea, by cowhands of the West, by lumberjacks in the North Woods, and in all sorts of places, among all sorts of men. "Casey Jones" is a virile song that appeals strongly to men—men of the outdoors—and, naturally, strongest of all to railroad men.

The hero of the famous ballad has come to occupy a unique place in American folklore. He has come to symbolize the courage and the devotion to duty of the men who work night and day, braving all conditions of weather, enduring all the discomforts of the road, to put the trains through on time, regardless of obstacles.

To many Americans Casey Jones typifies the spirit of the rails—a romantic, adventurous, appealing figure, more glamorous by far than the mythical Paul Bunyan of the lumber camps or the fabulous Mike Fink of the flatboats. Contrary to a widespread impression, Casey Jones was not a mere figment of the imagination. He was a popular locomotive engineer on the Illinois Central Railroad in the days when every trip at the controls of the Iron Horse was a hazardous adventure. A strapping, dashing figure—black-haired, gray-eyed, six feet four inches tall—Casey Jones was the eldest of four brothers, all crack locomotive engineers, all employed on the Illinois Central.

Casey's real name was John Luther Jones. Several towns in Kentucky have claimed the honor of being Casey's birthplace, but his biographer, Fred J. Lee, a former train conductor on the Illinois Central, who knew the famous engineer personally, wrote that Casey was born

---

From *Main Line of Mid-America,* The Story of the Illinois Central, by Carlton J. Corliss, pp. 301–311. Copyright, 1950, by Carlton J. Corliss. New York: Creative Age Press.

Diagram on p. 45 by Ralph Graeter from *Life,* Vol. 12 (January 26, 1942), No. 4, p. 63. Copyright, 1942, by Time, Inc. New York.

in southeastern Missouri on March 14, 1864, the son of a country school teacher, and that at the age of thirteen he moved with his family to Cayce, a little town in the southwestern corner of Kentucky, a few miles from Fulton. At Bird's Point, opposite Cairo, the boy was fascinated by the Illinois Central engines scurrying back and forth on the Cairo levee. They were the first locomotives he had ever seen. He watched their every movement and thrilled at the sound of their whistles and clanging bells as they darted to and fro like mammoth ants, loading and unloading the huge ferry boats, "H. S. McComb" and "William H. Osborn," that transferred cars across the Ohio to and from the Kentucky shore.

Was it here that the impressionable lad made up his mind that he would become a railroad man? At any rate, two years later, at the age of fifteen, the boy became an apprentice telegrapher on the Mobile & Ohio Railroad at Columbus, Kentucky, then the northern terminus of that road. There he obtained his nickname "Casey," after the sound of the name of his home town, to distinguish him from other railway employees named Jones. The nickname stuck with him for the rest of his days.

Casey astonished his fellow workers by the speed with which he mastered the art of telegraphy, but almost from the first day he entered railway service his aim was to become a locomotive engineer. . . . No sooner had the lad reached the age of eighteen than he applied for a fireman's job. Never was Casey happier than the day, several months later, when he passed the examination and started to fire.

While Casey was thus employed on the Mobile & Ohio, a devastating yellow fever epidemic visited central Mississippi and took an especially heavy toll of train crews on the Illinois Central. Hearing that many Illinois Central firemen were being promoted to engineers, Casey lost no time in applying to the Illinois Central for a job. He didn't have long to wait. On March 1, 1888, he entered the service of the Illinois Central as a fireman on a freight run between Jackson, Tennessee, and Water Valley, Mississippi. Casey fired locomotives for nearly two years, and then in February, 1890, while less than twenty-six years of age, he realized his boyhood ambition! He successfully passed the examination for the responsible position of locomotive engineer.

When Casey reached his twenty-sixth birthday he was a full-fledged engineer, assigned to a fast freight run over the 119 miles of main line between Jackson and Water Valley with an occasional run pulling "hot shot" banana specials from Jackson to Mounds, Illinois, over the new and majestic Cairo bridge. . . . Then, in the winter of 1892–1893, in response to a call for help north of the Ohio, Casey moved to Centralia, Illinois, pulling freights northward and southward out of that terminal for several months. In those days Casey's fireman was a young chap named Perry L. Walker, who later became one of the best-known locomotive engineers on the St. Louis Division. Walker recalled Casey as a "long, lean, lanky man who was so tall that he couldn't stand up in the engine cab without sticking his head outside a foot or so, reminding some of his friends of a young giraffe." Walker and other men who worked with Casey Jones described the latter as a friendly, good-natured, likable man, agreeable to work with, efficient, and determined to rank among the best engineers on the road.

That Casey was highly regarded by his superior officers as early as 1893 is attested by the fact that he was assigned to one of the fast specials which shuttled back and forth in Chicago that summer between Van Buren Street and the grounds of the World's Columbian Exposition in Jackson Park. . . . The Exposition played a major role in Casey's career. It was in the Transportation Building of that fair that Casey fell desperately in love for the second time in his life. His first love was Miss Janie Brady of Jackson, Tennessee, whom he wooed and won in 1886 and to whom he remained faithful to the end of his days. But this *affaire de Transportation Building* was of another sort. Casey promptly wrote his wife Janie and made a clean breast of it. His second love was the most beautiful locomotive he had ever seen—a huge Consolidation-type engine with eight drive wheels and two pilot wheels, known to railroad men as a 2-8-0. The shining new engine, representing the last word in steam locomotive development, was the central attraction of the Illinois Central exhibit. Again and again Casey visited the exhibit. He dreamed about the engine at night and talked about it by day. He pictured himself in its cab streaking through Tennessee and Mississippi.

How Casey managed it no one seems to know, but on the closing day of the fair, October 31, having completed his suburban train assignment, Casey appeared at the Illinois Central exhibit with formal credentials directing that the prize locomotive—officially identified as No. 638—be delivered to him personally for transfer, first to Burnside shops for reconditioning and second for a special run to Water Valley, Mississippi, where it was to be assigned to him for regular freight service out of that terminal.

Never before in the memory of railroaders had one man been directed to run a locomotive such a distance—over five operating divisions! Casey's fame was spreading.

For nearly seven years—from the fall of 1893 to the end of 1899—Casey Jones and Engine 638 were as inseparable as Casey and his wife Janie. When he was not with one he was usually with the other. He followed the engine to the roundhouse or shop and saw to it that repairs and renewals were properly made. In those days enginemen were permitted to decorate their locomotives in almost any way that pleased their fancy. An engineer who was fond of hunting might display a pair of antlers above or below the headlight; a Mason or a war veteran might adorn his engine with the emblem of his lodge or post. Casey's distinctive mark was his six-tone calliope whistle, which made his "whippoorwill call" known to every railroad man, plantation owner, and cotton-picker along his route.

> The switchmen knew by the whistle's moans
> That the man at the throttle was Casey Jones.

An old-timer once said: "The 'whistle's moans' in the song were right. Casey could just about play a tune on the whistle. He could make the cold chills run up and down your spine with it."

Out over the countryside would go the cry, like the voice of a great whippoorwill, which seemed to say

KAAAAAAAAAA SEEEEEEEEEE JOOOOOOOOOONES

And all up and down the Illinois Central, from Jackson to Water Valley, as he drove his engine through the night, people would arouse from their slumbers and say, "Ah, there goes Casey Jones!" and turn to sleep again as the familiar, friendly voice of his engine faded away in the distance.

Casey was in his twelfth year on the Illinois Central, principally on freight runs, when he was offered about the highest honor that could come to a locomotive engineer—the privilege of piloting the Illinois Central's fastest Chicago-New Orleans passenger train, known officially as No. 1, the New Orleans Special, but popularly known as the "Cannonball." The north bound "Cannonball" was officially No. 2, the Chicago Fast Mail. Casey's run was to be 190 miles in length, between Memphis and Canton. It necessitated moving from Jackson to Memphis and giving up No. 638, but it also meant better pay, a faster run, greater prestige, another step up the ladder; possibly it meant that Casey was on the road to further promotions.

Casey talked it over with Janie, and they decided the only thing to do was to accept the job. On January 1, 1900, Casey reported to Superintendent King at Memphis and was temporarily assigned to freight runs between Memphis and Canton to familiarize himself thoroughly with the road before taking the passenger run.

The record in the superintendent's office showed that in years past Casey had been disciplined nine times for infractions of the rules, each of which had drawn a suspension of from five to thirty days. All these infractions had occurred in freight service. Casey was not proud of this record; but he was proud of the fact that during his ten years as a locomotive engineer he had never been involved in a train accident that had resulted in the death of a fellow employee or a passenger. His record was also clear with regard to sobriety. Indeed, Casey Jones never frequented saloons or used alcohol in any form, and a responsible writer who interviewed many of Casey's personal acquaintances declared that "there was not a whisper of loose moral conduct in the innumerable recollections and anecdotes concerning him." Therefore, the term "rounder" in the song—if taken in its modern connotation—might convey an erroneous impression of Casey's character.

On the evening of April 29, 1900, Casey and his fireman, Sim Webb, brought the northbound "Cannonball" into Poplar Street station, Memphis, exactly on time and promptly backed their engine, No. 382, out to the South Memphis Yard roundhouse.

There they found that the engineer who was scheduled to take the "Cannonball" south that night was on the sick list. Since no other engine crew was available, Casey and Sim were asked to "double out" without sleep or rest. They consented on one condition—that their engine, No. 382, be conditioned and made ready for the trip. Agreed, Casey and Sim made off for food and coffee. When they reached Poplar Street station they learned that the southbound "Cannonball" was running late. The train was due to leave Memphis at 11:15 P.M., but it was not until 12:50 A.M., ninety-five minutes later, that Casey opened the throttle of 382 and the six-car train of mail, baggage, coaches, and sleepers pulled out of Poplar Street on its history-making run.

> Through South Memphis Yard on the fly,
> He heard the fireman say, "You've got a white eye."

It was a murky night, but Casey knew the road. Every station, bridge, switch, and plantation home along the route was a familiar landmark. Casey's orders were to run into Grenada thirty-five minutes late, into Durant twenty minutes late, and into Canton on time. Old 382 was steaming unusually well; Sim was on his toes, and Casey Jones was in his glory.

From Memphis to Grenada there were 100 miles of fairly straight, fairly level, single-track road, with no scheduled meets and no station stops. The regular running time for the "Cannonball," including a five-minute stop at Grenada, was two hours forty-five minutes. Casey pulled out of Grenada at 2:35 A.M., thirty-five minutes behind the schedule, as covered by his orders. He had made up sixty of the ninety-five minutes. Canton was 88 miles ahead.

South of Grenada, Casey poked his head out into the mizzly and murky dampness and signaled Sim for co-operation. When the "Cannonball" passed Winona, 23 miles south of Grenada, she had made up all but fifteen minutes, and when Casey pulled into Durant, 30 miles south of Winona, he was running practically on time. Here Casey received orders to meet No. 2 at Goodman and to "saw" through a flock of freights and passengers at Vaughan—22 miles south of Durant and 14 miles north of Canton. After meeting No. 2 at Goodman, Casey again pulled the throttle wide open and headed for Vaughan at a speed that has been estimated at seventy miles an hour. He was bent on reaching Canton on schedule. All the way south Casey had been practising on his six-tone calliope whistle.

"We're going into Canton on time!" Casey shouted to Sim. "That is, if we're not delayed by that mess of trains at Vaughan. And Canton will hear plenty of this whistle!"

Meanwhile things were happening at Vaughan station. On the east side of the single main track was a passing track, 3,148 feet in length. The station was about 2,000 feet south of the north switch. On the west side of the main track, near the station, was a short business track used for loading, unloading, and storing freight cars. Just north of the north switch of the passing track was a curve.

This was before the days of block signals on most roads, and the track was without signal protection of any sort. The safety of trains was dependent upon strict adherence to rules, obedience to train orders, alertness, and quick thinking.

Ahead of Casey's southbound "Cannonball" that night were two trains, also southbound—freight train No. 83, with forty-four cars and a caboose, pulled by two locomotives, and New Orleans-bound passenger train No. 25.

Somewhere south of Vaughan, headed north, were freight train No. 72, with thirty-six cars and a caboose, northbound "Cannonball" No. 2, and two sections of another Chicago-bound passenger, No. 26. All these trains were running late.

The first train to reach Vaughan was southbound freight No. 83, which had been delayed north of Pickens by a broken air hose. On arrival at Vaughan, 83 turned into the passing track at the north switch. When northbound 72 arrived it took the same (and only) passing track through the south switch. The two freights together were about four car-lengths too long to clear both switches. Flagman Newberry from 83 was sent north to place warning torpedoes on the track and signal the two southbound passengers, Nos. 25 and 1, that they were to be "sawed" through Vaughan. According to the usual procedure under such circumstances, Nos. 72 and 83 moved southward together, thus clearing the main line at the north switch, but putting

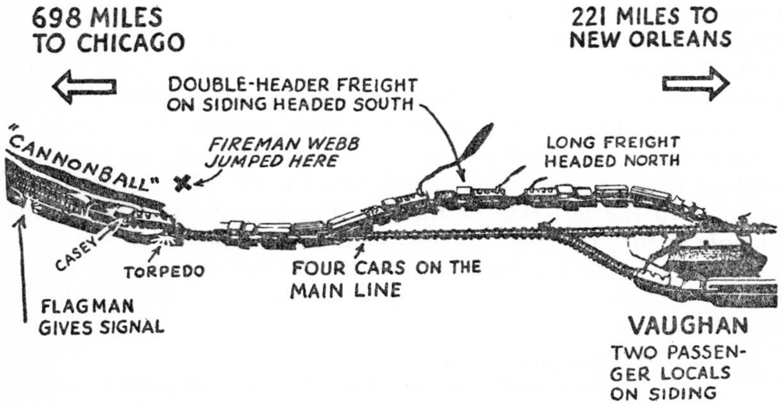

the rear cars of 72 out on the main line at the south switch. Southbound passenger train 25, properly warned by the flagman stationed about 3,200 feet north of the north switch and by a torpedo which had been placed about 500 feet south of that position, pulled cautiously into Vaughan station and stopped. After 25 had passed the north switch, the two freight trains "sawed" back north, clearing the main track at the south switch, but putting the rear of 83 out on the main line at the north switch. Then 25 proceeded south toward Canton. The two freights remained in a "north-saw" position, so as to leave the main line clear for No. 2 to pull past the south switch and proceed past the station. This gave the two freights time to "saw south." The moment the main line was clear and the north switch was properly set, No. 2 sped north to meet Casey's "Cannonball" at Goodman, 14 miles up the line, which it did. The freights were then in a position to enable Casey's approaching "Cannonball" to enter Vaughan and run down past the station while the freights executed the "north saw" to give the fast train a clear track south.

The freights would no doubt have remained in their "south-saw" positions had it not been for the arrival of two sections of Chicago-bound passenger No. 26, due at Vaughan at 1:05 A.M. Hurriedly the freights were "sawed north" to enable the two sections of 26 to take the business track and thus get out of the way of the "Cannonball." This done, the two freights started to "saw south" again, to make ready for Casey and the "Cannonball." But this move was delayed by the bursting of an air hose near the rear of No. 72. This left four cars of 83 fouling the main line at the north switch.

It was at this juncture that Casey's "Cannonball" came thundering down the two-mile stretch of main track approaching the curve just north of Vaughan. Casey pulled the throttle wide open to make up the last few minutes needed to put the "Cannonball" on time. Three thousand feet north of the north switch. Newberry waved his lantern frantically as Casey approached and shot past at seventy miles an hour. A few hundred feet beyond, Casey's engine detonated the torpedo which Newberry had placed on the track. The torpedo was heard by Casey's fireman, Sim Webb, by Newberry, and by other members of 83's crew. According to Webb, Casey applied the brakes and began to slow down immediately after passing the torpedo, but for some reason he failed to sound his famous whistle on passing the whistling board a few hundred feet beyond. On hearing the torpedo Sim went to the left side of the cab and peered into the darkness. Suddenly as they rounded the curve Sim saw the lights of 83's caboose on the track a few hundred feet ahead. He yelled to Casey to jump for his life. Casey applied the emergency brakes and yelled back: "You jump; I'll stay!"

> Fireman jumped, but Casey stayed on;
> He was a good engineer, but he's dead and gone!

Eye-witnesses estimated that Casey had reduced the speed from seventy to fifty miles an hour when Sim leaped, and in the next 300 feet Casey managed to cut the speed considerably more, but not enough to prevent the crash that turned his engine over on its side after demolishing the caboose and a car of hay and damaging two other cars loaded with hay and corn.

Casey had stuck to his post, and when his body was found in the wreckage of Engine 382, one hand was clutching the throttle and the other the air-brake control. Casey was the only person killed. No passenger or other member of the crew sustained more than slight injuries. And when the last rites for Casey Jones were said in the little church at Jackson, Tennessee, where he and Janie had pledged their troth fifteen years before, Casey's record of never having been in an accident which involved the loss of a fellow railway employee or a passenger still stood. Had Casey leaped when he had the opportunity, instead of sticking to his post and doing all he could to bring his passenger-laden train to a stop, his safety record might have been sadly different.

One question—never settled to this day—was why an alert and able engineer like Casey Jones did not heed the flagman's warning and slow down in ample time to bring his train to a full stop before reaching the north switch. The only explanation is that he had received orders to "saw" 83 and 72 at Vaughan and took it for granted that the north switch would be clear for the "Cannonball" to slow down all the way to the station. This would have been the case, according to Conductor J. R. Hoke of Train 72, had not the air hose burst on his train. Hoke made the further observation that "if the dispatcher had not given Casey the message at Durant that he would be 'sawed' at Vaughan, the chances are he would have stopped and picked up Flagman Newberry to ascertain the cause of his signal and would have avoided the accident."

But Casey Jones could not return to make his defense or give his version of the accident.

Probably the best immediate newspaper account of the accident was written by Adam Hauser, a passenger aboard the "Cannonball" and a former employee of the *New Orleans Times Democrat.* Hauser's account, which appeared in that newspaper on the day after the accident, said:

> If the speed of the train after the torpedoes went off was accurately judged by the mail clerk . . . Engineer Jones did a wonderful as well as an heroic piece of work, at the cost of his life. The trainmen said that he thought the torpedoes were for the south switch, and maybe they're right; and at any rate that theory puts the blame where it can do little harm, for Jones has finished his interpretation of train signals.

The marvel and mystery is how Engineer Jones stopped that train. The railroad men themselves wondered at it, and of course the uninitiated could not do less. But stop it he did, in a way that showed the complete mastery of his engine, as well as his sublime heroism.

And then Hauser added prophetically:

> I imagine that the Vaughan wreck will be talked about in roundhouses, lunchrooms, and cabooses for the next six months, not alone on the Illinois Central, but [on] many other roads in Mississippi and Louisiana.

Indeed it was talked about. But it was left for Wallace Saunders, a humble Negro engine-wiper in the Illinois Central shops, to bring immortality to the memory of Casey Jones. Saunders knew and loved the colorful and friendly engineer—thought he was the greatest engineer on the railroad—and when Saunders heard that his hero had been killed he began to chant, in a fashion characteristic of his race: "Casey Jones—Casey Jones . . . He was all right . . . Stuck to his duty both day and night . . . Casey Jones . . . Fireman say, Casey you'se runnin' too fast . . . out-run yo' signal last station yo' passed . . . Casey Jones. . . ."

Saunders' chantey, picked up and passed on in time by fellow workers, had gained wide circulation when one day a professional song writer "polished it up a little" by changing a word or line here and there, set it to music, and had it published. The ballad was a hit almost from the start, with the results already mentioned. Lee's biography of Casey Jones was followed by a full-length motion picture featuring the hero of the song. And in April, 1950, on the fiftieth anniversary of the dramatic incident described above, the Post Office Department issued a special postage stamp ["Honoring Railroad Engineers of America"] and bearing the likeness and name of Casey Jones—the first and only railroader ever to be so honored. All of which have had the effect of giving Casey Jones undying fame—along with such fabulous figures as Davy Crockett, Buffalo Bill, Johnny Appleseed, and "Wild Bill" Hickok—as one of the great characters of American folklore.

Casey Jones's Fireman

Sim Webb sits in the warm sunshine on the porch of his little shotgun house, sniffs the coal smoke drifting from the railroads to the west, and goes back in memory to that tragic night thirty-six years ago when death rode the Cannonball with Casey Jones and himself—

Casey Jones—mounted to his cabin—
  Casey Jones—with his orders in his hand—
Casey Jones—mounted to the cabin,
  Took a farewell trip to the Promised Land.

By Eldon Roark. From *Railroad Stories,* Vol. XIX (March, 1936), No. 4, pp. 36–38. Copyright, 1936, by the Frank A. Munsey Company, New York.

For the facts of Wallace Saunders' connection with *Casey Jones,* see p. 457n. below.

Sim was Casey's colored fireman. He was the man who kept No. 382 hot as they roared through the dark, ominous night, hitting eighty miles an hour at times while making up an hour and a half.

Sim is no longer a railroad man. In 1919 he asked for a leave of absence because of ill health—and he never went back. "But I see now I made a mistake," he says. He loved the life, and there are times when he gets mighty homesick. But now, of course, it is too late. Sim is still tall and straight and trim, but the years are beginning to creep up—he is 61—and there are little fingers of frost in his hair. . . .

Sim Webb grew up among the railroad shops and shanties at McComb, Mississippi. His father, John Webb, was with the Illinois Central Railroad for forty-eight continuous years as a carpenter. John Webb was able to provide well for his children, and Sim was sent to school in New Orleans. There he learned a trade—bricklaying—as well as reading, writing, and arithmetic. But young Sim was too crazy about locomotives to think about laying brick or doing something else equally unromantic. He just couldn't leave the railroad yards, and in time he got a job as a call boy. He held it down for more than a year, and then he started firing a switch engine.

Sim smilingly explains that he wasn't supposed to get a job like that till he was 21, of course, but on account of his father's fine record it was "all fixed for him." He fired there in the yards two years, and then came the big day when he was transferred to road service. For the next six years Sim fired freights on the Louisiana, Mississippi, and Tennessee Divisions of the IC.

January 1, 1900, John Luther (Casey) Jones and Sim were transferred from Water Valley to Memphis to go into passenger service. Up to that time Casey had been on freights with a white fireman named Wesley McKinney. Sim had never fired for Casey.

"The reason we were transferred," Sim explained, "was that Engineer William Hatfield and his colored fireman, George Lee, were giving up their run. Bill Hatfield was in poor health, and Lee was getting along in years. Firing a passenger in those days was considered hard and dangerous. Railroading wasn't as safe as it is now.

"We were assigned to No. One out of Memphis, known as the Chicago and New Orleans Fast Mail. Some folks called it the Cannonball, just like they called almost any fast train a cannonball. The run was to Canton, Mississippi, 188 miles. Then coming back we pulled No. Four.

"On the night Mr. Casey made his last run, we were called at Memphis at 10 P.M. That was Sunday, April 30th, 1900. No. One was reported to be thirty minutes late. We had doubled over on Mr. Sam Tate's run on No. Three and No. Two, and had come into Memphis that morning at 6:25. But that gave us time to get a good rest and get ready for our regular run, and we were both feeling good when we answered the call that night.

"We reported at the McLemore Avenue roundhouse and found old 382 hot and ready to go. The 382 was known as a ten-wheeler engine, with six drivers and four truck wheels. Well, we looked her over good, saw that we had tools, plenty of oil and everything, and got ready. The regular time for us to leave the Poplar Street depot, which was the main station in those days, was 11:35 P.M., and thirty minutes late would have put us out at 12:05. But it finally turned out that No. One was an hour and thirty minutes late.

"We got going, ran down the tracks along the river, over the Beale Street trestle, and on into the Central Station where we had to stop five minutes. We held a late order saying that we were running ninety minutes late from Memphis to Sardis. There was a freight train coming north, and that was the only thing in front of us.

"We had been having rainy, foggy weather for two weeks, and the clouds were mighty dark and low that night. But Mr. Casey's spirits were high. He seemed to be in an extra good mood. As we pulled out of Central Station he opened her up.

" 'We're going to have a pretty tough time going into Canton on time,' he said, 'but I believe we can do it, barring accidents.'

"And I replied: 'You can depend on me. I'll sure keep her hot.'

"Sardis was our first stop. That's about fifty miles. It took us one hour and two minutes from the Poplar Street Station in Memphis to Sardis, which included the stop at Central Station, Memphis. Our actual running time was between forty-five and forty-seven minutes.

"On south we roared, with everything working just fine. At some places we got to clipping off a mile every fifty seconds. Old 382 was steaming exceptionally well that night—and using very little fuel. I hadn't even taken down the top coal gate. We made Grenada—fifty miles from Sardis—in what seemed like no time.

"Then came Winona, twenty-three miles from Grenada, and next Durant, thirty-three miles from Winona. Everything was still going fine. We were whittling that lost time away to nothing, and Mr. Casey was still in high spirits. As we left Durant, he stood up and hollered to me over the boiler head. He said: 'Oh, Sim! The old girl's got her high-heeled slippers on to-night. We ought to pass Way on time.'

"Way was just six miles north of Canton, and he had it figured out that we'd be back on time when we hit there and could coast on in. We hadn't received any more orders.

"Well, what Mr. Casey hollored to me—that joke about the high-heeled slippers—was the last thing he ever said.

"Down the track we went, approaching Vaughan, which is twelve miles above Canton. Vaughan was at the lower end of a double 'S' curve. The north switch was just about the middle of the first 'S', and as we roared down on it I looked ahead and saw two big red lights. They appeared as big as houses to me, and I knew it was a train not in the clear.

"I could see the lights and Mr. Casey couldn't, because it was a deep curve to the fireman's side. I hollered to Mr. Casey, 'Look out! We're gonna hit something!'

"He was sitting down at the time. I heard him kick the seat out from under him and apply the brakes and emergency. About that time I swung down as low off the engine as I could and hit the dirt. When I came to thirty-five minutes later I was on the floor of the station. Mr. Casey was dead—broken all to pieces.

"Our engine had plowed through the caboose of the freight and two other cars—a car of corn and a car of hay. But the engine didn't leave the track. It was just stripped. They found Mr. Casey down by the back driving wheel of the engine—out in the clear. Our coal tender was turned at right angles across our boiler head, and one end of our mail car had climbed up on our water tank.

"Mr. Casey was the only one killed. Nobody else was even hurt very bad. I was just badly shaken up and bruised.

"What had happened was this: The freight had sawed No. 25 by just a little while before. No. 25 was a New Orleans-bound train, too, running from Jackson, Tennessee, to New Orleans by way of Water Valley. Well, the freight had pulled out some drawheads in sawing No. 25 by, and they hadn't got in the clear for our train. The caboose and two cars were out on the main line. The crew was chaining up the drawheads, and apparently had forgot to put out a flagman. There were two freights at Vaughan—one northbound and one southbound. The northbound was at the south switch.

"It was all too bad. Mr. Casey was a fine man—a good man to fire for. If you kept 'em hot for him, you got along. Running on time was his hobby. Like he said when we pulled out, 'We'll go into Canton on time.' We hit that caboose at 3:52 A.M., and we were due at Vaughan at 3:50. We would have passed Way on the dot.

"I was out of service about three months, and then I went back on that same run. Mr. Harry A. Norton took Mr. Casey's place."

Sim looked westward from his house at 246 Iowa Avenue, toward the railroad yards, and gazed at the smoke plumes.

"Since 1919 I've been laying brick, but work in the past few years has been mighty scarce. Yes, sir, I can see now I should never have left the road."

Jesus Garcia, the Hero of Nacozari

. . . On Nov. 7 each year, just about everyone except operating personnel on the National Railways of Mexico is given a holiday in commemoration of the hero who died on that day in 1907. . . .

From *Tracks,* Chesapeake and Ohio Railway Magazine, Vol. 35 (April, 1950), No. 4, pp. 3–5.

This is the story of the Hero of Nacozari:

It was a little past noon on Nov. 7, 1907, when Jesus Garcia seized the throttle of his engine in Nacozari's railroad yard and shouted to his fireman and brakemen:

"Go away . . . leave me alone!"

Then he rolled out of the yard to his death and to immortality, desperately hauling away two carloads of burning dynamite, enough to blow the whole place to smithereens.

Jesus Garcia was born in Hermosillo, in the Mexican state of Sonora, in 1883, one of seven brothers. The family moved to Nacozari, where a newly-discovered copper strike was attracting workers to the mines. In 1900, Garcia's father died and the boy went to work to help support his family. He applied for a position as fireman with the Moctezuma Copper Company, owner of the Nacozari Mining Railroad, and got the job.

The young fireman was especially fond of reading and when he could spare a little time, eagerly devoured heroic tales about daring men. Those stories undoubtedly influenced and prepared him for what one day would give him a place among railroading immortals.

Garcia displayed early signs of his courage and quick-wittedness. In time he was promoted to engineer. One day as he was inching his locomotive and its consist of ore cars down a steep grade to El Porvenir, seven miles from Nacozari, the air brakes failed and his train began to run wild. It took all of the young hogger's ability to keep the train from plunging to destruction. That bit of expert railroading won for him the good will of James Douglas, president of the company, who afterward considered Garcia one of his best friends.

At twenty-four, Garcia made a dashing young engineer. Strong, healthy, dark complexioned, he was good humored, enjoyed life and mixed easily with his railroad comrades in the little mining camp. And like many another young swain, he courted his sweetheart and fiancée Jesusita Soqui with *gallos* and *mañanita*. (*Gallo* is a serenade and *mañanita* is a special morning concert Mexicans give to amuse their friends on their birthdays.)

Garcia was something of a socialite, too. His presence was a must at every event and sometimes the engineer would report for work at six A.M., still wearing his best go-to-party clothes.

The Nacozari Mining Railroad's motive power consisted of two coal-burning locomotives, No. 2 and No. 3. On Nov. 7, 1907, after making three trips to the ore mine, Garcia was ordered down to the lower yard to bring back gondolas loaded with merchandise and two cars carrying dynamite for the mine.

A witness to the terrible blast that day tells how he was working in the engine pit in the lower yard when No. 2, driven by Garcia, approached and the engineer, with his usual good humor, motioned him to clear the track where the other Nacozari locomotive was being cleaned. Antonio Elizondo, the witness, moved the engine off the track. Garcia picked up his cars and started back up the hill.

The train had just reached the concentrating plant switch when an American named Phelps noticed that the dynamite in one of the cars was afire and called out to the train crew. The train stopped while brakemen frantically attempted to extinguish the fire. But to no avail. The blaze was growing and those near the scene raced about madly shouting hoarsely for help. Then over the uproar, a single voice cried out:

"Go away . . . leave me alone!"

It was the engineer, telling his men to seek safety for themselves. Garcia had made his decision.

The town of Nacozari lay just in front of the train. Garcia realized the explosion might come at any minute. As soon as one of the brakemen uncoupled the cars of merchandise, Garcia pulled away with the dynamite cars, and raced up the hillside as fast as his engine would go. Apparently, his intention was to reach a siding on a level stretch of track about three miles away.

Had Garcia hoped to jump from his death-laden train when he reached the siding? No one will ever know. The train was only 100 feet from the switch, and just opposite the section house, when the flames reached the percussion caps and Garcia, his locomotive and cars disappeared in an earth-splitting blast of fire, earth, and steel.

The explosion was heard miles away. Nacozari was shaken to its foundations. Thirteen persons were killed, among them Garcia, an American boy who had been waiting for a train and several members of the section workers' families.

Garcia's body was finally found, horribly broken and identified only by his short miner's boots. The engine and cars were almost totally destroyed. Many of their parts were found later in neighboring hills. Fortunately, the blast had occurred in a cut in the hillside and its walls had shielded Nacozari from the direct concussion. Had the explosion been any nearer the town, Nacozari would have been erased from the face of the earth. Jesus Garcia had sacrificed his own life to save his mother, his sweetheart, his family and the village where he had enjoyed life so much.

America's Casey Jones was a more glamorous figure as a mainline engineer than our Mexican hero, the gay, good-natured boss of a little mining railroad's switcher. To-day, Casey's fame has taken on a tinge of legend; probably few of those who chorus the famous song about him know the whole story of his exploit.

In Mexico, they don't call "come all you rounders" when Garcia's memory is celebrated. Instead, the big railroad offices shut down. Rows of silent desks in railroad terminals pay homage to him, while in chapels and cathedrals railroaders and their families offer a prayer for the young yard engineer who forty-three years ago challenged Death with the cry:

"Go away . . . leave me alone!"

New England Hurricane

Though it was not yet five P.M., daylight saving time, [September 21, 1938], darkness had fallen when I stuck my head out of the window to pick up a clear signal. *Maybe it won't ever come,* I was thinking. In the gloaming, however, a very faint clear board shone. We swished past Mystic at barely twenty miles an hour and were soon near the Stonington causeway, a strip of double track laid across an arm of the ocean on boulders and ballast. Creeping up on this structure, I could see that breakers were hitting the rocks and tumbling across the iron. As I distrusted those submarine rails, I brought Number 14 [*The Bostonian*] down to eight miles an hour. When we had navigated about half of the causeway, Dennis Horan, [my fireman], shouted: "Yellow board!"

"Yellow board it is," I replied.

Cutting down to the pace of a slug, I glanced at the water, now boiling over the track. You could feel the train shiver as waves smashed against the car sides. *Not a good place to be stopped,* I was thinking. *The track won't hold out.*

Just then it happened. When we were about six hundred feet from the mainland, a spot of red stabbed me in the eye. My heart sank as I cut out the air and let the brakes clamp down.

"In a jam," runs a certain motto, "a rail should keep his head and use it." Here was a chance to test my saying before the water reached the fire box. Seconds were precious. I pulled down the whistle cord; but the shrieks could not have reached the towerman, as the signal stayed red.

"There's only one thing to do," I said to Denny. "With luck I'll get to the tower."

Down the rungs I climbed into the knee-deep, boiling briny. Surf sprayed and blinded me, soaked me to the skin. As the wind caught at my clothes, I wrapped my fingers around the streamlined apron, feeling my way in the dark over dubious ground to the pilot. Then I walked out into the hurricane.

From "New England Hurricane," by Harry W. Easton, *Railroad Magazine,* Vol. 32 (July, 1942), No. 2, pp. 76–79. Copyright, 1942, by the Frank A. Munsey Company. New York.

For every step I took forward, the wind blew me back a yard. Two or three times I stumbled. A storm-driven log cracked me in the knee and threw me down, almost submerged, but instinct set me on my feet and pointed me toward the red signal. At length I slogged ashore, bruised and dripping, almost out of breath.

The tower looked like some gaunt ruin of No Man's Land, for all of its windows had been blown out. Upstairs I found the towerman, H. F. Thomas, staring at glass scattered over the floor mixed with books and records, while the wind continued to blast through the windows, shaking the structure to its foundations.

"You've got to give me a signal to get off the causeway," I shouted. "Our train is about ready to topple into the ocean."

"Okay," he yelled back, "but don't go beyond the station. Too much risk!" When I left the tower, so quickly was the water rising that the ground had turned into a waist-deep torrent. Six hundred feet to the rear my headlight was a lonely beacon. I waved a signal to Denny to come ahead, but was disappointed. He evidently couldn't see it. Plunging ahead for a long way, I observed that several of our coaches were leaning far over toward the seas.

"What are you going to do?" asked Conductor Barton, who had come up to the locomotive.

"Get out of here," I replied, "whether there are any tracks or not. The passengers don't sense the danger. Herd them into the deadhead baggage car, and we'll cut it off."

As I stepped around the cab, water gurgled from my shoes and my clothes dripped like sponges. The crew went through the cars chanting, "Everybody up front and make it snappy!"

As the two hundred and seventy-five passengers poured into the aisles, some began to shove; others opened doors and leaped into four feet of moving water. I saw a Negro porter wading waist-deep with a small child on each shoulder and a woman clinging to his coat tails. He got them safely aboard the baggage car. We did not know it then, but one of the dining-car employees lost his life when he plunged in to save a drowning woman. The name of Chester A. Walker has been added to the long list of railroad heroes.

Up to the cab came John Greenwood, the flagman. "We'll have to move fast," he said grimly. "The roadbed is gone from under the three rear cars."

By that time Denny, Barton, and a trainman named W. F. Moore were boosting passengers up on the engine, since the baggagemaster, A. N. Layton, could not find another inch of space in his car. People were crowding into the cab, perching on the tank, clinging to the hand-rails. When Barton had made a rough count of passengers and crew, a car inspector named Arthur D. Dooley tried to unlock the couplers; but there was no slack and he couldn't lift the pin. Several men floundered about trying to loosen the couplers.

Some one came wading in water almost to his chin. We recognized him as William Donoghue, general chairman of the Engineers' Brotherhood for the New Haven. Seeing the trouble, he swam between the two cars and tried to budge the couplers.

"Give me a lift!" he yelled to three trainmen. They pulled him into the vestibule. "Hang on to me!" he ordered. Lying flat on the vestibule floor, Donoghue shoved his hands into the water and tautened his muscles until, with a mighty tug, he loosened the jaws of steel and set us free.

As Conductor Barton gave the highball, large hunks of debris were whirling in front of the pilot. I pulled back the throttle, but we had barely started when—*bang!* A booming to the rear was followed by a jolt which rocked the engine and brought us to a dead stop. Some floating colossus had struck the baggage car, fouled the train airline, and locked the brakes in emergency. Some one behind me sobbed, pounded my back, and entreated: "Please make him go, mister!"

I turned around to see a gray-haired, elderly lady whose eyes were dilated with terror. Faces of other passengers were drawn and white. They were counting on me, but the waves seemed to taunt, "Pull through if you can." Again I shoved the throttle. The engine bellowed an angry staccato as her drivers churned, but the locked brakes held. Angrily I pulled the throttle back as far as it would go. The big modern engine bolted, groaned, and to my great relief slowly moved, dragging the car despite its locked wheels.

A light rowboat drifted into our path; we cracked it like a shell. Something began to drag us. Telegraph wires, thrown down by the storm, were tangled around our boiler. A mass of them held us in their fingers, slowing the beat of our exhaust, but they quickly let go as we snapped the pole. Water was now rising close to the firebox, sparks were shooting from the stack as the engine put forth her noblest efforts, drivers churning like the side wheels of an old-time steamboat.

Just as I thought all might be clear, a large hulk loomed in the darkness ahead. Several passengers spoke in alarm: "What is it?"

My heart sank when I saw it was a house which the storm had thrown on our track. I kept right on, thinking: *If I can't shove this house out of the way, we're cooked.* We neared the rising and falling structure until our pilot gently touched it. The cab shivered and windows rattled, but we kept on pushing, and every muscle in my body grew tighter. The hulk turned just a little and stopped. Then the gale caught the house and drove it into fast-gliding water, which carried it crazily out to sea.

Crates, logs, and small boats kept smashing against our pilot. Just as I thought the worst might be over, something heavy thumped the front end. A full-sized sailboat, tilted to one side, was lodged on the track. The old woman began to cry.

"If we can take care of a house, we can handle a ship," I consoled her; but the vessel disputed our efforts. Slowly our wheels ground forward. The boat was firmly wedged. Slower came our exhaust beat, then faster as the drivers spun free. My hand could feel the deep vibration as the engine's power drove against the heavy barrier of wood. Timbers grunted. Spray was dashing over the passengers who clung to the hand-rails; wind was lashing at them. We were stopped now, maybe for the last time.

But no; something snapped—I don't know what. The craft revolved sickly, turned bottom up, and began humping rapidly for shore. That boat started a rumor that Train Number 14 had been struck by a ship and demolished with heavy loss of life. This threw the general offices into a panic which lasted till wire service was restored.

Roaring her triumph, the big engine nosed ashore and passed the signal tower, now pierced with holes. When I looked back I could see sparks streaming from the wheels, but I kept right on to the crossing near the station before I stopped and thanked God we were safe. The lady beside me was smiling and wiping her eyes. Bedraggled passengers jumped out of the baggage car, among them a dapper gentleman who flopped into a puddle three feet deep and emerged a mass of mud. We just had to laugh.

None of us will ever forget the kindly people of Stonington, Conn., blasted though it was by the elements. They threw open their homes, halls, and churches for us. In a few hours the winds had died, but the storm had made such a hash of the roadbed between Providence and Bristol, R. I., that no trains could run over it for three weeks. . . . At Providence the waters had risen so fast that several people were trapped and drowned near the Union Station.

To-day I'm handling a juice engine between New Haven and New York. So many kind things have been said about the causeway run that I ought to explain. The credit belongs to an old lady who kept pounding me on the back and urging: "Please make him go, mister!"

The Runaway Federal Express

It was the night of January 14, 1953, 11 o'clock. No. 173, the *Federal Express,* was off on time for its 459-mile 8-hour 40-minute overnight run to the nation's capital. It was a routine beginning to what apparently was a routine trip. But at 8:38 the next morning in the Union Terminal in Washington the *Federal* was to turn into a hurtling juggernaut, a train out of control.

Abridged from "Runaway," by E. John Long, in *Trains and Travel,* Vol. 13 (August, 1953), No. 10, pp. 18–23. Copyright, 1953, by Kalmbach Publishing Co. Milwaukee, Wis.

Inspectors noticed nothing wrong with the *Federal* during its 15-minute stop at Providence. It pulled out of the depot at 12:05 A.M., on time.

But then the flagman noticed a few sharp jerks—brakes were sticking somewhere on the train. It seemed to be the rear two cars. He told Conductor Ralph Ward, who pulled the communicating cord. The *Federal* ground to a stop at Kingston Swamp, 27 miles out of Providence.

Ward made a rapid check along his train. The brakes on the two rear cars were very hot. He bled them off and signaled for a series of brake tests. Meanwhile Engineer Matta had sent the fireman back to see what was going on. The fireman decided that everything was all right and returned to the engine, telling Matta that it was O.K. to go ahead. But the train wouldn't budge.

Matta himself left the engine and found that the brakes on the first three cars were released but those beyond were jammed. He soon located the trouble—the angle cock was closed at the rear of the third car. The angle cock is the valve which closes the main brake pipe at each end of each car. With the valve closed, the brakes behind the third car were inoperative. Something or someone had closed the valve since the *Federal* had left Providence.

Matta figured the rear car brakes had remained off while the normal air pressure was in the trainline; but when air had leaked out and could not be replaced from the engine, the brakes automatically had begun to take hold.

At any rate, it was an easy matter to open the valve again, which Matta did. In a few minutes all the brakes released. Conductor Ward, puzzled as to the cause of the trouble, was working his way forward, examining the brakes and other equipment of each car. Before he reached the troublesome third car he was told the difficulty had been found. The flagman was whistled in and the *Federal* proceeded, 56 minutes late. Matta promptly made up 11 minutes of the loss in the 86-mile stretch to New Haven, Conn., using the brakes several times. They worked fine.

At New Haven the diesels came off and an electric locomotive was put on. Matta, the diesel engineer, switched his unit off without seeing Conductor Ward—who was continuing on to New York—or the new engineer. But this does not necessarily seem to be a dangerous act. The first engineer on the New Haven discovered the closed angle cock, and subsequent use of the brakes indicated that he had satisfactorily remedied the cause of the brakes' sticking on the rear cars. He had no particular reason to believe that his experience would be of value to other crews of the train on its journey to Washington, nor was he required to make such a report.

Two sleepers and a coach were added to the *Federal* at New Haven, bringing the consist up to 16 cars. While his men were making their inspection of the train, Chief Car Inspector William Pennepaker asked Ward why he was so late. Ward explained that the brakes on the rear Pullmans were sticking. Pennepaker says he was not told about the closed angle cock. However, he and his assistants made an extra check of all the brakes and found everything in order. He was certain that all angle cocks were noted.

With Engineer John D. Rowland at the controller, the *Federal* raced down the four-track Shore Line, blue sparks from the catenary lighting up the dark Connecticut countryside. Clipping minute after minute off the Kingston handicap, Rowland popped out of the East River tube into Pennsylvania Station, New York, at 4:28 A.M., only 38 minutes late. During the 75-mile trip he applied the brakes 14 times and they functioned perfectly.

Rowland's motor was uncoupled and run into a siding; Pennsylvania Railroad GG-1 electric No. 4876 was backed on. Harry W. Brower, the engineer, did not see Rowland nor was he told why the train was late. However, he did make the usual terminal check of the brakes and found them fine.

Between New York and Baltimore, with stops at Philadelphia and Wilmington, Brower applied the brakes 14 times. He had no trouble. At Baltimore the *Federal* had gained another three minutes. Once clear of the yard limit, Brower gave the big electric the gun. He bareled along at the usual 80-mile-an-hour clip. With clear signals all the way, Brower had no occasion to use the brakes.

Not until he saw ahead of him signal 1339, a little more than two miles out of Washington Union Station, did Brower make the first brake application. At this time his estimated speed was 60 to 70 miles an hour. As the engine flashed past the signal the cab signal changed to "Approach" and the signal whistle sounded until Brower acknowledged it with a movement of a lever. Brower moved the controller from the tenth or twelfth notch to the fifth, and made a split-pipe reduction of 17 pounds in the brake pipe. He did not notice that the exhaust from the brake valve was unusually short. The train slowed a little on the slight upgrade but not enough for a safe approach to the interlocking just ahead.

"I looked out and thought, 'This isn't holding at all,' " Brower recalls.

By now the train was a half mile beyond the signal. Brower quickly threw the controller off, opened the sander valve, and set the automatic brake valve in emergency. This action should have jammed all brakes and brought the *Federal* to a jarring halt. But the exhaust from the brake valve was only a short sigh. Emergency had little or no effect. The *Federal Express* was without brakes!

Around the bend and under the New York Avenue overpass the *Federal* swayed, cresting the rise and beginning the downgrade to the station. Brower was certain now that his train was out of control. He called to Fireman John W. Moyer and began to sound the engine's pneumatic horn. Moyer had already noticed the excessive speed. When he saw Brower sweating with the controls and heard him call, Moyer threw the emergency valve on his side of the cab. No exhaust, no brakes!

Meanwhile the 66-year-old veteran engineer stuck by his throttle. He had no idea what was wrong, except that his brakes weren't holding. He gritted his teeth and hoped for a miracle. As his engine lurched past C Tower, Brower again yanked at the whistle cord. Raucous blasts, one after another in quick succession, shattered the morning air. To those who saw the heavy train racing into the complicated pattern of track it added up to the one word that railroaders dread most: *runaway!*

Let Brower describe the next few seconds: "When I came under New York Avenue I started to blow the horn on the engine to notify people that we couldn't hold the train, to scare them away from the platform. . . . I was just hoping something would stop her. . . ."

Back in the train, Conductor Thomas J. Murphey heard the warning whistle at about the same time that he realized the train was rolling altogether too fast. Murphey was in the ill-fated third car. As luck would have it he hastened to the front vestibule and opened the conductor's back-up valve. Had he gone to the fourth car or been in the fourth car or beyond and opened the valve, the train might have been slowed or perhaps even stopped when he let out the air from the line holding the brakes released in the last 13 cars.

As it was, Murphey unfortunately got no brake action at all. "There was no air in the line," he said. "I warned the passengers in this [third] coach to lie on the floor or hold their seats, that the train was out of control. That was the best I could do."

Brakeman Fred E. King, in the fourth car, was about to lock the toilet when a sudden swerve of the train threw him off his feet. "When I got myself straightened out . . . I headed right back to the rear platform. I glanced outside and realized that we had no brakes and were not stopping. I made an attempt for that [emergency brake] valve on the platform. By that time we were coming into the interlocking right there at C Tower. It threw me around and I do not know whether I really did get that valve on. . . . I could not stay on my feet, to be frank about it."

It is apparent that King did not succeed in opening the valve. Asked later if he heard the warning blasts from the engine, he was not sure.

Far back at the rear of the train Flagman John H. Meng heard no whistle, but he knew something was wrong when the brakes did not begin to grind. At the time he was in the center of the rear car, a sleeper. Because passengers were in the aisle preparing to leave the train, he was unable to reach the emergency valve at either end before the crash came. As the train whipped through a crossover "the car swayed violently . . . causing me to lose my balance," he said.

Thus far the train crew had been waging a lone battle to save the train and passengers. To make matters worse, the mile from C Tower to K Tower descends at a grade of 0.73 per cent. Engineer Brower felt he had operating brakes on the engine and maybe the head car. The rest of the heavy train seemed to be pushing them to destruction. He attempted to reverse the motors, but the overload relays blew and his last hope was gone.

As No. 173 rolled down the home stretch, however, Train Director Harry S. Ball in C Tower made a split-second decision. The *Federal's* route had been set up along main track No. 41, then through a facing-point crossover to track 40, which becomes station track 16. The stub of track 16 is in the exact center of the station's concourse. A worse possible target for a runaway could hardly be imagined!

Ball knew there was no way to line up a new route to shunt the juggernaut into a siding. Once the interlocking is set, it takes several minutes to change the switches and signals. Ball had only seconds to act. He grabbed the phone. K Tower was just beyond the crossover. If the train hit the crossover too hard, it might jump the track and plow into the tower.

John W. Feeney, train director at K, answered the phone. He heard Ball shout, "One-seventy-three's out of control! She's running away!" If anything more was said it was lost in the frantic bleating of the onrushing engine's horn. The train lurched drunkenly on the crossover, but it did not leave the rails. Onward it rushed, sparks flying from its engine's wheels.

Seconds were precious. Feeney snatched the phone to the stationmaster's office. Although it was slowing, the racing monster had only 1500 feet to go! When Clerk R. A. Klopp answered, the usually calm and imperturbable Feeney wasted no words: "There's a runaway coming at you on track 16—get to hell outa there!"

Klopp didn't wait to look. He knew the train was aimed right at where he and the others in the office were sitting. "I yelled at the others in the office. I ran into the telegraph room next door and shouted at them to get out. I ran out the door and saw the train bearing down just a few car-lengths away, and I yelled at the people standing at the gate."

The careening engine smashed the stationmaster's office, completely demolished the newsstand, and just when it seemed certain that it would plow right into the waiting room, the floor of the concourse suddenly gave way. Like a dying animal, the heavy engine sank into the basement baggage room, dragging two cars with it. From the jumbled confusion of the hole great clouds of dust and steam billowed. There was a moment of strange stunned silence.

Klopp, meanwhile, was running to a telephone booth. Before the terminal's chief operator could learn what caused the earthquake-like shock she had felt, Klopp was urging her to send fire and rescue squads. Moments later, while others still gazed dazedly at the wreck, Klopp was in the station drug store carrying out a plea from nurses and doctors to get all the morphine he could.

The nimble wits, resourcefulness and devotion to duty of a handful of railroaders, plus a large measure of luck, prevented a major tragedy and loss of life that morning. . . . By a miracle no one was in the baggage room directly under the engine. The injured totaled 87, one being the fireman. Property damage was estimated at nearly a million dollars.

Clocks in the stationmaster's office stopped at 8:38 A.M., setting the time of the accident. The *Federal,* therefore, had arrived only 18 minutes late!

For the Washington Terminal Company, the short-line railroad operating Union Station, the accident could not have come at a worse time. Swarms of visitors were pouring into the city for General Dwight D. Eisenhower's inauguration five days later. But by sundown more than 600 men, including expert wreckers and engineers, were hard at work cleaning up the mess.

The plunging locomotive severed some of the station's power cables, so as darkness fell the job proceeded in the eerie glow of portable floodlights punctuated by the glare of acetylene torches and sparks from portable saws. It was a strange, unearthly sight to those arriving in a holiday mood for the week's festivities. When they learned that Washington had also had an explosion in a battery-service plant and a collision between two ambulances the same day, one of the visitors asked facetiously if this were "the departing Democrats' scorched-earth policy."

Most of the train could be hauled back to the yard, but the two coaches that had followed the engine into the hole had to be coaxed out inch by inch with cables strung from giant cranes. It was an all night job.

By 7 o'clock the following morning, however, all rolling stock except the locomotive had been removed from the scene of the accident. Like a housewife confronted with an unexpected emergency with company coming, Wreckmaster J. F. Swafford decided to sweep the engine under the rug. His crews lowered the locomotive fully into the basement and built a temporary plank floor right over it. A newsstand appeared as if by magic on the flooring. Wooden grille painted to match the steel train fence and gates went up at the same time.

In 72 hours only a keen observer would have known where the accident occurred, thanks to a truly remarkable bit of reconstruction. By January 28, the last piece of the locomotive was removed from the basement. They couldn't do it sooner, according to inaugural wits, because no one could find the baggage check for the engine!

How did the wreck affect inauguration traffic schedules? "Hardly at all, except for some slight delays on the 15th itself," said S. Kerl, manager of the Washington Terminal Company. "In fact, the whole thing put the Terminal boys on their mettle. As a result we had the most successful handling of heavy extra traffic in the station's history."

* * * * *

The *Federal's* runaway was historic also because, in the words of one veteran railroader who surveyed the scene, "It just couldn't happen! Brake valves just don't do those things!" Yet they did, twice on the same run! Railroaders will be debating about that for years to come. But they will also be recalling with probable pride that, thanks to a few brave and alert souls, death did not ride the rails that day!

PART TWO

Apprentice Years

Introduction

"The year 1835," wrote Charles Francis Adams, Jr., in 1880, "marked an historical dividing line. The world we now live in came into existence then; and, humanly speaking, it is in almost every essential respect, a different world from that lived in by the preceding six generations." [1]

In naming 1835 as the turning point, Adams was thinking of Boston, which completed its first three little railroads in that year. For other parts of the Atlantic seaboard, the time came a little earlier. For Albany and Philadelphia, for Baltimore and Charleston, it was 1830–31, when their first little locomotives tottered forth like babies just learning to walk. But these were all parts of the same epochal Rubicon of "Operation by Trial and Error" through which the young Nation plunged with the light-hearted determination, the quick perceptiveness and grasp of technic which became characteristic of America.

But this quick trend to railroads had not been achieved without loud but unavailing vocal opposition. The Nation had just gone through three increasingly vigorous decades of canal building, and for many, inland waterways seemed to carry the promise of national future prosperity. This belief had been strengthened in recent years by the coming of steam navigation. But the anti-railroad group was swept aside in the wave of enthusiasm set going by the steam locomotive. Here people rightly saw the real developer of the Nation.

"No generation had yet grown up accustomed to wealth from its birth," continued Adams. "There was no class of men of leisure. The railroad changed all this. Business vocations not only diversified themselves, but they increased in volume. New branches of industry came into existence. A wholly new America was meanwhile shaping itself. New York remained the financial center of the whole; but Chicago, in 1835 a mere outpost town on the shores of Lake Michigan, was transformed into the chief distributing point" of a vast interior.

Railroading began to be something of a prideful profession; it began to accumulate a lore. A passion for traveling had quickly developed among the populace. "The Americans are indeed a locomotive people," mused the editor of *Ariel,* a literary magazine. They were joined by great numbers of European tourists, especially British, many of whom wrote books that give a vivid, often comic picture of the years when we were learning how to operate railroads and build equipment. They were often, but not always, critical; they were enthusiastic, for example, over our system of baggage checking, long unknown in England.

And then came the War Between the States ("The Iron Horse Goes

[1] "The Canal and Railroad Enterprise of Boston," in *The Memorial History of Boston,* by Justin Winsor (Boston, 1881), Vol. IV, pp. 148–150.

to War"), to which the railroad promptly adapted itself. This was the first war in history in which the railroad played a large part—moving troops, moving ordnance, equipment and provender, carrying out or thwarting the plans of generals. Adversely, locomotives, cars, track and bridges were destroyed ruthlessly and recreated with marvelous celerity. Bridges hundreds of feet long and high were rebuilt in 24 to 48 hours, so that heavy trains rolled over them in safety. When the war ended, the South was left with an almost ruined railway system, which impeded its recovery by many years. Another effect of the war was the creation of the tramp (the word "hobo" originated later). Thousands of men, torn from long-established moorings, made restless by four years of motion and excitement, became drifters, a nuisance and a menace to the railroads, which were affected in another way, too; some of their employes became "boomers," that footloose, capricious type who never stay long on any job, disturbing yet likable phenomena to this day.

Meanwhile, the great westward movement of population and railroads, following "The Advancing Frontier," was steadily under way. Even during the war the transcontinental line was being planned; all through the latter 1860's the flying hammers of Irish and Chinese navvys drove the railheads of the Pacific Railway westward and eastward. Their joining at Promontory in 1869 was an event which still looms large in our literature and legend. But it was no more significant than the spreading in those post-war years of the great iron network, steadily changing to steel, over the vast central valley, to the Mississippi, to the Rockies, and beyond them to the coast, planting little germs of population or nourishing villages into great cities—St. Paul, Minneapolis, Omaha, Kansas City, Denver, San Francisco, Portland, Seattle; tapping every field, mine and forest in the valley and beyond it, carrying their products to market and bringing other markets to their doors; taming the wilderness, building new States. No other Nation on the globe in all history has such a railroad story.

In such high-powered development as this, there must inevitably be clashes, "Grand Strategy," among the promoters, the empire-builders, and between them and the city and state governments which sometimes wisely, sometimes unwisely, sought to curb their activities. The great promoters may not have been saints, but while building their own fortunes, they also contributed towards the building of the Nation, to an extent equalled by few, if any, other groups.

A. F. H.

I. OPERATION BY TRIAL AND ERROR

A Canal Stockholder's Outburst

"I see what will be the effect of it; it will set the whole world a-gadding. Twenty miles an hour, sir! Why, you will not be able to keep an apprentice boy at his work; every Saturday evening he must take a trip to Ohio to spend the Sabbath with his sweetheart. Grave, plodding citizens will be flying about like comets. All local attachments will be at an end. It will encourage flightiness of intellect. Veracious people will turn into the most immeasurable liars; all their conceptions will be exaggerated by their magnificent notions of distance. 'Only a hundred miles off? Tut, nonsense, I'll step across, madam, and bring your fan!' 'Pray, sir, will you dine with me today at my little box at Allegheny?' 'Why, indeed, I don't know. I shall be in town until twelve. Well, I shall be there; but you must let me off in time for the theatre.' And then, sir, there will be barrels of pork and cargoes of flour, and chaldrons of coal, and even lead and whisky and such-like sober things, that have always been used to sober traveling, whisking away like a set of sky-rockets. It will upset all the gravity of the nation. If two gentlemen have an affair of honor, they have only to steal off to the Rocky Mountains, and there no jurisdiction can touch them. And then, sir, think of flying for debt! A set of bailiffs mounted on Bomb-shells would not overtake an absconded debtor, only give him a fair start. Upon the whole, sir, it is a pestilential, topsy-turvy, harum-scarum whirligig. Give me the old solemn, straightforward, regular Dutch canal—three miles an hour for expresses and two for ordinary journeys, with a yoke of oxen for a heavy load. I go for beasts of

This appeared, with variations, in several newspapers, one of the earliest to print it being the *Western Sun* of Vincennes, Indiana, July 24, 1830.

burden; it is more primitive and scriptural, and suits a moral and religious people better. None of your hop-skip-and-jump whimsies for me!"

The Wagoner's Curse on the Railroad

This ballad dramatizes the Conestoga wagoners' plight when the railroad doomed their calling. I first learned of it in the twenties when a copy of the text came to me from an anonymous correspondent in Lancaster County [Pennsylvania]. An accompanying note explained that it was sung to the tune of "Green on the Cape." Later, after a determined search for other versions, I located an old man, the son of a miller who had done business with Conestoga wagoners. He supplied the following text and tune:

May the devil get the fellow that invented the plan.
It'll ruin us poor wag'ners and every other man.
It spoils our plantations wherever it may cross,
And it ruins our markets, so we can't sell a hoss.

If we go to Philadelphia, inquiring for a load,
They'll tell us quite directly it's gone out on the railroad.
The rich folks, the plan they must justly admire,
But it ruins us poor wag'ners and it makes our taxes higher.

Our states they are indebted to keep them in repair,
Which causes us poor wag'ners to curse and to swear.
It ruins our landlords, it makes business worse,
And to every other nation it has only been a curse.

From "Conestoga Wagoners," by Howard C. Frey, in *Pennsylvania Songs and Legends,* edited by George Korson, pp. 255–257. Copyright, 1949, by University of Pennsylvania Press. Philadelphia.

It ruins wheelwrights, blacksmiths, and every other trade.
So damned be all the railroads that ever was made.
It ruins our mechanics, what think you of it, then?
And it fills our country full of just a lot of great rich men.

The ships they will be coming with Irishmen by loads,
All with their picks and shovels, to work on the railroads;
When they get on the railroad, it is then that they are fixed;
They'll fight just like the devil with their cudgels and their sticks.

The American with safety can scarcely ever pass,
For they will blacken both his eyes for one word of his sass.
If it wasn't for the torment I as lief would be in hell,
As upon the cursed railroad, or upon the canal.

Come, all ye bold wag'ners, that have got good wives;
Go home to your farms and there spend your lives.
When your corn is all cribbed and your small grain is sowed,
You'll have nothing else to do but just to curse the damned railroad.

By Treadmill and Sail

. . . A competitor that steam had to contend with on the Baltimore & Ohio Railroad was "horse-power." A horse was placed in a car and made to walk on an endless apron or belt, and to communicate motion to the wheels. . . . The machine worked indifferently well, but on one occasion, when drawing a car filled with editors and other representatives of the press, it ran into a cow, and the passengers, having been tilted out and rolled down an embankment, were naturally enough unanimous in condemning the contrivance. And so the horse-power car, after countless bad jokes had been perpetrated on the cowed editors, passed out of existence, and probably out of mind.

Following the horse-power car came the Meteor, a sailing vehicle, the invention of Mr. Evan Thomas. . . . The Baltimore & Ohio Railroad, being the first in operation in this country, and almost the first in the world for the transportation of passengers and merchandise, was visited by crowds from almost every portion of the United States, as well as from Europe. Among these was Baron Krudener, envoy from Russia, who, by invitation of Mr. Thomas, made an excursion on the sailing car, managing the sail himself. On his return from the trip, he declared he had never before traveled so agreeably. Mr. Thomas caused a model sailing-car to be constructed, which he presented to the baron, with the respects of the company, to be forwarded to the emperor. . . .

From *The History of the First Locomotives in America,* from Original Documents and the Testimony of Living Witnesses, by William H. Brown, pp. 123–124, 138–139. New York: D. Appleton and Company. 1874.

A sailing car, or a car propelled by the wind, was also tested in 1829–30. . . . We copy from the Charleston *Courier,* March 20, 1830:

SAILING ON LAND.—A sail was set on a car on our railroad yesterday afternoon, in the presence of a large concourse of spectators. Fifteen gentlemen got on board and flew off at the rate of twelve to fourteen miles an hour. Thirteen persons and three tons of iron were carried about ten miles an hour. The preparations for sailing were very hastily got up, and of course were not of the best kind; but owing to this circumstance, the experiment afforded high sport. The wind blew very fresh from about northeast, which, as a sailor would say, was "abeam," and would drive the car either way with equal speed. When going at the rate of about twelve miles an hour and loaded with fifteen passengers, the mast went by the board, with the sail and rigging attached, carrying with them several of the crew. The wreck was descried by several friendly shipmasters, who kindly rendered assistance by rigging a jury-mast, and the car was again soon put under way. During the afternoon the wind changed so as to bring it nearly ahead when going in one direction; but this did not stop the sport, as it was ascertained that the car would sail within four points of the wind. We understand it is intended by some of our seamen to rig a car properly, and shortly to exhibit their skill in managing a vessel on land.

Peter Cooper Builds "Tom Thumb"

The Baltimore & Ohio Railroad had run its tracks down to Ellicott's Mills, thirteen miles, and had laid "snakehead" rails, as they called them, strap rails, you know, and had put on horses. Then they began to talk about the English experiments with locomotives. But there was a short turn of 150 feet radius around Point of Rocks, and the news came from England that Stephenson said that no locomotive could draw a train on any curve shorter than a 900-foot radius. . . . The directors had a fit of the blues. I had naturally a knack of contriving, and I told the directors that I believed I could knock together a locomotive that would get the train around Point of Rocks. . . .[1]

So I came back to New York and got a little bit of an engine, about one-horse power (three and one-half inch cylinder and fourteen-inch stroke) and carried it back to Baltimore. I got some boiler iron and made a boiler about as big as an ordinary washboiler, and then how to connect the boiler[2] with the engine I didn't know. . . . I had an iron

Interview with Peter Cooper in *Boston Herald,* July 7, 1882.

[1] After a lapse of fifty years, Mr. Cooper's memory was at fault regarding the point which threatened to give the engines trouble. It was not the one officially designated by geographers as Point of Rocks; that point was not reached by the rails until several years later.

[2] For this boiler, made vertical, see E. R. Hewitt, *Those Were the Days* (New York, 1943), pp. 48-50.

foundry, and had some manual skill in working in it. But I couldn't find any iron pipes. The fact is, there were none for sale in this country. So I took two muskets and broke off the wood part, and used the barrels for tubing to the boiler. . . . I went into a coachmaker's shop and made the locomotive, which I called the "Tom Thumb," because it was so insignificant. I didn't intend it for actual service, but only to show the directors what could be done. I meant to show two things; first, that short turns could be made; and secondly, that I could get rotary motion without the use of a crank. I changed the movement from a reciprocating to a rotary motion. I got steam up one Saturday night; the president of the road and two or three gentlemen were standing by, and we got on the track and went out two or three miles. All were much delighted, for it opened up new possibilities for the road. I put the locomotive up for the night in a shed. All were invited to a ride Monday—a ride to Ellicott's Mills.

Monday morning, what was my grief and chagrin to find that some scamp had been there and chopped off all the copper from the engine and carried it away, doubtless to sell to some junk dealer. The copper pipe that conveyed the steam to the pistons was gone. It took me a week or more to repair it. Then . . . we started—six on the engine, and thirty-six on the car. It was a great occasion, but it didn't seem so important then as it does now. We went up an average grade of eighteen feet to the mile, and made the passage . . . to Ellicott's Mills in an hour and twelve minutes. We came back in fifty-seven minutes. Ross Winans, the president of the road and the editor of the Baltimore Gazette made an estimate of the passengers carried, and the coal and water used, and reported that we did better than any English road did for four years after that. The result of the experiment was that the bonds were sold at once and the road was a success.

A Setback for Steam

. . . This was in the summer of 1830, but the triumph of the "Tom Thumb" engine [on the B&O] was not altogether without a drawback. . . . The great stage proprietors of the day were Stockton and Stokes; and on that occasion a gallant gray, of great beauty and power, was driven by them from town, attached to another car on the second track—for the company had begun by making two tracks to Ellicott's Mills—and met the engine at the Relay House, on its way back. From

---

From *The History of the First Locomotives in America,* from Original Documents and the Testimony of Living Witnesses, by William H. Brown, pp. 119–120. New York: D. Appleton and Company. 1874.

Related by H. B. Latrobe, famous engineer and counsellor of the B&O, who was a passenger on the train.

this point it was determined to have a race home; and the start being even, away went horse and engine, the snort of the one and the puff of the other keeping time and time.

At first the gray had the best of it, for his *steam* would be applied to the greatest advantage on the instant, while the engine had to wait until the rotation of the wheels set the blower to work. The horse was perhaps a quarter of a mile ahead when the safety-valve of the engine lifted and the thin blue vapor issuing from it showed an excess of steam. The blower whistled, the steam blew off in vapory clouds, the pace increased, the passengers shouted, the engine gained on the horse, soon it lapped him—the silk was applied—the race was neck and neck, nose and nose—then the engine passed the horse and a great hurrah hailed the victory. But it was not repeated, for just at this time, when the gray's master was almost giving up, the band which drove the pulley, which moved the blower, slipped from the drum, the safety-valve ceased to scream, and the engine, for want of breath, began to wheeze and pant. In vain Mr. Cooper, who was his own engineer and fireman, lacerated his hands in attempting to replace the band upon the wheel; in vain he tried to urge the fire with light wood; the horse gained on the machine and passed it, and, although the band was presently replaced, and steam again did its best, the horse was too far ahead to be overtaken, and came in the winner of the race.

What Happened to the "Best Friend"

Mr. W. H. Brown
Dear Sir:

. . . In the spring of 1830, Mr. E. I. Miller of our city entered into a contract to furnish the South Carolina Railroad with a locomotive that should travel ten miles an hour and draw three times its own weight. Under this contract Mr. Miller brought out his engine ("Best Friend") which was built at the West Point Foundry in New York City. . . .

When I run the best friend I had a Negro fireman to fire, clean, and grease the machine. This Negro, annoyed at the noise occasioned by the blowing off the steam, fastened the valve-lever down and sat upon it, which caused the explosion, badly injuring him, from the effects of which he died afterward, and scalding me. . . .

Yours with great respect,
Nicholas W. Darrell,
First Superintendent of Machinery,
South Carolina Railroad

Charleston, Sept. 2, 1869.

Ibid., pp. 150–151.

For some time after this accident, a flat car loaded with baled cotton was coupled between the locomotive and passenger cars, for the safety of the passengers. A small circular design picturing this arrangement was made by a New York engraver for the South Carolina Railroad's checks, bonds and stock certificates; and the engravers continued to use this design on the documents of other railroads, even in the North, far from the cotton country and long after the fear of explosion had subsided.

The "DeWitt Clinton" Launches the Mohawk & Hudson Railroad

This locomotive, the "DeWitt Clinton," stood upon the track [at Albany], already fired up and with a train of some five or six passenger coaches attached to it. (Two only were represented in our sketch, from lack of room.) These passenger coaches were of the old-fashioned stage-coach pattern, with a driver's seat or box upon either end outside. They had hitherto been used upon the road for passengers, and drawn by horse-power. At this early day, when the road was just built, passengers took a car at the foot of the inclined plane in Albany and were drawn up by a stationary engine to the top of the hill, where the regular track commenced. Horses were then hitched to the cars and proceeded to the other end of the road, where another inclined plane lowered the cars into Schenectady.

. . . A tin horn was sounded, and the word was given, "All aboard," by Mr. John T. Clark, the master of transportation, who acted as conductor. No such officer as conductor had been required upon a railroad before locomotives and long trains of cars were adopted. Before this event, in place of conductors the drivers of the single-horse cars collected the tickets or fares as omnibus drivers do at the present time.

[After the omnibus-shaped cars in the train] the remainder of the cars on the train were surmounted with seats made of rough plank to accommodate the vast crowd of anxious expectants assembled to witness the experiment and participate in this first ride on a railroad train drawn by a locomotive. The cars were crowded inside. Not an available position was unoccupied. Two persons stood ready for every place where one could be accommodated, and the train started on its route, leaving hundreds of the disappointed standing around.

As there were no coverings or awnings to protect the deck passengers upon the tops of the cars from the sun, the smoke, and the sparks, and as it was in the hot season of the year, the combustible nature of

Ibid., pp. 170–174.

their garments, summer coats, straw hats, and umbrellas soon became apparent, and a ludicrous scene was enacted among the outside excursionists before the train had run the first two miles.

* * * * *

On this first excursion [in the State of New York] on the 9th day of August, 1831 . . . Mr. John T. Clark, as the first passenger conductor in the North, stepping from platform to platform outside the cars, collected the tickets which had been sold at hotels and other places throughout the city. When he finished his tour, he mounted upon the tender attached to the engine, and sitting upon the little buggy-seat, as represented in our sketch, he gave the signal with a tin horn and the train started on its way. But how shall we describe that start, my readers? It was not that quiet, imperceptible motion which characterizes the first impulsive movement of the passenger engines of the present day. Not so. There came a sudden jerk, that bounded the sitters from their places, to the great detriment of their high-top fashionable beavers from the close proximity to the roofs of the cars. This first jerk being over, the engine proceeded on its route with considerable velocity for those times, when compared with stage-coaches, until it arrived at a water-station, when it suddenly brought up with jerk No. 2, to the further amusement of some of the excursionists. Mr. Clark retained his elevated seat, thanking his stars for its close proximity to the tall smoke-pipe of the machine, in allowing the smoke and sparks to pass over his head. At the water-station a short stop was made, and a successful experiment tried, to remedy the unpleasant jerks. A plan was soon hit upon and put into execution. The three links in the couplings of the cars were stretched to their utmost tension, a rail, from a fence in the neighborhood, was placed between each pair of cars and made fast by means of the packing yarn for the cylinders. . . . This arrangement improved the order of things, and it was found to answer the purpose, when the signal was again given and the engine started.

In a short time the engine (after frightening the horses attached to all sorts of vehicles filled with the people from the surrounding country, or congregated all along at every available position near the road, to get a view of the singular-looking machine; after causing thus innumerable capsizes and smash-ups of the vehicles, and the tumbling of the spectators in every direction to right and left), arrived at the head of the inclined plane at Schenectady, amid the cheers and welcome of thousands. . . .

Boss of the Train (The First Bell Cord)

In the early days of the railroad in this country the locomotive engineer was master of the train. He ran it according to his judgment, and collecting fares, superintending the loading and unloading of freight, and shouting "All aboard!" were all that the conductor was expected to do.

The Erie Railroad was then the New York and Erie Railroad. There was no rail connection with Jersey City in 1842. Boats carried passengers from New York to Piermont-on-the-Hudson, which was then the eastern terminus of the road. Turner's, forty-seven miles from New York, was as far west as the railroad was in operation.

One of the pioneer conductors of this line was the late Capt. Ayres. He ran the only train then called for between the two terminal points. It was made up of freight and passenger cars. The Captain frequently encountered a fractious passenger who insisted on riding without paying his fare. As there was no way of signaling the engineer, and the passenger could not be thrown from the train while it was in motion, the conductor in such cases had to let him ride until a regular stop was made. Capt. Ayres procured a stout twine, sufficiently long to reach from the locomotive to the rear car. To the end of this string next to the engine he fastened a stick of wood. He ran this cord back over the cars to the last one. He informed the engineer, who was a German named Abe Hammil, that if he desired to have the train stopped, he would pull the string and raise the stick, and would expect the signal to be obeyed. Hammil looked upon this innovation as a direct blow at his authority, and when the train left Piermont he cut the stick loose. At Turner's he told Captain Ayres that he proposed to run the train himself, without interference from any conductor. The next day the Captain rigged up his string and stick of wood again.

"Abe," said he, "this thing's got to be settled either one way or the other today. If that stick of wood is not on the end of this cord when we get to Turner's you've got to lick me or I'll lick you."

The stick was not on the string when the train reached Turner's. The Captain pulled off his coat, and told Hammil to get off his engine. Hammil declined to get off. Capt. Ayres climbed to the engineer's place. Hammil started to jump off on the opposite side. The conductor hit him under the ear, and saved him the trouble of jumping. That settled forever the question of the twine and stick of wood. The idea was quickly adopted by the few roads then in operation, and the

---

From *The Fast Men of America;* or, Racing with Time from Cradle to Grave, The Romance and Reality of Life on the Railroad, Illustrated with Pen and Pencil, by an Old Railroader, [Alfred Trumble], pp. 14–15. New York: Published by Richard K. Fox, Proprietor, *Police Gazette.* [1882.]

bell or gong in time took the place of the stick of wood. Henceforth the conductor was boss of the train, and the engineer took orders from him.

The First Mile-a-Minute Run

It was in 1848 and over the Boston & Maine's western division that the first mile-a-minute run of history was achieved. . . .

The road had become the delighted possessor of a new locomotive built to its order in England. It weighed ten tons, could develop, with a good hardwood fire, power equal to a team of thirty-five horses, and was called the "Antelope." Charles Minot, General Superintendent of the line, was an astute fellow, and even in the days before high-pressure promotion and press agents, was aware of the uses of publicity, and he summoned to his office his veteran engine driver.

"Pemberton," he said, abruptly, "can you make the Lawrence run in twenty-six minutes flat?"

"Twenty-six miles in twenty-six minutes? It's as good as taking your life in your hands," was the reply.

"You take it and I'll ride with you," said the General Super, and the next day the most intrepid reporter from each local paper showed up in Haymarket Square, his will neatly filed with his editor and a large bandanna handkerchief in his pocket with which to secure his best hat to his head. All along the line the switches had been spiked to prevent spreading. Every crossing was guarded by railroad men and local constables, and the populace were out along the line to see what they might see. Largely, it is reported, they were skeptical.

With a terrific amount of snorting and a shower of sparks that sent neighboring shopkeepers hastening to their roofs with wet mops, the Antelope got under way. There was no securing the cylinder cocks from the engine cab in those days, and after the train had run a few yards to gather momentum, the fireman dropped off, ran ahead, closed them and leaped aboard again as the drivers passed him. The reporters held onto their seats and grew pale. Somebody produced a flask of Old Tannery Dew, and at Somerville crossing, Charlie Minot was wheeling her at a breathless forty, and Pemberton was aiding the fireman to toss dry pine into the firebox.

At Malden the single coach was felt to be on the rails only at infrequent intervals, and the reporters were lying on the floor, inquiring of one another and of God why they had ever embarked on this ultimate folly. At South Reading the Antelope came into view on the

---

From *Boston and the Boston Legend,* by Lucius Beebe, pp. 133–135. Copyright, 1935, by D. Appleton-Century Co. New York and London.

Crystal Pond stretch in such a blaze of brass, red paint and rolling woodsmoke that Cyrus Wakefield, the town's first citizen, was observed jumping up and down in his congress gaiters from sheer delighted excitement. At Reading the village drunkard took one look at the demon that streaked across his vision and was strictly sober for a fortnight thereafter. At Ballardvale Minot leaned far out on the pounding gangway and smelled hot metal. In the course of which discovery he lost his hat, a new white beaver that had been brought him from Locke in London by Mr. Bartlee, the bookseller in Cornhill. The Dreyfus self-feeding oil cups had yet to be invented, and when the steam chest became overheated, the fireman crawled out on the running board with an oiler in his teeth, and clung precariously to the cowcatcher while sousing the running parts with liquid paraffin. As the Antelope sounded a piercing scream on her whistle for North Andover crossing, a loose stretch of track was encountered, and the strap-iron rails, torn from the ties by the speed of the train, flew up behind in a shower of curling snakeheads. It was, too, just twenty-six minutes to Lawrence. The reporters were in no shape to write their copy until they had been treated at the nearest sample room by the populace, and most of the gilt and red lacquer was blistered off the Antelope. It was the first time mankind had ever achieved a mile a minute over a protracted run, and the passengers said they never purposed to duplicate the performance. It was plainly against the will of God.

Snakeheads

The first railroads that were built in this country were built with flat iron bars laid on longitudinal timbers. Very few locomotives were over ten tons weight, but with this light weight the bars would often tear out the spikes and the end of the bars would turn up and we used to call them snakeheads. They were very dangerous. There was always a spike hammer and spikes on the locomotive, and when a snakehead was seen ahead it would be necessary to stop the train and put in a plug and spike down the rail before the train could pass. I have seen the bars thrown twenty feet high, when the forward wheel of the engine would run under the snakehead.

One day one of the snakeheads ran right up through the floor of the car and passed up through the fleshy part of a stout young lady's thigh without touching a single blood vessel, and passed through the roof of the car about four feet, so that the lower end of it was clear

---

From *Seymour's Reminiscences,* An Interesting Condensed History of Jay Gould and James Fisk, Jr.'s Mismanagement of the Erie Road in contrast with the Management of Commodore Vanderbilt, with Other Interesting Reading, pp. 104–105. Copyright, 1893, by A. B. Seymour. Fairfield, Connecticut.

of the track timber. The train was immediately stopped and the ladies in a house nearby came with camphor and stimulants, and a doctor was hastily procured who had to press with his greased hands the flesh of her thigh away from the bar of iron which was one inch in thickness, and then we had to cut away the wood of the floor and some of the roof so as to have no jar. Several men held the bar perfectly still between the doctor's hands until entirely clear of the lady's thigh. Such courage and fortitude was never exceeded, for the lady never uttered a word of complaint and it took one hour's time to carefully accomplish the work. The lady recovered and was married within a month.

Six Days a Week or Seven?

I [1]

Erastus Fairbanks of St. Johnsbury, Vermont, scale manufacturer, was also president and chief stockholder of the St. Johnsbury & Lake Champlain Railroad and a strict observer of the Sabbath. No trains were scheduled for Sunday operation, and his orders were that not a wheel should turn on that day. The operating officials, however, sometimes found it necessary to do some shifting of cars on Sunday, occasionally to run a work-train or in winter to send out a snow-plow to keep the line open. It behooved them to do this very early in the morning or as quietly as could be, so that Mr. Fairbanks in his mansion would not hear the noise. Accordingly, engineers were warned to "hook her up" as near noiselessly as possible, not to use the bell, blow off steam or blow the whistle, though there were some crossings where these warning sounds were legally required. As the railroad leaves town westward up a stiff grade, noiseless operation took some doing, but they often got away with it. They well knew that if Mr. Fairbanks heard so much as a whisper from an engine on Sunday, he would go down to the office on Monday morning and severely reprimand all parties concerned, with a threat of discharge if it happened again.

II [2]

. . . One Sunday morning at Galesburg's reddish-brown railway station a little drama was enacted that marked the end of an era. When

---

[1] Communicated by John S. Kendall, St. Johnsbury, Vermont, 1953.

[2] From *They Broke the Prairie,* by Earnest Elmo Calkins, pp. 219–220. Copyright, 1937, by Earnest Elmo Calkins. New York: Charles Scribner's Sons.

on the first Sunday the train arrived and departed according to its week-day schedule, those of the citizens who had in their keeping the sanctity of the Puritan Sabbath were too surprised and shocked to do anything about it. But on the following Sunday morning among the goodly crowd assembled at the station was a tall, commanding figure in a long frock coat, distinctly clerical, and otherwise clothed with unmistakable authority, his jet black hair slicked back, his heart filled with high purpose, his supporters, in their 1850 costumes, standing by ready for any emergency.

There was the engine with steam up, smoke pouring from its enormous top-heavy stack, its tender full of cordwood, its sweeping cowcatcher—so necessary in a country where livestock ran loose even in the village streets—drawing a string of short, square, flat-topped box-like cars—all as if just steamed out of a Currier & Ives print. Before the conductor could shout his "All aboard," and the engineer grab the bell rope, the tall, commanding figure stepped from the crowd, raised his hand, and bade the engineer take the engine to the roundhouse.

"Who are you to give me such orders?" asked the astonished engineer.

"I am President Blanchard of Knox College, and again I order you to take that engine to the roundhouse, and not run this train on Sunday."

"Well, President Blanchard of Knox College, you can go to hell and mind your own business, and I'll take my train out as ordered."

And that is what the engineer did. The town had asked for transportation and it had got it. The railroad was no longer a neighborhood enterprise, controlled by the little group of pious men who had founded Galesburg to be a Christian town after their own ideal. Blanchard had worked for the railroad and contributed to it from his meager salary, but stern moralist that he was, he would no doubt have foregone all its material benefits rather than yield one jot or tittle of the strict observance of the Sabbath which he and the founders of the town had thus far been able to maintain. But President Blanchard was as powerless to stem the tide of liberal ideas which came rolling in with the advent of the railroad as old King Canute had been to halt the inrolling breakers of the North Sea. Galesburg was never the same again.

Railroads and Community Intimacy

In our country, we look upon a railroad as something apart, awful, different from a common road. . . . It is railed in and fenced in, and

From *Across the Atlantic,* by the author of "Sketches of Cantabs" [John Delaware Lewis], pp. 160–161. London: George Earle. 1851.

walled in and banked in from the fields on each side; . . . intersecting roads and lanes must be either elevated out of reach of the formidable locomotive by means of a bridge, or carried beneath it by means of a tunnel. . . .

In America the difference is amusing. *There* the iron trams are laid down and by consequence, the trains rattle on, straight across lanes and roads and thoroughfares, without any other notice to the persons who may happen to be walking or riding or driving on them, than "Look out for the locomotive" painted up on a board which is elevated on a high pole. You might be walking in a shady lane, of a dark night, unconscious that there was a line of railway within a hundred miles, and suddenly hear the engine turn in out of a field behind you, and see it whisk past you or feel it go over you according as you did or did not get out of the way in time. As for villages and country towns, it rattles right up their main streets, not infrequently stopping at the door of the hotel or in front of the church, by way of a station. On these occasions, you might sometimes shake hands with the people on each side of you, who stand at their shop fronts to see you go past. Once indeed, being with a friend in a light "wagon," and finding by experiment that the distance of the rails apart tallied with the width of our vehicle, we continued to drive straight on it, being our shortest way to our destination. . . .

Indiana for Indianans

We renew an idea which we have propounded before, but which has been lost sight of by Railroad managers and by our citizens—namely, that an unnecessary number of trains are run on our railroads to accommodate travellers from distant States, and that one train daily would be all the passenger business that is now done on any of the roads. This extravagance is wrong and ought not to be continued. I have no doubt that to change it would add 8 to 10 percent to the dividends of these railroads. They should arrange their running and time to suit the citizens of Indiana, and not those of Massachusetts or Texas. All trains should arrive in this city between 11 and 12 A.M., and leave from it at 1 or 2 o'clock P.M.

Editorial in *Locomotive,* Indianapolis, Indiana, May 19, 1855.

American Chivalry

[En route from Chicago to Detroit.]

The cars were very full and were not able to seat all the passengers. Consequently, according to the usages of American etiquette, the gentlemen vacated their seats in favor of the ladies, who took possession of them in a very ungracious manner, as I thought. The gentlemen stood in the passage down the centre. At last, all but one had given up their seats, and while stopping at a station, another lady entered.

"A seat for a lady," said the conductor, when he saw the crowded condition of the car. The one gentleman did not stir. "A seat for a lady!" repeated the man in a more imperious tone. Still no movement on the part of the gentleman appealed to. "A seat for a lady! Don't you see there's a lady wanting one?" now vociferated several voices at once, but without producing any effect. "Get up for this lady!" said one, bolder than the rest, giving the stranger a sharp admonition on the shoulder. He pulled his traveling cap over his eyes and doggedly refused to stir. There was now a regular hubbub in the car. American blood was up, and several gentlemen tried to induce the offender to move.

"I'm an Englishman, and I tell you, I won't be browbeat by you beastly Yankees. I've paid for my seat and I mean to keep it!" savagely shouted the offender, verifying my worst suspicions.

"I thought so!—I knew it!—A regular John Bull trick!—Just like them!" were some of the observations made, and very mild they were, considering the aggravated circumstances.

Two men took the culprit by the shoulders, and the others, pressing behind, impelled him to the door amid a chorus of groans and hisses, disposing of him finally by placing him in the emigrant car, installing the lady in the vacated seat. I could almost fancy that the shade of the departed Judge Lynch stood by with an approving smile.

I was so thoroughly ashamed of my countrymen and so afraid of my nationality being discovered that if anyone spoke to me, I adopted every Americanism which I could think of in reply. . . .

Birth of the Ticket Punch

In the early days of the passenger business on the Erie, the cost of passenger tickets was no inconsiderable item, hence heavy card tickets

---

From *The Englishwoman in America,* [by Mrs. Isabella (Lucy) Bird Bishop], pp. 160–161. London: John Murray. 1856.

From *Between the Ocean and the Lakes; the Story of Erie,* by Edward Harold Mott, p. 413. Copyright, 1899, by John S. Collins. New York.

from and to the various stations were used. The signature of the general ticket agent was attached, and they were taken up by the conductor, returned to the general ticket office, and sent out to agents for resale so long as they remained undefaced.

After a time an important discovery, seriously affecting the revenue of the Erie, was made. A resident of Andover, on the Western Division, will be used as an illustration. He purchased a ticket to New York. The conductors run by divisions. The passenger's ticket was ex amined and honored by the conductor between Andover and Hornell ville, Hornellsville and Susquehanna, Susquehanna and Port Jer At the latter station, the passenger pocketed his through ticket a purchased a ticket from Port Jervis to New York, which was taken by the conductor on the Eastern Division. Returning, the passen bought his card ticket from New York to Andover. At Hornellsv he bought a ticket from that station to Andover and retained through ticket. After the foregoing description, it will be clear tl thereafter that person could travel between Andover and New Y as often as he might desire, paying fare only between Port Jervis a New York east bound, and between Hornellsville and Andover, w bound.

This fraud on the Company was in existence a long time before was discovered. Then a system of cancelling the tickets by divisio by the conductors was adopted. At first they were simply marked wit a pencil. This was not a success, and the emergency led to the making and introduction of the ticket punch.

The First Train Dispatching by Telegraph

To Charles Minot belongs the honor of having made the first practical application of the telegraph to railroading, either in this or any other country, by his adopting it in the early autumn of 1851, as near as the date can be now fixed, to the running of a train by telegraphic order, which led to a system that was adopted by railroads throughout the world, and remained the standard signal and reporting system on railroads until the block system began to take its place. Up to the time of Minot's initial experiment with telegraph orders, trains on the railroad were run on what was called the "time interval system." The rule was that a ruling train had right of one hour against the opposing train of the same class. Trainmen were anxious to get through. As an instance of this, once Conductor Henry Ayres had lost his hour at Pond Eddy. He took the switch, and after waiting ten minutes, as was the rule, and the opposing train not being in sight or hearing, he

Ibid., p. 420.

started a brakeman with a red flag, and giving him twenty minutes start, followed with his train. A little west of Shohola he caught the flagman, who had stopped on enough straight line to make it safe. The exhausted man was taken aboard the train and a fresh man started on with the flag, which operation was repeated until the train expected was met at Callicoon, 34 miles from Pond Eddy. Captain Ayers used to say that he had flagged the entire length of the Delaware Division more than once.

W. H. Stewart was running the west-bound express train on the day when Superintendent Minot made his astounding innovation in railroading, he happening to be going over the road on that train. The train, under the rule then existing, was to wait for an east-bound express to pass it at Turner's, 47 miles from New York. That train had not arrived, and the west-bound train would be unable to proceed until an hour had expired, unless the tardy east-bound train arrived at Turner's within that time. There was a telegraph office at Turner's, and Superintendent Minot telegraphed to the operator at Goshen, fourteen miles further on, and asked him whether the east-bound train had left that station. The reply was that the train had not yet arrived at Goshen, showing that it was much behind its time. Then, according to the narrative of the late W. H. Stewart, given to the author in 1896, Superintendent Minot telegraphed as follows, as nearly as Stewart could recollect:

To Agent and Operator at Goshen:

Hold the train for further orders.

Chas. Minot, *Superintendent*

He then wrote this order, and handed it to Conductor Stewart:

To Conductor and Engineer, Day Express:

Run to Goshen regardless of opposing train.

Chas. Minot, *Superintendent*

"I took the order," said Mr. Stewart, relating the incident, "showing it to the engineer, Isaac Lewis, and told him to go ahead. The surprised engineer read the order, and handing it back to me, exclaimed:

" 'Do you take me for a d——d fool? I won't run by that thing!'

"I reported to the Superintendent, who went forward and used his verbal authority on the engineer, but without effect. Minot then climbed in the engine and took charge of it himself. Engineer Lewis jumped off and got in the rear seat of the rear car. The Superintendent ran the train to Goshen. The east-bound train had not yet reached that station. He telegraphed to Middletown. The train had not arrived there. The west-bound train was run on a similar order to Middletown, and from there to Port Jervis, where it entered the yard from the East as the other train came into it from the West."

An hour and more in time had been saved to the west-bound train, and the question of running trains on the Erie by telegraph was at once and forever settled.

When the system of running trains on the Erie by telegraph was well established, a code of signals or signs for stations was adopted, such as "PO" for Port Jervis, "XN" for Lackawaxen, and so on. With some modifications this abbreviated nomenclature is in use today.

A Primitive Headlight

That the locomotive was to be used in the night, and during the whole night, was plainly to be anticipated. [On the South Carolina Railroad] it was thought well to make trial of such running by night, that it might be known what it was necessary to provide. For such trial two platform cars were placed in front of the locomotive. On the forward platform was placed an inclosure of sand, and on the sand a structure of iron rods somewhat of urn shape. In this structure was to be kept up a fire of pine-wood knots. Suitable signals as to the rate of speed, etc., were provided. The day preceding the evening of the trial closed in with as heavy a fog as I have ever seen, and I have seen a first-class London fog. But the fog did not prevent the trial when the appointed time came.

The country to be run through was a dead level, and on the surface rested this heavy fog; but just before we were ready to start, the fog began to lift and continued to rise slowly and as uniformly as ever curtain left surface of stage, until about eighteen feet high; there it remained stationary, with an under surface as uniform as the surface it had risen from. This under surface was lit up with radiating lines in all directions with prismatic colors, presenting a scene of remarkable brilliancy and beauty.

Under this canopy, lit on its under surface, the locomotive moved onward with a clearly illuminated road before it; the run was continued for some five miles, with no untoward occurrence, and I had reason to exclaim, "The very atmosphere of Carolina says, 'Welcome to the locomotive.' "

From *The Railroad Era, First Five Years of its Development*, by Horatio Allen, pp. 28–29. Copyright, 1884. by Horatio Allen. New York.

The First Sander

The origin of the sand-box on locomotives was due to a plague of grasshoppers in Pennsylvania in 1836. They covered the ground in myriads, and seriously interfered with the running of trains on the railroads then in operation. For a week or two the roads employed men to walk back and forth along the tracks and sweep the insects off the rails with brooms, but this expedient was unavailing, for no sooner were they displaced from one point than the little pests jumped back again after the track sweepers had passed. Scrapers were then installed on some engines and small brooms on others, but these attempts to remedy the trouble also proved useless, since the brooms were worn out in a short time and the contact between scrapers and rails made it necessary to run the trains at a crawling gait. Finally some genius whose name has been forgotten hit upon the plan of attaching sand-boxes to the locomotives in such a way that streams of sand should be automatically deposited on the rails in front of the wheels. The scheme proved an unqualified success, was adopted by other existing roads, and used thereafter by all new ones.

In the Days of the Wood-Burners

. . . There was one advantage in wood-burning—you always had a tenderful of "replacers," and what those old-timers could do with engine wood, in the way of rerailing, was astonishing. And the wood served equally well to fill a gap in a broken rail (and there were many of these) to permit a train to pass over. Engine wood served almost as varied purpose, in its way, as the ladies' hairpin of today. . . .

* * * * *

. . . Even the picturesqueness of "wooding up" was as nothing to "watering" when as not infrequently happened in the dry season, that fluid had to be taken at some between-stations brook, and all hands formed a line, the leathern buckets were unhung from the rear of the tender, and the aqueous supply therewith transferred to the tank.

* * * * *

From *A History of Travel in America,* by Seymour Dunbar, pp. 1032–1033. Copyright, 1915, by the Bobbs-Merrill Company. Indianapolis.

From "Railroad Reminiscences," by J. H. French, New England Railroad Club, Proceedings of the Meeting Held at Pierce Hall, Copley Square, Boston, on Tuesday Evening, November 13, 1900, pp. 4–10, 24. [Boston: The New England Railroad Club.]

The author was a veteran of the Old Colony Railroad.

. . . Freight trains began carrying cabooses, affording a crumb of comfort to the poor brakemen who, before, had no shelter for themselves or their clothing, and whose frozen dinners in the winter time were only made eatable by first stuffing the pails down the engine's escape pipes. A tough time those poor fellows had, and the freight man who did not carry one or more marks of injury must have borne a charmed life.

* * * * *

. . . For many years such a thing as a smoking car was unknown, and passengers went into the baggage car to indulge in the weed.

Time-tables were crude affairs. Instead of train numbers, conductors' names were used on some roads, and the schedules stated that "Jones" would meet "Brown" at Jericho. Jones might die the day the time-table took effect and Brown be discharged, but "Jones" and "Brown" met regularly at the appointed place, day by day, notwithstanding. . . . In the timetables of some roads, the schedule merely gave the leaving time at the initial point, and not a figure or other indication to denote where the train went, or when it might be expected to get there, and yet the run covered the whole length of a single-track road!

* * * * *

One superintendent issued time-tables only to trains whose time was changed; and a very important train which, because of uncertain connections, was required to keep clear of all other trains, happened to have no change in its schedule. Fortunately, its conductor learned of the new time-table, borrowed a copy, made the run (which, by the way, was on single track), and called at the office to ascertain why he was not supplied. He was informed that there was no change in his time. "No," said he, "but the time of every other train on the road is changed, and I have to dodge them all." He was immediately provided.

* * * * *

The runs of certain trains of my division extended over some miles of single main line of a connecting road whose trains, whether passenger or freight, had absolute right of track over my trains by rule. It was desired to reverse their rights as to one train and give us the preference, and the superintendent of that road accomplished this important change by an obscure footnote to which attention was called by a reference mark, made by upsetting a type and using the bottom imprint which resembled a couple of fly specks.

The same official so timed some of his trains that they "crossed" midway between stations on single track, and then applied a corrective in the form of a special rule saying that they wouldn't so cross.

And this rule was almost the only one of a large page of rules that did not end with the phrase "unless otherwise ordered." . . .

. . . Upon the advent of air brakes the average engineman stood aghast, and seriously claimed increased compensation for manipulating them. . . .

* * * * *

What would the men of today think of running over an unlighted single track, upon a dark, gloomy night, with a "doubleheader" of 36 cars—mixed passenger and freight—loaded with troops, horses, cannon, caissons, ammunition, camp equipment, and accoutrements—with the old-fashioned car platforms and loose-coupled—at a speed of 40 miles, with neither a train brake, a signal cord, a semaphore or mast signal, nor a spacing signal at a station? And yet this was common practice in Civil War times.

In the early days, extras were seldom, and the trackmen did not always let their work suffer (nor their dinners oftentimes) from any fear of them. Irregular trains usually followed some train that could "flag" them, and the trackmen mostly relied upon such signals being carried. A leading railroad man of our city recently told me that when he was a track hand up country long ago, they never displayed danger signals to protect their work, and sometimes the gang would go quite a distance to dinner, leaving a rail out and unprotected. X

But there was another kind of "flagging" that did have to be complied with, and that was against opposing trains in cases of delay, in the days before the telegraph, when a train had to work its way in this manner for a score of miles perhaps and the flagman's lot was not a happy one.

Southern Railroading in Ante-Bellum Days

I. Train Dispatching As It Might Have Been [1]

Train dispatching by wire, as carried on now, was hardly thought of then, and all trains were intended to be moved on time card figures,

---

From "The Savor of Old-Time Southern Railroading, A Choice from Workingmen's Memoirs," edited by Jesse C. Burt, Jr., *Bulletin No. 84,* The Railway & Locomotive Historical Society, Inc., pp. 37–38, 40, 41. Copyright, 1951, by the Railway & Locomotive Historical Society, Inc. Baker Library, Harvard Business School. Boston.

The "Old Guard of the NC&StL Railway" was a group of twenty-two men gray in the service of the Nashville, Chattanooga, and St. Louis Railway [which lasted from May 9, 1907 to 1933] when it was kept out by the penury of depression and the depletion of the grim reaper. . . . There are two of these minute books, but the editor has only extracted material from the first such volume, a book covering the period 1907 to 1915. The memoirs in that latter collection are of rich interest for they cover the ante-bellum period dealing for the most part with actual railroad operations and practices, and such data are comparatively rare.—J.C.B., Jr.

[1] Address by W. L. Danley, May 9, 1907, Old Guard Minute Book 1, p. 10.

under the prescribed rule to keep on the safe side; consequently they were frequently hung up, delayed and held out waiting schedule requirements, and much trouble was experienced by the operating department. When Col. [E. W.] Cole was Superintendent one of the telegraph operators suggested to him that the difficulty of passing trains on the line could be overcome by running all trains southbound one day and northbound the next. This was a bright idea.

II. Brandy in Tin Dippers [2]

In earlier railroad days there was not much said in regard to the use of whisky and sometimes it was forced on us in place of water. In 1854 a bad cholera epidemic was raging in Nashville and when we roustabouts had nothing else to do we had to work in the freight house and were not allowed to drink water but instead a bucket of French brandy and a tin dipper were at each door and we had to drink that or nothing.

III. The Strike That Failed [3]

There never was but one strike on the old Nashville & Chattanooga road. When old man Hayne was set up as conductor he employed six decrepit old men as brakemen; they had heard of strikes and they talked it over. One old man by the name of Perry said he would go and tell the Superintendent [E. W. Cole] and he would raise their pay, so he went up in the office and found the Superintendent at his table writing and said, "Mr. Cole, I strike." Mr. Cole said, "You strike for what?" Perry said, "Better pay." Mr. Cole told him to strike out of there and strike home afoot . . . and ended one of the greatest strikes in ancient or modern times.

IV. Human Nature [4]

Some of you will remember the engineman, whose conductor, not doing to suit him, wanted to add too many cars, or something of that sort, was left standing on the main track, the engineer deliberately pulling the pin out from behind the tender, and going on with a light engine to the terminal. . . .

Another instance some of you will recall. An engine had stalled on the mountain; the engineer, whom you all know well, tied down the safety valves—there were no pops in those days, put on the blower,

---

[2] Paper read by William Lynch, May 13, 1909, Old Guard Minute Book 1, p. 46.

[3] Paper read by Lafayette Lynch, May 12, 1910, Old Guard Minute Book 1, p. 61.

[4] Address by John W. Thomas Jr., May 9, 1907, Old Guard Minute Book 1, p. 18. Thomas was president of the NC&StL 1907–1914. He really began his work on the railway in 1872 as a fireman, later became engineer, assistant superintendent, superintendent, and president. His father before him, John W. Thomas, Sr., was president of the road from 1882 to 1906.—J.C.B., Jr.

sanded the rail, pulled the throttle wide open, pirched [*sic*] himself on the side of the cut, and threw rocks at the old kettle, abusing her all the while, until presently the steam pressure went away up beyond the limit, and the train moved off. What would we do with a fellow who would be guilty of a trick like this now? . . .

V. The Perils of Operation [5]

. . . You will understand we did not use the telegraph in running trains, and if for any cause a freight schedule was abandoned, you would receive no notification of it, and on one occasion I was coming from Chattanooga to Nashville—I had a meeting point at Smyrna with Decherd Night Freight; we arrived at Smyrna on time, pulled on side track, and being about midnight and all pretty well worn out, we all went to sleep—when I awoke I found the entire crew asleep, and no one knew whether the opposing train had passed or not. . . . While I knew that frequently this train was abandoned, yet I did not know whether it was on this particular night or not, so I adhered to the main old rule (take the safe side) and we flagged all the way Smyrna to Nashville; on our arrival the night man in the office asked the questions [*sic*] what delayed you, my answer, doing work on and off the rails a few times—that was the end of it— But I was anxious to know if the train passed us in our nap, but I was afraid to ask this night man anything about it, so in the afternoon when I came down to the Train Master's office, I casually remarked who went out on Decherd night freight last night. Why, he remarked, there was none went out last night— "That's so, I did not meet any at Smyrna last night." In those days it was indeed a rare thing to run a round trip from Nashville to Chattanooga without a run off, however in those days we made such slow time that we seldom did much damage when we did leave the rail.

Pre-Pullman Sleeping Cars in 1860

I am going—say from Albany—at the head of the Hudson—to Buffalo, near Lake Ontario. The conductor, seeing me walk about the platform and eye the several carriages, says to me with sagacious forethought, "Sleeping car, mister? Going through, stranger?"

I reply, Yes, and follow the quiet sallow, lean man into the last carriage, which is lettered in large red letters on a sunflower yellow ground, "Albany and Buffalo Sleeping Car." I go in and find an ordi-

---

[5] Address by J. H. Latimer, May 9, 1907, Old Guard Minute Book 1, p. 22.

Anonymous. Abridged from *All the Year Round,* January 12, 1861, pp. 322–331. London.

nary railway carriage; the usual filter, and the usual stove are there; and the seats, two and two, are arranged in the old quiet procession, turning their backs on each other glumly, after their kind. I ask how much extra I must pay for a bed.

"Single-high, twenty-five cents; yes, sir," says the officer on duty. "Double-low, half a dollar; yes, sir."

I order a single-high (without at all knowing what I mean), and as I pay my twenty-five cents the bell on the engine begins to get restless, the steam horses snort and champ and struggle. Ten other persons enter, and order beds and pay for them, with more or less expectation, regret and wrangling.

More bell, more steam, smothering us all with white—a wrench, a drag, a jolt back half angry, as if the engine were sulky and restive and we are off. The signal-posts stride by us, the timber yards fly by, and we are in the open country, with its zigzag snake fences, and Indian corn patches and piles of orange pumpkins. Now ladies come in from other carriages, for the restless or seeking traveller can walk all through the American train. We are seated in twos and twos some musing, some chatting, some discussing "the irrepressible squabble," many chewing or cutting plugs of tobacco from long wedges, produced from their waistcoat-pockets. The candy boys have been around three times, the Negro with water can twice, the lad with the book basket once. One hour from Albany we are at Hoffman's; twenty minutes more, at Amsterdam; fifty minutes more and we have reached Spraker's —pure Dutch names all as though old Hudson christened them. Now we are between Little Falls and Herkimer, the officer of the sleeping car enters, and calls out:

"Now then, misters, if you please, get up from your seats, and allow me to make up the beds."

Two by two we rise, and with neat trimness and quick hand the nimble Yankee turns over every other seat, so as to reverse the back, and make two seats, one facing the other. Nimbly he shuts the windows and pulls up the shutters, leaving for ventilation the strip of perforated zinc at the top of each. Smartly he strips up the cushions and unfastens from beneath each seat a cane-bottomed frame, there secreted. In a moment, opening certain ratchet holes in the wall of the carriage, he has slided these in at a proper height above, and covered each with cushions and sleeping rug.

I go outside on the balcony, to be out of the way, and when I come back the whole place is transformed. No longer an aisle of double seats; like a section of a proprietary chapel put snug for sleeping, with curtained berths and closed portholes.

Oh, dexterous genius of Zenas Wallace and Ezra Jones, conductors of the New York Central Railway! The lights of the candle lamps are dimmed or withdrawn; a hushed stillness pervades the chambers of sleep; no sound breaks it but the clump of the falling boots, and the button slapping sound of coats flung upon benches. Further on, within a second enclosure, I hear voices of women and children. A fat German haberdasher, from Cincinnati, is unrobing as if he were performing a religious ceremony, and, indeed, sleeping is a rehearsal of death, and seems rather a solemn thing, however we look at it.

The bottom berths are singularly comfortable. There is room to wander and explore, to roll and turn, and the curtains hush all sound, and keep off all inquisitive rays from Zenas or Ezra's portable lamps. There is, indeed, twice the room I had in the Atlantic steamer that brought me over, for, in that berth, I could not sit up at night without bumping my head against No. 46's bed planks, and could not turn without pulling all the scant clothes off me. As for a heavy sea, why then there was no keeping in bed at all without being lashed in.

Now, I mount my berth; for sleep is sympathetic, and when everyone else goes to sleep I must, too. There are two berths to choose from, both wicker trays, ledged in, cushioned and rugged, one about half a foot higher than the other. I choose the top one as being nearer the zinc ventilator.

Several have turned in, and are snorting approval of themselves and of sleep as an institution generally. Others, like young crows, balancing on the spring boughs, swing their Yankee legs, lean and yellow, from the wicker trays, and peel off their stockings or struggle to get off their boots. . . .

I clambered to my perch. The tray was narrow and high. It was like lying with one's back on the narrow plank thrown across a torrent. If I turned my back to the carriage wall, the motion bumped me off my bed altogether; if I turned my face to the wall, I felt a horrible sensation of being likely to roll down backwards to be three minutes afterward picked up in detached portions.

I lay on my back and so settled the question; but then the motion! The American Railways are cheaply made and hastily constructed. They have often, on even great roads, but one line of rails, and that one line of rails is anything but even. . . .

Then the stoppages, the clashing of the bell on the engine at "Chittenango," "Manlins," "Canton," "Jordon," "Canaserago" and all the other places with Indian, classical or scriptural names. When I peered through the zinc ventilator into outer darkness, a flying scud of sparks from the engine funnel did not serve to divest my mind of all chances of being burned. Then there were blazes of pine-torches as we neared a station, fresh bell clamor and jumbling sounds of baggage, slamming doors and itinerant conductors. . . .

I lay on my back on that wicker shelf of the "American Sleeping car," and in vain offered up prayers to the great black King Morpheus of the mandragora crown and ebon sceptre. . . . No, zigzag goes the car, rush, jolts, and now I begin to believe the old story of the stoker and engineer playing cards all night, and now and then leaping the train over a "bad place," crying, "Go ahead; let her rip!"

At last a precarious and fragile sleep crusts me over, but it is like workhouse food; it keeps life together, but not amply or luxuriously. So blessed daylight reluctantly and sullenly returns, one by one we wake up, yawn and stretch ourselves. There is something suspicious in the haste with which we all flop out of bed; no really comfortable bed was ever left with such coarse ingratitude. Presently to us enter Zenas and Ezra, not to mention a new passenger from Crete, regardless of the somewhat effete atmosphere of our carriage, and proceed to adjust the seats.

Beds, in a few minutes, will be invisible. Slide out those wicker trays—strip off the rugs and cushions—furl back those curtains—ratchet up to the roof those supporters—push in those underpinning bolts—click, jolt, they are chair seats once more. And now, through the open windows comes a draught of pure air that freshens our frowzy and disheveled crew.

Now repair we to the washing room and the one dirty brush fastened to the wall by a chain, giving the whole place the appearance of the cell of a dead barber. We wash with scanty rinsings of water, always tilted up at one corner of the basin, as if we were in the desert and water was scarce on "t'other side of Jordan." I didn't feel as if I had washed, or as if I had been asleep, but that is no consequence. I feel tired, flabby, dirty, grimy and low.

Let me, however, remember to mention that the second time I took a railway sleeping car, I really did sleep, and the third time, I slept well. So much for habit.

II. THE IRON HORSE GOES TO WAR

The Secret Entry into Washington

The guests in the brilliantly lighted dining hall of the Jones House, Harrisburg's leading hotel, were startled when President-elect Abraham Lincoln rose before he'd finished dinner. Pennsylvania's Governor Andrew G. Curtin rose with him. Guests whispered that Mr. Lincoln had a headache and wanted to retire early. There were murmurs of sympathy.

Mr. Lincoln and Mr. Curtin walked quickly to the hotel's door. They were joined by a tense-looking young man, Ward H. Lamon, an attorney who was to be Lincoln's bodyguard for the night.

A black, curtained carriage waited outside. As the three men entered it, Governor Curtin loudly ordered the driver to go to the Executive Mansion. But a moment later he quietly told the driver to go on to the Pennsylvania Railroad tracks.

There, at the edge of town, stood a train, a locomotive and tender, and a single passenger car, without a light showing. Mr. Lincoln and Mr. Lamon stepped aboard. Instantly the train, still not showing a light, chugged away into the darkness. Scarcely a dozen persons in the country knew of this sudden trip of the new President, that night of February 22, 1861, when civil war seemed imminent.

The secrecy resulted from the report of a plot to assassinate the President-elect. The report had come from Allan Pinkerton, the noted detective, who had been hired by the Philadelphia, Wilmington & Baltimore Railroad, now part of the PRR, to investigate threats of Southern sympathizers in Baltimore. Pinkerton, doing undercover

---

From *The Pennsy,* Vol. 2 (February, 1953), No. 2, pp. 6–7. Philadelphia: The Pennsylvania Railroad Company.

work, had learned a band of conspirators planned to murder Mr. Lincoln as he came through Baltimore on his way to Washington on February 23. Mr. Lincoln, at the insistence of his close friends, accepted the detective's advice to leave for Washington secretly the night of the 22nd, even though he disliked, as he said, going into the capital "like a thief in the night."

The success of the plan depended almost entirely on the efficiency and discretion of Pennsylvania Railroad men. Riding with Mr. Lincoln to take care of any emergency were Enoch Lewis, general superintendent of the Railroad; G. C. Franciscus, superintendent of the Philadelphia Division; T. E. Garrett, general baggage agent; and John Pitcairn, Jr., telegrapher. Back at Harrisburg, Thomas A. Scott, vice-president of the Railroad, who was later to help the Railroad serve the Union spectacularly, had cleared the tracks to Philadelphia. He also had personally superintended cutting of the telegraph wires to prevent word going to the conspirators; and he stayed to make sure the wires stayed cut.

No stop delayed the swift passage of the train except a brief halt at Downingtown for water. The train pulled into the PRR station in West Philadelphia at 10 P.M. Two men hurried toward it. They were Allan Pinkerton and H. F. Kenney, superintendent of the PW&B.

There was still an hour to go before the PW&B night express left for Baltimore. Mr. Pinkerton hurried Mr. Lincoln and Mr. Lamon into a carriage and had the driver take them through the dark streets of Philadelphia. They pretended to be looking for a friend.

At 10:55 P.M. the carriage was driven into the shadow of a fence flanking the yard of the PW&B station at Broad Street and Washington Avenue, still in use today as a PRR freight station. The rear door of the last car had been left open to accommodate an "invalid." Messrs. Lincoln, Lamon, and Pinkerton were quickly settled in a compartment with the shades drawn. Armed Pinkerton operatives, one a woman, had the compartments on either side.

None of the secret travelers slept as the blacked-out train moved through the night. At Havre de Grace, where the cars were ferried across the Susquehanna, a lantern flashed from the bushes. It was a Pinkerton man signaling all-clear.

The train reached President Street Station in Baltimore at 3:30 A.M. Here, as was the practice then, the cars were detached and hauled by teams of horses on tracks through Pratt Street to the Camden Station of the Baltimore and Ohio. They were promptly coupled to the waiting Washington train.

The sun was rising over the unfinished Capitol dome when the train pulled into Washington. Lincoln slowly unfolded his 6-foot-4-inch frame and gave a weary smile. "Well, boys," he said "thank God this prayer-meeting is over."

In Harrisburg, haggardly watching the sun come up, Thomas Scott ordered the telegraph connections restored. Then came the code message he was anxiously awaiting from Pinkerton:

PLUMS (Lincoln) ARRIVED HERE WITH NUTS (Lamon) THIS MORNING—ALL RIGHT.

Stonewall Jackson's Ruse

From the very beginning of the war the Confederacy was greatly in need of rolling-stock for the railroads. We were particularly short of locomotives, and were without the shops to build them. Jackson, appreciating this, hit upon a plan to obtain a good supply from the Baltimore and Ohio road. Its line was double-tracked, at least from Point of Rocks to Martinsburg, a distance of 25 or 30 miles. We had not interfered with the running of trains, except on the occasion of the arrest of General Harney. The coal traffic from Cumberland was immense, as the Washington government was accumulating supplies of coal on the seaboard. These coal trains passed Harper's Ferry at all hours of the day and night, and thus furnished Jackson with a pretext for arranging a brilliant "scoop." When he sent me to Point of Rocks, he ordered Colonel Harper with the 5th Virginia Infantry to Martinsburg. He then complained to President Garrett, of the Baltimore and Ohio, that the night trains, eastward bound, disturbed the repose of his camp, and requested a change of schedule that would pass all east-bound trains by Harper's Ferry between 11 and 1 o'clock in the day-time. Mr. Garrett complied, and thereafter for several days we heard the constant roar of passing trains for an hour before and an hour after noon. But since the "empties" were sent up the road at night, Jackson again complained that the nuisance was as great as ever, and, as the road had two tracks, said he must insist that the west-bound trains should pass during the same two hours as those going east. Mr. Garrett promptly complied, and we then had, for two hours every day, the liveliest railroad in America. One night, as soon as the schedule was working at its best, Jackson sent me an order to take a force of men across to the Maryland side of the river the next day at 11 o'clock, and, letting all west-bound trains pass till 12 o'clock, to permit none to go east, and at 12 o'clock to obstruct the road so that it would require several days to repair it. He ordered the reverse to be done at Martinsburg. Thus he caught all the trains that were

From "Jackson at Harper's Ferry in 1861," by John D. Imboden, Brigadier-General, C.S.A., in *Battles and Leaders of the Civil War,* Being for the Most Part Contributions by Union and Confederate Officers, based upon "The Century War Series," edited by Robert Underwood Johnson and Clarence Clough Buel, of the Editorial Staff of The Century Magazine, Vol. I, pp. 122–123. Copyright, 1884, 1887, 1888, by the Century Co. New York.

going east or west between those points, and these he ran up to Winchester, thirty-two miles on the branch road, where they were safe, and whence they were removed by horse-power to the railway at Strasburg. I do not remember the number of trains captured, but the loss crippled the Baltimore and Ohio road seriously for some time, and the gain to our scantily stocked Virginia roads of the same gage was invaluable.

The Andrews Raid

On the 8th of April, 1862—the day after the battle of Pittsburg Landing [Shiloh], of which, however, [General] Mitchel had received no intelligence—he marched swiftly southward from Shelbyville and seized Huntsville, in Alabama, on the 11th of April, and then sent a detachment westward over the Memphis and Charleston railroad to open railway communication with the Union army at Pittsburg Landing.

Another detachment, commanded by Mitchel in person, advanced on the same day 70 miles by rail directly into the enemy's territory, arriving unchecked within 30 miles of Chattanooga. In two hours' time he could have reached that point, the most important position in the West, with 2,000 men. Why did he not go? The story of the railroad raid is the answer.

The night before breaking camp at Shelbyville, Mitchel sent an expedition secretly into the heart of Georgia to cut the railroad communications of Chattanooga to the south and east. . . .

In the employ of General Buell was a spy, named James J. Andrews, who had rendered valuable services in the first year of the war, and had secured the confidence of the Union commanders. In March, 1862, Buell had sent him secretly with eight men to burn the bridges west of Chattanooga; but the failure of expected coöperation defeated the plan, and Andrews, after visiting Atlanta, and inspecting the whole of the enemy's lines in that vicinity and northward, had returned, ambitious to make another attempt. His plans for the second raid were submitted to Mitchel, and on the eve of the movement from Shelbyville to Huntsville, the latter authorized him to take twenty-four men, secretly enter the enemy's territory, and, by means of capturing a train, burn the bridges on the northern part of the Georgia State railroad, and also one on the East Tennessee railroad where it approaches the Georgia State line, thus completely isolating Chattanooga, which was then virtually ungarrisoned.

From "The Locomotive Chase in Georgia," by Rev. William Pittenger, 2d Ohio Volunteers, *ibid.*, Vol. II, pp. 709–716.

The soldiers for this expedition, of whom the writer was one, were selected from the three Ohio regiments belonging to General J. W. Sill's brigade, being simply told that they were wanted for secret and very dangerous service. So far as known, not a man chosen declined the perilous honor. Our uniforms were exchanged for ordinary Southern dress, and all arms, except revolvers, were left in camp. On the 7th of April, by the roadside about a mile east of Shelbyville, in the late twilight, we met our leader. Taking us a little way from the road, he quietly placed before us the outlines of the romantic and adventurous plan, which was: to break into small detachments of three or four, journey eastward into the mountains, and then work southward, traveling by rail after we were well within the Confederate lines, and finally meet Andrews at Marietta, Georgia, more than 200 miles away, the evening of the third day after the start. When questioned, we were to profess ourselves Kentuckians going to join the Southern army.

On the journey we were a good deal annoyed by the swollen streams and the muddy roads consequent on three days of almost ceaseless rain. Andrews was led to believe that Mitchel's column would be inevitably delayed; and as we were expected to destroy the bridges the very day that Huntsville was entered, he took the responsibility of sending word to our different groups that our attempt would be postponed one day—from Friday to Saturday, April 12th. This was a natural but a most lamentable error of judgment.

One of the men was belated and did not join us at all. Two others were very soon captured by the enemy; and though their true character was not detected, they were forced into the Southern army, and two, who reached Marietta, failed to report at the rendezvous. Thus, when we assembled, very early in the morning, in Andrews' room at the Marietta Hotel for final consultation before the blow was struck, we were but twenty, including our leader. All preliminary difficulties had been easily overcome, and we were in good spirits. But some serious obstacles had been revealed on our ride from Chattanooga to Marietta the previous evening. The railroad was found to be crowded with trains, and many soldiers were among the passengers. Then the station—Big Shanty—at which the capture was to be effected had recently been made a Confederate camp. [But it still had no telegraph connections!] To succeed in our enterprise it would be necessary first to capture the engine in a guarded camp, with soldiers standing around as spectators, and then to run it from 100 to 200 miles through the enemy's country, and to deceive or overpower all trains that should be met—a large contract for twenty men! Some of our party thought the chances of success so slight, under existing circumstances, that they urged the abandonment of the whole enterprise. But Andrews declared his purpose to succeed or die, offering to each man, however, the privilege of withdrawing from the attempt—an offer no one was in the least disposed to accept. Final instructions were then given, and we hurried to the ticket office in time for the northward-bound mail train, and purchased tickets for different stations along the line in the direction of Chattanooga.

Our ride as passengers was but eight miles. We swept swiftly around the base of Kenesaw Mountain, and soon saw the tents of the forces camped at Big Shanty (now Kenesaw Station) gleam white in the morning mist. Here we were to stop for breakfast and attempt the seizure of the train. The morning was raw and gloomy, and a rain, which fell all day, had already begun. It was a painfully thrilling moment! We were but twenty, with an army about us and a long and difficult road before us crowded with enemies. In an instant we were to throw off the disguise which had been our only protection, and trust our leader's genius and our own efforts for safety and success. . . .

When we stopped, the conductor, engineer, and many of the passengers hurried to breakfast, leaving the train unguarded. Now was the moment of action! Ascertaining that there was nothing to prevent a rapid start, Andrews, our two engineers, Brown and Knight, and the fireman hurried forward, uncoupling a section of the train consisting of three empty baggage or box cars, the locomotive and tender. The engineer and fireman sprang into the cab of the engine, while Andrews, with hand on the rail and foot on the step, waited to see that the remainder of the band had gained entrance into the rear box car. This seemed difficult and slow, though it really consumed but a few seconds, for the car stood on a considerable bank, and the first who came were pitched in by their comrades, while these, in turn, dragged in the others, and the door was instantly closed. A sentinel, with musket in hand, stood not a dozen feet from the engine watching the whole proceeding, but before he or any of the soldiers and guards around could make up their minds to interfere, all was done, and Andrews, with a nod to his engineer, stepped on board. The valve was pulled wide open, and for a moment the wheels of the "General" slipped around ineffectively; then, with a bound that jerked the soldiers in the box car from their feet, the little train darted away, leaving the camp and station in the wildest uproar of confusion. The first step of the enterprise was triumphantly accomplished.

According to the time-table, of which Andrews had secured a copy, there were two trains to be met. These presented no serious hindrance to our attaining high speed, for we could tell just where to expect them. There was also a local freight not down on the time-table, but which could not be far distant. Any danger of collision with it could be avoided by running according to the schedule of the captured train until it was passed; then, at the highest possible speed, we would run to the Oostenaula and Chickamauga bridges, lay them in ashes, and pass on through Chattanooga to Mitchel, at Huntsville, or wherever eastward of that point he might be found, arriving long before the close of the day. It was a brilliant prospect, and, so far as human estimates can determine, it would have been realized had the day been Friday instead of Saturday. On Friday every train had been on time, the day dry, and the road in perfect order. Now the road was in disorder, every train far behind time, and two "extras" were approaching us. But of these unfavorable conditions we knew nothing, and pressed confidently forward.

We stopped frequently, at one point tore up the track, cut telegraph wires, and loaded on crossties to be used in bridge burning. Wood and water were taken without difficulty, Andrews telling, very coolly, the story to which he adhered throughout the run, namely, that he was an agent of General Beauregard's running an impressed powder train through to that officer at Corinth. We had no good instruments for track-raising, as we had intended rather to depend upon fire; but the amount of time spent in taking up a rail was not material at this stage of our journey, as we easily kept on the time of our captured train. There was a wonderful exhilaration in passing swiftly by towns and stations through the heart of an enemy's country in this manner. It possessed just enough of the spice of danger—in this part of the run—to render it thoroughly enjoyable. The slightest accident to our engine, however, or a miscarriage in any part of our program, would have completely changed the conditions.

At Etowah Station we found the "Yonah," an old locomotive owned by an iron company, standing with steam up; but not wishing to alarm the enemy till the local freight had been safely met, we left it unharmed. Kingston, thirty miles from the starting-point, was safely reached. A train from Rome, Ga., on a branch road, had just arrived and was waiting for the morning mail—our train. We learned that the local freight would soon come also, and taking the side track, waited for it. When it arrived, however, Andrews saw to his surprise and chagrin that it bore a red flag, indicating another train not far behind. Stepping to the conductor, he boldly asked, "What does it mean that the road is blocked in this manner when I have orders to take this powder to Beauregard without a minute's delay?" The answer was interesting but not reassuring: "Mitchel has captured Huntsville and is said to be coming to Chattanooga, and we are getting everything out of there." He was asked by Andrews to pull his train a long way down the track out of the way, and promptly obeyed.

It seemed an exceedingly long time before the expected "extra" arrived; and when it did come it bore another red flag! The reason given was that the "local," being too great for one engine, had been made up in two sections, and the second section would doubtless be along in a short time. This was terribly vexatious; yet there seemed nothing to do but wait. To start out between the sections of an extra train would be to court destruction. There were already three trains around us, and their many passengers, and others, were growing very curious about the mysterious train which had arrived on the time of the morning mail, manned by strangers. For an hour and five minutes from the time of arrival at Kingston, we remained in the most critical position. The sixteen of us who were shut up tightly in a box car, personating Beauregard's ammunition—hearing sounds outside, but unable to distinguish words—had perhaps the most trying position. Andrews sent us, by one of the engineers, a cautious warning to be ready to fight in case the uneasiness of the crowd around led them to make any investigations, while he himself kept near the station to prevent the sending off of any alarming telegram. So intolerable was our suspense that the order for a deadly conflict would have been felt as a relief. But the assurance of Andrews quieted the crowd until the whistle of the expected train from the north was heard; then, as it glided up to the depot, past the end of our side track, we were off without more words.

But unexpected danger had arisen behind us. Out of the panic at Big Shanty two men emerged, determined, if possible, to foil the unknown captors of their train. There was no telegraph station, and no locomotive at hand with which to follow; but the conductor of the train, W. A. Fuller, and Anthony Murphy, foreman of the Atlanta railway machine shops, who happened to be on board of Fuller's train, started on foot after us as hard as they could run! Finding a hand-car they mounted it and pushed forward till they neared Etowah, where they ran on the break we had made in the road and were precipitated down the embankment into the ditch. Continuing with more caution, they reached Etowah and found the "Yonah," which was at once pressed into service, loaded with soldiers who were at hand, and hurried with flying wheels towards Kingston. Fuller prepared to fight at that point, for he knew of the tangle of extra trains, and of the lateness of the regular trains, and did not think we would be able to pass. We had been gone only four minutes when he arrived and found himself stopped by three long, heavy trains of cars headed in the wrong direction. To move them out of the way so as to pass would cause a delay he was little inclined to afford—would indeed have almost certainly given us the victory. So, abandoning his engine, he, with Murphy, ran across to the Rome train, and, uncoupling the engine and one car, pushed forward with about forty armed men. As the Rome branch connected with the main road above the depot, he encountered no hindrance, and it was now a fair race. We were not many minutes ahead.

Four miles from Kingston we again stopped and cut the telegraph. While trying to take up a rail at this point, we were greatly startled. One of the rails was loosened and eight of us were pulling at it, when distant, but distinct, we heard the whistle of a pursuing engine! With a frantic pull we broke the rail and all tumbled over the embankment with the effort. We moved on, and at Adairsville we found a mixed train (freight and passenger) waiting, but there was an express on the road that had not yet arrived. We could afford no more delay, and set out for the next station, Calhoun, at terrible speed, hoping to reach that point before the express, which was behind time, should arrive. The nine miles which we had to travel were left behind in less than the same number of minutes! The express was just pulling out, but, hearing our whistle, backed before us until we were able to take the side track; it stopped, however, in such a manner as completely to close up the other end of the switch. The two trains, side by side, almost touched each other, and our precipitate arrival caused natural suspicion. Many searching questions were asked which had to be answered before we could get the opportunity of proceeding. We, in the box car, could hear the altercation and were almost sure that a fight would be necessary before the conductor would consent to "pull up" in order to let us out. Here, again, our position was most critical, for the pursuers were rapidly approaching.

Fuller and Murphy saw the obstruction of the broken rail, in time to prevent [a] wreck, by reversing their engine; but the hindrance was for the present insuperable. Leaving all their men behind, they started for a second foot-race. Before they had gone far they met the train we had passed at Adairsville and turned it back after us. At Adairsville they dropped the cars, and, with locomotive and tender loaded with armed men, they drove forward at the highest speed possible. They knew that we were not many minutes ahead, and trusted to overhaul us before the express train could be safely passed.

But Andrews had told the powder story again, with all his skill, and had added a direct request in peremptory form to have the way opened before him, which the Confederate conductor did not see fit to resist; and just before the pursuers arrived at Calhoun we were again under way. Stopping once more to cut wires and tear up the track, we felt a thrill of exhilaration to which we had long been strangers. The track was now clear before us to Chattanooga; and even west of that city we had good reason to believe that we would find no other train in the way till we had reached Mitchel's lines. If one rail could now be lifted we would be in a few minutes at Oostenaula bridge, and, that burned, the rest of the task would be little more than simple manual labor, with the enemy absolutely powerless. We worked with a will.

But in a moment the tables were turned! Not far behind we heard the scream of a locomotive bearing down upon us at lightning speed! The men on board were in plain sight and well armed! Two minutes —perhaps one—would have removed the rail at which we were toiling; then the game would have been in our own hands, for there was no other locomotive beyond that could be turned back after us. But the most desperate efforts were in vain. The rail was simply bent, and we hurried to our engine and darted away, while remorselessly after us thundered the enemy.

Now the contestants were in clear view, and a most exciting race followed. Wishing to gain a little time for the burning of the Oostenaula bridge, we dropped one car, and shortly after, another; but they were "picked up" and pushed ahead to Resaca station. We were obliged to run over the high trestles and covered bridge at that point without a pause. This was the first failure in the work assigned us.

The Confederates could not overtake and stop us on the road, but their aim was to keep close behind so that we might not be able to damage the road or take in wood or water. In the former they succeeded, but not the latter. Both engines were put at the highest rate of speed. We were obliged to cut the wire after every station passed, in order that an alarm might not be sent ahead, and we constantly strove to throw our pursuer off the track or to obstruct the road permanently in some way so that we might be able to burn the Chickamauga bridges, still ahead. The chances seemed good that Fuller and Murphy would be wrecked. We broke out the end of our last box car and dropped cross-ties on the track as we ran, thus checking their progress and getting far enough ahead to take in wood and water at two separate stations. Several times we almost lifted a rail, but each time the coming of the Confederates, within rifle range, compelled us to desist and speed on. Our worst hindrance was the rain. The previous day (Friday) had been clear, with a high wind, and on such a day fire would have been easily and tremendously effective. But today a bridge could be burned only with abundance of fuel and careful nursing.

Thus we sped on, mile after mile, in this fearful chase, around curves and past stations in seemingly endless perspective. Whenever we lost sight of the enemy beyond a curve, we hoped that some of our obstructions had been effective in throwing him from the track and that we would see him no more; but at each long reach backward the smoke was again seen, and the shrill whistle was like the scream of a bird of prey. The time could not have been so very long, for the terrible speed was rapidly devouring the distance, but with our nerves strained to the highest tension each minute seemed an hour. On several occasions the escape of the enemy from wreck seemed little less than miraculous. At one point a rail was placed across the track so skillfully on a curve that it was not seen till the train ran upon it at full speed. Fuller says that they were terribly jolted, and seemed to bounce altogether from the track, but lighted on the rails in safety. Some of the Confederates wished to leave a train which was driven at such a reckless rate, but their wishes were not gratified.

Before reaching Dalton we urged Andrews to turn and attack the enemy, laying an ambush so as to get into close quarters that our revolvers might be on equal terms with their guns. I have little doubt that if this had been carried out it would have succeeded. But Andrews—whether because he thought the chance of wrecking or obstructing the enemy still good, or feared that the country ahead had been alarmed by a telegram around the Confederacy by the way of Richmond—merely gave the plan his sanction without making any attempt to carry it into execution.

Dalton was passed without difficulty, and beyond we stopped again to cut wires and obstruct the track. It happened that a regiment was encamped not a hundred yards away, but they did not molest us. Fuller had written a dispatch to Chattanooga and dropped a man with orders to have it forwarded instantly while he pushed on to save the bridges. Part of the messages got through and created a wild panic in Chattanooga, although it did not materially influence our fortunes. Our supply of fuel was now very short, and without getting rid of our pursuer long enough to take on more, it was evident that we could not run as far as Chattanooga.

While cutting the wire we made an attempt to get up another rail, but the enemy, as usual, were too quick for us. We had no tool for this purpose except a wedge-pointed iron bar. Two or three bent iron claws for pulling out spikes would have given us such superiority that, down to almost the last of our run, we would have been able to escape and to burn all the Chickamauga bridges. But it had not been our intention to rely on this mode of obstruction—an emergency only rendered necessary by our unexpected delay and the pouring rain.

We made no attempt to damage the long tunnel north of Dalton, as our enemies had greatly dreaded. The last hope of the raid was now staked upon an effort of a different kind. A few more obstructions were dropped on the track and our speed was increased so that we soon forged a considerable distance ahead. The side and end boards of the last car were torn into shreds, all available fuel was piled upon it, and blazing brands were brought back from the engine. By the time we approached a long covered bridge the fire in the car was fairly started. We uncoupled it in the middle of the bridge, and with painful suspense awaited the issue. Oh, for a few minutes till the work of conflagration was fairly begun! There was still steam-pressure enough in our boiler to carry us to the next wood-yard, where we could have replenished our fuel, by force if necessary, so as to run us as near to Chattanooga as was deemed prudent. We did not know of the telegraph message which the pursuers had sent ahead. But, alas! the minutes were not given. Before the bridge was extensively fired the enemy was upon us. They pushed right into the smoke and drove the burning car before them to the next side-track.

With no car left, and no fuel, the last scrap having been thrown into the engine or upon the burning car, and with no obstruction to drop on the track, our situation was indeed desperate.

But it might still be possible to save ourselves if we left the train in a body and took a direct course toward the Union lines. Confederate pursuers with whom I have since conversed have agreed on two points—that we could have escaped in the manner here pointed out; and that an attack on the pursuing train would likely have been successful. But Andrews thought otherwise, at least in relation to the former plan, and ordered us to jump from the locomotive, and, dispersing in the woods, each endeavored to save himself.

The question is often asked, "Why did you not reverse your engine and thus wreck the one following?" Wanton injury was no part of our plan, and we could not afford to throw away our engine till the last extremity. When the raiders were jumping off, however, the engine was reversed and driven back, but by that time the steam was so nearly exhausted that the Confederate engine had no difficulty in reversing and receiving the shock without injury. Both were soon at a stand-still, and the Confederates, reinforced by a party from a train which soon arrived on the scene—the express passenger, which had been turned back at Calhoun—continued the chase on foot.

It is easy now to understand why Mitchel paused thirty miles west of Chattanooga. The Andrews raiders had been forced to stop eighteen miles south of the same town, and no flying train met Mitchel with tidings that all the railroad communications of Chattanooga were destroyed, and that the town was in a panic and undefended.

A few words will give the sequel to this remarkable enterprise. The hunt for the fugitive raiders was prompt, energetic, and successful. Several were captured the same day, and all but two within a week. Even these two were overtaken and brought back, when they supposed that they were virtually out of danger. Two who had reached Marietta but had failed to board the train . . . were identified and added to the band of prisoners.

Now follows the saddest part of the story. Being in citizens' dress within an enemy's lines, the whole party were held as spies. A court-martial was convened, and the leader and seven out of the remaining twenty-one were condemned and executed. The others were never brought to trial, probably because of the advance of Union forces and the consequent confusion into which the affairs of the Departments of East Tennessee and Georgia were thrown. Of the remaining fourteen, eight succeeded, by a bold effort—attacking their guard in broad daylight—in making their escape from Atlanta, Ga., and ultimately in reaching the North. The other six, who shared in this effort, but were recaptured, remained prisoners until the latter part of March, 1863, when they were exchanged through a special arrangement made by Secretary Stanton. All the survivors of this expedition received medals and promotion. The pursuers also received expressions of gratitude from their fellow Confederates, notably from the Governor and Legislature of Georgia.

Destroying a Railroad

The cutting of railroads was, from the outbreak of the war, encouraged on both sides, and by this time had developed into an important military industry. Various implements and appliances, to facilitate the havoc and make it as effectual as possible, were part of the equipment of every army.

"Now we're goin' ter have some fun, Shorty!" exclaimed Si, as the 200th Indiana stacked arms beside the track and the specific duty to be performed became apparent to all. "I hain't never fergot the time the Johnnies cut *our* cracker-line, 'n' I've allus been hopin' we'd git a chance ter pay 'em back. 'Sides that you 'n' me's got a pertickler spite agin this 'ere railroad, 'cause it's the one 't tuk us down ter that measly place 't we had sich a time gittin' 'way from. I've got a fust-rate stummick fer pitchin' inter this job!"

Five thousand men were thickly distributed on both sides of the road for a mile. They did not lay off their accouterments, and their muskets were within grasp, should there be occasion to stop work and go to fighting. Axes, sledge-hammers, levers, and "claws" were plentifully supplied. A few spikes were quickly drawn at intervals of two or three hundred yards. Then the men laid hold of the rails on one side, gave a mighty yell, and in an instant the track was turned over into the ditch. Vigorous blows with the sledges rapidly detached the ties from the rails. Meanwhile others had started a hundred fires all along the line. Upon these the ties were loosely piled, with quantities of fence rails and dry limbs and brush to feed the flames. The long, clumsy iron rails were picked up, with a dozen men to each, as if they were feathers, and laid across the blazing heaps. In half an hour they were at a red heat, for six or eight feet in the middle. Then came the final process by which the devastation was made complete. With grappling-irons, made for the purpose, the rails were twisted two or three times around, as Si had often seen his mother twist doughnuts. The still glowing rails were then bent entirely around the trunks of standing trees, where they were left to cool.

It was a scene of wild and furious tumult, never to be forgotten—the yelling, scrambling, sweating men, their faces begrimed with dust and smoke, lifting, prying, pounding, and chopping, the shouts of the officers directing the operations and urging up the laggards, and the blazing, crackling fires, stretching far along the track on either side. A few hours sufficed to utterly destroy miles of the road—the ties in

---

From *Corporal Si Klegg and His "Pard,"* How They Lived and Talked, and What They Did and Suffered, while Fighting for the Flag, by Wilbur F. Hinman, pp. 648–652. Copyright, 1887, by Wilbur F. Hinman. Cleveland: The Williams Publishing Company.

ashes and the twisted, shapeless rails transformed into rings encircling the trees.

When an undertaking of this kind was thoroughly carried out it caused, in many cases, serious embarrassment to the Confederate army. The vast mineral resources of the South were then almost entirely undeveloped. Before the war all iron for railroads in that section was obtained from the North or imported from Europe. The South had no means to make good the wear of constant use and the ravage of war. If rails were merely heated and bent it was possible to straighten them so that they might be relaid, but when they were fantastically twisted by the grappling-irons of well equipped raiders, they were made valueless except as they might command the market price for "old iron." The frequent raids upon the lines of supply of the Union army, though annoying, were far less disastrous than was the destruction of railroads to the enemy. The government kept at all desirable points abundant supplies of rails, ties, spikes, etc., and the engineer corps repaired the breaks with a rapidity that was amazing. Not infrequently this was done under fire, the men toiling with their muskets slung over their backs, part of them keeping back the enemy while the others pushed forward the work. There seemed to be nothing impossible to the intelligent soldiers of the Union army.

Railroads were invaluable for the speedy transportation of troops and supplies. At times, when extraordinary facilities were needed—as when two corps were sent from the Army of the Potomac to reinforce the Army of the Cumberland at Chattanooga—the government took possession of the necessary roads with all their rolling stock, and as many engines and cars of other roads as could be used; and for the time all private business had to give way. The Southern roads, in the territory occupied by the Union army, were in many cases laid with new rails, the gauge being changed when necessary, and stocked with engines and cars owned by the government. These were all designated "U.S.M.R.Rds."—United States Military Railroads. During the last year of the war the military railway service reached the height of efficiency. Plenty of engineers, conductors, and trainmen were found, who took their lives in their hands as truly as did the soldiers who marched to battle.

While the 200th Indiana and the other wreckers were engaged in their work, they were more than once called into line with loaded muskets by sharp firing on the outposts, where there was constant skirmishing with the enemy's cavalry. At length a horseman came galloping in with the intelligence that a large body of Confederate infantry was approaching with rapid strides. The bugles sounded the "fall in" and away went the Union force, leaving the road for miles a smoking ruin. Through the night, stumbling along in the darkness, the men pushed on, harassed in front, flank, and rear by the rebel riders. Morning found the corps safely back in its place behind the great line of intrenchments.

New Gages to Order

. . . The War played havoc with the Southern railroads in more ways than one. Today a company would be doing business on a standard-gage scale; early next morning the Union army would sweep into town, and by noon the railroad men found they had a narrow-gage road on their hands. A few days later the Confederate soldiers would chase the Yankees off the property, and *they* would promptly rebuild the line to a *broad* gage.

Many stories are told down there of this shifting of gage, mostly as a military measure to prevent a pursuing army from getting too close, but sometimes as an economic necessity to continued operation. If their own engines and cars had been destroyed or carried off by some marauding army and there was no locomotive on hand for the morning train, the super would call the boys together, hurry them over to a neighboring town where there was a railroad of totally different gage, but owning some fine equipment. Then, with a couple of engines and a few cars under their arms, so to speak, the crowd would hurry back home. While one crew busied itself with setting up the borrowed equipment, another gang would hurriedly change the road's gage to fit the newly-acquired rolling stock, and the Morning Mail would leave town on time! And then, when the War was over, many a Southern railway official found his yards full of decrepit equipment of several different gages, due to all this juggling, and probably his line of track was broken in several places by changes in gage. Because he was hard put to decide which of these gages to adopt in the rehabilitation program, it is likely his decision came after a survey of the equipment there. Choosing the best of the lot, he would rebuild his road to fit it. In view of the fact that the South was a muddle of broad, narrow and all the in-between widths, it must have taxed the official mind sometimes to know how to choose.

From "The Muddle of the Gages," by Linwood W. Moody, in *Bulletin No. 47,* The Railway & Locomotive Historical Society, Inc., September, 1938, pp. 62–63. Copyright, 1938, by the Railway & Locomotive Historical Society, Inc. Baker Library, Harvard Business School. Boston.

War-Time Expressmen

Expressmen were exempted from military service by both Northern and Southern governments. The companies, while garnering large profits on the one hand, on the other often displayed fine public spirit, sometimes in special emergencies placing their facilities at the disposal of cities, states, or organizations, free of cost. They were officially thanked on several occasions for patriotic services.

The Adams and Southern Expresses formed the only feasible means of communication by letter or of transportation between North and South, and that, of course, was necessarily desultory and unreliable. The privations of prisoners in their dismal places of detention during the war were pitiful, and people on each side strove to alleviate the sufferings of their own men by sending them clothing, food, and other comforts by express. Adams and Southern agents exchanged such shipments whenever possible. The same was true of letters. There was of course no postal communion between the warring sections, and the expresses did the best they could at transmitting letters (though sometimes forbidden and always subject to censorship) between friends, kinsmen, and business associates who were separated by the red line of war.

The Adams was the dominant company in the city of Washington and along the war front, and it did an enormous business for the Government. Adams special messengers on some occasions carried official documents from Washington to army commanders in the field. . . . In the sorely harassed South, when the freight service had broken down, heavy materials, even up to bales of cotton, were occasionally seen traveling by express. When the Union troops had overspread Kentucky and Tennessee, the Adams frequently carried a carload of army or sutler's supplies to some of the camps in that area. The car would be sidetracked at the camp and the messenger made his way back as best he could.

The business done with the soldiers was immense, and the Adams showed remarkable efficiency in expanding and extending its service to every headquarters in the field. Its messengers waited at bivouac fires for letters, perhaps scribbled on a Bible or prayer-book flyleaf, and on more than one occasion took last messages from dying soldiers —messages sometimes left unfinished.

The expresses shipped packages addressed to soldiers at half rates. The Adams advertised that donated blankets for the soldiers, if addressed to a United States quartermaster, would be carried free. From home, packages of warm under clothing, shoes and good things to eat

---

Abridged from *Old Waybills,* The Romance of the Express Companies, by Alvin F. Harlow, pp. 290–300. Copyright, 1934, by Alvin F. Harlow. New York and London: D. Appleton-Century Co., Inc.

were hopefully forwarded to the loved ones in the ranks and garrisons, and the expresses did the best they could. The returning business was as large or larger. On payday officers and privates sent shares of their modest salaries home to families who in many cases sorely needed it. There were privates who sent the whole of their tiny $13 monthly pittance to needy wives and children, blithely relying on foraging and pillage to supply what extra comforts they hoped to enjoy. And the doughboys of the first World War were by no means the first to send home souvenirs. By express (charges usually to be collected from the home folks) went thousands of articles picked up on the battlefield or in "Rebel" territory, and therefore considered legitimate spoil.

The two companies, Adams and Southern, flowed back and forth as liquidly as water as the armies moved this way and that. When Lee or Bragg advanced northward, the Southern Express followed and the Adams fell back. When the gray-coated hosts retreated southward, the Adams, almost before the smoke of battle had cleared, retook possession of the disputed ground, and even penetrated Southern territory wherever Union troops led the way. The Adams had the better of the argument, particularly in the West. On landing, the messenger would have a tent assigned to him by the commanding officer, and with a plank across two barrels as a counter, he would deal out boxes, parcels, letters, and home papers to eager inquirers.

When the Union fleet captured Memphis in June, 1861, Charles Woodward, superintendent of the Adams second military division, and his men were close behind. The Southern Express had made a futile attempt to remove some of their equipment, but the Confederate troops had seized their horses, and the evacuation was so sudden that they could take away almost nothing. Woodward and his men took over their office, with its furniture and a large quantity of undelivered freight, some money (mostly Confederate), and the wagons. The railroads into Memphis had been torn up or were held by Confederate troops, and the Adams could for a time enter the city only by the river.

Adams representatives traveled with Grant's army and had an office at Pittsburg Landing during the Battle of Shiloh, where a shell crashed through the log building which housed it, half wrecking it. The two men in charge were pressed into service (as they frequently were during the war) to help drag heavy siege guns up the bluff. At Helena, Arkansas, in 1863, when 7,600 Confederates were trying to capture the town, an Adams messenger and Superintendent Woodward were pressed into the ranks, and served for two hours with the artillery before the attack was beaten off.

After the Battles of Shiloh and Corinth in the spring of '62, Tennessee towns along the Mobile & Ohio Railroad were occupied and Adams offices opened. The railroads had been frequently torn up and relaid, they were dilapidated and dangerous, and most of the inhabitants were hostile and in communication with guerrillas and Confederate cavalry who roamed the country, burning trains and stations, cutting telegraph wires and lifting rails. Trains were frequently fired upon; messengers dropped to the car floor at the sound of shots, and they had a habit of piling the car door half full of heavy freight behind which to dodge if attacked at a station. Messengers were frequently seized and haled before Confederate commanders, but as a rule, soon released. One messenger was captured four times on one trip between Corinth and Memphis. The company held back money shipments, for fear of confiscation.

An interesting snapshot of wartime conditions even in classic Indiana is the story of the shipping of $2,000,000 in cash in the winter of 1863–64 for the payroll of the Army of the Cumberland, then lying around Chattanooga. The cash was packed in a heavy wooden box about two feet square and four or five feet long, which disguised its nature. From Cincinnati it traveled under the unostentatious care of a special messenger and two guards over the Ohio and Mississippi Railroads (delayed en route by two freight wrecks) to Seymour, where a long and anxious wait ensued. Southern Indiana was then a dangerous territory. That "copperhead" organization, the Knights of the Golden Circle, flourished there; thieves and counterfeiters pestered the countryside, and near Seymour lived the Reno family, who were to become notorious three years later as bank and train robbers.

There was no bridge across the Ohio at Louisville, and the messenger learned that the river was full of floating ice and no ferries running. He meditated returning to Cincinnati with the box, but knowing its vital importance to the Army, he feared not to go on. When the Jeffersonville and Indianapolis train came, "crowded, filthy and odorous," they set forth again, but two more freight wrecks delayed them, and the box, which had left Cincinnati on Friday, did not reach Jeffersonville, on the Ohio River, until Wednesday at daybreak. From there the messenger wired Louisville of his arrival. The river above the falls was almost jammed with ice, but below the falls it was freer. The agent at Louisville took a wagon downstream, succeeded in getting a boat to ferry him across below the falls, drove up to Jeffersonville, and finally relieved the grateful messenger of his onerous charge.

In the East during the latter years of the war, the railroads had a rough time of it. Southern Express messengers between Richmond and Wilmington, N. C., were four or five days in making the trip. When Grant was converging on Petersburg in 1864, trains from the south, because of the furious bombardment, would not approach nearer than two miles from the city; and the messenger, to reach the office, had to make a four-mile detour in a wagon, most of the time within range of the Northern fire. Messengers and drivers were wounded at times, and once the Appomattox bridge was destroyed by a shell just as the wagon left it.

A forgotten incident in war history has to do with a small express founded in 1845 by N. G. Howard, which for 46 years handled the business over the Reading Railroad and parts of some adjoining systems. When Lee's Confederate army invaded Pennsylvania in June, 1863, burning a bridge over the Susquehanna and thrusting northward to Gettysburg, all eastern Pennsylvania fell into a panic. The banks in Pottsville cleaned out their vaults and entrusted all cash and negotiable securities to Abner Mason, a messenger for Howard's Express, who took the treasure to New York and deposited it in various banks, where it remained until the scare was over.

The saddest of all traffic which occupied the express companies during the war was that of the carriage of bodies of soldiers slain by disease or enemy bullets. Many who died on the battlefield were buried where they fell; but when kinsmen could locate the body and were able to pay the high cost of shipment home, it was in many cases sent back to be buried in the family plot. After a battle, it was no uncommon thing for a messenger to have 200 or more coffins in his car—perhaps a special car for them.

At the beginning of the war, many bodies were shipped in wooden coffins, and the hot weather and the long delays brought such unpleasant results that the Adams notified its agents that nothing but metallic coffins must be received thereafter. At the time, many wooden coffins were coming into Wheeling from the West Virginia battlefields, and as the agent there could not forward them, he started a little private cemetery, and in the course of a few weeks, buried between forty and fifty. He carefully recorded the name, regiment and home address of each fallen hero, and at the close of the war the express company saw to it that the bodies were disinterred, recoffined and sent to the kinsmen who mourned them.

The well-to-do parents of a Federal soldier killed in western Tennessee ordered his body shipped in the finest metallic casket available at the time. The shipment had to lie overnight at Jackson, Tennessee, and as the casket was so heavy that it was not supposed that anybody could steal it, the agent left it on a truck on the station platform outside his office. Fancy the agent's horror next morning when he found the soldier's body lying on the truck and the coffin gone! The thieves coveted that fine sarcophagus, but their consciences would not permit them to bereave the parents of the body.

A strange instance of human callousness was related in the *Express Gazette* in 1882 by a veteran who was a clerk in the Baltimore office of Harnden's Express early in 1865. There were several army hospitals around Baltimore then. A man came in and asked the rate on a corpse to a town in Massachusetts. "Thirty-four, fifty," replied the clerk after consulting his book. "Give me a receipt," said the stranger, counting out the money. "Have you a medical certificate?" asked the clerk. "No, the man ain't dead yet." The clerk was astonished. "Now, see here," said the stranger. "I've got to settle this thing and get away on the next train. The man is my brother; I've been down here nursing him until I'm sick and tired of this town, and I've got important business at home, and I've got to get away. So give me a receipt and the steward will bring you a certificate when he brings you the body." The clerk hinted that it might be a long time. "No, you'll get your shipment," said the man. "He'll probably die by six o'clock this evening." The clerk gave the receipt, though protesting that the affair was very irregular. Next morning the hospital wagon backed up to the express office with the expected body and several others. "When did this man die?" asked the clerk of the steward. "About 6:45 last evening," replied the other, laughing. "He kept his engagement pretty well."

III. THE ADVANCING FRONTIER

River vs. Rail: Lincoln and the Rock Island Bridge Case

The first bridge that ever spanned the mighty Mississippi was a splendid wooden structure containing more than a million feet of timber and several hundred thousand pounds of iron. It stood on five stone piers poised thirty-five feet above mean water level and resting on the solid bed rock of the river.

This great connecting link between the East and the potential West, built by the Rock Island Railroad, was 1582 feet long and extended between Rock Island, Ill., and Davenport, Iowa. The first shovelful

From "Lincoln and the First Mississippi Bridge," by Bernie Babcock, *The Railroad Man's Magazine,* Vol. IV (February, 1931), No. 3, pp. 328–332. Copyright, 1931, by the Frank A. Munsey Company. New York.

of earth excavated for a pier was turned on the Iowa side, July 16, 1853. The corner stone was laid in September, 1854, with a great celebration at Davenport. Flags waved and bands played. Cannon boomed, speeches were made.

Almost since the beginning of American history the Mississippi River had been the great artery for north and south trade. Merchants and manufacturers did not want to lose established markets. Boats and barges operating on the river did not want to lose trade. Nothing so threatened a revolution in established traffic as did the meeting of East and West which this bridge was certain to bring about.

Already opposing forces were actively at work. The matter was taken up with the Secretary of War, Jefferson Davis, who later became President of the Confederate States. Mr. Davis refused the Rock Island the grant it asked for. Not only this, but he directed the United States attorney for the Northern District of Illinois to apply for an injunction to prevent the construction of a railroad bridge across the river.

For a time hopes for the proposed span were dim. If the court upheld the ruling of the Secretary of War there would be no bridge and the great West must lie undeveloped for perhaps a decade.

Fortunately for the Rock Island and the future of the West, the decree of Mr. Davis was not upheld by the court. Building continued. In April, 1856, this great structure stood fully completed; and great was the joy and excitement when, on April 22, three locomotives, with two tenders and eight passenger cars, crossed the new bridge.

Everything seemed rosy for the future of the bridge when, in a day, destruction came, and from a quarter wholly unexpected.

A new boat named *Effie Afton* had been added by the New Orleans & Louisville Packet Company to its number. Two weeks after the Rock Island bridge had been opened for traffic, the *Effie Afton* made her virgin trip north, out of St. Louis, on the morning of May 6. The boat had gone about two hundred feet above the draw pier, when, one of her wheels stopping, she swung against the bridge. How it happened that, as the boat struck, its stove turned over, will never be known. New, and shipshape, there was no reason why the stove should upset.

As a result of this "accident"—for such the ship owners called it—the boat took fire, and in its burning destroyed the bridge span where it struck.

Owners of the *Effie Afton* brought suit against the bridge construction company for damages. What they wanted to do was prove the Rock Island, or any other agent building a span across the Mississippi, guilty of creating a material obstruction to river traffic.

Litigation was now in sight, and plenty of it. It seemed likely to Norman B. Judd, solicitor for the Rock Island, in a conference with Henry Farnam, chief engineer, and officials of the Rock Island, that the lower court would decide against the railroad. It was decided that, when the case came into the United States Court, a strong and popular man would be needed to present the railroad's case.

"Gentlemen," Mr. Judd said, "there is only one man in this country who can take the case and win it. This man is Abraham Lincoln."

"And who is Abraham Lincoln?" questioned Mr. Farnam.

"A young lawyer from Sangamon County. One of the best men to state a case forcibly and convincingly that I have ever heard. I heard him first in the waterway convention here in Chicago back in 1847 when we were after President Polk's scalp for vetoing as unconstitutional the bill which Congress had passed for the improvement of rivers and the construction of harbors in our Lake Michigan."

It was agreed to employ Mr. Lincoln if, after looking the case over, he cared to take it. The suggestion was made that Mr. Judd's private car be taken to Springfield to bring Mr. Lincoln to Chicago for a conference.

That was not Mr. Lincoln's way. How he arrived on the scene is not told. In the story, however, it happened that, a few days later, a boy sitting out from shore on one of the bridge spans, watching driftwood run with the river current, was surprised by a caller. A tall man he was with plenty of dark hair, a big nose, and a friendly smile. He asked the lad if he lived around there.

"Yes, sir. I live in Davenport. My dad helped build this railroad."

"I see," said the tall man, and, taking a seat beside the boy, he dropped his long legs down over the bridge tie and was ready for conversation.

"I suppose you know all about this river?"

"I guess I do. It was here when I was born, and it's been here ever since."

"Well, well!" laughed the long-legged man. "I'm mighty glad I came out here where I can get a little less opinion and more fact. Tell me now, how fast does this water run under here? Have you ever thought it out?"

"Never have. But I know how to find out."

"I knew you could do it. Tell me how, will you?"

"Got a watch?"

"Right here." The stranger drew a big silver timepiece from his pocket.

"All right," said the boy. "I'll spy a log swinging out from the island. I'll tell you, and you take the time. When it goes in under us you can take the time again. Then we've got the distance and the time. Can't we figure it this way?"

Mr. Lincoln agreed they could. So it was the big-brained, big-hearted Lincoln got this and much other information about the current of the river, its speeds, its eddies, its traffic, from a boy afterward well known as Benjamin R. Brayton, for many years a Rock Island engineer.

In his speech to the jury Mr. Lincoln said he did not propose to assail anybody, but intended to be much in earnest, since much was involved bearing vitally on the future development of our country.

"The plaintiff must establish," he argued, "their contention that the bridge is a material obstruction and that they managed their boat with reasonable care and skill. As to the last point, high winds had nothing to do with it, for it was not a windy day. They must show due skill and care. Difficulties going downstream will not do, for they were going upstream. My investigation of river currents shows they help, instead of hinder, the passage of boats."

Mr. Lincoln said much more. He accused no man of intentionally wrecking the *Effie Afton,* but his facts and arguments had great weight. And one by one the jurymen came to Mr. Lincoln's viewpoint.

Other litigation followed, and bills were introduced in Congress. But the facts and reasoning of Mr. Lincoln could not be set aside nor outreasoned. The end of it all was told in the words of Judge Grant, who, years before at the laying of the corner stone of the wooden bridge, had said, "Never in the history of time will this vast expanse of water be void of this crossing which is in building at this time."

General Dodge Discovers a Pass through the Black Hills

One of the great problems that confronted our early surveys was the crossing of the Black Hills, a spur of the Rocky Mountains. There was no trouble in obtaining a line from the summit of the range and descending to the west into Laramie Plains, but the country on the east dropped off so rapidly there was no stream or any divide we could find that was practicable for a 116-foot grade; the engineers had examined nearly every stream and every divide. The divides from the summit for a long distance down were favorable, but where the division of the granite and sedimentary formations joined there would be a drop of 500 feet to 1,000, and we could not find supporting ground to hold our grade to overcome this great fall.

In 1865, as I was returning from the Yellowstone country, after finishing the Indian campaigns, I took my command along the east base of the Black Hills, following up the Chug Water, and so on south, leaving my train every day and going on to the summit of the Black Hills with a view of trying to discover some approach from the east that was feasible. When we got down to the crossing of the Lodge

From *How We Built the Union Pacific Railway,* and other Railway Papers and Addresses, by Major-General Grenville M. Dodge, pp. 85–87. 61st Congress, 2nd Session, Senate, Document No. 447. Washington: Government Printing Office. 1910.

Pole, I knew the Indians were following us, but I left the command with a few cavalrymen and guides, with a view of following the country from the Cheyenne Pass south, leaving strict orders with the command if they saw smoke signals they were to come to us immediately. We worked south from the Cheyenne Pass and around the head of Crow Creek. When I looked down into the valley there was a band of Indians who had worked themselves in between our party and the trains. I knew it meant trouble for us; they were either after us or our stock. I therefore immediately dismounted, and giving our horses to a couple of men with instructions to keep on the west side of the ridge out of sight and gunshot as much as possible, we took the ridge between Crow Creek and Lone Tree Creek, keeping upon it and holding the Indians away from us, as our arms were so far-reaching that when they came too near our best shots would reach them and they soon saw their danger.

We made signals for our cavalry, but they did not seem to see them. It was getting along in the afternoon, as we worked down this ridge, that I began to discover we were on an apparently very fine approach to the Black Hills, and one of the guides has stated that I said: "If we saved our scalps I believed we had found a railroad line over the mountains."

At about 4 o'clock the Indians were preparing to take the ridge in our front. The cavalry now saw our signals and soon came to our rescue, and when we reached the valley I was satisfied that the ridge we had followed was one which we could climb with a maximum grade within our charter and with comparatively light work.

As soon as I took charge of the Union Pacific I immediately wired to Mr. James A. Evans, who had charge of that division and who had been working on this mountain range for nearly a year, describing this ridge to him, as I had thoroughly marked it by a lone tree on Lone Tree Creek, and by a very steep cut butte on Crow Creek, and a deep depression in the ridge where the granite and sedimentary formations joined. He immediately made an examination and discovered a remarkably direct line of only a 90-foot grade reaching from the summit to the valley of Crow Creek, near where Cheyenne now stands, and this summit I immediately named for my old commander, General Sherman. The Union Pacific is constructed over this line and it is one of the two 80-foot grades now left on the Union Pacific that they were unable to reduce during the reconstruction of the road.

An Indian's Account of the Plum Creek Wreck

In the late summer of 1867, some Cheyennes succeeded in what was perhaps the only attempt to disable a railroad ever made by Indians. General Custer's summer campaign on the Republican and Smoky Hill Rivers had proved futile. The Indians continued to raid unchecked in Kansas and Nebraska and on the South Platte in Colorado. In the early days of August a camp of Cheyenne Indians under Turkey Leg [the actual leader of the party that ditched the train was Spotted Wolf] came to the Union Pacific Railroad, near Plum Creek, and by interfering with the rails threw a hand-car off the track, and subsequently ditched a freight train. A number of men were killed, and one, William Thompson, was scalped alive, recovered, and as recently as 1912 was still living, in England.

The printed accounts state that the Indians took out a culvert and broke the track in that way, but the narrative of Porcupine, then a young man in the Cheyenne camp, gives the facts about it.

* * * * *

The story of the wreck is told at length by Stanley.[1] The men he interviewed were perhaps not in a position to make very careful observations of what happened at the time, and we may prefer the story told by Porcupine. Stanley, however, quotes the story of Thompson, who was one of five men who started up the track on a hand-car to repair telegraph lines. When the hand-car was thrown from the track by the obstruction, the men ran. Thompson was shot through the arm, knocked down and partially stunned by an Indian, who jumped from his horse, scalped him, and remounted to ride off. Thompson saw the scalp slip from the Indian's belt and regained it, and later set out for Omaha, carrying his scalp in a pail of water, in the hope that it might be reattached to his head. He was treated by Doctor R. C. Moore, of Omaha. The operation was not successful, and Thompson finally went to England, and later sent back to Doctor Moore, the scalp, which had been tanned. The scalp, preserved in alcohol, is now in the Omaha Public Library Museum.

Porcupine's story is the only ever told by an eye-witness of the train wreck. We may imagine that the plundering of the train, and the acquiring of what to the Indians must have seemed an inexhaustible supply of extraordinary and valuable plunder, made a wild scene. It is related that young men tied to their ponies' tails the ends of bolts of calico and muslin, and amused themselves by careering over the

---

From *The Fighting Cheyennes,* by George Bird Grinnell, pp. 254–258. Copyright, 1915, by Charles Scribner's Sons. New York.

[1] *Early Travels and Adventures,* Vol. I, p. 154.—G.B.G.

prairie with long streamers waving behind them, each boy trying to ride over, tread upon, and so tear off the adornment of one of his fellows.

Porcupine's account, with some interpolations, is as follows:

We had a fight with the soldiers on [near] Ash Creek, which flows into the Arkansas. There were Sioux and Cheyennes in the fight, and the troops had defeated us, and taken everything that we had, and had made us poor. We were feeling angry.

Not long after that we saw the first train of cars that any of us had seen. We looked at it from a high ridge. Far off it was very small, but it kept coming and growing larger all the time, puffing out smoke and steam, and as it came on we said to each other that it looked like a white man's pipe when he was smoking.

The soldiers had beaten us in the fight and we thought that perhaps it was because of the way in which they rode and carried themselves, and we determined that we would try to imitate the soldiers, so we rode two by two in double file. One of the men had a bugle and from time to time he blew it in imitation of the bugle-call of the troops.

After we had seen this train and watched it come near us and grow large and pass by and then disappear in the distance, we went down from the ridge where we had been, to look at the ground where the train had passed, to see what sort of trail it made. When we came near to the track we could see white people going up and down by it, riding in light wagons. We were riding two by two and when we had come near to the track the man with the bugle sounded it, and the Indians spread out and formed a line and for a little way marched with extended front, and then again formed by twos. The white people paid no attention to us. Perhaps they thought that we were soldiers.

We crossed the track, looking carefully at it as we passed, and then went and crossed the river.

Not long after this, as we talked of our troubles, we said among ourselves: "Now the white people have taken all we had and have made us poor and we ought to do something. In these big wagons that go on this metal road, there must be things that are valuable—perhaps clothing. If we could throw these wagons off the iron they run on and break them open, we should find out what was in them and could take whatever might be useful to us."

Red Wolf and I tried to do this. We got a big stick, and just before sundown one day tied it to the rails and sat down to watch and see what would happen. Close by the track we built a big fire. Quite a long time after it got dark we heard a rumbling sound, at first very faint, but constantly growing louder. We said to each other: "It is coming." Presently the sound grew loud, and through the darkness we could see a small thing coming with something on it that moved up and down.

It was a hand-car with two men working it.

When the men on the car saw the fire and the Indians, they worked harder so as to run by them quickly, but when the car struck the stick it jumped high into the air. The men on it got up from where they had fallen and ran away, but were soon overtaken and killed.

On the hand-car were two guns, and in handling them the Indians pulled something and the guns broke in two in the middle and the barrels fell down. The Indians said: "It is a pity that these are broken; if they had not been, we should have had two good guns."

They were Spencer carbines, the first breech-loaders these Cheyennes had seen.

After their success in ditching the hand-car they thought they would do more. They took levers and after pulling out the spikes at the end of a rail, they bent the rail up a foot or two in the air. The next train came from the side of the bent-up rail. Porcupine said that the weight of the train ought to have bent back the rail in place; but in raising it they must have given it a sidewise twist, so that when the rail came down on the ties, the ends of the two rails did not meet, and the train jumped the track.

Looking over the long level plain, we saw a small light close to the horizon, and some one said: "The morning star is rising." "No," said another, "that is one of those things that we have seen." "No," said a third man, "the first one has gone and another one is rising."

It was learned afterward that they had seen the headlights of two trains that were coming, one following behind the other.

They sent men on the best horses they had eastward along the track to find out what these lights were and to come and report, telling them also to yell and shoot, in the hope that they might frighten it. The men went, and as soon as they saw that the first light was on a train, they started to return, riding as hard as they could, but before they had reached the place the train overtook and passed them. Some of them fired at the train and one tried to throw a rope over the engine, but when they got close, the horses were frightened and ran away. When they fired, the train made a loud noise—puffing—and threw up sparks into the air, going faster and faster, until it reached the break, and the locomotive jumped into the air and the cars all came together.

After the train was wrecked, a man with a lantern was seen coming running along the track, swearing in a loud tone of voice. He was the only one on the train left alive. They killed him. The other train stopped somewhere far off and whistled. Four or five men came walking along the track toward the wrecked train. The Cheyennes did not attack them. The second train then backed away.

Next morning they plundered and burned the wrecked train and scattered the contents of the cars all over the prairie. They tied bits of calico to their horses' tails and galloped about and had much amusement.

As they were going away with their plunder, another train came up from the west and many soldiers got off it, but they did not attack the Cheyennes. Later some of the Cheyennes went back for more plunder and were attacked by the Pawnees and driven away. An old man was killed and a woman and a boy, Pawnee, and a girl, Island Woman, were captured.

Strobridge Beats Casement in a Track-Laying Contest

I drew from Mr. Strobridge the story of the famous day in which he laid ten miles of rails between sunrise and sunset. He said:

In the rush to make distance, Casement brothers had laid in one day seven miles and eighteen hundred feet on the Union Pacific end, a feat which T. C. Durant, vice-president of the Union Pacific, offered to bet ten thousand dollars could not be beaten. I said to Mr. Crocker, "We can beat them but it will cost something." "Go ahead and do it," said Crocker, and this is how we did it. The two lines . . . were only twenty-five miles apart in April, 1869, so I knew if I beat them Casement would have no room to come back, even if he tried. I had five trains with five thousand men at my command, as well as plenty of iron, ties, spikes, and material, and I got everything ready just in time. Tuesday was the 27th, so I picked my men, arranged my plans and got them properly placed to start at the foot of Promontory mountain. I took two miles of material loaded on a train with a double header to push it up ahead of the engines, so it could be unloaded close to the end of the last rail laid in the track. On Wednesday the whistle blew right on time, the two engines gave a lurch, the push bar broke, and we were laid up for the day, helpless. We waited a day and on Thursday, the 29th, I put the two engines in front to pull instead of to push the train. With a will the men went to work, laying six miles in six hours and a quarter, two miles at a time. We changed horses every two and a half miles, but they were all tired and we gave them a good rest after that.

We had kept them on the run, and at six o'clock we quit with a record of ten miles and two hundred feet. Every bolt was screwed up, every spike driven home so that we backed down over that sixty-foot of grade at the rate of twenty-five miles an hour, twelve hundred men riding on the empty flat cars. Two Union Pacific engineers were there with their surveying chains, so there was no guess work and no contradictions. Our organization was as well drilled as any military company. Each rail was handled by eight men, four on a side. They ran it out to the edge of the car, dropping it into place for the spikes to be driven, a man for each spike. When it was down the men walked to the same spike on the next rail, drove it and on to the next, all day. Thus there were a thousand tons of rails, thirty-five hundred in number in the ten miles. H. H. Minkler was the foreman laying rails, and the men who handled them were Mike Shay, Mike Kennedy, Mike Sullivan, Pat Joyce, Tom Daily, George Wyatt, E. W. Killeen, and

---

Fred McNamara. There were men following up the trains, surfacing the track, filling in the dirt and making it ready for business. Nobody was crowded, nobody was hurt, nobody lost a minute. General Casement, who laid the Union Pacific Iron, told me that they had laid every rail they could under their system and he owned up beaten. But he said he would beat me on the Northern Pacific. I said, "Then I'll beat you on the Southern Pacific." This record stands unparalleled in railroad building anywhere in the world.

"Hell on Wheels"

I. "The Wickedest City in America"

There were . . . those recurrent stations of greed, the "roaring town" terminal points—each a brief supply quarters from which end o' track was fed with iron ammunition and stimulus for man and beast until, 100 or so miles out, Jack Casement or Charles Crocker stamped his foot and another thistle burst into full bloom from some seed waiting in the apparently sterile soil.

Upon the Central Pacific mountain and desert trail which when first projected might sight only one white man along its route of 575 miles from the California boundary to central Utah, there flourished, for heyday short or long, the terminal bases of Cisco, Truckee, Lakes Crossing rechristened Reno, Wadsworth, Humboldt, Lovelocks, Winnemucca of French Ford, Argenta, Carlin, Elko, Wells, Toano—semicolons of the railroad history. Upon the Union Pacific trail, where for 400 miles at a stretch the rails needs must bring their own company with them, there burst upon the astonished sunrises North Platte, Julesburg, Sidney, Cheyenne, Laramie, Benton, Bryan, Green River, Wasatch, Corinne, Promontory Point. And these were the epitome of "roaring towns" whose like has been matched only by a Virginia City, a Deadwood, a Dodge City, a Leadville.

"Hell on Wheels" was the title accorded them; whether reported first by journalist Samuel Bowles, their observer in 1868, is not stated, but at any rate the phrase has come down uncensored as a current coinage of the day. They successively irrupted along the Union Pacific like malignant sores upon the surface of a hectic westward-hurrying civilization, only to disappear again or form into healthy flesh. They were a phenomenon.

* * * * *

Julesburg had been founded, the third of its name, 377 miles out, as removed from the stage line south of the South Platte to squat be-

From *Building the Pacific Railway,* by Edwin L. Sabin, pp. 254–256. Copyright, 1919, by J. B. Lippincott Company. Philadelphia and London.

side the rails and brag of its well-earned title, "The Wickedest City in America." What a fresh nucleus of the bizarre and vice rampant this was, where North Platte experience joined force with Denver's and all the hard-bitten tail-twisters of old Julesburg (toughest of Overland stage stations) migrated, jealous of opportunities!

In June new Julesburg had a population of forty men and one woman. By the end of July it had 4000 transient residents. Town lots, staked off by the land agent of the railroad, were selling at $1000. The streets, ankle deep in sand, were lined by warehouses, saloons, gambling joints, and stores piled with goods fresh from New York and Chicago. The people trudged, laughed, whooped, bargained, joked and cursed and shot, in the exuberance of life at high tide: soldiers, teamsters, graders, merchants, clerks, gamblers, tourists; the "expensive luxuries" of women in Black Crook dresses, with fancy derringers daintily dangling at their ribbon and rattlesnake-skin belts; Mexicans, Indians, half-breeds, horses, oxen, and dogs—all these swirled in this eddy of the northern plains.

The "upper tendom of sinful Julesburg," as young Henry M. Stanley called them, dined at the Julesburg House, selecting from a menu of "soups, *fricandeaus,* vegetables, game in abundance, pies, puddings, raisins, apples, nuts, wine, and bread at discretion for the moderate sum of twelve bits."

By their gold watches and expensive chains, their modish clothes and their patent-leather boots, he thought them to be capitalists and was amazed to find that they "were only clerks, ticket agents, conductors, engineers," and the like.

At night the great dance hall, "King of the Hills," was ablaze with the brightest of lights; the strains of music, the shuffle of feet, the clamor of voices, almost deafened. Along the shallow Platte, beyond the kerosene-illuminated streets, myriad camp-fires twinkled. In the mornings the customary dead man was buried.

The Union Pacific had laid out the town. The gamblers and gunmen anticipated owning it cheaply, for a human life was worth less than a bottle of wine. When on the survey west of Salt Lake City, General Dodge heard of the defiance of law and order, he wired General Jack Casement to go back with his track force and help the officers.

In the fall they visited Julesburg together. General Casement acted as guide.

"What did you do, General?"

"I will show you," he said.

He led straight to the graveyard, and indicated by a wave of his hand: "There they are, General. They died with their boots on, but they brought peace."

Peace indeed! There was nothing else here. Of all the "roaring" town of Julesburg, Wickedest City in America, there remained only the graveyard, the station agent, heaps of tin cans, and the undisturbed prairie dogs and ground owls. After its five months' existence, like a May-fly, Julesburg had dried up. Its progeny had folded their tents and departed.

II. "A Quiet and Moral Burg"

Cheyenne, "Magic City of the Plains," was booming, 140 miles westward again. Hell on Wheels had hit the trail, amazing the sage and the very heavens.

Casement brothers' portable warehouse, store and dining-room; all the other knock-down contraptions of canvas, rough lumber, and sheet-iron; the imitation stucco-front buildings, collapsible into sections numbered with the convenience of a pack of cards; the gamblers' lay-outs, the saloon bars, the merchants' counters and desks, the various commodities of trade and housekeeping—all these, accompanied by owners and employers, had been loaded upon flatcars for the next end of creation. And up the trail wended horse, buggy, wagon, and foot—man, woman, and child astride, atop, within, without, dust-drenched, expectant, cheering, peering, following the pay-car to Cheyenne.

Midway, depleted Sidney sat, a minor quantity. Who cared for Sidney and its pretensions as a terminus when Cheyenne awaited?

Cheyenne, located by General Dodge July 4 here upon the dun flatness in a bend of Crow Creek, an elevation of 6000 feet, already was accoutred complete, from spurs to helm; had a city government duly elected, two daily papers, 4000 people, and a brass band, with which to welcome the first influx on November 13.

Town lots sold by the railroad company at $250 were being resold at $3500. The post-office was ten by fifteen feet, the Headquarters Saloon thirty-six by 100 feet. A store building fifty-five by twenty-five feet, of rough lumber from Denver, had been erected in forty-eight hours. There were two two-story hotels—the Rollins House hostelry catered to only the élite, including Chief Spotted Tail and Mrs. Spotted Tail, recent arrivals "in our midst." There were the Great Western mammoth corral, three banks, a stone warehouse costing $20,000, one hundred saloons, gambling joints, dance halls, a medley of shanties, dugouts, and tents, a town site of four sections of land, a military reservation four miles square, and a "man for breakfast" every morning.

Great was Cheyenne, the Magic City and the winter terminus of the Pacific Railway on the plains. Before spring it was headquarters for 10,000 men and women of all degrees, and the *entrepôt* for all degrees of business. Every known gambling device was in lucrative operation, and legitimate merchants themselves reaped at the rate of $30,000 a month.

The value of the city scrip had been raised eighteen cents on the dollar by Magistrate Colonel Murrin, who required every man who had indulged in a gun-play to pay a fine of $10, "whether he hit or missed." The city treasury was plethoric.

"Your fine is ten dollars and two bits."

"Yes, your Honor; but what's the two bits for?"

"To buy your honorable judge a drink in the morning."

* * * * *

In Cheyenne the Vigilance Committee arose; the military of General J. D. Stevenson marched down from Fort Russell; culprits were paraded, criminals hoisted. Life ceased to boil and only simmered. In April 1000 grading teams toiled out for Sherman Summit and beyond. Five thousand chastened graders and track-layers followed. In May Hell on Wheels was rolling again into the west; and with its 10,000 souls concentrated to 1500, Cheyenne (lucky at that) settled down to be a "quiet and moral burg."

The Last Spike

I. As It Was [1]

I saw the Golden Spike driven at Promontory, Utah, on May 10, 1869. I had a beef contract to furnish meat to the construction camps of Benson and West. . . .

* * * * *

On the last day, only about 100 feet were laid, and everybody tried to have a hand in the work. I took a shovel from an Irishman, and threw a shovel full of dirt on the ties just to tell about it afterward.

A special train from the west brought Sidney Dillon, General Dodge, T. C. Durant, John R. Duff, S. A. Seymour, a lot of newspaper men, and plenty of the best brands of champagne.

Another train made up at Ogden carried the band from Fort Douglas, the leading men of Utah Territory, and a small but efficient supply of Valley Tan.

It was a very hilarious occasion; everybody had all they wanted to drink all the time. Some of the participants got "sloppy," and these were not all Irish and Chinese by any means.

California furnished the Golden Spike. Governor Tuttle of Nevada furnished one of silver. General Stanford [Governor Safford?] presented one of gold, silver, and iron from Arizona. The last tie was of California laurel.

When they came to drive the last spike, Governor Stanford, president of the Central Pacific, took the sledge, and the first time he struck he missed the spike and hit the rail.

---

[1] From *Reminiscences of Alexander Toponce, Pioneer,* pp. 177–179. Copyright, 1923, by Mrs. Kate Toponce. Ogden, Utah: Privately printed.

What a howl went up! Irish, Chinese, Mexicans, and everybody yelled with delight. "He missed it. Yee." The engineers blew the whistles and rang their bells. Then Stanford tried it again and tapped the spike and the telegraph operators had fixed their instruments so that the tap was reported in all the offices east and west, and set bells to tapping in hundreds of towns and cities. . . . Then Vice President T. C. Durant of the Union Pacific took up the sledge and he missed the spike the first time. Then everybody slapped everybody else again and yelled, "He missed it too, yow!"

It was a great occasion, every one carried off souvenirs and there are enough splinters of the last tie in museums to make a good bonfire.

When the connection was finally made the Union Pacific and the Central Pacific engineers ran their engines up until their pilots touched. Then the engineers shook hands and had their pictures taken and each broke a bottle of champagne on the pilot of the other's engine and had their picture taken again.

The Union Pacific engine, the "Jupiter," was driven by my good friend, George Lashus, who still lives in Ogden.

Both before and after the spike driving ceremony there were speeches, which were cheered heartily. I do not remember what any of the speakers said now, but I do remember that there was a great abundance of champagne.

II. As It Wasn't [2]

Although Colonel Savage's wet plate is the standard record of Promontory and one of the world's most celebrated news pictures of all time, it never quite pleased Leland Stanford, President of the Central Pacific. For one thing, he wasn't in it. For another, the picture seemed raffish, uncouth, and, to a man in politics, a trifle boozy. At least three bottles showed in the photograph and the presence of others was strongly suggested. Stanford therefore commissioned Thomas Hill, an understanding artist, to recreate the scene in a cleaned-up version which should plainly depict Stanford, always a candidate for public office, in association with Rev. Todd who spoke the invocation. Stanford's commission also stipulated the inclusion of a good many people who had conspicuously not been at Promontory; the long dead Theodore Judah, first engineer of the railroad, Collis Huntington who was in New York at the time, Charlie Crocker and Mark Hopkins, who had been in San Francisco, and Brigham Young, who had emphatically refused an invitation when the railroad avoided passing through Salt Lake City. Upon its completion the massive scene included seventy likenesses painted from life, making it one of the greatest portrait studies in the history of art. Stanford refused to accept it. Several per-

[2] From *Hear the Train Blow,* A Pictorial Epic of America in the Railroad Age, by Lucius Beebe and Charles Clegg, p. 153. Copyright, 1952, by E. P. Dutton & Co., Inc. New York.

sons he thought might be useful to him politically were placed behind people of less importance. It hangs today in the State Capitol at Sacramento, a bogus re-creation of one of the epic carouses of American history.

Moving a Court House

When the Burlington built a line through Box Butte County (Neb.) in the late '80s, it little dreamed it was starting a bitter tri-cornered feud, which the railroad itself would have to end by turning house-mover.

A natural site for the commercial center of the county was the junction of two small railroad lines, both Burlington subsidiaries. At this point the Lincoln Land Company plotted a town and called it Alliance; 19 miles to the northwest they laid out Hemingford as the prospective county seat. Nonpareil, which had held that distinction, was now considered out of the running, as the railroad passed it up by five miles.

To determine the county political center, a special election was held on March 7, 1890, but as none of the three towns received the necessary three-fifths of the vote, the citizens went again to the polls on April 8th. This time Nonpareil failed to get even the two-fifths of the vote required to stay in the race, and after the regular November election, the county seat was moved to Hemingford by a majority of sixteen votes. Immediately the local townsmen constructed a new court house with the financial backing of the Lincoln Land Company, and for the ensuing nine years they were able to hold their political advantage.

Refusing to admit defeat, however, the persistent Alliance voters finally had their way in 1899, and the county seat found its third home. This time the economy-minded county commissioners decided it would be cheaper to move their comparatively new court house over the intervening 19 miles than to build a new one. So they bought the building from the people of Hemingford for $1,500. The Lincoln Land Company now undertook to have the hundred-ton court house firmly set on a new stone foundation and ready for business at Alliance thirty days later.

After ten days had passed, however, the total progress achieved by the house-mover who had taken the job was twenty feet. At this critical moment, J. R. Phelan, superintendent of the Burlington, offered the facilities of the railroad to the worried company president, and the offer was accepted. The building was two and a half stories in height

---

From the publicity files of the Chicago, Burlington & Quincy Railroad. Chicago.

and nearly 40 feet square. It was rolled to the track, carefully balanced upon four 50,000-pound capacity trucks, with guy ropes extending from each side of the structure to coal cars in front of and behind it, to steady it. The 19 miles of track were across an almost dead-level prairie, with no truss bridges to be passed over, and only two shallow cuts whose banks could be shaved a little. Within six hours from the start, Alliance had the court house for which it had been battling since it was scarcely more than a paper plat in the Land Company's office.

The Pond Creek-Jefferson Depot Fight

Two months after the opening of the Cherokee Strip I carried mail back and forth from Pond Creek to Jefferson twice a day, in a hack. I had to ford the Salt Fork of the North Canadian. One time the water was so high I stood up in the hack and held the mail on my shoulders to keep it from getting wet.

Instead of locating the land offices and county seats at the railroad towns of Jefferson and Enid, the government put them in, in each case, three miles from the depots. The settlers began building a town at a place called Pond Creek, three miles south of the depot town at Jefferson in L County. (When the Strip was opened to settlement, it was divided into sections known as K-L-M-N-O and Q counties.) About the same distance south of Enid another town sprang up in O County. The two Enid towns were known as North and South Enid.

The government established its post offices at Pond Creek and South Enid but the railroad refused to stop trains at either place. Just before trains got to Pond Creek, the engineer would turn on the throttle and go through the town sixty miles an hour. They had instructions from the railroad bosses and were afraid of losing their jobs if they didn't obey them.

Ill feeling arose between the residents of the old and North towns and the new and South towns. What began as a controversy turned into a fight with the government and the South towns on one side, the railroad and the North towns on the other side.

Mail addressed to the South towns wasn't put out there but was carried through and dumped on the depot platforms of the North towns. Then it had to be taken back in hacks to the South towns. Passengers had to be transported back and forth likewise. The Salt Fork of the Canadian River separated Pond Creek and Jefferson. There was only a railroad bridge, and the river bed had to be forded each trip.

By F. P. Rider. From *Southwestern Folk History*, Dramatic Material for Writers, Told by Those Who Lived It, Compiled to Stimulate an Interest in Regional Drama, pp. 85–92. Publication No. 19. Oklahoma City: Research Department, Federal Theatre of Oklahoma, Works Progress Administration. April, 1939.

The worst inconvenience was getting and shipping produce and supplies, groceries, dry goods, etc. When the Salt Fork was high they had to wait until it went down before loads of supplies could be taken back and forth from Pond Creek to Jefferson.

Trains were going through Pond Creek so fast that it was dangerous. After the town was incorporated the citizens held a meeting to discuss what to do about it. The City Council passed an ordinance that all trains passing through the town must slow up to eight miles an hour. That would give passengers a chance to step off the train and time to throw mail off and on the train.

The Railroad Company's answer was to instruct its engineers to neither stop nor slow down.

The citizens of Pond Creek became desperate. One day the city marshal stopped me just as I was starting to Jefferson with the mail. "Halt!" he says. "We're going to enforce the law today, and make the trains slow up through here to eight miles an hour. I deputize you and every man in Pond Creek to help."

"Can't do it. I'm carrying the U. S. mail."

I drove on to Jefferson. When the train came in, I told the conductor and engineer about the ordinance, that they'd have to slow down to eight miles an hour when they went through Pond Creek, and what they told me won't do to print.

I got the mail and started back to Pond Creek. The train went on ahead of me. Men from Pond Creek had been stationed all along the track north of town to flag the train. When the engineer saw them he had the train crew put on the "high balls" and speed up the train. The men along the track waved and signaled for him to stop. They yelled, "Slow up to eight miles going through Pond Creek."

Trainmen hollered back, telling the men where they could go to.

At Pond Creek the citizens had laid some long heavy planks across wagonwheels. A bunch of them hoisted an old flat-topped house on to the boards. They hitched a team to the wheels and stood ready. When they saw the train speeding down the track they pulled the house on the middle of the track right on Main Street. Then they unfastened the coupling pin, ran their horses away, and everybody scattered. The engineer saw it and whistled. Then he shut his eyes, ducked his head, and turned on the throttle. The engine hit that house broadside at sixty miles an hour. Boards and splinters flew everywhere.

Everybody was excited and mad. A fellow by the name of Williams stopped me and says, "Come and help us, Rider. We're going to tear up this track."

"For God's sake, boys, don't do that," I says, "for there's a train coming from Kremlin." I knew this train was due in Pond Creek before very long.

The men began to tear up that track with sledge hammers and picks. They went wild. I grabbed the mail out of the hack, gave it to a fellow, and told him to take it to the post office. I unhitched my team and started back to Jefferson bareback. I rode as fast as I could and swam the horse across the Salt Fork. I hoped to get to Jefferson in time to have the telegraph operator there send a message to Kremlin and stop the next train.

As soon as I got there I ran into the depot and says to the agent, "Stop all trains coming from Kremlin. They're tearing up the track at Pond Creek."

"Can't do it. The train's just gone," he says.

We stood on the depot platform—it was about noon—and watched. Pond Creek was three miles away across the prairies but when that train went off the tracks we could see smoke, splinters, and rails fly up into the air.

The train that hit the house was going north. Somewhere on the way, the engineer on the southbound train had told the engineer on the train coming from Kremlin not to stop. He says, "They'll try to stop you, put something on the track, but you can go right through it." Some of the rails had been braced together and stood up in the air. When this engineer saw them he thought it was a frail windmill tower, and that he could go through it, same as the other engineer had done.

The engine went off the track with such terrific force it was half buried in a steep bank on the east side. The cars turned over on the west side of the track. There were twenty-seven cars of cattle on that train.

I rode back to Pond Creek. That wreck was an awful sight. They were digging the engine out, and the engineer was trying to pull himself through the cab window. I says, "Are you hurt?"

"No!" He could laugh!

He got out and went back to help get the imprisoned cattle out. Some were already loose and were running wild through the streets. Crazed with fright, they'd lower their heads and bellow. Men, women, and children climbed up on lumber piles, telephone posts, buildings, anywhere to get out of reach of those cattle.

The owner of the cattle, who had been riding in the caboose, was wringing his hands and crying. He didn't have any insurance on them. The man later went crazy over it.

The railroad company laid the blame for the wreck on Pond Creek. Many of the cattle were killed outright, more of 'em died later from injuries. People stole and butchered a lot of them. The conductor telephoned the territorial governor to send fifty U.S. marshals to Pond Creek to arrest the citizens there for delaying the U.S. mail.

We spent that night getting the wounded and dying cattle out of the box cars. They were a pitiful sight, mangled, legs broken, horns smashed. They lowed and bellowed all that night.

The next day, Sunday, Gentry and I took a bunch of men to the country. They helped burn the dead cattle. Cowboys rounded up the loose cattle, running over the country. Lots of them died out on the prairies from their injuries. We had a big dinner out in the country that day.

Gentry, who afterward run a Pony Show all over the country called "The Gentry Pony Show," had tried to flag that cattle train. He lived near the track, and when he saw that train coming he grabbed his wife's petticoat off a chair. The petticoat was sort of a reddish color and Gentry ran down the track and signaled the train to stop, but the engineer wouldn't heed the signal.

Only one person was killed—a tramp, who had stolen a ride on the train.

Meanwhile, the Pond Creek folks got ready for the U.S. marshals. They knew they were coming and planned a big banquet.

From El Reno the train came as far into town as the broken track. The marshals got off and started to walk the rest of the way. I went down the track to meet them.

One of the marshals got out his gun and says, "Stand back. You're under arrest for delaying the mails."

I told him that we (the Pond Creek citizens) were not delaying repair on the tracks or bothering the section men who were doing it; that we were going to give them a banquet at the Wichita Hotel. The business men would make speeches explaining all about the wreck and why we did it.

We had the banquet and the leading men of Pond Creek made speeches explaining the situation. Everybody had a good time. The marshals went back to El Reno but they didn't find out who actually did the wrecking. After the track was fixed trains still roared through the town at sixty miles an hour. War was on. Something was happening every minute. Neither the railroad nor the government would make any concessions.

Some time after the cattle train wreck and after the track had been repaired, one afternoon about four o'clock I started out of Pond Creek with the Jefferson mail. I saw two men going down the track south of town with what looked like two sticks of dynamite on their shoulders. I hurried on to Jefferson, and when the train came in I said to the conductor, "Don't cross the bridge south of Pond Creek. I saw two men carrying dynamite going down the track and I know they're going to blow the train up."

"You're lying, there's nothing to it," he says.

Some one hollered, "Arrest this man."

Several men started toward me. I had been a Pinkerton detective and gave the sign, hoping the railroad detective would see it and protect me. The train detective was on the platform and I gave him the sign. He came forward and says to the conductor, "This man's all right. He's one of us. I believe he's telling the truth."

The conductor took a lantern and led some of the train crew down the track to the railroad bridge, about two hundred yards from the depot at Jefferson. He felt sure that was where the dynamite would be, but they couldn't find anything, so he ordered the engineer to go on.

I threw the mail in the hack and started. I knew there was going to be another wreck. A traveling man got off the train and rode with me to Pond Creek. We heard the boom of the explosion before we got there. It was about nine o'clock in the evening when we pulled in at Pond Creek. I didn't go through town to deliver the mail but drove straight on south to where the wreck was, south of Pond Creek. A hundred men had already gathered there, and when they saw me coming, the railroad men thought I was the one who had planted the dynamite. Two men grabbed my horses and run them into a wire fence. Another one hit me over the back of the head. I heard some one say, "There's the ——! We've got him." A crowd began to gather around me.

The railroad detective pushed his way through and says, "He's all right, men. You've got the wrong man. He tried to warn you about this wreck."

I told them that I was carrying the U.S. mail and warned the conductor but he wouldn't listen. I was glad I had the mail with me, to prove I was telling the truth.

About this time a gang of about one hundred and fifty men, led by the sheriff, was coming from the north. They all had guns. I started toward them and the detective jerked me back. He says, "Get back, they're going to shoot."

I said, "Let me go. I'm the only man here who can give the Pond Creek password and talk to them." I started toward them.

"Halt!" the sheriff yelled.

I gave the password sign for that day and said, "Sheriff, halt! The train's blowed up! Don't shoot!"

The Pond Creek sheriff explained to the conductor that he was there to help protect the railroad property and find the men who placed the dynamite.

The detective and I started back to see what the wreck looked like. Just then I saw the conductor give a man a note and the man stick it in his shoe and start running north toward Jefferson.

"There goes a man running north with a message. Get him," I called.

They ran after him and got the message. It was to the governor. "Send troops at once. I won't move this train till troops come."

They had heard the boom of the explosion at Jefferson and sent twenty-four section hands down to repair the track. The dynamite had been placed on the tracks to blow up the train, but the only damage done was to blow off part of a wheel. The train didn't go off the track and no one was hurt. The section hands repaired the damaged wheel and the train went on.

It hadn't no more than started till the trainmen saw a blaze a little down the track. They stopped the train to investigate. Some one had piled lumber under a little culvert and set it afire in an attempt to burn the culvert. Probably the same ones did this who tried to wreck the train with the dynamite. The trainmen saw it in time and put the blaze out. The train was, "On again, gone again."

About a week later some one sawed three pilings in half under a trestle that went across a little branch across the bluffs near South Enid. They sawed them obliquely. A lumber and wheat train came along. The engine got across before the trestle crumpled in half. The cars filled with wheat and lumber went into the ditch. The wheat was scattered everywhere. They gave it to the farmers. They could come and haul away as much as they could use.

North and South Enid were fighting just like Jefferson and Pond Creek. This same week two fellows carried some dynamite in a beer keg down to the tracks and blew up the track between Jefferson and Pond Creek. I saw the men from my house. I saw them go under a bridge. Pretty soon I heard the boom of the explosion and saw the blue smoke. A train came along but got across before the explosion. I started to flag the next train. I met a handcar that had been sent out from Jefferson. They'd heard the boom there too. The men asked, "What's up?"

"They've blowed up a bridge," I told them and got in the handcar with them. We went back where the track had been blowed up. We found the fuse and took it along with us.

That's where I began to get in bad. The Pond Creek bunch began to suspect me of helping the north town (Jefferson) and playing traitor to them. They knew I'd tried to warn the trainmen before the other wrecks. When they saw me coming back on the handcar with the Jefferson crew they decided for sure I was standing in with the north town.

I was in a devil of a mess. The railroad had it in for me because I was a Pond Creek man and, they supposed, in on the wrecking. I was working for the government and it was my duty to help protect the U.S. mail.

A crowd had gathered around the wrecked track. Pond Creek men began to say, "One of the trainmen must have dropped a bomb off the back end of the train." They were trying to clear the Pond Creek citizens and put the blame for the wreck on the railroad company.

All the men in Pond Creek were deputized to help hunt and arrest the men who blowed up that track. We went down into a ravine and found a railroad guard who'd been stationed along the track north of town. He was scared to death. When the two men who blowed up the track passed him, as they went down the track, he told them to halt and asked them what they were going to do. They had answered, "If you don't want to get blowed up like we're going to blow this bridge up, you better run." He ran as fast as he could and stayed in this ravine till the sheriff's men found him.

With the track at South Enid out of business and the one between Pond Creek and Jefferson out, trains beyond these two towns couldn't run any farther north or south. The track was good between these towns and a train could run from one town to the other but no farther. We called it "The Oregon Short Line Track."

After the tracks were fixed, an engine and a caboose came up from the south one Sunday. Three men kidnapped the Pond Creek city marshal, arrested him, and were going to take him away with them. The citizens tried to get bond for him, so the three men, the marshal, and the citizens all went to the courthouse. While they were in there, some Pond Creek men went up on the top of the courthouse with a long rope. They walked out on some big planks that reached across to another building. When these three men came out of that courthouse and passed under the planks they let the rope down and dangled it over their heads like they was going to hang 'em. They let the marshal go, and left town on the caboose and engine.

By this time the railroad situation had become desperate. People were afraid to ride or ship cattle on trains going through the Strip. The railroad company stationed men to patrol the tracks between Pond Creek and Jefferson and beyond the towns. Guards were stationed outside the city limits on all roads leading to Pond Creek. They halted every one before allowing him to enter the town. If they couldn't give the Pond Creek password, they were questioned.

Pond Creek was under martial law. Something was happening all the time. One night after I'd put my team up, I heard a boom and saw a blaze on the track close to the barns. Then I saw a man running down the track. I started after him but couldn't catch him.

One morning when I was waiting for the train at Jefferson, I saw twenty-seven soldiers going through a drill near the depot at Jefferson. I could hear the captain say, "Step, step, forward march." I asked the agent what it was all about. He told me they were doing it to attract attention and get us over there, that the soldiers were coming to Pond Creek from the south and [would] take us by surprise. That fellow lost his job for telling that.

I got my mail and galloped my horses back to Pond Creek. I told Johnson, the sheriff, "The soldiers are coming here from El Reno and there's going to be a battle. The agent had told me the town would be running blood before night."

"Rider, you're a liar," he said. "You're always starting something to stir people up." I told him to get up on the courthouse and see for himself. We climbed up there and he could see them with his field glasses. About that time we heard a lot of whistles and several trains pulled in loaded with soldiers. The sheriff says, "Rider, I appoint you as a deputy. Get down in the street and take all men who have guns. Put them in a wagon and take them outside the city limits." He was afraid there'd be bloodshed if he didn't. He knew it would go against Pond Creek if the citizens put up a fight with firearms.

The soldiers formed two lines, one on the east and one on the west, and came marching down the track toward the town. Crowds began to gather. Everybody in town, men, women, and children, came to see what was going to happen.

When they got down town where the crowd was, the captain of the soldiers wanted to scare us, I guess. He had the soldiers on the east get down on their knees, the soldiers on the west stand behind them. He yelled, "Halt, fix bayonets, charge." They charged the crowd and ran us all back about sixty feet. I saw the muzzle of a gun stuck in my face and stepped back behind a printing press.

The city marshal came up. They grabbed him and run him on the train. His wife came running across the street after him, screamed, and fainted. Dr. Marsh started toward her. The captain told him to halt, but the doctor says, "I'm going to do my duty. I'm a doctor." Then a woman started across. The soldiers yelled at her to halt. She turned on them and says, "Shoot, you cowards, shoot. That's my sister and I'm going to her."

A meeting had been scheduled to be held in the courthouse that day to fix taxation for bridges, schoolbuilding, etc. A fellow from Jefferson was there, working against Pond Creek, and trying to break us up. He turned in the names of a whole bunch of us Pond Creek men to the captain of those soldiers.

It looked as though the soldiers planned to take us by force. A fellow by the name of Scoggins got up on some scales and yelled above the noise of the crowd, "Captain, don't shoot. If you'll call the names of the men you want, I'll point them out and guarantee they'll respond and come forward."

The captain began calling names. Scoggins stood up there on the scales and pointed us out like this: He'd say, "That's one, and that's one." They arrested fifty-seven men from Pond Creek and put them on the train to take to Kingfisher for trial.

I heard F. P. Rider called. I jerked loose and ran. I wanted to get back to the post office, get my mail, and clear out of town before they got me. I hitched up my team and drove down an alley to the post office, knocked on the back door, and yelled, "Give me my mail." They handed it to me and I started toward Jefferson.

I didn't see the train that left Pond Creek with the prisoners. When I got to Jefferson, I grabbed the Pond Creek mail and threw it in the hack. I saw what looked like a big bonfire and I said to the agent, "You folks must be celebrating because they've arrested all our men."

He says, "No, that's the soldiers cookin' supper for the prisoners and they're waitin' for you."

I said, "They wasn't smart enough to catch me."

Just then an officer stationed there to catch me yelled, "Is that Rider?"

Somebody hollered, "Yes."

The officer says, "Rider, you're under arrest."

I hollered back, "Not me." I jumped in the hack, whipped my horses and away I went to Pond Creek but I didn't go my usual route. When I got home that night I asked my wife if they had been looking for me. She said, "Yes." I told her I wouldn't stay at home that night.

I slept in a ravine. Before daylight the next morning I got my team and drove to the back of the post office for my mail. The agent says, "Rider, haven't they got you yet?"

I says, "No, they wasn't smart enough."

I went on to Jefferson. A traveling man stood on the depot platform. He asked me if I was going to Pond Creek. I says, "Yes." He asked me what I'd charge to take him to the Wichita Hotel there. I told him fifty cents.

When we got to Pond Creek, I took the man into the hotel. The landlord came out and said, "Rider, didn't they get you?"

I says, "No, they wasn't smart enough."

The traveling man paid me, and I put the money in my pocket. A man with glasses was sitting on the hotel porch in shirt sleeves. He pulled his glasses down over his nose, looked at me, then walked over to me and said, "Good morning, Mr. Rider."

I says, "You've got the advantage of me, brother. I don't know who you are."

He says, "Yes, I guess I have. I've been layin' for you all night. Come on with me." I told him he couldn't take me, that I was carrying the U.S. mail. "Some one else can carry the mail."

I told him to take care of my team. He says, "Here's a boy who'll take care of your team."

I asked him if I couldn't go home and kiss my wife good-bye. He says, "No, come with me."

"I ain't got no coat on."

"You don't need no coat." He took me to Jefferson, put me on a train, and took me to Kingfisher. That's where they'd taken the other fifty-seven men from Pond Creek.

When we got to Kingfisher, they took me off the train between two officers. We crossed a swinging bridge west of the jail next to a ravine. Names of all the Pond Creek men taken in there as prisoners were printed in white chalk on the outside walls. Way down near the bottom I saw "F. P. Rider." The cells down there were called dungeons.

Two government men came and asked who I was, then told the officers I was a government man carrying U.S. mail, and they couldn't arrest me. They took me away from the officers to the best hotel in town and said, "Rider, you'll be our guest while you're here. Order anything you want, fried chicken, beer, cigars, whisky."

They took everybody to court the next morning for trial. Pond Creek had an attorney named Mackey who was a smart man. He made a motion that according to the organic act, we had to be tried in the town where the act was committed. The judge said, "You can't show that organic act, and I overrule your motion." Mackey got out a lot of law books showing that he was right.

Mackey says, "We're going back to Pond Creek. These men must be tried in the town where the act was committed."

The judge says, "You can't show us."

"I can't?" Mackey says. He sent a telegram to Washington to find out if he was right about the act. Court was adjourned until the next day.

Next day he got an answer from Washington, and the telegram stated he was right, that the trial must be where the crime was committed.

So they took us all back to Jefferson. We had to walk from Jefferson to Pond Creek. Guards were stationed all along the bridge there. We had to give a countersign to get across.

The next morning we all appeared in court in Pond Creek. The judge got a telegram from the governor saying, "You can't try those men till the fall term of court."

Every man went somebody else's bond for one hundred dollars, and we were all turned loose. Meanwhile the governor, Mayor Moore of Pond Creek, and a council man named Gregg went to Washington to work for passage of the depot bill.

When the fall term of court was in session, the prosecuting attorney got up and says, "Gentlemen, I've got good news for you. The President has ordered there are no charges against you. The cases are dropped. You are free men."

We started to cheer, but the judge shouted "Order."

When the depot bill was passed in Washington, the railroad was ordered to begin work on depots at Pond Creek and South Enid, and pay five hundred dollars [each] day they missed stopping.

The first time the train had to stop, everybody in Pond Creek was down on the tracks to meet it. The people took charge of the train, jumped on, and got a free ride to Jefferson. The train crew was good-natured about it, and everybody was happy.

We had a big jubilee in Pond Creek to celebrate our victory. The high school band at Enid came down. We marched around the town pushing a wagon. My wife was in that wagon. The Enid high school kids would yell: "Pond Creek, zip, boom! Pond Creek, Enid, rip, zip, boom!" A few days after that we had another jubilee in Enid with free ice cream, candy, and pop.

IV. GRAND STRATEGY

The Erie Gage War

Between Buffalo and Toledo (1842–51) there developed a gaggle of little railroads. No stretch of road on the continent was so bedeviled by differences in gages. First of all to be authorized was the Erie & North East, projected from Erie, Pa., up the lake shore to the New York state line, and intended to bring the New York & Erie railroad on from Dunkirk to Erie, but that company had all it could do to stagger into Dunkirk in 1851. A separate company, the Dunkirk & State Line, was organized to bridge the gap, but found difficulty in getting on its legs.

A serious complication was in the making. Another railroad was promoted in 1848, the Buffalo & State Line, which was to some extent being backed by the Albany-Buffalo chain of railroads (already becoming known as the Central Line), which were of standard gage—4 feet, 8½ inches. The Erie was a six-footer and the Erie & North East and the Dunkirk & State Line were planned to be of the same width. On the other side of this little neck of Pennsylvania were the Ohio railroads, of 4 foot, 10-inch gage, established by State law in 1848; to which Pennsylvania retorted by forbidding a mile of track of the "Ohio Gage" to be built within her borders. As for the city of Erie, it was at first not at all interested in being connected with Ohio by railroad. If Ohio wanted an outlet to the Atlantic seaboard, let her get it in some other way; a not infrequent example of community thinking in those days.

Abridged from *The Road of the Century,* The Story of the New York Central, by Alvin F. Harlow, pp. 267–274. Copyright, 1947, by Alvin Fay Harlow. New York: Creative Age Press.

Some miscreant stole into the Legislature in 1848 and procured a charter for the Erie & Ohio Railroad, to cover that thirty-mile stretch between Erie and the Ohio boundary, but the Legislature hastened to undo its error by repealing this charter, thus rearing, as it modestly boasted, what it believed to be "an insurmountable barrier to the progress of the New York Railroads west."

For five years Pennsylvania was kept busy repelling insidious invaders. Then a new idea dawned on Erie; let the railroads come, but make the break in the gage at her own depot. This brilliant conceit flowered in a law on March 11, 1851, which provided that all railroads from the city of Erie to the New York border must be of either 6 feet or 4 feet-8½ inches gage, while all from that city to the Ohio line must be 4 feet-10 inches in width. This would compel a change of trains by all passengers at Erie, possibly a layover of a few hours, and the inevitable spending of some money there. As the mayor of Erie said:

> The Roads of New York sought to pass through a portion of Pennsylvania without conferring any advantage upon the State—in fact, drawing away trade from her own metropolis and conferring no local advantage even upon Erie, unless there was a break of gauge. . . . If the foreign companies succeed in their schemes, there is one great monopoly of railroad interest from Albany to Chicago, rich and powerful enough to buy out or trample upon any rival interest, combining a moneyed power which is without a parallel in the history of the country. We propose making at Erie a break in this interest, and it is this in reality which the railroads fear.

Erie believed that the people of the entire lake shore region would some day thank her for saving them from this vast monopoly. Whilst the law of 1851 was in effect, said the Erie mayor, that city was "safe"; the interests of Pennsylvania were protected, and the selfish, aggressive schemes of the New York Companies were checked. But the repeal of the law "by any means, fair or foul," had been resolved upon by the "foreign railroads" . . . and "to the lasting disgrace of the Legislature of Pennsylvania," the law was repealed on April 11, 1853, and "Erie was thus left singly and alone to battle for her interests and those of Pennsylvania."

Matters were now rapidly approaching a climax. As the railroads said, "The selfishness of Pennsylvania prevents a uniform gage through the borders of the State," and compelled the transfer of passengers and freight twice within twenty miles; for the Buffalo & State Line, which had absorbed the unborn Dunkirk & State Line, was of standard width, the 19-mile Erie & North East was six feet, while at Erie you encountered the Ohio gage. But on November 17, 1853, the Erie & North Eastern and the Buffalo & State Line both agreed to change their tracks to the Ohio gage, thus making possible real through service between Buffalo, Cleveland and Toledo. The two companies—now both well under the control of the newly-organized New York Central —planned joint operation.

The railroads acted swiftly. On December 7 they put a large force to work, changing the track to the Ohio gage, and it was rapidly done. Nine days before this, the City Council of Erie, expecting the action, had named a heavy fine for "obstructing the streets," and called on the High Constable to remove the obstructions. The H. C. did not lack possemen. Crowds of citizens, whom the railroads called mobs, demolished two of the company's bridges which spanned streets, and tore up the tracks at other street crossings. At Harbor Creek, seven miles to eastward, where the railroad had crossed a highway in a long diagonal, the citizen mob ripped up a long stretch of track and destroyed a bridge. They were quickly replaced, and in one night destroyed again; once more replaced and again dismantled—"abated by order of the Commissioners." A gap of seven miles was thus made in the railroad in midwinter, and at first many passengers walked the whole distance. Then some enterprising neighbors began operating vehicles, some of which were open to the weather, some curtained, between Harbor Creek and Erie, charging a dollar for the trip. At least one passenger, a woman, had her feet frozen during the journey in an open wagon.

Governor Bigler of Pennsylvania was in full accord with these doings. He telegraphed to Erie that "My sympathies are with the people of Erie and whatever my duties and the laws permit, shall be done for them." He told the Legislature that "Pennsylvania *holds the key* to the important link of connection between the East and the West, and when no principle of amity or commerce is to be violated, it is the right and duty of the State to turn her natural advantages to the promotion and welfare of her own people."

The next incident was on December 27, when "an armed force" invaded the state from New York, and in the words of a member of the Erie Bar, found "a number of the citizens of Harbor Creek assembled for the purpose, in a peaceful and legitimate way, of protecting their rights and preventing the unlawful encroachments of the railroads upon their public thoroughfare." There was a scuffle, and two citizens were slightly wounded by pistol shots fired, it was said, by a Buffalo & State Line conductor. Four Harbor Creek residents were arrested by a United States marshal and taken to jail at Pittsburgh.

A few nights later a gang drove the employees from the depot at Harbor Creek and cut the telegraph wires. The marshal and his deputies, under order of a federal court, were superintending the relaying of a track at Erie when they themselves were arrested on a warrant from a local judge on a charge of false imprisonment, but gave bail and were released. Now the High Constable at Erie ordered the tracklayers to quit work and they did so. Three days later a mob of women, "mostly German," it was said, marched to the State Street bridge, which had been built under the marshal's direction, and destroyed it. They were making slow progress with the job when they were joined by others, said to be men wearing dresses, and the task was hastened.

While the war was in progress, Alfred Kelley, the Ohio railroad promoter, visited the home, near Erie, of Judge James Miles, who had aided him in obtaining a right of way. Hearing that threats had been made in Erie that he would be mobbed if he showed his face there, Kelley with Judge Miles drove into town and walked calmly about the streets. Nothing happened save that one brick was thrown, which struck the Judge, but did not injure him seriously. There were those in Erie who did not share in the anti-railroad sentiment, and factional ill-feeling in the town did not disappear for years. Old friends became bitter enemies, church congregations were split, and merchants who leaned towards the railroad cause—"Shanghais," they were called—were boycotted by the "Ripper" or anti-railroad element.

Long litigation in the State and United States courts ensued; but Kelley had gotten an order which threw the federal Government's protection over the railroad on the valid ground that it was a post road, and it continued to operate. Pennsylvania, finally seeing that it was licked, gave in and chartered the railroad from Erie to the Ohio Border. But resentment over the affair smoldered for long afterward, and the derailment of a train in 1860 was attributed to the old grudge.

The Commodore and the Conductor

In 1853, while Commodore Vanderbilt was only a steamboat boss, he was riding from Albany to New York on the Hudson River Railroad, when he became tired of sitting and concluded to go into the baggage-car and enjoy a cigar. In those days, they had no smoking-cars, and whenever a passenger felt like turning a little of the weed into ashes, he had to do it on the platform, as the regulations of most of the roads forbade smoking in the baggage-car. As a rule, there was more chewing than smoking in those days.

But the commodore concluded that the baggage-car was good enough for him, and thither he went. Seating himself on a trunk, he began pulling away at a cigar with great delight and finally became lost in thought.

Allen Conrey was the conductor of the only express train that ran on the road. Thousands of travelers, at the mention of his name, will remember "Al," as he was always called. Well, after collecting his tick-

---

From *Humors of the Railroad Kings,* Authentic and Original Anecdotes of Prominent Railroad Men, [by George G. Small], pp. 3–4. New York: Published at the Office of "Wild Oats." [Collin & Small.] [1872.]

ets on leaving Poughkeepsie, "Al" went into the baggage-car to count them and arrange his other business relating to the trip.

Noticing an old fellow seated there, smoking, with his white hat pulled down over his eyes, he turned to the baggage-master and asked who he was.

"Blessed if I know," said the trunk-burster. "He is either somebody in authority or somebody with a good deal of cheek; for I told him that it was against the rules to smoke here, and all the reply he made was, 'All right, young man'; and there he is. Suppose you tackle him," he added.

"Al" looked at him for a moment, and then turned away to finish counting his money and tickets, after which he approached and tapped the stranger on the shoulder.

"It is against the rules to smoke here, sir."

"So that young man told me. Nothing like enforcing the rules, conductor," said he, emitting a mouthful of smoke.

"That's just what I intend to do in your case," said "Al" firmly. "So you must budge. Come."

"Oh, that's the word, is it? Supposing I don't budge?"

"Then I shall assist you, that's all."

"You look as though you would make a good assistant. I rather like you, young man."

"All right, but I shall think more of you if you save me the trouble of ejecting you."

"I'll do all I can for you. Do you know who I am?"

"Haven't the remotest idea, sir; but I know what the rules of this road are."

"Well, sir, read that," he said, handing him his card.

"C. Vanderbilt," said "Al," looking from the card to the renowned steamboat man. "So you are Commodore Vanderbilt, are you?"

"I am," replied the old smoker.

"Well, you must stop smoking, nevertheless. I will not allow you to break a rule of this road any more than I would allow any other man to do it—not even if you owned it."

"That's good; I like your style," said Vanderbilt, throwing his cigar from the open door. "Do you know I have a great mind to buy this road just for the sake of getting you? I will, by thunder!"

"All right; but I wouldn't allow you to smoke even then unless you abolished the rule."

"Correct! young man. Come and see me at No. 9 Battery Place. Here is a cigar for you."

This ended the interview, and not long afterward the old steamboater had control of the great river road, and "Al" Conrey was long held in his place of trust as conductor of the famous express train between Albany and New York.

What Brought About the Pennsylvania Turnpike

In 1880 the New York, West Shore & Buffalo was chartered. Read the list of its incorporators, and you will find there scarcely anyone who is remembered today. Who or what was back of them? William H. Vanderbilt reddened with anger and his blood-pressure rose as he thought he saw through the whole scheme. One of the directors was General Horace Porter, vice-president of the Pullman Company. George M. Pullman was furious because Vanderbilt had shoved his cars off the Fitchburg, the Michigan Central, and the Northwestern and replaced them with Wagner cars, in which the New York Central was interested. Pullman was now out for revenge.

As the plot unfolded, Mr. Vanderbilt was confident that he saw a still more powerful hand in the background, that of the Pennsylvania Railroad. It angered him as nothing else had done. In an interview with a New York *Tribune* reporter in August, 1884, he said, "The West Shore was built as a blackmailing scheme, just as the Nickel Plate was." With a track sticking like its own shadow to the New York Central up the Hudson and Mohawk, through Utica and Syracuse to Buffalo, it might cut so heavily into the Central's business as either to cripple it or force it to buy out the interloper.

Its first passenger service—between Jersey City and Newburgh—began on June 4, 1883. But for several reasons it was doomed from the beginning. On the last day of 1883 its bonds fell to 68. William H. Vanderbilt's rage over the building of the West Shore, coming right upon the heels of the Nickel Plate provocation, stung him into committing the only act of his life which seemed to border upon madness. He had once toyed with the idea of controlling the Baltimore & Ohio, but gave it up. Now he decided to invade the Pennsylvania's territory, to parallel it with a line shorter and of lower grades, and therefore a fatal competitor. He had already a majority interest in the Philadelphia & Reading, which carried with it control of the Central of New Jersey, leading into New York; and beyond Harrisburg he had discovered another blueprint ready to his hand.

[As early as 1837 a survey had been made from Pittsburgh to Chambersburg, and one corporation after another was reorganized with the idea of building the road, eventually as far east as Harrisburg. The company was incorporated in 1863 as the South Pennsylvania Railroad, though not a stroke of work was ever done on it.]

It was natural that William H. Vanderbilt should hear about this South Pennsylvania dream, and suddenly see a great light. In 1882 he

---

Abridged from *The Road of the Century,* The Story of the New York Central, by Alvin F. Harlow, pp. 321–336. New York: Creative Age Press.

bought the franchise and all rights of the sleeping company for what was a mere song to him. He then laid before Andrew Carnegie—whose Homestead steel works had developed into one of the nation's great industries and would be right in the path of the proposed railroad—his plan for a line to the seaboard which, according to the latest survey, would be from forty-six to forty-nine miles shorter than the Pennsylvania between New York and Pittsburgh, and would avoid many of the road's heavy mountain grades and curves. East of Harrisburg, it would use the Reading and the Jersey Central. At its west end, it would join, near McKeesport, the Pittsburgh, McKeesport & Youghiogheny, then nearing completion, which Vanderbilt had aided to the extent of $4,500,000, and which was destined almost immediately to become a part of the Pittsburgh & Lake Erie, which both Vanderbilt and Carnegie had helped to finance. The PMcK&Y track ran right through the yard of the Homestead plant.

"What do you think of it?" asked Vanderbilt of Carnegie.

"I think so well of it," replied the latter, "that I and my friends will put five million into it."

"All right, then I will put in five million," rejoined the railroad magnate. He signed up the Rockefeller brothers for another million, and yet other millions came from New York and Pittsburgh. He sent 300 engineers and helpers into the territory that autumn of 1883 for a complete resurvey. Contracts were quickly let, and thousands of workmen began grading and drilling the tunnels. So strong had the emphasis become on directness and low grades that the line was going to pierce the Appalachian ranges instead of going over them or wriggling along stream beds. There were to be nine great tunnels, from 700 to 6,662 feet in length.

Announcement of the project threw the Pennsylvania offices in Philadelphia into turmoil, and they began buying West Shore bonds in order to weight the club with which to clout the audacious interloper. Here also is a partial explanation of the sanguinary rate-cutting into which the West Shore launched itself at the time.

Piers for the bridge across the Susquehanna near Pittsburgh were being built and the nine tunnels were all well under way. The rate war, however, was playing hob with both West Shore and Central. West Shore bonds had fallen to 57 in June, 1884, and were down to 28½ in April, 1885, while NYC&HR stock, for the first time since its organization, slipped below par, as the result of the halving of the dividend. In April it touched 81¾.

Morgan was in England when he heard of it, the stockholders there grousing bitterly to him about the situation. He hurried home, and in July, 1885, with something of the air of a schoolmaster, summoned Depew, George B. Roberts, and Frank Thomson of the Pennsylvania to a conference on his yacht, the *Corsair*. There, during a considerable part of a day, while the boat cruised slowly in the East River and the Sound, the new dictator of Wall Street demanded in effect that the West Shore and South Pennsylvania nonsense be halted and matters restored to normality. He simply threw the problem into the laps of his guests and told them to get together. While they wrangled, he disposed his six-foot frame comfortably in a deck chair, smoking one of his huge, black, deadly cigars, listening and now and then putting in a biting sentence to keep them on the track. The NYC didn't want the decadent West Shore, and the Pennsylvania wasn't keen on buying off the South Pennsylvania. Roberts was the most difficult to handle, and Morgan practically refused to let him go ashore until he was willing to compromise. Finally, near nightfall, he yielded.

Under the agreement then made, the Pennsylvania was to take over the South Pennsylvania, with its capital written down to $3,500,000, and the New York Central was to lease the West Shore after it had gone through the wringer. On July 27, Morgan made public announcement of the plan. But the Pennsylvania was not to gain control of the many-tunneled competitor so easily. On August 25, the Attorney General of Pennsylvania brought suit, asking for an order to prevent the absorption, as contrary to state law forbidding the buying by a railroad of a parallel or competing line. The testimony in the case, which was quickly tried, filled a thick volume. Morgan was a prominent witness, and he was strenuously grilled as to that conference on the *Corsair*, and why it was so secret. In the end, the court blocked the Pennsylvania's taking possession. Whereupon, on September 12, work ceased forever on the South Pennsylvania Railroad. About 62 percent of the tunneling had been bored, and the piers and abutments of the Susquehanna bridge were ready for the superstructure.

On December 5, 1885, the New York, West Shore & Buffalo was sold under foreclosure to J. Pierpont Morgan, Chauncey M. Depew and Ashbel Green as joint tenants. Papers were all ready, and as quick as a wink they had organized a new corporation, the West Shore Railroad Company, with a capital of only $10,000,000—all owned by the New York Central—and had leased it to the Central for 475 years.

As for the forsaken South Pennsylvania Railroad, the large Pittsburgh stockholders tried unsuccessfully to revive it in 1887. In 1899, when the railroads raised rates to the seaboard, Carnegie sent surveyors over the route at considerable cost to himself, but once more the plan was dropped. For almost another forty years the bridge piers, grade, and tunnels lay sleeping, with Nature chipping away at them, trying to restore her ancient landscape. Meanwhile came the automobile, and in 1938 the idea of constructing a motor highway over the course and using six of the nine tunnels was adopted. And so, after fifty-five years of slow decay, they were bored through, and the great paved speedway (the Pennsylvania Turnpike) was opened in 1940.

Houck versus Jay Gould

Houck was the principal in a big lawsuit here in the '80's, which is recalled by some of the older citizens of the county. The litigation resulted from the efforts of the Goulds to obtain possession of the Cape Girardeau Southwestern Railroad, Houck's first project, extending from Cape Girardeau to Delta. Houck had taken over the building of the railroad after two companies had failed to construct the line, and a substantial bonus was to be paid him if a train was operated between Cape Girardeau and Delta by January 1. Houck conquered numerous difficulties, one of which was the lack of capital, to make good on the work. He bought his rails second-hand from the old Iron Mountain, and deliveries were made to him at Delta in small lots. A few days before the work was to have been completed, deliveries stopped and the work came to a halt. Whether or not this was a premeditated scheme on the part of the Iron Mountain to ruin Houck and obtain control of the road has always been a moot question. At any rate, Houck lacked a mile or so of rails of having enough to reach Cape Girardeau, and seeing failure facing him, he started his train from Delta, pulled up the rails behind him and carried them to the Cape Girardeau end, the last yard of track being completed and the first train operated into Cape Giradeau just ten minutes before the contract required. Some time later the Iron Mountain demanded payment for the rails furnished, and Houck refused, on the ground that the company had failed to fulfil its contract to make proper deliveries.

The suit came to Charleston for trial, and so important was it that Jay Gould, then the principal owner of the Iron Mountain, came down on a special train and spent a week here while the case was on trial. Houck served as his own attorney, and his ability is shown by the fact that he won the suit, although opposed by some of the leading railroad lawyers in this part of the country. After the trial, Gould is said to have walked across the courtroom and congratulated Houck on his victory.

"You are the first man that ever beat me in a railroad fight," Mr. Gould told him. "I have seen your railroad at Delta and I have heard you conduct your case, and I want to say that you are a d—— poor railroad man, but a d—— fine lawyer."

Houck later had another brush with the Goulds when he attempted to cross their tracks with his Missouri & Arkansas Railroad at Morley.

Abridged from the Charleston (Mo.) *Enterprise-Courier,* February 26, 1925, in the library of the State Historical Society of Missouri, Columbia, Mo.

Louis Houck, a versatile genius—lawyer, journalist, historian—wrote a good three-volume history of Missouri and built most of the network of railroads in southeast Missouri in the latter 19th century. A county newspaper relates some of his exploits as follows.

The Iron Mountain, to block the crossing, built a switch and filled it full of cars. Houck, however, went to the town board and conveyed his right of way, crossing the Iron Mountain, to the town for a street, with the proviso that he might run his tracks through the street. He then had the town authorities inform the Iron Mountain that they were blocking a public thoroughfare, and in this way forced the Iron Mountain to move the cars from the crossing location.

Houck's railroads were never model lines, but they opened up some of the finest country in southeast Missouri. . . . For some years we lived at Benton, on his HM&A line, which is now the Gulf line of the Frisco. This road was known locally as the "peavine," because it was so crooked, and sometimes for days at a time there would be no trains, because the one engine and coach had jumped the track. At one place just south of Benton, Houck had felled two trees and laid them across a small creek, laying his rails on this structure instead of the regulation trestle. This caused the track to rise up to get on the trestle, and we recall the warning which the conductor always gave the passengers, "Look out, she's going to jump!" so that they might prepare themselves for the sudden change in level.

Harriman and the Runaway River

Readers who picked up the Los Angeles newspapers one day in 1906 found themselves confronted by shocking headlines. All of Southern California might slip into the Pacific Ocean!

Down in the Imperial Valley, a strange and unbelievable event was taking place. Where there had once been only dry desert, a vast inland sea had appeared and was now growing with alarming swiftness. Somehow, cried the newspapers, water was seeping in through some subterranean passage from the ocean. Before long, Southern California might be part of the sea floor.

Though the reporters turned out to be wrong about their explanation, they were right about the menace to a huge area of California. A disaster that would soon grip the attention of the nation was in the making, and it was going to lead to one of history's strangest battles between man and nature. What gave it an odd twist was that man, not nature, had started the trouble, with an engineering mistake.

It all began in the late '90s when adventurous promoters set out to turn the Imperial Valley into a garden spot by building a canal from the mighty Colorado River. As life-giving water poured in, so did thousands of settlers, and the desert, which had been virtually uninhab-

---

From "The Battle to Save Imperial Valley," by Norman and Madelyn Wood Carlisle, *Coronet*, Vol. 32 (May, 1952), No. 1, pp. 82–85. Copyright, 1952, by Esquire, Inc. Chicago.

ited, sprang into life. By 1904 it boasted a population of 15,000, with more coming every day. Imperial, Holtville, Brawley, El Centro, Calexico sprang up overnight. Lavish crops of alfalfa, cotton, melons, and grapes were making the valley an agricultural wonderland.

For a few years the Colorado rolled calmly through the canal, a red and sleepy giant, willing to play along for a while with this man-made scheme. But there was trouble ahead. Its waters were carrying tons of sand into the opening of the canal, building up a giant levee, 20 feet high, 20 feet wide, and a mile long. Finally the first four miles of the canal were blocked and Imperial Valley's water supply was almost cut off.

Meanwhile the merciless sun continued to beat down, shriveling the crops. Frantic farmers threatened to lynch the development-company officers who had lured them into the desert with promises that there would always be water.

Something had to be done fast, and that something was to dig a ditch that by-passed the blocked section of the canal. Later, the engineers figured, they would build a control gate; the need for water was too desperate to worry about that now. Right there came the mistake that cost millions, frightened all Southern Californians, and almost destroyed the richest agricultural valley in the world.

More and more water began to flow into the ditch. By August, 1905, the stunned engineers were able to see catastrophe taking shape. The Colorado River, which for millenniums had flowed into the Gulf of California, had changed its course. The whole river was now roaring through the ditch, thundering along, not south but north—into the Imperial Valley. The engineers had to get the river back in its original course—but how?

Development officials begged the Southern Pacific Railroad, with its big stake in the Valley, to step into the picture. The railroad had already given some financial help, but more was desperately needed. E. H. Harriman, famed head of the railroad, sent an engineer to take a look. When he saw the red tide ripping through the cut, he sent a frantic wire to Harriman. The job would cost millions. "Stop it at any cost!" Harriman wired back.

So the fight began. They tried several dams, with no success. Then, engineers based their hopes on a scheme to dig out the original channel with a giant dredge from San Francisco. But on April 18, when the dredge was loaded in a flatcar, ready to be shipped, nature struck at that city with the great earthquake and fire. Tumbled under tons of debris was the dredge so desperately needed in the Imperial Valley.

Numbly, the engineer in charge stared at the telegram from Southern Pacific headquarters. "Deeply regret this act of God destroys your hopes. Advise you to fight on as best you can."

By now the waters had created a vast lake, called the Salton Sea, which covered almost 800 square miles. Reporters sent out disturbing reports of what was happening, among them the theory that all that water couldn't be coming just from the river, but must be seeping in from the ocean. Fifty top engineers reported that the job was too big for the railroad—maybe too big for anybody.

Harriman roared with rage at that verdict, and sent a new engineer, Harry Cory, who plunged into the job with furious urgency. He wasn't sure he could lick the Colorado, but nobody was going to say he hadn't tried. He would need a railroad first, a branch line from Yuma to haul in supplies. In six weeks it was built. At the scene of the river break, workmen's barracks, a hospital, a roundhouse were set up. Labor was scarce so Cory brought in six tribes of Indians from Mexico and Arizona. For a time, it seemed, he was winning. He even got a gate installed in the face of the tearing current—only to see a flash flood wash it away.

As the situation grew more desperate, mass meetings of angry citizens were held. Heated telegrams began to pour into Washington, landing on the desk of Theodore Roosevelt. Angrily he sent a wire to Harriman. Why hadn't the railroad stopped the river?

Harriman shot back a wire saying that the railroad had already spent more than a million dollars of stockholders' money. It would spend no more. Why didn't the government do the job?

For days the telegrams went back and forth, while the nation looked on in amazement at this strange tug of war between a famous businessman and the President of the United States. Finally Harriman gave in, and the President gratefully promised to do all he could to get Congress to reimburse the railroad.

Harriman himself rushed to the scene. He shook his head when he saw the fury of the waters as they rushed through the cut. Then he whirled to face his engineers. "Turn it at all costs," he said shortly. "Forget the money. Stop the river!"

Engineers in huddled consultations decided that there was only one way to challenge the flood. Out along 1,200 miles of the main line went electrifying orders. The railroad was to be mobilized to haul rock to beat the Colorado. Every available flatcar was to be pressed into service. All trains were to be pushed onto sidings to give the rock cars the right of way.

The whole Southwest was in an uproar. At San Pedro, second largest port on the West Coast, shipping came to a halt; freight shipments on the Southern Pacific's entire western division were stopped. Night and day, the long rock trains rolled from the quarries, some of them hundreds of miles away.

Meanwhile, at the roaring crevasse there was a scene of furious activity. Fifteen hundred workmen were gathered at the spot and more volunteers were pouring in. This was no mere engineering job; this was a battle for survival, and the Southwest knew it.

Cory was fighting to get a trestle built across the crevasse before the rush shipments of rocks began to pour in. Five huge piledrivers went to work to smash massive 90-foot pilings into place. Hardly had a trestle been completed when a flood swept down and carried it away.

A second trestle was completed and it, too, was washed out. Hardly were the piles for the third trestle in place when sweating gangs of track layers swarmed out to fasten down stringers, ties, and rails. In a matter of hours trains were rolling onto the trestle. Gangs of men lifted the huge rocks by sheer brute force and rolled them into the waters.

At night the work went on in the bright glare of searchlights. The whole operation was a bedlam of noise in which the shouts of men were drowned by rumbling freight trains, shrieking locomotives, and the angry thunder of the river itself.

While the world watched this strange drama in the desert, the end came suddenly on February 11, 1907. The water rushing into that fatal ditch slowed to a trickle and then stopped. The Colorado, finally thwarted by the barrier of rock, went back into its ancient bed.

Years later, Harriman, whose railroad still had not received a cent of government compensation for its gigantic battle, visited the valley. Had he ever regretted his gift to the nation?

For answer, Harriman looked out over the lush green acres that, except for him, might have been just the desolate floor of an inland sea.

"The Imperial Valley was worth it," he said simply.

Jim Hill in Action

During all of this battle for rights-of-way, of titans jousting, of big-time financing and immense strategy, Jim Hill still had time to permit play of his minor likes and passions. I think several incidents are revealing of his character and of his insatiable and immediate interest in anything pertaining to his railroads. One glimpse of Hill in action comes from Lee Howard. Mr. Howard, later a celebrated pilot on the Yukon, and still rugged in 1946, told me of working in a Hill track gang in Dakota, in the late Seventies.

From *The Story of American Railroads,* by Stewart H. Holbrook, pp. 179–180. Copyright, 1947, by Crown Publishers. New York.

In the course of a revival meeting a Swede was exhorted: "Won't you come forward, Ole, and work for Jesus?" The unemotional Ole shook his head. "Naw, I got good yob with Yim Hill."—*Railroad Stories,* Vol. 21 (February, 1937), No. 3, p. 48.

During a sizable blizzard . . . Jim Hill came out in his special car to where a crew of us were trying to clear the line. He didn't stay in his car, either. He grabbed my shovel and started tossing snow, telling me to go back to his car and I'd find a pot of coffee there. I did, and spent half an hour drinking coffee and resting. Mr. Hill spelled off first one man, then another. My, but he was tough! He must have shoveled snow two or three hours that day.

It has been told of Jim Hill that he knew all of his superintendents and chief foremen by name. Hell, he even knew the first names of all of the older shovel-stiffs! He cussed us impartially when things went wrong, or we weren't working fast enough to suit him. He was obviously a man who was used to having his own way. When he didn't, he got hot under his collar, and I'm telling you he wore a powerfully big collar.

One of the remembered great snows of the prairies came in 1897. At that time, and among many other things, Hill had the contract to carry the mails between Ortonville, Minnesota, and Ellendale, North Dakota. The railroad was paralyzed by six feet of brand-new snow. The story goes that the Post Office Department wired Hill, after several days of no mail at Ellendale, saying they were going to fine him $5,000 for breach of contract. Hill wired back: "Gladly pay you ten thousand dollars if you will get this line open and keep it that way."

Of Jim Hill's vindictiveness many a town has a story to tell. One of the best of the authenticated stories, and perhaps as typical as any in the lot, concerns Wayzata, on the shores of Lake Minnetonka, celebrated by Longfellow, and comes from Mrs. Thelma Jones, a resident of the town.[1]

In the days before malarial control, . . . many rich Southern families, particularly from New Orleans and St. Louis, came north to Lake Minnetonka, with their colored servants, to escape the fever season. For these people large wooden hotels sprang up all around the lake. Two of these hotels, the Gleason House and the Minnetonka House, were right in the village of Wayzata, and almost upon the water's edge. Almost, but not quite, for between them and the beach ran the Great Northern tracks.

The through trains would go past at quite a clip, whistling. Added to that was a good deal of switching of cars, some of it at night, right between the aristocratic guests and the beautiful lake. Hotel guests were annoyed by the noise and the obstruction of their view, and the townspeople also became incensed.

Some time in the Nineties, the Wayzata mayor, E. B. Sanders, who perhaps not incidentally owned the Gleason House, brought some sort of injunction against the railroad, and it was fined. Jim Hill was pretty mad about it, and he is said to have vowed to wipe Wayzata

---

[1] In letters to the author, 1946.—S.H.H.

off the map. He immediately had the Wayzata station taken down and moved to Holdridge, a mile or so to the east.

Many of the villagers lined up to watch the first train that was to pass them by. She went through with the bell ringing and the whistle blowing derisively, and with the big stack throwing smoke and cinders over everything, including the water tank, which caught fire. From that day on, for about fifteen years, according to old-timers here—although one insists it was longer, lasting until Hill's death in 1916—Wayzatans had to take livery service, at fifty cents a head, to ride to Holdridge to catch the train. The livery service did very well because, of course, all freight for Wayzata was also put off at Holdridge.

It was pressure brought by influential families, including the Pillsburys, the Peavys, and Lorings—who had estates in the neighborhood—that ultimately got Jim Hill, or his son Louis, to restore service at Wayzata, and when this was finally done, the GN put up one of the finest small stations along its line.

Why Danville Lost a Railroad

Dressed as a plain surveyor, bespattered with muddy water, a stranger registered in the old Gilcher House, Danville, Ky., and was assigned to an attic bedroom with a dormer window, a shuck-mattress bed, and a tallow-dip candle, in the late '60's. The unknown guest demanded a decent room for the night. This infuriated the clerk, who sized up the stranger and exclaimed: "That room is plenty good for the looks of you."

Thereupon the infuriated "surveyor" wrote across the page of the hotel register:

"Surveyors: locate the road just far enough away from Danville so its citizens can barely hear the whistles blow.

(Signed) E. D. Standiford, President of the Louisville & Nashville R.R. Co."

Sequel to the above: To this day, sixty odd years later, Danville passengers must hire taxis and drive three miles to catch an L&N train for east or west. To assuage their grief, awakened citizens of Danville induced the Cincinnati Southern Railway to survey its municipally owned "Queen & Crescent" route via Danville. . . .

By Col. C. E. Woods, youngest L&N station agent to 1884, Sidney, Illinois, in *Time*, reprinted in *Railroad Stories*, Vol. XV (October, 1934), No. 3, p. 64. Copyright, 1934, by the Frank A. Munsey Company. New York.

How the Nickel Plate Got Its Name

I[1]

The Nickel Plate was built in 1881 and 1882 to be a competitor of the Lake Shore & Michigan Southern. But within a month after it had begun operation, it was purchased by the Vanderbilt interests, which already controlled the Lake Shore, and William H. Vanderbilt became its president. An old yarn has it that one of its purchasers remarked, "Well, for the price we paid for it it ought to be nickel plated," and thus christened the infant. But the fact is that "nickel plated" was at the time an expression with about the significance of "nifty" or the "cat's whiskers" today. And where, if it had been built in 1905, it might have been named the Blue Ribbon Road or in 1920 the Gold Bond Road, it became in the Eighties the Nickel Plate. It was called that by itself to convey the general idea of unparalleled excellence.

II[2]

The name "Nickel Plate" found its origin in a remark made by Jay Gould. When the road had failed and was placed on sale, Gould entered a bid for it. The bid was considered unsatisfactory, and Gould was urged by the interested parties to increase the amount. Though the road had not proved very profitable, it was a splendid piece of construction and worth much more than he had bid. Gould tersely replied that his bid was the maximum and that he wouldn't raise it if the old line was "nickel plated."

III[3]

In speaking of the road, its glittering prospects, the brilliant possibilities of trade opened up for the cities through which it operated, together with the gilt-edged character of its financial backing, the Norwalk (Ohio) *Chronicle* in its issue of April 14, 1881, called the institution the "Nickel Plate" road, the term being intended as expressive of the bright and substantial attributes of the enterprises. Through circulation of the Great American Newspaper the name became popular and the line was generally spoken of as the Nickel Plate Road.

---

[1] Service News of the Nickel Plate Road.

[2] From the Portland [Me.] *Express and Advertiser,* February 15, 1912.

[3] From Memorandum from J. H. Day, Vice President, Traffic Department, NYC&SLRR, December 29, 1943, to Carlton J. Corliss.

Collection of Carlton J. Corliss, Association of American Railroads, Washington, D.C.

In recent years, the name has been used officially by the Company in every department as the trade mark.

IV [4]

The unusual circumstances by which the New York, Chicago and St. Louis Railroad came to be known as the Nickel Plate Road was broadcast throughout Ohio early in June. The story of the name's "christening" was told on "The Ohio Story," a radio program carried on a state-wide network of 19 stations under the sponsorship of the Ohio Bell Telephone Company.

Nelson Olmstead, nationally known radio and television personality, was the narrator. He explained that the name had its origin back in March, 1881, when the railroad was planning to lay tracks through northwestern Ohio. The Ohio communities of Bellevue and Norwalk competed strenuously to persuade the railroad to build within their respective boundaries.

At a special council meeting Norwalk declared the contemplated route through the city as a public thoroughfare and deeded it to the railroad. Bellevue counter-attacked by sending a representative to officials of the railroad with pledges of $10,000 to route the rails through that community. When Norwalk heard of this, a mass meeting was called to meet the emergency.

To publicize the meeting F. R. Loomis, editor of the *Norwalk Chronicle,* was commissioned to put out a handbill outlining the purpose. When he wrote the text, it sounded good, but the headline needed punch—something short that would fit into one line. The name of the railroad was too long and people wouldn't understand the abbreviation, NYC&StL.

Then he recalled that when it was said the railroad would have all-steel tracks, palace cars, and the world's fastest locomotive, some one had remarked, "To hear 'em tell it, you'd think the whole thing was going to be nickel-plated."

Editor Loomis decided people would understand that. Ever since the nickel-plating process had been discovered, the phrase had been used as a synonym for quality. So when the handbill hit Norwalk's streets, it carried the headline, "The Nickel Plated Railroad."

In the end Bellevue won out over Norwalk in getting the railroad. But the editor's name for it spread, and so today the railroad is known to the world as the "Nickel Plate Road."

---

[4] From *Nickel Plate Road Magazine,* Vol. 4 (June, 1952), No. 6, p. 13. Cleveland, Ohio.

PART THREE

Vanishing Types

Introduction

With the passing of steam, an era—for many, the great era—of railroading came to an end, and passed into folklore. "Those were the days"—the "roaring days," the restless, reckless, harum-scarum days when rules (including Rule G) were too often honored in the breach rather than the observance, while speed, comfort, and safety (the triple goal of railroad competition and public relations) often got in each other's way. Those were the days, too, of simple pleasures, the Age of Innocence, symbolized by the leisurely casualness and neighborliness of poky little locals on branch and short lines and old-fashioned deepos in inland communities ranging from a "one-horse flag station" in the middle of the prairie to a bustling "railroad town." If there were giants in those days, there were also "little fellers"; and the latter have a special place in the memories of old-timers because, among other reasons, "He who travels by rail over the lesser lines of the U.S.A. clangs and shunts straight into his own childhood." [1]

Not only that, but "the local runs through another century," when a railroad was a country thing, an eccentric thing, and a neighborhood institution. In the old days, when an engineer had his "own" engine, he took a personal pride in its appearance; it had a personality and was almost human, living and breathing. In the same way a railroad is a "living thing. . . . Its financial and personal roots go deep into local history and pride." [2] Like the men who worked the trains, small roads were friends and neighbors; they brought the world to one's door and, like the deepos, were social centers. And the history and folklore of American railroads are written in the lyric and idyllic terms of the little pikes as surely as in the epic and heroic terms of the high iron.

In the early days of the railroads a great deal of thought was given to their "morality," their influence on manners and morals, including the problem of Sunday operations (pages 78-79). The railroad was also seen as the Great Leveler, as "The rich and the poor, the educated and the ignorant, the polite and the vulgar, all herd together in this modern improvement in traveling." [3] If the railroad joined and amalgamated men, they in turn humanized it. In America, as British travelers noted with their sharp eye for differences, the open right-of-way gave the roads a special community intimacy (page 79). All this—miracle and myth—was not lost on that traveler in little things, Thoreau.

The Fitchburg Railroad touches the pond about a hundred rods south of where I dwell. I usually go to the village along its causeway, and am, as it

---

1 Editorial comment on "The U.S. Depot, A Portfolio," by Walker Evans, *Fortune* (February, 1953), p. 138.

2 Archie Robertson, *Slow Train to Yesterday* (Boston, 1945), p. 4.

3 *Recollections of Samuel Breck,* with Passages from His Notebooks (1771–1862), edited by H. E. Scudder (Philadelphia, 1877), p. 275.

were, related to society by this link. The men on the freight trains, who go over the whole length of the road, bow to me as to an old acquaintance, they pass me so often, and apparently they take me for an employee; and so I am. I too would fain be a track-repairer somewhere in the orbit of the earth. . . .

When I meet the engine with its train of cars moving off with planetary motion . . . ; when I hear the iron horse make the hills echo with his snort like thunder, shaking the earth with his feet, and breathing fire and smoke from his nostrils (what kind of winged horse or fiery dragon they will put into the new Mythology I don't know), it seems as if the earth had got a race now worthy to inhabit it.

. . . They [the trains] go and come with such regularity and precision, and their whistle can be heard so far, that the farmers set their clocks by them, and thus one well-conducted institution regulates a whole country.[4]

A typical "slow train" of yesterday is the Texas railroad of 1866 described by R. H. Williams in *With the Border Ruffians:*

Slowly we crept along for about twelve miles; then came to a sudden halt, and discovered we had been left standing on the line, while the engine was steaming off by itself! Many were the surmises as to the cause of this extraordinary proceeding, and most were of the opinion that it was a practical joke on the part of the "drunken" engineer. Some of the more truculent passengers began to handle their six-shooters, and talk ominously of what they would do to him if, and when, he did return; and all took a gloomy view of things in general, for we were eighteen miles from Victoria and twelve from Lavacca, and, except one man who had brought two bottles of champagne, no one had anything either eatable or drinkable with him. Moreover, between us and Victoria was nothing but open prairie, with not a single house upon it.

At last the conductor—who, by the way, was a lieutenant in a black regiment of U.S. infantry, the line being run by the Government—informed us that it was the water difficulty that was stopping us once more. The "engineer," bemused as he still was, had neglected to take in enough at Lavacca, and had now gone on six miles to a waterhole, where he *hoped* to find sufficient. "And if he didn't find it?" we asked. "Waal, then he's got to go on to Victoria to get it, I reckon."[5]

A typical "cracker-barrel railroad" of today is the Belfast & Moosehead Lake, as seen by W. I. Hall, General Auditor:

Ours is one of the very few remaining short lines to operate a Railway Mail car. One day, a few years ago, there was a flag out at City Point Station, two miles from Belfast [Maine], where there is no agent. The train duly stopped and a lady came out, with a letter in her hand, and said she wanted a ticket to Waldo, the next station. The conductor sold the ticket and then prepared to help the lady aboard. She said, "Oh, I'm not going. I just wanted to stop the train to mail this letter."[6] . . .

---

[4] *Walden* (Boston, 1854), pp. 125–130.

[5] London, 1907, pp. 455–458.

[6] Letter to Alvin F. Harlow, July 3, 1953.

Even among city commuters today one encounters frequent throwbacks to the old individualism and neighborliness. In 1949 Harold Ross of *The New Yorker* led an embattled "captive audience" of Connecticut and Westchester suburban riders against the barbaric invasion of Grand Central Terminal by loud speakers blaring commercials and canned music. In both Grand Central and Pennsylvania Stations commuters racing for trains pay telephone operators in attended stations to relay last-minute messages to wives or husbands stating, simply, "6:02," or, "Tell Mama to put on the steak." In times of emergency and disaster, the community spirit is all the stronger. On January 17, 1952, when the Southern Pacific streamliner, *City of San Francisco,* was snowbound in the Sierras, not far from the scene of the Donner tragedy, a Republican National Committee woman told a *New York Herald Tribune* reporter of "bundling" and swapping stories ("some of them you can't print") with men she had never seen before and distributing '52 Elephant buttons to fellow passengers. On the night of the Big Snow of December 26, 1947, the writer was marooned for thirteen hours on a multiple unit train bound from New York to Croton (a trip that normally takes from fifty to seventy minutes); and the misery of that cold and hungry sleepless night was dwarfed by the commuters' intimate, wisecracking camaraderie; e.g., "If there was any way we could shoot a railroad!" "The people you meet when you're stuck on a train like this!" "I know I should have gone to church four times Christmas." "Is any one of the fifty-two vice-presidents of the road on this train?" (Answer) "No, they're all home in bed."

"Journeys are where stories live when they're at home." Journeys are also "swift reagents upon human nature." Perfect strangers confide their life stories to one another. In the days before radio and TV, Pullmans, side-door Pullmans, and smokers were among the chief distributors of floating stories, songs, and sayings, and they still are important "grapevine" routes. Train butchers still entertain passengers with kibitzing sales spiels, like the comedian on the Montreal Limited, before departure from Grand Central Terminal: "Nothing sold after the train leaves. Very little is being sold before. . . . Orangeade—it'll fill you, chill you, and thrill you. Eat, drink, have fun, live, and let live. . . . No ham sandwich? Not kosher? For another nickel I'll say a blessing and it will be kosher." And commuters on the New York Central Electric Division ride to the cheerful tune of a wise-cracking conductor who announces Philipse Manor as "Mortgage Manor" and Tarrytown as "The Garden Spot of Westchester County! The best people here are in the cemetery!—Sleepy Hollow!" "Express to the next station!" "Same at this end!"

Institutions may pass and types vanish and Railroad Nostalgia may replace Railroad Fever, but human nature still rides the cars.

B.A.B.

I. BOOMER AND HOME GUARD

Men Who Work the Trains

Away back in the beginning days, that is, in the 1830s, when the engineer had no cab, but stood on a little open platform connecting engine with tender and took the weather as it came, sheltering his eyes in time of severe storm with a shingle; when cars were lighted by candles if the train was caught out after dark, which wasn't often; when the Michigan Central's water tank at Chicago was filled by a windmill, and many others by horses walking on treadmills; when there were turn-tables like that at Batavia, N. Y., so small that even the little engines of that day and their tenders had to be turned separately; when the rule was that in case of a breakdown en route, the brakeman must borrow a horse from the nearest farm and go in search of "help," whatever that might be (perhaps a blacksmith), and in case a train didn't show up at a terminal for a couple of hours after it was due, the agent was to go out along the line on horseback, looking for it—in those days, there were some bizarre practices in the matter of employing trainmen, too.

On the Schenectady & Troy Railroad, in its very early years, the trainmen were elected by the Board of Directors. In the archives of the New York Central, inheritor of the little S&T, one may read in the minute books that, "On motion, Resolved that this Board now proceed to the election by ballot of a Ticket Agent & Clerk at Troy," and N. S. Hollister receiving all six votes was declared elected; salary $450 a year. Then they just as solemnly proceeded to the election of a conductor and baggage master (they needed only one of each). After

---

By Alvin F. Harlow. A compilation from various sources.

electing a superintendent, they seem to have permitted him to choose the other functionaries.

We hear of other curious practices before the railroads settled down into the modern routine: of conductors choosing their own brakemen, engineers hiring their own firemen. Throughout most of the Nineteenth Century, an engineer had his own engine, which nobody else was permitted to touch, save the wipers who cleaned and polished its gorgeously painted surfaces, its boiler (perhaps Russia iron), its brass and sometimes "German silver" mountings. Operating it just wasn't done by anybody but its own appointed engineer. He it was who sometimes mounted a brass spread-eagle on the sand dome, deerhorns on the headlight (some engineers claimed to own their headlights and took them home with them), in some cases a cast-iron figure about three feet tall of a Negro jockey, such as were mounted on stone bases at the curb in front of residences to serve as hitching posts. The figure always had an arm outstretched, with a ring at the end through which the hitching strap was reeved; and we hear of an engineer who placed a bouquet of flowers in the ring at the start of every run, though we cannot believe that much of it would be left at the end of the run.

On the Erie it required a trial of strength between conductor and engineer to determine who was master of the train. But on the New England roads, the conductor became the top authority at an early date, and was sternly ordered never to leave his train. The tendency to compare a train with a ship was manifest, when the conductor began to be called "captain" by the passengers, as many still do, though foreign tourists persisted in thinking of him as the guard. In the typical American way, he considered himself on a social level with the passengers. Dickens, going down from Hartford to New Haven, notes that "The guard and I were formally introduced to each other (as we usually were on such occasions) and exchanged a variety of small talk." A conductor on the Boston & Worcester, swapping gossip on the end platform of the car with Alexander Mackay, another tourist, offered him a chew of tobacco from his tin box.

As the conductors collected a great many fares on the trains, some of them became suspiciously prosperous. William Chambers, a British visitor, said, "The American railway conductor is a nondescript being, half clerk, half guard, with a dash of the gentleman. He is generally well dressed; sometimes wears a beard, and when off duty, he passes for a respectable personage at any of the hotels, and may be seen lounging about in the best company, with a fashionable wife. No one would be surprised to find that he is a colonel in the militia. . . . At all events, the conductor would need to be a person of some integrity, for the check upon his transactions is infinitesimally small. One thing remarkable about him—you do not catch sight of him until the train is in motion, and when it stops, he disappears. I can account for this only by supposing that as soon as he touches *terra firma,* he removes from the front of his hat the word blazoned in metal which indicates his office; and so all at once becomes an ordinary human being." [1]

As this indicates, the trainmen then wore no uniforms. The conductor wore a top hat, his only badge of office being a metal strip with the word "Conductor" on it attached to the front of his hat by an elastic. He wore broadcloth, the aristocrat of clothing in those days, and as time went on, in the '60s and '70s, he might wear yellow or lilac kid gloves when on duty, with wisps of paper money between the fingers of his left hand and plenty of coin in his pockets. His lantern might be silver plated, the upper half of its globe blue or green, clear glass below, with his name or his lodge emblem etched on the glass. The very swankiest sometimes had gold-plated ticket punches.

Freight conductors also collected the charges on freight, often by guesswork, as there were seldom any scales in the stations, and quite as often no tariff sheets. A conductor on the Boston & Lowell collected $500 in charges on one trip and put it into a bank which did not open its doors next morning, so his company lost the money. For a long time, some roads got along with very few station agents, and freight conductors often had to seek out the consignees, perhaps far out in the country, to collect charges on a shipment, while the train waited. They collected in advance whenever possible.

Conductors varied in character and temperament as widely as human beings do in any other walk of life. Inevitably, there were some unpleasant trainmen, but there were many of the other sort, too, such as John B. Adams, veteran conductor on the Western Railroad (Mass.), who in 1852 was given a $200 silver tea set by a group of his patrons. "There is hardly a man," said a newspaper notice of the presentation, "living upon the line of the railroad between Springfield and Albany who is not indebted to Mr. Adams for kind attention to his wife, mother, or sister."

Mrs. Isabella Bird Bishop, another traveler, going west from Albany on the New York Central in 1855, found the conductor very gracious. "He turned a chair into a sofa and lent me a buffalo robe (for hot though the day had been, the night was intensely cold), and several times brought me a cup of tea." They fell into a discussion on the comparative "breakage power" on English and American railroads, and he was so absorbed that he "forgot to signal the engine-driver to stop at a station." Looking out of a window, he said, "Dear me, we ought to have stopped three miles back"; but consoled himself with the thought that "Likely, there was no one to get out." [2]

---

[1] William Chambers, *Things as They Are in America* (London and Edinburgh, 1857), p. 331.

[2] *The Englishwoman in America* (London, 1856), p. 87.

Then there was jolly Dave Pratt on the Portland Division of the Grand Trunk, who genially teased his passengers about their propensity for doing the wrong thing. "Ladies and gentlemen, this is Lewiston Junction, not Danville Junction. Watch where you go." And they laughed and liked it. And there was the rare precisian-like Henry Banks, the first conductor on the Danbury & Norwalk, who would intone from the platform at leaving time, "Those who are about to proceed on the train will please take their seats." Approaching Norwalk, he would announce impressively, "The train will presently reach Norwalk bridge"; and after leaving Bethel, northbound, "We are now approaching the village of Danbury, which is the terminus of the road." Concord (N. H.) historians report that as a train on the Concord Railroad drew into the capital city, "The conductor alighted in the grand manner from the head of the train, and announced the station at some window of each car as they all went by."

The checks (in reality his receipt for tickets), which the conductor stuck in passengers' hat-bands or in later years thrust into a crevice in the seat-back, were of varied colors, sometimes blank, sometimes with a list of the stations on his run printed on one side. Many conductors had their own printed. Some read: "Keep this check in your [picture of a plug hat], to avoid the too frequent visits of [signed] John Smithers, conductor." John Bradley, conductor on the Hartford & New Haven around Civil War time, devised rebuses which were printed on his checks for the entertainment of his passengers, and a whole carful might be seen puzzling delightedly over them.

Perhaps the most famous conductor in American railroad history was Asa R. Porter, of the Old Colony's Steamboat Express, popularly known as the Boat Train, which for ninety years (1847–1937) left Boston daily in late afternoon to dash non-stop down to Fall River and catch one of the famous Fall River Line's big Queens of the Sound for New York, returning next morning upon the arrival of the New York boat. It was a favorite way of overnight travel between the two cities in those less hurried days. For thirty-two years, from 1864 until he died in harness in 1896, Asa Porter shuttled back and forth on that train between Boston and Fall River, save for times when he might be called upon to take charge of a President's special—and he was the one always billeted for such a task. His great popularity began with his kindness to sick and wounded soldiers during the Civil War. A dignified but genial figure in his frock coat, always with a flower in his buttonhole—at first a pink, it grew to a carnation in later years—with shaven upper lip and short beard which gradually turned from brown to white, he was not only the master of the train but the host. Even company officials called him Mr. Porter. Evenings at Fall River, as the passengers moved from the train to the gangplank, he stood shaking hands with scores of them—many through frequent trips had become friends or acquaintances—with a smiling word for each: "Good-night, ma'am—and a pleasant journey!" "Good-night, sir, hope to see you again"; "Good-night, Mr. Lyman, take care of yourself"—and all with a sincere heartiness which never seemed to slacken. It used to be said that he had much to do with making the Fall River Line the great success that it was. He was more than once offered a higher position by the company, but he could think of no happier life than the one he was living.[3]

In a more modest way, many conductors on short runs and ambling locals are fondly remembered as friends and neighbors, who would sometimes trust a passenger who had forgotten or lost money and ticket, and who were skilful at taking a cinder out of your eye—and cinders were omnipresent in those pre-diesel, pre-air-conditioned days. Conductor Charlie on the Long Island, a rotund, genial friend of two generations of commuters, was an example of this type.

West of the Mississippi, until well into the 1870s, you were apt to encounter some unscrupulous and roughneck conductors. Twain and Warner in *The Gilded Age* picture one throwing a passenger off the train on very slight provocation, and a local newspaper treating the matter quite merrily. Travelers, especially women, over the Overland Route to California sometimes encountered conductors who extorted additional moneys from them, although their fare was supposed to have been paid through to San Francisco. Happily, such characters became less numerous and vanished as the rough edges of the West were smoothed.

In the South, in the latter part of the century, where and when tenures were long and retirement was not forced upon a man at a stipulated age, one encountered some of the finest specimens of the old-time conductor and gentleman of yesteryear—slender, white-haired, some with the pale, waxen flesh of advanced years, yet maintaining their poise in the swaying car with the aplomb of youth, frock-coated, gravely courteous yet affable, with statesmanlike manner. The traditional Southern reverence for age made him the unquestioned though gentle autocrat of the train crew and passengers. Even the brashest drummer called him "Cap'n" with unwonted respect.

Electric lighting having not yet been developed, the conductor of those days went through the cars at night with his lantern in the crook of his left arm, so that he might examine tickets by its light.

As for the engineer, "Perhaps no other occupation," says Lucius Beebe, "ever fetched the American fancy as did that of the locomotive engineer. Not even the cowboy, the Indian scout, the godlike vision of Washington at Valley Forge or the swift facility of 'Tinker to Evers to Chance' quite so effectively captivated the national imagination as the steam locomotive, its drive-rods flashing obedient to the cross-heads in their guides and the dynamic whole obedient to the

---

[3] Alvin F. Harlow, *Steelways of New England* (New York, 1946), p. 231.

visor-capped man at the throttle. His eagle eye pierced the impenetrable storm and saw to the furthest horizons, his controlling hand on the air brake lever was the hand of Fate itself. The aviator of a later generation, a mere mechanic cleaving his wide blue yonder, was never in the same league with the brave engineer." [4]

What a long, long way the engineer has come—from the poor fellow shivering on that open platform in a New England blizzard—and why the idea of a cab didn't occur to anyone sooner, we can't imagine—down past the man who spent his days twisted sidewise on his seat, hurling a heavy Johnson bar back and forth, peering from a smaller and smaller window-slit past a bigger and bigger, longer and longer, boiler, and frequently having to poke his head out into the storm, and keeping tab on an increasing number of gadgets on his instrument board, to the sybarite of today in spotless jumper and overalls—he could almost do it in a dress suit—reared back on his red-leather-padded chair in his weather-proof cab, flicking a lever back and forth, and considering an extremely limited number of miles a day's work. But he is still the devotee of duty, the man who, with no ado about it, feels the weight of the whole massive fabric, with its hundreds of passengers, on his conscience and brain and good right arm, and lives up to the best traditions of his profession.

The fireman and brakeman—they have come a long way, too. The firemen on the early wood-burners had it easier, one thinks, than those later ones, after coal came in. Locomotives and trains were smaller, and tossing in sticks of wood wasn't so hard. The wood was soon burned, of course, but they stopped every few miles to wood up, and everybody joined in the chore, even the passengers. The firemen on the coal steamers needed—already we begin to speak of him in the past tense—a strong body—back, legs and arms—especially if he was on a hill or mountain run. He shoveled many a ton of coal in a week, and if he didn't keep a good head of steam on, he heard from the engineer in good, round terms. Some engineers could and did make it hard for a fireman, out of pure cussedness. There, in the most dangerous part of the train, the fireman was often a hero in emergency, alongside the engineer. Then came the oil burner and the automatic stoker, and now the diesel—and the fireman is no longer a mere coal-heaver but an artisan.

The passenger brakeman of the first two or three decades was a busy little cup of tea, indeed. He must help to stop the train at stations by twisting the brake-wheels—and the brakie who couldn't wind 'em tight enough to slide the wheels of his car wasn't considered up to his job—until headquarters began warning against sliding them; it made flat wheels. Between trips he was expected to keep the cars in good

---

[4] Lucius Beebe and Charles Clegg, *Hear the Train Blow* (New York, 1952), p. 198.

order, which meant sweeping, dusting, occasionally mopping the floor and washing the windows. He must clean and fill the lamps, the signal lanterns and the conductor's lantern, fill the big wood boxes at each end of the car, keep up the fires during the run and string up the bell-cord from car to car. He had to assist the yardmen in assembling the train, and when they stopped at wood stations, he must help toss wood into the tender. He assisted the conductor in collecting tickets if the train was long, and at the termini hauled the baggage on trucks between the station baggage room and the car door. Gradually, one by one, these duties were taken from him as the years passed.

By custom, he wore a black oilcloth cap, trousers tight from waistband to knees, and flaring, sailor-fashion, below the knees; a short, close-fitting coat, and thick-soled boots.

As for the freight brakeman, of other days, his lot was almost too pitiable to contemplate; skidding about, perhaps in zero weather, on the roofs of wildly swaying freight cars, often covered with ice or snow, twisting brake-wheels for dear life; and in early decades with no caboose in which to take shelter, nothing but the little engine cab—after they appeared—which was usually pretty crowded; losing a finger or two, perhaps half a hand in a link-and-pin coupling or missing his footing and losing a leg or his life. Today the air takes care of his braking, and he rides in a caboose which has many of the features of a club car.

Boomers

. . . The boomer was an itinerant railroader who traveled light, skipping at short notice from one road to another, from one job to another. . . . His uniform was generally a black "thousand-miler" shirt, so called because he was reputed to wear it on about a thousand miles of rail travel before sending it to the laundry.

The boomer's heyday was the period of national expansion between the Civil War and World War I. He was bred of wanderlust, wars, strikes, depressions, seasonal rushes, liquor, the desire to avoid shotgun weddings, and often just plain bad luck. Most boomers were actuated by a restless desire to see what lay beyond the next hill or to follow the wild ducks northward in the spring and southward in the fall. Others had an irresistible urge to punch some trainmaster on the jaw for a real or fancied insult and then collect their pay. Still others hit the bottle too much, or carelessly let a boxcar roll off the dock, or per-

---

From "Railroaders," by Freeman H. Hubbard, in *Pennsylvania Songs and Legends,* George Korson, editor, pp. 319–323. Copyright, 1949, by University of Pennsylvania Press. Philadelphia.

haps caused a wreck by failing to deliver a train order, and flew the coop, leaving the "home guards" (company men) to face the music.

* * * * *

A million railroaders were uprooted by the Civil War, the violent strikes of '77, '86, and especially '94, and a succession of panics and business slumps. They became floaters. Blacklisted as strikers or furloughed when traffic fell off, they roamed to areas where work was to be had, at least temporarily. But the top factor in creating boomers was the seasonal rushes—moving the various crops as soon as they were harvested. Drifters worked while the rails were hot and then rambled on to localities where new rushes were just beginning.

Nowadays the periodic needs of railroad companies for additional help to wheel the seasonal crops is met by recruiting local workers—men on the extra list who are laid off when the feverish activity subsides but who can be depended upon to stick around as long as it lasts. The old-time boomer did not worry about being given the gate. He would leave town in the firm belief that some road, somewhere, was bound to hire a capable man and that he could eat off a "pie card" (meal ticket) while waiting for his next pay. When a drifter "pulled the pin" (resigned), he would tell his pals that he was "going to the Indian Valley Line," that mythical "pike" (short railroad line) where a good job with ideal working conditions could always be found.

* * * * *

One of the boomer's most useful possessions was his paid-up membership card in some railroad brotherhood. During his frequent lean periods he would shove this under the nose of a worthy brother when he wanted to eat, sleep, ride, or all three, and it usually achieved the desired result. . . .

* * * * *

As railroading lost its pioneering quality and fell into the groove, as locomotives grew heavier, trains longer, traveling safer, and the competition for jobs more keen, the independent order of boomers gradually faded away. Thus passed a rugged era. Boomers were generous, worldly-wise, self-assured often to the point of insolence, humorous, resourceful, and given to braggadocio, but withal a likable lot. They knew railroad operation better, perhaps, than the home guards did, because they circulated widely and were continually picking up new kinks. They took chances and they often thumbed their noses at officials. Many of them chewed tobacco. As they drank too much, the company liked to blame its wrecks on booze rather than on equipment failure. Still, it required plenty of red-eye to make some fellows even want to railroad in the rowdy wooden-axle days when the industry was young, hard as steel, and sprinkled with blood.

Pie-Card

. . . An old American custom much patronized by this [boomer] breed was the "pie-book," a card or booklet good for a certain number of meals at a given restaurant. "Pie-book" was the magic word whereby a boomer could get his watch out of hock, a bottle of red-eye, a few dollars to send to the little lady, or his grub and lodgings. One of these talismans usually could be obtained by a new man as soon as he got his name on the pay roll. Many men older in service drew them regularly. Coupons in the book could be used as a medium of exchange at almost any store or gin mill on or near Railroad Avenue. Some were even traded off for cash payment.

"A trick of certain established railmen whose wives insisted on seeing their checks," Hugh F. O'Neil informs me, "was to draw four or five coupon books valued at $20 to $25 and then sell the books at a heavy discount. Thus they got pocket money without the knowledge of their wives."

Some roads would permit a man to sign for a pie-book even before he had made one trip or day's work. Others required that a man have one trip made or a day's work in the yard before he could sign. Some roads limited their issue to employees of less or not more than ninety days' seniority. Others would permit the oldest hogger or conductor on the road to sign, if he desired to do so—in other words, no time limit.

"These coupons were good to purchase any article, save one, liquor," Bill Knapke recalls. "Pardon the snicker. Sometimes one or more of the Brotherhood lodges would keep a pie-book at an eating and rooming house, generally run by a brother of that particular organization, and any traveling brother having proper credentials was entitled to three meals and a bed, when in need and seeking employment."

The Crane with a Broken Neck

After the [American Railway Union] 1894 strike, the GMA [General Managers' Association] refused to let the strikers return to their old jobs, instituting the most effective blackball system ever known in railroad history. Blacklisting was an old established custom. At least one rail labor union had practised it openly. A man expelled from

---

From *Railroad Avenue,* Great Stories and Legends of American Railroading, by Freeman H. Hubbard, pp. 184–185. Copyright, 1945, by Freeman H. Hubbard. New York: Whittlesey House, McGraw-Hill Book Company, Inc.

Ibid., pp. 178–182.

that group for drunkenness would have his name and offense printed in its monthly journal, copies of which went to mechanical department officials on roads all over the United States and Canada, to prevent his getting an engine-service job elsewhere, on the ground that alcohol and locomotive operation did not mix. That was before Rule G, forbidding employees to drink liquor while on duty, became standard in the railroad industry. Today, other forms of transportation have a similar code. Take motoring, for instance, where intoxication may make you forfeit your driver's license; that is really a legalized blacklist in behalf of public safety. The GMA action, however, was not on behalf of public safety. It was more like revenge, coupled with fear of what might have happened if the strike had succeeded.

Not all companies belonging to the GMA concurred in this policy. Among the few exceptions was the Rock Island. To its lasting credit, this line rehired more than 4,000 of its 4,500 striking employees. On most roads that served Chicago the breach was not so easily healed. ARU men seeking employment from lines that had not even been involved in the walkout were stymied because their bosses refused to verify the extent of their railroad experience.

This obstacle was overcome by one of the victims, who sued a railroad company to get a service letter. The fellow won his case and was awarded damages as well as the letter. Thereupon the GMA roads saw the light. Any erstwhile employee requesting a clearance could get it. The letter set forth his record, ending with these words, "Left the service of his own accord." But there was a catch in this sudden change of heart. The trick was revealed to me years ago by several old-timers who had been through the Pullman strike. One of them, a retired boomer named William F. Knapke of East St. Louis, Ill., . . . puts the situation as follows:

Two young brakemen, Smith and Jones, both of whom had been strikers, walked into a trainmaster's office looking for a job. Smith asked the trainmaster's clerk, "Hiring any brakemen?"

"Let's see your service letter," was the noncommittal reply.

Smith handed him the clearance. The clerk took it into the next room, returned in a few seconds, and handed it back, saying, "Sorry, can't use you."

The same process was repeated with Jones, except that the clerk said to Jones, "Come back this afternoon and fill out an application."

Since both brakemen were about the same age and had about the same length of railroad experience and both service letters read very much the same, the applicants naturally wondered why Smith had been rejected and Jones hired. They puzzled over this matter for quite some time. At length, in comparing the two letters, one of the men happened to hold them up in front of a strong light, and the mystery was solved. He noticed watermarks in the paper. Both depicted a crane; but Jones's bird, the trademark of a famous paper company, stood proudly with head erect, while Smith's had its head hanging down as though with a broken neck. According to Bill Knapke:

> Crane watermarks appeared on *all* the clearances of some roads, but "head-up" letters were given to those men, whether strikers or not, who had not been ARU leaders, agitators, or saboteurs. This symbol said, in effect: "If you want to hire this applicant, it's all right with us." But in the case of strikers who, like Smith, had been too active to please the brass collars, the "crane with a broken neck" constituted a warning to prospective employers that his services were undesirable.

Other strike veterans tell me that the droopy-necked bird was used for *all* American Railway Union members, regardless of their conduct during the early summer of 1894. Among those who take this view is Arthur B. Clark, a boomer now living in retirement at Stockton, Calif.

> The blacklisting watermark was all too real, as many an old ARU man will testify. It was pointed out to me by my brother-in-law, E. W. Waddell, master mechanic on the Rock Island at Fairbury, Neb. Waddell died some years ago. The "crane with a broken neck" was then dim but could be discerned by holding the service letter to the light. I had been in the Pullman strike myself and carried one of those letters in my pocket for months, until I learned from Waddell that it was my death warrant insofar as getting a railroad job was concerned. Then I disposed of it in short order, as did other strikers branded with the same outlaw stigma when they learned the truth.

Is such a letter now extant? If so, it should be preserved. It belongs in the permanent museum of railroadiana maintained by the Railway & Locomotive Historical Society in the Baker Library of Harvard University Business School. I myself have never seen this odd watermark. I cannot even produce indisputable evidence that it actually served as a blackball device and asked [Almont] Lindsey what he thought of it. Lindsey is a professor of history at Mary Washington College in Fredericksburg, Va., as well as author of *The Pullman Strike.* He replied as follows:

> I regret that I can neither affirm nor deny the story of the "crane with a broken neck." In my research on the Pullman strike I found no reference to this matter, although I encountered plenty of evidence that blacklisting was used with a vengeance by various railroads against the strikers in 1894. The story is, indeed, an interesting one and, in view of the techniques used by management in that period, could easily be true. However, I am afraid it will be extremely difficult to prove.

We now hear from Charles Anthony Roach, nicknamed Silent Slim. Roach is a watchman in a Portland, Ore., industrial plant. For the best years of his life he boomed around the United States and Canada as a brakeman, conductor, locomotive fireman, and switchman. He was even shanghaied in Mobile, Ala., awaking from a drink that had been doped, to find himself an involuntary seaman aboard a ship bound for Australia and New Zealand. . . .

As one victim of the American Railway Union strike in 1894, I will testify to the validity of those service letters watermarked with a crane whose neck appeared to be broken. I was working as a switchman for the Louisville & Nashville out of East Nashville, Tenn., at the time the strike order was issued; but instead of walking out with the other ARU members I reported sick and did not show up in the yards again until I knew the cause was lost. The general yardmaster, Billy Yater, said he would not put me back on the pay roll until I got a clearance from Nashville. I knew what that meant.

After shoving my socks into a bundle and putting on a thousand-mile shirt, I applied for a service letter. Well, they gave me one. I toted it around for nearly a year, until I met another boomer in Springfield, Ill., at a hobo jungle fire. There was quite a gathering of us and we got to talking about jobs. I showed my companion the service letter and mentioned the negative results I'd had when applying to several trainmasters for jobs. They would tell me, "Sorry, Mr. Roach, we're all filled up. We were short-handed a few days ago." I forget the fellow boomer's name, but I remember distinctly that he guffawed and answered, "Let's see that letter." I passed it over. Holding it to the light, he grunted, "Just like thousands of them. Look at this, Slim!" Then he showed me, through the firelight, the faint outline of a broken-necked frog catcher. The rest of the gang stared at it also, and there was general indignation at the dirty trick played on us.

Roach is trying to get one of those letters for me but doubts that he'll ever succeed, because more than half a century has elapsed since they were issued and, especially, because so many of them were thrown away when the men found out what the watermark meant.

"Pocatello Yardmaster"

There was a term used some years ago that has since gone into the discard. I am referring to "Pocatello yardmaster," which arose during the phony-clearance period that followed the ARU strike. I have heard the term used in several ways, but I believe the true origin was that a clerk in Pocatello, [Idaho], who made out service letters would for a small remuneration add to the man's service, "as night yardmaster." That was supposed to give the bearer a somewhat higher distinction. Then there was the gag that a man was not a real railroader unless he had been night yardmaster at Pocatello or trainmaster on the Lucin cutoff. Whatever its origin, it didn't go far as a distinction, for eventually any one who popped off too much without knowing the score was given the title.

Ibid., p. 200.

Spotters

"Spotting" . . . had its hilarious aspects, but it put the black check against the name of many a good railroader whose only fault was a soft heart. The spotters weren't much of a menace to engineers who didn't spend too much time crooking the elbow; they were after those minority fellows who glanced stealthily about a saloon before they ordered a glass of beer and, if they thought they saw a suspicious customer, said in a loud voice, "Hey, can you lend me a match?"

The case of Ed Saunders, a conductor of high rating and a very good friend of ours, haunted Dan and me for days. The spotter who got Ed was a pretty young woman with a couple of little children. She was riding without a ticket, and when Ed tried to collect her fare, she had no money. Looking up at him with tears in her eyes, she said that she had to get to Norwich to take care of her sick mother and that she would surely be at the station to give him the money on his return trip. Ed knew he oughtn't to do it, but he was a soft-hearted fellow and couldn't stand to see a woman cry; so when both of the children set up a howl, he said, "All right, you can go ahead, but don't forget."

The next day Ed was on the carpet, fired, although he didn't have another black mark against his entire record. Dan and I both worried about Ed, but I tried to shake us out of it. . . .

Leaves from a Callboy's Notebook

As callboy [on the Denver & Rio Grande in Grand Junction, Colorado, beginning in 1906], I called many a man without his having been formally hired. All I had to do was to ask to see his service letter (phony or good), tell him to see the doctor when he got back from his first trip, and get his name on the callbook. I knew one brakeman who worked for three months before we found out he had an artificial leg. He said the only time it bothered him was when he tried to dance. I discovered it one night when I went into his room to call him and saw his leg, from the knee down, lying on a chair by the head of his bed.

From *Clear the Tracks, The Story of an Old-Time Locomotive Engineer,* by Joseph Bromley, as told to Page Cooper, pp. 284–285. Copyright, 1943, by Joseph Bromley. New York and London: Whittlesey House, McGraw-Hill Book Company, Inc.

From "Callboy and Boomer," by William A. Lynch, *Railroad Magazine,* Vol. 59 (January, 1953), No. 4, pp. 66–67. Copyright, 1953, by Popular Publications, Inc. New York.

One night when I was in a big hurry, I rushed into a room to call old Newt Moreland for Number 2 at 3:20 A.M. Most of the men were sound sleepers, and as we were pushed for time we did not fool around with formalities but simply walked right into their rooms, turned on the light, touched the man on the arm or shoulder, and if necessary, shook him more or less gently (usually less), announced the train and time of his call and got his signature on the callbook.

The reactions of different men to this approach were sometimes amusing, and sometimes startling. Some of them merely grunted and tried to go back to sleep. Others would mumble sweetly how much they loved us or literally curse hell out of us. Then there were others who would sit bolt upright and commence stammering. But old Newt Moreland had a reaction peculiar only to himself. We had been cautioned always to awaken him gently, but in my hurry I forgot and gave him a sort of "bum's rush." As he jumped up his hand came out from under the pillow with the biggest forty-five I've ever seen. Since I had been cautioned about him, I knew just what to do. I was much larger than Newt and very quick, so I grabbed his wrist almost simultaneously with his movement and shoved it way above his head. He was unable to pull the trigger and in just an instant was awake enough to realize what was going on. He then told me emphatically never to awaken him like that again. He had had some trouble, and I believe that the story was he had killed one or more men but had been completely exonerated.

Most of the boomers quit after their first full payday. Others worked until their references caught up with them, and nearly all the rest of them got fired for violation of Rule G. But every once in a while one of them would find the "right" girl, get married, and settle down, so gradually the boomer disappeared from the job. It was strictly against the rules for us to call a man out of a saloon or a dance hall, but if we had not violated this dictum, I fear that very few trains would have run. However, we did not violate it for nothing. We had a sort of fixed schedule of fees or charges. If we found a man in one of these places and he accepted the call, it was good for one dollar (pie-book or cash); but if he did not accept the call and we reported him as "sick" or "unable to find," the fee was two dollars.

Then the gals had quite a lot of errands to run, for which they paid rather well, especially immediately following the monthly payday. Also, some of the gals (and wives) tipped quite lavishly to be kept posted on the arrival and departure time of the boy-friends or husbands. A discreet callboy not only made good money, but could also have been a rare source of luscious scandal!

Pay Car

On the Lackawanna the ghost walked near the tenth of the month. At the beginning of the second week, we watched the morning passenger out of Utica, to see if her pilot carried the red flag, which meant that the pay car would be along to-morrow. After paying off the men in the shops, it started down the line, calling at every station with wages for the stationmaster, the section crews, the gandy dancers who came in on handcars, and whatever trains happened to be due.

The minute we saw the red flag, we began to figure our earnings. The married men counted that the pay for their extra runs was so much velvet, not to be included in the accounting to the wife. It was held out for a poker game, a bet on a cock fight, or a visit to John Collins' in the evening.

When we happened to meet the pay car in the home yard, there was the additional drama of wives and the installment collectors gathered around the steps. Our pay car was no fancy rolling bank, with crimson stripes, lettering in gold leaf, and counters of solid mahogany, like those in the West (if you could believe the boomers); but the money that jingled inside made the same authentic clink. Ours was an old railroad coach with a cage at one end and a long table at the other, where the superintendent sat when he went along for an inspection of the road. Bill Clark, the company policeman, guarded the door, with a revolver in his belt; and in the cage, the paymaster stood behind a counter piled with stacks of silver dollars and fifty-cent pieces, quarters, and nickels, which he replenished from the iron box beside him on the floor.

One by one, we came up to the window.

"Thomas Schnell, conductor, sixty-three dollars and fifty cents." The clerk called out the name and ticked it in his big ledger; the paymaster repeated it and pushed the coin through the hole in the cage, along a groove in the counter that must have been worn a quarter of an inch deep.

"Henry Millgate, engineer, sixty-one dollars and seventy-five cents." Generally Henry was in line, full of importance, ready to make a dash through the yard before the installment agents (who weren't allowed inside the car) could get up their wind. But when the odds were too heavy, Mrs. Millgate signed his name and raked in the coin. She marched out boldly, clutching it in a shabby old silk bag, and there wasn't a collector in the State of New York who dared to halt her progress.

From *Clear the Tracks!* The Story of an Old-Time Locomotive Engineer, by Joseph Bromley, as told to Page Cooper, pp. 100–102. Copyright, 1943, by Joseph Bromley. New York and London: Whittlesey House, McGraw-Hill Book Company, Inc.

Train "Butch"

The news butcher, or "butch," as he is popularly called, is apparently a descendant of the water boy of early days. This youth of tender years, usually white, though sometimes colored, went through the coaches from time to time, offering the passengers a drink of water. On the more elegant lines he had a tray of glasses or one of those revolving devices known as a castor, and it was considered the decent thing to acknowledge the service by dropping a penny or two in the tray or castor. On some trains he just had a jug and single glass out of which everybody drank. Whether the glasses were ever washed and by whom, we shall never know. The Michigan Southern directors in the 1840s enjoined on the conductors great courtesy to passengers and a plentiful supply of good, *cold* ice water.

As for the selling of edibles and other things on the trains, that was taken care of by outsiders, who swarmed onto the train at any stop of ten minutes or more (and these were frequent) and bawled the merits of their wares. The railroads decided that they might as well have a little profit from this, so they forbade the selling of anything in the cars by any but authorized newsboys; outside peddlers were sometimes tossed off the trains pretty roughly. And so came upon the scene the butch, with his newspapers, magazines, paper-bound novels, fruits—fresh and dried—candies, cigars and cigarettes. Later on, he added sandwiches and ice cream, vended from a container in which dry ice smoked invitingly.

As might be expected, the butcher appeared in great variety, aged anywhere from thirteen to thirty, and of all manner of morals and temperament. He usually became more or less of an imp of Satan. Robert Louis Stevenson in his emigrant journey, *Across the Plains,* encountered two widely divergent types. Says he, "The newsboy with whom we started from the Transfer was a dark, bullying, contemptuous, insolent scoundrel, who treated us like dogs." (Obviously an adult.) "On the other hand, the lad who rode with us in this capacity from Ogden to Sacramento made himself the friend of all, and helped us with information, attention, assistance, and a kind countenance." One has a cynical notion that that charming boy did not always remain like that; his environment would be too much for him. If RLS had encountered him three or four years later, he wouldn't have recognized him.

Short-changing drunks and elderly people and selling bogus goods were among the rackets practised by the tougher sort of butcher, especially in the early West. They were up to all sorts of games, too. One of the less harmful was that of going through the car with a stack of

---

By Alvin F. Harlow.

paper-backed novels which wouldn't have sold for more than a quarter at the outside, offering them at fifty cents each, on the ground that there was a $10 bill concealed in one of them. In those free-and-easy days it was popular to take a chance. Some passengers bought a book by the title, but for those who took a second look at the stack, the butch had laid a trap. A small bit of stiff paper had been artfully placed between the leaves so that only a slanting corner of it peeped out by the thinnest of margins—as if in hastily placing the bill in the book, it had not quite all been covered.

"Le's see the titles of those books," the gull would say, elaborately casual, then select the one from which the tiny edge of paper protruded. Of course he never complained when he found that he had been "sold." It would have been too humiliating, and he had no ground for complaint.

William A. Brady, theatrical producer and boxing promoter and father of Actress Alice Brady, got his start in life as a news butcher in the West, where it is said, he sold even canned goods and bedding on emigrant trains. Thomas A. Edison was another; his deafness is said to have been the result of his having been pulled onto a moving train by his head, by a trainman when he seemed about to be left behind. Another was Tom Taggart, butch on the old Bee Line, who in comparatively early life, leased the Union Station restaurant in Indianapolis, then took over the Grand Hotel, became Democratic boss of Indiana, National Democratic Chairman and owner of French Lick Springs, for many years the Democratic Mecca.

Station or Depot?

Judging by what we hear, the railroad stations in this country must have been the last consideration of the early railroad magnates. Their chief aims were to build a track and put a train on it, and how the traveler was to obtain passage and where he was to wait for the train was something they couldn't be bothered with. For several years, each little railroad was a monopoly in its own territory, and didn't have to pamper the passenger. Furthermore, the first little lines thought only of their termini, as the Boston & Lowell did, and prepared to run their trains through without stopping. It startled them when they discovered that there was business to be had in between, and that some local trains were advisable. Even then, they couldn't see much importance in the local business, and for years, small-town passengers were well-nigh ignored.

In the smaller towns, the railroad's representative was often the nearest storekeeper, and passengers had to await the trains in the

---

By Alvin F. Harlow. A compilation from various sources.

store, and buy tickets there, too, after tickets began to be used. Towns large enough to be called cities had real depots, barnlike structures through which the track or tracks ran as through a tunnel. Seats and a ticket office were close along the track. For winter days, huge swinging doors closed the openings at each end of the depot, though plenty of cold wind wailed under and around them for the discomfort of the passengers shivering in the seats, awaiting a train which might be belated from half an hour to half a day—one never knew what to expect, because there was no telegraph to report its progress.

These structures were not infrequently fired by sparks from locomotives passing through them, and why they were not all destroyed thus is a mystery. The one built by the Eastern Railway at its East Boston track-end, across the narrow harbor from Boston proper, caught fire and burned on the first day of its use. Now and then, too, an engine crashed through the closed doors of one such depot and made no end of a mess.

An entertaining controversy raged for several years over what to call the stopping-place. In 1849 *Horn's Railroad Gazette, American Tourist, and Merchant's and Travellers' Guide,* said, "The Northern papers are discussing the feasibility of using the French word *dépôt,* to express the point of departure of trains. They recommended the English word 'station' as more expressive and better English. Some of them express the hope that within two years there will not be a single 'depot' in the United States." Horn endorsed this and began calling it "station." But there were dissidents. The *Locomotive,* the weekly railroad newspaper published in Indianapolis, sneered at these faddists and said Noah Webster, who regarded a depot as, among other things, a railroad stopping-place, should have consulted them before he compiled his dictionary. And so depot, or rather "deepo," has held the upper hand to this day.

For thirty years and more the advisability of placing the names of towns on the stations for the information of travelers did not occur to early railroad operators. Louis A. Godey, publisher of *Godey's Lady's Book,* was an innovator, as was his famous editor, Mrs. Sarah Josepha Hale. He didn't travel often, but when he did, he had some good advice to give railroad magnates. Returning from a trip to the Middle West in 1863, he asked:

> Why don't all the railroad stations have the name of each distinctly and conspicuously put up for the information of passing travelers? . . . Is every stopping place supposed to be so well known to strangers that exhibiting its name might be a superfluous accommodation? Or is the accommodation of strangers a matter of no consequence? What a business idea! Reform it altogether, gentlemen. Put up the names—put up the names!

Station bells often warned of the approach of a passenger train which didn't appear, maybe for hours; but they did give timely warning of the train's departure. The sweet-toned bells of three impoverished old churches or convents in Spain had been sold in some European market for junk, when they were spied and bought by the President of the Eastern Railroad for its depots at East Boston, Salem and Newburyport, where they for years rang out the comings and goings of trains.

The New York and Harlem, then coming under Vanderbilt influence and moving towards a junction with the Hudson River, had its main station on Fourth Avenue, from 26th to 27th Streets in Manhattan. Fifteen minutes before leaving time of a train there, a starter seized an iron bolt about a foot long with a nut on the end, and banged violently on an iron plate set in the top panel of the door leading from the waiting room to the platform. He then opened the door, allowing passengers access to the train if it was ready. At five minutes before leaving-time, a bell hanging in the roof of the train-shed was struck once, and this was continued at intervals of one minute until, on the sixth stroke, the train was supposed to start.

The coming of a new era, one dominated by telegraphs and time-tables, is seen in an item in the Woburn (Mass.) *Journal* in July, 1880, to the effect that "The ringing of the depot bell to announce the departure of trains is discontinued, as it interferes by its noise with the telegraph." In fact, it had long been unnecessary. The bell was bought by the Swedish Lutheran Church and may still be around somewhere. But it is refreshing to report that at a very recent date one might still hear a sweetly pleasant reminiscence of old times at the Atlantic Coast Line station at Wilmington, N. C., where the depot bell rang in warning of a train's departure.

In Boston it became the fashion to have an assembly hall on the upper floors of the large stations being built during the first half of the century. When the Old Colony built its "large and splendid depot" there in 1846, it announced that upstairs there would be a convention hall "with suitable drawing rooms connected," with the floor mounted on coiled springs, to make dancing less fatiguing. When the Fitchburg erected its granite castle on the North Side, it too contained an auditorium, and Jenny Lind sang there in 1850 to a packed house, including persons from as far away as Portland, Montreal and Quebec.

Boston South Station (New Haven and New York Central), in its 600-seating capacity waiting room, has a unique community friendship promotion idea. Thirteen of the big double benches have signs mounted over them, bearing the names of the Massachusetts counties—Essex, Barnstable, Plymouth, Bristol, Norfolk, Suffolk, Dukes, Middlesex, Franklin, Hampshire, Hampden, Berkshire and Worcester. If you wish to join a friend at the station, you say, "Meet me in Plymouth" or "See you in Middlesex." Out of town folk naturally drift towards their home-county bench and look around to see if there is anyone on it they know. Acquaintances are struck up there, they discover perhaps that they are neighbors, and friendships develop. Maybe you wouldn't expect to find this in Boston, but there it is.

Towers used to be considered an important part of railroad terminal architecture. A New Haven official made a trip to Italy one summer, fell in love with the tall, slender Mangia Tower at Siena, and upon his return, to the amusement of some other executives, saw to it that the new station at Waterbury was crowned with a replica of that campanile. But sad are the mutations of this automobile age! That building was recently sold by the New Haven to the local newspaper, the Waterbury *Republican-American*, for its publishing plant, the railroad renting space in it for modest station purposes.

In New England the village stations continued to be just a building near the track, also housing a grocery store or perhaps a saloon or barber shop (though in a separate room); in numerous cases, the business and perhaps the building itself being the property of the railroad agent. There is record of a Connecticut agent who was notified by the company that they were sending a man to replace him on the first of the month (they thought he was growing too old); to which he retorted tartly that if they sent a new agent they'd better send a new depot, too, as the one now in use was the property of the undersigned. Very often the station was the agent's living quarters, too; in a few cases, some are still. There is a vice-president of the New Haven, as this is being written, who was born upstairs in the station at Newtown, Connecticut, where his father was agent.

In other places, especially outside of New England, the village "deepo" became a familiar pattern; a long wooden platform with a two-wheeled or four-wheeled truck glumly inert somewhere; a little wooden building with projecting eaves (they're even abolishing those on the new stations), sometimes, though not always, a semaphore signal that would show red and white. Inside, there would be a stuffy little waiting room with a cast-iron coal stove, sometimes with the name or initials of the road cast in the door. Recently there were a few of these still around, though not infrequently the name on the door was an unfamiliar one to travelers; it was that of the company which preceded the present one. Wooden seats with iron arm "rests" allotting the space bordered the walls. Tacked on the wall beside the ticket-window would be one or two bunches of long bills advertising excursions, perhaps one of a local church supper or sociable for money-raising purposes.

Inside the agent's quarters would be a table with telegraph instruments, jars of acid, a wall clock, a chair with each leg set into the socket of a glass telegraph insulator in case of storms, another chair not so protected for qualified callers, a small safe, lantern with red and clear globes, red and white flags, handled hoops for passing orders up to engineers and conductors of moving trains, rate books, ticket stamp, sealing wax, brass seal, torch for melting wax, Official

Guide, Bullinger's Postal and Shipper's Guide (both out of date), broom and duster, and other odds and ends according to the personality of the agent. On the other side of his quarters from the waiting room there was a windowless cubicle, supposed to be always locked, seldom if ever swept, for baggage and express.

An anonymous writer in *Fortune* sings the swan song of the "small town railroad stations . . . now about fifty years old":

> By association these simple boardings bespeak the Saratoga trunk, the gold-mounted elk's tooth, calico and horsewhips and eight course meals. Such walls and such rooms may have caught their dimmest tones from the lone wayfarer's dark projected moods, but if the atmosphere of local railroad stations today is one of crushing serenity, this was hardly the aim of the builders. These places were to be the very pivots of life in all its most tumultuous departures and arrivals. Now, in unfolding history, they are a chapter called, The Economic Conquest of the Automobile.[1]

Man against Baggage

For weeks past the railroad men and baggage masters connected with the great lines centering in this city have been engaged in the preparation of a matter which, to them, was paramount, even to the proposed reduction in their wages. A chief baggage master on one of the lines penetrating the great Northwest had publicly announced that "little Jake Riter was the best baggage handler in this town, and could chuck a Saratoga trunk into a car with more force and greater damage than any other baggage wrestler in the city."

This excited the ire of an agent of one of the southern lines, and he then and there was willing to wager $100 that Billy Traquer, "Sickly Bill," as the boys called him, "could fire more baggage into a car in five minutes than Riter could in half an hour." Before a week had elapsed, the men were pitted against each other, and a day was fixed for the contest—Saturday last, when travel was great and baggage plenty.

---

[1] Editorial comment on "The U.S. Depot, A Portfolio," by Walker Evans, *Fortune* (February, 1953), p. 142.

From *The Philadelphia Record,* June 24, 1877.

Before the days of steel-framed trunks, the havoc wrought by baggage-handlers among travelers' wooden and leather luggage was frightful. Railroad baggagemen became commonly known as baggage-smashers, and many were the journalistic jokesters' quips about them.

At one of the great depots could have been two immense piles of miscellaneous baggage, and gathered about them two factions of railroad men, glaring at each other, for the excitement had grown to the point of bitter enmity. There were in the piles elegant canvas-covered trunks and sickly old residenters bound with ropes. There were small trunks and large trunks, countrymen's valises, ladies' traveling bags, sewing machines and baskets, awaiting their turn in the affray shortly to begin.

At 3:26 P.M. the train backed into the depot and the two baggage car doors were thrown open. In a few moments Riter put in an appearance and smiled blandly at his admirers and at the pile of baggage he was to tussle. It was some time before the tall, lank form of Traquer came on the scene. The preliminaries were soon arranged, and at half-past three o'clock precisely the contest opened. The baggage had been sorted out about equally, and the first man who succeeded in smashing the most material—which, it should be stated, means "loading" in the profession—in the least time was to win the stakes and the honor of being the champion baggage smasher of the consolidated railroads of Pennsylvania.

Time was called and Riter, to freshen himself for the work, pounced upon a good-sized, old-fashioned valise, bound together with a clothesline, and after spinning it over his head two or three times, hurled it into the car, much to the damage of the valise, but greatly to the edification of his friends.

Traquer had not been idle. He had humped himself over a three-story Saratoga trunk with a mansard roof, and bending his muscle to the work, sent the bulky article to the very rear of the car. It was admirably done, and it would have taken hours to collect the splinters and wearing apparel that he had scattered in one brief moment.

This spurred Riter to greater efforts. He sprang lightly to a sewing machine, and raising it upon his shoulder, winked confidentially to the boys and let her go. It was a beautiful feat. Pieces of fancy cast iron and woodwork lay in profusion over the floor, but the machine was loaded.

Then "Sickly Bill" snatched a bundle of bandboxes and four ladies' valises, and without apparent effort put them into the car. The flowers and fancy underwear looked beautiful with the other debris, and bets were in favor of the tall man. But Riter had succeeded most admirably in making kindling wood of two small trunks, and had one corner of the car completely filled with wearing apparel, broken umbrellas and cooking utensils. Perspiration was pouring from the contestants, but they lost none of their vigor.

In fifteen minutes Traquer had enough material in his end of the car to open up a junk shop, and made a strong impression by whizzing two small trunks into the car simultaneously and converting them into splinters.

Riter had gained on him steadily, and was heaving spring bonnets, panniers and feminine dry goods in the wildest profusion. The men showed their greatest ability in handling large trunks, but the crowd enjoyed it most when they gathered up an ancient valise belonging to some rural citizen. The men themselves smiled when they grasped one of these articles and "let 'er go." When the dry goods and two-dollar shoes and tinware and groceries burst their bonds, the enthusiasm was unbounded.

The train departed at 4:45, and when she moved slowly out of the depot, Bill Traquer was struggling with a second-hand black trunk without handles, and Riter was being rubbed down externally with towels and internally with beer by his jubilant friends on the very spot where once stood the pile of baggage which he had so successfully loaded and smashed. It is announced that Riter will challenge any other baggage-smasher in the United States for the honor of Champion of America and for $500 a side.

Commuters' Lanterns

Here is a picture of suburban travel as it was practised by the hardy pioneers of the seventies [on the Chicago and North Western]. Town dwellers who occasionally went to Winnetka or Palatine just for the ride were generally surprised at the large collections of oil lanterns on the station platforms. Word got around that in railroading the wear and tear on lanterns was terrific and that every switchman had to carry a spare.

The largest string of lanterns was outside the Davis Street station in Evanston. And a stranger, who inquired about them, discovered that they belonged not to the railroad personnel but to commuters, men who had taken the early morning trains to Chicago.

"Raymond Park," says the antiquarian who looked into the matter, "was a thickly wooded section in the 1870s, and on an early winter morning, those woods were as dark as the inside of a fireman's glove. . . ."

* * * * *

Survivors of those fascinating days say that the lanterns of commuters loping over the snow trails for the 7:23 were generally so thick

---

From *Pioneer Railroad,* The Story of the Chicago and North Western System, by Robert J. Casey and W. A. S. Douglas, pp. 277–278. Copyright, 1948, by the McGraw-Hill Book Company, Inc. New York and Toronto.

that the woods seemed to be swarming with fireflies. During the day the station attendant would service the lanterns, trimming the wicks, and filling them with oil so that the owners would be able to find their way home in the evening.

"E" for Eats

There was something very human and appealing about the [Minneapolis &] St. Louis Road; a warmth and friendliness which pervaded its operation. Most of the division points and many of the terminals had lunch counters, where every one from the engineer to Aunt Mary stepped off the local for a cup of strong coffee, a sandwich, and a generous cut of pie. Albia, Oskaloosa, Marshalltown, Albert Lea, Waterville, Fort Dodge, Winthrop, Morton, Conde, and Aberdeen were, and some still are, depots where passengers could "pick up a bite" between trains or during a lunch stop. No matter what train one took on the Louie, one could bank on the funny little mark or a suggestive "e" on the timecard. On close inspection one found that it stood for meals or, as the youngsters said, "eats." M&StL trains have been known to pass up coal and water, but to skip a lunchstop—never!

Sometimes when it was time to eat, a train pulled into a town which had no restaurant in the station. Such was the case of No. 2, *The St. Louis & Kansas City Mail,* on its arrival at Grinnell, Iowa. There was an "e" on the timetable, however, and long before that college town was reached a brakeman would come through the cars very solicitously inquiring how many wanted supper. Then, upon ascertaining the number, he would wire ahead to the station agent, who thereupon contacted Hotel Monroe on the west side of the tracks. When No. 2 pulled into Grinnell, the passengers walked across the street to the inn and a hot meal. The brakeman, for his bit of salesmanship, was given dinner on the house.

But, it may be asked, suppose there were no hotel or restaurant near the railroad? This contingency, too, was provided for at such stops as Livermore and Hampton, Iowa, and St. James, Minnesota. Trainmen merely wired ahead, and when the coaches came to a grinding halt at the respective communities, there would be a townsman with plate dinners, all prepared and packed in market baskets. The meal might consist of roast beef, pork, or fried country chicken, vegetables, a salad, rolls, and hot roasted coffee. Price: fifty cents.

From *Mileposts on the Prairie,* The Story of the Minneapolis & St. Louis Railway, by Frank P. Donovan, Jr., pp. 147–148. Copyright, 1950, by Frank P. Donovan, Jr. New York: Simmons-Boardman Publishing Corporation.

The "Deepo" and the Town

Some envious neighboring hamlets quipped that there was more railroad than town at North Vernon; a sneer such as you might expect from less fortunate burgs like Osgood and Seymour. Why, we were an incorporated city—yes, yes, I know the census of 1890 gave us only 2,012 population, but anybody in town could tell you that that figure was grossly inaccurate; we had at least 3,000 and the newspapers usually claimed 4,000. And up to the minute! Why, we had the Cincinnati and Louisville and Indianapolis papers, morning and evening, hot off the press, so we knew what was going on as well as anybody.

We were so used to trains that their noise and smoke didn't bother anyone save a few housewives with the usual strange feminine phobia against dirt. The staffs of our several hotels, all planted as close to the track as they could get, could sleep right through the nearly-all-night clatter of passing trains and switching, and hear none of it. But their guests often came forth in the morning looking haggard and sometimes complaining of cinders in their beds. True, there was comparative quiet for a couple of hours just after midnight; but even then a big consolidation might come storming up the grade to westward at the head of a long freight train, its thunderous exhaust awakening an occasional sound sleeper with a shriek and a leap upright in bed, under the impression that the engine was coming right through his bedroom.

Runners from all the hotels met all the trains. The observant traveler had only to look at them to know what he was getting into, for they fell into three classes. Two were always colored, and the one who bawled somewhat arrogantly, "Grand Hotel! Grand Hotel, here!" wore a gold-braided cap with the name "Grand Hotel" on it in gold, albeit all slightly tarnished. The Grand was our leading hotel—brick, and part of it three stories high! The other colored functionary announced, "Hotel! O'Dillon House! Hotel!" and his cap—worn and its gold threads very tarnished indeed—had no legend on it at all. His was a second-grade house. The other three or four bare, smelly little hostelries—for one or another was sometimes in a state of desuetude for months on end—were represented by the innkeepers themselves—discouraged-looking, shoddily dressed, middle-aged white men, who merely uttered the word, "Hotel," in varying shades of timidity, apology and ineptitude. The moneyed traveler or the "drummer" promptly surrendered his bags to one of the two colored representatives of the upper levels. The traveler, usually from the country, who couldn't afford to spend more than 25 or 35 cents for a bed, feared these pal-

---

Abridged from "The Deepo," by Alvin F. Harlow, *Railroad Magazine,* Vol. 39 (April, 1946), No. 5, pp. 110–114. Copyright, 1946, by Popular Publications, Inc. New York.

pable, living evidences of high overhead, and after careful inquiry and dickering as to prices, gingerly permitted one of the seedy Bonifaces to take over his valise or telescope (remember that old, expanding canvas carryall, the telescope?), though walking near him and keeping a wary eye on his property all the way to the hotel.

Yard? Of course we had a yard; two of them, you might say, east and west, with tracks named for animals—cow track, calf track, horse track, pig track, etc. Old 51, the maid of all work, a retired passenger junk-pile, had little more than a couple of hours' rest consecutively at any given time. It seemed hard to imagine her as having once been a queen of the road.

One day an embarrassing thing happened to her, one which she could never laugh off. When Number 17 pulled out for Louisville, late in the afternoon, 51's day stint was over, and she retired to a three-stall "roundhouse" to rest for an hour or so before being taken over by her night crew. Her last chore was that of hooking a Pullman from St. Louis to the tail of 17. As the latter's course lay right past the roundhouse, the old lady would go along, "helping" to push 17 up the gentle grade out of town, making a big fuss about it as she came by the deepo.

This show impressed the onlookers no end. On the afternoon in question, she was storming along, showering red-hot cinders all over the business center, when, just as they were passing the Grand Hotel, the train ran right away from her, leaving a slowly but steadily widening gap, and she never did catch up; nor did her crew ever hear the last of that story.

In a railroad town such as ours, one knows the trains familiarly—no countrified allusions to "the 9.30" or the "down train" or the "express," as the chaw-bacons in some hick town would call them. No, to us they were Number 1, Number 4, Number 20; they had personalities. We spoke of going to Seymour tonight on Number 3. . . . Is 16 in yet? . . . Whatsisname came out last night on 19. . . . They're going down to camp meeting tomorrow on 105.

Railroads being the life of our town, we paid them high respect and deference. If a train stopped on a street crossing for ten or twenty minutes, other traffic just had to wait, but did so more patiently than it would now. Again and again we told each other, "They can't block a crossing more'n ten minutes, accordin' to law," but they did it. Sometimes pedestrians in a hurry, even prominent citizens, if not too fat, crawled under freight trains on all fours, choosing, of course, a car which wasn't too low-slung and hadn't its under-belly all cluttered with air-brake gadgetry.

No town horse would pretend to be scared at sight or sound of a train. Once I saw Mort Rash, the drayman, leave his rig so close to a track that the nag had to turn its head aside to avoid being hit on the nose when the yard goat came by with a couple of cars; did it casually and with no sign of alarm, not even taking the trouble to back away.

The importance of the railroad station in a small town of the 1890s cannot be comprehended by a generation brought up on the automobile. In those days the rails were just about our only means of long distance land transportation. Even if we were going no further than Osgood, twenty-two miles distant, we never thought of going otherwise than by train. To drive it, even with good horses, would have required at best a long, tiresome half-day over rough, hilly, winding roads.

Therefore, the deepo was our leading social center. No one came into or left town unnoticed; he or she was sure to be seen boarding or leaving the train. There most of our farewells took place. It was a friendless soul, indeed, who left town unescorted to the car steps. There friends and kinsmen often looked into each other's eyes, touched hands, kissed, and heard the well-loved voice for the last time in life. You saw tears at the deepo more often then than now; tears perhaps for a son or sister going no farther than to Cincinnati. We realized more keenly then the ominous significance of "Good-bye." Today we say it lightly, for travel has become a commonplace.

Yes, yes, we promised, I'll come for a visit next summer—all the time painfully aware that probably few of us would get any farther away from that summer than the Deputy Camp Meeting (yes, Deputy was the name of the village), or the Sand Crick Baptist Association meeting at Zenas, or one of those half-cent-a-mile Sunday excursions to Cincinnati or Indynoplis in long trains of grimy old crates of Civil War vintage. Now and then there would be a five-dollar excursion to Niagara Falls, and maybe one or two of us who were in the dough might wangle that by riding in day coaches both ways and carrying almost enough lunch to last through the whole goshdinged trip, piecing it out with cinnamon buns and bananas picked up along the way at five to ten cents a dozen.

A common sight around our deepo was that of one or more kinsmen—father, mother, brother, sister, wife—snatching a precious moment or two of conversation with one of the passing trainmen who had been born and reared in our midst. Maybe they would give him a package of something that would taste all the better because it came from home; one of Mother's cakes, some garden strawberries or peaches from that favorite tree back by the woodshed. A railroad town develops railroad men. They graduated from our baggage room and express office to jobs on the road. They went to work in the yards, presently became brakemen or firemen, and some of them eventually engineers and conductors. We were proud of Frank Evans, engineer and native son, the acknowledged speed king of the Ohio & Mississippi. We repeated to each other his alleged remark that he'd never yet seen the machine that was too fast for him.

Frank had a little joke that was characteristic. As Number 1 came in from Cincinnati around 10:30 A.M., when they were both on time, the southbound JM&I train would be standing right across the O&M tracks west of the deepo. If Frank was at the throttle, he liked to sweep past the station at about twenty mph., giving the passengers on the other train the impression that he was going to knife right through them. However, in the last two or three seconds, he would use his air with that delicate touch in which he excelled, and while some of the JM&I passengers were screeching and jumping from their seats to run for their lives, Frank slowed to a quick but remarkably smooth stop with the tip of his cow-catcher almost under those frightened folk.

When word came down to him that the JM&I brass collars were squawking about it, Frank appeared very much surprised. He said he hadn't been aware that he was guilty of anything but routine stuff; he thought he'd always come into town in a quiet, conservative way.

At the deepo you saw a year-round pageant which old Cy Wimble—whom we usually had to shoo off a truck before we could use it—said was "educational." Changing from train to train or walking the platform while the trains paused or Pullmans were shifted, we saw at one time and another some of the great ones of earth—mostly, come to think of it, in the athletic line, though I do recall old Senator "Pitchfork Ben" Tillman, glaring ferociously at me with his one eye. A brakeman tipped us off one day that Jim Corbett was in a parlor car, sitting on this side, and a knot of us gathered on the platform and stared at the great boxer until the train pulled out.

And of course we knew from the papers exactly when a big league baseball team would pass through (remember that Louisville was a major league town then). Their trimly dressed figures, many carrying their own private bats in cloth bags, were recognizable by the few of us who had been fortunate enough to attend games in one of the cities. Then there was Sandow, the strong man, a massive figure, so bulky with muscle that it made him seem short—good-looking Germanic face, blonde hair and mustache—standing on the platform, watching—seemingly placid, though probably with a blend of amusement and anxiety—four or five baggagemen and helpers wrestling with his 250-pound dumbbells.

How thrilling the great truckloads of shiny, steel-bound trunks marked "Henry Irving Company, Hotel" or "Theatre!" What cursing and girding of loins among the baggagemen when word came that Powers' *Ivy Leaf* company was on Number 2 with sixty-five pieces of baggage and no end of scenery to be transferred to 17! Both trains would be delayed while all those trunks, the flats—looking so shabby and unreal by daylight—the sixty-foot rolled drop-curtains were handled, the drops passed endwise out of and into car doors and hastily stowed.

There was local color, too; Dr. Fosseps, for example, with tool-bag and foot-power drill, boarding a train for some near-by hamlet, for with so much competition in town, there was hardly enough business to keep a dentist in luxury. He had been preceded by paragraphs like this in the Paris Crossing and Queensville correspondence of the county papers:

> NOTICE: On the first Tuesday of each month, I will be at Mrs. Swingle's Hotel at Paris Crossing from 10 A.M. to 6 P.M., where I will do all sorts of fine dental work at the very lowest rates. Call and consult me.
>
> J. D. FOSSEPS

In July the long, thin figure of Dr. John Plato Hackbury, President of Moore's Hill College, on his way to the Deputy Camp Meeting, dancing, frantic with worry, at the sight of us expressmen rough-handling his boxes of canned (in glass) fruit, jellies and pickles, intended for the recuperation of the flesh while the spirit soared at the revival meetings. In mid-December we transferred the annual Christmas gift from the White Lick Baptist congregation, down in the country, to its pastor, Brother Pounder, who lived at Franklin—a newkilled hog, pinkly scalded, vest unbuttoned and all interior furnishings removed, traveling by express flat on his back, with his destination tag tied to one leg.

Stand there at our deepo long enough, and practically anything might come by; for example, trainloads of delegates going to St. Louis in 1892 to renominate Grover Cleveland for the Presidency, and coming back a few days later flaunting the red bandana which was the Democratic gonfalon in that campaign. And in March, '94, an ominous threat of depression years; hundreds of men roosting on the car roofs of freight trains rumbling eastward—Kelly's division of Coxey's army, on its way to Washington to demand help for the unemployed. Three months later the great rail strike led by Gene Debs halted all our freight trains for days on end, though mail trains continued to run; and then sweating expressmen struggled in quickstep time with what was ordinarily freight-train cargo—stoves, furniture, barrels of whisky, pianos, huge castings, farm machinery.

At our deepo in 1896 and 1900 the Boy Orator of the Platte, Mr. Bryan, displayed his oratory and his broad grin from a car-tail. From there, too, our few volunteers went away to the Spanish War in '98, and returned so disgusted with typhoid and the muddling in Cuba that in the words of Al Gookins, "If the USA was in trouble this minute, right out in the middle of that there railroad track, I wouldn't move a step to help 'em."

Yes, sir, a deepo is the place to see things, especially at our town, which was, as you might say, the crossroads of the world.

II. BANDITTI OF THE RAILS

The First Train Hold-Up

Less than a month after Appomattox, Cincinnati was startled by the first railroad train hold-up in history. Shortly after dawn on May 5, '65, an Ohio & Mississippi train en route from St. Louis to Cincinnati was derailed by an obstruction at North Bend, fourteen miles from the city, the engine and the baggage-and-express car being overturned. A gang of roughs promptly took over the train, some robbing the passengers—gallantly sparing the ladies—while others looted the express safes, making off with a large amount in cash and bonds. They were said to have escaped across the river in skiffs which seemed to confirm the belief that they were guerrillas, the irregulars who had been ravaging parts of Kentucky for years and continued to do so for several months more.

The Reno Gang

Southern Indiana around Civil War time and for some years thereafter was checkered with some pretty tough neighborhoods and pestered by some highly undesirable characters. Among these were Pete McCartney's gang of counterfeiters, some of whom did not scorn to take a hand in horse-stealing, burglary, or petty thievery at times,

---

From *The Serene Cincinnatians,* by Alvin F. Harlow, p. 239. Copyright, 1950, by Alvin F. Harlow. New York: E. P. Dutton & Co.

From *Old Waybills,* The Romance of the Express Companies, by Alvin F. Harlow, pp. 331–337. Copyright, 1934, by Alvin F. Harlow. New York and London: D. Appleton-Century Company, Inc.

along with the Rittenhouse brothers, John Dean, alias California Nelse, Bill Hopkins, and the four Reno brothers. Jackson County was the center of operations of some of the worst of these gentry, including the Renos, who lived near Seymour, in the eastern edge of the county, where the Ohio and Mississippi Railway crossed the Jeffersonville, Madison and Indianapolis. It was those two roads which suffered all or nearly all the train hold-ups of the Reno gang, the first organized band of train robbers in history and one of the most daring.

There were six Reno children, five boys and one girl, sprung from a father of Swiss descent and a Pennsylvania German mother. Four of the boys, John, Frank, Simeon and William and the girl, Laura, were of the same hard, comely, stalwart, reckless type. Laura could ride and shoot as well as her brothers. The fifth boy, Clint, was known to the amazed citizenry as Honest Reno, because he was so different. The other four brothers became notorious during the Civil War as "bounty-jumpers" and associates of McCartney and other crooks. After the war, a humdrum, honest means of livelihood was evidently out of the question for them.

For years after the war, certain portions of southern Indiana were plagued with this type of rapscallion. . . .

On that evening of October 6, 1866, an Ohio and Mississippi passenger train had scarcely pulled out of Seymour, headed eastward, when two masked men entered the express car from the coach behind it—for it had not yet occurred to expressmen that car doors should be locked—took the messenger's key from him at the gun-point, opened his safe, and robbed it of $13,000. They then pulled the bell cord, dumped an unopened safe out of the car door and dropped from the train themselves as it slowed up. The crew feared to oppose them, and after a momentary pause, the train went on, to the next station. From there a hand car full of armed men was sent back to the vicinity of the stop. They found that the robbers had decamped, leaving the safe, which was too heavy to carry conveniently and which they lacked key or tools to open, beside the track.

For this crime John and Simeon Reno and Frank Sparks were arrested some time later. A Grand Jury indictment was found against them, and then the influence of the rougher element over the county became apparent. They were promptly admitted to bail; from time to time their trial was postponed, and in fact, never did take place.

On September 28, 1867, the same eastbound train was robbed just outside Seymour in precisely the same manner by two men, who were, however, mere imitators of the Renos—local toughs named Walker Hammond and Michael Collins or Collerain. Their haul was somewhere between $6,000 and $7,000. Legend has it that the Renos knew they were going to make the attempt; that they waited in the woods east of the town, and when Hammond and Collins dropped from the train with their loot, the sardonic brothers in turn held them up and took it away from them. They then procured the arrest of the pair for the robbery, and though it was pretty widely known that they themselves had finally pocketed the money, they went unscathed.

The gang now extended their operations farther afield. In a raid into Missouri they robbed the county treasurer's office at Gallatin, Daviess County. Pinkerton was set upon the trail here and decided that the Renos were the perpetrators. Believing that it would be difficult to get them arrested in their home county, he arranged to have John virtually kidnapped. An assistant was planted in Seymour to make his acquaintance and lure him to the station when a certain train passed through. Requisition papers had been prepared, and half a dozen husky Missourians were on the train. These men stepped off and mingled with other passengers and the crowd on the station platform. Just as the conductor shouted, "All aboard!" and raised his hand in signal to the engineer, a dozen strong hands seized John Reno, clapped handcuffs on him and with guns against his ribs, hustled him aboard the train before his friends realized what was happening. Despite the outcry of his brothers and allies that he had been illegally kidnapped, Missouri held him and sentenced him, together with some minor members of the gang, to twenty-five years in prison.

This was the first break in the ranks of the band, and as if infuriated by it, the others set out to make the year 1868 one of unprecedented activity in their war on society. They first staged a raid across southern Indiana and Illinois, robbing small banks and county treasurers' offices. In one case, they held up the treasurer's office and, in fact, the whole town, in broad daylight, in the manner lately adopted by the James boys, and which the Daltons tried with such disastrous results at Coffeyville.

The Renos now dropped from sight for a very brief period; but in March, in western Iowa, two county treasurers' offices were burglarized —a type of crime which by that time had come to be regarded as bearing the Reno trade-mark. Allan Pinkerton's son, William, now a detective of rapidly growing reputation, was sent to the neighborhood. A few days later he and his assistants captured Frank Reno, Albert Perkins, Miles Ogle (later a notorious counterfeiter) and Michael Rogers, a well-to-do and reputable citizen of Council Bluffs, at Rogers' home, and charged them with the two recent crimes. They were placed in a county jail, but on April 1st, all of them escaped.

Nothing more was heard of the Renos until May 22nd, when they struck again, back in their old home bailiwick, and made their biggest haul. A northbound train on the JM&I Railroad was boarded late at night by a considerable group of armed men while the engine was taking on wood and water at Marshfield, a little station twenty miles south of Seymour. One man uncoupled the express car from the rest of the train; two others entered the cab, driving out the engineer and fireman, and started the engine and express car ahead while others forced their way into the car. The messenger made a brave resistance, but was beaten almost into insensibility and thrown from the car door down an embankment while the train was in rapid motion, sustaining injuries from which he finally died. From the Indianapolis and New York safes in the car the gang took $96,000, mostly in cash. Early in the morning, the locomotive and car were found deserted about a mile south of Seymour. The Renos had actually had the nerve to ride almost all the way home on it!

This robbery was promptly reported to Pinkerton as a Reno job by three operatives whom he had placed in Seymour, one posing as a gambler, while two others had found work, one in the railroad yards, the other as bartender of a low saloon. But before arrangements had been perfected to make arrests, some of the lesser lights of the gang attempted another robbery, but were thwarted. While taking wood and water near Brownstown, the capital of Jackson County, a westbound O&M engine and express car were seized by five bandits, who pursued the same technic as in the Marshfield affair—driving off the engine crew, detaching the express car, and pulling forward with it about eight miles. But when they made their assault upon the car, they found the express company, now anticipating trouble, had posted armed guards inside it; and in the ensuing pistol battle, the robbers were driven off, leaving one of their number, Val Elliott, a former O&M brakeman, wounded.

Elliott was taken to Cincinnati in custody, and two other men, Phil Clifton and Charles Roseberry, known to be Reno henchmen, were also arrested for the crime. Pinkerton charged that it was the Reno gang who had committed a robbery on the Cincinnati, Hamilton and Dayton Railroad, north of Cincinnati, a few weeks before. He and his cohorts were by this time in full cry after the lawless crew. But the irritated citizens of Jackson County, and vicinity, fearing that justice would be delayed or frustrated as it had been in the past, had now decided to take matters into their own hands, and make sure of retribution. Ten days after the attempted robbery, as officers were taking Elliott, Clifton, and Roseberry by rail towards Brownstown, the train was boarded at a small station a few miles east of that place by a large and determined party of men who seized the three prisoners and hung them to a tree not far from the track.

Disorder and corruption had brought the Vigilantes into being in Indiana, just as one or the other or both of those causes had done in California and Idaho and Montana; and the Indiana regulators were no less determined, ruthless, and efficient than those in the states farther west.

Three other men, Frank Sparks, John Moore, and Charles Gerroll or Jerroll, had been arrested in Illinois on a charge of being implicated in the attempted O&M robbery. They were brought to Seymour by rail, and thinking to elude the Vigilantes, the officers placed them in a wagon after darkness fell and started towards Brownstown. But at the same hamlet where the other miscreants were lynched, a small army of men seemed to spring from the ground, took the prisoners from their guards and hung them, so the story goes, to the same tree from whose boughs the other three had dangled only three days before.

The Renos had by this time decided it would be wise to vanish from their home at Rockford, near Seymour, and their old haunts in general; in fact, Frank had not been heard from since his jail escape in Iowa on the first of April. But Pinkerton's men were not baffled long. They located and captured Bill and Simeon rather easily in Indianapolis, and learned that Frank was in Windsor, Ontario, living and operating with one Charles Anderson, burglar, safe-blower and swindler, who had been associated with him in the United States. Requisitions were procured, though Frank made a hard fight against the move, and the two men were brought back to Indiana. It cannot be imagined that either the Pinkertons or the Adams Express Company were much grieved over the sudden elimination of six previous prisoners by the unauthorized rope of the Vigilantes; nevertheless, as a gesture towards maintaining the majesty of the law, the four latest prisoners were not returned to Jackson County, but were taken to a stronger jail in New Albany, Floyd County, across the Ohio River from Louisville.

The final act in the tragic drama was played only a few weeks later. One day late in November, 1868, a JM&I train dropped an empty passenger coach on the siding at Seymour. That night another train, southbound, hooked itself to the coach and took it away; and two or three citizens who happened to be in the vicinity reported that the car, when it departed, was full of men—at least fifty of them—all wearing caps and masks, and evidently under the command of a tall, dark man whom they addressed as "No. 1." The most curious feature of the episode was that the conductor of the train could remember nothing of the incident; he had not entered the car and did not see the men—in fact, did not even know that the car had been attached to the train!

But other observers noticed that the men remained quietly inside the car during the journey southward, and strove diligently to avoid notice. Reaching New Albany at 2 A.M., the train dropped the car and the men flowed out of it as noiselessly as they had entered. At a low-toned command from "No. 1," they marched to the jail, not far off, and demanded admittance to the cells. The Sheriff refused and made a brave resistance with firearms, wounding several of the mob. But he too was wounded and two city police taken prisoners, after which the attackers battered their way into the jail and seized the three Renos and Anderson. Frank begged that his younger brothers be "given a chance," but in vain. The Vigilantes had brought ropes ready noosed, and in a few minutes the bodies of the prisoners were swinging from the beams in the jail corridor.

The regulators now filed silently back to their car, and a north-bound train leaving at 3:30 A.M. took it to Seymour, where it was left just before dawn, and the mysterious avenging host melted away in the darkness. It was discovered that all telegraph wires leading out from New Albany had been cut, and the outer world did not hear of the hanging until twelve hours after it had occurred. The tall dark leader of the mob was described by witnesses as having worn a fine diamond ring on the little finger of his left hand. It was whispered that the description of his person fitted that of a prominent railroad official, and some importance was attached to the fact that he ceased to wear that ring for years afterward.

Laura Reno, after some empty threats against the Vigilantes, subsided into quieter ways, married a respectable citizen, and became, as far as known, a good wife and mother. Her brother John returned from the Missouri penitentiary fifteen years later, likewise a reformed character. The bandit career of the Renos had lasted less than two years, and today they are almost forgotten, even in Indiana; but their deeds entitled them to a high place in the criminal hall of ill fame.

Jesse James's Last Three Hold-Ups

I. The Glendale Robbery

[From the confession of Dick Liddil]

The first time I saw Jesse James was after the Northfield Bank robbery [September 7, 1876, at which time the gang was wrecked] at Ben Morrow's, in Jackson County. I met Ben and he told me Jesse was to be at his house that evening, and he had said he wanted to see me. About 2 o'clock I went to Ben's and found Jesse in the yard. We went out to where his horse was tied in the woods and had a little chat. He said he was broke and wanted to make a raise, and wanted me to help him. I agreed. This was Sunday. We separated then and met at Ben's the next Wednesday evening, and he told me he wanted to rob a C&A or Missouri Pacific train. He said he had two other men beside himself. . . . We went up to Jim Hulse's, getting there about 1 o'clock at night. We found Ed Miller there. Hulse entertained us as friends. I had no arms at the time. Jesse had a pair of Colt's 45-calibre, and Ed Miller had a breech-loading shot gun, a pair of Smith & Wesson 44 calibre and an old-fashioned Navy pistol. We went from there the

---

Abridged from *The Trial of Frank James for Murder; with Confessions of Dick Liddil and Clarence Hite,* from Official Records, pp. 284–288, 39–46, 315–318. Columbia, Missouri, 1898.

next night to old Thomas Eddington's, not to the house, but hitched our horses in the woods. Next morning I went up to get some food for us. I told them for whom I wanted it. After eating breakfast, Ed Miller started over to Clay County for Wood Hite and a man named Smith who lives about three or four miles from Mrs. Samuels [mother of the James brothers]. Miller was gone two days, and returned with Hite and Smith. During this time Jesse was hiding at Ben Morrow's, and I was at old man Eddington's. Upon Miller's return I told him to hide out in the brush and I would go after Jesse, which I did. When Jesse and I returned Smith had run off and left. He was afraid he would be killed. He thought Jesse was going to do it. After he left, we disbanded—Hite and Jesse going over to Mr. Ford's, near Richmond, Ray County, and Miller to see what had become of Smith. I stayed at Lamartine Hudspeth's.

About three days after this Jesse and Hite came back, and we three went back to Jim Hulse's. A little after this Ed Miller came up there also. The next morning I came up to Independence, took the train for Kansas City, and bought me a pair of Smith & Wesson pistols, forty-four calibre, from Blitz the pawnbroker in the Times Building. I went back, mounted my horse and rode to Independence, rode down towards Dick Tolley's, and met Jesse and Ed Miller on the road. We went off by the creek in the woods, where we found Hite and Bill Ryan. We talked the matter over, and determined to rob the C&A train at Glendale. We then broke up that night. Miller and I went to Tucker Basham's house—I don't know where the others went, but we were all to meet at the schoolhouse, several miles from Glendale. I did not know at that time who Basham was, and we did not know his real name until after he was arrested. They called him "Arkansaw." The next evening, about sun down, Miller and I started for the schoolhouse, and "Arkansaw" was to follow. The schoolhouse is about one mile from Basham's house. We met at the schoolhouse, and all went to Glendale together. We arrived there between six and seven o'clock on October 8, 1879, and hitched our horses about thirty yards due south of the station. Basham, Ryan and myself captured Joe Molt's store, and some men who were in it; and Jesse James, Ed Miller, and Wood Hite captured the depot. Jesse, who was the leader, then sent word to us to bring our prisoners over to the depot, which was done—and we put them all in the depot and guarded them. I think Jesse tore the telegraph apparatus to pieces. Basham thought it was a sewing machine, and wanted him to stop—as destroying it would do no good. A little east of the depot, obstructions were placed upon the track to stop the train in case flagging failed. When the eastern bound train came in sight we made the operator signal the train to stop.

Our plan was this: I was to capture the engineer and fireman, Bill Ryan was to uncouple the express car from the train, so that we could after backing the train run the engine forward again and leave the passenger coaches all to themselves. Basham and Hite were to keep the passengers on the train, while Jesse and Ed Miller robbed the express car. The cars had a patent coupling, so that Ryan could not unfasten them; so he helped Basham and Hite keep the passengers in. We carried out our respective parts with the above exception. Fifteen or twenty shots were fired in all—most of them in the air, and a few of them at a man with a lantern at the rear part of the train. Jesse said he fired three times at this man. Ed Miller got a sledge hammer out of the engine and struck the door of the express car several times before the express messenger would open it. They went in, and I think the messenger tried to get out and James struck him with his pistol. After the car was robbed, we were all standing on the depot platform together, when some one fired a shot from the train which went through the drawers and pants of Wood Hite, on the outside, between the ankle and knee of the right leg. Jesse remarked, "They are firing on us and we had better leave." We went to our horses, carrying our plunder in a common meal sack. We mounted and rode about six or seven miles south, to a little old log cabin, uninhabited, where we dismounted. Ed Miller carried the plunder. Here we divided the plunder equally, each getting about $1,025. There were a great many bonds, etc., and these were all destroyed. We left there all together, and retraced our steps several miles, when we began to break up, Ryan and Basham going home. We took Hite into the Kansas City road, about half way between Independence and the bridge over the big Blue, and left him. He went to Kansas City, I think, to Charlie McBride's.

* * * * *

II. The Winston Robbery

[*Here Frank James returns to the gang after an absence of five years. Two men were killed in this holdup—July 15, 1881—the train conductor and a passenger named McMillan. It was for the murder of McMillan that Frank James was being tried at Gallatin, Mo., in July, 1883, more than a year after Jesse's assassination. Following is a portion of the testimony of Dick Liddil during this trial.*]

. . . At Mrs. Samuels' I found Frank James and Wood and Clarence Hite. Jesse came along afterward. Jesse had bought a horse from his half-brother, Johnny Samuels. We started out about a week after, four on horseback—Frank, Jesse, Wood, and myself. Clarence went on the cars to Chillicothe. We were going there to take a train. I rode the sorrel, Jesse rode a bay, and Frank and Wood Hite rode horses that Wood and I took from a rack in Liberty. From Mrs. Samuels' we started to Ford's in Ray County, and got there about three o'clock in the morning, and left there the next morning. The Widow Bolton, sister of Charley Ford, lived there—a mile and a half southeast from

Richmond. From there we went to Chillicothe, stopping a mile and a half from town in the timber. Wood Hite went in after Clarence; but the roads were so muddy that we went back, Jesse and myself to the old lady, Wood and Frank to the Fords', and Clarence to Mrs. Samuels' also. We stayed there three or four days.

Shortly after this we started out again. Four went horseback and one on the cars, Wood going on the train. We came up to this county to look out a place to take a train. Frank was riding a roan pony. He took her at Richmond, and Wood Hite had a little bay mare, taken at the same time. Jesse and I had the horses we rode on the previous trip. The horses gotten at Liberty were turned loose at Richmond. We started that night, and camped out before daylight somewhere in the woods. We were to meet Wood Hite at Gallatin. We stopped and had dinner with a Dutchman in a one-story frame close to the road. . . .

We met Wood at Gallatin. Jesse got sick with toothache, and the creosote he used swelled his jaw and his face and he had to go back. Clarence went on foot, and Frank, Jesse, Wood and myself went on and stopped with a man named Wolfenberger, some sixteen miles from there. I helped him load up a load of wood next morning. We had supper and breakfast there, and left next day. Clarence stayed somewhere else. Jesse was very sick and we had to wait on him. We started for Mrs. Samuels', and Jesse was so sick we had to stop at an old stockman's. Jesse got the stockman to take him in a buggy to Hamilton depot. The others then started for Mrs. Samuels', but Frank and I went to Mrs. Bolton's, in Ray County. We stayed there a week, and then met Jesse, Clarence, and Wood at Mrs. Samuels'. In about a week or ten days we went on another trip.

We started from Mrs. Samuels' at dark, and when we came into a skirt of timber, we stayed all night till sunrise. Next day we scattered. Frank and Clarence went together, and I, Jesse and Wood Hite together. We three ate dinner at a white house on the road. There we met Frank and Clarence late in the evening. That night we stayed in the timber. We didn't get supper that night. We left next morning, Frank and Clarence together, Jesse and Wood together and I by myself, all different routes. We were to meet about a mile from Winston. I got dinner on the way, and went on to meet the boys in a skirt of timber near where the road crosses the track. We waited till dark, hitched our horses and went up on foot to the train. Wood and I went together, and met Frank, Jesse and Clarence at the depot.

The arrangement was as follows; that I and Clarence should capture the engineer, fireman, and engine and start it or stop it as we might be directed by Jesse and Frank. Jesse, Frank, and Wood were to get into the passenger cars and at the proper time rob the express car. We carried out the program when the north bound C.R.I.&P. passenger train came along. After getting outside of town, Clarence and I got up back of the tender, and went over on top to the engine. We had two pistols.

We kept quiet till the train stopped; then we hollered to go ahead. We shot to scare those fellows, who both ran onto the pilot. The first run was about two hundred yards, then a stop. About this time one of the boys pulled the bell rope and the engineer stopped the train, and firing back in the cars commenced. Don't know how many shots. Jesse got into the express car through the rear door and Wood and Frank tried to get in through the side door. The baggageman was standing in this side door and Frank seized him by the leg and jerked him out of the car and left him on the ground. He, Frank, dived into the express car and he or Jesse hollered to us to go ahead. The engineer pretended he could not move the train as the brakes were down. We then struck him with a piece of coal and told him we would kill him if he did not start the train. He then threw open the throttle and started it under a full head of steam. The engineer and fireman then got out of the cab and hid in front of the engine. We, firing a number of shots to frighten them, did not aim to hit them, as we could have easily killed them, being most of the time within a few feet. I then started back to the express car, but Clarence called to me and I returned to the engine. Frank came out and shut off steam, and as she slacked we jumped off while it was running. Frank and Clarence got off first, I went back after Jesse who was still in the express car, Jesse jumped first, and I followed. We got $700 or $800 that night in packages. It was all good money. Frank talked to me about the robbery afterward. He said he thought they had killed two men. Jesse said he shot one, he knew, and that Frank killed one. He saw him peep in at the window, and thought he killed him. From there we went to our horses, taking our time. We went to Crooked River. The money was divided in a pasture. Wood and I went to Ford's, the others went towards their mother's.

Cross examined: I went back to Jefferson City with Sheriff Timberlake in 1882, in January or February. I was there shortly after that with Mr. Craig, of Kansas City. I saw Governor Crittenden both times, first at the depot and the other time at his office. I don't remember telling the Governor at either of those times that after the Winston robbery Frank James upbraided Jesse for killing any one, or reminded him of the agreement before the robbery that no one should be hurt or killed.

[*Here Governor Thomas T. Crittenden of Missouri was called to the stand and testified as follows.*]

Liddil did make such a statement to me as propounded just now. I think it was the second time he was at Jefferson City. It grew out of asking him why they killed an innocent man engaged in his duties. He said that it was not the intention to do it; that the understanding was there was to be no killing; that Frank had said there was to be no blood shed, and that after it was over Frank said, "Jesse, why did you shoot that man? I thought the understanding was that no one was to be killed, and I would not have gone into it if I had known or thought there was to be anything of that sort done." To which Jesse said, "By G—d, I thought that the boys were pulling from me, and I wanted to make them a common band of murderers to hold them up to me."

[*But as to the killing, note this from the confession of Clarence Hite.*]

Jesse said that the conductor started to draw his pistol and he (Jesse) told him if he drew it he would kill him. He did not desist, and was shot. Jesse did not know the conductor. There is no truth in the story that Jesse killed him because he supposed he (the conductor) had carried Pinkerton's detectives out to his mother's (Mrs. Samuels) house. The stonemason was shot accidentally.

III. The Blue Cut Robbery

[*From the confession of Clarence Hite*]

Jesse wrote to Charlie Ford to come over to where they separated near Independence, which he did in a few days. He was then met near Independence by Jesse and Frank.

The object of this meeting was to plan another robbery. Charlie then went back home and got Dick and my brother, and we were all to meet at the same place three or four nights afterward, which we did. Six of us went there to rob the Chicago & Alton train. That night we came down between Kansas City and Independence and stayed in the woods. We intended to rob the Chicago & Alton train the next night—the western bound train, I mean. We would have robbed the east bound train, but there were two of them, and we did not know which of them had the most money. Jesse was our leader here also. The arrangement was as follows: We were to blockade the track with rock and stop the train if possible by waving a lantern with a piece of red flannel around it. Jesse and myself were to take the north side of the train. We were to keep the people from coming out by firing, etc. Frank and Dick were to take the south side of the train, and Wood and Charlie were to flag the train, take out the engineer, make him break open the express car door, and then they, Charlie and Wood, were to rob it. This arrangement was carried out on the night selected; next night. That was September 7, 1881.

When the Chicago & Alton train stopped at Blue Cut, Charlie and Wood made the engineer get his hammer and knock on the express car door (side door, the side Jesse and myself were on). After knocking several times the express messenger opened the door and jumped out and sat down on the bank. Charlie and Wood then went in, but they couldn't find the messenger, they supposing that the man who jumped out was the baggage man. One of them (Charlie and Wood) called out to Jesse that they could not find the messenger. Jesse than said: "There he sits on the bank with the engineer and fireman. Kill him if he does not get in and open the safe."

The messenger said: "I am not the messenger."

Charlie and Wood then covered him with their pistols and said: "Get in or we'll kill you."

The engineer said: "You had better get in. They have found you out."

He then got up and went in, opened the safe and I think they made him put the contents in the bag. We had a bag for the plunder. Then they accused him of hiding part of the contents, and Charlie hit him over the head with his pistol once or twice and fired it off for the purpose of scaring him. He was scared. They made a further search and found the messenger's pocketbook, containing about $60 (a $50 and a $10 or two $5's), and his watch and chain.

After Charlie and Wood came out of the car they told Jesse they did not have any money. Jesse then said: "We had better rob the passengers." They then started through the train, beginning at the smoker and going to the rear. Wood carried the bag (a common meal sack). Charlie went in front with a pistol in each hand and made the passengers deliver up their valuables and put them in the sack. I stood at the front door of each car as Charlie and Wood went through to prevent their being shot in the back. When we reached the chair car Frank got on. He did not go through the car, however. Everybody was badly scared. As we were coming back through the sleeper Charlie found a bottle of wine and took a drink. We also got some cake out of a basket. We got five watches, including the expressman's. Wood took the one which I have spoken of. Charlie Ford got two, one a fine gold one and chain (English make) and a silver one. I got a silver one and Jesse got the conductor's, a nickel, open-faced, stem-winder. We settled the division of jewelry as follows: Each article was sold to the highest bidder, and his bid was put in as so much cash and then the cash divided equally. Frank in this way got a set of Mexican jewelry. To go back a little. After we got through searching the passengers, Jesse came into the sleeper from the rear, and told the porter if he didn't hunt up all the money that was hid he'd kill him. The porter said he hadn't hid any, that they had gotten it all. Jesse then went to the first seat, turned it up and got about $60 and a gold watch. He then went to a brakeman and told him the same thing. The brakeman said "I gave you 50 cents—all I had." Jesse then gave him $1 or $1.50, saying: "This is principal and interest on your money."

We then released the prisoners, and waited until they had removed the obstructions, shook hands with the engineer and fireman, and the train moved on. We all then went north of the road, about half a mile, in a big bottom and divided the proceeds as I have said. Each man's share was estimated to be worth about $140.

Rube Burrow's Raids

Rube Burrow, the noted outlaw, train robber, and murderer, was born in that wild region which skirts Missouri and runs into Alabama. From youth up he was a bold and adventurous desperado. He roamed around the country and finally struck Silver City, Arkansas, a mining camp, which then abounded with a large and variegated collection of toughs and adventurers. In those diggings Winchester rifles cracked merrily day and night, and Rube Burrow was no less active than the majority. Rube Burrow drove a team in Silver City, Arkansas. He was a great, rawboned, strapping fellow, with a cold blue eye and a nerve like iron. He didn't care any more for death than most men do for missing their dinner. Two men as tough as Rube Burrow, and who had long had a grudge against him, one night poked a brace of 44's plump into his face. Rube was leaning against the bar and reflecting upon the uncertainties of playing faro by systems. There was a game in full blast at the back, and Rube had just been cleaned out. This pair of ruffians caught him just that way. Rube never moved a muscle or an eyelid. Those fellows thought he would go for his gun—and Rube was devilish quick on the trigger—but he didn't. If he had tried that, he would have been riddled. The unexpected always happened, and it did then. Rube looked the toughs straight in the eyes, and the pistols might have been so many cucumbers as far as he was concerned. Then he laughed contemptuously and told the barkeeper to set up three drinks. The toughs were dumfounded at Rube's nerve, and drank. They drank so much that they both got dead drunk. When he had them groggy, Rube Burrow shot both of them and then calmly lit out.

Then Rube Burrow began his adventurous career in earnest.

He robbed an Illinois Central train of $17,000 and escaped.

With three confederates Rube Burrow held up at different times seven emigrant trains, four way trains in Texas, three trains in Alabama and Missouri.

He robbed the Southern Express of $50,000, and they spent $20,000 to capture him.

On one of these expeditions, as he was robbing an express train, he shot two men and wounded them.

But Rube Burrow was not without chivalry. Tim Leary, one of his

From *Rube Burrows'* [Burrow's] *Raids; Historic Highwaymen; Night Riders of the Ozark, or, The Bald Knobbers of Missouri,* [by Richard K. Fox], pp. 4–16. New York: Richard K. Fox. 1891.

pals, one night brought in bound and gagged a young man. It was in the underbrush of Arkansas, in a log cabin. Rube Burrow was sitting at a deal table drinking whisky. He looked at the prisoner.

"Why, it's Joe Hackett, I'll be blowed!" he exclaimed. "Cut him loose, Jim. He's all right."

It appears that Hackett, in an encounter three years before, had shot Burrow in the arm so as to render him helpless, and then nursed him in his pain; Rube, touched by this chivalry, never forgot, and on the occasion in the log cabin, the three desperate men drank to each other's health.

Anecdotes of Rube Burrow's daredeviltry are rife all through Arkansas and Missouri. For years he terrorized whole counties.

One of the earliest robberies was this: Nip Thornton and Harrison Bromley's gang of train robbers were operating in northern Texas and Arkansas. Rube and his brother, Jim, who had returned to Texas with him, joined them in the fall of 1886. Their first trip with the gang was into the Indian Territory, where they went to rob an old Indian woman. The trip was, however, a failure. On the return, Rube did his first work as a train robber. Here is his own account of it, given a year ago: "On our return through the Panhandle," he said, "we came upon a Texas [and] Pacific train from Fort Worth taking on water. There were two passenger cars. Jim and myself took one and Nip and Bromley the other. In our car Jim kept the crowd covered while I took up the collection. There were four soldiers in our car, but they were so scared that we had no trouble in unarming them. We didn't get much, though. I believe we got only about $200."

Two weeks later the same gang held up another train on the same road at Ben Brooke. Rube and Thornton went through the express car and secured about $4,000. These two robberies were so easily performed that Burrow became enthusiastic, and a week later they held up another train at the same place, this time, however, getting only about $500. Rube then went home and remained quiet until the excitement of the robberies had blown over. Nobody suspected him. A few weeks later, however, the gang met again and decided to hold up another train on the Texas [and] Pacific. This time the four robbers, armed only with pistols, boarded the train at Gordon. When a few miles out, Bromley covered the engineer while the others went through the express and mail cars. The outlaws met with no resistance, and were not even chased. They remained in the neighborhood for three days thereafter. On the night of the third day the gang held up the same train again. This time it was going northward. The same crew was aboard, and when the engineer was covered by Bromley's revolver he turned sullenly and asked: "Well, where do you want me to stop this time?"

"Just the other side of that trestle," said Bromley, "and be sure you do it."

The engineer stopped as ordered, and the gang made quick work of going through the express and mail cars. They secured about $8,000. As they were getting off, some one on the train opened fire on them, and winged Nip Thornton, the ball going through his arm. Thornton and Bromley were captured a few days later but Rube and Jim Burrow left the state for their home in Alabama. The detectives did not suspect them.

The next time Rube appeared was in December, 1887. The St. Louis, Arkansas and Texas train was held up at Genoa, Arkansas, a few miles north of Texarkana. The work was done principally by Rube Burrow, assisted by his brother Jim and a fellow named Brock. They did not get much in this haul, but their robberies had become so frequent that the Southern Express Company sent a corps of their own detectives and Pinkerton men on the trail of the gang. The chase became so hot that Rube and his brother returned to Alabama. Brock was captured, and he "peached" on the Burrow boys, telling of the robberies in which they had been implicated, and that they had gone to Lamar County, Alabama. Four Pinkerton men went after them, and in Lamar County, with Sheriff Jasper Pennington, organized a posse. They first went to Jim Burrow's house. He saw them coming, and ran for the woods. A number of shots followed him, but he escaped and made for his father's house, where Rube was hiding. Hardly had he reached there when the posse arrived. The two outlaws, however, escaped without being seen, and commenced making their way toward Montgomery. On the train their actions aroused suspicion, and the conductor telegraphed ahead to the Chief of Police of Montgomery that two suspicious characters, supposed to be Rube and Jim Burrow, were on his train. They arrived in Montgomery late at night. It was raining hard. As they alighted in the depot a dozen policemen in rubber coats that hid their uniforms walked up, and the leader asked where they were going.

Rube knew at once who the men were. He was well armed, but Jim did not have even a knife. Rube, therefore, decided to await a better opportunity to escape.

"I want to find a cheap boarding house," he said.

"All right, I will show you to one," said one of the policemen.

Surrounded by the policemen, the two outlaws started for the police station. They walked along quietly for a few blocks when Rube signalled to Jim, and the outlaws made a break for liberty. The policemen opened fire. Rube returned it as he ran. Before they had run fifty yards, however, Jim fell wounded, but Rube, who could run like a deer, escaped. Neil Broy, a printer, who attempted to stop him, received a bullet hole in his chest. Jim Burrow was sent to Arkansas. He died in the penitentiary before his trial.

The chase after Rube was not renewed that night. He did not leave Montgomery, but went to the outskirts of the town and spent the night in a Negro's cabin. The Negro, who suspected Rube's identity, sent a messenger into the city to notify the Chief of Police. At daylight the next morning a large posse of policemen and men about town, armed with all kinds of weapons, were on hand to either capture or kill Burrow. The house was almost surrounded. The Negro who owned the cabin went in to Rube and said: "Boss, dere's some white men out here dat wants to see you."

"Well, they can't do it," said Rube.

He went to the door and peered out, but jumped back in time to escape a volley of bullets and shot. Rube returned the fire with a revolver through a crack in the logs, and the posse hastily sought cover. Then Rube removed his shoes, hung them over his arm, and with a pistol in each hand made a break through the rear door for a swamp about 200 yards off. He shot at the posse while running. The fire was returned, and just as the outlaw entered the swamp he received a lot of bird shot in the back of his neck. The police did not dare follow, and the chase was given up. Rube went to a country doctor and had the shot picked out of his neck.

About the middle of December, 1888, the Illinois Central Express was held up at Duck Hill, Mississippi, and $18,000 was stolen. Rube Burrow, of course, had a hand in the robbery, and another fellow, Joe Jackson, was his accomplice.

The station at Duck Hill, Mississippi, is a small one in a sparsely settled part of the country. The train was due there at midnight. As it stopped, Rube and Jackson jumped on the front platform of the express car, which was next to the engine. As soon as the train was well started, Rube crawled on the tender, covered the engineer and fireman, and ordered the engineer to come to a stop at a big pine near the track, two miles from Duck Hill, and which was a well-known landmark. The train came to a stop exactly opposite the pine. In an instant Rube jumped back on the platform, and the two robbers bolted into the express car to find the sleepy messenger rubbing his eyes and wondering at the cause of the stop. Finding himself covered by two rifles, however, he was wide awake in an instant and trembling with fear.

"Open that iron box and be quick about it," Rube demanded, as he pressed the muzzle of his rifle against the messenger's head.

The messenger hastened to obey. Then he drew back and, with both hands raised above his head, stood by and watched the robbers as they ran through the valuable packages, selecting only those that contained paper money. At first the conductor and the passengers thought there had been an accident. Then, as if prompted by instinct, the conductor cried out in the smoker: "Train robbers!" Two young men on a rear seat jumped up. One had a Winchester rifle, the other a revolver. They were Chester Hughes and John Wilkinson, two as brave and gallant young fellows as ever lived. Through the car they rushed and out on the platform, pushing open the door of the express car just as Rube Burrow had placed the last envelope in his coat.

Hughes and Wilkinson opened fire as they rushed into the car, but Rube was too quick for them, and Chester Hughes fell back with a bullet through his heart. Wilkinson dropped his revolver when Hughes's body fell against him, and the robbers jumped from the side door of the car and escaped.

The robbery aroused the express company and the Governors of some of the Southern states, and a large reward, aggregating $7,500, and including $1,000 offered by the United States Government, was offered for the capture of Rube Burrow, dead or alive.

Rube and Jackson returned to Lamar County, Alabama, and remained for several months. The few people in the neighborhood knew they were there, but none dared to breathe it. Indeed the Burrow family is related to nearly everybody in the county, and most of the men in that section were Rube's friends. Detectives disguised as peddlers occasionally went through the county. One who was known to be in search of Rube and the reward is yet missing. However, a little Irish detective named Burns, who is the shrewdest of all who ever tracked the outlaw, did go through the county in April, 1889, and even succeeded in spending one night at old man Allen Burrow's home and selling Tim Cash, Rube's brother-in-law, a pair of trousers. Burns gained a great deal of valuable information about Rube's habits on this trip. He, however, did not know that Rube and Joe Jackson were quietly spending their time at the home of John Thomas Burrow, only a mile distant from the old man's house, but in a piece of dense woodland; the house which was the ordinary backwoods cabin, made of planks instead of logs, somewhat in the shape of the letter L, had a secret room in the end, about three feet by nine, in which Rube slept. In the heavy walls of three sides were holes that could be opened from the inside. Rube thought he was safe from any attacks that might be made upon him, and his friends and relatives were continually on guard and ready to give him notice of the appearance of any stranger in the county.

Burrow met his fate in Alabama, in October, 1890.

He had just robbed the Southern Express Company. They offered a big reward for him. The particulars of the capture, as near as can be gathered, are as follows:

Rube was in the neighborhood of Beckley's landing on a place worked by Jesse Hildreth, colored. Jesse had by some means gotten into his good graces, if he had any; at least he had so gotten into his confidence that he did not fear to trust him some. By instruction of Messrs. Carter and McDuffee, Jesse and another Negro named Frank Marshall engaged to decoy Rube into a cabin occupied by George Ford. They succeeded in this, under the pretense that while they stopped in there out of the rain, they might be able to get him some eggs, for which he had expressed a desire. Rube entered the house, and when the two Negroes came in, he was wrapping up his gun in his coat, preparatory to leaving. Jesse remarked, "Boss, let me wrap it up for you." Rube consented and handed him the gun. The brave Negro performed the service deliberately, and having securely wrapped the weapon so it could not be used, handed it back to its owner. As Rube took the gun, somewhat off his guard, the Negro, with the determination born of true heroism, flung himself on the outlaw with all the strength at his command, and pinioned both arms in a vise-like grip. There was no use to struggle, the Negro was the stronger, and with his pistols and gun on him Rube found himself captured at last, and that by a Negro. Finding his inability to extricate himself, Rube exclaimed with an oath, "Don't hug me to death," to which his captor replied with characteristic frankness, "Boss, I can't turn you loose. I'se just got to hold you now." The other Negro then came to Jesse's assistance. Rube, in his rage, reached over and fastened his teeth on the shoulder of this Negro, nearly taking a piece out. Between the two they soon had him on the floor and called for McDuffee and Carter, who were waiting outside. The white men then came in, disarmed Rube, and securely tied him across McDuffee's saddle, in which position he was taken to Linden to jail. This all, we are informed, occurred near the site of the old mill on the George Payne place, near Beckley's landing.

Rube, when he arrived in Linden, was not locked in a cell, but was lodged in the Sheriff's sleeping room, which is a part of the jail, and was securely handcuffed and shackled, guarded by McDuffee and Jesse Hildreth. During the night he asked for something to eat. McDuffee replied that he had nothing to give him. Rube then asked that the Negro hand him a sack in which he had some gingersnaps and other things, and his request was granted. His hands were freed so he could use them in eating. In this pastime he engaged for some time, carrying on at the same time a pleasant conversation with his captors, until suddenly McDuffee and the Negro found themselves looking down the barrels of a couple of pistols in Rube's hands, now free. With deliberate coolness, Rube then compelled the Negro to take the shackles off his feet and put them on McDuffee. He then remarked to the Negro: "I'll take you along with me, and if you fight well, I'll keep you, and if you don't, I will send you home."

The Negro, of course, followed, and the two left the jail. Not satisfied with his liberty, Rube then went to look for Carter, who had his rifle and $178 in money that was found on him. In this he showed astonishing recklessness and daring; told several people that he was Rube Burrow and that he was going to "paint the town red and give 'em h——!" He inquired at several houses for Carter and found him at last at Glass's store, where Carter was sleeping. Carter came to the door with his pistol, and was informed by the Negro that the expressmen had come, and that he was wanted over at the jail at once. This was just before daylight. Carter opened the door, and as he did so Rube thrust his pistol into his face and demanded the rifle and the money. Surprised but not paralyzed, Carter refused, and firing commenced on both sides, Rube retreating into the street and Carter following. When Rube had nearly crossed the street, he turned and fell dead; Carter also fell with an ugly flesh wound in the shoulder. Only two shots took effect out of the six fired by Rube and five by Carter; the latter was not mortally wounded, as at first reported.

There are two singular facts connected with the capture and killing which are worthy of note. Rube was overpowered by a Negro, whose bravery he despised; he was killed by a ball from a .32 calibre pistol, a weapon he designated and laughed at as a mere toy or plaything.

It was through the intervention of Mr. E. B. McCarty, the *Mobile Register's* enterprising and talented correspondent, that the public was allowed to view the body of the outlaw. At his request, Mr. Fisher allowed the coffin to be opened on the depot platform and kept open for an hour or more. Hundreds of people, men, women, and children, crowded around to look upon the form and into the wide-open eyes of the man that twelve hours before some of them could not have been coaxed within a mile of. The body was placed on one corner of the platform and the crowd made to form into a procession as near as could be, and pass around the depot to the body and then out of the way.

If the reader had been present, he would have seen a man six feet one inch tall, weighing between 160 and 180 pounds, dressed in a coarse brown suit, checked homespun shirt, and with all the appearance of a common tramp; not the ideal hero of romantic minds, but just a plain, coarse, common looking man. A study of his face, though, could not fail to impress one. His forehead was high and rather broad, crowned with a mass of long, unkempt hair, eyes blue-gray, expressive even in death, and betokening a man of more than usual shrewdness, if not intelligence. His whiskers were slightly lighter than the hair, his mouth covered by a thin moustache. His complexion was rather swarthy; cheek bones high, and lower jaw exceedingly square and massive; mouth large, measuring three inches from corner to corner; lips very thin. There were several visible small scars on the forehead, said to be from gunshot wounds received when he escaped from the Montgomery police several years ago. The wound which caused his death was about the pit of the stomach, and was rather insignificant looking for its fearful consequences to Rube. The doctors say death was caused by the ball piercing the liver and breaking the abdominal aorta.

Considerable interest was manifested in examining his weapons, clothing, etc. Many people tried to secure locks of his hair, buttons from his clothes, and pieces of the coffin, to keep as mementos, but some had to be disappointed. A .38 calibre Marlin magazine rifle, 1887 patent, two Colt's .44 navy sixes, and the .38 Colt's five shot taken from the express messenger at Buckatunna, constituted the arsenal he had on him when taken.

The body was shipped in an express car to Lamar County, where his people consigned to mother earth all that remained of Alabama's notorious outlaw.

The Strange Case of Evans and Sontag

A series of California train robberies [was] followed by a chain of the most spectacular man hunts and by two of the most amazing examples of human endurance and physical courage in history. And after the evidence is all in, the proof is not absolutely convincing that the men who were accused, hounded, imprisoned, shot to pieces, were the men who actually committed the crime.

The prologue of the story is found in the building of the Southern Pacific Railroad from San Francisco southeastward up the San Joaquin Valley in the 1870s. As usual in those days, the railroad had been subsidized by the Government, receiving free large tracts of land on each side of its right of way. Anxious to realize on this land, it offered low fares and other facilities to settlers, promising that as soon as its government grants were surveyed and its titles validated, it would sell the land to homesteaders at $2.50 an acre. Some of the new emigrants had already "squatted" on the land, and some had already begun proceedings to obtain titles of their own from the Government. Most of them were quite willing to buy from the railroad at the price named; but after the road had perfected its title, the price leaped to $10, $15, and a year or two later to $25 and $30 per acre.

It was not only in California that this thing took place. It was a favorite game of the day. In other Western states railroads were pursuing similar tactics, and much bitterness was engendered. Settlers' Leagues were organized, communities were divided into railroad and anti-railroad factions, fighting and sabotage occurred, and frequently lives were lost. A Settlers' League was organized in the San Joaquin, and even attacked the railroad's title to the land, as its charter had specified that it was to run along the coast. Both the local land offices and the Department of the Interior at Washington ignored the settlers' pleas, and the Federal courts regularly threw out their claims. One can prove little now, but those were crooked days at Washington, and it is a sinister fact that the railroads, with their powerful lobbies and

---

From *Old Waybills,* The Romance of the Express Companies, by Alvin F. Harlow, pp. 408–422. Copyright, 1934, by Alvin F. Harlow. New York and London: D. Appleton-Century Company, Inc.

subsidized government officials, always had the better of it in a dispute with homesteaders.

The ill feeling of the period found a climax in the dreadful Mussel Slough tragedy of May, 1880, when a Federal marshal and three deputies killed five ranchmen, three of them unarmed, at a barbecue where no one was expecting trouble. For this the farmers were punished, seventeen of them being sent to prison for resisting a Federal officer!

There were other oppressions—exorbitant freight rates and many more too numerous to list—which you may find described in Frank Norris's novel, *The Octopus,* whose title very aptly describes the railroad of those days. Fortunately, that dynasty [C. P. Huntington, et al.] passed from the Southern Pacific management long ago. But as long as it existed, as long as men lived who had known its oppression, there was hatred of it in California. And a dozen years after the Mussel Slough killing, that hatred made it difficult for officers to capture two men accused of robbing Southern Pacific trains and committing murder while so doing.

[On the evening of February 22, 1889, Southern Pacific passenger train No. 17 was held up and the express car robbed two miles southeast of Pixley, a village just south of the Mussel Slough.] Reports of the loss placed it variously from $500 to $5,000. Had it not been for the killing of Gabert [a railroad employee], the bulk of public opinion would have inclined to rejoicing because of the assault upon the railroad. There was little sympathy with the officers in their search for trails, and they soon gave up the chase.

Eleven months passed by, and on the night of January 20, 1890, southbound train No. 19 was stopped north of Pixley on the very edge of the Mussel Slough country by two bandits in precisely the same manner. . . . [A tramp who had been riding between the cars was fired on by the brigands and mortally wounded while attempting to escape.]

The loot in this second hold-up was rumored to be $20,000. Excitement now rose high in the vicinity, and some of the better citizens, despite their hatred of the railroad, began to deplore these instances of violence. Officers of justice and their own detectives were berated by railroad and express company, but though they made several arrests, they were evidently at a loss for clues, and once more the chase of the phantom bandits petered out in flatulence and ridicule.

A trifle more than a year later either these robbers or others struck again. On the evening of February 6, 1891, train No. 17 was again attacked, this time near Alila, a few miles south of Pixley. . . . And lying on the ground by the side of the express car was Fireman Radcliffe with a fatal wound in the abdomen.

The countryside was now in wild excitement. All three of the fatal hold-ups had taken place in Tulare County, though the last was near the border of Kern; and the sheriffs of Tulare and Kern, with special posses, rushed to the scene by special train and followed what they believed to be a trail leading westward towards the Coast Range. It was presently announced that the villains were surrounded; but if so, they must have evaporated into the ether, for within a week or so the sleuthhounds came back with tails between legs, shrinking from the chorus of derision and vituperation which arose from public, press, railroad and express officials.

* * * * *

Now the local law officers, hearing of the rude escapade of some of the Dalton boys in New Mexico and remembering that rowdy Grat Dalton was visiting his brother Bill in the vicinity and had been engaged in some disorderly affairs, they decided to pin the robberies on those gentlemen . . . so Bill and Grat were arrested. Bill was presently released on bond; but with Grat in jail, a fourth hold-up took place nine months later near Modesto, in Stanislaus County, a full hundred miles north of the scene of the other three.

The method in this case was so like that of the preceding ones that there was little doubt in the public mind that all were committed by the same men. . . .

Nearly a year had passed since the last attack when the fifth and most spectacular of all the robberies took place. About midnight on August 3, 1892, near Collis station, a few miles west of Fresno, two men appeared in the engine cab of train No. 17, and the usual routine was followed. As the train was slowed to a stop, it crossed a county road, and here one bandit fired three shots, believed to be a signal to a confederate waiting near by with a buggy and team. Here there was a variation. The fireman, under duress, uncoupled the engine from the train and remained with the bandits, while the engineer was ordered to pull a quarter of a mile down the track and wait.

The express car was of a new type, of very stout construction. Without even warning the messenger, the men exploded bombs on the sills of the two left-hand side doors, damaging them badly but making no opening large enough for a man to pass through. The right side doors were then bombed with similar results. George D. Roberts, the messenger, had doused his lights when the train stopped, and crouched in one end of the car with his heavy revolver. The second or third blast hurled him against the side of the car and dislocated his shoulder. After the four doors had been assaulted, the attackers poked a fifth bomb through one of the shattered doors. Roberts attempted to kick it back, but it escaped from him and rolled across the floor. He threw himself flat just as the explosion occurred. It dazed him so that one robber crawled through the now enlarged opening unmolested.

Though battered and half stunned, the messenger still tried to be defiant, but the marauder struck him over the head with a pistol and took the safe key from his pocket. Three forty-pound bags of silver coin and a small bag of gold were found in the safe. The man demanded that Roberts open three large safes with combination locks which stood against the wall and beat him again with the gun when he declared that he could not, but finally accepted his story. With the enforced aid of the messenger and fireman, the 125 pounds of coin were carried to the buggy waiting in the road near by, and the thieves disappeared in the darkness.

The most authoritative report of the loss placed it at between $2,000 and $3,000, though round-eyed local gossip boosted it as high as $50,000. There was difference of opinion among the witnesses, too; the fireman was positive that there was an accomplice, a third man taking care of the waiting buggy; but the messenger saw no such man. But there could be no doubt as to the violence of the attack. A large area was strewn with débris from the damaged car, and even the track and earth under it were scarred by the blasts.

Again came sneers from the populace, demands from express and railroad officials that something be done. Again some of the sleuths mentioned the name of Dalton, which by this time was beginning to sound rather silly, inasmuch as the Daltons were at the moment very busy robbing trains a thousand miles away in Oklahoma. But within forty-eight hours after the crime, new suspects had been found and accused, and with lightning suddenness the great man hunt was on.

Christopher Evans, aged about forty-five, a native of Vermont and pioneer in the San Joaquin, and John Sontag, an ex-railroad employee, born in Minnesota, were the latest to be accused, while the latter's brother, George Sontag, played a subordinate role.

Evans had gone to California in his twenties and first tried gold-seeking, without results. Later he took up a claim in the San Joaquin Valley on the supposition that he could buy it from the railroad at $2.50 an acre; but after two or three years of struggle, just when he seemed to be getting a foothold, he learned that the price would be $10. He could not pay it and lost his little farm, with all the improvements he had put on it.

Happily married but impoverished and embittered, he struggled as best he could to provide for his growing family. That he was a loving and beloved husband and father is proven by their devotion to him during the years that followed and by the letters which passed between them while he was hiding like a hunted animal in the wilds or incarcerated in prison. He still owned some horses, and with these he did hauling and grading jobs. He was also superintendent for a time of three large grain warehouses, one each at Tulare, Goshen, and Pixley. By a sinister coincidence, the first two of the five robberies were perpetrated near the two latter towns. Here he saw more railroad oppression.

Next he tried running a livery stable in Modesto. But he was not a good business man; he overreached himself in the venture, and only a few months after he had begun, the stable burned one night, and with it most of the horses. While the cries of the tortured animals sounded from the flames, he sat on the curb across the street with his face in his hands, sobbing—not only because of his broken hopes, but out of sympathy for the tortured animals he loved. Some folk remembered that afterward and argued that Evans would never have taken human life unless unjustly hounded and driven to it.

Evans, his nerve now shaken by his misfortune, returned to Visalia, Tulare County, and started farming a small tract nearby. He had been there for some months prior to the Collis robbery, and was considered a thoroughly upright citizen. It is asserted in his favor that it was while living there that he was first introduced to John Sontag on the street one day by an acquaintance. Sontag was lame and ill. While he was working for the railroad as a brakeman, his ankle had been badly hurt, and he said he had been neglected and ill-treated in the company's hospital at Sacramento. Railroad hospitals in those days were often crude and dreadful places as compared with those of today. Sontag, suffering great pain after weeks of indifferent treatment, cursed the house surgeon and the railroad one day, and in retaliation, was turned out of his bed a week later, though he could only hobble painfully on the injured leg. He asked the railroad for work, but they offered him only his old job as a brakeman or a place on a track gang, and he, protesting that he was too lame to handle either, was roughly invited to clear out then and take care of himself. Another bitter enemy for the railroad!

Sontag had come from Minnesota several years before with his brother George, who was smaller than he, dapper and talkative. George's loose tongue was probably responsible for the fate which overtook all three men. The three were seen together about the streets of Visalia during the day or two after the robbery, denouncing the railroad so acridly that the attention of railroad detectives was attracted to them. The sleuths claimed later that Evans had been under suspicion since the robbery attempt at Ceres, which took place only a few days before the burning of his stable near by, at Modesto, but they did not adduce the reasons for this. It was found that on the day of the Collis robbery, Evans and John Sontag had hired a buggy and team from a livery stable, ostensibly to go to the mountains to eastward on a prospecting trip. It was claimed also that the trail of the Collis robbers had been followed almost to Visalia.

These circumstances cast suspicion upon the trio, and when George Sontag bragged of having been a passenger on the train which was robbed at Collis, Detective Will Smith of the Southern Pacific decided to catechize him. Under a fire of questions as to his knowledge of the robbery and his recent whereabouts, he became confused and contradictory and was finally put under arrest. Smith and a deputy sheriff named Witty then started for Evans's home on the edge of town, intending also to look up John Sontag, who was rooming at the home of Evans's mother-in-law. The call at Evans's house ended in a gunbout, from which the officers fled, slightly peppered with shot. The Evans side of the story was that it started when Smith called Evans's sixteen-year-old daughter a "damned little liar" because she said, thinking that she was telling the truth, that Sontag was not on the place.

Months later, when he lay dying from his wounds, John Sontag, denying any part in the robberies, said that Evans had advised him not to surrender to the detectives, as they would probably maltreat him because of his slurs on the railroad. But neither Evans's nor the accused men's side of the rencounter was made public until seventeen months later, at Evans's trial. As C. B. Glasscock, who has made a careful study of the case, says, "That five minutes of melodrama, in public opinion, convicted Evans and Sontag of the robberies more definitely than did all the evidence submitted in the course of the murder trial later. Indeed, it was their only conviction of robbery, and that entirely unofficial."

As Smith and Witty fled into town, Evans and Sontag, now outlaws, leaped into the sheriff's spring wagon and without equipment drove rapidly eastward towards the Sierra. And so began a chase which lasted, all told, a year and a half, and proved the two hunted men to be masters of strategy and marksmanship. They proved their strategy at the very beginning by driving into a meadow only a few miles from Visalia and hiding themselves and their horses and wagon behind some haystacks while the pursuers galloped by. After dark they returned quietly to Evans's home and were loading provisions and extra clothing into their wagon when they were challenged by a deputy sheriff who had suspected some such move and had approached the house with two other possemen. In the gunfight which ensued, one of the officers was killed, and the accused men again escaped.

For ten months thereafter they seemed almost to lead charmed lives, mostly in the Sierra foothills; often aided by sympathizers who were enemies of the railroad, sometimes by persons who did not know them and again by others who had heard of their prowess and feared their vengeance. Meanwhile George Sontag was brought to trial. His attorney complained—and justly, too—that nearly all the evidence adduced was against Evans and John Sontag rather than his client; but no protest availed. On the flimsiest of circumstantial evidence, which at another time and in another place could not have prevented an acquittal, he was convicted and sentenced to prison for life.

Shortly after the trial, Evans and his partner stopped at a ranch house near Visalia for dinner one day, and the chase received new impetus. A posse of ten men, railroad detectives, deputy sheriffs, Indian trackers, and others, ran upon the outlaws in Young's cabin, an isolated shack in the hills, and after a spirited battle, retired with the loss of two of their men and one horse.

The pursuit with hired man-hunters went on through the autumn. The railroad spent enough on the case that year, says Glasscock, to have pensioned the two men for life. Now and then they dropped in, bearded, ragged and haggard, at some farm or lumber camp in the hills for a meal, always comporting themselves quietly and genially, but never letting their guns out of their hands for a moment.

Evans was in constant communication by letter with his family—letters full of love on both sides, and on the part of the family, of perfect confidence in the husband's and father's innocence. Eva Evans, at her father's instigation, arranged an attempt at escape from Folsom prison for George Sontag. With the help of sympathizers, some guns were hidden in a stone quarry where the prisoners worked; but when the break came, there was a slip-up—three prisoners were killed and six wounded, among them George, who became a cripple for life. He now made an alleged confession, in which he admitted complicity in the Collis robbery and knowledge of his brother's and Evans's having committed the others.

One day in April, 1893, Visalia was stunned when school-children reported that two bearded men had driven into the Evans yard in broad daylight, put their horse into the barn, and entered the house. The sheriff posted a cordon around the house, at a respectful distance, and guarded every road leading from town with men armed with guns and flares. Such was the awe in which the outlaws were held that no attempt was made to rush the cottage. Nothing could be seen of them behind the drawn shades of the house; the afternoon and evening passed, and suddenly at midnight there came the whack of a whip, clattering hoofs, rattling wheels, a shout; a flare flamed as the buggy whirled into the road, shots rang out, bullets whined and thudded into fences—and Evans and Sontag were gone again!

But a few days later came their Waterloo. All unsuspecting, they walked up one afternoon near sunset to a deserted cabin known as the Stone Corral, where United States Marshal Gard and a large posse were concealed. An overenthusiastic deputy precipitated the battle by firing at once, shattering Evans's right arm. He and Sontag dropped behind a low pile of straw and manure some seventy-five yards from the house and from that poor shelter fought their enemies until darkness fell. Sontag, receiving a bullet through the right arm and another in the side, begged Evans to kill him; but when the latter refused, he continued firing with his left hand. A bullet from a posseman crawling through the weeds raked across Evans's back, another crippled his left arm, and a spatter of buckshot riddled his right eye. He could no longer use a gun, but Sontag continued firing wildly at intervals until another ball shattered his shoulder, when he sank unconscious in the litter. At dusk, Evans's crouching figure was seen stealing away at the edge of the clearing. An officer fired at him, but missed him; and thus, his clothing soaked with blood from the gash in his back, both arms hanging useless, one eye torn to pieces, and three buckshot embedded in the brain cavity, he tottered through rocks and brush to a cottage six miles away. No more amazing instance of human endurance and will power is on record.

Such was the fear of the two men that no attempt was made to rush the little fortress of stable litter that night. Next morning it was cautiously surrounded, and Sontag found still faintly alive. He had a pistol in his hand, with which he had made a feeble attempt to commit suicide during the night. Before anything was done for his relief, a photographer, who had rushed out from town, took a picture of him with the proud manhunters posing behind him. The broken body was removed to Fresno jail, where Sontag died a few days later.

Evans, unable to carry on longer, sent word to the sheriff that day from the cottage where he had taken refuge, offering to surrender and asking that the rewards be divided between the person who was sheltering him and his own family. He recovered his strength slowly, but it was necessary to amputate his left arm. In November he was brought to trial, not for robbery, but for the murder of one of his pursuers in the fight at Young's cabin. But despite the protests of his attorney, the state persisted in adducing so-called evidence, all totally irrelevant, as to the train robberies. Detective Smith exhibited bits of the black cloth of which the robbers' masks were made, which he claimed to have found in Evans's house, and he and another detective asserted that they had dug up in Evans's yard some Peruvian dollars taken in the robbery at Collis. It appeared that there was no one else present at this ceremony, and defense attorneys hinted that the dollars had been "planted."

Nevertheless, the prisoner was convicted and returned to jail to await sentence. Fifteen days later, with the aid of one Ed Morrell, waiter in a small restaurant in Fresno, he escaped one evening when Morrell brought in his supper from the cafe. Morrell also brought two pistols, with which he and Evans cowed the jailor; they walked out, seized a horse and cart from a boy driver, and galloped away in the darkness.

The chase was begun all over again, and Evans, now handicapped by an artificial arm and the loss of an eye, again displayed his iron nerve and fiendish cleverness in standing off and outwitting his pursuers for several weeks. But the law was bound to win at last. A new device was tried—a spurious message to Evans to the effect that one of his younger children was ill. That brought the anxious father home hotfoot. A small army quickly surrounded the house, and the weary fugitive saw that the game was up.

He was sentenced to prison for life, and taken to Folsom in 1894. In 1911, after years of effort in his behalf on the part of his wife and children (in which even the poet, Joaquin Miller, took a hand), he was paroled by Governor, afterwards Senator, Hiram Johnson, himself one of the bitterest enemies of the Southern Pacific. Evans came out an aged and palsied man of sixty-four and joined his wife in Oregon. His palsy grew worse and an operation was decided upon. Embedded in the edge of the brain the surgeon found the three buckshot which had riddled his eye in the fight at the Stone Corral nearly twenty years before. He lived almost six years longer, dying in 1917, and denying to the end his having had any part in the Southern Pacific robberies.

Boxed Bandits

It was during those years [the latter Seventies] that crooks conceived the device of having themselves shipped in coffins as corpses, with the idea of attacking the messenger en route. One who tried this in Wisconsin in 1886 quickly aroused the suspicion of the messenger who piled several hundred pounds of freight on and around the box. At the next stopping place it was taken out and placed on the station platform. "Is there a man in that box?" asked the express agent. "If so, he'd better speak. I'm going to fire through it." At that the corpse admitted, "I'm in here; don't shoot." The side of the box, held in place by buttons, dropped and a sheepish-looking crook rolled out, to receive a three-year prison term.

When Messenger Axley on the Union Pacific one day in 1879 was helping to load a supposed corpse into his car at Ogden, he remarked that the coffin didn't fit the box very well, as he felt a slight reacting movement inside. A weeping old woman in a heavy mourning veil and two plainly dressed men, said to be the mother and brothers of the deceased, wanted to ride in the express car with the remains, but were forbidden, as it was against the rules.

Just before the train pulled out, Axley, who had $35,000 in his safe, went to Frye, the baggageman in the next car, and told him that he suspected a robbery plot, but that he dreaded having the box examined, lest he be laughed off the road. After the train had started, Frye went to Axley's car and found him pale and perspiring. "There's a live man in that box," said he, "I know it." Frye thereupon notified the conductor. "Yes," commented the latter, "and that reminds me that the old lady weeping back there in the coach has rather ponderous feet for a woman."

Taking his pistol, Frye went to ride in the express car. Presently some one pulled the bell-cord, and the train slackened speed. Axley kept his eyes riveted on the box. Suddenly the lid flew up, and the

---

Ibid., pp. 436–437.

primordial countenance of a heavily armed bandit known as Utah Charley appeared, only to receive a bullet in the neck from the messenger's pistol. The lid dropped again. "Watch the door!" cried Axley, none too soon, for at that moment the end door flew open, and "Mother" appeared. "Hands up!" shouted Frye, and up went two large, hairy paws, one clutching a pistol. A minute later a stringy little man appeared, bringing the two "brothers," handcuffed. He was a United States Marshal who had guessed their errand. All received prison terms save Utah Charley, who had need of a real box this time.

Shaming a Train Robber

[Colonel Samuel W. Fordyce, president of the Cotton Belt, and directors were on an inspection trip north of Texarkana, when they were stopped at Red River Bridge.]

Colonel Fordyce stepped out onto the platform and found himself face to face with a masked man who pointed a pistol in the Colonel's face. . . . As the Colonel backed into the lighted room, the masked man started—he seemed to recognize Colonel Fordyce. At the same time Colonel Fordyce knew that voice. The bandit was an old friend of the Colonel's named Shang Doland. Shang had been a freight conductor when the Colonel was station agent back in Ohio before the Civil War. Shang had turned up in Hot Springs, while Colonel Fordyce was living there, and he had found him a job on the police force. Later Shang had killed a man and was sent to the penitentiary at Little Rock. After he had served a short time, Colonel Fordyce had obtained a pardon for Shang. Since that time the Colonel had lost track of his colorful friend.

Colonel Fordyce said: "Shang, aren't you ashamed of yourself to come over on the Cotton Belt and try to rob a road as poor as this one? Don't you know that no one with any money ever rides on the Cotton Belt? Why don't you go over and hold up the Iron Mountain?"

The bandit was floored. He pulled off his mask and extended his hand, saying: "Excuse me, Colonel, if I had known this was your special I never would have held it up. I'll go out and stop the boys and let you go. Good-bye."

Shang took the Colonel's advice, and a few nights later he and his boys held up a northbound Iron Mountain train out of Texarkana.

From *A Brief History of the St. Louis Southwestern Railway Lines*, by Jacob E. Anderson, reprinted, 1947, from the *Cotton Belt News*. Cited by Richard C. Overton, *The Westerners Brand Book*, Chicago, Illinois, Vol. V (January, 1949), No. 11, p. 63.

The Buried Treasure of the Overland Express

In the black hour that immediately preceded the dawn of October 11, 1894, two masked men halted the Overland Express just two miles outside of Sacramento. At rifle point they forced the engineer and the fireman to detach the locomotive and the express car from the rest of the train and to move it forward. Then the bandits got into the express car and, catching the messenger off guard, bound him hand and foot. They then looted the car at their leisure. The prize was $51,000 in gold. In all the history of train robbery no one had succeeded in capturing so large a haul. Just in terms of weight, the gold was over 200 pounds. It was a troublesome load and so, after getting the gold out of the express car and sending the *Overland* on its way down the Big Hill they wondered what they should do with it. In a brief time it would be known all over Sacramento that the Central Pacific *Overland Express* had been held up and plundered. Posses would be scouring the countryside for the men and, with their heavy load, it would be an easy matter to catch up with them.

So, as the fog and darkness gave way to the dim early morning, the two men dug a deep hole, not far from the point of the hold-up. Into this hole they dropped their loot and quickly covered it with the soft, fresh earth. They marked the spot in their memory, sprang quickly to their horses, and rode away. As they did so, a man crept out of the fog and feverishly began to remove the earth from the hole they had just filled.

If the state of California considered that its reputation for law and order and the protection of property had been violated, how about Wells Fargo whose express lines criss-crossed the entire state? It was the express company that would either have to recover the gold or make up the loss—as it always had. There was, in addition, a matter of reputation. For forty years it had been said throughout the West that there were two institutions dangerous for bad men to tinker with. One was the Federal Government and the other, Wells Fargo. This Sacramento robbery was not the Government's affair but the company's. Moreover, it was the worst of a group of robberies. Within a few months, two of the express company's messengers had been killed in defense of its treasure. This robbery was the last straw.

"It's a job for Jimmie Hume," said [San Francisco Superintendent] John Valentine. "It will be about the biggest job he's ever tackled," he added.

The two men who had held up the train returned to the spot where

---

From *Wells Fargo, Advancing the American Frontier,* by Edward Hungerford, pp. 156–159. Copyright, 1949, by Wells Fargo & Company. New York: Random House.

they had buried the gold. They dug all about the area but didn't find it. When, after repeated attempts to locate the gold, they realized that it was gone, they turned to robbery again. So, a few months later, they held up another train, not far from Redding. This was to be a complete job. The first of the bandits, named Browning, tackled the express car while the other, Brady, went into the sleeping cars. The passengers tumbled out of their berths, held up their hands while Brady removed their watches and wallets. One man, whom novelists might describe as "big and upstanding," said that he would die rather than surrender his valuables to the outlaw. He was the sheriff of Tehama County and he had a reputation to maintain. He maintained it, for he died with his boots on, in the aisle of the Pullman sleeper. But the outlaw who killed him paid the price for his crime right there. The rest of the passengers took courage from the sheriff, fell on the murderer, and filled his body with bullets. The other bandit heard the commotion in the sleeping car and quickly rode off into the brake, leaving his booty and dead partner behind.

A telegram was sent to Captain Hume in San Francisco and he hurried up to Redding. He proceeded to the scene of the crime and then he left it and rode off in search of the second bandit. He was gone for three days and, when he returned, it was with Jack Brady's body. He had killed the man when he resisted arrest. But, before he died, Brady had made his confession. He also told Hume that the gold from the *Overland* had disappeared and that he and his partner never got it.

Hume had known this fact all the time. By a slow, laborious painstaking method of piecing together clues, Hume had found the man who had stepped out of the fog as the bandits had gone off. This man was a tramp. His name was John D. Harms who had been born Karl Heerman in Hamburg, Germany. He admitted that he was a hobo who slept under the stars and who measured off railroad miles as his daily exercise. He had set up his tiny pup tent at Sheep Camp just outside Sacramento on the night of the first robbery. Awakening just before dawn, he had been disturbed by men talking beside the railroad embankment near by. Slowly he crept through the bushes and watched while Brady and Browning buried their gold. In their haste they made a bad job of it and, after they rode off, Harms came over and finished it for them. He made a very good job of it and later he came back and took the gold bars for himself.

There were several things that Harms might have done instead. He *might* have reported the discovery of the gold to Wells Fargo and collected a large reward for his honesty. He might have forgotten what he saw and headed along down the tracks. But dazzled by the size of the haul, he took it and placed part of it in a bank. Then he purchased a fine, new outfit for himself, including three mustache curlers. After that he rode to New York in style and blew in $11,000 on wine, song, and a voluptuous blonde from the Tenderloin. When his money was gone he returned to San Francisco and there Wells Fargo finally caught up with him. He was tried but, in the eyes of California justice of that day, his offense was not too bad and he was sentenced to only three years in Folsom Penitentiary.

This case marked the practical end of train robbery in California. The empire of the Pacific had grown up. The Golden Gate had law and order. San Francisco wore spats and it took afternoon tea.

Canada Bill and Three-Card Monte

The king of all monte throwers was known as "Canada Bill." Where he came from or who he was, no one ever knew. He had no bad habits, never indulged in profanity or vulgarity. He possessed what is known as a poker face; there was no change of expression in his countenance, either in success or defeat. He was liberal to a fault, gave lavishly from his winnings to those in need, and prided himself in the philosophy that money had no value unless it was kept in active circulation. This was fully demonstrated, for in dealing his final game, he was penniless, and the sporting fraternity provided the necessary funds for his burial somewhere in Pennsylvania.

Bill posed as a Texas cattle man, and was either born with or acquired a Southern dialect which added a peculiar zest to his quaint expressions.

The laws in effect in those days west of the Mississippi applying to games of chance were not overly severe. . . . For a long period the officials of the Union Pacific Railroad were embarrassed by complaints from their patrons, which called for positive instructions to prohibit passengers from being buncoed, even if necessary to tender the gamester his fare and eject him from the train. This occurred a number of times, but never before sufficient time was allowed to separate the tenderfoot from his surplus funds. After this was done, the order would become immediately effective. Bill would put up a bluff in the form of a protest, then leave the train and hire a native to drive him to Omaha, where the "con" would casually meet him, and the proceeds would be divided on a fair and equitable basis.

On one occasion, coming from Grand Island, Bill capped a game with a party of over-sanguine San Francisco mining men, who failed to turn up the eagle bird, and quit losers by $3,300 in the coin of

---

From "Tales from Old-Timers, No. 18," by W. H. Hurlburt, *Union Pacific Magazine,* Vol. 3 (December, 1924), No. 12, pp. 12–13. Omaha, Nebraska.

Cf. Allen Pinkerton's account of Canada Bill in *Criminal Reminiscences and Detective Sketches* (New York, 1878), pp. 177–206.

the realm, which at that time brought a premium of sixty cents on the dollar over greenbacks. The losers, realizing that they had been flimflammed, wired Omaha for Bill's arrest upon arrival. This was done, and he was taken before Judge John Porter, who required $100 cash bail for his appearance next morning. On his appearance, the following took place; "Judge, I plead guilty. How much is the fine?" "Ten dollars and costs," which amounted to approximately sixteen dollars. Bill then turned to the Judge and said, "Judge, where does all this money go?" "To the expenses of the city and the maintenance of the schools," the Judge replied. "Do I understand that it goes to educate the children?" "Yes, that is included in the expenses." Quietly peeling off another $100 note, Bill remarked, "Judge, put that with the other money, and let's educate all the children."

On another occasion, going west from Omaha, while a game was in progress in the smoking car, a young man ventured $50 on the turn of the card and lost; then another fifty, then ten, which was all the money he possessed. Walking back to the coach, he returned with his mother, who was in tears. Approaching Bill, she asked if he would not return the money, as it was all they had in the world, and they were on their way to Schuyler to take up a homestead. "My good woman," said Bill, "you have a fine boy, and if you will make him promise before us both that he will never bet another dollar on another man's game, I will give you back the money." The promise was made, and Bill took from his roll three $50 bills and handed them back. The woman said, "I have no change," to which Bill replied, "You don't need any; keep it all, and when you are settled on the homestead, use the surplus to buy a mule."

The Kansas Pacific (now the KP division of the Union Pacific) was also seriously annoyed by monte and confidence operators on their trains. To give protection as far as possible, the officials caused to be installed in each day coach, printed in heavy type, the following:

BEWARE OF THREE-CARD AND CONFIDENCE MEN!

Passing over the line shortly after these signs were prominently displayed, the writer's attention was called to the system adopted by Bill to use the company's precautionary method as a medium for enticing the unwary. His custom was to seat himself in the smoking car, fronting the hanging notice, and in due time begin a long, hearty laugh, with his eyes riveted on the caution sign. After having attracted attention by his mirth, he would say, "Well, I suppose you-all think I'm crazy, but I ain't. Of course you-all can read that sign; everybody can read. I can read myself, and yet that sign was right in front of me, same as now, when one of those fellows done me out of five hundred so slick that I can't help laughing when I see it."

He then explained that the game was played with "three tickets," and that this time, on his trip to Chicago to sell a few cars of steers, he had bought a set of the tickets to have some fun with the cow-punchers when he got back to Texas. Here he would produce the cards and begin explaining how the eagle-bird won and the stars lost, during which time the winning card had one corner crimped silghtly upward. At this point he would suggest that as you would naturally think it easy, suppose you just try it for fun. Someone, always venturesome, and perceiving the crimped card, would turn it to win, then try it again and again, winning each time, until Bill would appear discouraged at his failure to do aught but lose, and would then suggest trying it for ten cents. The result was the same; again and again it was tried, until Bill would pretend to be disgusted at his lack of ability to deftly throw the cards to win. Growing excited, he would offer to wager all the money he had received for his steers or any part of it, that they couldn't do it again. It appeared such a sure thing and the gamester such a chump that there was no reason why he shouldn't be permitted to part with a portion of his capital. So a pool of the available cash would be made up, and one of the number selected to turn up the winning card. The result was a foregone conclusion. The deft fingers of the thrower had transferred the crimp to another card, and the eagle bird and their money had disappeared.

As the trainmen found it inconvenient while attending to their duties, and unprofitable as well, to protect the traveler, detectives were placed in service on the overland trains, who finally compelled the King of the Game to capitulate. Realizing that he was under constant surveillance and further effort was useless, he decided to play his trump card by calling upon the manager and pleading his case from another angle. Presenting himself at the general offices, he was informed by the manager's secretary that the chief was engaged, and possibly he could attend to his requirements. Bill replied that his business was personal, and his time was not valuable, and if permitted, he would wait for an audience. After a brief delay, he was admitted to the manager's office, where he accosted that official as follows: "Are you the manager?" "Yes, sir." "Well, my name is Canada Bill, and I dropped in to make you a business proposition."

The manager was taken by surprise to be confronted by this man whom he had never seen, but whom he had caused to be trailed for months. "May I ask what is the nature of your proposition?" he asked. Said Bill, "I would like to make a contract with your company, I to put up a bond for $10,000, whereby I agree to pay yearly the sum of $10,000 for the privilege of throwing the cards on your trains; and under the terms of the bond, I agree not to throw cards with any passengers except ministers of the gospel."

Naturally, the contract was not executed. . . .

III. RAIL STIFFS

Road Kids

On the sand-bar above the railroad bridge we fell in with a bunch of boys likewise in swimming. Between swims we lay on the bank and talked. They talked differently from the fellows I had been used to herding with. It was a new vernacular. They were road kids, and with every word they uttered the lure of The Road laid hold of me more imperiously.

"When I was down in Alabama," one kid would begin; or, another, "Coming up on the C. & A. from K.C."; whereat, a third kid, "On the C. & A. there ain't no steps to the 'blinds.'" And I would lie silently in the sand and listen. "It was at a little town in Ohio on the Lake Shore and Michigan Southern," a kid would start; and another, "Ever ride the Cannonball on the Wabash?"; and yet another, "Nope, but I've been on the White Mail out of Chicago." "Talk about railroadin' —wait till you hit the Pennsylvania, four tracks, no water tanks, take water on the fly, that's goin' some." "The Northern Pacific's a bad road now." "Salinas is on the 'hog,' the 'bulls' is 'horstile.'" "I got 'pinched' at El Paso, along with Moko Kid." "Talkin' of 'poke-outs,' wait till you hit the French country out of Montreal—not a word of English—you say, 'Mongee, Madame, mongee, no spika da French,' an' rub your stomach an' look hungry, an' she gives you a slice of sow-belly an' a chunk of dry 'punk.'"

And I continued to lie in the sand and listen. These wanderers made my oyster-piracy look like thirty cents. A new world was calling to me in every word that was spoken—a world of rods and gunnels, blind

From *The Road*, by Jack London, pp. 158–159. Copyright, 1907, by International Magazine Company and The Macmillan Company. New York.

baggages and "side-door Pullmans," "bulls" and "shacks," "floppings" and "chewin's," "pinches" and "get-aways," "strong arms" and "bindle-stiffs," "punks," and "profesh." And it all spelled Adventure. Very well; I would tackle this new world. I "lined" myself up alongside those road kids. I was just as strong as any of them, just as quick, just as nervy, and my brain was just as good.

Hoboes and Trains

When occasion demanded it, hoboes [1] used stratagem to flag down a train that otherwise would not stop where the boes waited. The late Jerry Springer, long-time locomotive engineer on the Soo Line, told of such an incident one night in Wisconsin.

"We left Weyerhaeuser on time," he related,[2] "but were held up at Ladysmith a little longer than usual. When we left, I pulled her open to make up for lost time. Just as we passed the station at Tony, the glare of the headlight picked up what looked to me like a railroad tie across the rails ahead. I slowed down, then came to a full stop, and hollered to my fireman to get down and take the tie off the track.

"He jumped off and removed the obstruction. When he got back into the cab, he said to me, 'That wasn't a tie. It was an inch-board the length of a tie and placed on edge across the rails to look thick like a tie.' I gave the matter little thought until we got to Pennington and stopped for water. Then I noticed two hoboes who were riding on the blind. I was sure they hadn't got aboard at Ladysmith, our last stop. The fireman was going to put them off, but I told him to let them ride. Any two boes as smart as they were, I said, were entitled to ride blind the whole division, if they wanted to."

* * * * *

The more reflective hoboes occasionally applied the science of mathematics to their routes of travel, according to A-No. 1, a far-ranging man who bummed his way, apparently, chiefly for the purpose of putting his experiences into print. A-No. 1 was of the opinion that one

From *The Story of American Railroads,* by Stewart H. Holbrook, pp. 390–396. Copyright, 1947, by Crown Publishers. New York.

[1] Tramps are often called hoboes or bums, but although all three are migrants, they are not the same thing. Ben L. Reitman, who tramped a good deal himself, remarked that a hobo works and wanders, a tramp dreams and wanders, and a bum drinks and wanders. Migratory workers, if they apply any of the terms to themselves, are more likely than not to say they are hoboes.—S.H.H., p. 309.

[2] In a letter to his son, George T. Springer of Minneapolis, who permitted its use here.—S.H.H.

of the busiest hobo junctions in the United States was Mattoon, Illinois, where the east-west tracks of the Big Four crossed the north-south line of the Illinois Central. Both main lines were double-tracked to handle the great volume of traffic.

All trains stopped at Mattoon for varying lengths of time. Other than the Lake Shore Division of the New York Central, the Chicago-St. Louis route of the Chicago & Alton, and the Chicago-Kansas City route of the Santa Fe, no other carrier in the country was so plagued with hoboes, says A-No. 1, as the two systems crossing at Mattoon.

The boys had the percentages all figured out. The chances of a bo being arrested for trespass on the Big Four stood at something like 107 to 1, in the bo's favor. This ratio was arrived at by multiplying 535, the mileage between Cleveland and St. Louis, by 2, the track count on this double-tracked line, and again by 20, the average run of daily trains, then dividing 21,400, the product obtained, by 200, a number representing the actual track mileage patrolled by each agent in the road's police department, each agent being assigned to guard 100 miles of the line.

The Illinois Central of the time, it seems, presented an even better break. You multiplied 363 (Chicago to Cairo mileage) by 2, again by 35, and divided the product of 25,410 by 100, giving the bo the better of the deal by 254 to 1. It is amusing to think of those genuine bums, dodgers of work, scorners of education, sitting around some jungle fire while the mulligan stewed, applying the science of numbers to their daily occupation of getting from where they were to somewhere else, free of charge.

This A-No. 1 tramp seems to have got around a good deal. During the first decade and a half of the present century, a common sign seen on western railroad underpasses and bridges, on warehouses and even depots, was A-No. 1, painted in huge letters, sometimes in red. Whether these moniker marks were left by the A-No. 1 who wrote the paperbacks published in Erie, Pennsylvania, or whether a number of hoboes were using the same moniker, as in the case of "T-Bone Slim" of the Wobblies, isn't to be known. The literary A-No. 1 claimed to have traveled "500,000 miles for $7.61," and turned out at least an even dozen of atrociously written and printed books which were sold through the American News Company. He seems to have done for tramps what Thomas L. Jackson did for drummers—I mean the Jackson of "On a Slow Train through Arkansas" celebrity.

From around 1906 until 1923, men riding freights in the West found it advisable to carry a Little Red Card, showing membership in the Industrial Workers of the World. Somehow a red card came in time to be the badge of the honest if migratory worker, and trainmen were prone to be easy on such men, even to letting them ride free of charge. So, naturally, even the lowest of the bums tried to get and carry a Wobbly card.

The 60,000 tramps estimated by Flynt in the Nineties grew after the turn of the century to probably fifteen times that number. In 1921, for instance, 20,643 "undesirable persons" were removed during the one month of October from "trains and property" of one company, the Southern Pacific, according to Dan O'Connell, chief special agent for that carrier. In times of depression more than a million men were probably moving somewhere in the United States by other than orthodox tickets on railroads. Various hobo organizations flourished, then faded, and here and there a man like Jeff Davis—said to be moving still, in 1946, though feebly—set himself up as King of the Hoboes and made an occupation of being king.

By the turn of the century the chief job of railroad detectives or police was to keep tramps off the trains and away from the railroad yards. Civil police were not greatly interested in how a migrant traveled. In fact, more often than not they arrested a tramp only to tell him he must "leave town on the next train." So the railroad bulls came into being. Their job was not simply to make arrests but primarily to keep to a minimum the number of men trespassing on company property, trains, or land. Hence railroad bulls endeavored to put fear into the hearts of all migrants who rode rods, blinds, bumpers, and decks. They accomplished this in various ways, by tossing tramps off moving trains, by shooting at and sometimes hitting them, by beating them up with fists or saps.

* * * * *

Although no one knows how many men are riding about the country on freights, or in blind baggage, at any one time, it is not difficult to know in a general way the rise and fall of the population of hoboes, tramps, and bums. Their number probably slowly decreased throughout the 1920s; then, after about 1930, it increased quickly and enormously, and this time to the number of males were added many thousands of girls and women. Before the 1930s were out, however, the number of railroad tramps had unquestionably fallen, and meanwhile the number of auto tramps had increased and they were being discussed in serious study and fiction as the new American problem. The railroad had helped to create the Weary Willie; the automobile was creating the Okie and Arkie. Then came the busy war years, when few men or women rode freights. Not until 1946 did the number of freight riders increase appreciably.[3]

---

[3] According to Special Agent G. H. Hobbs, Omaha railroad detective, "'riding the rods' has become a lost art and the hobo is the real 'vanishing American.' . . . He says that only about one man a day is booted off trains in the 500 miles of track in his area. And Agent Hobbs can remember when, a couple of decades ago, there were as many as 5,000 to 6,000 a month."—Harold Helfer, in "Short Ties," *Railway Progress,* Vol. III (May, 1953), No. 3, p. 45.

Transient Trackmen

The men who ride the freights are a class without which North America couldn't have been built to its present greatness. They shipped out from their homes for extra gangs—lumber camps and road work; they settled the sparse and scattered communities. Yet these men were victims of so much graft that some became permanent wanderers.

Most authors paint these men who ride "boxcar Pullman" as ne'er-do-wells and bums. Many of them, however, became unsettled mainly because of the rackets to which they were subjected. There was the shakedown from collectors of easy money; then too there was the question of employment. For extra gangs used to have three complete crews: the first working, the second coming, and the third going. The foreman on the job and the employment shark in town saw to it there were always three. You paid the town shark a fee for the job, you shipped out, and you were allowed to work—but only for a short time. Soon you were fired to make room for the new crew. The foreman and the employment agent split the fees.

Other jobs were located in barren country where you saw nothing but sand and sagebrush and drank alkali water for months at a time. Or you might be exposed to highjackers who operated in the wheat belts at harvest time, preying on the hands who had accumulated stakes. Minot, North Dakota, and other belt cities, the Great Northern hump out of Whitefish, Montana, and the Blue Mountain hump on the Union Pacific between Pendleton and La Grande, Oregon, were favorite spots of these men. They would board trains at division points with the gang of transients, and when the train dragged on the grade they did their work. The UP between Pocatello, Idaho, and Butte, Montana, was so full of highjackers that it was called the "Silver Dollar Route."

The migrating worker faced unsanitary camps or barracks. Some roads in the West required you to carry your own blankets, while others supplied them for a fee. These blankets were used over and over again without laundering or fumigating. I once got a job in Schodack Landing, New York, as brakeman on a work train of the Walsh Construction Company during the building of the Castleton Cutoff near Albany. Finding myself assigned to a lousy bunk, I proceeded to clean it up. Two days later, after I'd freed it of livestock, I was fired for running two cars through a derail due to a sleepy switchtender.

From "On the Spot," *Railroad Magazine*, Vol. 37 (January, 1945), No. 2, pp. 103–104.

Reminiscences of Elmer Graff, Madison, Illinois.

Frisco, the Tramp Royal

When I knew him, Frisco was twenty-five years old and had been on and off the Road since he was ten. His father was an Irish sea-captain named O'Hearn, his mother a dissolute Indian woman who had deserted him after his father had been stabbed to death in a drunken fight. He was nine years old at that time. Then an old worn-out prostitute adopted him and led him around the streets of San Francisco to help her beg. He ran away from her after a time and started traveling around through the West.

"Slim," he said to me once, "I started bummin' before I was dry behind the ears yet. Used to hide under seats in the day-coaches, and old ladies would cover me up with their skirts and feed me when the con wasn't around, and I'd tell them blubber stories to get money out of 'em. I traveled over most ever' State in the Union before I was sixteen. Out West I was a punk, or beggin' kid, for a guy name o' Seattle Tom. He had only one eye, and, believe me, he took damned good care o' that. I never could slip anything over on him. He used to beat the tar out o' me if I didn't bring him good lumps. So I couldn't steal much out of 'em. I got what he left. Finally I run away from him. So you see I'm what they call an ex-Proossian.[1] Seattle Tom learned me a lot about the Road, though, and he learned me to read and write. He was rotten cruel, but did somethin' for me, after all.

* * * * *

"Four years ago, I got a crazy notion I wanted to go to college. But, Jeeze, think what I was a-buckin'. High school trainin' had to come first. I got me a job herdin' sheep one summer. It was lonesome as hell. Stuck it out two months. Saw nobody; heard nobody. Only sheep. Baa, baa, baa, all day and night. Then I got to baain' myself, tryin' to hold a conversation with 'em. That scairt me I was goin' nuts; so I quit and went to Los, where I got knocked on the head and rolled for every nickel I had.

"Last time I tried a long-stake job, I shipped gandy-dancer with a railroad construction outfit. Shovel stiff, y' know. Guineas! The bunk-car stunk. Oh, *boy!* And shirt-rabbits in the blankets. Say! They made themselves right at home on your hide, no mistake. They scoffed off o' me till I was so damned thin I coulda turned a handspring in a flute. Every mornin' I'd turn out and take muh shot of black cawfee, and choke down rye bread greased with sowbelly. Sowbelly with the buttons on too! Then I'd mosey out and say 'Good morning' to the

---

---

[1] Ex-prushun or ex-punk. See "The Rating of the Tramps," below.

pick, and 'Howdy' to the shovel and hop to it. I lasted a month; then I got greased for bustin' the foreman. Big husk, but yella as a duck's foot. He kicked me one day, and I crawls him. When they pulled me off muh meat, I had 'im bloody as a hawg. Course then I had to get muh time and beat it. When I got back to Los, the bright lights looked so good after that hard life with the gandies, I got drunker than a fiddler's bitch, and blowed all my jack. Two days later I was headed for Chi in a battery-box of the Golden State Limited."

. . . Without some account of riding battery-boxes, no book on the Road would be complete. Frisco, as I have already mentioned, had a weakness for crack trains; and when he wanted to make a long jump he rode in a battery-box.

The battery-boxes are those oblong wooden boxes which hang beneath passenger-coaches midway of the car-length and just over the rails. Such boxes usually carry storage-batteries which furnish power for the lighting system of the train; but occasionally a box contains no battery, and then a tramp may stow himself away in it and sometimes hold the train down for hundreds of miles.

But the trick of hiding oneself without assistance in one of these empty boxes is not so simple as it might at first seem. If you examine a battery-box as you pace along the depot platform, you may observe that the door is flush with the side of the car and that it opens outward and downward. It is secured by a hasp on the outside, and when you open the door it swings down on its hinges so that its lower edge almost scrapes the ties outside the rail.

Now, the tramp who crawls into the box, unless he has a confederate to lock him in, must make shift from the inside to pull shut the flapping door, and somehow to keep it shut until he reaches his destination. If he is possessed of Frisco's resourcefulness, he provides himself with a piece of pliable wire and a screw-eye. He fastens one end of the wire in the outer staple of the door through which the hasp slips, and yanks the door shut with the free end of the wire. Next he inserts his screw-eye, often an awkward and laborious process, into the upper beam of the box just above the crack formed by the top edge of the door and the sill. Then he secures the wire, which moves freely through the crack, to the screw-eye. The hobo is all set now. If he has supplied himself with plenty of poke-outs and a bottle of water, he has an excellent chance of holding down the train as far as it goes.

That afternoon as Frisco and I sat in the spool-car on our way south from Portland he told me of that first battery-box trip of his from Chicago to California over the Santa Fe.

"Some trip that was. I'll never forget it. I had a lot o' trouble gettin' in the box without somebody seein' me, and I went down to the yards hours before the train pulled out too. I had a bunch o' sandwiches on me, and a bottle o' water with a little sugar in it. I just laid quiet till the train clicked out of Chi. Three days I was in there. The grub and the water lasted me two days, so I had to go hungry the rest of the time. I don't mind that so much, but the cramps in my back tortured me till I nearly went bughouse. You know, you're doubled up like a jack-knife and ain't got room to stretch."

"I suppose you couldn't read in there?"

"Read? Hell! Do you think I had a study-lamp or somethin' in there? I had a deck of cards with me, and once I tried to play solitaire; but the dust was too thick and the dark strained my eyes. Nothin' to do but sleep and think. I had no idea of time or where I was. I knew when it was daylight and when it was dark; that's all. After I had been there a week, it seemed, it got infernal cold in the night, and I figured I was crossin' the mountains somewheres in Arizona or New Mexico. I shivered till I thought I'd shake myself to pieces. Then suddenly, *z-z-z-z-z-z-z-zt-zt!* the damned screw-eye flew out, with my wire wrapped in it. The door flopped open, and the wind came at me ice-cold and yelpin' like a pack o' dogs. The limited was hittin' her up fifty miles an hour anyway. The door slammed up and down, and I thought every second she'd strike a high tie, and rip the ol' battery-box, with me in, right out from under the car and send us a-smashin' to hell. Holy Smokes! I was scairt. Then the train hit a curve so fast I had to fight like a whitehead to keep her from pitchin' me out. I was paddlin' and clawin' with both hands and feet, like a damned mouse on a tread-wheel. She straightened purty soon, and I was all right. Then I pokes my head out a little ways, and the wind almost blinded me while I was grabbin' for that jumpin' wire. Before I knew it though, *zowy!* the door flew up and caught me right on the bean. Knocked me silly. By and by the door flew shut with an awful wham. I was in a daze, but I managed to get my hooks on that wire before she blew open again. And I swung on to her most of the night just like a guy that's tryin' to hold a bull calf that's rippin' and rarin' and lungin'. My head ached fierce, and a bump crowned the top of her the size of a half a grapefruit. When the train slowed down at a town I got the screw back in place, but I was nervous as hell and couldn't sleep all the rest of the trip."

"And you made Los all right?"

"Sure! Crawled out humpbacked, though. My ol' spine had sprung a reverse curve, like a croquet wicket. It took me a week to spring her back in place, and she was sore. Six months later I went through the whole thing again on the return trip to Chi. I had a guy lock me in the box from the outside that time, and when I got to Chi I hammered like hell with my fists and a car-knocker let me out. Works all right long as a dick ain't the one to raise the latch. That happened once. On the second trip when I landed in Los, it was a long time 'fore I could make any one hear me. Then a dick came and assisted me p'litely from mv carriage. When we was goin' to the booby-hatch together, I gave him such a spiel that he got interested and turned me loose with his blessing—and a swift kick in the pants."

Frisco paused, ruminated a moment, then continued: "Guess the bull was irritated because I'd talked him out of a pinch. I'm not *quite* sure, but I think that was the hardest kick in the pants I ever got."

Frisco had ridden in every place on a train where a hobo could possibly hang on by the eyelids. When he was younger in years and smaller in bulk he had ridden the steps, the little compartment whose ceiling is the movable floor of passenger-coach vestibules. It exists, of course, only when the doors are closed. You have to hop off whenever the train stops. Frisco was familiar with all the tricks of gunnel or rod riding. A hundred times he had trucked it, or ridden in the trucks between the wheels. He was always prepared for the trucks, and carried in his pocket a piece of wood about ten inches long and grooved down the center. This he clamped on the small lateral rod between the wheels, so that he could perch there with more comfort. This device he called his ducket or ticket.

Then, he had ridden on the tender of the engine, and down in the water-tank, and on the pilot or cow-catcher. He was always surreptitiously examining locomotives, because he had heard a rumor somewhere that there was a place under the boiler of certain types of engines where a tramp could ride without much discomfort or danger. He never discovered it, at least not while I was hoboing with him. I'll bet if he ever found that place, he took a chance on riding there. What a great old train-barnacle he was, that Frisco!

When I asked him once about cow-catchers, he said:

"I rode a cow-catcher just once. Never again, unless I have to. It was out o' Eldorado, Kansas, over the Missouri Pacific. While the engine was in the station, I pipes the engineer comin' out of his cab with a little broom, and I see 'im dust the cow-catcher off nice and clean with it. I thinks to myself: 'Well, ain't that fine? He's dustin' her off for me.' So when his back was turned, I hops on the cow-catcher and crouches under the overhang of the boiler. I got by with it. Nobody saw me, and when the engine snorted out, there was yours truly smilin' like a basket o' chips on the cow-catcher. But I didn't smile long. That engine was a passenger-engine and kicked up an awful wind. Open yer mouth and she'd blow you wrong side out, and so cold she felt like an icicle laid agin your eyeballs."

"Didn't hit anything, did you?"

"Oh, boy! Wait a minute! I'm comin' to that. Well, as I set there slappin' myself, tryin' to keep warm, the headlight sprayed out across the prairie and attracted all the bugs in Kansas. My mouth and eyes and shirt got full of 'em, and them big shiny black bugs hurt too when they hit you between the eyes. The light was so bright I could see big bloaty-hoptoads pantin' along between the rails twenty-five yards ahead. Purty soon a quarter-mile away, at a crossing, I see an old white cow with her calf standin' on the track. The light didn't seem to bother her none. She just stood there munchin' her cud and blinkin' as we bore down on her. The old engine began tootin' like you hear 'em on New Year's eve. I sort o' slid down on the back of my neck, and h'isted my heels up in the air so's bossy would hit them first. Well, just before we reached her, she ambled calmly off the track flickin' her tail—and the calf nosin' her in the flanks as she went. Say, I was so weak for a little while I couldn't sit up. I just laid there on my neck prayin' for strength. Don't never mention cow-catcher to me again. It makes me nervous to talk about it."

Jeff Carr, Hobo-Stalker

. . . Jeff was the notorious hobo-stalker of Cheyenne, Wyoming. I inquired if either of them had ever run afoul of Jeff Carr.

"Well, I should snigger and spit and smile on meself," piped the Runt. The Runt's voice was more like a strangled whistle than a voice, two missing front teeth still further impairing a vocalization which at best was excruciatingly reedy. He instituted himself as spokesman on the subject of Jeff Carr.

"Me and Frost here lit in Cheyenne one mornin'. Kee-reyest! It was cold! A guy couldn't wiggle his eyebrows. Well, we bummed a little slum at a railroad eatin'-house, an' while we was eatin' dis Jeff Carr walks in an' bought hisself a cup of coffee. He didn't say nuttin' to us, but he sure looked us over hard. A big goof he was wid a slouch-down mustash, cowboy hat, coupla guns strapped on 'im—"

"Naw! one gun," interrupted Frosty. The Runt insisted it was two. They argued until the Runt, vanquished by his opponent's superior lung-power, gave in and got his squeak-whistle narrative moving again.

"Well, boy, we rode a blind out o' Cheyenne dat same night, and dey was tree ginks on it wid us; and purty soon a guy comes ridin' up side o' de train like hell splittin' tan-bark on a wite horse. He reaches fer one o' de ginks and yanks him off'n de blind, and den ketches an-udder one by de belt and trows 'im across de horse's neck an' starts shootin'—"

"Dat's de night I lost de pint o' whisky," Frosty boomed in reminiscently. Then, ignoring his companion, he took up the story at this point. "Runt hops off'n de train soon as ole Jeff Carr starts a-shootin' an' catches de second blind on de udder side o' de train, but me like a damn fool scrooches down on a side stirrup to hide, me tail a-bumpin' de ties. Course de bottle o' red-eye slips out o' me pocket. Good night!

Ibid., pp. 286–287.

An' all we had was a little kiss apiece off'n it. An' I had a dirty fight wid a dyno to get dat goods too."

"What became of Jeff Carr?" I interposed, bustling Frosty away from his pet theme. "Is he still in Cheyenne?"

"Naw," growled Frosty with a hint of irritation, "some bums ganged up an' croaked 'im. He follered 'em in a box-car an' one of 'em laid 'im out cold with a couplin-pin. Man! he was sure dead when dey got tru workin' on 'im."

The gory details of Jeff's taking off I had heard before with all sorts of ghastly variations. What the real facts were concerning Jeff Carr's career I do not pretend to say; but from Maine to Texas wherever I had foregathered with hoboes his name had been spoken with dread. He must have been a terrific personage to have cast shuddering ripples to the most remote shores of Hoboland. Sometimes he was represented as dead, sometimes as still alive murdering and maiming every hobo he could lay his hands on, shooting them off decks or rods, fiendishly manhandling them in cells. Among the 'boes he came to be a symbol of cunning and ferocity; even the white horse came to be possessed of demoniac powers. Let us hope that some hobo bard of the future shall do full epic justice to the Jeff Carr cycle of legends.

Nailing a Drag

We crawl on our hands and knees and ease up towards the yards. It is so dark you can hardly see your hand in front of you. We can hear them banging these cars around inside this high board fence that separates us from the yards. We can hear the switch engines chugging as they make up our drags. We do not have long to wait. We hear this drag give the high ball. We ease up as close as we can get without being seen by the bulls. We scrape our knees and our hands on the sharp pebbles in the tracks and stumble over the ties that are higher than the rest. We cuss under our breath. We crawl to the side of the tracks and press up tight against these piles of ties. We are nervous. A stiff is always nervous when he knows he has to nail a drag in the dark. This drag is pulling out. We see this shack on the tops wave his lantern to the engineer. We can hear her puffing as she comes. I cock my ear and listen to the puff. You can judge how fast a drag is coming by listening to the puff. This one is picking up fast. She will be balling the jack when she gets to where we are. I keep one eye peeled for the bulls. If they are riding this drag out, they will be laying for us. I have too many scars already from being sapped up by the bulls.

From *Waiting for Nothing,* by Tom Kromer, pp. 149–154. Copyright, 1935, by Alfred A. Knopf, Inc. New York.

I can see her coming now. I can see the sparks that fly from her stacks, and the flames that leap above her. She is puffing plenty. She is a long drag, and a double header. I can make out the sparks from the two engines. That is why she is balling the jack so much. This is a manifest. She won't lose any time going where she is going. Passenger trains will take a siding and let these red balls through.

This old stiff picks up his bindle, and starts back towards the jungle.

"This one is too hot," he says. "There will be another drag to-morrow. I do not like to sell pencils."

Four or five stiffs follow him. They know when a drag is too hot, too. They do not want to sell pencils either.

I crouch here in the dark and wait. Farther up the track I can see these other stiffs crouching beside the tracks. They are only a shadow through the dark. I hope I can make it, but I am plenty nervous. It is too dark to see the steps on the cars. I will have to feel for them. I pick me out an even place to run in. I look close to see that there are no switches to trip me up. If a guy was to trip over something when he was running after this drag, it would be just too bad. That guy would not have to worry about any more drags.

These engines bellow past us. I can see now that I have waited in the cold for nothing. I can see that a guy can't make this one. It is just too fast. The roar she makes as she crashes over the rails, and the sparks that shoot from her stacks, tell me she is just too fast. A stiff is foolish to even think about nailing this one. Christ, but I hate to wait all night for a drag and then miss it because it is too fast.

This stiff in front of me does not think this drag is too fast.

"Brother," I think, "I hope you are right, because if you are wrong you will not do any more thinking."

I see him run along by this drag. I see him make a dive at this step. He makes it. It swings him hard against the side of the car. I can hear the slam of his hitting from where I am. He does not let go. He hangs on. I see him begin to climb the steps to the tops. Damn, but that was pretty. No waiting all night for a drag and then missing it for this guy. He is an old-timer. I can tell by the way he nailed this drag that he is an old-timer.

Another stiff runs along by this drag. I can tell that he is scared. He reaches out his hand after this step as this drag flies by, and then he jerks it away. This stiff will never make it. I can tell. He has not got the guts. A stiff has got to make up his mind to dive for those steps and then dive. This stiff makes up his mind to take a chance. He reaches out and nails this step. The jerk swings him around and slams him against the car. He hits hard. If he can hold on, he is all right, but he cannot hold on. He lets loose and flies head-first into the ditch at the side of the track. The bottom of that ditch is cinders. Christ, but there's a stiff that's dead or skinned alive. I cannot tell if he is moving in the ditch or not. It is too dark to see. I cannot go over there and see. I have waited all night in the cold to make this drag, and I am going to make it. That first stiff made it. If he can make it, I can make it. I have nailed as many drags as the next stiff.

"Be sure and nail the front end of the car," I tell myself. "Be sure and nail the step on the front end of the car. If you lose your hold, you will land in the ditch like that other stiff. That will be bad enough, but if you nail the rear end and lose your grip, you will land between the cars."

It is just too bad for a guy when he goes between the cars. I saw a stiff once after they pulled him out from under a box car. The stiff did not need to worry about nailing any more red balls at night.

I judge my distance. I start running along this track. I hold my hand up to the side of these cars. They brush my fingers as they fly by. I feel this step hit my fingers, and dive. Christ, but I am lucky. My fingers get hold of it. I grab it as tight as I can. I know what is coming. I slam against the side of the car. I think my arms will be jerked out of their sockets. My ribs feel like they are smashed, they ache so much. I hang on. I made it. I am bruised and sore, but I made it. I climb to the tops. The wind rushes by and cools the sweat on my face. I cannot believe I made this drag, she is high-balling it down the tracks so fast. I am shaking all over. My hands tremble like a leaf. My heart pounds against my ribs. I always get nervous like this when I have nailed a drag at night going as fast as this one is.

I lie up here on the tops in the rush of the wind and wonder about that poor bastard over in the ditch. I wonder if he was killed. I know that these other stiffs who missed the drag will see to him, but I cannot get my mind from him. A stiff like that has no business on the road. That guy should be a mission stiff. He has not got the guts to nail a drag at night. He should stick to the day drags. A stiff can't expect to reach up there and grab hold of those steps. You have to feel them brush your fingers, and then dive for them. If you make it, you are lucky. If you don't make it, well what the hell? What difference does it make if a stiff is dead? A stiff might just as well be dead as on the fritz. But just the same I am glad I am here on the tops and not smashed all to hell underneath those wheels that sing beneath me.

The Hobo and the Brakeman

Hobo always havin' hard time. Ketch it tough no matter which way you go. Brakeman put you off thirty or fohty miles from nowhere. So

From *Rainbow Round My Shoulder,* The Blue Trail of Black Ulysses, by Howard W. Odum, pp. 226–227. Copyright, 1928, by the Bobbs-Merrill Company. Indianapolis.

this time I says ain't no one brakeman can put me off an' I packs gun along with me. I didn't have but 'bout fifty cents, got broke gamblin' with them dam' Texas roustabouts befo' I lef' Galveston. So I would ketch freight an' ride a while on different branch of road, I would stop an' ketch 'nuther train. Then I got on through-freight an' got in empty car 'bout six or seven cars from cab. I rode long time an' thought nobody was goin' to bother with me when front brakeman come along an' say I have to git out an' off. So I says to him:

"Now, white folks, I ain't gonna git down an' out. I'm ridin' jes same as you."

Brakeman begin cussin' an' tellin' me he give me five minutes to git off an' if I ain't off then he gonna throw me out door while train's runnin'. So I looks at him while, an' he looks at me. I see he mean business so I says:

"Well, Mr. Whiteman, s'pose you sit down here with me while. I'm goin' same place as you is, an' we might jes well set together."

So I draw my gun an' makes him set down in front o' me. Eve'ytime whistle blow brakeman say he got to go now, an' I says to him he ain't goin' no dam' place, 'cept where I'm goin', we's passengers together. So I snaps my pistol an' made him set there an' wouldn't even let him git up for nothin'. After while train blowed for big town an' begin slowin' up. So I gits up an' backs off to door holdin' gun on brakeman an' when train stops I slips out an' goes over on other side o' town an' caught 'nuther train. I guess that brakeman still lookin' for me, but wasn't my fault. I was gonna be decent to him, an' he wouldn't have none of it. He can take what he got.

Hobo Hero

No other class of people has more contempt for the tramp than the railroad men. The great railroad companies wage ceaseless war upon him. Yet many times from the ranks of these outcasts a hero has appeared to save a train from destruction and crew and passengers from death.

* * * * *

Modesty seems to be a prevailing characteristic of the tramp hero. . . . Among the tramp heroes of the railroads, "Springfield Mike" Rolland should not be passed by unmentioned. He it was who, on the morning of May 23, 1908, saved a crowded express train on the New Haven Railroad from disaster.

From "Hobo Heroes Who Have Saved Trains," by E. L. Bacon, *The Railroad Man's Magazine,* Vol. VII (November, 1908), No. 2, pp. 198–201. Copyright, 1908, by the Frank A. Munsey Company. New York.

While strolling along the tracks near Dutchman's Curve, in Torrington, Connecticut, he discovered that a foot of rail had either been cut or broken. Almost at the same moment he heard the whistle of an engine. It was the express that was due in Torrington soon after seven o'clock.

Running forward toward the curve, he heard the roar of the train only a short distance off. He pulled out his red bandanna and, as the engine hove in sight, waved it above his head and shouted with all the strength of his lungs.

The engineer stopped the train, and the passengers flocked out on the tracks. Then "Springfield Mike" told of his discovery. A few seconds more and the train would have plunged into the ditch.

Conductor Dailey and the crew and passengers, when they realized how near they had been to death, showered "Mike" with thanks and spoke of rewarding him.

"Reward!" cried "Mike." "Why, I owe the railroad this much. Many's the time I've hit the rods or the blind baggage, and I guess this makes it square."

Million-Dollar Mulligan

In boomer days, an unemployed switchman or brakeman who was broke was not too proud to stop in at a hobo *jungle* (camp) to eat, sleep, wash up, or merely stick around between trains. Such a character was Charles B. Chrysler, an old-timer now living at . . . Los Angeles, California. Looking back through the years, Charley recalls a certain time when he, a dirty, hungry boomer, wandered into a jungle, some distance from the rail center at San Bernardino. We'll let him tell us what happened, in his own words:

"Howzit for camping and cutting in on the mulligan?" says I.

Mulligan, in case you don't know, is hobo stew. It consists of *hoppins* (any and all vegetables that can be bought, begged, borrowed, or stolen), together with meat acquired the same way, or maybe *gumps* (chickens) or other fowl, the whole savory mess cooked outdoors.

My question was answered by the camp bully, a big carrot-topped boomer of philosophical bent, who liked to hear himself talk. They called him "Rhode Island Red."

"The camp belongs to God almighty," says Red, "and if you're all right with Him you're all right with us. There's plenty of timber, straw, moss, water, fire, and plenty of alky [alcoholic liquor]. But mulligan—well, that's something else again. The law of compensation

---

From "On the Spot," *Railroad Magazine,* Vol. 39 (February, 1946), No. 3, pp. 89–92. Copyright, 1946, by Popular Publications, Inc. New York.

says you can't take something out unless you put something in. I didn't make the law—it was made by the camp—I enforce it. You can stay here as long as you like; but if you want to eat, you'll have to hustle some hoppins. Unless you're a Johnnie Newcomer you know this as well as I do."

As I said, the guy liked to chew the rag, so I listened.

"All right, all right," he says. "You're hungry. Well, I'm gonna show you how you can eat. See that tar kettle there? It holds about a barrel of anything you want to put into it. Right now it contains hot water, but to-night I'm taking a detail of men out to fill it. Now, here's the layout. . . ."

Red explained there was a carload of live chickens on a sidetrack by the depot in town. All kinds. Big ones, tall ones, fat ones, Plymouth Rocks, Leghorns—all in crates. A whole express car full. A score of volunteers would sneak out of the jungle at night, go down to the depot, and grab as many of the crates as they could get away with. Some crates had only a pair of chickens in them; others had six or eight. The plan was for each man to pick out a crate containing a large number of chickens.

"If you fail," Red warned, "don't come back to the jungle and expect to eat. If your conscience bothers you, you needn't trail along."

So that night twenty or so unshaven stalwarts disappeared in the darkness toward San Bernardino. A war council was held in the underbrush. Red spoke up again.

"Two of you men go down the track a few blocks, pick up some dry leaves and straw, place them in an empty boxcar, and set them afire. Then return here. When it's smoking good, you, Dutch, run over to the depot and tell the agent there's a boxcar burning down the track. When they leave the station to put out the fire, the rest of us go into action. It's every bozo for himself. Grab a crate, take to the brush, and hike for camp."

There were two men in the station and both of them ran over to the smoking car. The denizens of the hobo camp moved with trained precision. Each grabbed a pen of squawking chickens, four men lugging the big containers, one or two lugging each of the small ones.

The raiders solemnly toted the crates down to the river bank near the jungle and there they held sacrificial rites. Then they dumped the slaughtered fowl back into the crates, took them to the campfire, and scalded them in the tar kettle. One squad neatly picked off the feathers, another degutted and cut up the poultry, a third buried the feathers and refuse. Each job was handled efficiently. After that, all hands went back to the stream and washed up in cold water. Finally, after cleaning the kettle, we plopped the chickens into the great pot. Then we broke up the crates to feed the roaring flames.

By that time the midnight prowling detail had returned with paper bags full of cabbage, potatoes, onions, chili peppers, tomatoes, and parsley. Somebody even brought along a bag of salt. At two in the morning our mulligan started to simmer. By sunrise it was prime. And we were famished! Bowls and spoons mysteriously appeared and we dug in.

The stew lasted us three days. Tramps for miles around heard of the feast and drifted into camp. They tried to wheedle us into sharing with them, but only those who brought along dessert for the gang or other food to vary our diet were permitted to more than sniff the mulligan.

Meanwhile, there was hell to pay at San Bernardino. It seems that a lot of pedigreed chickens had been stolen from an express car. The loss was terrific. Those fowl had been the result of years of scientific breeding and had been exhibited all over California. In fact, at the time of the theft, they had been awaiting shipment to the Los Angeles County Fair at Pomona, where they were expected to win medal cups, blue ribbons, and cash prizes in addition to the long list of awards they already held. These haughty birds were rare breeding stock. But by the time railroad bulls reached our camp there was no trace of them, and most of the men had scattered.

Even to-day, if you chance to visit hobo jungles on the West Coast, you are likely to hear men around campfires tell about the "Million-Dollar Mulligan," as it was called. Many a wandering brother will claim that he was either a night yardmaster at Pocatello or else was "in on" the greatest stew of all time. But Rhode Island Red, "Circus" Doyle, "Fishmouth" Ferguson, and other famous boomers—if they are still living—will tell you there were less than twenty-five men in that raid, and Charley Chrysler was one of them.

The Rating of the Tramps

1. Plinger .... solicited alms at stores, offices and residences.
2. Moocher .... accosted passers-by in the street
3. Flopper .... squatted on sidewalk in business thoroughfares
4. Stiffy .... simulated paralysis
5. Dummy .... pretended to be deaf and dumb
6. Wires .... peddled articles made of stolen telegraph wire

---

From *Mother Delcassee of the Hoboes and Other Stories,* by A-No. 1, The Famous Tramp [Leon Ray Livingston], Written by Himself from Personal Experiences, pp. 43–44. Copyright, 1918, by the A-No. 1 Publishing Company. Erie, Pa.

7. Mush Faker [1]	umbrella mender who learned trade in penal institution
8. Mush Rigger	umbrella mender who learned trade in penal institution
9. Wangy	disguised begging by selling shoe-strings
10. Stickers	disguised begging by selling court plaster
11. Timbers	disguised begging by selling pencils
12. Sticks	train rider who lost a leg
13. Peg	train rider who lost a foot
14. Fingy or Fingers	train rider who lost one or more fingers
15. Blinky	train rider who lost one or both eyes
16. Wingy	train rider who lost one or both arms
17. Mitts	train rider who lost one or both hands
18. Righty	train rider who lost right arm and leg
19. Lefty	train rider who lost left arm and leg
20. Halfy	train rider who lost both legs above knee
21. Straight Crip	actually crippled or otherwise afflicted
22. Phony Crip	self-mutilated or simulating a deformity
23. Pokey Stiff	subsisted on handouts solely
24. Phony Stiff	disposed of fraudulent jewelry
25. Proper Stiff	considered manual toil the acme of disgrace
26. Gink or Gandy Stiff	occasionally labored, a day or two at the most
27. Alkee Stiff	confirmed consumers of alcohol
28. White Line Stiff	confirmed consumers of alcohol
29. Rummy Stiff	deranged intellect by habitual use of raw rum
30. Bindle Stiff	carried bedding
31. Blanket Stiff	carried bedding
32. Chronicker	hoboed with cooking utensils
33. Stew Bum	the dregs of vagrantdom
34. Ding Bat	the dregs of vagrantdom
35. Fuzzy Tail	the dregs of vagrantdom
36. Grease Ball	the dregs of vagrantdom
37. Jungle Buzzard	the dregs of vagrantdom
38. Shine or Dingy	colored vagabond
39. Gay Cat	employed as scout by criminal tramps
40. Dino or Dynamiter	sponged food of fellow-hoboes
41. Yegg	roving desperado

[1] Hoboes term umbrellas "mushrooms." Hence the itinerant umbrella mender came to his odd moniker "mush faker" or "mush rigger."—L.R.L.

42. Gun Moll .... dangerous woman tramp
43. Hay Bag .... female stew bum
44. Jocker .... taught minors to beg and crook
45. Road Kid or Prushun .... boy held in bondage by jocker
46. Punk .... lad discarded by jocker
47. Gonsil .... youth not yet adopted by jocker

Monicas on the Water-Tank

Water-tanks are tramp directories. Not all in idle wantonness do tramps carve their monicas, dates, and courses. Often and often have I met hoboes earnestly inquiring if I had seen anywhere such and such a "stiff" or his monica. And more than once I have been able to give the monica of recent date, the water-tank, and the direction in which he was then bound. And promptly the hobo to whom I gave the information lit out after his pal. I have met hoboes who, in trying to catch a pal, had pursued clear across the continent and back again, and were still going.

"Monicas" [more recently, "monikers"] are the nom-de-rails that hoboes assume or accept when thrust upon them by their fellows. Leary Joe, for instance, was timid, and was so named by his fellows. No self-respecting hobo would select Stew Bum for himself. Very few tramps care to remember their past during which they ignobly worked, so monicas based upon trades are very rare, though I remember having met the following: Moulder Blackey, Painter Red, Chi Plumber, Boiler-maker, Sailor Boy, and Printer Bo. "Chi" (pronounced *shy*), by the way, is the argot for "Chicago."

A favorite device of hoboes is to base their monicas on the localities from which they hail, as: New York Tommy, Pacific Slim, Buffalo Smithy, Canton Tim, Pittsburgh Jack, Syracuse Shine, Troy Mickey, K. C. Bill, and Connecticut Jimmy. Then there was "Slim Jim from Vinegar Hill, who never worked and never will." A "shine" is always a Negro, so called, possibly, from the high lights on his countenance. Texas Shine or Toledo Shine convey both race and nativity.

Among those that incorporated their race, I recollect the following: Frisco Sheeny, New York Irish, Michigan French, English Jack, Cockney Kid, and Milwaukee Dutch. Others seem to take their monicas in part from the color-schemes stamped upon them at birth, such as: Chi Whitey, New Jersey Red, Boston Blackey, Seattle Browney,

---

From *The Road*, by Jack London, pp. 125–128. Copyright, 1907, by International Magazine Company and The Macmillan Company. New York.

See also "Monika Songs," in George Milburn's *The Hobo's Hornbook* (New York, 1930), pp. 25–37.

and Yellow Dick and Yellow Belly—the last a Creole from Mississippi, who, I suspect, had his monica thrust upon him.

Texas Royal, Happy Joe, Bust Connors, Burley Bo, Tornado Blackey, and Touch McCall used more imagination in rechristening themselves. Others, with less fancy, carry the names of their physical peculiarities, such as: Vancouver Slim, Detroit Shorty, Ohio Fatty, Long Jack, Big Jim, Little Joe, New York Blink, Chi Nosey, and Broken-backed Ben.

By themselves come the road-kids, sporting an infinite variety of monicas. For example, the following, whom here and there I have encountered: Buck Kid, Blind Kid, Midget Kid, Holy Kid, Bat Kid, Swift Kid, Cookey Kid, Monkey Kid, Iowa Kid, Corduroy Kid, Orator Kid (who could tell how it happened), and Lippy Kid (who was insolent, depend upon it).

On the water-tank at San Marcial, New Mexico, a dozen years ago, was the following hobo bill of fare:

(1) Main-drag fair.
(2) Bulls not hostile.
(3) Round-house good for kipping.
(4) North-bound trains no good.
(5) Privates no good.
(6) Restaurants good for cooks only.
(7) Railroad House good for night-work only.

Number one conveys the information that begging for money on the main street is fair; number two, that the police will not bother hoboes; number three, that one can sleep in the round-house. Number four, however, is ambiguous. The north-bound trains may be no good to beat, and they may be no good to beg. Number five means that the residents are not good to beggars, and number six means that only hoboes that have been cooks can get grub from the restaurants. Number seven bothers me. I cannot make out whether the Railroad House is a good place for any hobo to beg at night, or whether it is good only for hobo-cooks to beg at night, or whether any hobo, cook or non-cook, can lend a hand at night, helping the cooks of the Railroad House with their dirty work and getting something to eat in payment.

IV. CRACKER-BARREL RAILROADS

A Short Line Is a Country Thing

The definition of a short line is precisely what its name implies, and it is not to be confused with the branch lines of a main-line railroad. It is independently operated with motive power and rolling stock bearing its own name or insigne, even though it may in some cases be owned or controlled through stock ownership by a great railway system. Almost invariably short lines connect and exchange traffic with a main-line railroad and in some cases they are themselves fed and nourished by other connecting short lines. The Southern Railway, traversing as it does a territory more opulent than any other in short lines, connects with no fewer than fifty-seven, all various, like the pickles, all operated independently and in patterns of their individual devising, while the Rock Island and Northern Pacific, operating in regions where feeders are few and far between, connect with but one each, and the Boston and Albany with none! A short-line map of the United States reveals that independence and individuality, so long considered essentially Yankee qualities, in the field of railroading at least, flourish most luxuriously in the Deep South, overflowing in eccentric and florid abundance into Texas, Arkansas, and North Carolina.

But the happy hunting ground of the ultimately sophisticated connoisseur of short-haul railroading is in Colorado, Nevada, and California, where the little roads are fewer and farther apart than in Georgia, Alabama, South Carolina, and Mississippi, but are richer than any others in fragrant souvenirs of the heroic youth of the land.

From *Mixed Train Daily,* A Book of Short-Line Railroads, by Lucius Beebe, pp. 3–4, 241, 243. Copyright, 1947, by E. P. Dutton & Co. Inc. New York.

The historian or minstrel, as the case may be, is warmed by the names of the Smoky Mountain or the Live Oak, Perry and Gulf, and he will shed an unhappy tear for the little Lawndale or other tragic abandonments, but his pulse quickens at the mention of the Virginia and Truckee, the Midland Terminal, the Rio Grande Southern [all now abandoned] or the narrow-gauge division of the Southern Pacific.

* * * * *

. . . In the most general imagining the railroad is a country thing. Its operations are rural and the vistas from the windows of its cars are those of fields and fertile meadows, grazing cattle, tall trees, barns, silos, and homesteads. Within the memory of almost all Americans, the railroads of their youth skirted the streams of boyhood, penetrated delightfully through shady woods, and paused briefly in their going at forgotten crossroads and improbable and isolated spots.

The railroads of later worldly experience may thunder through tall stacked factories, past steel mills and the massed refineries of giant industry, but it was not always so. The first railroads were part of remote landscapes and country backgrounds, and the first train brigades swam gently through the rank grass of meadowlands and under the curving branches of groves of friendly trees. In the distance thunderheads piled up in summer skies and in the evening their headlamps shone yellow and wavering in the gathering darkness. Their bells were a country sound, one with the church bells that are so intimately and dearly involved in the lives and imaginings of country people.

So, to achieve its ultimately proper setting, the short-line railroad must be removed and essentially divorced from the contrivings of industrialization. Its concern must be with agriculture or with the resources of nature even as the dominant traffic of the Durham and Southern is Carolina tobacco, of the Clarendon and Pittsford the quarried marble of Vermont, and of the Bath and Hammondsport the wine grapes of upper New York. The Unadilla Valley lives almost alone by the dairy products of its region, and the Atlantic and East Carolina is known as "The Mullet Line" by reason of the quantities of fish it carries. The East Broad Top is a coal railroad, and without the peanut crop of rural Georgia the Sylvania Central would have scant reason for being. The tally is a long one and would of necessity include the Louisiana and North West, whose freight is almost exclusively lumber, the Frankfort and Cincinnati, whose lifeblood is the bourbon whisky of Kentucky, and the Prescott and Northwestern, which annually hauls out the richest portion of Arkansas' peach crop.

And to all of these in varying degrees is added the traffic in passengers, express, and the government mails.

Thus it is apparent that the archetypal little railroad is predominantly a country concern. It may be the Smoky Mountain or the San Luis Central or the Arcade and Attica or the Moscow, Camden and

San Augustine. Or it may be the Weatherford, Mineral Wells and Northeastern, which deals largely with Crazy Water, a product of Texas mineral spas, or the Sumpter Valley, which carried nothing but the pine of Oregon.

But its right of way will run through cornlands or orchards or past meadows and grazing lands fenced with wooden rails and through grass which in some places will grow so tall as to hide the flashing cross heads in their guides and the radius bars of its locomotives in passing. The smoke of its going will roll richly from the stacks of its engines, uninhibited by fear of operating executives, and there will be the personal touches of the crew visible in the form of stag horns on the headlamp, a braided bell cord or a bronze eagle with wings spread on the top of the smokebox. Its rails will in no way resemble those of main lines, and here and there the ties will have merged themselves with the elemental earth on which they are laid. The whistle posts will have known their most recent coat of paint when Taft was in the White House, its trestles will be of wood and very susceptible to fire, and its passenger coaches will be of at least Edwardian origin, perhaps Victorian, with stained glass in their clerestory windows, open platforms, Pintsch lamps, and wood-burning stoves of the type long since outlawed for interstate commerce.

Here is the Happy Valley Railroad, the legendary short line of Never Never Land which is to railroaders the mythical equivalent of the Big Rock Candy Mountain of hobo dreams. And it is the Happy Valley Railroad of which we sing.

Short Line Eccentricities

The short line is the negation of regimented uniformity and it survives as a triumph of individualism and even eccentricity in a world grown gray from the breath of assembly-line efficiency. Largely, the employees of short lines shun the collectivist infamies as well as the forged and fictional usufructs of unionism; mostly their operations are innocent of the trammeling devices of signaling, dispatching and traffic control of any save the most primitive sort. They run on the basis of a sort of synthesis of whim of their immediate operatives and shippers and passengers without too much hindrance from the fiat idiocies of the I.C.C. and other and allied super-nuisance agencies. And in their rolling stock and motive power may be discerned the ultimate triumph of individuality, of ingenuity combined with caprice and the evolution of character from the circumstance of necessity.

* * * * *

Ibid., pp. 275–276, 286, 302–305, 320.

Short-line operations in themselves offer a fruitful field for the amateur of heterodoxy. There are, for example, the roads which run only at night, such as the Yreka Western in California, the Oregon and Northwestern in southern Oregon, whose handsome black and gold 2-8-2's with tender cabs for the head brakeman will never be photographed in the main line, since their run from Hines to Seneca and back is over before daybreak, and the Trona, a mining road in the most desolate reaches of the Mojave Desert which only ventures out of the ore tipples to meet the Southern Pacific at Searles, California, in the darkest hours of early morning. Most such roads occupy their daylight shifting cars within the premises of mills, lumber yards, mines, smelters and manufactories.

There are the roads, like the Chestnut Ridge in Pennsylvania, the Manistee and Northeastern in northern Michigan and the Trinidad Division of the Colorado and Wyoming, a property of the mighty Colorado Fuel and Iron Company, which possess neither wye nor turntable, with the result that an even fifty percent of their operations are accomplished backward while the other half of the time their engines run pilot first as their builders intended. The Tooele Valley, only passenger-haul short line in Utah, although it might well turn its motive power at either end of its run, always heads its engines east and pushes its passenger coaches ahead of them. The reason is that from Tooele, where its rails run down the main street of the town, to the Anaconda Copper Company's smelter at International five miles away, the grade is a steady two and a half percent. "We run 'em like this," the conductor told us of his three aged wooden coaches, "because if they ever got away on the grade they'd take most of Old Town and New Town with 'em and jump the whole kit 'n' caboodle over the U.P. rails down in the valley."

* * * * *

The foibles and eccentricities of individualism, to which the short lines, even at the advanced date of this survey, are subject, are almost as numerous as their separate entities. There is, for example, the Roscoe, Snyder and Pacific in Texas, which was built less as a common carrier than as a spite railroad or nuisance value to interfere with the Santa Fe by crossing its right of way a maximum number of times instead of paralleling it; there is the Colorado and Wyoming, which operates in three separate and unconnected divisions, the farthest from each other being several hundred miles apart in two states; there is the White Sulphur Springs and Yellowstone Park in Montana, which unaccountably turned up in the estate of John Ringling North, the circus heir; there is the Narragansett Pier Railroad in Rhode Island which operates highway buses with rubber tires combined with flanged wheels and which leaves the rails for the highway when fancy dictates; and there is the East Washington, the old "Chesapeake Beach line," which was originally built by Otto Mears, who was a good deal better known for his Rio Grande Southern in the Colorado San Juan.

Connoisseurs are familiar with the Norwood and St. Lawrence in upper New York State, which is so attached to its single passenger coach that it is never uncoupled from it even during yard operations; with the Kelley's Creek and Northwestern which advertises freight service only but nevertheless carries passengers; with the Wyoming Railway running between Clearmont and Buffalo, Wyoming, whose train crews stop their trains and open gates whenever the right of way crosses the pastures; and with the Apache in Arizona, which makes a practice of starting its trains about an hour ahead of schedule to preclude the possibility of any passenger business whatsoever.

On the Grasse River Railroad in the north woods of New York the authors discovered a stoutly built little Black Maria coach in which the lumber company which controls the road is accustomed to bring back its timber workers from town on Saturday night after the saloons close, first taking the precaution of locking them in. The Hartwell Railroad in Georgia is owned and operated by the proprietor of the local newspaper who contrives to make a good thing out of both, while on several roads, notably the Warren and Oachita Valley in Arkansas, the Huntingdon and Broad Top Mountain in Pennsylvania and the Ferdinand in southern Indiana, there are one-time self-propelled gasoline-motor coaches with their engines removed in service as passenger cars. On the Rockdale, Sandow and Southern Railroad in Texas, passengers who once rode in the caboose when the trains were steam powered now ride in the operating cab of a gas-electric along with the crew, and the same is true of the Stewartstown in Pennsylvania.

Probably no portion of the country is so fertile in the business of trading locomotives as the Pacific coast, from the tall-timber lands of Oregon and Washington as far as the border of Old Mexico. Among the short lines and lumber-dominated railroads of the region there can scarcely be found an engine in service on the road for which it was originally built, and many have changed hands so often that their pedigree is lost in the mists of comparative antiquity.

* * * * *

Some short-line trains have never achieved the final terminal of their last run. Judgment Day will dawn to find them still unreported at Okay Depot crossover and they will spend all eternity half way between nowhere and nowhere, in the ditch or through the weakened trestle, as the case may be. There were savage wrecks in the high ramparts of the Colorado Rockies in the narrow-gauge seventies and eighties from which the debris was never recovered and whose traces in the form of rusted trucks and shattered engine frames are visible to this day.

In June of 1933, Engine No. 8 of the Wiscasset, Waterville and Farmington Railway, a narrow-gauge pike still surviving in Maine, on the down run from Albion broke a rail just below Whitefield and went over the fill for the last time. That afternoon the railroad, which . . . dated [its charter] back to 1854, suspended operations and closed its books forever.

Six miles from Eagle Gorge, Washington, on the Northern Pacific, a fir tree grows through the tender of the last train over the right of way of the Buffellen Lumber and Manufacturing Company which jumped the tracks on the trestle a quarter of a century ago, never to be rerailed. A once-resplendent combine from the New York Central, during the presidency of Chauncy M. Depew, and a few twisted remains of the boiler of a Mason-built engine at Steadman in the Mojave Desert are all that exists today to show where once the Ludlow and Southern Railroad's last train in 1925 burned with the mines it served before its engineer could crack the throttle. The annals of the little railroads are freighted with the records of last runs which were never made.

The Pontchartrain Railroad

The Pontchartrain could rightfully claim to be the first railroad west of the Appalachians, for it was chartered on January 20, 1830, just one week sooner than Kentucky's Lexington & Ohio, the next nearest claimant. When it was dismantled in 1935, it could also claim to be the oldest railroad on the continent still operating under its original name.

New Orleans wanted a shorter outlet to the sea than the hundred-mile, sinuous Mississippi River, and the thought was that through Lake Pontchartrain and its outlet to the Gulf this might be obtained. A railroad connection to the lake shore was necessary, however, and in 1829 the New Orleans Railroad Society, organized for the purpose, promoted it after several meetings. The road was built from downtown New Orleans through a generous, 150-foot right of way directly to the lake shore, 4½ miles distant, where there was no town at all, but on land belonging to one Milne, a village sprang up called Milneburg. Horses were the motive power for a short time, and then a locomotive was purchased.

An assistant general manager in its latter days, a Colonel Morton, declared that the Pontchartrain was "the most unique and correct from an engineering viewpoint ever constructed, since it was entirely free from curves or grades, this being possibly due to the fact that the

---

Compiled from articles in the *L. & N. Employes' Magazine* by Kincaid Herr, October, 1928 and January, 1930, and by C. H. Phares, April, 1932. Louisville: Louisville & Nashville Railroad Co.

Pontchartrain antedates the active practice of railroad civil engineering." Also due to the flat, open terrain through which it ran. You could stand at one terminus on a clear day, and if your eyes were good, you could see the train leaving the other end, 4½ miles away and watch it through its entire course.

Milneburg was on swampy ground, and for years the tender of the railroad's one locomotive was the only water supply the citizens had. It was their custom, on the arrival of a morning train, to flock to the station or along the trestle extending some distance into the lake with buckets, tubs or handy culinary containers, and take home enough water to last until next day—for drinking, of course. For bathing, there was always the lake. No charge was ever made for this service.

As the years passed, a pleasure resort appeared at Milneburg. A hotel was built there and Novelist William M. Thackeray loved its cuisine in 1855. Said he, "At that comfortable inn in Pontchartrain, we had bouillabaisse (a goulash of fish and vegetables, highly seasoned with onion, orange peel, oil and whatever else lying around that was in the chef's way) than which a better never eaten at Marseilles, and not a headache in the morning, upon my word, on the contrary, only awoke with a sweet, refreshing thirst for claret and water."

By that time, the railroad was riding high on prosperity. In 1838 it had four locomotives, and its original capital of $150,000 had been raised to $500,000. In 1855 it was upped to $2,000,000 (the country thereabouts is extremely well watered). The resort, which came to be known as Boudreau Gardens, was a favorite haunt of pleasure-loving New Orleanians. In fact, it became too popular; a class of citizens highly undesirable sometimes made the conductor's job so difficult that he had to be accompanied by a policeman or two on his rounds to enable him to collect his fares. It also became the custom for the first train out to Milneburg in the morning to set a box car on the siding there, into which from time to time during the day, drunk or disorderly persons were tossed by the constabulary to get them out of circulation. This car was attached to the last train into New Orleans at night, where they were transferred—often not without considerable disturbance of the peace—to the parish bastille.

The road was taken under the wing of the Louisville & Nashville, its big connection, in 1880, though still maintaining its corporate existence. It was then at the height of its prosperity, had a 15-cent fare and sometimes ran fifty trains on a summer Sunday. But with the improvement of roads and the coming of the automobile, its traffic steadily declined. At last, just one little engine was left, whose genesis went so far back into antiquity that there were those who swore she had begun with the railroad itself in the 1830s. Could she have been the one offered by William Norris, the Philadelphia locomotive builder in a telegram in the archives, dated Feb. 26, 1848, giving price and terms?—

"Mr. Norris can ship at once a superior engine, $7,000, four, six, eight and twelve months, with interest. Answer by telegraph." Anyhow, known lovingly to at least three or four generations as "Smoky Mary," she was in 1930 making eight round trips on week-days and twelve on Sundays.

At last the end, as far as passenger train operation was concerned, came at 6:25 P.M., March 15, 1932. The *Mobile Press* of March 16 described the occasion thus (quoted in part):

"Amid outbursts of hilarity, intermingled with loud weeping, 'Smoky Mary' passed on to the scrap-heap last night, ending 102 years of service (!) as a locomotive on the nation's second oldest railroad. Three hundred passengers paid the 15-cent fare and made the last trip over the ancient line last night. J. K. Ridgely, president of the Pontchartrain, was among the passengers, and he passed up and down the aisles, shaking hands with old-timers, many of whom wept.

"The line, established in 1830, was dissolved by Federal Court authority on March 4th. Seven times a day Smoky Mary has been making the 4½-mile trip, 20 minutes each way, running backward on the inbound trip because there was no turntable at the other terminus.

"A. R. Smith, vice-president of the Louisville & Nashville Railroad, came from Nashville to make the last run. C. McD. Davis, vice-president of the Atlantic Coast Line, and Charles Barham, vice-president of the Nashville, Chattanooga & St. Louis, were among the passengers.

" 'Smoky Mary' was known to every resident along the route between Milneburg and Pontchartrain Junction. 'She was just like one of the family!' wailed Mrs. F. Roma, 70, who rode the last trip from Milneburg. School children at Milneburg met the train there, spread lilies on the tracks and stood with bowed heads as the last return trip was started. Automobiles lined the full 4½-mile stretch of right-of-way, and the din of horns, fireworks and a huge bonfire saluted the passing.

"For the past 37 years Engineer John Galivan has been in the cab of 'Smoky Mary.' His errands of mercy, with water during the drought of 1924, with doctors for almost every stork in the past quarter-century, had become part of the traditions of Milneburg. Regular time over the run was 20 minutes each way. Once in 1912 Galivan made the run in nine minutes, bringing a dying policeman into New Orleans. Once during the storm of '89, the train was caught in a snowdrift and arrived ten hours late.

"The train served at various times as jail, ambulance and hearse to residents of the settlement. Formerly, all funerals to Hebrew Rest had to go by the train."

The L. & N. operated freight trains irregularly over the track for three years more, finally closing it in 1935. The right of way was made into a boulevard, called, with typical Crescent City floridity, Elysian Fields Avenue.

Decline and Fall of the West River Railroad

It was originally planned in the 1840s as a standard gauge, to cross the Green Mountains to Lake Champlain. The folks up the West River Valley above Brattleboro fought from 1867 to 1876 to get something under way, and finally compromised on a 3-foot gauge, to be called the Brattleboro & Whitehall. After some optimistic and precarious financing, they began grading in 1878, and slowly pushed up alongside the West River through West Dummerston, Newfane, Townshend, West Townshend, Jamaica, and Windhall to South Londonderry, 36 miles from Brattleboro, where they halted—forever, as it afterward appeared. . . .

Its best years were its earlier ones, though even in those years it had begun to lean on the Central Vermont, whose main line passed through Brattleboro; eventually it borrowed $150,000 from the CV and gave a mortgage on its property. . . .

Its biggest days were those of the Brattleboro Valley Fair. The entire West River Valley or as much of it as could get aboard the trains went down to the big town, and all rules were cast aside. Every piece of rolling stock was in use. Before a train pulled out of South Londonderry, all passenger cars were jammed, and passengers down the line sat on crude plank benches in box cars. At that, by the time the train reached Brattleboro, some were sitting on top of the cars, hanging on the sides, bulging out of the doors.

In the evening, those who hoped to have a seat on the ride home were at the Brattleboro depot hours ahead of time, standing in line until the cars were brought to the platform. Once when the crowd was extraordinary even for a Fair day, rain started and there was a stampede for the shelter of the platform roof, far from adequate. One woman fainted. Another drew her hat pin and began jabbing those pushing behind her, who were being pushed themselves. It took the police department to quell the disorder.

Second to the fair was the annual stockholders' meeting, the main feature of which was a free dinner at a Brattleboro hotel. The shares were transferable, and anyone who presented a certificate to a conductor on annual meeting day had a free ride. A share was likewise a dinner ticket, and everybody who could beg one was in the crowd. Many families held five or ten shares or more, so they turned out in full strength, along with their cousins. About 300 shares were privately owned, and few of them were not represented at the dinner. The other 1700 were held by the towns, and by various acts of official legerdemain, these got into numerous hands on that day.

Abridged from *The West River Railroad,* by Victor L. Morse, first appearing serially in the *Brattleboro* (Vt.) *Reformer,* and later in pamphlet form (Brattleboro, 1939).

Every year the Central Vermont turned $400 into the B&W treasury, but nothing else; as often as $2,000 accumulated, a dividend was declared. This, distributed about half a dozen times, was all the stockholders ever got.

Quickly the railroad became a community fixture. It was seldom spoken of as the Brattleboro & Whitehall, or the Central Vermont, or the West River, which finally became its corporate name. Instead, it was "the narrow gauge," which before long was shortened to "the gauge." Even after it was widened to standard gauge, it was still "the gauge"; and gradually the valley it served came to be known by the same name. To this day [1939] a trip up the valley is often called "going up the gauge."

The three original locomotives were wood-burners, and the crew alone had to spend half an hour wooding up; with passengers helping, it could be cut to ten minutes—and passengers were glad enough to save the time. Governor Fuller once joined the other passengers at the woodpile. His beaver hat fell off at every throw, and he gave it to a passenger to hold while he pitched on his share.

Waits were common for the mixed and heavy passenger trains at the foot of the hills on either side of Newfane. Frequently the engine could pull up only half the train at a time. So it would have to put one section on the Newfane siding and go back for the other. One trainman was said to leave the train when the first section got to Newfane, to pay a half hour's court to a widow. At Williamsville the crew also took the time to pass around water from a cold spring. In deer season the crew and sometimes passengers carried rifles in case a buck came into view. Not infrequently the train stopped for a volley, and the railroad carried a lot of venison without bills of lading.

To get the line built at all required severe economy, and the roadbed wasn't made an inch wider than necessary, nor any ledges cut away that could be left. For much of the distance the roadbed was a narrow path cut in the side of ledges, and when the locomotive started swaying, it would bump into projecting rocks. More than once it limped home with some vital part knocked off in this manner. In the course of time the biggest projections were worn off and less trouble was experienced.

Bridges were cheaply built of wood, and soon began to fail under pressure of freshets, until by the turn of the century, every major bridge had been replaced. Most disastrous was the collapse with a mixed train of the bridge across West River near Brattleboro, which took two lives. Some others were destroyed by fire, some carried out by ice and flood. One day in the late Nineties, a train stopped at the end of the West Dummerston bridge when the engineer saw it swaying and trembling under the battering of flood waters. Soon the southbound train reached the other side, and passengers, taking their nerve in their hands, walked across. One was still on the bridge when it began to sink, but he leaped to safety.

In 1896 a serious spring freshet caused two washouts, tore out two trestles, and left a landslide fifteen feet deep on a section of track north of Townshend. A train which left South Londonderry when the flood was at its height got no farther than Wardsboro, and five days later its mail came into Brattleboro on a hand car. Passengers waited in Brattleboro from Monday until Thursday, when a train took them to Townshend, and teams transferred them to another train at Wardsboro.

Blizzards frequently tied up the road. One Saturday evening in March, 1887, three coaches laden with men and women, most of whom had spent the day at a horse show, left Brattleboro. The wood-burner plowed through the snow until it reached West Dummerston, where it stuck. A small hotel could take in only eight women; the rest of the female passengers and all the men did the best they could in the cars, waiting for an engine to come with a snow-plow—for luckily the telegraph line was still working. They were still waiting next morning, and most of them waded through the snow to church services. About noon the engine and plow arrived; with everybody aboard, they surged ahead a little way and stuck again. With crew and passengers shoveling, they labored a little farther—and stuck again. But passengers toiled manfully alongside the crew, and late in the evening they reached Jamaica, a comparative metropolis, where the hotel was large enough to accommodate all the women; the men spent another dismal night in the cars. Shortly before noon on Monday they reached South Londonderry.

Sometimes when a bad storm struck, the engines just remained cosily in the roundhouse. Once a large crowd from various stations was waiting at Brattleboro on a stormy evening when word went out that the train wouldn't leave. It was two days later when they left town, but the Brattleboro hotels were more comfortable than the cars, and the meals were served more regularly. In such cases the railroad company paid the bills and light-hearted passengers made a lark of it. It was once remarked that the only reason Newfane had two hotels was to take care of stranded trains. But in winter it was unfortunate that hotels weren't closer together, for locomotives sometimes went to sleep between towns. One day in March, 1900, a train which left Brattleboro in the morning wasn't heard from after it left Townshend. Another sent to its rescue came on it stuck in a ten-foot drift below Jamaica. Both spent the night there, and on the next day crew and passengers shoveled their way into Jamaica, slept there, and next day reached South Londonderry.

On another occasion three locomotives, two snow-plows, three train crews, and two days were required to convey four passengers from Brattleboro to South Londonderry. The four left on the regular train

Tuesday afternoon. Until midnight it bucked the snow, and finally gave up at Jamaica. A call to Brattleboro for help, and an engine and snow-plow left there at 1:30 A. M., but a few miles up the line the plow ran off the track and wrecked itself. Another engine and plow left the roundhouse and reached the stalled train by midnight. With the four passengers blistering their hands on the shovel-handles, they worked their way to South Londonderry by Thursday noon.

Worst of all was the blizzard of '88, which engulfed two trains for eight days. A mixed train which left South Londonderry on Monday and was snowed in half a mile above Jamaica, didn't reach Brattleboro until Tuesday of the following week. A relief train had left Brattleboro with a snow-plow early on Monday afternoon, and at nightfall had made it to the vicinity of Williamsville. The crew of seven elected to spend the night there. Three of them waded through the snow to a farmhouse half a mile away for food. It took them five hours to get there and back, and they had to dig snow from the door to get in.

Daybreak found the engine almost completely buried. In the whole day it advanced little more than a mile. The toil and endurance of the devoted trainmen are almost beyond belief in the present age. Tuesday night was spent by the crew at a farmhouse, and on Wednesday night they were still near enough to stay at the same house. Thursday night they slept at Newfane, and on Friday they reached the stalled train which had struggled through the snow to Jamaica. The two locomotives got behind the plow for a final push. By this time the two crews, passengers and recruits from near by had augmented the shovelers to thirty. On Saturday the plow went off the track and one engine had to go back to Williamsville for tools. By the time the plow was back on the rails, night had fallen. Late on Sunday, South Londonderry was reached. On Monday the engines were turned around and started for Brattleboro with the mixed train. They tooled along to Williamsville, where the lead engine jumped the track and into a snow-bank, and there they spent most of the night. Early on Tuesday morning the train pulled into Brattleboro—36 miles in eight days, an average of a quarter of a mile per hour.

The crews soon learned which farmhouses were the best eating places. When houses were not convenient, there were usually shipments of eggs in the express car. Some of these were taken over and quickly hard-boiled in steam from the boiler. When boiled eggs palled on the taste, the crew washed off the fire-shovel and fried a few thereon in the fire-box. Finicky passengers learned to follow the crew's example when they grew hungry enough.

By 1895 deterioration of the line was far advanced. Rotten ties let the rails spread until trains went off the track with annoying frequency. The trainmen had long since become skilful in rerailing engines and cars, and always carried tools for the purpose. Rumors of a change to standard gauge increased. By 1898 several wooden bridges had been replaced by iron ones of standard width, and others were promised. The *Brattleboro Reformer* and the *South Londonderry Sifter* continuously lambasted the company and the Central Vermont, which was a sort of stepfather. In 1902 a third rail was laid, increasing the width to standard gauge, but it was a poor makeshift; the ties were so rotten that the third rail wouldn't stay in place, and continually let cars down on the ground, usually laden with granite from a West Dummerston quarry.

The Brattleboro & Whitehall now petitioned for receivership and asked that the Central Vermont lease be set aside, saying that the track was unsafe, the cars and locomotives old and worn out. The CV countered with a petition for foreclosure of the $150,000 mortgage, alleging that the line had never earned the interest on the mortgage, and in fact, had been operating at a loss. For two years the litigation moldered in the courts, while the Brattleboro & Whitehall did the same in the valley. Finally, after long negotiation, the B&W agreed to consent to foreclosure, on condition that the CV broad-gauge and repair the road. The CV handed the company $5,000 to finance the preservation of its corporate structure, then organized the West River Railroad as the nominal owner and promptly put it in debt to the parent company by $75,000 for the track-widening job. The roadbed was cleared and widened, and on Sunday, July 30th, 1905, the track was made standard gauge.

The run of the first broad-gauge train was reminiscent of the opening of the road a quarter-century earlier. A big crowd was at Brattleboro to see it off, and all along the way the populace turned out as for a gala. The road began its new life with three locomotives and an assortment of cars from the CV, which made it a sort of Old Folks' Home for discarded equipment. But the cheaply ballasted track sank frequently under the weight of trains and there were several fatal accidents. The *Reformer* charged that the track let a train down sometimes two or three times on one trip. On one occasion all three of the company's locomotives were on the ground at once. Automobile roads crossed the track frequently, and the motor cars began to be a nuisance. Many a time an engineer had to brake to avoid an auto at a certain crossing above Brattleboro where he needed all possible speed to get over a grade, but sometimes had to back up a mile or two and get a fresh start.

One cold day a passenger car tipped over near West Dummerston and the stoves in each end of it set the car afire. Nine or ten disgruntled passengers scrambled out of the windows and went back to Brattleboro in a box car. One December morning a passenger train's engine broke down; a relief engine known as "the scrap heap" went to its assistance, and it, too, broke down. A third engine managed to win through and brought train and passengers into Brattleboro after thirteen hours.

A blizzard once tied up the line for several days, with trains waiting at each end, knowing that it would be foolhardy to start with the feeble engines to buck the snow. When the storm subsided a bit, a locomotive with a snow-plow in front and a caboose behind left Brattleboro to break out the road. Several miles up the country a brakeman looked out of a caboose window and asked idly, "What's that little house out on the river?" It was the snow-plow, which had left the track and skidded out on the ice, with two men in it. The engine went back for another plow before dragging the stranded one ashore.

Once a deep snow fell, a thaw turned it to slush and then it froze, coating the track with ice. Not a train ran for three weeks.

One night a group of Brattleboro Odd Fellows were rash enough to charter a special train to attend a fraternal festivity at Wardsboro. They didn't start home until 2 A.M., and stalled on Newfane hill, where the sickly locomotive had to take the train apart and draw it up the hill one car at a time. They reached Brattleboro at 5:10 A.M., a "record-breaking run of 23 miles in three hours," jeered the *Reformer*. Shopmen often toiled all night, trying to patch up an engine so that it could take out a train in the morning, and then it might break down on the way. The cars became so leaky that water sloshed around the floor in a rainstorm, and passengers sat with umbrellas raised.

The Central Vermont had become a part of the Grand Trunk system, and some West River parishioner, forgetting that the valley road had been broadened, wrote a poem on it, the first stanza of which was:

We've got a little railroad
  And it isn't very wide.
We put in twenty thousand
  And quite a lot beside.
They took all our money—
  It was something of a chunk;
It is now being run
  By the old Grand Trunk.

On one occasion, all of the mixed train but the engine left the rails near Townshend, and some of the passengers rode into South Londonderry on the cow-catcher. Another day, the engineer of a mixed train was dashing across a bridge, getting up speed to climb a grade on the other side, when, just as it reached the bridge, the one passenger car left the rails and went bouncing along on the ties. The passengers, panicky with visions of going into the river, ran wildly hither and yon, colliding and falling in heaps. An elderly character, who had been slumbering peacefully, awoke and asked, "What station is this?"

"It's an accident!" yelled a wild-eyed brakeman.

"I thought this was the way you always stopped," said the old gentleman.

Leaving the bridge, the passenger car jumped back on the rails, and the engineer was unaware that it had ever been off.

After the widening of the track, the number of trains was increased to three and then to four a day; at least, that many were scheduled, though the last one often didn't arrive until next morning. Then the automobile cut into the business, and by 1920 passenger service had ceased altogether. The great flood of 1927, which carried away long sections of track, was almost a death-blow. Thirteen box cars stranded on bits of track stood there until the next train ran, four years later.

Valley citizens wangled a $200,000 loan from the State and put the road in repair again. Then a man named Ashley, with an ambition to be a railroad magnate, took a 25-year lease on it, and with a rail bus and decrepit locomotive, proceeded to lose his life's savings. The staff was finally reduced to himself and his wife, she operating the engine and he throwing the switches. In 1936–38, the road was dismantled, and the State managed to salvage $30,000 of its loan.

At the Sign of the Moosehead

. . . For the last twenty years, the life of Belfast has depended on the Belfast & Moosehead Lake Railroad [one of the few municipally owned railroads in the country]. Twice a day it highballs across thirty-three miles of Maine hills from Belfast, quiet and snug on Penobscot Bay, to Burnham Junction, where it connects with the Maine Central Railroad and the outside world.

If you're going to Belfast, you get the B&ML passenger special at Burnham Junction. You clamber off Maine Central's streamlined coaches and walk a few yards to where the B&ML train waits—a puffing, 50-year-old freight engine with six white drive wheels, a mail car, and a wooden, old-fashioned, open-vestibule passenger coach painted a rich brown and trimmed in black. The fresh paint and white tires of the engine give the little train a certain impudent gaiety as it stands across from the long, all-steel, modernized Maine Central train.

Inside its wooden coach, this gaiety reaches thumbed-nose proportions. The color scheme would shame the most modern of roads; its walls and ceilings are a yellowish cream, the seats a bright blue plush, and the brown-painted floor is spotlessly clean. In one corner sits an old-fashioned, egg-shaped coal stove, glorified by a coat of aluminum paint and trimmed in black.

It was at Burnham Junction that you first saw Conductor Pat Shaw [now retired], a jovial, roly-poly man of fifty-odd years who obviously has been railroading all his life. He was the head man of the B&ML passenger and freight crews. He also helped make the Belfast & Moose-

From "Cracker-Barrel Railroaders," by Harry Henderson and Sam Shaw, *Colliers*, Vol. 115 (January 13, 1945), No. 2, pp. 16, 66. Copyright, 1945, by the Crowell-Collier Publishing Company. New York.

head Lake different. He knew nearly all his passengers, tousled the heads of small boys, kidded with regular customers. No woman got on the train carrying her bags while Pat was around, and he was a sort of unofficial welcomer for Belfast to strangers.

On that cold 5:30 A.M. trip, he was apt to brew a pot of coffee on the coal stove and serve it. He would stop the train to let a mother and her kids off near their house and sometimes, in hunting season, he would make a special stop to give hunters a lift or let them off at a point where he had seen deer.

Until recently Pat wore a freight brakeman's work cap on both his daily runs. Then a retiring Maine Central conductor gave him a regulation conductor's cap. The B&ML came through with a resplendent brassplate reading: "Conductor, Belfast & Moosehead Lake R.R." . . . He wore his brakeman's cap on the morning freight and his conductor's cap on the passenger train.

Life on the Belfast & Moosehead Lake, Pat says, is never dull because the "country's too wild for it." Once a moose got on the tracks ahead of the train and wouldn't get off. The engineer blew his whistle, made his engine snort and bellow white clouds of steam. All the moose did was break into a lope and run a couple of miles down the track just ahead of the engine. Finally he came to a clearing and stepped out of the way.

The toughest experience Pat remembers was the time seven freight cars were derailed on a bridge near Burnham Junction. Luckily, they all remained upright. Lacking the wrecking equipment the big railroads have, the Belfast & Moosehead Lake solved the problem with the same ingenuity that has made the road a paying proposition.

"What we did was simple," Pat says. "We simply jacked up one car at a time and laid track under it. When we got all the track laid, we put in a switch, and then just switched her back on the regular track. It took us over twenty-four hours, though, and no one got any sleep."

Old Peppersass

Bretton Woods, N. H., July 20.—"Old Peppersass," famous mountain-climbing locomotive, plunged off a trestle far up the side of Mount Washington and blew up [1] this evening as it was descending the cog railroad of the mountain at the end of ceremonies rededicating it as an historic relic. One man, Daniel Rossiter, a photographer, was killed, three others in the engine cab were injured, and the lives of

---

Abridged from dispatch in the New York *Times,* July 21, 1929.

[1] It did not explode. A small cloud of steam arising from a broken pipe as it rolled over gave this erroneous impression.

half a dozen State Governors and other persons of prominence who were in trains following Old Peppersass down the mountain were imperiled.

Old Peppersass, one of the famous locomotives of American railroad history, was especially built in 1869 to climb Mount Washington from the base here. It attracted wide attention as "the locomotive that built its own track," for the cog road over which it ran was built just ahead of it as it pushed its way up the mountain. It burned wood in its vertically hung boiler and spouted smoke from a mushroom stack. It derived its nickname from a remark made by an acquaintance to Sylvester Marsh, its designer and builder of the railway, who, on his first view of the "contraption," said, "Looks like a peppersass bottle, don't she, Sylvester?"

Three Presidents—Grant, Hayes and Cleveland—were drawn to the summit of the mountain by the old engine, besides such other notables as Oliver Wendell Holmes, James Russell Lowell, John G. Whittier and Harriet Beecher Stowe. It was withdrawn in 1893 to make way for newer locomotives, and was taken to Chicago to be exhibited at the World's Columbian Exposition, and then at the Field Museum. Later it was acquired by the Baltimore & Ohio Railroad. Today's ceremony marked the presentation of Old Peppersass by the B. & O. to the Boston & Maine Railroad, which in turn presented it to the State of New Hampshire. Then the venerable locomotive was to be placed on a pedestal alongside the station at the foot of the mountain.

A notable gathering was here for the ceremony. It included Governors Bibb Graves of Alabama, John Hamill of Iowa, Theodore Christiansen of Minnesota, Henry C. Caulfield of Wisconsin, George H. Dern of Utah, John E. Weeks of Vermont and W. G. Conley of West Virginia. Senator George H. Moses of New Hampshire was one of his State's delegation. Many of the prominent participants in the rededication had come during the day from Boston in a special train and were to have returned on it to-night.

Former Governor J. J. Cornwell of West Virginia, general counsel of the Baltimore & Ohio, made the presentation speech for his road, and George Hannauer, President of the Boston & Maine, accepted Old Peppersass in behalf of his road. He in turn presented the locomotive to Governor Tobey of New Hampshire.

The presentation being completed, it remained for the old engine, repainted in the design it had worn on its service so many years ago, to climb its old track on one last symbolical journey before going into permanent retirement on its pedestal. Six trains carrying the Governors and other distinguished guests and the crowd of general spectators ascended the mountain to the Summit House. Old Peppersass, with its veteran engineer, E. C. "Jack" Frost come out of retirement to pilot it, and fireman W. J. Newsham, both of Concord, followed.

The engine had been reconditioned and thoroughly tested, both in the shop and on the mountain.

At the summit, Old Peppersass paused a while, then began its descent, with Photographer Rossiter and Winston Pote in the cab with the crew. Five miles up the mountain side and not far from the top, the line crosses a great gully known as Jacob's Ladder on a trestle 75 feet above the rugged rocks below. As the locomotive reached the trestle, something went wrong—a wheel broke, it was reported here—and Old Peppersass left the rails and plowed over the ties. Frost tried to check it but saw that it was out of control. He and Newsham called a warning and jumped from the cab to rocks alongside the track. Pote jumped, too, and struck on his face, breaking his jaw. Rossiter delayed to get his camera, and when he jumped the engine was out over the gully. He fell into the gorge and was killed.

With no one aboard it, Old Peppersass rumbled along the ties a half mile, then broke across the rails and shot out into space. . . .

Meanwhile, the trains had left the mountain top to follow it. The first train, carrying many of the most distinguished guests, had gotten 200 yards out on the trestle before the crew saw the ties which had been torn and split by the old engine. It was brought to a stop within fifty feet of the point where the damage to the track would in all probability have derailed it. The trains were sent back to the mountain top, and automobiles were sent from the bottom of the mountain to bring down the distinguished guests and spectators. It was cold on the mountain top, yet many, including several women, walked the five miles back to Bretton Woods.[2]

"Tweetsie" and Her People

On a May evening in 1932, young and broke, I parked on the crest of the Blue Ridge to watch the sunset. . . . A sheep bell tinkled a thousand feet below. Smoke curled from an invisible cabin under the lean of Grandfather Mountain. A shotgun echoed against rocks a long way off, and then from an unexpected direction I heard a high, thin whistle, almost too childlike for a train, and with it the distant breathing of an engine climbing a hill.

* * * * *

---

[2] Old Peppersass, almost a ruin, was picked up from the mountain side, rehabilitated and put on her pedestal, after all.

From *Slow Train to Yesterday,* A Last Glance at the Local, by Archie Robertson, pp. 65-88. Copyright, 1945, by Archie Robertson. Boston: Houghton Mifflin Company.

[I] walked down the hill to the freight yards at the back of the Appalachian Teachers' College. In the dark, panting from her run up the mountain, stood the shortest, slimmest train I had ever seen. On the three-foot track was a single car carved in four slices: United States Mail, express, and passengers, white and colored. It was coupled to a ten-wheel steam engine with a slender smokestack and a flaring cow-catcher. In the glow from the fire-box green paint shone on the lettering, "East Tennessee & Western North Carolina R.R." The driving-wheels were painted red, as in a Currier & Ives print. I fingered a wheel-spoke lightly; it was clean as a wedding present.

* * * * *

At Banner Elk that winter I handled publicity, took long walks, and taught Sociology. . . .

The faculty planned an excursion on the evening train to Boone. The girls packed a box-supper, and we set forth across the bottomless winter mud to Linville Gap. When we asked a woodcutter when the train was due, he squinted at the heavens.

" 'Bout the time the shadow hits the near peak of Grandfather," he said. "Hit's nigh due now."

In Tweetsie's small passenger compartment, filled with warm comfort, we turned the seats and began our deviled eggs as the conductor called for fares. When he told me the amount, I counted my change and followed him to the rocking open platform. Three and a half cents a mile, I said, seemed a bit steep when all other roads in the South charged a cent and a half.

"You know," said the captain, "hit *is* too much. I've always thought so. The company sets 'em high on purpose so folks'll ride their buses. You just give me what you've got there and I'll punch your tickets from Shulls Mills, instead."

* * * * *

The narrow-gauge served principally a few hamlets and isolated cabins not reached by the highways, yet it was held in considerable esteem by the mountain people far and wide. It was a reminder of the days when men first came seeking the timber on the hillsides and the ore in the mines, before the first farm family from the Blue Ridge went begging for work in the orchards of California.

None of them could tell you in so many words what the railroad meant to them. To do the job properly took pictures or poetry. On a lazy spring day we would walk out to see old Mrs. Judkins, near Linville Gap, who painted free-hand water-colors. In Mrs. Judkins's pictures, Tweetsie, with no sense of gravity or perspective, leaped over the top of Grandfather Mountain, or puffed on a siding, her windows filled with happy children waving. I asked her why she always chose the same subject.

"I dunno, unless it's the onliest train there is around here."

They had a poet, too. Anywhere in the Grandfather Mountain country if you saw a little old man with a fringe of gray hair around his bald head and the smooth bland face of a child, you stopped to visit with Shepherd Monroe Dugger, author of *The Balsam Groves of the Grandfather Mountain,* [including]:

* * * * *

THE COMING OF THE IRON HORSE

Yes, the iron horse is coming, and that's good news.
It will cure hard times and drive away the blues.
Awake from your slumbers, ye good mountaineers,
You'll hear the mighty whistle in two or three years.
Ring the bells of welcome, let your cheers go round,
Our wealth will come forth, our wealth is in the ground. . . .
And joy will kindle in the good farmer's eye
When he can buy so cheap and can sell so high,
His cabbage, potatoes, his turnips and fruits,
His bacon, beef, butter and milk from his brutes. . . .
And everything he buys from a railroad store
Will come much lower than it came before;
His clothing and coffee, his sugar and flour,
Will all testify to the iron horse's power. . . .
How the merchant will smile when the railroad comes
And brings cheaper goods to his customers' homes. . . .

* * * * *

Tweetsie, like many another, had set forth in the first burst of hope at the end of the Civil War. From Johnson City, Tennessee, in 1866 five miles of solid iron rail were laid down toward the towering Blue Ridge wall of North Carolina, its summit crowned with virgin balsam groves and iron mines. More cautiously, the promoters built the next eleven miles of wood, covered with strap iron. Then the grades grew really steep—the motorist along the highway which parallels the track is still endangered by falling rocks—and for the twenty years of the Reconstruction period the project was at a standstill.

* * * * *

By 1882, however, most of the bitterness had begun to fade with the uniforms, and, as part of a general renaissance in which the old captains of the South cheerfully borrowed Northern money to build new industries and railroads, Tweetsie set forth again. Yankee capitalists purchased her franchise from General R. F. Hoke, of North Carolina. For the climb which lay ahead, they narrowed her gauge from five feet to three. Thus prepared, and at a cost of a million dollars, she pushed up through the bottom of the spectacular Doe River Gorge, crossed the state line at an elevation close to four thousand feet, and, at the time Mr. Dugger's book was published, had reached the [magnetic] iron mines at Cranberry, North Carolina, some six miles from Banner Elk.

Beyond the Cranberry mines a lumber company gradually extended the rails from one sawmill to another. In 1917, when the sawmills were operating lines fairly close to Boone, Dr. B. B. Dougherty, president of the State Teachers' College, rallied his fellow citizens to persuade the railroad to come into Boone. The town, of less than a thousand population, offered the line a present of a thirty-five thousand dollar bond issue, taxing themselves to pay principal and interest. Nor was this all. Before the management of the logging road would agree to come into Boone and become a common carrier, hauling passengers and freight, they required the townspeople to get up the right-of-way, to secure contracts for the cutting of the desired timber and for its hauling over the narrow-gauge, and to obtain the franchise for the United States mail. The weather was cold and the snow was deep, but all these things the school-teacher did, tramping the mountains to get the necessary signatures.

The Linville River Railway, extending from Cranberry to Boone, was incorporated as a common carrier and operated jointly with the East Tennessee & Western North Carolina Railroad by the Cranberry iron mine corporation, which owned them both. Thus, after some twenty years, the hopes of the Bard of the Highlands were partially fulfilled.

Boone held a banquet to celebrate, at which Mayor Shull, of Banner Elk (which, unfortunately, was left some four miles off the line), was asked, after a round of gloating speeches, to extend congratulations from his town.

Mr. Shull rose and remarked, "I remember when the only way a man could get into Boone was to be born there," and sat down.

Beyond Boone, the westernmost terminus of the line, the Blue Ridge drops precipitately and the narrow-gauge was never extended to form a through rail connection with the eastern seaboard. Yet for a while, I understand, there was a period when local agriculture and industry prospered from the line. Summer hotels and homes were built throughout the region, and the supply of lumber seemed inexhaustible. Enrollment rose at Doctor Dougherty's Teachers' College at Boone and Edgar Tufts's little mission school at Banner Elk. Material and spiritual progress seemed linked in those days as they have not been since.

During the nineteen-twenties, the stemwinder—its later nickname of Tweetsie was conferred by the boys and girls in summer camps near Banner Elk—hauled out satisfactory loads of freight, although gradually the passenger business, and much of the lighter freight, began to go to the highways.

For now the coming of the "hard road" aroused the same hopes which had once been pinned to the iron horse. To this day, North Carolina and Tennessee are joined by only one through railroad, the Southern from Asheville to Knoxville; it was the highroads which opened the Blue Ridge Mountains all the way from east to west, giving the farmers and other shippers a direct connection with the lowland. Whatever plans Tweetsie's management may have had for making a through rail connection were thwarted.

It seemed plain enough, however, in the early nineteen-thirties that she could not last much longer. The iron mines at Cranberry were already closed down, and the balsam groves at the Grandfather Mountain lived only in Shepherd Dugger's curious book. With the exhaustion of its natural resources, the mountain region had its own private collapse within the larger depression.

* * * * *

[After I left North Carolina] I did not see Tweetsie for many years. Throughout the nineteen-thirties her whistle continued to blow for mountain dignity, independence, and pride, and when at last she went on trial for her life, these qualities were richly displayed.

In the summer of 1940, a heavy flood struck Western North Carolina and East Tennessee. Downstream cities were efficiently protected by the huge dams of the TVA; but on the upper reaches of the mountain streams its programs of soil and forest conservation had not yet made enough headway to hold back the waters. I read in the *Watauga Democrat* that the part of the narrow-gauge line between Cranberry and Boone had been heavily damaged and that the owners, who lived in Philadelphia, were not disposed to rebuild. Week by week the *Democrat* reflected growing excitement. The merchants' association wired their Congressman. In order to show their need for keeping the railroad running, local committees were formed and petitions circulated. The Interstate Commerce Commission, which has authority in such matters, agreed to hold a public hearing in November at Johnson City, Tennessee. On this hardened Government agency the little train at least left its mark. When I asked the I.C.C. in Washington to see the record, the clerks could not at first locate the docket until I described the line.

"Oh," they exclaimed, "you mean Tweetsie!"

In general, Tweetsie's case followed the set pattern of such proceedings. First, the railroad official must apply to the I.C.C. for permission to abandon, then he must fill out exhaustive questionnaires. The I.C.C. notifies the Governor, the State Railroad Commission (which control such matters as the discontinuance of passenger service, but cannot grant permission to abandon a line), and other interested parties. The railroad brotherhoods write asking to be advised of the proceedings, which in this case was as far as they went, as the brothers concerned were assured of jobs on the remaining part of the line.

Some months after the hearing, the I.C.C. issued a certificate of public convenience and necessity allowing the owners to tear up the damaged track. Passenger service was abandoned on the rest of the line between Johnson City and Cranberry. That is all there is in the docket, except for one thing.

In the Grandfather Mountain country, when some one dies, it is customary to write a few lines of appreciation and send them to the county paper. Thus Annette Vance, of Minneapolis, North Carolina (population, 53), who wrote to Examiner Schutrumpf during the hearing, asking him not to permit abandonment, enclosed a poem which has been placed in the official record. It is called "A Hill Billie's Lament":

In Carolina how it did rain,
It took from us a little train.
So long it seems since we heard her blow
I wonder why it could thus be so.
Our Tweetsie whom we loved so dear,
Her coming and going we have ceased to hear,
Our little train we loved so well,
And our love for her in our hearts doth dwell.
Dear God, is this hope in vain?
Send us back our little train.
The waters rose and took her track,
We want our little Tweetsie back.
What could we do or what could we say
To get her back the same old way?
Are we civilized, oh, who can know
Now we can't even hear a train blow.
When she passed, we stood amazed,
We admired her so, we stood and gazed.
Her loss we pine, we loved her so.
To think we will never hear her blow.
Our memory of her is clear and plain.
Please send us back our little train.

This would be the logical ending of the story, and if it were any other train but Tweetsie, it would certainly be the end. But in the Grandfather Mountain country we believe in a power which is higher than the Interstate Commerce Commission, and sometimes our prayers are answered. Gradually, so to speak, on the original thirty-three miles of line between Johnson City and Cranberry, Tweetsie came to life again.

All during the summer of 1942, following a national magazine article which mentioned her fate, pilgrims came to Johnson City begging to be allowed to ride on a Sunday excursion, a freight train, a handcar, anything.

"There was a man and his wife came from the Pacific Coast and waited a whole week in their trailer waiting for a train to go up," Mr. Blackwell told me in Johnson City in the spring of 1942.

Mr. Blackwell obliged the fans when he could by hooking a passenger coach, but he said frankly that he hoped they would never have to run regular passenger service again.

So far as miracles can be analyzed, the same world forces which helped to kill Tweetsie likewise helped to raise her up. The high price of scrap iron, brought about through the activities of the Germans and Japanese, unquestionably contributed to the desire of her owners to abandon the line after the washout. And by the late summer of 1942, the rubber and gasoline shortages for which these same foreign gentlemen were responsible made it necessary to resume train service between the rayon plants at Elizabethton and the North Carolina mountains where many of the mill workers live. Most of Tweetsie's passenger equipment had already been sold to South America, but the management purchased three wooden coaches from the Boston, Revere Beach & Lynn, a narrow-gauge, which had likewise been recently abandoned. One of its three remaining ten-wheel engines pulls this sizable train on three round trips a day between the mills near Elizabethton and Elk Park, North Carolina, twenty-four miles each way. Because there is no Y or turn-around, at Elk Park, the train backs up. They had rather have the engine in front going down, because of the air-brakes. Her manners are no more formal than they used to be. When a passenger wants off, he tells the brakeman who signals with his fingers to the engineer.

What will happen to Tweetsie in the future? I don't know, but I am willing to leave her fate, and ours, in the hands of the Providence which has revived her.[1]

---

[1] A hint of the reverence with which rail enthusiasts regarded "Tweetsie" is found in Lucius Beebe's whimsical comment; "To the reverent pilgrim, to have seen Tweetsie is, in a manner of speaking, to have beheld the Veronica, to have bathed in an antiquarian's Ganges. It is the true and the absolute of ferrophilia, and we left No. 12 reluctantly, to dine off chicken pot pie and coke at the Coffee Shop in Roan Mountain. Perhaps, we remarked conversationally, we were entitled to wear a bordered toga or other emblem of accomplishment, as having made the Pilgrimage, the Golden Journey to Samarkand." (*Mixed Train Daily*, p. 82)

A few miles of track and a whole train of Tweetsie were saved from destruction by a trio of rail fans, and may now be ridden by all who wish on the farm of Dr. Paul S. Hill, near Harrisonburg, Va.

Otto Mears and the Rio Grande Southern

I [1]

. . . A gold rush was on in southwestern Colorado, where six mountain ranges, jammed tightly together in a mighty granite uplift, throw up no less than fourteen summits to a height of fourteen thousand feet or more above sea level, a hundred more above twelve thousand feet.

It was a brawling time. Prospectors' diggings by the hundreds perforated the shadowy gorges and the Technicolor amphitheaters above timber line. Lawless mining camps bulged with new wealth counted in millions, and some of the nation's great present-day fortunes—notably that of the late Evalyn Walsh McLean—were being founded here by those who were lucky. The San Juan country was a road builder's greatest opportunity and his greatest challenge.

Before Otto Mears other builders, using brawn and black powder, had completed the all but absurd task of driving a railroad north from Durango up the mile-deep gorge of the Rio de las Animas Perdidas (River of Lost Souls) to alpine Silverton, 9,300 feet high. There they stopped. Ouray, railhead at the northern edge of the range, was only twenty-four miles away, but getting there would involve a tortuous struggle up into the arctic boulder fields, a crossing of the Continental Divide at 12,000-foot Red Mountain Pass, then a plunge down the bare and awesome declivities on the northern side. Couldn't be done, the surveyors decided. Not even a wagon road could be put through *that.*

Otto Mears thought otherwise. Already a road builder without rival in a state where roads were everything, he had gouged out fourteen toll roads for the supply wagons, spanning 430 miles of supremely difficult terrain.

With his wonted disregard of engineer fellows, Mears began by blasting out of the raw rock walls above Ouray a Glory Road such as even he had never before attempted. As a wagon trail, it was frightening enough to evoke instant, meditative sobriety in the most blasphemous of bottle-belting mule skinners. As an automobile road today, it's the broad, paved shelf of one of the most thrilling of modern highways, marked near the summit by a monument to its builder.

But he was bound to put a railroad through. He gained experience by building several short lines to mines above Silverton—one of these

---

[1] From "A Railroad under Her Arm," by Elvon L. Howe, in *Rocky Mountain Empire,* Revealing Glimpses of the West in Transition from Old to New, from the Pages of the Rocky Mountain Empire Magazine of the *Denver Post,* edited by Elvon L. Howe, pp. 41–49. Copyright, 1946, 1947, 1948, 1949, 1950, by Post Printing and Publishing Company. Garden City, N. Y.: Doubleday & Company, Inc.

an incomparable little spur built on a seven per cent grade. (On that, one engineman testified, his locomotive could barely pull one car of coal and one "empty" up to the mine; the return was a matter of setting the brakes at the top and kneeling in prayer all the way down.)

Then Mears tackled Red Mountain and managed to reach the pass. But the cliffs below stopped him cold. The engineers were right: it couldn't be done.

But Otto Mears was no man to be pushed around even by a mountain range. He took note of the fact that other mining camps lay just a few miles across the impassable ridges to the west. Rico, Matterhorn, Ophir, Placerville, and canyon-locked Telluride, where an explosive porridge of immigrant and native American humanity seethed and bubbled like the restless mash at the bottom of a high-walled brewer's vat. If he couldn't push a railroad down the last twelve miles through the center of these mountains, he'd drive another 172 miles around the western flank of the range, where the San Juans shoulder against the La Platas and the majestic peaks of San Miguel. Just like that.

Again the engineers laughed. The proposed route, they pointed out, was not only many times longer but beset with difficulties hardly less formidable than the descent from Red Mountain Pass.

Mears built it in two years—a railroad without counterpart. Not one of its 172 miles was on level ground. It toiled up and over four mountain passes, the highest a 10,250-foot crossing under the sunset shadow of a huge, reptilian spear of rock named Lizard Head. It required no less than 132 bridges, many of them lofty wooden trestles over booming freshets. And the total climb and curvature of its twisting tracks were the equivalent of a staircase of eighty spirals, 8,000 feet high!

It was a summer day in 1891 when a bunting-draped inaugural train chuffed out of the terminus at Ridgway, beyond the range just north of Ouray, to show the state's notables what had been done. Up the piñon-covered slopes of Dallas Divide the tiny engine (second-hand—the Southern never owned a new one) fought for every precious foot of altitude, then quickly lost it all on the descent to swarming Placerville. Thence it started up again, winding the ocher and purple gorge of the San Miguel River, and took the spur to Telluride, coming to a dead end and a celebration that echoed to the top of the 1,000-foot, blue-veined cliffs overhanging the town.

A retreat to the main line and eight hard miles of climb brought the top-hatted guests into sight of Otto Mears's all-time wonder of mountain railroading: the Ophir Loop. Here, under a cluster of rock pinnacles fully a half mile tall, the rails crossed the canyon on an astonishing wooden trestle 450 feet long and almost a hundred high. Station house and dwellings of a tiny village were hung on the cliffside, accommodating themselves to the tight curve of track as it doubled the end of the canyon and climbed back several hundred feet above itself on the slopes of Yellow Mountain.

From there it was a goatlike scramble along the curving face of the cliffs and across six more frightening trestles to Matterhorn, a steep-rooted village straight from Baedeker's Tyrol.

Two panting miles and a full half hour farther was Trout Lake, a sapphire expanse set in the vermilion cirque of the peak named just that. Then a labyrinthine series of switchbacks that straightway acquired the nickname "Mears's Puzzle," and finally the Lizard Head summit.

Fourteen miles and a dozen more trestles farther down the southern side, festivities were waiting.

Rico, then the world's largest silver camp, had already welcomed another train that had climbed over two lower passes and up the grassy valley of the Dolores River on the southern half of the route. Now it riotously feted conqueror Mears as the customary golden spike was driven.

Shouted to his feet for a speech, Mears rose and proclaimed himself absolutely terrified, declared that no man in his right mind would ride on the railroad he had just built, and roared for horses and wagon to continue his journey!

Despite such deplorable salesmanship, the Southern had been instantly prosperous. Passes of sheet silver and gold, delicately filigreed to Mears's personal order by a Denver goldsmith, were dispensed to local notables with a free hand. Many a miner, scorched by the bright lights of pistol-packing Durango, rode back to his job upon nothing more than his promise to buy a ticket from friend John the conductor next payday. (Rumor had it that friend John himself often neglected to turn in even what passenger fares the more conscientious had paid. The Southern was too busy hauling ore to care greatly about such minor revenue.)

But good times lasted a mere two years. Panic and the federal demonetization of silver in 1893 spread sudden paralysis over the whole Silver West. The boom was over. In a few months the Southern was in receivership.

* * * * *

Hardly had the Denver and Rio Grande Western Railroad taken over the little road in the nineties as a rather unwanted subsidiary than the mountain goliaths began to swing massive punches at their impudent little adversary.

Five times roaring spring floods carried away almost the entire trackage on the thirty-mile river-bottom stretch between Dolores and Rico. Once the dam impounding Trout Lake went out and the flood took with it twenty-two miles of track. Seldom was there money for new rail; the old was fished out, straightened, and patched together almost yard by yard to keep the cars rolling. Ties rotted, bridges sagged, tiny 30- and 42-pound rail warped until it was hardly straighter than so many lengths of ribbon laid through grass.

Slides joined the floods. Once a huge boulder tumbled down on a moving freight, neatly removed two cars at the center of the train, and deposited them on the bottom of the canyon a thousand feet below. The wreckage is a thought-provoking sight for train crews passing today.

At Ames siding, where a mountainside is moving, a section of track has been doggedly rebuilt almost every year. Once a full half mile of track slid 750 feet down the slope and traffic over the pass stopped for twelve months. But receiver Victor Miller found the money somehow and rebuilt the gap.

Snow was annually an almost insuperable problem. Frequently the Southern's entire fleet of engines united behind one rotary snowplow to ram through drifts higher than the smokestacks. Five engines once required seven sixteen-hour days to open a thirteen-mile stretch. Sometimes the tightly packed snow had to be dynamited. Brakemen kept their cabooses well provisioned, ready any time to be stranded in the snow for days. In prolonged storms, they often had to open the baggage car and help themselves to provisions consigned to the little grocery stores up the line. Fifty-foot drifts and seventy-mile gales are not uncommon.

In very recent times a dozen passengers were stranded nine long days near Lizard Head, surviving on food dropped from airplanes.

Nor does the coming of spring bring much relief. Down on the lower passes near Durango the mud is almost worse than snow. Here Otto Mears had built his railroad "around the alfalfa patches, not through them" (since his route was financed by the mile, he had to put in many extra low-country miles to pay the tab for such endeavors as the Ophir Loop), and the unballasted ties sank into the soft goo. Rails, too, spiked as they were to the gradually rotting wood without tie plates, spread or turned over on slightest provocation.

Derailments occurred almost as often as trains went out. Trainmen merely took down the "frogs" from the back of the caboose and wearily pulled the cars back onto the tracks. The veteran freight conductor, J. H. Crum, whose wife Josie is the Southern's most faithful historian, recalls one memorable sixty-mile trip from Dolores to Durango when he had to uncouple his engine and haul derailed cars back onto the tracks no less than twenty-six times.

Engineers and firemen have learned to stay well inside the cab so as not to be crushed when the engine drops off the track and the tender climbs onto its back. There is hardly an engineman on the Southern who has not, several times, "bailed out" of a locomotive which had suddenly decided to take a roll down the mountainside. They ride always ready to take sudden departure.

Fatalities were entirely too frequent. At Bilk Creek one night in 1910, the first of two engines coasting downhill by the light of their kerosene headlamps plunged through an S-shaped trestle. Engineer Al Bickford was killed and Fireman Jasper Compton, scalded and pinned beneath the engine with a broken leg, lay waiting for fifteen minutes for the second engine to tumble down on top of him. It did, with two cars of the train behind it, but Compton survived. The uninjured fireman of the second engine lit running, and, so far as local records indicate, is running yet. He completely disappeared.

Hard times of the thirties brought monumental improvisation but no abandonment. To cut down expense in passenger and baggage schedules, the Southern's miracle machinists procured an aged [Pierce-Arrow] automobile engine, fashioned a ten-passenger cab on trucks behind it, and articulated a baggage car to that. Out on the main line this clattering nonesuch instantly acquired the name and fame of "Galloping Goose." Six of them still ply the passes daily with steam-powered freights operating about three times a week.

II [2]

Probably no other narrow gauge went through such agonies at the end as the Rio Grande Southern, the last of whose tracks were being torn out [in the] summer [of 1952]. Its fight for life was symbolic of many roads. . . .

Cancellation of the Goose's mail contract in 1950 prove the coup de grace. For years it hadn't even paid any taxes. Stock and bond certificates had sentimental value only.

A discontinue service order turned out by the Colorado Public Utilities Commission on St. Valentine's Day, 1951, became the Goose's obituary. Also, in a sense it was a requiem for all narrow gauges.

Commissioner John R. Barry, a native of the area, wrote the death sentence. How he felt about it can be summed up from a closing passage, describing how the elements seemed to feel about man's intrusion into the mountains:

> In the winter they heaped snow to unimaginable depths. Then they sent snowslides crashing down their bare surfaces to cover up, bury, and kill those who were disemboweling them. In the summertime, they did the same with torrential downpours of rain. These were not the only weapons they used. Rock slides, lightning, biting cold were also their weapons. . . .
>
> It has been a long and arduous fight, but we, as well as the others who made the fight and lost, must admit that those mighty mountains have conquered us too.

---

[2] From "The Obituary of the Goose," by Gordon G. Gauss, *Omaha World-Herald Magazine,* June 28, 1953, p. 8–G.

The Rawhide Railroad: Short Line to Tall Tale

... [Dr. Dorsey S.] Baker had a railroad, hardly a first class one, and to keep it alive and operating he was forced to use stringent economies —a nice phrase for makeshift methods. That the Walla Walla and Columbia River lacked certain of the conveniences for smooth running could not be denied. It was about twenty miles long, but it had no turntables and it had no water tanks. When the little engines needed water, the engineer stopped on a bridge or by a creek, and the fireman took a bucket tied to a rope and dipped up water, pouring it by bucketfuls into the tank until he had enough. The bucket was an old tin oil can, salvaged from the junk pile. Regular bearing oil was expensive, but hog lard, made locally, would do, and so hog lard, poured out of another tin can, lubricated the locomotives and cars.

* * * * *

The thin line between the truth and the tall tale on the Walla Walla railroad is sometimes hard to locate. Once running regularly, the little engines on the strap rail did not turn in a spectacular performance. Hitched to a string of homemade flat or box cars, they huffed and wheezed their way back and forth, now and then tearing along at four or five miles an hour, for ten miles an hour was their best speed—downgrade and running light. One otherwise trustworthy narrator told how he rode to Walla Walla, or to within six miles of the place, as he found eventually. He paid two dollars for the privilege, but was warned that he would be safer riding a flatcar than the coach. The strap iron had a nasty habit of working loose under the train and rising up until it poked its way through the floor of a car, forming the familiar snakehead, known on eastern roads thirty years before. When a long strip of iron came prodding through a car, it was time for the passengers to scatter, if they did not want to be stuck like a bug in a collector's cabinet. Then the train stopped—it had to, for the snakehead simply pinned the whole outfit to the track—and the crew went for the blockade with sledge hammers and cold chisels. It was only a hazard of travel, and passengers watched the floor rather than the scenery.

From *Railroads down the Valley,* Some Short Lines of the Oregon Country, by Randall V. Mills, pp. 16–25. Copyright, 1950, by Randall V. Mills. Palo Alto, California: Pacific Books.

For "The Rawhide Railroad," see *A Treasury of American Folklore* (New York, 1944), pp. 520–524. For its author, George Estes, see Stewart H. Holbrook, *Far Corner* (New York, 1952), pp. 86–92, which answers the attack on Estes by W. W. Baker in his life of his father, *Forty Years a Pioneer* (1934).

Anyway, the traveler (who was an innocent stranger in those parts) climbed onto a flatcar and waited for the train to leave Wallula. Eventually the Conductor came by and told the Engineer to go ahead, that the Conductor had some business at hand but would catch up with them before too long. The little engine gasped, clattered and shuddered; the whistle bleated in pain, and the trip started. Within a short time the whole shebang was rocketing along at a steady two miles an hour, swaying and jolting on the uncertain track "like a canoe in a cross sea," a plaintive pling-pling-pling coming from the strap iron under the wheels, a cloud of drifting smoke and lively sparks from the engine, a breeze from the river and the rear to cool the travelers. Within an hour the Conductor came sauntering up the track, passed his laboring train, and nodded to the Engineer. But did he get aboard? Certainly not. It was easier to walk, and besides, how could a conductor maintain dignity while hanging onto that rocking, teetering contraption? Soberly, calmly, he walked by his train, like the captain of an overland caravan, guiding and soothing, and paying no attention to the ribaldries of teamsters driving their ox-teams along the dusty, paralleling road to Walla Walla. Scornfully he ignored their challenges to race. Their taunts fell on deaf ears, and they got no satisfaction. Besides, in a race, the oxen probably would have won, and the Conductor would have been diverted from his patient, careful watch for derailments.

A story like that rather stretches credulity and could be put down as just another good lie, except that Dr. Baker's son tells one nearly as big—and tells it solemnly. One day a freight train to Walla Walla jumped the track, as it frequently did, when Dr. Baker was along. While the crew was at work chivvying the cars back onto the rails, a pedestrian sauntered up, saw what was happening, and amiably skinned off his coat to help. When the train was ready to go again, the Doctor thanked the stranger for his aid and invited him aboard to ride the rest of the way. The stranger was polite. "No, thank you, Doctor," he said. "I'm in a hurry."

As the twenty miles often required seven hours of riding, the stranger had an argument, but now and then a lightning express made the whole run in three hours and scared everybody to death. Trains might be freight or mixed or passenger, but whatever they theoretically were carded to be, they were all accommodations. If a farmer had freight to load, the train stopped at his farm and loaded it. If some one wanted to ride the train, he stood by the track and the train stopped for him. If he happened already to be aboard and wanted to get off, he yelled at the engineer, who stopped the train—and waited, if the pause were only that which refreshes.

At the end of the train rambled the passenger equipment, either coach, or both of them, though usually one was quite enough. There were two coaches: the prefabricated job and a homemade affair, but between them there was little to choose, and their arrangements and comforts were about equal. The boughten one was square and boxy, rather short, with a curved roof, of a style familiar a couple of decades earlier. Along its sides were small, narrow windows, and inside were wooden seats running lengthwise of the car, so that passengers were ranged along the sides, facing each other; at the time, the problem of cross seats in narrow-gauge coaches had not been entirely solved, and the cars, without much overhang, probably were not over six feet wide. The home-made coach was simply a boxcar, its sides pierced for the same narrow windows, and its seats were planks fastened to the sides. Cars like that were operating on some California narrow gauges, and the Walla Walla jobs, while uncomfortable, were not unique. In them the passengers sat tense, waiting for warning that the car was off the track or that a snakehead was crunching through the floor beneath them. Mainly women and children rode the coaches; the men preferred airy perches on the flatcars or the roofs of the boxcars. One rider, who took the coach, remembered how, on the way, the coach was full of dogs, each secured by a leash to its owner. One pup, unaccustomed to riding, suddenly became carsick; the other dogs watched it, and the epidemic spread. The rider promptly decamped, to a less odorous place on the flatcar ahead. Another remembered how he rode up from Wallula on the morning train.

At Wallula was a sort of hotel, a glorified deadfall run in connection with a roaring saloon where, rather than risk the hardships and livestock of the hotel beds, the men collected to pass the hours, soaking up red-eye and figuring chances in poker. By morning the passengers were a bit bleary, some with eyes that were red, others, who had had opinions they expressed too loudly, with eyes that were black. Uncertainly all made their way to the train and limply poured themselves aboard. That morning had followed a particularly lively night at Wallula, and the passengers were suffering the torments of glorious hangovers. As the train chugged up the valley, few watched the scenery, such as it was. Then a woman asked the Conductor how she might get a drink of water for her little girl. The coach, she pointed out, lacked certain facilities, like a water-tank and a tin dipper on a chain. The Conductor, always ready to help, waved at the Engineer, and the train stopped. A quarter of a mile away was a spring, and he would fetch some water, he assured the lady. Then taking a bucket, he started back down the track. The gentlemen passengers watched him leave, and fell in behind, in uncertain procession, looking for cool water. In an hour they were back, heads dripping, but not aching too much; the Conductor brought in the bucket, improvised a cup, and the baby had a drink. Then the train started again its slow journey toward Walla Walla, the baby asleep, the hangovers abated, the little engine refreshed. Service—that was the motto of the Walla Walla flyer.

Naturally the Walla Walla railroad was not fenced, and as some cattlemen ran their herds thereabouts, now and then some stray cow or indignant steer wandered onto the track. The cattlemen, too, did not love the railroad; often they had run freighting teams in connection with their ranches, so when a cow died, it became notable how frequently it died on the track, often when there was no train for miles. When a train came upon a defunct critter, it had to stop while the crew hauled the corpse off the track and into the brush alongside, a job that somehow amused the cowboys. As the railroad ran no trains at night, it was reasonably easy for the cowboys to see that dead cattle would be on the track in time for the morning train.

Live cows were less predictable, unless they were staked out, but that was too obvious; still, they could be depended upon, in their bovine stupidity, to be where they were not wanted when they should most desirably not be there. They seemed to be fascinated by the track, and quite regularly a train crawled around a curve to find a browsing cow blocking the way. Neither the *Walla Walla* nor the *Wallula* had a cowcatcher on the front, and besides, one would have been sheer ostentation because in a clash between cow and locomotive it was an open question which would win, though betting generally favored the cow. Still, something had to be done, and again Dr. Baker turned his mind to the problem. It resolved itself fairly simply. Live cows had to be removed from the track in advance of the locomotive's coming. They could be chased away either by a man or a dog. Dogs were cheaper, and dogs were used. And so before each train ran a dog, trained to go up and down the track and snap and bark at stray cows until the critter either got out of the way or the engineer, thus warned, stopped the train and had a brakeman pry the cow away with a brake-club. Later, so says the legend, onto the front of the engines were built small platforms on which the dogs rode until they spotted a steer and leaped forward into frenzied action.

In time the dogs got used to riding and, discovering that they were too frequently summoned to duty, they learned to hide behind a bush until the train went by and then leap onto the platform of the coach, where they might sleep undisturbed, lulled by the click of wheels and the swaying of the car, at least until a brakeman found them and booted them off into action. That ruse discovered, the dogs found another; they would rush down the track, belling and snarling, around a curve and out of sight, whereupon they would lie down, scratch fleas or doze until the train caught up. One of them worked it too often; he could judge to the second how long it would take the train to catch up, and he could time his naps beautifully, rising only when the engine was close upon him. Then the road was relaid to T-rail, oil replaced lard as lubricant, trains speeded up, and one day an engine arrived too soon. The Walla Walla railroad had outgrown its primitive ways, anyway, so the dog's demise was only mildly lamented by the officials.

Somehow the strap-iron railroad became, in the telling, the rawhide railway, with the story that the rails were covered by strips of rawhide that dries and becomes as hard as iron. Next came the story, by logical progression, that during a famous hard winter hungry wolves came down from the hills and ate the rawhide, thereby tying up the line. The myth of the rawhide started early; it is told in a book published in 1911, and then was expanded by other writers until a magazine article in 1922 gave it the final and probably ineradicable stamp.

In the Far West rawhide was used for everything. It held together timbers in buildings when no nails were available—and still does in the Mormon Tabernacle at Salt Lake. It patched wagons and went into harnesses. An old story tells of a team hauling a load when a sudden shower of rain fell, wetting the harness. The team kept going while the harness stretched, leaving the load back in the woods, but the unworried driver on reaching camp unharnessed the team and tossed the collars over a stump. When the sun came out the rawhide dried, shrank, and pulled the load home. Then there was the chap whose leather breeches shrank while he was drying out before a fire, and before he could cut the elegant straps under his shoes, they lifted him into the air and sent him whirling endlessly through space. The folklore of rawhide in the West is common; besides, rawhide was usually cut into straps, and since the railroad had straps on the top of its wooden rails, the identity could be made.

But rawhide had some other meanings. As a verb, it meant to treat harshly, to oppress, to overwork, and as the Walla Walla railroad kept its crews busy, it was a rawhide line. Moreover, rawhide, from its widespread use to patch, fix, and improvise anything, came to mean a makeshift, so that a rawhide outfit meant cheap or improvised, much as haywire, from its equal availability to repair anything, came to be used. A rawhide railroad was a road that depended on cheap substitutes or extreme economies, just as a haywire outfit was one that had inadequate equipment. And no one would deny that the Walla Walla road could qualify as a rawhide railroad. It was a rawhide railroad, figuratively, not literally, but the confusion is the stuff from which folklore develops.

The Serio-Comic Lancaster & Chester

One railroad around which a real comic sketch has been written is the Lancaster & Chester in South Carolina, chiefly owned by Col. Elliott White Springs, soldier of World War One, fiction writer, third-generation railroader, but above all, principal owner of what he modestly admits to be the largest cotton mills in the world—as they certainly

---

Compiled from the Lancaster & Chester Railroad's literature and other sources.

look to be. The 29-mile railway is his favorite jape and most useful tool, connecting as it does, several of his cotton and finishing mills with major rail systems and with each other; an efficient and hard-working organism, with handsome stone terminal buildings, topped with a cut-out locomotive weather-vane, but no passenger trains. Its full-page spread in the deadly serious *Official Guide* at first glance looks as matter-of-fact as the rest of that august publication, until you notice the unusually long list of officials and read the names—Lowell Thomas as press agent, R. J. Reynolds, tobacconist, as marine superintendent, Clair Maxwell as news butcher, et cetera; three surgeons located in Columbia, S. C., Charlotte, N. C., and Cheyenne, Wyoming, respectively, and Bobby Jones, retired golfer of Atlanta, as one of the attorneys. Among the thirty-odd vice-presidents one finds such names as Sam Hopkins Adams, James Warner Bellah, James Montgomery Flagg, General Frank O'D. Hunter, John Reed King, Charles MacArthur, Gypsy Rose Lee, "vice-president in charge of unveiling," and Lucius Beebe, "vice-president in charge of the internal audit."

If this sounds a bit cracked, the printed matter privately circulated is more so. There is a large and gorgeous timetable scheduling three westbound trains, The Blue Blazes, The Purple Cow and The Black Label, and three eastbound, The Red Rose, The Shrinking Violet and The White Horse, all with colored pictures of the various namesakes heading the columns. There are more parenthetical letter references than any other railroad can boast. An (a) over The Blue Blazes and The Red Rose means, so we are told at the bottom of the page, "Private cars only"; (c) over The Black Label and The White Horse (which claim to cover the 29 miles in 30 minutes), "Run only by a Vice President." Other letters at certain stations indicate connections with other railroads, but at Richburg (j) means "bad connection," and at Knox (k) means "not the slightest connection." Among the standard equipment on all trains are Diesel locomotives and "combination caboose-lounge-observation cars." On the back of the folder is a map of the eastern United States, with a great railway network in the usual heavy black lines, which upon analysis proves to be the Southern and Seaboard systems, with a double track leading all the way to New York. It takes reading-glass scrutiny to discover Lancaster and Chester in the midst of the tangle. The map is labeled

LANCASTER AND CHESTER
RAILWAY SYSTEM
and connecting lines

Calmly ignoring the absence of passenger trains, the road issues a handsome menu folder for "Dinner—a La Carte or by Express," with some 120 items. Among the soups are

Diamond Back Terrapin with drawn butter	$ .75
Bareback Taxpayer with drawn blood	.50

Split Pea	.85
Split Infinitive	.85
Split Dixiecrat with frozen assets	.20

Oysters are quoted:

On the half shell	$ .65
with Artificial Pearl	1.65 plus tax
with Cultured Pearl	2.65 plus tax
with Oriental Pearl	3.65 plus tax
with Mother of Pearl	4.65
with Pearl	$4.65 plus $15.35 tip.

Under Sea Foods we find, among the rest,

Fillet of Flounder		$ 1.00
Floundering Filly	New York	20.00
	Southampton	40.00
Deep Sea Scallops, with Salty Accent		1.00
Back Bay Trollops with Harvard Accent		2.00 plus tip
English Sole Armenonville		.75
English Heel Newport		20.00

Among the more than fifty entrees are these:

Fricassee of Fabulous Fanny, Broad Gauge		$ 6.00
Pork Chops stuffed with Frozen Spinach		2.50
Pork Barrel stuffed with Republican		3.50
with Apple in Mouth		4.00
Drawn and Quartered Democrat Roasted in own Jacket		2.00
Mutton Chops stuffed with Union League		3.00
Hot Dogs with Sanforized Skins		.60
Breast of Chicken on Television		3.50
Breast of Peasant stuffed with Russian Propaganda		10 Rubles
Long Island Ugly Duckling stuffed with Turnip Greens and Pearl Onions		1.50
Lame Duck stuffed with Long Green and Perle Mesta		.30
Unicorn Steak with Lionnaise Potatoes		2.00
Baron of Beef with Duchess Salad	New York	1.00
	Palm Beach	1000 Lire

And so on and on. It must have required several hours of Col. Springs's leisure time to think it all up.

Rail Fans

Amateur Firemen

. . . The term "railroad fan" takes in as many kinds of people and attitudes, fake and genuine, rich and poor, sane and goofy, serious and

From "The Iron Hobby Horse," by J. C. Furnas, *The Saturday Evening Post*, Vol. 210 (August 21, 1937), No. 8, pp. 11, 49–50. Copyright, 1937, by the Curtis Publishing Company. Philadelphia.

frivolous, as the word "artist." King of them all may be the amateur railroad fireman, the spiritual heir of the Regency buck who, out of sheer love of driving horses six-in-hand, used to pay high for the privilege of taking the ribbons on the box of the Brighton-to-London stagecoach. His modern counterpart is so keen on real railroading that he curries favor with train crews and officials until they let him spend his week ends and holidays firing locomotive boilers on regular runs. The regular fireman merely sits and looks on, astonished, no doubt, but also approving, for a good fireman is proud of his job and can readily understand its fascination for outsiders.

"I tell you that was the happiest moment of my life," testified one amateur. "It was a cold day, with the train eating up steam, and I was already having to help the self-stoker along a good deal, and then she goes haywire on us right on a long, tough grade, and the fireman and I both had to pitch in and shovel like hell. Boy, you shoulda seen that coal move into that firebox—it was a caution!"

Amateur firemen are relatively rare. There may be a dozen in the country, of whom the largest group, some four or five comradely maniacs, inhabit Boston and environs. Now and again one of them gets so well established with the engine crew that they let him handle the throttle. That is equivalent to the Victoria Cross melted down with the Congressional Medal of Honor.

Lazier types, of course, might not enjoy having hurriedly to move several tons of coal from a tender to a roaring, flaming firebox by hand. But anything is fun if you get a kick out of it, and the beauty of railroad fanning is that it presents as large a variety of opportunities for special tastes as book collecting, and usually costs far less. . . .

Collectors

Practically any kind of railroad fan has a junk-heap complex similar to what a horse lover feels when he sees old Baldy being driven off to the glue factory. The only fans who don't share it are the collectors of engine bells, badges, headlights, and other such detachable, but barely portable, parts of old-time locomotives. Even a bell collector shakes his head and sighs on general principles when, after months of searching, he finally runs down the carcass of an old Mother Hubbard engine. But, after he has dried his eyes, you will find him astraddle of the boiler, using a cold chisel to cut off the bell, which weighs some two hundred pounds along with its yoke, and displays, round its lip, certain grooves which, to the connoisseur's eye, mean it was cast before 1880. It sometimes worries the junk dealer, yard master, president's secretary, or what not to think of allowing a man who collects locomotive bells for a hobby to wander round the place with a dangerous weapon like a cold chisel in his hand. But, if the secretary or what not only knew it, screwier things than that are collected in the name of railroad fanning, collected so earnestly and widely that many of them acquire a considerable commercial value.

One man in Connecticut, for instance, has over ninety different types of old railroad lanterns. Others go in for oil cans, sections of old rail, rear-end lanterns, old tickets, railroad stocks and bonds—canceled, since this is not a gag—timetables, flagstaffs, and the grand old colored lithographs that pre-Civil War locomotive makers used to put out as advertising, which last may be worth as much as $150 apiece. An eminent fan out in Jersey has planted, in his back yard, two genuine railroad block signals, operating from remote control and in crack working order, which fascinate not only him but every kid in the neighborhood. Another recently insisted on renting a suburban house down by the tracks so he could wave to the train crews as the trains went by. A third has, for years and years, walked two miles every day in a small upstate New York town to see the Century go by.

Miniature Railroaders

The granddaddy of them all was a wealthy old gentleman in Pennsylvania in the last century, who died gloriously in the cab of his own 9 7/16″-gauge engine one night, when she turned over as authentically as if she had been the old Ninety-Seven herself. He was particularly fond of using his two engines to buck snowdrifts, they say. You could go on forever. When the late William Gillette's will was probated, the wire-service reporters had themselves a field day over the fact that one solid paragraph of it was devoted to cautioning his executors against allowing "sapheads" to lay hands on the miniature railroad which ran round his estate at Hadlyme, Connecticut, in the cars of which Mr. Gillette's guests often rode with Sherlock Holmes himself at the throttle, garbed in overalls and a blue-denim cap and yellow wash gloves.

That railroad of Sherlock Holmes', however, tactlessly brings up the subject of the contempt that each kind of amateur railroader feels for the others. Mr. Gillette's miniature layout had cars, roadbed, ties, and rails. But one of its locomotives made the social error of being storage-battery powered, a dodge which is anathema to those aristocrats among private railroaders, the seventy-odd members of the American Brotherhood of Live-Steamers, all of whom own and operate—many of whom are capable of building with their own hands—exact-scale locomotives run by real steam. Vincent Astor, for example, has a miniature railroad with a live-steam loco at his place at Rhinebeck, New York. Up in Westchester is another prosperous man whose proud possession of a two-inch-gauge live-steamer results from a history of youthful frustration. As a boy, he was wild to own a toy train, but his parents, who had ideas of their own, never supplied one. So, when he grew middle-aged, he made it up to himself gorgeously, with any amount of track curling round the back premises and, chuffing along its rails, an engine which is a patrician even among live-steamers, because, instead of alcohol, it burns actual coal in a firebox of about the size of a cigar case.

Model Railroaders

Live-steamers look down not only on battery-powered locomotives, but also on the electric-driven miniatures of steam locomotives that model railroaders make, fondle, and use. Yet model railroading is one of the two major sects of railroad fandom, and its numerous and genial tribe of fans, in turn, look on fanatical live-steamers as worthy, but unhappily idealistic, maniacs. For the model railroader doesn't worry about what moves his loco so long as she moves. What he wants is small-scale realism, and that is what he gets by the sweat of his brow, the expenditure of much pocket money, and the exercise of an ingenuity that would do credit to the inventor of the wasp's nest.

Practically every big city in the United States has at least one model-railroad club which maintains a first-class pike in addition to the numerous private pikes that individuals run in their own basements, in the teeth of protests from their wives. Occasionally a wife who protested bitterly about cluttering up the basement with toys succumbs to the same fever as her husband, and is presently found lettering boxcars and spiking rails to ties as neatly as she ever darned socks. Few outsiders feel the fascination of collecting old timetables right off the reel. They react much more quickly to their first glimpses of a first-class model railroad in operation.

Everything is made to [gauge] scale. . . . The advertising posters on the station walls are match covers glued up and shellacked, the shrubs along the cuts are twisted bits of sponge painted green—and the language of the operators, whose ages range from seventeen to seventy—is the purest of railroad jargon: "Hog" for engine, "pike" for railroad line, "reefer" for refrigerator car, "brownie" for demerit mark, "hotshot" for fast train, "drag" for slow freight, and so forth. "Brownies" are frequent. A real model railroad runs to a split-hair schedule like the real thing. Each evening the members of a model-railroad club take on regular railroad jobs as brakemen, dispatchers, and conductors. The dispatcher who brings a train in late, the yardmaster who gums up the assembling of a mixed freight, gets enough "brownies" to demote him to section hand next evening.

The mere names of these railroads are a delight. The Interstate Commerce Commission knows nothing of the Sierra Pacific, the Keystone Central, the Hudson Central & Atlantic, the Allegheny Southern. But the readers of model railroaders' fan magazines know them, are aware that the New Hampshire Central is building a new Pacific-type loco in its shops, and that the Union Connecting has recently acquired four new reefers and a "crummy"—meaning caboose. They take all that just as soberly as the fan magazine's advice to build umbrella sheds at suburban stations because "it isn't fair to your passengers to make them wait in the rain."

Even though the name of the pike is often humorous, its operator stands on the dignity appropriate to railroad men. The Alhambra & Lilliputia, the Diminutive & Obstinate, the Hell West & Crooked, the Bigbee Littlin, or the writer's own favorite among them, the Sfarze Looville & Nawlins, cut just as much ice as something calling itself the International Midland, and you will get into just as much trouble by calling them "toy railroads." To the model railroader "toy" means "tin-plate"—what you buy in a department store for Junior's Christmas, all off-scale, incapable of giving the observer that illusion of miniature actuality that the modeler craves. If you are going to call it "toy railroading," what was the point in the long hours the club members spent over a workbench making a mikado loco to exact scale from the manufacturer's own blueprints, in the joy they felt in discovering that the bell-shaped dingus on the end of an old electric-light cord is the exact scale size for the bell of an 0-gauge engine, in the nerve-shattering delicacy of painting one-quarter-inch-scale lettering on the side of a new boxcar for the Mason & Dixon Lines? A miniature railroader has his reward when, putting his eye down to track level—the track being an exact scale miniature of the real thing, rolled out of the same steel and spiked to the ties at the same intervals—he sees his home-built mikado coming round the corner at a scale-speed of fifty-five miles an hour, with a mail car and five vestibule Pullmans of his own manufacture following behind in gliding dignity. If you listen, even the clickety-click of the rails is just the same, and, if you look, the lights on the signal bridge up ahead are dead ringers for those on a main line.

Tin-Platers

The next step down in the scale is the "tin-plater," who runs a miniature railroad, but with bought rolling stock and right of way, which, scandal of scandals, is not even intended to be scale stuff. At least this is the next step down in the model railroader's estimation. The tin-plater in turn professes to be amused by the modeler's toploftiness because, he says, model railroaders learned everything they know from tin-plate pioneers. An outsider has no business in that fight, except to note that tin-platers also have their fan magazines and that, in this field, collecting reaches astounding refinements. Tin-plate collectors not only rake out old-time toy rolling stock and track from garrets, junk shops, and bankruptcy sales but ardently collect the obsolete catalogues of manufacturers of toy trains, some items of which are worth as high as ten dollars. The prize tin-plate item, however, is the oldest known tin-plate engine, a live-steam affair, which is so far from trying to be a scale model of the real thing that its safety valve consists of a spring-and-split arrangement of the cylinders against the steam intake, so that, when pressure gets too high, the cylinders are pushed away and the steam escapes prematurely. Only two of these weird little things are known to exist. Their owners would probably not listen to much under $1000.

Fan Trips

Fan trips, being, by all odds, the strangest thing in the whole kingdom of railroad fandom, call for a lot of explanation. The idea is for a batch of admirers of railroading, usually connected with some railroad-fan organization, to charter a train collectively and have an orgy of railroading under special circumstances. A fair sample would be the annual junket of the Boston chapter of the Railroad Enthusiasts over the Hoosac Tunnel and Wilmington Railroad, locally known as the Hoot, Toot and Whistle, which trickles up into Vermont from the northwest corner of Massachusetts. The HT&W carries passengers on only this one day a year, when its forty-four-year-old engine couples on to an old day coach and two flat cars, studded with chairs and benches for open-air observation, and transports the Enthusiasts over a route famous for one of the few switchbacks in the East, and often affording fans such informal delights as derailments and cows on the track. The engine is fired by an eminent amateur fireman who, in private life, runs an elevator factory in Cambridge, Massachusetts. There was a similar spirit last year about a fan expedition over the Ma & Pa Railroad—officially the Maryland & Pennsylvania—admirers of which swear its right of way is so crooked it makes horseshoe bends to avoid all trees over a foot thick. A recent fan trip over an old-time one-horse California railroad was so popular that the passengers were twice too many for all the available cars and had to sit on the roofs, with the conductor profanely climbing up there to collect his tickets.

Other fan trips climax in visits to the main shops of some big-time railroad, where there are engines standing with steam up so the fans can climb into the cabs and blow the whistles, ask questions of company guides, and generally wallow in backstage stuff.

The Engine Picture Club

. . . These heterogeneous fans are zealous railroad experts, they are talking railroad, living railroad for the time being much more earnestly than if it were their job. Many a real railroader will admit that a really ardent fan knows more about the organization, both technical and administrative, of the modern railroad than anybody in the business who gets paid for knowing it. Amateurs devour professional magazines from cover to cover, whereas actual railroaders pick out what interests them and cast the rest aside. A member of the national Railway and Locomotive Historical Society, which has some eight or nine hundred members throughout the country and boasts of a considerable museum in the Baker Library of the Harvard University School of Business Administration, can probably tell you absolutely everything about the history of the railroad in which he specializes, clear down to the names and dates of and scandals appertaining to the numberless small local roads that were consolidated in 1867 to make up its trackage. A crack member of the Engine Picture Club, concentrating on photographs of engines of some particular road, will often be consulted by its engineering department as to just what plant built the diamond-stacked 4–4–0 that the line bought second-hand from the Dutch Gap & Points-west in 1879. He usually knows and has photographs to prove it.

At that, the Engine Picture Club may be the weirdest detail of all, outstripping even the amateur firemen. The engine picture business has nothing to do with the modern cult of arty amateur photography, any more than railroad fan trips have anything to do with modern hobby trains, for skiers, bicyclers, folding-canoe nuts, and photographers, with which enterprising railroads step up operating revenue. What the engine-picture fan wants and gets, by swapping, by pestering railroads, and by wearing out his own camera, is a photograph as much like a blueprint as possible, which enables him to check that queer proportion of the smokebox which distinguishes this particular 4-4-2 from the loco that preceded it in the road's affections. To be called sizable a collection of engine pictures should number over 10,000 items.

The Fans and the Railroads

. . . Some fan organizations actually go to bat for the railroads before public-service commissions and legislatures. Not long ago, when a small Vermont railroad was losing its milk-hauling business to cut-rate truck competition, railroad fans in the vicinity rallied round to do such a fine job of plugging the railroad among local business men and politicos that the legislature reduced its taxes and the day was saved. One organization even assigns a certain member to look after the interests of each railroad in the vicinity.

Suspicious as it all sounds, however, granted that it would have been dramatically to the railroads' benefit to plant, cherish, and develop it, the railroad fan movement arose as spontaneously as a waterspout. In fact, its phenomenal growth has occurred largely in spite of the railroads' earnest efforts to discourage it.

* * * * *

Only in the last few years, since the era of greater speed, new trains, and lowered fares opened the railroads' eyes, have they even tried to cooperate with their fans at all. . . .

The changing nature of the iron horse himself is another potential source of headaches for the enterprising publicity man. After spending any amount of time and money on the build-up of modern motive power, the roads are presently going to find that it flouts the fundamental prejudices of railroad fandom. For fans are practically unanimous in looking distastefully at the kind of locomotive that the lines have been plugging in the public eye for the last two or three years. New-fangled engines make pretty posters, says the fan, but they don't satisfy the longing for thundering, vibrating, visible action which he gets in such overflowing measure from the spectacle of a big, square-fronted, snorting steam job trampling down the track with connecting rods churning and drivers rolling regardless. In comparison with that, the silent rush of an electric "jack" or the pulsating grumble of a Diesel is tame. Even a stream-line job, for all that she sounds and feels the same, is shrouded in metal that masks all the significant detail of pipes and valves and rods and domes, makes a kind of parlor decoration out of the imperiously utilitarian ugliness of an honest boiler.[2]. . .

Collector of Railroads

Rogers E. M. Whitaker stands unique among rail fans; he has an ambition—or to be more precise, he would like to ride over every mile of track on the North American continent. He knows that this cannot be accomplished as to track currently in use, for every little while another branch or small railroad is abandoned—the 12.7-mile Hooppole, Yorktown & Tampico in Illinois, for example, which just the other day folded its hands so suddenly and quietly that the world never noticed it. These abandonments annoy Whitaker as much as anyone of his placid temperament can be annoyed. He has been nibbling away at his hobby at odd moments for 18 years, and at the last audit had racked up more than 400 railroads, big and little, and traversed some 900,000 miles of track, much of which he traveled in reaching other railroads which he wanted to add to his score.

Whitaker is one of the editors of that smart magazine, *The New Yorker;* a big fellow with a quiet, diffident manner which conceals a dogged persistence in getting what he wants. For some years past he has been dashing out of New York on week-ends—by plane since avi-

---

[2] For the fads and foibles of model railroaders regarding stream-lining, among other things, see Doug Welch's story, "Mrs. Union Station," in *Headlights and Markers,* edited by Frank P. Donovan, Jr., and Robert Selph Henry (New York, 1946), pp. 250–278.

From interviews with Rogers E. M. Whitaker by Alvin F. Harlow, New York City, 1953.

ation became not too desperate an adventure—often to annex just one short railroad. For example, he recently flew to California to add the McCloud River Railroad (49.5 miles, Mount Shasta to Hambone) to his list, after hearing that it is soon to be dieselized. Like all dyed-in-the-wool rail bugs, he likes them in steam. His shortest single pickup for a cross-country flight was the Camino, Placerville & Lake Tahoe—8 miles—in the Sierra foothills. During his vacations he really goes places, and may gather in short lines by the dozen. And in emergencies—for he has friends in rail circles who tip him off to sudden, rare opportunities—he may leave his desk in mid-week and rush off somewhere.

He has covered every major main line on the continent—including those in Canada and Mexico—though it took some doing in several cases, for what were once important arteries of travel, traversed by jaunty, busy passenger trains, now, in deplorably too many instances, know only the plodding tread of freight trains. Permission to ride on them isn't easy to obtain, and the ride is often somewhat of an ordeal when it is permitted. Some short lines which are "captive" roads, that is, owned by big iron, steel or copper companies, are simply inaccessible to the traveler, no matter what sort of plea he puts up; though Whitaker still ponders possible ways of reaching, wheedling or bringing pressure to bear—some of these days. . . .

He had a small but unexpected windfall once in the Northwest when he was cruising about there, picking up little rails; he heard of a two-mile branch of the Union Pacific which hadn't felt the pressure of wheels for months on end, but over which, two or three days later, an engine was to venture to bring out two flat-car loads of timber. He rushed by car to the division superintendent's office, explained his hobby, and the good-natured official gave the desired permission, though probably warning the train-crew privately to keep an eye on that fellow, as he might be a little off his rocker. That nameless little streak of rust was to Whitaker what the Bay Psalm-book is to a book collector; a poor thing intrinsically, but a jewel in its rarity.

Many of the little railroads which are Whitaker's chief objectives nowadays make a brave show in the *Official Guide*. It is not uncommon to find one occupying a quarter of a page in the *Guide* with its list of officers—President, Vice President, Secretary, Treasurer, Auditor, Superintendent, General Manager, Purchasing Agent, Traffic Manager and Master Mechanic, and then discover further down that the road is 7.6 miles in length and has only irregular freight service. The Southern Iowa, a freight-only line with 18 miles of trackage and Centerville and Moravia as its principal cities, spreads over more than a half-page of the *Guide* a map of a considerable portion of the Middle West, with the numerous lines which contribute to the S.I.'s traffic, and the statements, "Fast through service from all parts of the United States," and "Freight terminals on paved streets in the heart of the business sections."

Whitaker's smile over these immodesties is not merely tolerant, it is affectionate. He is all for these brave little pikes, which, like the old steam locomotive, so typify the hard-to-daunt American spirit, struggling against heavy odds to do its job, holding its head high, putting its best foot forward and contributing its bit, however small, to the functioning of the national economy.

There are dozens of midget railroads, one, two or three miles long, each functioning sturdily in its own little ant-hill. Name one, and the odds are in favor of Whitaker's being able to tell you about it, for he knows the *Official Guide* better than some preachers know their Bibles. There used to be a one-miler—but is no more—which bore the name, New York Central, Hudson River and Fort Orange without tottering, extending from Castleton on the New York Central to a paper mill. There are others, too, which overload themselves with name; to mention only one, the Waco, Beaumont, Trinity and Sabine, whose 17.7-mile line touches none of those points but Trinity.

The railroads that Whitaker really loves are the little 5, 10, 20 and 30-mile pikes, many of which own no cars and use cast-off engines from bigger roads—sometimes owned, sometimes borrowed, permanently or temporarily from a larger neighbor, frequently breaking down. The quainter they are, the better. One of the real peaks of enjoyment in Whitaker's travels seems to have been reached when, at the terminus of a little forest-and-swamp line in New Brunswick, the vehicle which met the train to receive the mail and express was a creaky wagon with a rough plank bed, drawn by a yoke of oxen.

Some of these little roads run mixed trains, some nothing but freights; some have alleged schedules, of others the *Guide* says, "Service irregular." They are quite prepared to violate their schedule—if they have one—when it's a matter of bread and butter to them. For example, let us say a certain one, as the Book shows, runs a mixed train on Tuesdays and Fridays. Whitaker flies down to some express plane stop in the Carolinas or Georgia, takes a train or two, maybe loses a night's sleep and arrives at the terminus on Tuesday morning, only to be told, "Well, y'see, the cotton mill wanted to make a carload shipment on Monday without fail, so we ran the train yesterday insteader today." And they think nothing of leaving a half or three-quarters of an hour ahead of the scheduled time.

All sorts of things delay and tie them up—wrecks, floods, landslides, washouts, breakdowns. Once Whitaker started out on a train just after there had been a fall of snow, and they weren't far out of town before they began bouncing on the ties. Stopping, they found that two rails had been removed, and the snow had prevented its being noticed. Whitaker never did find out who had removed them, but the on-the-spot surmise was the section men needed them somewhere else.

On some of these minor railroads in the South—not the extremely small ones, but the somewhat larger ones which still run passenger or mixed trains—one frequently finds a coach of late Victorian make, with interior finish in fine cabinet work of the sort that isn't being done today; and more frequently an engine of the same period, the one which rail connoisseurs regard, in the matter of grace and beauty, as the Golden Age of locomotive building. And on a few roads such as the Aberdeen & Rockfish, the Georgia & Florida and others, one may find on the pilot one of those fiercely painted, sheet-iron cut-outs of an Indian in war dress, drawing a hostile bow.

For some little lines such as the twins, Louisville & Wadley and Wadley Southern, Whitaker's word is "gorgeous"—"from an antiquarian's standpoint, I mean," he explains. This is undoubtedly what Lucius Beebe means when he speaks of the Prescott & Northwestern in Arkansas as "indescribably beautiful." These two little roads running north and south from Wadley, on the Central of Georgia, are separate corporations, but with some mysterious umbilical tie by which they use the same rolling stock. The one mixed train performs a round trip over the 19.8-mile Wadley Southern in the forenoon, knocks off at Wadley for lunch, and then does the 10-mile L. & W. to Louisville and back in the afternoon. When something breaks down, they borrow from the Central of Georgia, under whose sponsorship they seem to be. The Wrightsville & Tennille and the Sandersville Railroad, near by, are in the same happy family of kinfolks.

Three weeks in succession Whitaker flew down to South Carolina to ride the 20-mile Buffalo-Union Carolina Railroad (now abandoned), but on the first tries, found that it wasn't going to run a train that week; nothing to haul, but was hopeful for next week. On his third trip he was lucky; they ran a train. This road had a nice brick depot at Union, but its locomotive was so asthmatic that when it had twelve gondolas of coal to haul to the cotton mill at Buffalo, it couldn't make the two percent grade with the whole shipment, but had to take them up four cars at a time.

One of his toughest assignments was the Smoky Mountain Railroad (Knoxville to Sevierville, 30 miles). The first time he reached Knoxville, he was greeted with the news that there had been a flash flood on the line and half a mile of the track was covered with gravel; "be several days before we get it dug out." He gave them two months and flew down again. This time he found a surgical operation in progress. "Sorry, Mister," was the news. "One side of our engine's broke down; be two or three days, maybe . . ." He flew back to New York, and came again the following week. He felt an urge because the Smoky Mountain company was trying to get permission to abandon its road (though the State Public Service Commission wouldn't allow it). This time it was bad flying weather, and he came down by train. Believe it or not, a freight wreck made him four and a half hours late in reaching

Knoxville, where he found that the Smoky Mountain had tooled grandly out of town right on time, an hour and a half ago.

He sought a taxi and said, "I know you'll think I'm crazy, but I want to catch that Smoky Mountain train," thinking he'd get at least a piece of the ride.

The driver gave him only one startled look; seasoned taxicab drivers have ceased being greatly surprised at anything. "Well, the highway crosses the railroad twice between here and Sevierville," he said. "I'll do the best I can."

But at each crossing of the track, they learned from people in the neighborhood that the train had passed; it was almost setting a record.

"Keep going," said Whitaker to the taximan. "I can ride back to Knoxville on it, anyhow."

They reached the terminal at Sevierville, and there was the train, the crew, greasy and sweating, laboring over what appeared to be a leaky steam-chest. In fact, steam was escaping in several places. They recognized him at once. It was too bad, the engineer said, but they were having trouble again. Just barely did get here.

"How long will it take to make repairs?" asked Whitaker.

"Coupla hours, maybe."

"Going back to Knoxville today?"

"Yes, sir"; and then, with the hasty stipulation, "if we get this thing fixed."

"Well, I'll ride back with you," said Whitaker.

"Here's my card," said the taxi driver, smiling. "Call me if you need transportation."

But that time—wheezing, coughing, sputtering, clanking, leaking steam at every joint and seam, so that Whitaker expected any moment to be the last, they finally won back to Knoxville and the indefatigable collector added one more to his score.

On the little five- and ten-mile roads, especially in the South, getting passage on the freight trains, their only service, isn't hard. No ticket to be bought, of course, and no stipulated fare. "I declare, it's been so long since we had a passenger," the conductor may say, "I hardly know what it would be right to charge." Once in a while he solves the puzzle by saying, "Oh, shucks, let it go," and collects nothing at all. As for the crews on these little drags, their life is a bit monotonous, and they are pleased to have a passenger, especially one from New York, who has travelled far and wide. "Lunch? Sure, go and eat your lunch," they tell him. "We'll wait for you. There's the lunch wagon right over yonder; food ain't bad. Take your time. Don't worry; we won't leave you. Sure, it'll throw us a little late, but," with a grin, "we can make it up next trip."

Here is one of the chief joys of knocking about on those little Southern punkin-vines; no studied, from-the-teeth-out courtesy for policy's sake, but old-time, homespun friendliness that comes from the heart in a land that still hasn't quite forgotten how to live with serenity and content.

Whitaker can tell you of some railroad curiosities which few Americans will ever see; the Camas Prairie road, up in Idaho and Washington, with thirty-one trestles in 25 miles of track, covering only ten miles in an air-line, before it reaches the prairie; the 69-mile stretch of the old Carson & Colorado narrow gage, in eastern California, north of Death Valley, which the Southern Pacific is keeping alive, as an official confessed, just because they are fond of it and its romantic past; the Nevada Northern which used to have all Japanese section hands, because it was hard to get white men to work in the desert—though the Japanese had to leave when the war came on; the Washington, Idaho & Montana, a 50-mile pike, of whose fourteen stations, eight are named Princeton, Harvard, Yale, Stanford, Vassar, Wellesley, Cornell and Purdue, this by the young engineers and rodmen who surveyed the line, honoring their own and their friends' alma maters, until it occurred to them that they were slighting the girls, upon which they added Vassar and Wellesley; of the Bellefonte Central on a Saturday afternoon, when half of the coach in which he rode was stacked to the ceiling with fiber boxes full of Penn State College students' soiled linen, going home to be washed; of the Western Maryland's big coal drags on its West Virginia division—the former West Virginia Central Railroad—which climbs to 4,000 feet above sea level, the highest bit of track east of the Rockies—where you may at times see—like a horde of ants dragging a huge beetle—as many as ten big steam engines pushing and pulling a 100-car train of coal—though this may be dieselized by the time this book is off the press.

Whitaker began too late to ride on the Jupiter & Lake Worth, the "Celestial Line," on Florida's east coast, whose 8-mile track touched four stations—Jupiter, Venus, Mars and Juno; and he wasn't quick enough to catch the Bartlett Western in Texas, known as "the Road of the Apostles" before it was dismantled during the recent war. Its 23.2 miles between its termini, Bartlett and Florence, were studded with four stations named St. Matthew, St. Mark, St. Luke and St. John, and copies of the gospels of each of those reverend authors were affixed to the walls of the waiting rooms.

Long Island Commuters

We are—and will you all please bow your heads for a moment—railroad commuters. There's nothing unusual about us except that

From *Slightly Cooler in the Suburbs*, by C. B. Palmer, pp. 19–28. Copyright, 1944, 1946, 1948, 1949, 1950, by C. B. Palmer. Garden City, N. Y.: Doubleday & Company, Inc.

we cringe easily. We wear plaid mufflers and snap-brim felt hats (on the male side) and mouton coats and galoshes (on the female side). We tend toward middle-aged spread and are possibly a little lopsided from carrying bundles home. We speak a fairly standard American, but—funny thing—our conversation seems to be rather limited. We're always telling people we're sorry to be late but something went wrong with the train we were on. And the response is always anything from a tired raised eyebrow to "Ah, your father's Hamilton Railroad Special!"

In this brief and troubled life of mine I have made excuses for a branch of the Boston & Maine, a branch of the New Haven, an interurban trolley line (which terrified me the way it went lolloping around curves), and I can't remember how many bus lines.

* * * * *

. . . All I can report on with any accuracy is what happens on the line my neighbors and I use now. This is none other than the world-famous institution known as the Long Island Rail Road.

We come in from The Raunt and Wyandanch and Copiague and East Williston and Baldwin and Floral Park. (At least, we come in when we can.) We feel, in a rather syllogistic way, that ours is the most important railroad in the world—New York the most important city, the Old LI bringing in the most people per day, *ergo,* and so on. We carry Ace Diplomats and Big Wheels in the thumbtack industry. We have Christopher Morley and Powers girls, Guy Lombardo and duck farmers. About 300,000 of us a day use the LIRR. (And, by the way, it's one of the few roads in the country that's an RR and not simply an R.) We travel on 967.5 miles of track over 370 miles of right of way, comprising—we are proud to say—twelve main lines and branches and, so somebody tells us, making up the largest passenger mile haulage of any RR lying within a single state.

We have steam lines, electric lines, and lines which, we've heard somewhere, are powered by a man pumping a bicycle arrangement in a compartment in the head car. We link up the Brookhaven atomic research thing with the rest of the world. We served the United Nations at both Flushing Meadow and Lake Success (change at Jamaica). We haul oysters and potatoes and airplanes in, and we haul coal and automobiles and flat cars loaded with funny-shaped boxes out.

So the Old LI is not anything to be sneezed at. ("For your own comfort kindly help us keep this door closed. Thank you.") We patrons know the line has its quirks and cranks and wanton wiles, but what hasn't these days? We know our RR and it means something to us. Whereas on the Lackawanna and the NYC the passengers talk about baseball and taxes, we of the LIRR talk about the RR.

* * * * *

Man from Douglaston tells how he didn't mind the night when the vestibule door came off in his hands. He just set it against the wall out of the way and got off. He did mind, though, the night the door wouldn't open at all and the train went wheep-wheep! and got under way while he was struggling with it. He hiked it back from Little Neck.

Man from Baldwin (change at Jamaica) says that's interesting, and take his case, for example. He thinks the engineer on his train either had an unhappy love affair in Baldwin or else owes money there. Anyway, he frequently skips the stop. The Baldwin man gets off at Freeport.

Man from Ozone Park (change at Woodside) says he never had that happen to him, but his wife gets upset sometimes when his evening train gets lost. Quite a mess of loops and spurs and crossovers and causeways out around the Rockaways, and sometimes the motorman has to get down at a crossing and ask the shanty man where he is.

* * * * *

Do any other commuters lead such interesting lives? We doubt it. Our very rolling stock has character. We have our Main Line with its steam locomotives and heavy cars and green plush upholstery that is preserved as a memento of Cleveland's second administration. We have the lighter electric cars, which impart that jiggle to our stride and whose basaltic seats of wicker are now gradually giving way to basaltic seats of tasteful plaid and herringbone. We have those doubledeckers in which we play kneesies with perfect strangers. (People on the Port Washington branch were awfully pleased to get some of the brand-new ones. They were hardly discouraged at all when one of the cars fell apart underneath on the first morning, shot sparks out twenty feet and filled with smoke. The passengers just climbed up over a retaining wall and took a bus.) And some of our cars now have overhead fans. They've been working fine on some of the coldest days this winter and presumably will when we need them next summer.

* * * * *

Certain of the younger element, unseasoned and with a narrow perspective, occasionally get a little bit irreverent. They spend the twenty-three minutes which we wait in the tunnel under the East River making up nicknames for the LIRR. Things like the Languid & Indolent. The Lazy & Impudent. The Late & Indefinite. The Lurid & Impish. The Lack of Interest. But they will lose that nervousness in time.

We old-timers—well, we never shot buffalo from the coach windows or had to fight off a wolf pack in the snowdrifts, but we're veterans—we old-timers don't get rattled so easily. We know the RR officials don't get upset, so why should we? Probes come and probes go, trains disappear, and seat backs fall off into the aisle. But the Old LI never loses its aplomb. . . .

PART FOUR

Main Line and Sidetrack

Introduction

In the old individualistic days, when "working conditions were more or less in the rough, as you might say," a freight yard foreman told me, "there were more happenings, both serious and humorous. In those days, when a freight man went out, he didn't know when he'd come back." And as men moved from one job, road, and region to another, often "traveling under a flag," or an assumed name, stories and characters traveled, too.

Years ago I knew a conductor named John Gorman. Around the fall he'd start to grow a beard to keep his neck warm. He was always fond of his liquor. He hated the engineer. He could bellow like a bull—you could hear him ten blocks away. One day he got mad at an engineer, who threatened to go without him; and Gorman threw himself across the track and dared the engineer to run over him.[1]

The question, "Are railroad men superstitious?," is capable of various interpretations. Herbert E. Hamblen answers both in the negative (inasmuch as "their entire training teaches them to look for the causes of things") and in the affirmative—what superstitions they do indulge in naturally pertain to their work.[2] In other words, the necessity of growing up in the business and "internal exclusiveness" (intensified in the early days by "social ostracism") have tended to put the mark of their craft indelibly upon them.

Among other traits the railroader's language sets him apart. It is both functional—"a workaday device for handling situations peculiar to the railroad"—and expressive of attitudes; a tool, along with whistle, lantern, and flag language, and a set of symbols and allusions, as eloquent and esoteric as the missing fingers on link-and-pin brakemen and the scars from flying sparks at the base of the old-time engineer's neck. An old word like "highball" points to the primitive days when a metal globe, originally a basket, was raised and lowered on a gallows-arm on a mast, just as stories of lost, runaway, and hoodoo trains (or cars) point to a time before modern safety devices and regulations made railroading a saner if tamer affair.

Railroad language sets the veteran apart from the newcomer as well as from the community; and the humor of the rails abounds in stories of greenhorns (including tenderfoot officials) who are victimized by tricky terms and pranksters alike. Railroaders as well as passengers

---

1 Alex MacKenzie, Harmon, New York, July 19, 1953.

2 *Munsey's Magazine,* Vol. 27 (July, 1902), No. 4, p. 596.

have fun with the initials of railroad names (see "Appendix," pp. 505–506) to express their uncomplimentary opinions of the lines; while derisive nicknames and jests express the strong clan feelings dividing old hand and new, boomer and home guard, trainmaster and trainman, brass hat or foreman and worker, and men of different crafts or neighboring roads.

When a train came into Boston from the North Conway line, the city fellows greeted the crew with such a welcome as "Here come the Bark Peelers. How are things in the woods?" [3]

The boilermakers called the machinists "nut splitters" and the machinists termed the boilermakers "lost motion machinists." All a machinist had to do to make a boilermaker mad was to say to him, "Listen, pal, you don't have a trade. All you have is a habit." [4]

The ultimate in habit, as far as language is concerned, was attained by "Gun" Gunderson, in one of John A. Hill's stories. Gun was an engineer who "always talked engine about his own anatomy, clothes, food, and drink."

His hat was always referred to as his "dome-casing"; his Brotherhood pin was his "number-plate"; his coat was "the jacket"; his legs the "drivers"; his hands the "pins"; arms were "side-rods"; stomach "firebox"; and his mouth "the pop." He invariably referred to a missing suspender button as a broken "spring-hanger"; to a limp as a "flat wheel"; he "fired up" when eating; he "took water," the same as the engine; and "oiled around," when he tasted whisky.[5]

The strongest of railroad feuds (and still going strong) is the feud between the engineer or "hoghead" (i.e., "no brains," says the conductor) and the conductor or "brains." ("An engineer is a fireman with his brains baked out.") Both engineer and conductor concur in their lack of respect for trainmasters, whom to-day "you can buy for a dime a dozen," according to the former, or who are mostly made out of old clerks, according to the latter.

So off the "Main Line" of modern railroading, with its "replacement of the fallible mind and hand by the infallible machine," folklore lingers on the "Sidetrack," as human fallibility vies with mechanical infallibility, humanizing the machine, with the partial acceptances and resistances that characterize all folklore and folk groups. The Age of Improvisation may be over in railroad technology, but its spirit is far from dead in railroad lore.

B.A.B.

---

[3] R. M. Neal, *High Green and the Bark Peelers* (New York, 1950), p. 223.

[4] Frank Cunningham, *Big Dan* (Salt Lake City, 1946), p. 97.

[5] John A. Hill and Jasper Ewing Brady, *Danger Signals* (Chicago, 1900), pp. 155–156.

I. TOOLS AND TRICKS OF THE TRADE

Transition

Yes, the old times were changing fast. There were new, clean bunkhouses at the terminals, where a man could catch an hour or two of sleep or wash the soot off his face without freezing his hands in outdoor faucet water squirted into a coal bucket. Little holes-in-the-wall that sold coffee and doughnuts and hamburgers were beginning to take the place of the free lunches in saloons.

Men were no longer hired at the nod of the master mechanic or the yardmaster; they had to fill out application blanks, pass examinations and show service letters from their last job. The service letters were supposed to catch boomers—the new crop of them that lost their jobs when they went out with Debs in '94. The roads were bitter about the strike of the American Railroad Union and wouldn't take the men back; so many a good railroad man hit the boomer's trail, wandering from road to road under one alias after another, trying to beat the blacklist. It wasn't etiquette in those days to address a boomer by name when you met him again after a year or two—he was most likely traveling under a new one.

The A.R.U. strike didn't affect our [Lackawanna's Utica] division; very few of the men went out. But we soon began to get the influx of boomers from the Middle West. A lot of them got around the service letter requirement by buying letters from a Negro named "Sugarfoot"

From *Clear the Tracks!* The Story of an Old-Time Locomotive Engineer, by Joseph Bromley, as told to Page Cooper, pp. 280-283. Copyright, 1943, by Joseph Bromley. New York and London; Whittlesey House, McGraw-Hill Book Company, Inc.

Burns in Chicago. For five dollars he sold a man the "secret works" of any brotherhood, a traveling card, and receipts for three months' dues. A service letter cost a buck.

The examinations weren't hard for the old-timers and the boomers who knew their stuff; but they liked to grouse about them—especially the boomers—and complain that it took a college education to get a job of heaving coal. They were always telling us about the wisecracks that they wrote in answer to such questions as "What would you do if the engine wouldn't steam?" or "What do you do when you find a dead body on the track?" The "dead body" was the favorite one. Every boomer claimed that he was the author of the famous answer, "Go through his pockets."

The physical examinations were a good innovation. The younger men got used to the idea of playing kindergarten with strands of colored yarn, to prove that they weren't color blind, and of submitting to examinations in the inspection car that carried an eye and ear specialist and a traveling office equipped with the latest eye charts and lenses and devices for testing the hearing. But to some of the older engineers, who were afraid to admit even to themselves that their eyes weren't so sharp as they used to be, or that they didn't always hear the first indications of trouble with the engine, this car grew to be a nightmare.

Nor did the old-timers take kindly to the standardization of everything, from the issues of waste per mile to the number of seconds to blow the whistle—so many seconds for the long toot, so many for the short. What was life coming to, they protested, when you couldn't play *Polly Put the Kettle On* as a signal to your wife, at your own home crossing? As the old engines were discarded and the new ones came in, each like every other of its class, they could no longer put blocks of wood in their whistles to give them a distinctive note. But regimentation has never yet defeated human ingenuity. Polly still recognized the toot and knew when to put the kettle on, even when her man drove a different engine every day.

Time was doing away with the romance and flamboyant individualism of the tough old days, when a man thought nothing of running sixteen or eighteen hours, catching a cat nap, and staggering, cursing, to the engine for another run—and made up for it with stolen time on the river catching butterfish or snoozing under an apple tree. And the jolly lies about losing time on account of a bunch of cows on the railroad track were outworn. But on the other hand, a railroad man had a much better chance of living to tell about his adventures than he did in the days when we were making legends.

The side-brakes were gone, and the vicious pin couplers; the brotherhoods had succeeded in making air brakes compulsory, required by the Interstate Commerce Commission. Every day new safety devices were giving us a better chance to enjoy our new pensions. There was a lot to be said for the new regime—the fair hearings, regular hours and vacations; but we often felt a twinge of regret for the grand, unregenerate era that produced the Old Man.

Tallow Pot on the Old Black River Line

I. Railroading Was in My Blood

As long as I can remember, railroading has been in my blood. The first sounds that registered on my ears were the whistles of the New York Central trains hooting for a crossing. They drifted over the hill to the farm, calling to me to follow the iron pike. When I was old and sturdy enough to walk six miles to the railroad, I sat on an embankment above the tracks and watched the trains go by, waved to the lordly creatures leaning out of the cab windows, with the wind parting their whiskers, and made up my mind that I too was going to run one of those snorting engines with red-and-yellow wheels and their names in gold letters on their sides.

* * * * *

For two months I had been callboy; already I was dreaming that John Bailey would let me go out on an engine as a student fireman, a "tallow pot," next spring, and then it would be no time until I was set up with an engine of my own, pulling freight over the hump of the Adirondacks and down into the valley of the St. Lawrence—following the river that cut rock gorges and snaked its tortuous, black way through forests toward Ogdensburg on the Canadian border, or hauling the timber from the sawmills of Watertown. And one day I would be on the best run of them all, a fast passenger carrying summer people to Cape Vincent and the Thousand Islands.

To hang out of the right-hand window of the cab of a through train and whistle an arrogant toot to the girls at the crossings then seemed to me a gallant adventure, and after sixty years the feel of the throttle under my hand and the shriek of the whistle still warm my blood. But we can't toot to the girls any more. Life is regulated: so many toots at a way station, so many long and so many short at a crossing. The "Book of Rules" took a lot of carefree individualism out of railroading.

But in the old days, when a train highballed out of the station, the engineer was on his own, a man who rode destiny and twisted her tail. To be sure, the fingers of the old brass-pounders were stretching out after him, trying to harness him to telegraph keys; but on the old Black River Line most of the operators didn't work after five o'clock,

Ibid., pp. 1, 3–4, 11–12, 40–41, 45–50.

and they weren't too scrupulous about the time they reported you out of sight. Sometimes they were almost human, and understood that a smoke-maker and his "brains," as we ironically called the conductor, liked to go fishing.

II. The Roundhouse

. . . I was finding twenty-four hours a day hardly long enough to cram into my head all the fascinating sounds and smells and lingo of the railroad. My trick was from six o'clock in the evening until six in the morning, but by running home the minute I reported off duty, gobbling the hot breakfast that mother had waiting for me, and promptly falling into bed, I was able to reach the yards again by three o'clock in the afternoon. John Bailey let me stay around the shops and the roundhouse, running errands for him and hunting up pieces of waste for the firemen who were polishing brass.

The roundhouse, which was the garage of the line's twenty-two high-stacked, wood-burning engines, was as murky as a pit in hell, and full of noise. Usually five or six engines were in—some of them just off the run, belching into the "smoke racks" over their heads (ventilators that stuck up through the roof and were supposed to carry off the smoke); others puffing a hot black breath as they got up steam. Above them hung a cloud of vapor that smelled of hot oil and steam, and good, pungent burning wood. On the tracks that spidered out from the turntable, Baldy and Rubberguts and the runners of the freights puttered about with oil cans, tinkering with their buggies. The engineer all but owned the engine and made it a glorified reflection of his personality. He bought it handsome tallow pots, bells, and whistles, pasted pictures in the cab, and adorned it according to his fancy. If Black River Jack wanted the high driving-wheels of his engine painted red or yellow or blue with white strips, he gave his fireman a can of paint; and sometimes he even sank a large hunk of his pay into real gold leaf for lettering on the cab.

When the engine was laid up for repairs, the engineer was laid off too; so he looked it over every time he came in off a run and tried to keep it out of the shops. Sometimes he trusted a fireman to grind a cylinder, but not often. His tallow pot was the engine's nursemaid; he kept her clean and polished the brass until it shone like gold. Sometimes a tallow pot let me wash down the jacket, but I was never allowed to touch the brass.

III. The Shop

. . . I was working in the shop until I could persuade John Bailey to send me out firing again. In slow seasons all the men who weren't on regular runs could work in the shop, but they didn't like it because of the poorer pay. A railroader in those days was so handy with the wrench and cold chisel that he could do almost everything short of making a new engine, and he wouldn't have been entirely hopeless at that.

The shop was a great, wide shack with the sun pouring in through the open door and windows all around. Clouds of dust and metal filings danced in the light, and the place was full of the sound of hammering and the grunts and shouts of men wrestling with heavy engine parts. The floor was cluttered with headlights, brass trimmings of engines, flat wheels, and dismembered boilers. It made you feel arrogant and at the same time sad to walk safely among these crippled hulks, which were usually so full of snorting power.

On one side were yellow passenger cars trimmed inside with carved curlicues, very elegant, and upholstered with bright blue plush. They were heated with potbellied wood stoves with silver rails and isinglass doors, which were shined until they looked like black diamonds. The box-cars were gaudy but not so interesting as those that I had seen on the New York Central line when I was a child. On their pale-gray sides were painted portraits in huge ovals, one to a car. I remember best the likeness of the Governor of Massachusetts against a turkey-red background—an overpowering fellow, looking out full face with a high white collar and black whiskers chopped off by the edge of the frame. The Governor of Maine was more of a dandy, a regular profile against robin's-egg-blue—his whiskers, like those of John Bailey, looking as if they had been waved with a curling iron.

But our own Black River cars were by no means subdued when they came out of the paint shop in new blue-and-yellow coats. I would have enjoyed slathering them with paint, but that was a specialized job, so I was put to unscrewing the bolts of crippled engines that had to be taken down. I liked the smell of turpentine and grease and the screeching of files on steel, and I would have been happy in the shop if I hadn't been so eager to get back on the high iron. Every morning I stopped by the board to see if John Bailey could have marked me up and the new callboy forgotten to let me know.

IV. Firing a Wood-Burner

I ran all the way and burst into the kitchen to tell mother that I must dress up, I was going out on the passenger. While I gulped my dinner, she laid out my best blue-and-white checked shirt and black bow tie. With my hair plastered with water and shoes shined, I hurried back to the roundhouse.

Number 22 was already on the turntable, spitting steam. In a few minutes Baldy came in. He and the conductor compared watches, picked up the orders, and we all climbed aboard the engine, the two brakemen riding on the steps. Baldy gave her a whisper of steam, and we slid into the yard to take on wood and water. At the woodpile, the whole crew worked, piling up logs in the tender. Baldy stacked them in the gangway and I filled the firebox. Gently we backed into the train: four bright yellow coaches trimmed with black, a mail car, and, on the tail, a "combo" (an express and baggage car). The head shack dropped in the coupling pin, and we strutted into the station.

* * * * *

After we got the highball and Baldy eased us out, picking up the slack without a bump, he nodded to the steam gauge. "Now, Nobby, you keep your eyes on the steam and see that we carry a hundred and forty pounds. When she gets high and ready to pop, you can open the door a little; but the minute she begins to drop, go to work. You'll have to fire like hell to pull us up to Remson."

Didn't I know it! On that hill I had slit my fingers almost to the bone. Marcy, Stittsville, Holland Patent—we made short, impatient stops, and I took advantage of every one to stoke the fire.

We had no air brakes but we coasted to a fine stop. The baggagemen and the trainmen manned the hand brakes and were so well trained that they turned the wheels on the instant that Baldy whistled for brakes. It was my job to tend the tank brake; so as we slid into a station, I grabbed the club (a tough piece of hickory shaped like a baseball bat), stuck it through the wheel, and at the signal from Baldy gave it a wrench that clamped the shoes tight on the resisting wheels. At Marcy I set the wheel so hard that Baldy had to climb down from his seat and throw his whole weight on one end of the club before we could get it loose.

Baldy didn't say anything or pay much attention to me, except to call orders, until we got up the hill at Remson. Number 17 didn't stop at Trenton Falls, except to leave passengers; and on this run we whistled through without cutting off steam. As we hooted in the outskirts of Remson (a large town with rows of little back yards and gardens flanking the tracks), Baldy shouted to me, "Open the firebox door." I threw it open and watched anxiously while the steam went down.

"It's all right, boy," he explained while we stood in the station. "Got to leave the door open to lower the steam pressure when we come into a big station. When she spits and pops, she's likely to scare the horses; and we can't take a chance of doing that. It's important. Don't you ever forget."

* * * * *

. . . When we had eased out of Port Leyden and picked up our speed, he leaned back in the window and called in an imperious tone, "Boy, my teeth!" I was eyeing the steam gauge, and as I looked around, I nearly tripped over the slash bar. He was holding out to me a set of false teeth—the uppers held gingerly by the points of his fingers. They were dripping with tobacco juice.

"Wash them," he ordered, indicating with his head the tap on the water tank. I put them under the spigot and washed them off. Then he returned them to his mouth and smoothed his beard in the little mirror hung on the front wall of the engine. Four times between Utica and Watertown—every time he finished a chew of tobacco—he held them out to me with that lordly gesture.

"What a man," I thought. "What fastidiousness!" And I burned with admiration.

As I examined him sitting on the high seat, solid and handsome, his heavy white arm lying along the window, with the sleeve meticulously folded back to cut off the head of a tattooed lady, I could find only one imperfection in his magnificent person, a row of little pits around the base of his neck. It seemed almost as if he had been marked with smallpox there and nowhere else. What hair he had left, he wore long over these scars. All the engineers, I had noticed, wore their hair uncut on the back of the neck. Before I got to Watertown, I knew why. The pits were scars from the red-hot sparks that flew down into their collars.

As we shot through this new country, whistling for way stations, I caught a glimpse of rowdy little falls tumbling over saw-toothed rocks, and watched the forest swoop down to little white villages. When Baldy cut off the steam to drift down to Lowville, he said that it was time to oil the valves and cylinders. I knew what I was to do; climb out on the running board of the engine and open the cocks, so that the oil could be sucked from the cups into the steam chest. It looked simple enough when she was standing on the roundhouse track.

From the shelf on the boiler head I took the tallow pot, a handsome one with a spout like a teakettle and shiny brass bands around its black iron mouth. The tallow was warm enough to pour, so I grabbed the hand-hold and climbed onto the board, clinging there for a dizzy moment, trying not to fall off onto the ribbon of ballast shooting by on the roadbed, or against the hot jacket of the boiler. The grade was not steep, but the rails swooped down and around a hill, and the runners pounded in my ears and screeched as they took the curve. Holding myself there, with the wind cutting my face and blowing out my hair in a fan, I thought I was riding a runaway train; but I glanced back and saw Baldy in the cab, resting against the window and smiling at me. This was nothing, nothing at all. Shutting the cocks, I climbed back and nonchalantly threw in a couple of logs.

The Track Man and the Section Foreman

. . . Thay sent a great big Irishman to take the section, and he whas a fine man. And, as Irishman, he would drink some, but he nevver did ask the section men to buy his whiskey. And I wear that summer the jack man on the track, and we wear just about half way betwen Bucklin and Marceline, the devision, one day, and thire whas not a shade tree in a mile of us, and it whas just about as hot a day as you evver see come in July. And when noon came we got our dinner pails, and as wear all used to the hot sun, we sit right down on the track and eat our dinners, and the boys had to, at that, had to have a game of cards. And the section foreman had his coat on the car, and he got it and throwed it down on the rail to keep the rail from burning him, as the hot sun had them rails as hot as a cooking stove. And when he throwed his coat down, it fell on the joint of the track, and as that joint had rusted so mutch that the hot sun hadent pushed [it] to geathor, and that joint whas open just about one inch ore maby more. And thay wear playing cards. And that morning I had broken the handle out of my spike mall, and I got it to fix while we wear at dinner, so I would have it when we started to work again. And knocked out the old stub, and had trimed my new handle down tell I could get it started on. And as I saw it would go by pounding it on a railroad tie, I nevver thought, and just raised up and hit the end of the handle on a tie right behind the boss, and that joint went to geathor and cought the flesh part of his backparts, and it just took out a slug as big as fifty cents. And we had to pull him off that joint, and he just holowed bludy murder and everything that he could holow.

And we had to then take him in, and he went to the hospital at Ft. Madison, Iowa, and he had a very bad time with it. And he showed it to me one day after it had heailed up, and you would have have nevver thought that it would have made the scar that it did. But that man did not get mad at me, and lots of times after that he would come to my house and stay all night, and whas one of the finest old

---

By Samuel M. Van Swearingen.

From "A Manuscript of the Folk Language," by Duncan Emrich, *Western Folklore,* Vol. XI (October, 1952), No. 4, p. 280. Copyright, 1952, by the California Folklore Society. Berkeley and Los Angeles: Published for the California Folklore Society by the University of California Press.

. . . Born in Chariton County, Missouri, in 1869, [he] was 72 years old in the Denver of 1941 [when] he . . . handed me a manuscript "pertaining to my life." . . . The spelling . . . reflects the pronunciation of Missouri. . . . I . . . encouraged Van Swearingen to go ahead. . . . In all, Van Swearingen typed 272 single-spaced pages. . . . I have punctuated, sentenced (sometimes with difficulty), and paragraphed. I have also reduced the capitals for easier reading. I have not touched the spelling, grammar, or syntax.—D.E., pp. 266-269.

men that I evver knew, for if he had a dollar and I whanted it, he has a nomber of times asked me if I needed eney money. And my wife and all the children just thought if that man dident eat XMAS dinner with us, we dident know what whas rong, for I don't think he mised beeing to hour house for XMAS dinner for five years in succession.

Pat's Storekeeping

The section foreman, Pat, or "Boss," as he was called, was one of the old capable Irish foremen of a type which has all but disappeared. He was about sixty years old and had spent his whole life in track work. He was witty, with an answer for every one and was popular with all the roadmen who made it a point to wave to him as they passed.

* * * * *

One morning, John was awakened before daylight by Pat who said to hurry as there was a wreck on the road and they were to go on the early morning train to help clear it. The gang, therefore, was ready at the station an hour before the usual time for going to work. He had told John to get a shovel and pick, and John reported at the station with the shovel and pick used in his daily work.

When John came up, Pat said, "You —— fool. What are you doing with that shovel and pick?"

"You told me to bring them."

"Not those. Take them back and go under the toolhouse and get an *old* shovel and an *old* pick, and when you come home to-night, bring back *good* ones."

On returning to the station, he found that the other men in the gang had learned their lesson at some previous time. All had old shovels and picks, and all brought back good ones, stolen from other gangs, that night.

* * * * *

While walking track one day, John found a broken rail and sent word to the foreman. While waiting for him to come up with the rest of the men, John wondered where he was going to get a rail to replace it, as from his knowledge there were no extra rails on mile posts on this section. This did not seem to bother the foreman in the least. He proceeded a short distance until he came to a swamp alongside

From *The Making of a Railroad Officer,* by Robert E. Woodruff, Superintendent, Erie Railroad, pp. 2-6. Copyright, 1925, by Simmons-Boardman Publishing Company. New York.

the track. He went over to the edge of the swamp and with a pick handle, started fishing, and finally located something hard. In a few minutes, he had recovered a brand new rail from beneath the water. Upon looking carefully, six more were sighted in the same place. Pat remarked, "When we unloaded the new rail here four years ago, I figured the time would come when we would need these rails, so I saved them."

John ventured, "Have you shown these on your book?"

He answered, "Do you think I am a fool?" And the matter was dropped. There were many other corners on the section where piles of spikes and bolts and other material were hidden which had been laid away for future use.

Toward the end of the month, knowing that Pat could hardly read, John offered to help him make up his monthly reports, as he was anxious to see what they looked like. Pat readily agreed. John first checked up the stocks on hand and reported at Pat's home that night. The books had printed headings showing the tools and material. The first column was "adzes." Pat said, "Put down two."

In reply to John's comment, "Why, we have four," Pat said, "That makes no difference. We are only supposed to have two, so put down two."

Next came the claw-bars. Again, "Put down three."

John said, "We only have two."

"That makes no difference. I gave one to another foreman, but we are supposed to have three, so put down three."

When it came to lining bars, the gang had eight. Pat said, "Put down six. The other two I stole from the B & O."

When it came to shovels, there were sixteen. Pat said, "Put down eight. The other eight are under the tool house and are not to be counted." The material scattered along the section in hidden places was not counted in the material book, as that was the section foreman's own private stock for use when he could not secure any more on requisition. Thus John learned storekeeping methods "in the rough," and something of the self-preservation instinct among foremen.

O'Callahan's Solution

X

"In the early days of the Illinois Central," said Conductor Meeks, at the [Illinois] Central Station [in Chicago], "I was working on the Louisville Division on construction work. We had a section foreman

---

From "Campaigning with a Railroad Army," by Gilson Willets, Second Series, No. VII, "Inner Life of Chicago Stations," *The Railroad Man's Magazine*, Vol. III (August, 1907), No. 3, p. 408. Copyright, 1907, by the Frank A. Munsey Company. New York.

named O'Callahan. One day the roadmaster ordered O'Callahan to build a tool-house at a spot exactly halfway between two particular mile-posts.

"To locate the desired spot midway, O'Callahan said to one of his trackmen: 'I'll walk south from the north mile-post and you walk north from the south post. We'll start at exactly the same time, and the place were we meet will be the halfway point.'

"This plan was carried out. At the spot where the two men came together O'Callahan proceeded to build a shanty for the storage of tools. Hardly had he finished the job, however, when along came one of the company's surveyors, saying:

" 'O'Callahan, I've heard how you located that midway point, and I want to tell you that you're off in your reckoning. You are a tall man with a seven-league-boot stride, while the man who did the walking from the other end is a sawed-off-and-hammered-down dub with a step like a dancing-master. Now, I've measured the distance, and find that your tool-house is ninety feet nearer to the south post than to the one at the north. You'd better fix the matter before the roadmaster hears of your blunder and calls you down.'

"A week later the roadmaster turned up.

" 'Well, O'Callahan, is that tool-house exactly halfway between the two mile-posts?'

" 'Yes, sir; precisely halfway.'

" 'But I hear that you built the shanty, at first, on the wrong spot, too near, by ninety feet, to the south post. Did you have any bother moving the house to the right place?'

" 'Not a bit of bother, sir. I didn't move the house. I moved the post.' "

Safety in Sleep

The foreman of a gang of railway men had more than his share of Irish wit. One day he was walking along his section of the line when he found one of his laborers fast asleep in the shade of a tree. Eying the man with a smile, he said:

"Slape on, ye idle spalpeen, slape on. So long as ye slape ye've got a job, but when ye wake up ye're out of wurrk!"

From *Along the Line,* reprinted in *The Delaware and Hudson Company Bulletin,* Vol. 7 (September 15, 1927), No. 18, p. 286. Albany, N. Y.

Economy

I [1]

James J. Hill, empire builder and founder of the Great Northern, was an extremely thrifty man. Making one of his periodic rounds of inspection one day, he discovered a new track spike on the roadbed. With fire in his eye and the spike in his hand, he sought the section foreman. The foreman, who must have been one of the quickest thinkers ever born, saw Mr. Hill approaching, saw the spike, guessed what was coming and hurried to meet him.

"Thank goodness you found that spike, Mr. Hill!" he exclaimed. "I've had three men looking for it for nearly a week."

II [2]

The Boggs River & Northern Railroad was putting into effect almost rigid practice of economy. Locomotives were patched and repaired with old parts and pieces until O'Leary, the shop foreman, threatened to break down under the strain.

To cap the climax, one day a worn-out-looking locomotive was placed in the shops. O'Leary was asked to give it a thorough examination with a view to ascertaining just what would be required to put it in first-class running shape. That same afternoon, O'Leary, having completed his review of the locomotive, dispatched the following laconic note to headquarters:

No. 36—in to-day. To put in complete repair: Jack up her whistle and build a new engine underneath.

III [3]

. . Dan was with the [Norfolk & Western] road foreman of equipment once when he was examining a new fireman. Included in the examination was the item of economy, especially of oil and waste. Safety was, of course, stressed. The road foreman asked the young fireman what he would do if he was running fifty miles per hour on a single track and saw another train approaching. Remembering the safety and economy angle, the fireman replied, "Why, I would grab the oil can and a bunch of waste and jump off!"

---

[1] Communicated by H. R. Wiecking, Public Relations Assistant, Great Northern Railway, St. Paul.

[2] From *Judge*, reprinted in *The Express Gazette*, Vol. 42 (July, 1917), No. 7, p. 202. Cincinnati and New York.

[3] From *Big Dan*, The Story of a Colorful Railroader, by Frank Cunningham, p. 197. Copyright, 1946, by Frank Cunningham. Salt Lake City: The Deseret News Press.

Yardmaster's Troubles

[On the St. Joseph & Grand Island] in the winter of 1871, I left Elwood at one o'clock in the afternoon, and was just eight days and nights getting through to Hanover. Never had my clothes off, never sat down to table to eat but twice, and what rest we got was sitting in the caboose. We would get into a snow bank, bucking snow all the time, and get our little eight-wheel engine stuck, and go down and shovel snow from around her, take the jacks and set under the engine and raise off of weights, so we could pump her up. The pumps were connected with the cross-heads, and we would shovel snow into the heater pipe in order to have water. We would dig coal out of the snow on the tender with our hands in order to keep the engine alive while she was stuck in the snow.

On one occasion our engine left the track in a cut and laid over on her side against the rock. We shoveled the snow out and leveled the engine up with jackscrews, and put her on with a hemp rope and incline and frog, with a baggage car. We left the coach back a distance and used the baggage car to jerk the tender on, and we dragged the engine on the same way. Had no ash pan on the engine, no pilot, no smokestack. We went up on the side of a hill and tore down a man's fence and built a fire in the engine, got a salt-barrel and put on for a smokestack, and took the train to Hanover.

Rock would fall off sometimes and break the oil-box on one side of the train. We would have to take off the brake-chain to fasten the pieces of oil-box together, so we could bring the train in. We had no telegraph and no telephones; if we got in trouble, we had to work out of it.

The St. Joseph & Grand Island had pretty hard sledding for the first four or five years. We worked six months in 1871 without pay. The company was short of equipment, and some of the fellows would get dissatisfied because of no pay, and they would sue the company, get judgment and levy on some locomotive or car, and tie up the little equipment the company had.

I recollect going west on a local freight when a sheriff got on at Hiawatha with a judgment against the engine. We told the sheriff he could not tie us up on the main line, but would have to get on the sidetrack. The sheriff said, "Well, I will get on and ride down to the switch"—but instead of stopping when we came to the switch and going onto the sidetrack, we kept on going and did not stop any more in Brown County. We took the sheriff to Nemaha County line and put him off and let him walk to Sabetha and buy a ticket back to

---

Abridged from "Tales from Old Timers—No. 22," by George L. Anderson, Retired General Yardmaster, St. Joseph Terminal Railroad, St. Joseph, Mo., *Union Pacific Magazine,* Vol. 4 (April, 1925), No. 4, pp. 18, 34. Omaha, Nebraska.

Hiawatha. We ran that crew and engine three or four weeks; would run them out of St. Joseph until we got to the Brown County line, then we would run through Brown County and get clear to Sabetha before we made any other stop. We would set the merchandise for Brown County out at Sabetha, and let the crew who was not in trouble do the local work for Brown County.

After I had taken over the yard in Elwood, they ran an attachment on my switch engine and chained it down to the rail. I went down the next morning, and Mr. Tuttle said to me, "They have got your engine tied up." I said, "Well, sir, I do not know whether she is tied up or not, but I will go down and open the switch." As I went by the engineer, I said to him, "I am going to open the switch, and when I give you the signal, I want you to come out." He pointed down to the drivers, but I shook my head that I did not know anything about that and said, "When I get the switch open, you come out." I opened the switch and gave him the signal, and he just took up the slack and broke the log chain and came out. The deputy sheriff came to me and said, "Did you know that engine was tied down?" I said, "No sir, I do not know anything about that, but I will guarantee you will never tie her again." He said, "I will tie her to-night." I said, "I will guarantee that you don't, as I will leave her on the main line all night." After that, I left a hostler with the engine all night on the main line, and they dared not tie anything to the main line.

Six of our box cars were attached and tied up in East St. Joseph and stayed there for fifteen or eighteen months. Mr. Tuttle and Mr. Hanson came to me and said, "George, can you get those box cars?" I said, "Yes." I went to Hi Alder, yardmaster of the Hannibal & St. Jo and I said, "Hi, you have six of our box cars tied up on Starch Factory Track. Will you give them to me at one o'clock today?" He said he would if I was there at one o'clock; and so I slipped across the river and got an engine out and came over and got the cars. In about twenty minutes after we got them, the letters and numbers on them were painted out; they were plain red. We used those box cars several months without any lettering or numbers.

Whenever we could get hold of an empty box car, we generally took it. If we could not get it farther than Elwood, we would take it there and keep it on the sidetrack until we could send it farther west. I recollect one day the Kansas City, St. Joseph & Council Bluffs yardmaster put eleven cars on a sidetrack near the east end of the bridge, while he went to dinner, after which he was going to take them to the freight house to load with freight for his road. While he was gone, I rushed an engine over the river and pulled those eleven box cars to Elwood and hid them in the woods, so we would have cars when we needed them. The only way we could move what little business we had to move was by hooking somebody's equipment to do it with.

The Origin of "Wabashing"

["Time-Check" McCuen] stated that during the "Q" strike he was switching in East St. Louis for the Bridge Terminal. One day, just as the strike was an assured stunt, the Terminal G.Y.M. gathered up every Q car, perishable and all, and rushed them for delivery, so as to clean the yard of hold cars, also avoid damage claims and such from thievery or rot, or other causes. He wanted to clean his hands of Q stuff before 12 midnight the night the strike took effect.

[Bill] was a drunken savage foreman on the goat that Time-Check was riding with that night, and they dragged a long string over the bridge for the Q East St. Louis yard delivery, and when they arrived at the transfer track, it was chockablock—not a damned car could this foreman shove in. He was about half shot then, so what did he do but couple onto the first car out on the transfer, with his own drag, then gave a signal to the hogger to go ahead. Naturally the slack was stretched well out of some seventy-five or eighty loaded cars, but that was all the goat was able to pull. However, this foreman didn't want them pulled, he wanted the slack that was in all those cars for a purpose. When he got it, he walked up to the hogger on the goat and said, "Hank, when I give you a backup signal, shove hell out of that drag you're coupled onto."

Bill sneaked down the string of cars on the transfer and with his own little footsies kicked off all the dogs he found holding a brake set for keeps, to ward off more cars. Not only was there going to be an embargo put out, but switches were to be locked and spiked, brakes set, and wheels chocked with ties, and everything to keep any more cars from arriving on the Q line.

After Wild Bill got all set he was way down out of sight of any Q trainmen or officials, but where he could see Hank. He then gave the big circle sign to back up. He embellished the signal with faster and faster swings of the lantern until his light made a complete ring of white, and Hank, having all that slack, gave the goat all she had in her. He shoved, and kept shoving, until the last car Wild Bill had in his cut was in the clear on the Q transfer; then he gave a stop sign, cut off and, stepping on the footboard, returned to the Terminal yard for other work, well satisfied with his delivery.

Now, as you probably know, the Bridge Terminal then was owned by, or controlled by, the Wabash system. It was affiliated in some way with Jay Gould's stock manipulations before the old Wabash went into the hands of a receiver.

From *The Railroad Man's Magazine*, Vol. IV (February, 1931), No. 3, pp. 475–476.

As told by "Time-Check" McCuen to Charles Anthony Roach ("Silent Slim"), Portland, Oregon, when the two worked together in the South.

So trainmen working on the Wabash or Terminal were like brothers. They rode and got passes and such over either line with little or no trouble, although there was no public knowledge of the interlocked associations. Anyway, Wild Bill received his time for that night's shove, and, like all nuts of that era when something they'd done came up against them, they demanded to know what they were fired for, and caused a lot of hot air to percolate around where they raved over a terrible insult of whatever had been perpetrated upon their lily-white characters.

Wild Bill naturally demanded to know why he was fired. The G.Y.M. was a level-headed, good-humored guy, and he'd received a report of the damage Wild Bill had done, shoving that string in the clear. So this G.Y.M. turned to a clerk and asked for the letter, which he showed to Wild Bill.

Pretty soon out rushed Wild Bill, cursing like a savage and frothing at the mouth. "I'll sue 'em for that, so help me, I'll make 'em weep over that word. There ain't no such damned word anyway—they reported me for 'Wabashing' that transfer track. Who the hell ever heard of Wabashin' cars?" And with that the men began to laugh over the strange charge.

It was learned that a chief clerk over in the Q yard office had named the stunt by reporting it to his superior in these words: "Last night some crew filled our yard with cars, piled 'em all over the yard, so that the wrecker will be busy for a month clearing up the mess. It was a Wabash stunt," he stated.

And with that, the term got started, so when any wild shoving was pulled off, or smashing of cars in an effort to push them in some place where they couldn't possibly fit, it was laughed at as Wabashing.

The Conductor and the Trainmaster

Many trainmasters today are made from office clerks instead of old railroad men. They take a clerical man who has the proper influence somewheres along the line, and appoint him a trainmaster. And it takes him years to accumulate experience in operations—you can readily see that. He has to go through the entire routine that a brakeman has to go through; for example, what constitutes switching, make-up of trains, trying of air brakes, and so forth. He has to learn that—he comes out of the office instead of off the road.

Generally speaking, a trainmaster has to be a friend to the men and still assert his authority to get the work out. There's no question about

---

As told by a conductor on the New York Central's Hudson Division, Harmon, New York, July 13, 1953. Recorded and transcribed by B. A. Botkin.

that. He has to have the cooperation of the men because, as you probably know, we have what is known as the Book of Rules (the railroad's bible), and in order to get these trains in and out at particular times, he's got to have the cooperation of the men. It's just a question—the way it is all over the railroad—of give and take.

I have an example of this. A number of years ago I was the conductor on a switcher in the Bronx Terminal Market, and we had this trainmaster (who was made from one of the yard clerks) come down and ride the job. And it just goes to show you how it worked out. He wanted to know what that hose was between the cars—which was actually the air hose. Those are the men that the management bring out. And, unfortunately, the management doesn't take those things into recognition—that the men don't know what it's all about and have to go through all the ropes.

Now I'll never forget one time this particular trainmaster I was talking about with this air hose business. He was there in the place we switch cars, which is BN, where the Putnam Division and the Hudson Division come together. The trains come down off the Hudson Division, and they leave their cars at Spuyten Duyvil. The switcher goes over to Spuyten Duyvil and hauls the cars into what we call BN yard, which has four tracks.

This particular trainmaster was obsessed with the fact that these crews were going to make overtime (the officials had probably hammered it into his head that he'd got to cut out the overtime). That particular morning there were four cars of kosher meat. This has to be delivered in Westchester Avenue yard in the Bronx before nine o'clock. If it's not delivered there before nine o'clock, it has to be rewashed by a rabbi, at a cost of $25 a car.

Well, this particular morning this trainmaster came over to BN, it happened that the conductor was on overtime. And he said to this conductor: "Take your caboose and go back to Kingsbridge freight yard and tie up. You're on overtime, and we have orders to cut it out." And the conductor tried to tell him what he had in his consist there. The trainmaster didn't want to know anything about it—about these cars going to Westchester Avenue with the kosher meat. The conductor just took his caboose, went over and tied up and went on home; that is to say, he terminated this particular day's work. Well, the repercussions of that were heard around the world, so as to say—all over the electric division—that this tied up four cars of kosher meat and it cost the railroad $100 to have the cars rewashed, whereas if they'd only let him go to the Westchester Avenue yard they would have made the deadline and it would have been easier all around. That's just an instance of what I mean.

Oh, there are quite a number of instances in relation to trainmasters. I was in the Croton West yard one time, a number of years ago. I was making up the Chevrolet train. I had about 46 cars to go to the Chevrolet plant in Tarrytown. I went in to write up the wheel report in the yard office, and this trainmaster came bellowing out. He says, "Why don't you get moving?" I had a 500 series diesel engine. "I can't possibly get moving," I said. "We've got to pump up the air in this train. We just coupled it all up." "Well, as soon as you get it," he said, "get moving. It shouldn't take long." I said, "We have, unfortunately, these diesels that take 30 minutes to pump up 46 cars of air. And," I said, "you'll have to bear me out in relation to time. You take your watch out, and while you're doing that," I said, "I'll be making up the wheel reports for these cars." And he was incensed. He was so mad he didn't know what to do—he really was mad. Well, actually it took 29 minutes to pump up the 46 cars of air before we could get out of the place. But that's just an instance of trainmasters.

There's an old expression among the train crews: As long as they make trainmasters out of clerks, train crews'll have good jobs. They'll always make a dollar. Because they always have repetition of things. For example, this particular trainmaster. He'd bring the first drag of cars from "Spike" [Spuyten Duyvil] over to BN—five cars. He knew darn well that the next train down from Selkirk was right on the heels of the first train. Why double back there and make a double move? No. He'd make us take the five cars and bring them over to BN, and by the time we got to BN—the switching point—it was time to go back and get ten more cars, whereas, if we had but waited another ten or fifteen minutes, we could have got the fifteen in one move and saved the extra switching move and the waste of time.

The best thing the trainmaster can possibly do is to leave the crews alone and let them do their own switching. They've been used to that. As to this particular trainmaster, one time I was switching there in BN. One of these trains come in there on DM 2, which goes into Westchester Avenue, and she dropped 56 cars. And he come down with the switch lists—four copies of them—and he started telling me here to make the cut, here to make the cut, here to make the cut, and double here. So I said, "Sounds very good, Mr. B. When you get through switching, let me know. I'll be upstairs in the tower." He says, "Why?" I says, "Well, there's only one conductor on the job. He's got to make the moves. We can't follow two bosses." "Well," he says, "here, here, here—you take the switch list, and do what you can." "Well," I says, "that's all there is to it. You go up there and watch."

Breaking the Rules in the Old Days

Every road in the United States has a written code of standard rules. Every employee in train and engine service must know these rules as well as he knows his A, B, C, but it's been my observation that the fellow who never violates one of those rules is the guy who is always looking for a job.

Every road puts out special orders and rules to cover extraordinary conditions on their pike, and these must not be violated—but they are! When you hear some division superintendent praising a conductor for getting over the road in short order, you can always put it down in the blue book that the conductor is lucky and is getting away with some long shots.

I am reminded of "Hard-Luck" Strenk, of the In and Out, in this particular. He never broke a rule in his life because he didn't know enough, and every pay-day the Old Man used to say that half of his check was made while he was on a siding. He never would get over the division on time, because he tried to clear every superior train by five minutes; and if he couldn't do it, he would stay in the clear just wherever he happened to be.

I have started out on a drag of cars, six hours behind that fellow, and beat him into the terminal by two hours, all because I had a conductor who took chances. When you take the chance and get away with it, you're a good railroad man; when you take the chance and fall down on it, if you don't play the principal part in a tragedy, you get a large piece of hardware tied to you and go out to hunt a new job.

Make the time, get over the road, that's what you have to do if you're going to keep your full name on the pay-roll; and you're expected to know that the standard rules are there just to keep the company in the clear. Here's a few things a good railroad man does every day of his life which are against the rules on almost all roads:

He will flag against trains; he won't clear by five minutes if he knows he can make a station by the leaving-time of a superior train; he won't brake the air-hose before he cuts off a car; he won't shove a car into the siding when he can kick it in just as well; if he's on a local, he'll run ahead of any old train, any old time, any old way, to get over the ground, and he gets away with it ninety-nine times out of a hundred.

It's the hundredth time when he don't make good that gets box-car letters in the newspapers.

When you take a chance, and the Old Man wants to know about it;

From "Being a Boomer Brakeman," by Horace Herr, *The Railroad Man's Magazine,* Vol. X (January, 1910), No. 4, p. 640. Copyright, 1910, by the Frank A. Munsey Company. New York.

when you fall down running ahead of the varnished cars and lay them out for ten minutes, of course you are supposed to have an argument more unique than logical. If you can't talk fast, you are supposed to take the "Brownies" without talking back and promise to be a good boy.

I'm reminded that Dennis Duleay illustrated the point very finely one morning when the Old Man found him going out on a drag without his conductor's badge on his hat. The Old Man made a bluff at being angry at such a flagrant violation of the rule-book. He walked up to Dennis, who was signing the register, and this is what followed:

"Dennis, where's your badge?"

"It's on me hat."

"It's not on your hat."

Dennis put his hand up to the front of his hat where the badge should have been, grinned at the Old Man a minute, and came back:

"Sure, it's on me hat. I have two hats."

And it's the same sort of an argument which gets a man out of trouble when he violates the rules in the interest of the company.

In the Link and Pin Days

. . . Freight cars had only hand brakes and link and pin couplers; this meant the cars had to be coupled by hand.

Dan watched a gang of boomer (transient) brakemen and switchmen come in the yards and ask for work. The yardmaster asked them to hold up their hands in lieu of references. If the applicants had several fingers missing, the yardmaster knew they were "old timers" and would be able to go on the job as experienced workers and not students.

On the Witness Stand

I [1]

A railroad switchman was a witness in an accident case arising out of a head-on collision. While on the stand, he described how he saw two trains bearing down on each other on the same track at a terrific clip.

From *Big Dan,* The Story of a Colorful Railroader, by Frank Cunningham, p. 97. Copyright, 1946, by Frank Cunningham. Salt Lake City: The Deseret News Press.

---

[1] Communicated by Nathan Frankel, New York City, October 5, 1953.

One of the lawyers asked him: "What went through your mind when you saw this?"

The switchman drawled, "This is one helluva way to run a railroad!"

II [2]

. . . On a certain piece of track used jointly by two railroads, a rear end collision occurred. A suit was filed as to responsibility for the damage. The engineer of the train that ran into the rear of the other road's train testified that he had not been flagged. The Negro flagman of the struck train swore he was back the proper distance and had swung his lanterns vigorously to stop the oncoming engine. The colored flagman was so apparently sincere and honest in his testimony that the jury believed him in preference to the engineer and awarded the suit to the struck train's road. After the trial, one of the winning road's attorneys complimented the flagman on his clear-cut testimony and for not being confused by the opposing attorney's questions. "Well, boss," said the flagman, "all I did was jest to stick right to the truth. But, boss, I was sure scared that gentleman was goin' to ask me, was them lamps lit?"

III [3]

At a railroad wreck official investigation recently, according to an exchange, the "Brakesey" on the carpet recalled his version of the story thiswise:

"The 'con' was flipping the tissue in the doghouse; the hind 'shack' was freezing a hot hub, near the hind end; 'tallow pot' was cracking diamonds in the tank; 'Eagle Eye' was down greasing the pig; and I was bending the rails, when they hit us."

Under a lengthy cross-examination this was translated to mean that the conductor was examining the orders in the cupola. The rear brakeman was cooling off a journal. The fireman was breaking coal. The engineer was oiling the engine, and the head brakeman was throwing a switch, when the collision took place.

---

[2] From "With Tongues of Fire," by Bill Knapke, *Railroad Magazine*, Vol. 59 (January, 1953), No. 4, p. 42. Copyright, 1953, by Popular Publications, Inc. New York.

[3] From *The Railroad Telegrapher*, Vol. XVII (March, 1900), No. 3, p. 221. Published monthly by the Order of Railroad Telegraphers. St. Louis, Missouri.

A Catch

An engineer had been running for some time when orders came through that all engineers had to pass an intelligence test. This one was not very bright and was afraid that he would fail the test, so he convinced the examiner that he would do better if he took the test on Sunday. "I have a family to support. I'd lose the day's pay. I can't afford it, and it would upset me so that I'd never pass the test. Let me take it on Sunday, and I know I can do better."

At last the examiner was convinced and gave the test on Sunday. "This test," said he, "is only one question. You are running a train from Rouses Point to Albany, stopping at Saratoga. Tell me where you would stop, sidetrack, and so forth, for other trains, signals, etc."

The engineer answered quickly, "I'd stop at Saratoga and Albany."

The examiner yelled, "Why, man, that's ridiculous! You'd have seven accidents. You'd hit the rear of the freight train, one place you'd hit a passenger train. You'd never make it. I never heard anything so foolish!"

The engineer said, "You said I'm running this train today, didn't you?"

"Yes."

"Well, today is Sunday and them other trains aren't runnin'."

The Last Desperate Expedient

An applicant was being examined for the position of tower man. The trainmaster had the neophyte up in a wayside tower, which controlled a passing track. He asked the young man what he would do if both switches were set for the main line, and two trains were in approaching each other at 60 miles an hour. The fellow replied, "I would throw a lever and put one of the trains on the siding." The examiner said, "Yes, but suppose when you try to throw the lever, the cable breaks. Then what?" The man answered, "I would run down and throw the switch by hand." The trainmaster said, "Suppose you found the switch locked?" To this the young applicant replied, "I would go to the section house, get a hammer and break the lock." But

---

From "Two Catches and a Tall One," *New York Folklore Quarterly,* Vol. III (Winter, 1947), No. 4, pp. 357-358. Copyright, 1947, by New York Folklore Society. Ithaca, New York.

As told by W. H. Dralle to Dorothy Dralle.

From *Big Dan,* the Story of a Colorful Railroader, by Frank Cunningham, p. 254. Copyright, 1946, by Frank Cunningham. Salt Lake City: The Deseret News Press.

the examiner wasn't satisfied. "Let's say the section house was locked. Remember, all this time the trains are coming closer at 60 miles an hour. Now what would you do?" The man sighed. "Well, I'd get on the telephone and I'd call up my wife. I'd say, 'Honey, get the hell down here as fast as you can, 'cause there's going to be the damndest wreck you've ever seen.' "

He Gave Himself Away

Dana Krum, one of the conductors on the Erie Railway, was approached before train time by an unknown man, who spoke to him as if he had known him for years. "I say, Dana," said he, "I have forgotten my pass, and I want to go to Susquehanna; I am a fireman on the road, you know." But the conductor told him he ought to have a pass with him. It was the safest way. Pretty soon, Dana came along to collect tickets. Seeing this man, he spoke when he reached him. "Say, my friend, have you got the time with you?" "Yes," said he, as he pulled out a watch. "It is twenty minutes past nine." "Oh, it is, is it? Now, if you don't show me your pass or fare, I will stop the train. There is no railway man that I ever saw who would say, 'Twenty minutes past nine.' He would say, 'Nine-twenty.' " He settled.

Argument by Analogy

A good story is told of a fireman who went to the Superintendent for a pass out on the road to his home, and the Superintendent declined to give it. The fireman thought and said that it was pretty tough after working several years for the company to be compelled to pay his fare home when he wanted to go, which was not often, and naturally he growled about it.

"Now look here," said the Superintendent, "suppose you worked for a farmer out in the country, would you expect him to hitch up his team and take you home for nothing every time you wanted to go?"

"Well, no," said the fireman, "but if he had his team all hitched up and was going out by the house, he'd be a damned hog if he wouldn't let me ride."

He got his pass all right and went home.

From *Railway Adventures and Anecdotes:* Extending over Fifty Years, edited by Richard Pike, p. 184. London: Hamilton, Adams and Co. 1887.

From *Early Day Railroading from Chicago,* by D. C. Prescott, p. 117. Copyright, 1910, by D. C. Prescott. Chicago: David B. Clarkson Company.

A Lesson in Etiquette

When Stuyvesant Fish was president of the Illinois Central Railroad he was sitting in his office one morning with the door closed. The door was suddenly opened and in came an Irishman with his hat on his head and pipe in mouth. Walking up to Mr. Fish, he said: "I want a pass to St. Louis."

President Fish, somewhat surprised, looked up and said: "Who are you?"

The man replied: "I'm Pat Casey, one of your switchmen."

President Fish, thinking it was a good chance to teach the man a little lesson in etiquette, said, "Now, Pat, I'm not going to say that I will refuse your request, but there are certain forms a man should observe in asking a favor. You should knock at the door before you come in, and when I say 'Come in' you should enter and, taking off your hat and removing your pipe from your mouth, you should say, 'Are you President Fish.' I would say, 'I am. Who are you?' Then you should say, 'I am Pat Casey, one of your switchmen.' Then I would say, 'What can I do for you?' Then you would tell me and the matter would be settled. Now you go out and come in again in a little while and see if you can't do better."

So the switchman went out, closing the door. About two hours later there was a knock on the door and President Fish said, "Come in." In came Pat Casey with his hat off and pipe out of his mouth.

Pat said, "Good morning, are you President Fish of the Illinois Central?"

President Fish said, "I am. Who are you?"

"I am Pat Casey, one of your switchmen."

"Well, Mr. Casey, what can I do for you?"

"You can go to h—–l. I got a job and a pass on the Wabash."

Ingalls and the Operator

Despite his distinctions, [Melville E. Ingalls, creator of the Big Four Railroad system, now a part of the New York Central] retained his sense of humor and relished jokes at his own expense. . . .

[An] incident to which he confessed—long afterward—was that of a

---

From *Merrill* (Ia.) *Record,* May 23, 1929, reprinted in *Kansas City Star.* Collection of Carlton J. Corliss, who notes that the story has also been told on President J. T. Harahan.

From *The Road of the Century,* by Alvin F. Harlow, pp. 389-390. Copyright, 1947, by Alvin Fay Harlow. New York: Creative Age Press.

night when a train, with his private car at its tail, was stalled alongside a lonely little station. The crew, with the exception of a rear brakeman, who had gone back with a flag, were all out ahead of the train somewhere. After some time had passed, Mr. Ingalls suggested to his son, a youth in his latter teens, that he go to the station and learn, if possible, what was the trouble. The son walked forward to the station, which was near the middle of the train, and found it tenanted by a lone operator in a green eyeshade, who was pounding a telegraph key like mad.

"Know why the train's stopped?" asked young Ingalls.

The operator ignored him and continued to hammer the brass. The boy, a bit diffident, stood irresolute for a few moments, then went back to the car. "Operator was so busy, I hated to bother him," was the report.

There was another wait in dead silence for several minutes, and then the impatient executive sent his son up to the station again, but with the same result. "Can't get a word out of him," he reported upon his return.

"Well, I will!" snapped his father. He swung down from the car steps and strode to the station. "Say, what's the matter?" he demanded. "Why are we hung up here?"

With a barely perceptible pause in the clicking, and the mere flick of a peevish glance aside at the questioner's legs, the operator grated, "If you G. d. s. o. b.'s will stay away from here and leave me alone, we'll get this thing straightened out."

After a moment's startled hesitation, the president turned and trudged meekly back to his car.

"Find out what was the matter?" asked his son.

"Oh, just a little trouble up ahead," replied the father, casually. "They'll have it cleared up directly."

The Red Flag

Samuel Breeton was the first agent of the railroad company (at Biggs, Cal., in 1870), and he was followed by a man named Cecil, who had opened a small store there, and was the first postmaster. Cecil, having a great many things to perform, was not thoroughly posted as to his duties. The conductor of a train presented him with a red flag one day, telling him to wave it and stop the train when there were any passengers who wished to get aboard. On the following morning the train was flagged; and to the conductor's query, "Where's your pas-

---

From *History of Butte County, California,* by Frank T. Gilbert, Harry L. Wells and W. L. Chambers, II, p. 246. San Francisco, 1882.

sengers?" Cecil replied, "There ain't any, but I thought maybe some would like to get off."

Washout

Tim Callahan got a job on the section working for a railroad. The superintendent told him to go along the line looking for washouts.

"And don't be as long-winded in your next reports as you have been in the past," said the superintendent, "just report the condition of the roadbed as you find it, and don't use a lot of needless words that are not to the point. Write like a business letter, not like a love letter."

Tim proceeded on his tour of inspection and when he reached the river, he wrote his report to the superintendent:

"Sir: Where the railroad was, the river is."

Finnigin to Flannigan

Superintindint wuz Flannigan;
Boss av th' siction wuz Finnigin.
Whiniver th' cyars got off th' thrack
An' muddled up things t' th' divvle an' back,
Finnigin writ it t' Flannigan,
Afther th' wrick wuz all on agin;
That is, this Finnigin
Repoorted t' Flannigan.

From *Everybody's Magazine,* reprinted in *Illinois Central Magazine,* Vol. 6 (March, 1918), No. 9, p. 75. Chicago, Ill. Collection of Carlton J. Corliss, Association of American Railroads, Washington, D.C.

From *Including Finnigin,* A Book of Gillilan Verse, by Strickland W. Gillilan, pp. 11–12. Copyright, 1908, by Strickland W. Gillilan; 1910, by Forbes & Company. Chicago.

This, probably the most famous railroad poem ever written, was knocked off one day in 1897 by Strickland W. Gillilan, when he was a reporter on the Richmond (Ind.) *Palladium,* with the glorified title of city editor. He was astounded by its instant and enormous popularity. *Life,* then a noted humorous weekly, reprinted it. From coast to coast, long afterwards, the seven words comprising the climax and close of the poem were on everybody's lips, and they are not forgotten yet. Overnight, Gillilan became nationally famous. He went to the Baltimore *American* as a columnist, and became a noted lecturer. He wrote many other poems, but as he himself said, "Not more than one Finnigan happens to one man in one lifetime."

Whin Finnigin furrst writ t' Flannigan,
He writed tin pa-ages, did Finnigin;
An' he towld just how th' wrick occurred—
Yis, minny a tajus, blundherin' wurrd
Did Finnigin write t' Flannigan
Afther th' cyars had gone on agin—
That's th' way Finnigin
Repoorted t' Flannigan.

Now Flannigan knowed more than Finnigin—
He'd more idjucation, had Flannigan.
An' ut wore 'm clane an' complately out
T' tell what Finnigin writ about
In 's writin' t' Musther Flannigan.
So he writed this back. "Musther Finnigin:—
Don't do sich a sin agin;
Make 'em brief, Finnigin!"

Whin Finnigin got that frum Flannigan
He blushed rosy-rid, did Finnigin.
An' he said: "I'll gamble a whole month's pay
That ut'll be minny an' minny a day
Befure sup'rintindint—that's Flannigan—
Gits a whack at that very same sin agin.
Frum Finnigin to Flannigan
Repoorts won't be long agin."

Wan day on th' siction av Finnigin,
On th' road sup'rintinded be Flannigan,
A ra-ail give way on a bit av a currve
An' some cyars wint off as they made th' shwarrve.
"They's nobody hurrted," says Finnigin,
"But repoorts must be made t' Flannigan."
An' he winked at McGorrigan
As married a Finnigin.

He wuz shantyin' thin, wuz Finnigin,
As minny a railroader's been agin,
An' 'is shmoky ol' lamp wuz burrnin' bright
In Finnigin's shanty all that night—
Bilin' down 's repoort, wuz Finnigin.
An' he writed this here: "Musther Flannigan:—
Off agin, on agin,
Gone agin.—Finnigin."

The Wind Was High

Old stories die hard. The rhyme of Finnigin and Flannigan has been ascribed to nearly every man in the United States—except the one who was actually responsible for it. Now there comes to the Editorial Carpet another old-timer, sent us by a correspondent in Pottsville, Pennsylvania. This time it is told of Billy Tuckens, a fireman on the Reading.

Billy forgot his fire, and his train was hung up for lack of steam, blocking No. 8, a fast passenger. The train-dispatcher demanded a reason for the delay, and Billy vouchsafed the following explanation:

The wind was high; the steam was low;
The train was heavy, and hard to tow;
The coal was bad and full of slate;
And that was the reason we blocked No. 8.

If Billy Tuckens was really the originator of this gem, there is a laurel waiting somewhere for his modest brow.

Racing Again

. . . A favorite [Mobile & Ohio] pastime was racing engines with men of the New Orleans & North Eastern (now in the Southern system), whose tracks paralleled those of the M&O for several miles through Mississippi cotton fields in the vicinity of Meridian. This sport was finally halted by the General Manager, who posted a bulletin forbidding such practice.

Shortly after his announcement an M&O runner received a challenge from an NO&NE man, which for the sake of his honor he would not refuse. When the two enginemen approached Enterprise, the first station south, the M&O hogger pulled into the lead, becoming the victor. His exultation was short-lived, however. On arriving at the next station he met the General Manager, who, unknown to the engineer, had boarded the train at Meridian. The G.M. strode forward, demanding: "Been racing agin, haven't you?"

The offender, recalling that the warning had threatened dismissal for all violators, quaked as he replied, "Yes, sir." He was greatly relieved to hear the brass hat comment:

From *The Railroad Man's Magazine*, Vol. III (August, 1907), No. 3, p. 573. Copyright, 1907, by the Frank A. Munsey Company. New York.

From "Rebel Route," by Stuart Covington, *Railroad Magazine*, Vol. 37 (January, 1945), No. 2, pp. 20-21. Copyright, 1945, by Popular Publications, Inc. New York.

"Well, I won't penalize you this time, seeing that you won, but if you had let that son of a biscuit on the NO&NE get ahead of you, there's no telling what I might do."

A Carload of Mules

A train dispatcher is a half-witted nincompoop who sticks you in a blind siding [a non-telegraph station] and forgets you. Ask any rookie tallowpot or brakie. . . .

For twenty years I was one of those half-wits, tucked away in an isolated attic bending over a train sheet daily for eight hours. And looking back over that feverish period I am inclined to agree with friend tallowpot and friend brakie.

But there is one thing to be said about a train dispatcher. He gets the whole picture. The train sheet is an accurate, ever-changing map of the division with its freight and passenger trains weaving in and out, working and worming in both directions from one end of the division to the other. And if the division be single track, look out. Tragedy lurks in the offing. Pathos is there, too, and humor. The latter helps a lot to ease the strain.

It was a hot day in August. I happened to be handling the Big Sandy Division, on the old Chesapeake & Ohio that day. Across the glass-partitioned table from me, George J. Derbyshire struggled and sweated with the single track Lexington Division, full of trains and everything going wrong.

Came a lull on the Big Sandy. I leaned back in my chair to catch my breath, at the same time automatically reading what the telegraph instrument on the other side of the table was saying. All was telegraph in those days. What I read was coming from the operator at Winchester, Kentucky, a hundred miles down the line.

"First 92 is here, dispatcher. Pop Berry says tell you he's got a carload of mules next his caboose and they've kicked four slats out of the side of the car. 'What must he do?' "

Now a helpless conductor, one who is eternally stopping a busy train dispatcher to ask about some minor detail, gets in a train dispatcher's hair worse than anything. I was watching Derby through the glass table partition.

"Tell him," he said, after swallowing hard, "to borrow a hatchet and nails from the agent, nail the slats back, and bring the car forward."

It was more than an hour later and again a lull had come in my work.

By William H. Overley, *Railroad Stories,* Vol. XIX (March, 1936), No. 4, pp. 76-77. Copyright, 1936, by the Frank A. Munsey Company. New York.

This time it was the operator at Midland, a coaling station, that I heard reporting to Derbyshire.

"Pop Berry on First 92 is here," he was saying. "He says tell you those mules are kicking worse than ever. Four more slats are kicked out and one mule has his leg caught in a crack. 'What must he do?' "

"Tell him," the dispatcher said tensely, "to bring that carload of jackasses to Ashland if it takes him all day and all night. We want to make conductors out of them."

The next day dispatcher Derbyshire was called into the superintendent's office. Pop Berry was there with dignified, white-haired superintendent John A. Fox.

"Mr. Derbyshire," the latter began soberly, "Conductor Berry is here with a serious complaint. He tells me that yesterday while on First 92 at Midland, doing his best to get his train over the road with a car of refractory—ah—animals next his caboose that you, in effect, called him a jackass. Conductor Berry feels humiliated and that an apology is due him. I agree with Conductor Berry."

The dispatcher looked hard at his old super, caught the faintest of twinkles, and came through like the good sport he was.

Five minutes later, after cordial handshakes and mutual assurances of good will and good feeling, Pop Berry marched out of the office with the air of a conquering hero. And the minute the door was closed, two tactful division officials, convulsed with laughter, bent double over a flat-topped desk. But Pop didn't know that.

Enough Was Enough

Cyrus H. Jenks was a division superintendent for the Great Northern Railroad at Crookston, Minnesota, in the early days.

En route to St. Cloud one day he received a message to the effect that a locomotive tender had fallen into the turntable pit at the Crookston roundhouse, and that a hand derrick was being used to extricate it.

A few miles down the line he received another message: "Hand derrick now in pit. Shall we send for steam derrick from Melrose?"

At that, the pressure in the Jenks boiler rose to the danger point. He wired his roundhouse, "Leave steam derrick where it is. No more room in pit."

Communicated by H. R. Wiecking, Public Relations Assistant, Great Northern Railway. St. Paul, Minnesota.

Tenderfoot Officials

A prominent Union Pacific official, in yellow gloves and blue glasses, once asked a brakeman why the coach in which he was riding was uncomfortably cold. The brakeman replied that the heater was in the rear instead of the front end of the car. That afternoon a sharp letter went to the superintendent of motive power and machinery, ordering the cold coach in the shops, in order that the heating apparatus might be taken out and put in the front end. The mechanical superintendent wrote, explaining that there was no front or rear end to a day coach; that all depended upon the direction in which the car was moving; that the heater had been all right going out that morning, but that this was a branch line, with no table or "Y" at the other end; but there is no evidence that the new official ever understood the letter.

Another importation was being shown over the road by the late "Tom" Potter, then general manager. Out on the plains there were a great many "Y's." At one point they backed in on a spur to allow a long train to pass. "I say," said the tenderfoot, looking about, "there's only one leg to this 'Y.' "

"Oh, damn it!" said Potter, "this is no 'Y,' this is a spur, and you must not talk that way before the trainmen or they'll insist upon tying you under the bridge till you get used to the cars."

The same official once wrote a letter, it is said, to the road master, reproving him for his wanton waste of steel. He had watched a yard engine for an hour going up and down the yards, and there were rails with bent ends spiked down among the switches, that were never touched by the wheels of the passing engine. He ordered these rails taken up, straightened out, and used in building side tracks.

The road master did not answer the letter. He called personally and explained to the thoughtful official that the rails referred to were guard rails, put there for the protection of the lives of employees and the property of the company.

Greenhorns

"We all have to learn," replied Boomer Bill. . . . "The first trip I made, we stalled on Gads Hill and when the conductor came around and said, 'The engineer's jerked out a lung,' I started off up the road

---

From *The Story of the Railroad,* by Cy Warman, pp. 38-39n. Copyright, 1898, by D. Appleton & Company. New York. 1906.

From *Boomer Bill, His Book,* by I. M. Brown, pp. 43-46. Copyright, 1930, by I. M. Brown. [No publisher, place, or date.]

to hunt a doctor. 'Come back here,' he yelled, 'where the blue blankety blazes you going?' 'Won't he need medical attention?' I asked. 'Medical attention, nothing,' he replied, 'all we got to do is to drag this half-ton chain about sixty car lengths and hook her around that draw bar, and get into clear at Des Arc for No. 4.'

"The biggest trouble with the student is he has to learn our language before he can get along on the railroad. When I was still making my student trips, we stalled one day and the engineer says, 'We'll have to back down a ways and blow up.' I started to join the bird gang, and he grabbed me by the arm and queried, 'What's the matter?' 'If this engine is going to blow up,' I told him, 'I'm going to get away from it.' I suppose you heard that story about the student fireman on the L&N. When they started out, the engineer told him to look out for the mail cranes. They went along about a hundred miles, and the engineer heard the fireman yell: 'Wait a minute, I missed one.' He looked back and saw that the fireman had the whole deck full of mail sacks he'd been grabbing off the cranes.

"Why, I was so dumb I thought a 'Riverton turn' was some kind of a vaudeville stunt, and the first day I caught the Hoxie local and Charlie Ketcham told me I would be the swing man,[1] I hunted all over the train for the swing. Finally I went over to the engine and asked Lem Fiske what the swing man had to do. Lem winked at his fireman and says, as solemn as an owl, 'Son, that's a pretty important job for you to tackle. You see, when we go around these curves and the cars swing to the low side of the track, you have to jump over on the high side and balance the train, so it won't tip over.' By the time we got over that curve track between Leeper and Hendrickson I had up a pretty good sweat.

"We were setting out a couple of empties at Neelyville one morning, and got a pair of trucks off. Charley sent one of the students after a pair of frogs. He was gone a long time, and just about the time the 'con' was ready to explode, he came back and said: 'I couldn't catch any frogs, Mr. Ketcham, won't a couple of toads do?' Another thing I'll never forget is the day I first tried to get off a moving train. I was calling nights at Poplar Bluff, and every morning I would take a ride on one of the gravel trains down to Harviell and back. Well, it looked so easy to see the old heads get off that I tried to do it, lit stifflegged and plowed up considerable of the right-of-way. 'Heinie' Heiligman was running the train, and he tied into me. 'What's the use of spreading gravel on this track, if you're going to come down here and scatter it all over creation?' He then proceeded to instruct me in the proper manner of alighting from a moving train, and since then I have caused the section foreman no extra work."

[1] Middle brakeman.

Student Switchman

. . . The yard crew [was] shoving a cut of cars onto a spur. This spur curved to the left so it was necessary to give signals on the fireman's side of the engine. One of the switchmen was a student, and after the cut had been shoved to the spot the foreman [conductor] had indicated, he told this student to set a binder [hand-brake] on the first car in. The student set his lamp on the ground and cooned the buggy [climbed the ladder to the hand-brake]. The foreman had been looking in another direction, but turned his head again just as the student got on top. "Hey!" said the foreman. "Don't ever set your lamp down this way, always take it with you." And he picked up the student's lamp and gave it an easy toss up to him.

Back in the engine cab the tallow was leaning on his armrest watching for a signal from the switch crew. Across from him the hogger was sitting sideways on his seat, his legs astride the Johnson bar, one hand on top of it and the other on the brake valve, all ready to move as directed. Suddenly, instead of the expected, "Easy, ahead," or "Take 'em out o' here," he heard the fireman muttering, "Holy cow! I wouldn'a believed it if I hadn't seen it."

"What's going on? Whatcha muttering about?" queried the hogger.

"By golly," said the tallow, "one of them switchmen out there stood flat-footed and jumped clean on top of a boxcar, and he had his lamp in his hand too."

They Didn't Speak the Same Language

Years ago Freight Conductor Henry Petrey, on the Cumberland Valley Division, between Middlesborough, Ky., and Norton, Va.—"Uncle Henry," as he was universally known—had a shrill voice that made it a distinctive one. . . . It was the usual practice of Uncle Henry's crew to head in on the wye at Appalachia, cut off their engine, do their station switching and then come back and pick up their train.

On this particular day, Uncle Henry's regular brakeman had laid off and he had the misfortune to catch a "boll weevil" (raw recruit) with only two weeks' experience. As somewhat of a sartorial offense to old hands, this new employe showed up, wearing a large black hat.

From "Tongues of Fire," by Bill Knapke, *Railroad Magazine,* Vol. 59 (January, 1953), No. 4, pp. 42-43. Copyright, 1953, by Popular Publications, Inc. New York.

From "Didn't Speak the Same Language," by John A. McGinniss, *L. & N. Employes' Magazine,* Vol. 27 (March, 1951), No. 47, p. 6. Louisville & Nashville Railroad Co. Louisville, Kentucky.

Subsequently, going down the hill into Appalachia, the green brakeman was on top of the train setting brakes, and to keep the wind from blowing his hat away, he stuffed it into his right hip pocket.

As the local neared Appalachia, Uncle Henry got out on top of the caboose and signaled the brakeman, patting the top of his head with his hand to indicate that they were to head into the siding. The brakeman, not knowing what the signal meant, and thinking Uncle Henry was solicitous about his hat, patted his right hip pocket.

At that, Uncle Henry exploded in choice expletives and lush descriptive adjectives, sputtering in his high-pitched voice:

"Look at that so-and-so-and-so-and-so brakeman! Been workin' here two weeks, and when I tell him to head in, he says run around and back in!"

The New Brakeman

I [1]

Years ago on the Knox & Lincoln, the little woodburner was having a hard time dragging the freight up Warren Hill. When at last she got 'em over, the engineer sighed: "I was afraid she'd stall and they'd run back with us."

"Nothing to worry about," the new brakeman assured him. "I went back and set all the brakes."

II [2]

One train ran into another one on the Harlem Division a couple of years back, and there wasn't much damage—just a shaking up of the cars. In the investigation the following morning the new rear brakeman of the first train was asked whether he had thrown off any fusees in the fog—it happened to be a foggy night. And the brakeman testified, "Yes." Later on in the hall the conductor said to him, "Hey, Bill, I looked back and I didn't see any red fusees. I didn't see any light." The brakeman said, "What! Are you supposed to light them?"

---

[1] From *Belfast & Moosehead Lake Railroad Waycar Magazine,* Vol. I (January, 1948), No. 4, p. 14. Belfast, Maine.

[2] As told by Harry Nestle to B. A. Botkin, Harmon, New York, October 12, 1953.

The New Fireman

The new fireman kept looking at the narrow pipes leading from the engine cab, and on asking the engineer what this particular pipe was, he was told it was the straight air pipe. After thinking for a moment, he asked: "How can they put straight air through a crooked pipe?" There are two kinds of air—one is for the automatic brake that operates brakes for the whole train; the other is straight air for the brake on the engine only. The pipe leading to it was bent all around, of course.

At Spuyten Duyvil bridge, the West Side freight trains get stopped to let the boats through. This particular time the new fireman got annoyed at being stopped because he was in a hurry to get home. He complained about being held up. So he was told they planned to do a dredging job and dredge the channel eight or ten feet deeper so the boats could get through without having to open the drawbridge.

Freight Car Repair Yard Pranks

Car repairers, or "car toads," as they are derisively called by trainmen and others of higher station and salary, are the aristocrats of their particular department. They put back into running order freight cars that have been damaged by wrecks or the effects of age. Lumber hustlers and helpers are next in station to the "car toads," and last of all are the laborers who carry away the waste material discarded from the cars and flung into the aisles between the repair tracks.

The apprentice "car toad" is often the butt of sardonic jokes perpetrated upon him by his superior, the journeyman car repairer, but seldom at the hands of lumber hustlers or laborers. The car repairer reserves the right to gull his own apprentice, but resents the playing of pranks by others.

One of the duties of the apprentice is to carry his superior's tool box about, and often it is filled in advance with coupling pins and other heavy articles so that the apprentice cannot lift it from the ground, let alone carry it. Again, an empty and locked tool box may be nailed through the bottom to a sill or box car floor, and the apprentice ordered to fetch it. While he tugs away in vain, the "car toad" cries on in affected impatience, expressing amazement at the delay in

---

As told by Alex MacKenzie, freight yard foreman, New York Central System, Harmon, New York, July 19, 1953. Recorded and transcribed by B. A. Botkin.

From "Chicago Industrial Folklore," by Jack Conroy. Manuscripts of the Federal Writers' Project of the Works Progress Administration for the State of Illinois. 1939.

bringing the tool box, which, according to the owner, is imperatively needed.

An apprentice is frequently sent to the store room with a material requisition calling for a "doogin pin," a "whilakaloo brace," a "half dozen rubber reamers," or a "pair of celluloid rivet tongs." Whenever the wrong material has been used on a job or any sort of botching done and the error is detected by the checker, the "car toad" sometimes protests that the apprentice selected the material and did all the work single-handed, and thus must bear full responsibility. This shouldering of the blame upon the assistant is not taken seriously either by the checker or by the car repairer, but is done to worry the apprentice, who may be severely reprimanded by the checker.

The beginning lumber hustler is subjected to an initiation designed to prove that "a weak mind and a strong back" are the only prerequisites for the job. Car wheels being delivered to the repairers are transferred from one track to another by way of a wooden platform bisecting the tracks. In order to turn the wheel about, one man thrusts a notched stick beneath one and elevates it into the air while his fellow workmen push on the other end. It requires some skill and practice to elevate one end of the wheel on the notched stick and to hold it balanced while the other end is being turned. If the wheel is traveling with sufficient momentum and the wheel stick man adept enough, the other end will whirl about under its own power. The newcomer is often assigned to the wheelstick when the wheel is going at a high rate of speed. As a result, he is often tossed into the air from the impact, or at least severely shaken.

Another ordeal for the lumber hustler is the siding or roofing board carrying test. The newcomer braces himself while two of his fellows pile board after board upon his shoulders. When his knees begin to sag, he is propelled forward for a few steps and then turned loose. If he walks a specified distance without falling or dropping his load, he has successfully passed the test. If he fails, he must try again.

The older type of box car is built on long wooden sills, and these are often carried on the shoulders of seven or eight lumber hustlers. The shorter men obviously have the better of it on such occasions, and the tall men are wont to insist that these make up the difference in height by wearing a shoulder pad surmounted by a wooden block. A new hand, however, may find himself burdened with the entire weight when he is placed in the middle and the others stoop simultaneously at a prearranged signal.

One of the least desirable jobs about the freight yard is that of the "dope pullers" who extract "dope" (woolen waste soaked with grease, which is packed inside the journal boxes to lubricate the wheels). The beginning "dope puller" must submit to a ritual which includes greasing various parts of his body with "dope." Since he must sit down on a low stool while either packing in fresh "dope" or pulling out the old with a steel hook, the "dope puller" usually has his back turned toward his wheelbarrow. An experienced man never picks up the wheelbarrow handles and pushes before he examines the wheel and extracts the long bolt which is almost certain to be thrust through it to hinder its turning. Another favorite trick is to mix a can of used "dope" with the fresh, thus spoiling the whole batch and earning the "dope puller" a bawling out from the man in charge of the "dope house," where the batches are prepared.

Laborers or lumber hustlers are not permitted to touch any work habitually performed by a car repairer or apprentice. A waggish car repairer may arrange himself beneath a box car under a sill or timber in such a position that the weight appears to be crushing him. When the prospective victim, a guileless laborer or lumber hustler, passes by, the car repairer summons him to his aid with loud cries of feigned pain. As soon as the victim lifts on the timber, the car repairer miraculously recovers and also begins to lift. At this point a foreman who is assisting in the joke makes his appearance and reprimands the victim for doing work forbidden him. The victim's protests that he thought he was helping an injured man are scoffed at, since the car repairer insists that the victim voluntarily offered to lend a hand at the repairer's regular work.

Pranking and Hazing Railway Mail Service Substitutes

Stories about new subs' inexperience make laughable reading. There are many versions of the tale in which the newcomer is told to stack numerous important bags of mail in a storage car or bin "with the labels out" (for quick perusal from the aisle); the sub reports to his chief with a whole pocketful of labels, necessitating opening and examining every pouch. Another classic: A sub is given a row of labels in proper order and asked to "put them in" a row of pouches to be locked out; not knowing about label holders, the young innocent drops them inside each pouch, locks the unlabeled pouches, and usually has them all in a heap just as the first throw-off point is reached! Then there was the sub instructed to "take down" a row of overhead boxes of mail, being given an empty pouch for the first box's contents as an example. Of course he puts the mails from every box into the one pouch, necessitating a frenzied reworking of the contents. Subs have sometimes made up a "junction box" for letters for all points

---

From *Mail by Rail*, The Story of the Postal Transportation Service, by Bryant Alden Long, with William Jefferson Dennis, pp. 51-54. Copyright, 1951, by Simmons-Boardman Publishing Corporation. New York.

which are R. P. O. junctions, just as they are required to do with junction cards on their examination practice case.

Harassed substitutes are sent from one clerk to another, in search of a sack stretcher, case scraper, or similar weird article, or are put to work counting locks when they've nothing else to do. But such jokes can backfire. When Boundary Line & Glenwood (MStP&SSteM) clerks used to run through to St. Paul, Minn., on Train 110, the second clerk would set a green sub to sandpapering the rust off locks as they ran into Minneapolis and St. Paul, giving the observant transfer clerks at both places a good laugh. But one day the district superintendent greeted the train on arrival and asked the sub what he was doing. Answered, he remarked, "Do a good job of it," and walked in for a quiet word with the clerk-in-charge. There were precious few locks sandpapered on that line after this.

One gag was to require a new sub to get off the train at each stop to announce its arrival in loud tones. W. F. Kilman tells how, on a MoPac train stopping at Poplar Bluff, Arkansas, he dutifully leaped to the crowded platform to cry out, "OH YES, OH YES, ST. LOUIS & LITTLE ROCK TRAIN 7 HAS NOW ARRIVED." On the same trip he learned that all sacks were to be "thoroughly washed and sacked twenty to the bundle with each layer sprinkled with talcum" before arrival at Little Rock. Fortunately for him, the basin and talcum could not be located.

Hazing new clerks has declined considerably following such tricks as that once played on the Rock Island & Kansas City (Rock Island) years ago, when a sub, awed at the huge piles of working mail, asked what would happen if it was not sorted in time. An old clerk cracked, "Oh, if we have a few left at the Mississippi, we just heave 'em overboard" —and a few minutes later, when the sub went stuck on an "East States" sack, he did just that! It was rescued by a fisherman, and the old clerk guarded his joking after that. (When the writer,[1] asked the same question as a sub, the old "head clerk" just straightened up and announced with set jaw, "Young man, this crew *never* goes stuck!")

On the old Davenport & Kansas City (CM&StP), in the days of "sack time" when clerks could sleep on duty, a clerk-in-charge asked a sub to awaken him at Dawn (a small Missouri town) to finish his reports —and, of course, was not awakened until daylight, at the very end of the run. Jokes about subs and others distributing mail "nice and evenly" among all sacks in a rack, without regard to destination, date back to the pre-R.M.S. "route agent" days. In the 1850s, W. H. "Hoss" Eddy (CB&Q agent, Chicago-Burlington) boasted of "the fairest distribution of mail ever made. As it came into the car I piled it all on a big table; when the engine whistled for a station, I looked . . . to see

[1] Professor Dennis here.—B.A.L. and W.J.D.

how big the town was, and poked into a mailbag what I thought was the town's share and put it off."

Railway Mail Catching Stories

Tales of "catching on the fly" are legion. A. D. Bunger, of the Oelwein & Kansas City (CGW), had a series of failures to catch at Peru, Barney, and Lorimer, Iowa. Although the headlight daily revealed each pouch landing in its place, he'd swing out his hook and catch nothing—the pouch would be nowhere, not even on the ground. His correspondence on the matter piled up, but when an inspector visited, the catch was normal. Next trip it happened again at Peru and Barney, but at Lorimer the train stopped for passengers and the station agent threw in the Lorimer pouch and the Peru and Barney pouches also. The fireman had brought up the other two, explaining that he'd found them on the end of his rake, which he'd left protruding across the end of the tender. The rake had acted as a catcher, holding each pouch for miles.

One clerk used to depend partly on a white horse in a certain field as a landmark for a catch—and missed it when the horse was moved to another lot. When Bert Bemis, now a well-known writer, was a clerk on the Omaha & Denver (CB&Q) he made a nearly fatal exchange near Lincoln, Nebraska. His key chain became entangled with the cords of a pile of sacks he was dumping out and they pulled him out to hang in space from the safety rod until pulled in by other clerks. One clerk on another run caught a small trunk off a truck instead of the intended pouch.

When a Texarkana & Port Arthur (KCS) train once stopped in Leesville, Louisiana, a young lad jumped up and hung on to the catcher arm, seeking to "bum" a ride that way. When the clerk opened the door to make the catch at the next town he saw the boy in the nick of time, for it would have been fatal if the prongs of the oncoming crane had hit him. Dragging the frightened youngster inside, the clerk undoubtedly saved his life.

A classic story tells about a substitute who missed the first catch, which made his station list one behind, and he later put off each local pouch one station ahead and was reported by thirty-two postmasters for missending their mail. And legend has it that on reaching the terminal of the run, he had up his catcher arm, since he thought one more town was due to be caught.

Ibid., pp. 88-91.

Pullman Porter Sign Language and Lingo

In the folklore that has grown up around porters is the belief that they have an elaborate sign language by which they communicate with each other as their trains pass in opposite directions. The only bit of sign language one reporter was able to unearth has to do with the hotel guide book that appears in a rack at the men's end of a sleeper. The male reader will have seen it often, a fat volume with a bright red cover. Well, if this book is held up to a window, flat against the glass, when two trains are passing, it means that a Pullman inspector, or spotter, is somewhere about, and the porter so warned had best see that his car is in fine condition.

Porters never lack for topics of conversation. Much of the talk takes place in the Pullman dormitories maintained by the company in all of the large terminals. Here in the barracks, between runs, porters discuss the ups and downs and exciting moments of life aboard a sleeping car. The talk fests are known in the trade as the Baker Heater League, so-called from the now obsolete type of heating apparatus once used in Pullmans.

In talk among themselves porters refer to a "boxcar," by which they mean the new type of all-room Pullmans. An observation car is a "buggy." A "tin can" is a buffet car. A "battleship" is the oldline 16-section sleeper. Like mariners with ships, porters have favorite cars, and then there are jinx cars, bad luck for any one. . . .

The Runaway Pullman Car

. . . A porter, Johnson, . . . in 1908 was in charge of a car on the Northern Pacific running between St. Paul and Seattle. Johnson left St. Paul on November 5, in the sleeper *Umpyna,* deadheading to Butte, where he arrived on the 7th and learned he was to remain there overnight. So, well content with the layover, he ate his supper, made up a berth in the empty *Umpyna,* and went to bed about eleven o'clock.

Sometime in the night Porter Johnson awoke to find that his car was in motion. This did not immediately worry him, for he believed, naturally enough from long experience, that for some reason or other the yard crew was shifting his car to another track. But he put up the shade and looked out. It was still dark, but he came to the conclusion

From *The Story of American Railroads,* by Stewart H. Holbrook, pp. 335-336. Copyright, 1947, by Crown Publishers. New York.

Ibid., pp. 336-337.

he was moving pretty fast, far too fast for yard switching, and he also saw what looked to be a small depot flash past.

"I lighted my lantern," said Porter Johnson in his report to the Pullman company, "and began to ascertain the situation of things. Went to front end of car and found nothing in front of me, no signals nor anything. So I says to myself, 'This is queer railroading,' and went to the other end of the car and found standard car *Kooskia* hooked onto me. I went through the *Kooskia* and found no porter or anybody else aboard, and kept on to the rear vestibule and found it same as front of my car *Umpyna*. . . ."

Porter Johnson thought it was time he did something. His two-car engineless train was doing, he calculated, about 75 miles an hour. He grabbed the brakes and began turning the ratchet. It didn't seem to do any good at all. "So," he reported later, "I then ran to front end of car and saw men piling ties and putting a rail across the track in order to ditch me, not knowing anybody was aboard. But me and my two cars was too slick for that game and broke the rail in two pieces and shoved the ties ahead near two miles, knocking down all the switches. The Butte & Anaconda freight had just pulled in below Durant, and they threw open their switch, which put me on their road and at the same time administering to me an upgrade. While otherwise I would have kept on the NP down grade to four miles beyond Durant, and as Number 2 *Northcoast Limited* was late, saved me from slapping them square in the mouth. So I am still alive but am awful scared. Cause of the runaway, brakes being released by some unknown person in the yards. They telegraphed all along the line to look out for runaway cars, but I was beating all telegraphic communications time."

"Operator's Fist" and the Phillips Code

The fact that the speed of the telegraph was kept within the limits of the ability of the receiver to copy in longhand tended to emphasize the need for more speed in this respect, so telegraph operators gradually abandoned the Spencerian and Palmer Systems of penmanship and devised one of their own, based entirely upon speed, with no thought whatsoever of beauty or legibility. This new type of penmanship did not come into being over night, you may be sure; in fact, it was developed slowly, over a period of years—one operator adding a little here and another adding a little there—until it emerged as a finished product, comparable to a stripped-down chassis of an automobile. Everything was eliminated that could be, and new ways of mak-

---

From *Working on the Railroad,* by O. H. Kirkpatrick, pp. 103-104, 106-107.

ing letters quickly were devised, the idea being to keep up with the speed of the sender. This new type of writing, in time, came to be known as the "operator's fist," and no more resembled Spencerian, or Palmer, penmanship, than day resembles night. It was hard to read, too—that is, until one became accustomed to it. Operators and trainmen and most of the other railroad men could read it, but it was a bit difficult for the uninitiated.

Now the race for speed between the sender and the receiver was on, and they were running neck-and-neck. There had always been in use in telegraphy a system of "cutting" known as the "Phillips Code," which was simply the abbreviation of certain words, and it was used continually in conversations over the wire, but it was useless in sending and receiving messages, as the sender could already send as fast as any one could copy. So its use was confined to casual conversations over the wire—those which did not have to be copied.

* * * * *

The following is an incomplete list of these abbreviations:

Anr	another
B	be
Bg	big
Bk	back
Bn	been
Bo	bad order
B4	before
C	see
Cl	carload
Cn	can
Cy	copy
Dh	deadhead
Dm	damn
Ds	dispatcher
Em	them
F	if
Fm	from
Fr	for
Ft	foot
Ga	go ahead
Gd	good, or God
Gm	good morning
Gn	good night
Gt	get
Gv	give
Hm	him
Hr	here, or hear
Hv	have
Hy	hurry
Jb	job
Jt	just
Kd	knocked down
Kp	keep
Lcl	less carload
Lk	look
Ly	lay
Md	made
Mk	make
N	in
Ng	no good
Nt	not
O	of
Oh	on hand
Ok	correct
Opr	operator
Os	report train
Ot	on time
Pk	pack
Pt	put
Qk	quick
Rj	relief operator
Sd	said
Sm	some
Sn	soon
T	the
Tk	take
Tp	top
Ts	this
Tt	that
Tts	that is, or that's

U	you	Ws	was
Vy	very	9	train order
Wb	waybill	25	busy on another line
Wh	who, or where	30	that's all, or the end
Wk	work	&	and

In addition to these, all those in general use such as Dr., Mr., Mrs., A.M., P.M., and many others were made use of.

Dots and Dashes

The operator always carries his dot and dash with him. You will find him making a key of his knife at the table, if his dinner is slow; and communicating with his wife in monosyllables, which he is taught to believe save both time and money. It is the ruling passion strong in death.

When we were summoned to the death-bed of poor Charlie Phillips at New Albany he had but an hour or two to live.

"No use, boys," said he; "no battery; no current; zinc's all eaten away, and no time to galvanize now. Guess I'll have to cut off."

* * * * *

Talking about fellows carrying the dots and dashes with them, I know two who made it pay. They left the Louisville office, and went down the Mississippi River on a sporting tour—playing cards for money. They managed always to sit opposite each other, and conversed freely with their fingers on the table. They won every time, and being apparently strangers, the trick was never suspected.

The Harvey Girls

[Fred Harvey] has been given credit by some hearty eaters for "civilizing the West." Doubtless he helped, but some of the honors should go to the famous Harvey Girls, who took a demure decorum into the wild places. Most of them married well-to-do Westerners and carried into their homes the culinary niceties and social poise that distinguished Harvey House staffs.

The Santa Fe got its Harvey girls by running ads in newspapers all over the East and Middle West. These called for "Young women of

---

From *Romance and Humor of the Road,* A Book for Railway Men and Travelers, by Stephe R. Smith, pp. 130, 131. Chicago: Horton & Leonard, Railroad Printers. 1871.

From *Sante Fe, The Railroad That Built an Empire,* by James Marshall, pp. 100–101. Copyright, 1945, by Random House, Inc. New York.

The Harvey Girls are also famous for their "cup-code": . . The first course [was placed] on the tables under the inspecting eye of the headwaitress, who was known as the "wagon boss." . . . Having seated themselves and decorously eaten their mush or fruit, the patrons were asked whether they preferred coffee, tea, good character, attractive and intelligent, 18 to 30." No experience was necessary, but the good character requirement meant what it said. In most places the girls were under the stern eye of a matron, slept in dormitories and had to be in by ten o'clock, except on special occasions.

The girls promised, when signing, not to marry for a year, but love often found a way. Harvey accepted the frequent weddings philosophically and often staged parties for the newlyweds. The experience was that if a girl got through her first six months at Dodge City or Las Vegas or Albuquerque unwed she—and Harvey—were pretty safe for three or four years. Harvey always congratulated a girl who got through her first half year without an engagement ring.

Many teachers, wearying of the schoolroom and yearning for the wild, free life of the West—advertised in some Santa Fe literature of the period as "unrestrained by the crass stupidities of boiled-shirt civilization"—became Miss Harveys. They were not extra welcome, usually being unwilling to conform to the strict discipline and the direction of the matron.

The standard uniform included black shoes and stockings, a plain black dress with an "Elsie collar," and a black bow. The hair had to be plainly done and ornamented only with a white ribbon neatly tied. The hours usually were regular, but in cases of delayed trains the staff was expected to work any hours to get the passengers fed. For all this the starting wage was $17.50 a month, plus tips, board and sleeping quarters, which was generous for the day. Most passengers left tips, and, as each girl waited on eight or ten people several times a day, her income was ample. Most girls saved considerable money.

Waitresses usually married well, many of them becoming brides of Santa Fe engineers, conductors, and station agents. It has been estimated that about 5,000 girls, of good character, attractive and intelligent, became wives as the result of acquaintanceships struck up in Harvey dining rooms and lunch counters.

There is a Western legend that more than 4,000 babies were christened Fred or Harvey or both, after these marriages, but there is no proof of this, and the original story was an invention of the late Elbert Hubbard.

In addition to the certified waitresses, there were hundreds of amateurs who, unable to pass the strict Harvey tests for neatness, poise, and morality, struck out boldly on their own and got jobs in frontier restaurants by claiming to be Harvey Girls. The behavior of some

iced tea, or milk. The waitress then fiddled with the cup before each patron and went away. Then there appeared the "drink girl," who magically poured the patron's preferred drink without even asking. This was accomplished by a cup-code. If the waitress left the cup right side up in its saucer, that meant coffee. Upside down meant hot tea. Upside down but tilted against the saucer meant iced tea. Upside down, away from the saucer, meant milk. Patrons who changed the positions of their cups were out of luck.—J. M.

of these brought no sheen to the Harvey escutcheon, but nothing could be done about it. It was one of the penalties of success.

So was a great deal of the poetry written about Harvey Houses and Harvey Girls. An early specimen was produced in 1895, by J. C. Davis, of Devore, California, described by the editor who printed his poem as "possessed of the Divine afflatus." Mr. Davis wrote:

Harvey Houses, don't you savvy; clean across the old Mojave,
  On the Santa Fe they've strung 'em like a string of Indian beads.
We all couldn't eat without 'em but the slickest things about 'em
  Is the Harvey skirts that hustle up the feeds.

Locomotive Bells

It's hard to say when bells were first used on locomotives, but probably around 1833, when whistles were introduced. Research was done on all kinds of materials—glass, iron, and steel—in order to determine which was best. Nothing equaled bronze. Glass gave a beautiful clear tone, but it was too brittle to be practical. And iron and steel bells were just the opposite—durable, but dull in tone.

For generations men have studied contour, weight, and texture, seeking to perfect the locomotive bell; and the result today is truly a masterpiece of acoustical design. All locomotives, from the smallest yard engine to the largest freight engine, carry the same size bell. The C&O did use smaller ones for a while on their Mallet type locomotives, because the bigger bells failed to make the proper clearance in certain tunnels. But now, because of larger tunnels, the regular size bells again are used.

Locomotive bells have changed very little in the last hundred years. The biggest change has occurred in the methods of ringing them. At first, they were swung by means of a rope attached to the crankshaft and threaded back to the engineer sitting in his cab—a method still in use today, but with two main disadvantages. The very moments when the bell should be rung—when the engine is approaching a road crossing or entering a passenger station or freight yard—are just the moments when the engineer has most to do. Then, too, the rope constantly gets tangled, which means that the engineer has to crawl out through his cab window to free it.

Today, most locomotive bells are equipped with an automatic ringer—a cylinder fastened to the bell frame and operated either by compressed air or by vacuum. In some cases the clapper moves, but the bell does not. In others, the bell swings just as it would if pulled by hand. The advantage in having the whole bell swing is that it

---

From "Hear dem Bells," by Mary Learned, *Tracks*, Chesapeake & Ohio, Nickel Plate, Pere Marquette, Vol. 30 (August, 1945), No. 8, pp. 24–25. Copyright, 1945, by The Chesapeake and Ohio Railway Company. New York.

See also Freeman H. Hubbard, "Romance of Locomotive Bells," *Railroad Magazine*, Vol. 49 (September, 1949), No. 4, pp. 8–31.

projects the sound in a broad arc. The main disadvantage is that the momentum of the swing can mount until it sometimes turns the bell completely around with such force that the clapper is plastered tight against the lip, and not a sound is made.

The scrap value of a locomotive bell before Pearl Harbor was around $35. However, all of them are not scrapped by any means. Railroads are constantly being approached by people who want a locomotive bell for some other purpose than use on a railroad. A pensioned road foreman of engines and motive power inspector of the C&O has a farm down in Virginia. Crowning a tall pole just outside the back door of his farmhouse is the old bell from an engine on the line he knew well and loved. Often, when he is off in the fields, he hears the clear ringing note of the old bell rising above the wind; and his heart lifts with it and with the memories it recalls—even though this time he knows it's only his wife calling him in for lunch.

* * * * *

It is said that the *Lewis Lawrence* locomotive, which was built in Schenectady, had an unusually beautiful-sounding bell. Mr. Lawrence, a stockholder for whom the locomotive was named, had put 28 silver dollars into the brass from which the bell was cast. And it was the silver, according to the men in the shop, that gave a tone higher and truer than any other bell.

Whistle Talk

I [1]

"Coming into Albert Lea from Des Moines," says George Nelson, retired from the Minneapolis & St. Louis, of the old Civil War veteran for whom he fired, "he would smile and rub his hands after he had whistled to his wife. . . . 'Hot coffee for John,' he'd say. And his wife never disappointed him."

* * * * *

Most engineers are family men (the railroads like them that way), but there was also many a gay blade who learned how to imitate his rival's whistle, as he rolled into town, to notify the lady to be ready for an evening out, or in.

One engineer on the C&O who switched at Lexington, Kentucky, invariably played "Home, Sweet Home" at midnight on New Year's Eve.

In Florida, trains coming from the North whistled to warn the farmers if a freeze was on the way.

As late as 1919, in Macon, Georgia, folks used to call up their aldermen at night, get them out of bed, and say "the whistles are blowing."

---

1 From *Slow Train to Yesterday*, A Last Glance at the Local, by Archie Robertson, pp. 176–177. Copyright, 1945, by Archie Robertson. Boston: Houghton Mifflin Company.

Most cities in recent years have put through ordinances prohibiting whistling in yards.

The trend, unfortunately, is against self-expression and toward uniformity. As long ago as 1895 the Fitchburg Railroad's general superintendent, E. W. Ewing, gathered a group of unhappy engineers around a table and conducted a "how-long-to-whistle" school. In succeeding years they became as scientific about whistles as about everything else on a railroad.

II [2]

. . . Back in the halcyon era when runners were assigned to regular locomotives and virtually owned them, and before brass hats cracked down on whistle tooters, every division of the Southern—not to mention other pikes—had its notable "musicians." Plenty of youngsters could tell you an engineer's name the moment they heard his whistle. Casey Jones was the classic example of a runner with a distinctive quill. As the song relates,

> The switchmen knew by the engine's moans
> That the man at the throttle was Casey Jones.

. . . His mournful locomotive whistle . . . was a home-made chime instrument, formed by six slender tubes banded together, the smallest being just half as long as the tallest one. It had a beautiful tone. Casey could make the thing say prayers or scream like a banshee.

* * * * *

Hard-earned money was spent for special casts from which mellow- or keen-toned instruments were bored, and no kid was prouder of a new toy than certain hoggers were of their whistles. Some gadgets were the tall bootleg type that gave forth a wailing sound. Others were stumpy, less than six inches tall and more than six in diameter, with tones resembling the human whistle. Then there were slender cylinders, not unlike a pipe organ's pipes, banded together in groups of four and six to form chime whistles.

To my thinking, the most popular quills were the three- four- and five-cell chimes, bored from blocks twelve to eighteen inches in length, which machinists were persuaded to tone to the notion of their owners by blocking the cells to various depths. . . .

[The] sound is produced by steam passing from the cup below to strike the edge of the bowl above. . . . The opening in the cup is regulated by plates bolted to the center of the cup. Often engineers

---

[2] From "Whistling Hoggers," by Herbert G. Monroe, *Railroad Magazine,* Vol. 37 (May, 1945), No. 6, pp. 10–31. Copyright, 1945, by Popular Publications, Inc. New York.

placed steel balls beneath these plates to help tone their whistle by steam bouncing them against the plates.

After the instruments were toned to suit the artists, many hours of patient practice were required to learn the technique of imitating birds or producing tunes. The story is told of a Macon, Dublin & Savannah engineer who was so good with the whistle cord that he called stations for his skipper.

C. E. Eiford, known as "Dutch," who wheels over the "Rathole" Division of the old CNO&TP, now the Southern, learned to whistle songs while pulling coal trains on the Louisville & Nashville through the Cumberland Mountains.

"It was a lonesome drag," Dutch explains, "and I passed the time playing with my whistle. I'll never forget the day the hind man kept signaling for more whistling; and not knowing the trainmaster was aboard, I almost killed the hog for steam. When we stopped, the brass hat strode over to the engine and tore into me, almost running me off the railroad. After that I made sure he wasn't along before I started my music."

One night a new preacher in Stearns, Kentucky, was in the middle of a sermon when the strain of *Oh, How I Love Jesus* drifted from the mountains. The parson stopped, raised his hand for silence, and listened to the engine music until its tones faded out in the distance.

"Brothers and sisters," he said, his voice trembling with emotion, "only a religious man could whistle a hymn as that engineer has done."

Dutch stood ace-high with the minister till the unfortunate Sunday night that he forgot himself and dropped through Stearns to the tune of *How Dry I Am*. Well, sir, that pastor was incensed and mortified. His letter to the Division Superintendent resulted in Mr. Eiford being advised to "use steam to pull cars instead of entertaining the citizens of Stearns."

Most whistling hoggers had only one call for which they were noted. . . . My brother-in-law, John Cheaves, was well remembered for his whippoorwill. I never heard of his whistling anything else. Claude Jones not only was a good whippoorwiller but could make you cry one moment and toss your hat in the air the next. One of his best incidents occurred in the summer of 1925.

"On a fine Sunday morning," he said, "I was to detour Number 6 over the Georgia Railroad to Madison, Georgia, after a pile-up on our line at Wrens Spur. It sorta got my dander up to reach the depot in Atlanta and learn that a conductor was going to pilot me the sixty-eight miles to Madison, where I'd then have to detour over the Central of Georgia to get back on my own pike at Athens. I told the big ox I wanted an engineer.

" 'That's all right, fella,' he replied. 'I know this road like a book and can even run the engine for you if necessary.'

"Now, after me pulling trains since 1892 I didn't need any one to do my running, and I said so in very few words; but as this was my first trip on the Georgia I'd have felt easier with a local engineer as pilot. Well, we got out of the yards, and as we were nearing Decatur, the first station out of Atlanta, the conductor told me I had better blow for the crossing. At the first sound of my whistle his mouth popped open and he stared.

" 'What a whistle!' he exclaimed as soon as I let go of the cord. 'Joe Hogan's got a honey, but yours is the prettiest quill I've ever heard!'

"In those days the order boards at all telegraph offices were out against us. We had to call for the board with four blasts of the whistle. When we saw a red semaphore drop, giving us a clear block, we answered the change with two short blasts. Calling for the board gave us an excuse for tricky whistling; and though the tallowpots cussed us under their breath for using their hard-earned steam, we generally strutted our stuff when we were approaching the telegraph office.

"Back in 1925, no freight trains were operated on Sundays on the Georgia, and as we went down the line we found that all telegraph offices below Decatur were closed. But when I started back that evening with the same conductor, I was surprised to see a red board at Rutledge, nine miles out of Madison. I did some fancy whistling and got a white board. I met another red one at Social Circle, the second station, and still another at Covington. Curiosity got the better of me.

" 'Do you have only night telegraph offices on your road?' I asked my pilot, and had the surprise of my life when he laughingly replied: 'Hell, those birds are not on duty! They heard you whistle when you went down this morning and have opened their offices just to hear you call for their boards. Seems like they've got an ear for music.' "

* * * * *

While the woods down South were full of lonesome whistlers, a handful of less serious minded hoggers beat drums, imitated bugle calls, or did a good job of tap dancing. There was one fellow whose wife quit him to marry another man. He kept the lady reminded of his feeling for her by calling her name with his whistle.

Gus Manning, who wheeled trains over the NC&StL, actually could laugh with his quill. His merry *ha-ha* echoed through the mountains of northern Georgia and Tennessee. But, like most whistlers, Gus had his troubles when the brass hats went on the warpath about excessive whistling.

One day "Little John" Thomas, General Manager of the road, was cooling his heels in his private car while waiting for Gus's train. Not knowing that the big chief was on the rails, Gus dropped down the Allatoona Mountains in a fit of laughter, his whistle whooping and hollowing like something wild. Little John was a stern, hell-roaring official who'd learned his railroading from the ground up. He nearly threw a fit when Gus went by with his whistle screaming *ha-ha,* and he later advised the hogger, in no uncertain language, to confine his activity to obeying company rules.

"With your kind of whistling," the G. M. rebuked, "no one would know or pay attention to any signal you might wish to give."

Grayheads living in the vicinity of Chattahoochee, Georgia, still shudder when they tell about my old friend Joe Herrick, who used to cross the Chattahoochee River bridge with his whistle screaming weirdly, like the laughter of an old hag in Grimm's fairy tales.

There was a reason for Joe's demoniac laughter, and as he told me the story he looked down from the bridge to a brickyard where hundreds of hapless souls, garbed in black-striped cotton suits, toiled from sunup to sundown making red mud bricks. Joe himself had spent three years in this hell-hole, and it seemed that the Devil was in him whenever he came in sight of the sprawling old shacks and the smoking kilns of the prison yard.

Track Torpedoes

About the smallest, yet most essential, item used in railroading is the track torpedo or, as it is commonly named by trainmen, the "gun" or "cap." The present type is a fiber-cased, slightly oblong package of loud noise which weighs about an ounce. Most torpedoes have two soft lead straps, one of which is bent around the head of the rail to secure the gun in position, and the second is a "pig-tail" extending toward the approaching wheel. The rolling of the wheel on this strap prevents the torpedo from being shoved ahead and displaced.

* * * * *

. . . The first I used in the summer of 1888 when I started braking on the L.E. & St. Louis Ry. (Air-Line) . . . were rather round, flat discs of paper that had been dipped in tar to make them waterproof. We had no scientific means of securing them to the rails, so we'd either heap a handful of dirt or, if mud were available, plaster a handful of that on top to hold them in place. In those days of light rails and poor ballast, the vibration would frequently dislodge them despite all our efforts. It was during that period that I first heard about the origin of the torpedo, and in the absence of authentic information to the contrary I imagine the information to be correct. At least it sounds logical to me.

From "Track Torpedoes," by William F. Knapke, *Railroad Magazine,* Vol. 52 (June, 1950), No. 1, pp. 36–39, 43. Copyright, 1950, by Popular Publications, Inc. New York.

One hot day, while I was straightening up the crummy, I found a bunch of torpedoes that were pretty well stuck together due to the heat's softening of the tar. I was braking for "Neighbor" Little, who had been in the Union Army during the Civil War. Neighbor noticed that the torpedoes had caught my attention.

"Do you know where those things originated?" he asked.

I replied that I didn't.

"Well," he said, "one stormy night back in the war a soldier, who was working as a brakeman, had to go back to flag a following train. His lantern failed him, and knowing the following eagle-eye would never see him in that rain, he took his tin box of musket caps and stuck it on the rail by plastering it with a handful of mud. Sure enough, the eagle-eye didn't see him but the box of musket caps busted with a loud bang and flash. The engineer thought that something had broken or exploded in his engine and stopped to see what was wrong. That's the origin of these torpedoes. I guess they found boxes of caps too expensive and some fellow thought up these to take their place."

* * * * *

In practically every one of the thousands of cabooses that roll the American railroads will be found, over or near the rear door, a red flag, tightly rolled on its staff. Attached to this staff are three torpedoes with their lead straps twisted around the flag staff or a "Bull Durham" sack containing the three torpedoes. An equal number of red lanterns will have from three to six guns fastened to their frames and probably a good half of the brakemen that use said flags or lanterns will have a handful of torpedoes in their coat pockets. . . .

Semaphores, flags, lanterns, fusees—all have their ordered places and are mighty efficient articles. But out in the storm and fog, there is nothing quite so reliable, that gives the flagmen such sense of security, as the good old properly placed track torpedo.

The Caboose

In the gaudy lexicon of railroad jargon it has more names than any other property in the economy of the high iron, even more than there are for engines and engine drivers. It is a caboose, crummy, way car, van, cage, doghouse, drone house, bouncer, bedhouse, buggy, chariot, shelter house, glory wagon, go-cart, hack, hut, monkey wagon, pavilion, palace, parlor, brainbox, zoo, diner, kitchen, perambulator, parlor,

---

From *Highball,* A Pageant of Trains, by Lucius Beebe, pp. 207–223. Copyright, 1945, by D. Appleton-Century Company, Inc. New York and London.

cabin car, and shanty. There are probably others in a variety only bounded by the limitations of human imagining and the vocabulary of profane and uninhibited men.

It is the freight crew's home away from home, a rolling microcosm of domesticity, a shelter against the blast, a premises as masculine in its implications as a corner saloon, a light to guide a man in the dark, the period and apostrophe at the end of the completed sentence of a train. . . . There can be no train, in the technical sense and as an esthetic entity, distinguished from a cut of cars, without a caboose complete with markers. There are, shamefully enough in a degenerate age, transcontinental Pullman trains without observation cars. There are also pork chops without apple sauce. Either is more thinkable than a freight, whether redball manifest or modest local, effacing itself on passing tracks for every other train on the employees' card, without a crummy.

Probably there is more warmth of homeliness and sentiment about a hack at the end of a string of high cars, a little self-contained world of animation and reality as it diminishes down the tracks behind a hustling symbol freight, than exists for any other of a railroad's tangible properties. Neither the drowsing water tank in the desert nor the semaphore giving green in a cut in the high hills nor even the glitter and crisp linen and fresh cut flowers of the de luxe dining-car are possessed of quite the qualities to captivate the imagining that belong to the red-painted caboose with a wisp of smoke from its disreputable chimney pot, canted at a rakish angle and secured against complete disintegration by a length of rusty baling wire.

Because of its unique status in the roster of railroad equipment, too, the caboose achieves an individuality unshared by rolling stock in any other category, freight or passenger. Because, unlike all sorts of freight and some passenger cars, a crummy seldom rides any rails but those of its home company, it is not subject to the qualifying regulations which govern the design and maintenance of stock cars, reefers, or tanks, which must operate over a vast multiplicity of different systems. It is an individualist, a maverick, proud of its own eccentricities of character and disdainful, in its usually shabby raffishness, of the well-bred uniformity of Pullmans and high cars alike. The caboose is the Bohemian of railroad rolling stock society.

For this reason it is possible to find on some roads, such, for example, as the Boston and Maine and Lehigh Valley, crummies equipped with the last word in high-speed passenger trucks and all steel construction, while on other systems there are still in service cabooses with wooden underframes which, when a pusher is used on grades, require that the engine be cut in between the hack and the last revenue car equipped, according to I.C.C. regulations, with steel frames.

. . . The caboose came into being conditioned by the imaginings and necessities of finger-shy link-and-pin brakemen and chin-whiskered freight conductors who required a shelter from the storm in which to light their ponderous globular lanterns and tally their way-bills, and who begged or stole a disused high car or rigged a precarious pavilion on a flat to serve their purpose.

Probably the first cabooses were much of a pattern with the shelter cars still current on the Terminal Railroad of St. Louis trains, a sort of rough-hewn gazebo erected and stayed in the middle of a flatcar. Or they may have been a simple boxcar with windows sawed to suit and a cannonball stove installed in a sandbox in the corner. Presumably they were side door crummies, without benefit of end doors and platforms, for the side door hack has only recently been more or less universally outlawed. Certainly the earliest of the tribe boasted no raised cupola or clerestory window, an innovation which may have been the invention of some Christopher Wren of the Illinois Central or a Bullfinch of the Camden and Amboy. Properly speaking, the Bullfinch or bay window hack is a very modern institution indeed and is standard practice only known to a handful of roads . . . which have found that a bulge on the side of a car is less conducive to falls and injuries to personnel than a perch on a vantage point poked through the roof.

Going to the other extreme, there are [in 1945] the crummies of the Rock Island which obviate all shelter whatsoever and provide the train crew with a sort of fore-and-aft love seat attached crosswise in the center of the roof, open to the elements and facing in both directions.

Probably the first refinement to appear on the converted boxcar caboose, the side door entry to which caused the loss of so many lives as to be of the classic menaces of railroading along with the lethal car stove and the pre-Janney coupling devices, was a simple one in the form of a curved grabiron which, it was discovered, helped swing a know-how brakeman up the step of a moving string of cars. The most modern innovations include solid steel construction, chromium trim on inside furniture, sponge rubber mattresses, stainless steel cooking facilities, built-in iceboxes, individual clothes lockers, and, on certain divisions of the Pennsylvania, caboose-to-engine telephone connections by short-wave radio intercommunication.

The word caboose in a variety of more or less germane meanings has been a part of several languages since it first appeared as *cambose* or *camboose* in the records of the French navy in the middle of the eighteenth century. Its initial appearance in English literature, according to the New English Dictionary, was when in 1805 in the record of a New England shipwreck the New York Chronicle reported that a member of the crew, "William Duncan, drifted aboard the canboose." In 1859 the word caboose, spelled as it is today and used in a railroading context, appeared in the litigation attendant upon a lawsuit against the New York and Harlem Railway, and Bill Knapke reports that in the same year a traveler visiting a New England town was struck by the sight of a flat car on which there was a sort of shelter or pavilion, and subsequently wrote: "The men had erected a caboose in which to cook their meals."

* * * * *

It was in the summer of 1863 that Conductor T. B. Watson of the very English Chicago and North Western was assigned to regular freight runs between Cedar Rapids and Clinton, Iowa, according to Mr. Knapke. His regular shack was being shopped and he was temporarily the unhappy captain of a somewhat disreputable boxcar which had, in some manner, come by a large circular hole in the roof. Shamed by his makeshift buggy and being something of a card or character, Watson determined to make the best of things and decided that comedy was indicated. As his consist clattered over the sixty-pound switch points into the Clinton yards, other trainmen and loiterers were fascinated to observe Watson's portly person, obviously supported by a requisitioned chair or packing case, protruding from the unseemly aperture while the fellow raised his hat and made courtly bows to all and sundry. In the course of his little act, however, Watson discovered that a clearance of a couple of feet above the roof of his car was an ideal vantage point from which to con the progress of his train, and he forthwith persuaded the road's master mechanic to enclose the position with glass against the weather and install a permanent deck underneath this clerestory. Thus the cupola was born.

The parallel between the caboose of railroad operations and the original and antecedent cook shack on the deck of a sailing ship is in no way merely one of etymology. Their exterior resemblance was obvious from the beginning and consideration of their function further heightens the resemblance. Both are designed as strictly functional parts in the integrated economy of travel. Both are made to withstand the assaults of nature upon man's inherent frailties, to stay and comfort him when the rains descend and great winds blow upon the earth. Both are destined to voyage into far places and see strange and wonderful things, and each of them nourishes and strengthens a breed of men at once individualistic and disciplined beyond the ordinary run. And, of course, the ship's galley and the little red caboose are both dedicated, primarily, to that great equalizer and most common of all human common denominators: food!

A great deal has been written and sung on the subject of waycar food, and it is probable that the legend increases in the telling, since the facilities of even the most elaborately commissioned shack can scarcely live up to the requirements, say, of a Scotto or Escoffier. But under unusual and peculiarly characteristic circumstances, even the simplest fare has been known to assume a certain charm, and the saga of caboose cooking would never have been firmly established if it had not exercised, for the men interested in its consumption, a considerable persuasiveness. The baked beans and bread puddings, the pork chops and pan-fried potatoes, and the illimitable varieties of hot breads evolved by generations of chariot chefs sustained many and many a famished brakeman and conductor on desert divisions before the days of Harvey Houses and in times when it was not uncommon to tie up for rest on the road miles from the nearest eating place. Then, too, old-timers can recall forgotten runs on Down East pikes and even on the great trunk lines of Canada where the train crew found it handy to take along a sporting rifle in the interest of venison and the engineer was known to have to make repairs with singular regularity adjacent to favored trout streams. Rule G is more widely and respectfully observed, in all probability, than any similar regulation on the subject of alcohol anywhere in the world, but that crummy ice boxes occasionally carry a consignment of the best Milwaukee or St. Louis beer in summer months is a circumstance which occasions surprise or agitation in few official breasts.

Least homely of the uses of the caboose, but of necessity a primary one, is that of office for the conductor and supply department for the entire freight crew. The train's operating headquarters is represented by the conductor's desk, among the pigeon holes and filing devices of which that functionary may spend as much as half of the running time of his trip receipting waybills, drawing up his wheel reports, which furnish the basis for the home office's statistical records of all freight and merchandise movement, and doing the other paper work necessary to the orderly conduct of a vast business enterprise.

Lockers, variously located in accordance with the details of the design of the individual hack, but all convenient to the hand of the crew, are provided for the storage of heavy supplies; chains, journal brasses, knuckle pins, rerailing frogs, and wrecking tools for emergencies. Signal fusees, torpedoes, signal flags, lanterns and fuel oil, too, are stored away as neatly and ready to instant use and availability as the signal flags and code books on the bridge of an ocean-going liner. There is also the conductor's emergency air control and in some cases an air horn for calling the attention of the engineer up ahead. This latter device is standard while old-timers recall that on some of the Western roads where drags were frequently more than a mile long from pilot to markers, caboose roofs mounted fixed-position semaphores for signaling the head end.

In addition to its function as a diner and dormitory for the train crew and a vantage point from which to watch for hot bearings or other operating irregularities, the caboose, in the days before air brakes, was one of the two important braking units of a train, the other being the locomotive and tender. When trains were lighter and hand brakes were standard equipment, it was seldom necessary to tie down more than the crummy and a car or so directly ahead of it and a few cars up forward next the motive power to bring the drag to a stop. To make the braking capacity of the shack more effective than its own light weight would be, it was the custom to load its lockers and spare space with pig iron or old scrap of any description in order to increase its braking effectiveness. This custom, of course, passed into the discard with the universal adoption of the Westinghouse system.

West of the Mississippi—as might be expected, where divisions are longer and cities fewer—cabooses are more than ever self-contained homes for train crews, and Bill Knapke recalls living and eating in a Southern Pacific crummy for a year on end without inconvenience of any sort. In such set-ups a good cook is beyond rubies and many a conductor has been known to ask to have assigned to his run brakemen who were noted more for their ability to run up a creditable tin pan of hot biscuits than for their railroading competence. In the West, too, cabooses are frequently made longer and more on the order of Pullmans to accommodate in folding berths the drovers who, on stock trains, ride to market with their cattle and sheep to assure their arrival in good order. Such elaborate cabooses are usually assigned permanently to a single train crew who spend their own money for their commissary and fittings with the result that shacks sometimes boast such details as radios and elaborate sets of cooking utensils.

One New York, New Haven and Hartford caboose, No. C-246, is famous wherever railroaders foregather for its elaborate collection of more than 200 railroad photographs framed and hung under glass on its walls. The modern streamlined brain cages of the Lehigh Valley are in reality small mobile apartments with electric iceboxes and sponge rubber mattresses on their berths. At one time when an enterprising youth named Robert Willier was handling publicity for the Wabash, he persuaded the management to turn over to him a company way car which he painted a bright Wabash blue of the same tone as the equipment of the road's crack Banner Blue and Bluebird and set up a complete publicity unit with typewriters, mimeograph machines, and other accustomed office equipment. An old wooden four-wheel hack from the Erie, No. 4259, accompanied Lieutenant Robert E. Peary on the trip to the North Pole aboard the Windward in 1899 and served the party as sleeping quarters at Etah in the ice fields.

* * * * *

If the caboose has figured in legend it has also been written large in the ballad lore of the land. It has probably been dramatized on the stage and it has certainly furnished a favorite theme for several generations of railroad artists and photographers. . . .

* * * * *

Be it, however, a swallowtail hack or a less fanciful model, it is probable that the crummy lies nearer to the heart of railroad men everywhere than anything except the wonderful steam locomotives that for many decades have rolled them over the main lines and short hauls, the standard iron and the slim gages of the nation's roads. The all-steel streamlined, airflow shacks of the Peoria Road, the Rock Island and the Erie, and the old-time four-wheel bouncers of the valiant little roads such as the Raritan River and the Morristown and Erie, the doghouses of the stormy mountain divisions of the Rio Grande, conditioned against the winters on the Great Divide, and the buggies of the Santa Fe rolling across the August wheatlands of Kansas, the bright painted way cars of the St. Louis Southwestern rolling south toward the heart of Texas, and the Tuscan red cages of the Pennsy hotshotting through the green fields of Indiana, all have been and still are, most of them, colorful players in the pageant of overland travel by the iron highroad. The saga of the high iron would be the poorer had they never been.

Railroad Slanguage

The shack was in the angel's seat of the ape wagon, blowing smoke to the Big-O of the time he was a baby lifter on the varnish. Or, to say it another way: The brakeman was in the cupola of the caboose, boasting to the conductor of the time he was a brakeman on a passenger train.

If you would talk like a railroader talks, just study the railroad slang terms published in some of the current railroad books. But please do not attempt to converse with the boys who run the trains in their own language. If you do, don't say we didn't warn you.

If you ever have occasion to locate the caboose on a freight train, don't ask the ORC (conductor) to show you the way to the ape wagon, bouncer, buggy, cage, chariot, dog-house, hack, hay-wagon, hearse, or louse-cage. Ask for the *caboose,* just like that, for that's exactly what railroad men call the little red car that rides the rear end of every freight train.

Since scanning a fresh book that lists anew many of the slang terms that have been kicking around, in print, for years—we can give you some further advice: Don't, no matter how colorful the terms may sound, call a roadmaster a butterfly boy, nor a special officer a cinder dick. A fireman will answer to his correct title, but you're asking for

From "Roundhouse Round-Up," *Tracks,* Chesapeake & Ohio, Nickel Plate, Pere Marquette, Vol. 31 (April, 1946), No. 4, p. 23. Copyright, 1946, by the Chesapeake and Ohio Railway Company. New York.

a dirty look if you call him greaseball. And a locomotive engineer is not going to love you if you call him hoghead [or hogger].

It is true that many of the so-called *slang* terms are used by railroaders, but, for the most part, they are abbreviations, or synonyms, of words in good usage, such as *combine* for combination (car), *age* for seniority, *mty* for empty car, and *gon* for gondola.

As long as railroad books are written, and railroad vocabularies are compiled, we may expect to hear brakemen called *block-heads, donickers, ground-hogs, shacks, snakes;* conductors, *Big-Os, ORCs;* bridge workers, *monkeys;* cooks, *lizard scorchers;* and yard clerks, *mud hops* . . . the engine house will go right on being the *pig pen,* a business car will be a *palace of justice,* and the passenger trainman's uniform a *harness,* or *monkey suit* . . . but in print only.

A Railroad Prayer

Every trade has its own peculiar vernacular. It is told of a railroad man's recent conversion when the pastor of his church called on him for a public prayer, he prayed as follows:

Now that I have flagged Thee, lift up my feet from the road of life and plant them safely on the deck of the train of salvation. Let me use the safety lamp of prudence, make all couplings with the link of love, let my hand-lamp be the Bible, and keep all switches closed that lead off the main line into the sidings with blind ends. Have every semaphore white along the line of hope, that I may make the run of life without stopping. Give me the Ten Commandments as a working card, and when I have finished the run on schedule time and pulled into the terminal, may Thou, superintendent of the universe, say, "Well done, good and faithful servant; come into the general office to sign the pay-roll and receive your check for happiness."

From *Topeka State Journal,* reprinted in *The Railroad Man's Magazine,* Vol. I (October, 1906), No. 1, pp. 133-134. Copyright, 1906, by the Frank A. Munsey Company. New York.

II. IT DID HAPPEN HERE

999

. . . Ninety-one and Ninety-two came and went, and then in 1893, passenger travel upon American railroads began to be greatly stimulated by the advent of another huge world's fair, this one at Chicago. The roads all made elaborate preparations for their part in this event. . . . It was a season all over the world when railroads were once again trying out their speed possibilities. . . . The New York Central . . . turned to its distinguished superintendent of motive power, William Buchanan, and asked him to design as fleet a passenger carrier as this country had ever seen—and then somewhat fleeter. . . . In a short time the historic shops of the road at West Albany were engaged in building the most beautiful locomotive that America had seen up to that time. "Greyhound hardly typifies the *999*. When she lightly touched her 84-inch [1] drivers to the rail, she fairly shot ahead. The world stood back and gazed, overwhelmed with admiration.

Hardly had the spring of 1893 fully come before they had *999* out of West Albany, trying out her pretty heels on the stoutly ballasted track of the New York Central. To every test she responded nobly. And finally the day came when she was hitched to the smart new *Empire State Express* and permitted to haul it over the smooth and almost gradeless Western Division, from Syracuse to Buffalo. Her supreme test came on May 10th of that spring. The *999* waited at the

From *Men and Iron,* The History of the New York Central, by Edward Hungerford, pp. 377–380. Copyright, 1938, by Thomas Y. Crowell Company. New York.

[1] An error. New York Central records give the diameter of her driving wheels as 86 inches.—A.F.H.

west end of the old Syracuse station, steam up and poised for her 150-mile run. In her cab was Engineer Charles H. Hogan. The day was perfect, and Hogan had been told that if he took the bridle off, so much the better.

The *Empire* came into Syracuse from the East just a few minutes late. It was a matter more of seconds than of minutes to detach the engine and put the *999* in its place. The platform was crowded as the train pulled out. Word had gone forth that this day there was to be a race to command the admiration of the gods.

To Rochester Hogan held the engine and train to their schedule. From Rochester to Batavia, up over the fairly steep Bergan Hill, the same. And then, for the final 36 miles of the Western Division, from Batavia to Buffalo, a fine straight line of railroad, Charlie and the *999* did their job. There is a slightly rising grade for two miles west of Batavia, then fourteen miles of perfectly level line, then a very slight descent into Buffalo. On this stretch the throttle of *999* came wide open. The train settled down with a sullen roar, a steady determination. The men back in the coaches caught their breaths. They had been told to expect fast time this day. Some of them held their stop watches in front of their astonished eyes. Fast time! Fast time is one thing, but this thing was speed! Watches do not lie, not all of them held together, at any rate. And watches that memorable quarter of an hour showed that one of those thirty-six miles between Batavia and Buffalo was covered at the astonishing rate of 112½ miles an hour! Other miles were covered in 38 seconds, 41, and 42 seconds respectively. The watches agreed. The world's record had been smashed.

And the saga of old Exchange Street Station was to relate that in those few minutes Charlie Hogan's hair had changed from its deep brown to snowy white.

. . . Hogan and the *999* in a minute became world-famous. . . . The *999* was immediately withdrawn from active service and sent to Chicago, where she became an outstanding feature of the great Fair. At its conclusion she was again put upon the *Empire State Express*. A very few years later, she was withdrawn, however. The *999* with its great drivers had speed rather than tractive power. Even after those wondrous high heels had been cut down, she still lacked haulage power. And fast trains upon the Central were rapidly growing longer and much heavier. For a time the famous engine was all but forgotten. Then, a score of years later she was discovered, under a different number, hauling the milk train from Watertown to Carthage. From this ignominy and the rapidly approaching scrap-heap the *999* was finally rescued by some of the officers of the Central and was restored to her former fine appearance, even to the restoration of her old number. Since then the locomotive has been carefully preserved. Upon certain occasions, this old belle of the rail makes her appearance again, to be greeted with all the great homage properly due her.

Disaster Made to Order

The city that came into being for the sole purpose of an exhibition train wreck was called Crush City, Texas.

Crush City, although it existed for only one day, boasted a population of 30,000, its own officers of the law, restaurants, first aid stations, jail and side-shows. No other railroad city in the world has mushroomed so fast—or faded away so quickly.

Back in 1896, W. G. Crush, general passenger agent of the Missouri-Kansas-Texas Railroad, dreamed up an idea for increasing passenger traffic—and revenue—for his company. He would stage an exhibition head-on collision, the first in America.

Huge billboards along the MKT right of way and advertisements in a thousand newspapers told the world of the coming event. And when the special excursion trains began pulling into Crush, Tex., that hot summer day, it seemed that the whole world had responded. Men, women and youngsters swarmed all over the place. The one-day police officers were kept busy collaring mashers, pickpockets, fighters, drunks and lost children. The jail and saloons did a thriving business.

The site of the exhibition was a basin about one-quarter mile across, with gently rolling hills surrounding it. The place was a natural amphitheatre for such a spectacle. At about 4:30 P.M. two old diamond-stack wood-burning locomotives, each pulling a tender and six box cars, were given right of way on the main line for a test run. Both trains were gaudily painted with enthusiastic advertisements of the Katy's service.

One engine that had been renumbered 999 had engineer Bill Staunton at the controls. The other, 1001, was piloted by Tom Caine. The engineers backed their trains until they were about two miles apart. Then, at a signal, they put them into motion and charged down the track, with whistles shrieking, towards one another. The spectators gasped as the two old kettles charged. It seemed impossible they would be able to stop in time. The engineers would be killed!

The screech of tortured brakes rent the air, and the cow-catchers clanked together as the trains shuddered to a stop. A mighty roar went up from the crowd. The real thing was going to be good. After their pictures were taken, the two old diamond-stacks were wheeled back to the starting points.

Once more the whistles let out a yell—this time a death scream—and the trains began to roll. Bill Staunton stayed with No. 999 until it had covered about 500 yards, then widened the throttle and hit the dirt.

Tom Caine in No. 1001 stuck with his engine for about one-half

---

Abridged from "Train Wrecks Made to Order," by Paul Norton, *Railway Progress,* Vol. 7 (May, 1953), No. 3, pp. 24–30. Copyright, 1953, by Federation for Railway Progress. Washington, D.C.

mile before jumping. He hit rolling and ended on his feet with a dashing bow to the crowd. The cheer for his daring was interrupted by a series of loud explosions. The track had been plastered with torpedoes.

A few seconds later the two trains came together with a mighty crash. A boiler explosion followed. Clouds of dust leaped skyward. A hail of broken metal was blasted aloft by the impact of liberated steam.

A man who had roosted in a tree near the track for a better view was struck in the head by flying iron. And a piece of chain tore through a girl's skull. These two died the following day. Several others were injured. It was a subdued crowd that climbed back into the excursion trains and deserted Crush City that night.

Several damage suits were filed against the railway company. Although considerable revenue had been gained by the special trains, W. G. Crush, who had promoted the dangerous spectacle against the advice of the more conservative railway officials, admitted the scheme had not been a smashing success. He had succeeded in getting a great deal of publicity for his line, but most of it was bad. This is the first and last instance of a railway company sponsoring a staged wreck in the United States and continuing in business afterward.

However, a character known as "Head-On" Joe Connolly earned his living for over thirty-six years, doing nothing but wrecking trains to thrill spectators. He started his career in 1896, the same year the Crush City fiasco took place, but a couple of months later, at Des Moines, Iowa. He approached the state fair board with the proposition that he would stage a head-on collision between two locomotives for a percentage of the admission fee.

Connolly then approached officials of the old Des Moines and Northwestern with an offer to buy two old, nearly worn-out engines. The proposition was a new one to the railroad's brass, and they required time to think it over. A few days later they told Connolly that they would lease him the locomotives more reasonably than he could buy them. Connolly was delighted. They apparently had the idea that the engines would not be damaged badly, and could be put back in good condition at a reasonable cost. However, they were in for a rude shock.

Connolly took twenty days for his preparations, spending $15,000 for equipment, trackage and labor. Temporary tracks had to be laid from the permanent line to the fair grounds. And at the fair grounds he laid 3,800 feet of temporary track from one side of the oval race track to the other, in front of the grandstand.

Engineers and firemen were hired to run the old engines and were carefully briefed in their roles. Connolly knew that a jittery engineer losing his nerve would spoil the whole show. He instructed them to stick with their engines until they were rolling at a good clip, then jerk the throttle open and jump.

Eighty-nine thousand people paid from 50 cents to $1.50 to see the show. The exhibition came off as planned, with 100 percent satisfied customers—and a fat profit for "Head-On" Joe.

But the two locomotives were mere piles of rubble, and Joe was never able to lease engines again. He had to buy them outright. His second exhibition took place in Kansas later that year, and "Head-On" Joe Connolly was on his way to a fortune. Detroit, Grand Rapids, Atlanta, Salt Lake City, Omaha, Lincoln, Tampa, Pittsburgh and many other cities witnessed "Head-On" Joe's handiwork. Crowds varied from 25,000 to a record 102,000 that plunked down their cash at Brighton Beach in 1911. The average number of paid admissions was about 50,000.

Connolly improved the exhibitions as he gained experience in crowd pleasing. He added coaches behind the locomotives to produce a greater thrill. Then he hit upon the idea of saturating the cars with gasoline and placing iron pots in the aisles filled with live coals. The impact of the collision upset the pots, and roaring flames immediately engulfed the trains, producing "gasps of awe" from the spectators.

Before his career was ended, when Joe was in his seventies, he had staged over seventy-five head-on collisions, and not a single person had been killed or even injured in the process. Joe Connolly was proud of this record, and at times held up the show for as much as two hours while mounted police herded the crowd back to a safe distance.

Connolly once told newsmen that he had hit upon the head-on idea because of a lifelong desire to see such a disaster without danger to himself, and thought many other people harbored the same secret desire and would be willing to spend money to satisfy the urge. How right he was!

One railroad ended its public service in just such a gasp-inspiring smashup. In 1931 the Rutland, Toluca and Northern, a short line in Illinois, found itself bankrupt. So the railroad staged a head-on collision between engines No. 50 and No. 51 near Magnolia, Ill. Admission was 25 cents per person, and enough money was raised to partially satisfy the RT&N's creditors.

A Monument to Rent

A few years after the Union Pacific tied itself to the Central Pacific with the golden spike in 1869, its officials began to think of erecting a suitable monument to its great promoter, Oakes Ames. Ames will be remembered as the man who became such a storm center because of the Credit Mobilier trouble, and who was so mercilessly assailed thereafter that he was driven from public life and hastened to his grave.

By Alvin F. Harlow. From *Trains,* Vol. 8 (October, 1948), No. 12, pp. 52–53.

However, not a few honest historians nowadays are admitting that he was to a considerable degree a victim of circumstances, and was not nearly as black as he was painted.

The monument was finally erected at a cost of $75,000 in the latter 1870's near the track on Sherman Hill, between Cheyenne and Laramie, and many travelers over the road have seen it. It is a stubby, rough granite pyramid with large bronze medallion busts of the two Ames brothers, Oakes and Oliver, set into its east and west faces. Relocation of the track in recent years has put it fully half a mile distant, but the passenger can still see it if he looks at the right moment.

At that time, many of the sections of land granted by the government to the railroad were still unsold, and the men sent out to erect the monument were of course expected to place it on one of the unsold railroad tracts. None of the land in that wild mountain area had yet been fenced or staked, and the builders had only crude maps and meager data to guide them. Even so, it seems scarcely credible that they could have made such an error as they did; but then, many important matters were carelessly handled in those days.

A few uneventful years passed. One day in the early Eighties Bill Murphy, jack of all trades and well-known character of Laramie, dropped into the county surveyor's office and asked for the exact location by township, section and range line of the Ames monument. The surveyor studied his plates and figured out that it was in Section 6 of a certain township. At that Murphy let out a whoop of joy and said, "Owens, help me out on this, and neither one of us need ever do another lick of work as long as we live."

He had developed a suspicion, now confirmed, that the men sent out by the railroad had by mistake placed the monument on government land still unsold. He therefore proposed to file a claim as a homesteader on the quarter section on which it stood. Once he had bought the land from the government, everything on it would become his property. It was his idea then to open negotiations with patent medicine concerns and other big advertisers, offering them space on the pyramid. Even in those early days, advertising signs were being painted on rocks, cliffs and farmers' barns all over the country.

"I think they'll grab for space and pay high rates," he said, "and when the railroad hears of it, they'll come a-runnin' and want to buy it back. I guess they'd give 'most anything to keep that monument from bein' plastered with signs. Why, folks all over the earth would laugh at 'em! So you see, there's big money in it, either way; and if you'll help me cinch that land and keep it a secret, Owens, I'll give you half of what we make."

Owens couldn't believe that Bill had the ghost of a chance. "It's ridiculous," said he. "The UP Railroad wouldn't make a bust like that. If that monument's not on railroad land, you will find they've bought the section from the government or reserved the right to move it when the land is sold or made it safe somehow. Big corporations ain't as careless as all that."

Nevertheless, he agreed to lend a hand. So fearful were the two that news of their project would leak out that they wouldn't trust any lawyer in Wyoming to look up the land office records and give them an opinion. But there was Bill Nye, formerly an attorney and newspaper man in Laramie, but who had now gone East to write comic stuff for the papers, and they knew they could trust Bill. They wrote to him, and he found, amazingly enough, that the section on which the monument stood was still the property of the government. Nye added in response to their query that when the government acknowledged the filing of Murphy's claim, the monument would by ordinary law pass into his hands just as if it had been a tree or a cowshed on the tract; but even he could scarcely believe that the railroad had not made some secret arrangement for retaining it.

Owens now filed on the desired quarter-section in Bill Murphy's name, appending his own name as one of the two witnesses, and Bill hustled to the branch land office in Cheyenne and presented it with his heart in his mouth. Without question the agent filled out and handed him his paper, and the Ames monument was in effect his property. He had three years in which to perfect his title by making improvements, such as digging a well or building a one-room shack, but that would be easy.

Negotiations were now opened with the leading advertisers of the day, mostly compounders of such nostrums as Hostetter's Stomach Bitters, Simmons Liver Regulator, India Cholagogue, Drake Plantation Bitters and such-like. Americans guzzled such stuff by the barrel in those days, and the manufacturers spent pots of money in spreading their claims over every cliff and dead wall between the oceans. The response was quick and enthusiastic; the big medicine men saw a fine advertising medium in the Ames monument. One company offered $25,000 for the whole side for a year, but the promoters sneered at this —mere cigarette money! They were asking $20 per square foot per annum, and as there was more than 5000 square feet of space on the three sides visible from the trains, they had more than $100,000 in sight if they could induce the advertisers to come across. And they did! It is said that bids sufficient to cover all the space had been received when Bill Murphy threw a wrench into the machinery.

Bill was a weak, inept sort of person who could be depended on to do the wrong thing about three times out of five. He was still a bit uneasy for fear the railroad company might have some way of getting back at him, while on the other hand, he wondered fatuously whether they wouldn't be willing to pay more to recover the monument unspoiled than the advertisers were offering him. The fact that this was only for a year's business and that he might go on collecting it year after year began to seem less desirable to him than having a nice big wad of folding money right in his hand, and be free of all fear of comebacks or consequences. Accordingly, without consulting his partner, he wrote to the railroad company, notifying the officials that they had built a monument on his land and asking what they intended to do about it.

As may be imagined, the letter was a bombshell at headquarters, particularly as Bill's advertising plans were learned shortly thereafter. At first his claim was received with incredulity, but a hasty investigation revealed that he was on firm ground. Brass hats turned pale, tore their hair, and ran around in circles. There's no telling how many were fired for the error. The company saw itself as a laughing stock for the nation, maybe for the world! The dictum went out that something must be done. Murphy must be bluffed out or bought out, even if it cost the price of a dozen passenger trains.

No reply was made to his letter, but two or three weeks after he had written it and when he was growing anxious as to the outcome, two important-looking men dropped from a train at Laramie, and were met by one Boswell, former sheriff, now a railroad detective. The strangers were the company's chief attorney and a prominent lawyer of Cheyenne. In company with Boswell they hurried to the local land office of the railroad, and from there a messenger was sent to Bill Murphy, asking him to step over for a few moments on a matter of business. Bill, who had long had his ear to the ground, guessed the subject of the coming interview, but he had no inkling as to the ominous turn it would take.

When Bill reached the office, he was ushered into an inner room where the two lawyers sat, looking as solemn as owls. The burly Boswell locked the door behind him and pocketed the key. This had a disquieting look, but it was as nothing as compared with what followed. The attorneys had asked Boswell whether he thought Murphy could be bluffed, and he unhesitatingly replied, "Yes"—that notwithstanding Bill's luck in discovering the company's error and his ingenuity in offering the monument as advertising space, he was more or less of a jellyfish. The lawyers had accordingly planned to lure Bill into their trap alone and scare him to death. They began by asking him in voices that trembled slightly with solemn emotion if he had the slightest notion as to the serious predicament into which he had gotten himself. Evidently not, or he would never have ventured upon such a course of procedure.

At this point, Bill began to break out in a light perspiration. Reason should have assured him that he had nothing to fear; but under the barrage of those two master bluffers, his reason fled from its throne. He tried to answer nonchalantly, tried to do a little bluffing himself, but failed. Remorselessly his torturers belabored him with Latin phrases of which he understood not a word, with the names of high crimes of which he had never heard, but which it seemed he had committed in buying that monument for his evidently nefarious purposes. Even his two witnesses on the filing papers had perjured themselves almost beyond hope of pardon. The doors of the penitentiary yawned for all of them, and Bill's own law-violations were so heinous that he might expect to be peering through bars for the rest of his natural life.

There was only one ray of hope for him. If he would sign over to the railroad his title to that tract containing the monument, the attorneys agreed to do what they could to save him from the consequences of his ill-judged attempt to blackmail the corporation. Bill was dazed and helpless. Alone with three overpowering brains, with no advocate, no friend to give him moral support, he collapsed and surrendered; and with an income of $100,000 a year practically within his grasp, he signed it all away by turning his quarter-section of land over to the company in exchange for two town lots of railroad land in Laramie, worth at a liberal estimate the princely sum of $300!

No sooner had the bamboozled dimwit tottered into the open air than his common sense began slowly functioning again, and he realized that he had let himself be bluffed out of a fortune. As for Owens, his fury was beyond description. But he was only a silent partner; the land had been taken out in Murphy's name, and he could do nothing but curse spineless Bill. This he did right heartily and at length.

The real cream of the jest remains to be told. Boswell told friends afterward that the Omaha attorney had with him in a handbag $15,000 in cash which he would have paid Murphy rather than let him get out of that room without a settlement; and if Bill proved unexpectedly stubborn, the attorney was authorized to write a check for twice that amount! It is reasonable to believe that in the last extremity the company would have gone much higher still, rather than let that monument be plastered with medicine signs. But even if he had sold at any price, Bill Murphy had tossed away the opportunity to make himself comfortable for life.

The First Cross-Continent Speed Test

The Jarrett & Palmer theatrical train left New York City June 1, 1876, and arrived at San Francisco June 4, covering the 3,313.5 miles in 84 hours and 17 minutes, thus maintaining an average speed of 40 miles an hour from ocean to ocean.

Abridged from "The Steam of '76," by Leo F. Creagan, *Union Pacific Magazine*, Vol. 2 (March, 1923), No. 3, pp. 6–9, Omaha, Neb.; and "The Jarrett and Palmer Special," by D. L. Joslyn, Bulletin No. 11, The Railway & Locomotive Historical Society, Inc., June 9, 1926, pp. 31–38, Baker Library, Harvard Business School. Boston.

The special was arranged and managed by Henry C. Jarrett, of Jarrett & Palmer, managers of Booth's Theatre, New York. Lawrence Barrett, the famous actor, Frederick Thorne and C. B. Bishop, were scheduled to appear in Shakespeare's "Henry V," at McCullough's California Theatre, San Francisco, on Monday, June 5. As the fastest regular schedule required seven days, the proposition to operate a through train on a schedule of three and a half days, undoubtedly appealed to the famous actor.

The railroads interested readily coöperated with Mr. Jarrett, and arranged a tentative schedule of 84 hours from New York to San Francisco.

Remember that in those days they did not have the heavy rails, the well-ballasted track, the automatic couplers and spring buffers of today, and the air brakes were not as up to date. The line was nearly all single track.

The New York *Herald,* the leading newspaper of the country, also took active interest in the plan and gave it their unlimited support. The New York Post Office also endorsed the idea, and made arrangements for the forwarding of mail to the Pacific Coast, and intermediate points on the train.

The fare from New York to San Francisco and return on the Jarrett & Palmer Special, including a week's board at the Palace Hotel, San Francisco, and return on regular trains within six months, was $500. The tickets were specially prepared, and were of exquisite workmanship, in book form, five by four inches. The outer cover was of solid silver, burnished in the center. Inside the cover were ten leaves, constituting the ticket and its various coupons. These leaves and coupons were all printed from engraved steel plates. Each book ticket was enclosed in a white satin casket, with lilac or ecru satin lining. The cost of each ticket book and case or casket was $40.

The special train, consisting of one Pullman hotel car, with 42-inch wheels, one combination passenger and smoking car and one baggage car all with the old link-and-pin couplings, left New York at 12:40 A.M., Philadelphia time, over the Pennsylvania Railroad, and the first stop was made at Pittsburgh at 10:58 A.M. Mark this: the distance between the points named is 439.5 miles, and it was covered by one engine, and without a single stop. The speed was not excessive, only an average of 43.5 miles an hour, but it wasn't bad for 1876.

Leaving Pittsburgh over the Pittsburgh, Fort Wayne and Chicago at 11:05 A.M., Philadelphia time [1] or 10:43 A.M. Columbus time, which was several minutes after the train's arrival, the run of 468.3 miles to Chicago was made in 11 hours and six minutes, at an average speed of 42.1 miles an hour. Four stops to change engines and 21 other oper-

---

[1] Observe this continual marking of time by cities. This was before the introduction of Standard Time by zones.

ating stops were made, and the train arrived at Chicago at 10:19 P.M., Columbus time, June 1. Here it remained for 31 minutes, leaving over the Chicago & Northwestern at 10:50 P.M. Columbus time, or 10:30 P.M. Chicago time.

From Chicago to Council Bluffs the train continued, meeting and passing thirty-seven trains on the single track, arriving at Council Bluffs at 10:00 A.M. Chicago time, June 2. Four stops to change engines and four other stops were made on the C. & N.W., one of which was to repair a broken air pump, one at the Mississippi River bridge and another for water. The fastest time made had been 62.2 miles an hour and the average speed for the run was 42.6 miles an hour.

Now for the run on the Union Pacific. The train left Omaha at 10:10 A.M., June 2, Omaha time, or 10:43 A.M. Chicago time, beginning the most difficult part of its journey, climbing from 966 feet above sea level at Omaha to 8,242 feet at Sherman, dropping down to 6,550 feet at Medicine Bow, up again to 7,030 feet at Creston, down to 6,140 feet at Green River, up to 7,835 feet at Aspen, Wyoming, and thence down to 4,310 feet at Ogden, involving stops to cool the wheels hot from frequent brake applications.

At Ogden Central Pacific locomotive No. 149 was waiting to take the train the entire 879 miles to Oakland. It left Ogden at 11:01 A.M. Laramie time, or 9:44 A.M. San Francisco time. A short distance out of Ogden, a hot box developed on the baggage car, and one of the men sent along by the C. P. road to take care of such cases, succeeded in breaking the cover of the journal-box while kneeling on the step of the car and holding on with one hand. He succeeded in getting hot-box dope and oil into the box, so that it cooled off in a little while.

The Central Pacific officials had platforms erected along the right of way where it was thought the train would require fuel and water, and on these platforms were men with bags or buckets of coal, and tubs of water on the other side, so that to coal and water the locomotive was the work of but a few minutes.

In stopping at Kelton, the air pipe on the Pullman was broken. The hand brakes were in good condition, so the train was handled largely by elbow grease the rest of the way except when crossing the Sierra Nevada, where a coach was added to give air brake power.

In passing Palisade, a box got hot on one of the wheels of the tender, and one of the engineers nursed it until Battle Mountain was reached, when a stop of 18 minutes was made and it was cooled off.

As the train approached Reno, Mr. Jarrett said he wanted to go through there like a streak of lightning; he brought out a lot of Roman candles, and prepared red fire on the tender. He mustered all hands on the Reno side of the train, each holding four Roman candles, and when near Reno, they were lighted, the red fire set off, and into Reno went the train, flames rolling out of the smokestack, an immense red fire blazing on the tender, and hundreds of balls belching out of the Roman candles. The whole town was up, and the train was received with bonfires and thunder of cannon.

At Truckee (1:31 A.M.) the town was alive with people, and everybody had a lantern. A coach was added so that air brakes could be used, and a locomotive was coupled on behind to help up the mountain. Gold Run was reached at 4:08 A.M., and the passengers began to bestir themselves, desiring to see Cape Horn, but the train flew by so fast in the morning haze that the view did not abide with them; the passengers declared the train was going too fast, that there was no particular hurry, that they did not desire to reach San Francisco before noon, but on rushed the train, and as it swung around the curves it threw them from their feet. The conductor himself was braking on the Pullman to hold her steady and keep her back. Colfax was reached at 4:30, people all along the way waving their hands and shouting "Go it!" and the train still going it.

The 879.2 miles of the Central Pacific was made with one engine, which, in spite of the severe handicap of inoperative air brakes for more than two-thirds of the distance, maintained an average of 37 miles an hour, though making sixteen stops. The last two miles into Oakland were covered in two minutes.

[Two newspaper comments follow.]

[From Fort Wayne (Ind.) *Gazette,* June 2, 1876:]

"For the first time in the history of the world, the New York morning papers were received in this city before sunset of the same day. On yesterday evening at 7 o'clock, we received the New York Herald of June 1, eighteen hours from the time it left the press."

[From the correspondent of the New York *Herald* aboard the train:]

"San Francisco, June 4, 1876

". . . As each station was passed, the excitement grew apace, and the party was received here with that enthusiasm and hospitality peculiar to the Pacific Coast. . . . The closing scenes of our journey were more exciting than any that preceded, for we were treated more like heroes from a battlefield than as men who had sat peaceably in a railroad car, to be whirled across the continent on half time. None of the passengers, sensible as they were that the achievement was wonderful, ever dreamed that the people of a whole city would turn out en masse on a bright Sabbath morning to welcome [us] . . .

". . . As the carriages were driven into the inner court of the Palace Hotel, the crowd burst out with enthusiastic shouts of welcome. Royalty could have received no greater respect and admiration than were showered upon every traveler as he alighted from his carriage. We found assembled the leading citizens of San Francisco, headed by Mayor Bryant, awaiting our entrance."

The South Carolina Earthquake of 1886

Just below the Ten-Mile Hill the first indication of the many railway disasters of the fatal night was seen. The engine, tender and cab of the train that left Charleston on Tuesday night at 9:35 o'clock were in the ditch. The engineer Burns and his fireman Arnold, colored, had been badly injured by the tremendous leap which the train took in the dark under the unseen influence of the shock that dismantled Charleston.

It is said that the earth suddenly gave way and that the engine first plunged down the temporary declivity. It was then raised on the top of the succeeding terrestrial undulation, and having reached the top of the wave, a sudden swerving of the force to the right and left hurled the ill-fated train down the embankment. How it was done was plainly indicated in many places along the track of the South Carolina and Northeastern Railways. For spaces of several hundred yards the dreadful energy of the earthquake was exhibited in two particular ways.

First, there were intervals of a hundred yards and more in which the track had the appearance of having been alternately raised and depressed, like a line of waves frozen in their last position. The second indication was where the forces had oscillated from east to west, bending the rails into reverse curves, most of them taking the shape of a single and others of a double "S" placed longitudinally. These latter accidents occurred almost invariably at trestles and culverts. There were no less than five of them between the Seven-Mile Junction and Jedburg. In other places the track had the appearance of being kinked for miles and miles, but always in these cases, in the direction of the rails.

At Summerville the first correct information was received about the delayed section of the Columbia train that was due in Charleston at 9 o'clock on Tuesday night. Owing to an ordinary accident above Summerville, the train did not reach Jedburg until about 9:45 o'clock. The train at the time of the earthquake was running at the usual speed, and when about a mile south of Jedburg it encountered a terrific experience. It was freighted with hundreds of excursionists returning from the mountains. They were all gay and happy, laughing and talking, when all of a sudden, in the language of one of them, "the train appeared to have left the track and was going up, up, up into the air."

This was the rising wave. Suddenly it descended, and as it rapidly fell, it was flung first violently to the east, the side of the car apparently leaning over at less than an angle of 45 degrees. Then there was a reflex action, the train righted and was hurled with a roar as of a discharge of artillery over to the west, and finally subsided on the

---

From the Charleston *News and Courier,* Friday, September 3, 1886.

track and took a plunge downward—evidently the descending wave. The engineer, Mr. Keyes, put down the brakes tight, but so great was the original and added momentum that the train kept right ahead. It is said that the train actually galloped along the track, the front and rear trucks of the coaches rising and falling alternately.

The utmost confusion prevailed. Women and children shrieked with dismay, and the bravest heart quailed in momentary expectation of a more terrible catastrophe. . . . The train was taken back to Jedburg, and on the way, the work of the earthquake was terribly patent. The train had actually passed over one of these serpentine curves already described, and . . . every soul on board was saved through the interposition of a Divine Providence . . .

The train then proceeded towards Summerville, and when within a mile of it was warned of impending danger by torpedoes that had been placed by Col. Averill. At this latter place, the track had been fearfully wrenched and twisted into reverse curves, and a similar accident occurred almost simultaneously at Lincolnville. [Hearing of the devastation at Charleston] the passengers all requested to be taken back up the track, and the train was again run up to Jedburg, where it remained until Wednesday evening, when it was brought to Summerville. . . .

The Deadly Drums

One Sunday night during the [second World] War, at nine-thirty o'clock, an official of the Office of Defense Transportation called an official of the Car Service Division [of the Association of American Railroads, Washington, D.C.] at his home, and stated that there were five cars of ferro-silicon in drums somewhere in the country, and that he had information this substance would explode and blow up the railroads at the points where they were in transit, if we did not locate the cars upon which it was loaded, sidetrack them, and have railroad employees shoot holes in the drums so as to permit the gas to escape. A check with the government agency responsible for shipping the freight developed that these five cars were part of a consignment not all of which had been shipped and that the drums remaining in the plant had exploded on that day. The official was able to furnish the initials and numbers of the five freight cars said to contain the sub-

---

From *Statement of Charles H. Buford, on November 28, 1949,* pp. 38–39. Association of American Railroads, Washington, D.C. Courtesy of W. A. Lockyear.

From October, 1939, to March, 1946, Mr. Buford, president of Chicago, Milwaukee, St. Paul and Pacific Railroad Company, was vice president in charge of the Operations and Maintenance Department of the Association of American Railroads, Washington, D.C.

stance, but he could give no information as to when they were shipped, where they were going, or over what roads they were routed. It was known only that the shipments originated at Permanente, California. The night force in the Military Transportation Section was immediately put to work locating these cars and within one and a half hours they had found all five of them and had instructed the railroads having the cars to shoot holes in the drums containing the ferro-silicon. The cars were located: one at Jersey City awaiting export, one at Chicago, one at Council Bluffs, Iowa, one at Reno, Nevada, and one at Roseville, California. The instructions were carried out and casualty avoided.

The Lost Freight Car

In the Union Pacific car service department the documents in this case make a paper monument more imposing than that which was upbuilt with all the deeds pertaining to the purchase of the whole line by Harriman. Yet, this is a simple little case of one empty box car that strayed, got lost, and was stolen.

In the Northern Pacific car service department there's a similarly imposing shaft of documents relating to that same lost, strayed, and stolen box car.

The documents include, principally, letters written by the two roads at the time the car disappeared. The tale has its beginning in the flood that brought devastation to Kansas City three years ago. In that deluge a freight-train of twenty cars, caboose and all, was washed from the tracks a short distance out of the city.

The cars were mostly empties, and all except one of them were afterward found, more or less unroofed, undoored, and untrucked, lying thus amputated and scattered over a square mile of Kansas landscape.

The one missing car, an empty, remained missing, despite the efforts of the parties that scoured the country in quest of it, with their very noses to the ground. That car was the property of the Union Pacific, and the road responsible for its return to its owner was the Northern Pacific.

Twenty days elapsed. Still no car! Whereupon the Harriman people, in accordance with number three of the "Per Diem" Rules for car service, made formal demand for the return of their car.

Thirty days passed without a sign of the lost car. And now, again in accordance with rule three, the Union Pacific notified the Northern

---

From "Lost and Stolen Cars," by Pearson Macintosh, *The Railroad Man's Magazine*, Vol. 12 (June, 1910), No. 1, pp. 169–171. Copyright, 1910, by the Frank A. Munsey Company. New York.

Pacific that it was liable to a payment of seventy-five cents a day in addition to the regular per diem charge of twenty-five cents.

Three months slipped by. By that time the car service departments of both lines had grown so literary, and had acquired so deeply the letter-writing habit, that great sheaves of correspondence were swapped almost daily.

Meantime that car had vanished, had melted away as if it had been a cake of ice in the warm waters of the flood; had disappeared as mysteriously as a card from the hands of a Hermann or a Kellar.

Six months! Still no trace, though the railroad people pursued the still hunt conscientiously. The Northern Pacific, according to per diem rule seven, might long ago have reported the car destroyed (and hence put a stopper on the avalanche of correspondence, and, incidentally, on the per diem charge), if only they had unearthed even the smallest evidence of destruction.

But not even a remnant was discovered—not a bolt nor a board that could be identified as part of that particular car.

Nine months! No car! But pigeon-holes were choked to death with correspondence. The Hill car service men raged impotently at the failure of their sleuths to locate the missing car, and Harriman car service men made further demands, just as impotent, for the return of their property.

A year slid into history, and thirteen months. By this time the Union Pacific men were injecting sarcasm into their literary productions, meaning, in effect: "What sort of fellows *are* you, anyway, that your search for our car is as futile as that for Captain Kidd's treasure?" In this way the correspondence grew into reams.

Now, in the fourteenth month, the Northern Pacific men, blue in the face at being so long baffled, decided to make one last systematic search for that car, even if they could produce only its dead body. Right and left, men were sent, and north and south, to scrutinize every square inch of that part of Kansas near the flooded district, to hunt as a man hunts for a lost collar-button.

One of the sleuths of the Northern Pacific, on the fourth day of the fourteenth month after the flood, spied some rusty car-trucks that were revealed by workmen in the process, who were removing the debris of a barn that had collapsed in the deluge.

The number on those trucks made the sleuth aforesaid whoop with joy. Here was part of the missing rolling-stock. The number was that of the car that was so badly wanted. And the trucks lay a quarter of a mile from the railroad track.

But the hunter was not satisfied. He wanted the *whole* thing. The other half, he bethought him, must be near. In casting his eye over the geography, he finally caught sight of the name of a patent cure for biliousness that was painted in large white letters on a black background, half a mile from the railroad track.

In his huntings and snoopings, he had passed that sign often. And as often he had ignored it as furnishing no clue to the lost car. Now, however, he recalled that the name of that patent medicine was emblazoned on the four sides of an improvised stable.

He sought the farmer who owned the nag that stood in the improvised stable.

"Where'd you get that stable?"

"Didn't get it. Just took it for my mare. It was once a box car, as any fool could see."

"You remember the car number?"

"No! Hadn't more'n located it 'fore a man came along and give me four bits just for lettin' him give her a nice coat of paint along with them bilious cure words."

"But don't you recall any railroad sign on that car—a shield, for instance?"

"Shield? Right, I do, stranger! A shield, and in it was the word 'Overland.' "

"Found! Found at last!"

"Found? You lost something, stranger?"

"Yes. We'll trouble you to hand over that stable. We'll send men to get it."

Forthwith the "stable" and the rusty trucks were sent to the repair-shop. There the patent-medicine paint was carefully scraped away, revealing, sure enough, the number identifying the "stable" as the long-lost car.

In the middle of the fifteenth month from the time of its disappearance, that car, now shiny in a coat of real freight-department paint, and otherwise renovated, was delivered to the Union Pacific. And with the receipt for the car in their possession, the Northern Pacific car service men danced a jig to the tune of a comic-opera ditty entitled, "And the Prodigal Came Back."

A few days later, however, consternation reigned in the Northern Pacific car service office. A bill had been received from the Union Pacific for the rent of that long-suffering car—a bill for twenty-five cents a day for the first thirty days, and one dollar a day for each day in the rest of the fifteen and a half months that the Northern Pacific was responsible for the car.

For the per diem rules permitted the Union Pacific to put in just such a bill, and it amounted to $442.50.

A Harriman man told me that, in an effort to get square, the Hill men sent the farmer who had taken possession of the car for his mare a bill for $442.50 for "a year's rent of stable." And that Harriman man had such a baby-blue eye, too!

The Runaway Freight Car

. . . Ever since the first water heater came down the railroad, there have been races, but one of the greatest ever staged was between a box car and a caboose. It's one of the best races I ever heard of and is the story of a brakeman who had a cast-iron nerve and was willing to try anything once. Here you are:

It was at the top of San Gorgonia Pass on the Southern Pacific that a freight train pulled a rear drawbar, or coupling, out of one of the leading cars. They had to set this defective car out on a passing track, which track was right alongside when the accident happened. So they did. A brakeman climbed up and tied her down with hand brakes, but the hand brakes wouldn't hold. The conductor got up to help him, but they couldn't hold her. They were on a 3.25 per cent grade. The car kept picking up speed, and the brakeman took to the air. The conductor left his lantern on top and unloaded. He figured that leaving the lantern there might do a little good and it certainly couldn't do any harm. There was a train, No. 244, coming up the hill below them, and the conductor hoped the engine crew might see the lantern come shooting around a curve and have time to take to the woods.

When the runaway car passed the caboose of the freight train a half mile below and broke through the switch and entered the main line, a brakeman named Kammerling, acting as rear brakeman, saw the lantern on top of the car and thought some one, probably the head brakeman, was on the car and couldn't get off on account of the speed. He pulled the pin, uncoupled the caboose—the automatic air was cut off because the caboose was behind the helper engine—and he lit out after the runaway car. He opened all the doors and windows to cut down the air resistance and let her roll.

The cars were on a 3.25 per cent grade all the way, and for twenty-five miles down the side of that mountain, around hairpin curves, Kammerling pursued that elusive runaway. They passed one telegraph station on the way down and the operator swore that they were doing not less than 125 miles an hour.

Twenty-five miles from where they started, Kammerling caught up with the car, coupled on, tied down the caboose hand brakes, stopped both cars, and prevented what would have been a collision to go down in history.

It took nerve. Kammerling had no idea where 244 was except that she was coming up the hill, and he might have met her on any one of

---

From "Comin' Down the Railroad," by A. W. Somerville, *The Saturday Evening Post,* Vol. 201 (September 15, 1928), No. 11, p. 165. Copyright, 1928, by the Curtis Publishing Company. Philadelphia.

the multitudinous curves that go to make up San Gorgonia Pass. It all occurred at night. Kammerling would have been killed had he stayed aboard in the event of meeting 244, and he would have had to be picked up in a basket had he jumped. But he kept after that runaway until he caught it because he thought there was a man aboard who couldn't get off—on account of the lantern the conductor left on top.

Engineer's Expedient

Between Buckley and South Prairie [Washington] the [Northern Pacific] track winds along a mountain-side at a considerable elevation. The grade here is about 80 feet to the mile. . . .

On this winter's night [January 2, 1892], about 8:55, I was skimming along down the upper stretch of track. It was quite cold, and snow covered the ground and shrouded the forests. We had been drifting along at good speed when I made a reduction to about 25 miles an hour because of a projecting bluff around which the track curved. We had just rounded the point when I released the air, and the train was quickly regaining its former momentum of about 40 miles per hour when, three coach-lengths ahead, I saw, to my consternation, that a rail had been removed!

. . . There appeared to be but one chance, and I grasped at it like a drowning man at a straw. Applying the emergency air and then instantly pulling the throttle wide open with the hope that the terrific shock and strain would break the train in two, in which event the engine and what cars happened to cling to it would dash into the trap and then on to destruction down the hill, while the rear portion would be brought to a sudden stop by the air-brakes. It will be understood that running on a downgrade, each car in the train will crowd forward on the car ahead, the slack being taken up by each car. Applying the emergency air under these conditions has the effect of pulling the slack out, and then the sudden opening of the throttle and the resulting forward bound of the heavy engine creates a strain that is bound to break one or more of the weaker couplings of a train.

In this instance, the train broke into three sections. Two rear Pullman cars broke off and stopped almost instantly; the next four cars left a gap of about forty feet between them and the Pullmans, the forward car just reaching the gap in the rails, where the front truck went off the track; while the engine, mail, express, baggage and an unoccupied tourist car dashed into the danger zone and went down

---

From *Forty Years a Locomotive Engineer,* by J. Harvey Reed, pp. 85–91. Copyright, 1915, by J. Harvey Reed. Prescott, Washington: C. H. O'Neil.

the hillside. . . . The twinkling stars looked down upon this scene of wreckage and disaster and witnessed a miracle; for of the men representing the engine crew, mail clerks, baggageman, express messenger and a brakeman, not one was seriously injured, although cars and engine were an indescribable mass of splintered wood and bent and twisted iron, and it was but a few moments ere the remnants were sending tongues of flame to the firmament above.

As the engine hit the ties after I had opened up and done all there was to be done, I stuck my feet out of the cab window to jump—I had shouted to the fireman when I first saw the open rail, and he made his getaway some time during the excitement, but I don't know when—just then she tore over the bank and down the hill, landing on her left side. I have no recollection of anything after I stuck my feet out until I found myself in a coach up on the track, but they told me that they picked me up about twenty feet down the hill from the engine.

It was never definitely known who removed the rail, but the supposition was that a gang of train robbers had undertaken the job for the purpose of robbing the wrecked express car, but witnessing the disaster, their hearts failed them and they slunk away into the night.

The Latest Train on Record

Some short lines run more or less if, as and particularly when it is convenient. None ever ran so late as Train No. 1 of the Gulf & Interstate (now Santa Fe) did on its 7 A.M. haul from Beaumont, Texas, to Port Bolivar, where it was due on the morning of September 8, 1900.

That was the day of the Galveston flood, which killed scores and destroyed millions of dollars' worth of property, but hardly anyone suffered so complete a catastrophe as the little Gulf & Interstate. Its engine No. 4, with a mixed consist behind it, fought along the Gulf coastline to within eleven miles of Bolivar, when a monumental wave came over the rip-rap and rolled the baggage car off the track and 500 feet inland across the tidal marshes. The engine and tender were half buried in sand and debris, and the crew and passengers fought their way to safety on the age-old basis of *sauve qui peut.*

After the flood the G&I's finances were in little better shape than its morning train. Thirty miles of track were gone, and No. 4 and its cars stayed immersed in the sand dunes of High Island for three years,

---

From *Mixed Train Daily,* A Book of Short-Line Railroads, by Lucius Beebe, pp. 320–321. Copyright, 1947, by E. P. Dutton & Co., Inc. New York.

Various versions of this story have appeared, with the train's lateness ranging from 2 years and 7 months to 8 years.—James Marshall, *Santa Fe* (New York, 1945), p. 228.

while citizens of Beaumont and Galveston raised $20,000 to float the railroad and its train. The line was rebuilt, the engine fired up and the train put back to Beaumont for repairs, including a fresh coat of paint and new cushions for the coaches. On the next run the railroad management offered to honor any tickets that had been punched three years before, but not picked up at the end of the run. Several hardy and venturesome souls showed up, according to James Marshall in *Santa Fe,* and Train No. 1 got to Port Bolivar at 11:10 on the morning of September 24, 1903—a total of three years, sixteen days and ten minutes late, probably an all-time record.

One irrepressible passenger who had expected to find breakfast waiting for him at the end of the original run stamped into his favorite Port Bolivar restaurant, screaming, "God damn it, aren't those three-minute eggs done yet?"

Hay-Burning Motive Power

Railway history offers many curious examples of motive power; none more so than that of a line operated between Marshall, Texas, and Shreveport, Louisiana, near the close of the Civil War. The ownership and management of the road were vested in one John Higginson. He was chairman of the board, president, vice-president, superintendent, trainmaster, freight and passenger agent, fireman, conductor, express messenger and master mechanic. His road was known as the Memphis, El Paso & Pacific, and was 40 miles in length. During the war, the soldiers took all the rolling stock of the road except three box cars. Motive power consisted of several yoke of oxen.

The road was operated on a tri-weekly schedule. When a cargo was gathered and—leaving Marshall, for example—the oxen were loaded into the first box car, the second was loaded with freight and passengers, while the third was occupied by the management. Leaving Marshall, there was a long downgrade, and the train coasted for several miles. After rolling as far as they could, the oxen were unloaded and hitched to the foremost car, and pulled along the level or up the next grade until the top was reached, when the oxen climbed aboard again, and once more they coasted. This was repeated until Shreveport was reached.

The passenger rate was a flat 25 cents per person. Freight charges were anything the owner of the line could get. Since there was no competition, Mr. Higginson did well. All freight was "Red ball," and handled as soon as received and the train made up.

From the *Express Gazette,* New York, April 15, 1911, reprinted from Fort Worth *Record.* [N.d.]

Rerailing a Locomotive

. . . After a bad storm, the sun would thaw the ice which, in turn, lost its hold on the mountainsides, and sheets thumped down on the railroad tracks. Often a sudden drop in temperature froze solid the mass of ice and water. . . .

One wintery day with the temperature around 45 below, Dan [Cunningham] watched a hostler run a steamed-up Mallet out of the enginehouse at Tabernash [Colorado] to connect it with an awaiting train. Shortly after the engine got into the open, it derailed on the heavy ice which was as hard as granite. The locomotive's momentum carried it across the ice to the track where the train was standing. The Mallet hit the track in a slow slide and all the wheels of the engine and tender settled exactly on the track. The startled hostler climbed from the Mallet to find it was rerailed satisfactorily and all he had to do was back the Mallet up and couple it on to the train. The whole action had taken less than two minutes. Such a method of moving a mighty Mallet from one track to another is not recommended by Big Dan!

Track Ballast

In Argentine, Kansas, about forty-five years ago, was a large lead and silver smelter. It used some silver and lead ores from Mexico and these ores were generally shipped to Argentine in sealed box cars. One day a coal car came to the Santa Fe terminal yard loaded with what yardmen thought was some kind of coarse sand. There was no bill with it, and the freight department knew nothing about it. It lay around for ten days or so, when finally the yardmaster switched it over to the sandhouse track, to be unloaded and dried for use on the engines. The roundhouse foreman, however, promptly hooked an engine onto it and shot it right back to the yard. He told the yardmaster that it was a cheap grade of sand and of no use to engines.

Next the yardmaster tried it out on a sand and gravel company, first spotting it with several cars of gravel and then switching it into their yard. The sand company promptly put up a howl about the yardmaster's passing off a bum car of sand, and for him to get that blan-

---

From *Big Dan,* The Story of a Colorful Railroader, by Frank Cunningham, p. 280. Copyright, 1946, by Frank Cunningham. Salt Lake City: The Deseret News Press.

By "Highball," John J. Burns, Phoenix, Arizona, *Railroad Stories,* Vol. XIII (March, 1934), No. 4, p. 45. Copyright, 1934, by the Frank A. Munsey Company. New York.

kety-blank car out of there and put clean sand in place of it. By that time the yardmaster was getting peeved. He was going around the yard just about biting the heads off the track bolts, batting his eyes, and talking to himself.

Finally he met a section foreman, and he asked the king snipe if he needed a carload of good track ballast. No railroad man in those days ever saw a section foreman when he couldn't use a carload of ballast, good or bad, rock or sand, cinders or brush. So it came to pass that the sand was unloaded at the west end of the yard. One more coal car went back into service; everybody, including the yardmaster, felt better.

About a month later a car tracer stepped off the morning passenger train and landed in the yardmaster's office with blood in his eye and plenty of hard words for the yardmaster. He was looking for a car of high grade silver ore from Mexico. It had been traced to the terminal yards, but the car was found to be loaded with a poor grade of soft coal slack. The car tracer wanted to know where the ore was! The yardmaster remembered the car of coarse sand, so he took the tracer by the hand and led him to the west end. The car tracer took one look and told the wide world what he thought of a dumb railroad man who would use $200 a ton silver ore for track ballast.

"Well," mused the yardmaster as he watched the section gang load the ore back into the coal car, "it was a damn rich piece of track while it lasted."

As I have said, usually silver ore was shipped in sealed cars, but this time there had been a wreck, and apparently the ore had been reloaded into an open coal car.

A Long Mile

One of the well-authenticated yarns that comes down to us from the days of wholesale railway construction deals with the foreman who estimated that his gang should be able to lay one mile of track per day. He forthwith made an agreement with the Italian gang boss that as soon as one mile was completed any day, the gang could quit. Things went along smoothly for a while and the men would finish ahead of time on most days. Then came the orders to finish the track-laying to a point we shall call Ashby before the following Sunday. The foreman was somewhat at a loss, since Ashby was five miles away and four days only remained until Sunday. But he was resourceful, and that same night he and a few cronies dug up the intervening mileposts and reset them in such a way that, according to the newly arranged mileposts,

---

By N. G. Near, *Railway Age*, Vol. 85 (November 17, 1928), No. 20, p. 978. Copyright, 1928, by the Simmons-Boardman Publishing Company. New York. Collection of Carlton J. Corliss, Association of American Railroads, Washington, D.C.

Ashby was only four miles away instead of five. Of course, the gang was obliged to put in considerable overtime, but they finished before Saturday night. When the gang boss complained that the miles seemed unusually long, the foreman admitted that they were longer in that locality, because of the climate, and he got away with it.

A Ride on a Handcar

It would not do, when story-telling is in order, to overlook the extraordinary adventure of Mrs. Carrie Chapman Catt, when that distinguished woman was stumping Colorado in the suffrage campaign. Mrs. Catt had been speaking at a jerkwater town in the mountains and was due in another berg of the same dimensions down in the valley the same evening. She made a wild race for the depot, but missed her train and was in despair. The distance to her destination was thirty miles down a mountain side and there was no means of transportation except a mule team, which could not have made it in time.

In this dilemma Mrs. Catt was rescued by a man—a mere protoplasm of the section-hand species. The great hairy fellow offered to get Mrs. Catt to Pilotville on time if she would entrust herself to his tender mercies.

"But how?" cried the lady; "good heavens, you can't carry me."

"Handcar," said the protoplasm, laconically. "Down hill all the way; do it in forty-five minutes."

"Saved!" cried the lady. "I'll go on the handcar."

Now a handcar skidding down a mountain side is a mighty uncertain sort of vehicle. As the protoplasm took care to inform Mrs. Catt, the handcar was liable to jump the track any minute. They often did it.

There wasn't a mortal thing to hang on by except the legs of the navvy, who for the first fifteen miles or so displayed a taciturnity of demeanor that forbade such a liberty. Mrs. Catt froze to the flat surface of the car as hard as she could, but remained in momentary expectation of sudden death.

A thousand feet below, on one side of the track, flowed a river. It looked like a typewriter ribbon with holes in it at the distance, but the river was seventy yards wide, with big boulders dotting its surface.

"What river is that?" inquired the frightened traveler, desiring to keep her mind off the apparently inevitable disaster.

"That," responded the protoplasm, "is called 'The River of Lost Souls.' "

"You don't mean it," said Mrs. Catt, with a shudder.

From *The Denver Times*, June 16, 1901. Clipping files of the Western History Collection, Denver Public Library, Denver, Colorado.

"On the level," reiterated the protoplasm.

"I wish I were," pursued Mrs. Catt; "but I'm afraid," she gasped, "that the end approaches."

The tacticurn individual at the brake deigned to smile. The car swung round a sharp curve and balanced on two wheels for an appreciable space of time. Then it righted and sped on. Under an hour the handcar jolted into Pilotville just in time for the meeting.

"How much?" said Mrs. Catt to the protoplasm.

"Not a cent," was the response. "Proud to have assisted you. By the way, remember you never could have reached this place had it not been for a man."

Mrs. Catt learned subsequently that she had been succored by a 'varsity graduate down on his luck. "But," said she, in relating the adventure, "I'd never ride down a mountain on a handcar again if Congress were waiting to hear me."

Nephi's Problem

. . . [The Denver & Rio Grande, now Denver & Rio Grande Western] railroad had a branch line on the Marysville route which ran from Manti to Nephi where the Rio Grande connected with the Union Pacific. After entering the town limits of Nephi, the D&RG tracks crossed a number of streets before reaching the depot. According to law, the engineer would blow a crossing signal of two longs and two shorts before entering each crossing. This train was scheduled into Nephi at 4 o'clock in the morning and the continual whistling of the locomotive awakened everybody in Nephi.

As time passed, there were so many babies born in Nephi the infant population created a problem. The town considered the matter and decided to send the railroad a request to set up its schedule an hour so the train wouldn't come in until 5 o'clock.

. . . The understanding management of the railroad granted the request.

Traveling Shoes

For many traveling men the Iowa communities of Oelwein and McIntire had a very special significance. It was at these stations that

---

From *Big Dan,* The Story of a Colorful Railroader, by Frank Cunningham, pp. 257–258. Copyright, 1946, by Frank Cunningham. Salt Lake City: The Deseret News Press.

From "The Great Western in Iowa," by Frank P. Donovan, Jr., *The Palimpsest,* Vol. XXXIV (June, 1953), No. 6, pp. 279–281. Copyright, 1953, by the State Historical Society of Iowa.

sleepers were set out or added. True, some trains managed to get by McIntire without shuffling equipment, but at Oelwein, never. On some runs the night train from Chicago set out a couple of cars at Oelwein for Kansas City; another car or two was shed at McIntire for Rochester, Minnesota. The balance of the train continued to the Twin Cities. On the eastbound trip, sleepers were added. The arrangement varied with the year, the season, and the railway. The point is that any evening train going through Oelwein was generally shunted around midnight or very early in the morning. The test of an experienced traveler was to sleep through Oelwein. If he succeeded, he was regarded as a 32-degree veteran by seasoned drummers.

Occasionally, switching cars at Oelwein caused complications. The late Siegmund Greve recalled a classic incident of this kind. On the day in question a porter took the shoes from his Twin Cities car into one of the other sleepers where he could have the companionship of a fellow-porter. After polishing the shoes, he started back to his Pullman but became confused and ended up in a Kansas City sleeper. Well, Oelwein came and went and so did the shoes—to Kansas City. Consternation reigned after the error was detected, but it was too late. When the train arrived in St. Paul the passengers were obliged to walk in their stocking feet about a block and a half to the nearest hotel. Here they were met by a passenger representative, who took their measurements and provided them with new pairs of shoes, compliments of the Chicago, Great Western!

Roy Bean's Party for Jay Gould

The rival giants of the Southwestern railway world at this time were C. P. Huntington and Jay Gould. Roy Bean's town was on the Huntington line and he was a loyal supporter of the SP, yet he had a great admiration for the physically weak but strong-minded Jay Gould, and had frequently expressed a desire to meet him.

Matters of high finance were in a state of considerable strain, and required constant attention from the heads of contending railroad interests.

On a certain day the rumor spread that the redoubtable Jay Gould and a party of friends would pass through Langtry on a special train within a few days on their return trip from the West. Roy was much interested. He sent to San Antonio for a case of champagne and had his place put in order. The animal, bird, and snake cages were renovated and trash burnt, and the broken bottles removed. He did not

From *Law West of the Pecos,* The Story of Judge Roy Bean, by Everett Lloyd, pp. 67–71. Copyright, 1936, by Everett Lloyd. San Antonio, Texas: The Naylor Company.

take any one into his confidence, and there was much speculation as to what was the matter with the Judge. Looked as if he were losing his grip—putting on all those airs.

Judge Bean learned from the telegraph operator when the Gould Special was to reach Langtry—and that it would not stop. He continued to say nothing; but listened for the engine whistle. At last the distant sound was heard, and the telegraph man said: "That's her." The train thundered up and the engine passed the station and the operator flashed the report to the Division Train Dispatcher that the Special had passed. Then he rushed out to see what was the matter; for the engine had shrieked and the brakes were set so hard that the wheels skidded and threw off showers of sparks as the train came to a sudden and crashing halt. Judge Bean desired to meet Mr. Gould, so when he saw Mr. Gould's train about to pass his place of authority, he calmly removed the red kerchief from around his throat and waved it a few times at Mr. Gould's engineer. The latter gentleman, seeing the signal of danger, jammed on the air and said things. As the train jarred to a stop several men on each side of the train poked out their heads and sawed-off shotguns. Only the station agent and a square-built middle-aged gentleman were in sight. The latter pulled off his sombrero and asked in a quiet voice if Mr. Gould was aboard. Before any one answered, a small jerky man with a beard stuck his head out of a window and asked, "What do you want?" The Judge looked him in the eyes. Those who were privileged to be present said that the air was full of electricity or something—as before a storm.

Presently the Judge said: "I guess you are Mr. Gould. I'm Roy Bean, the Law West of the Pecos, and I want to shake hands with you. Won't you get out and say howdy?"

Mr. Gould withdrew from the window and people stirred inside the car. In a moment Mr. Gould and his physician, Dr. Munn, and others, including Miss Helen Gould and a young lady friend, came down the car steps. Judge Bean shook hands all around and invited them over to his place. They read the signs and accepted the invitation. Bean also invited the agent to come and have a drink. He accepted. Once inside the saloon, the Judge ordered the barkeeper to open champagne. Dr. Munn examined the bottle and nodded and smiled at Mr. Gould. It was the one thing the professional man allowed his patient to use as a beverage. Every one present took a drink and the Judge proposed the health of the ladies in the party and Mr. Gould. The wind was just right and Mr. Gould couldn't refuse another glass. The ladies began looking at the eagles, the snakes, the deer, the Mexican lion. Mr. Gould sent some one to his car for some ladyfingers, and when they were brought he dipped them in champagne and ate them with gusto as he and Roy Bean talked.

In what seemed a short time Mr. Gould arose to depart, but the ladies had many questions to ask the Judge about his pets, his specimens, his dogs and horses, his official duties—including some unusual marriage ceremonies he had performed. At last Mr. Gould insisted that although he would like to stay longer they really must go, so with hearty handshakes, expressions of regret at leaving, and cordial good wishes for the future, the party entered the train and waved adieu to the wonderful Judge, who, hat in hand, waved his red neckerchief to those standing on the rear platform until the train was out of sight.

The Judge and the operator strolled toward the station, when suddenly the operator broke into a run. The telegraph key was frantically pounding out his "call." He answered, and was shocked at the message he received. It ran something like this:

Where the hell you been? What the hell matter Gould Special? Passed you three hours. Should been Del Rio two hours ago. Hasn't reached Comstock. Been calling. Why the hell don't you stay on job? Must be ditched. May have fallen off High Bridge. For God's sake get section crew and find out. Reported New York Gould killed in wreck. Stock Exchange wild. Trains piled up all over division. Answer quick.

So the agent ticked off:

Jay Gould been visiting friend Judge Roy Bean and me. Been eating ladyfingers and drinking champagne. Special just left.

The Self-Operating Railroad

Some years ago, a few days after I had sailed for Europe, a man went into my office and said:

"I want to see Chauncey Depew."

"He has gone to Europe," my colored porter told him.

"Well, I want to see his secretary."

"He has also gone to Europe."

"Then I want to see Cornelius Vanderbilt."

"He is in Newport."

"Oh, I guess I want to see W. K. Vanderbilt."

"He is also in Newport."

"You don't tell me. Well, may I see the first vice-president?"

"He is in Albany."

"How about the second vice-president?"

"No, he is out of town."

"Is the third vice-president in?"

"No, he is in Europe."

"Is the superintendent in?"

From *The Depew Story Book*, edited by Will M. Clemens, pp. 71–72. Copyright, 1898, by Will M. Clemens. New York and London: F. Tennyson Neely.

"No, he is up the road somewhere."

"How about the general passenger agent?"

"He has gone to Cape May."

"Who in thunder is running this road, anyway?"

"I guess it's running itself."

An Exchange of Courtesies

The president of the Waupaca and Nisha Railroad Company went to see the president of the Vanderbilt system.

"What can I do for you?" Mr. Depew asked, letting the smile he uses on such occasions have full swing at the visitor.

"I dropped in to see you, Mr. Depew, to ask for an exchange of courtesies. I am the president of the Waupaca and Nisha Railroad Company. I would like to have a pass over your road, and will extend the same courtesy to yourself over my road."

Depew looked thoughtful for a minute. Then he said:

"Where is your road?"

"Why, it's out in Wisconsin."

"Is it rated in Poor's Manual?"

"Oh, yes, indeed; we paid a nice dividend last year."

"Strange. I never heard of your road. How long is it?"

"We are operating sixty-seven miles this year."

"What, sixty-seven miles, and you call that an exchange of courtesy, and the Vanderbilt system has its thousands of miles?"

Depew assumed his most cavalier air as he launched that question at the head of the president of the Waupaca and Nisha, and then he waited for a reply.

"Well, Mr. Depew," said the Western railroad president, as he arose to go, "your road may be a little longer than mine, but it ain't any wider."

A. Lincoln Asks for a Pass

Some seventy years ago Abraham Lincoln, in need of a new annual railroad pass, wrote to an official of the Chicago & Alton at Bloomington, Illinois, according to a story in the Bloomington *Pantagraph,* which was reproduced in the *Chicago Railway Review* of December

Ibid., pp. 160-161.

From *The Railway Age,* Vol. 85 (December 1, 1928), No. 22, p. 1107. Copyright, 1928, by the Simmons-Boardman Publishing Corporation. New York.

28, 1878. The letter, which was at that time in the files of the superintendent's office at Bloomington, was as follows:

Springfield, Feb. 13, 1858.

R. P. Morgan, Supt. C. & A.R.—Dr. Sir: Says Sam to John, "Here's your old rotten wheelbarrow. I've broke it usin' on it. I wish you would take it and mend it, 'ca'se I shall want to borrow it this afternoon." Acting on this as a precedent, here's your old "chalked hat." I wish you would take it and send me a new one, 'ca'se I shall need to use it the first of March. Yours truly,

A. Lincoln.

Railroad Laws to End All Laws

There is a Kansas law still in existence which reads: "When two trains approach each other at a crossing, they shall both come to a full stop and neither shall start up until the other has gone."

A search through the statute books reveals that this is not the only loony law that applies to the railroader, railway companies and the traveling public. Some of them sound strange but do have a practical purpose—but others are fantastic.

An Indiana law forbids any one to attack a train. Texas has a law against the use of cocoa mats in waiting rooms. In Maryland it is illegal to "knock a train off the tracks." And Alabama solemnly warns "Do not shoot at an engine cab." In Rhode Island they're even more particular on this point, proclaiming, "It is unlawful to throw anything at locomotives."

South Dakota frowns upon its citizens placing firecrackers on railway and trolley tracks "especially if you touch a match onto it."

No one may legally show the movie, "The Great Train Robbery" in Montana. Pictures of train holdups are outlawed in that state. Somebody might get ambitious ideas. In some states the law has provided certain privileges for trainmen. For example, in Michigan, train and engine men are allowed to carry blank cartridges. And in Nebraska trainmen are permitted to go "muskrat hunting." The laws say nothing about the companies' points-of-view in these matters.

Louisiana feels strongly about the matter of cuspidors. A state law decrees that every depot shall be equipped with such a receptacle. (A tobacco-chewing senator or two must have felt the great public need for this one.) And in Texas the law says that there must be a cuspidor for every three seats in parlor cars and one for every two seats in the smoker. Also, in Texas the dressing rooms must have signs, coaches

---

By Paul Norton. From *Tracks,* Chesapeake & Ohio, Nickel Plate, Pere Marquette, Vol. 35 (July, 1950), No. 7, pp. 8–10. Copyright, 1950, by the Chesapeake & Ohio Railway Company. New York.

must be fumigated if germs are found, and blankets washed every ninety days.

A Los Angeles law prohibits "firing on jackrabbits from the rear platform of a train," and Idaho protects game birds with a similar law—but they neglect to say a single word in the jackrabbit's behalf.

Connecticut law frowns upon any one who lends a handcar to a friend, or any one who leaves a handcar on the highway.

Pennsylvania says it is illegal for a railroad to haul any vehicle except railway cars. Rhode Island has made it a crime to run a passenger coach between the locomotive and a carload of dirt.

Railroad laws can be somewhat contradictory from state to state. No Iowa state official is allowed to accept a railroad pass. On the other hand, New Jersey railroads *must* carry many officials free: the Governor, game commissioners, prison inspectors, and about fifty other people.

In Mississippi any conductor who puts a passenger into the wrong compartment can be fined $500. A conductor can go to jail in Minnesota if he doesn't eject a swindler or arrest a gambler on sight. And in Idaho there is a penalty for the conductor if he doesn't telephone ahead when his train is late.

In Alabama it is unlawful for any one to apply for freight cars unless the applicant intends to use them.

"Prize packages may not be sold on trains," states a Nebraska law. Texas prohibits dry cleaning on trains. In Michigan, passengers who have been exposed to certain diseases have to be disinfected.

The law makers haven't overlooked a bet. They've covered about every possibility on a train from caboose to cow-catcher.

In Arkansas no railroad company is allowed to let Russian thistles or Johnson grass go to seed on its right-of-way. It's a crime in Mississippi to soap railroad tracks, and in Alabama you are not allowed to put salt on tracks.

If you spot any one carrying opium on a train in Illinois and don't report it you are liable to a fine of $5000. If an unauthorized person uncouples a train in Iowa, he can be made to pay a fine of $1000.

Railroad trestles in Montana are required by law to have sidewalks for cattle. Arizona has a law that is humane in intent: "Any train that is flagged in a desert must stop and give water to any person who needs it." Florida trains must stop for a doctor at any place that he cares to get on or off. Alabama's citizens are not allowed to wave at a train with a red flag or a light if there is no danger present.

There are many, many other strange railway laws. Some of them make one wonder why any law-making body bothered their heads about the matter. One example is the Minnesota code which declares, "A railroad car is a building." And who would think Montana would find it necessary to legislate that "Children can not be employed to run trains."

The law that just about tops them all is one that was enforced in Washington state in the early days (and it has never been removed from the books): "A dog shall be carried on the cowcatcher of all trains. The dog is necessary to put to flight cattle obstructing the track." The old Walla Walla and Columbia roads were the only ones that ever complied.

The Railroad Conscience Fund

From the earliest days of railroading officials have received occasional letters from remorseful persons who, through carelessness or with fell design, received transportation for which they did not pay. And with that load of guilt removed from their shoulders, such persons presumably thereafter walked with a springier step.

What is done with this "conscience fund?" A ticket is bought by the system's passenger department, which turns the amount at issue into the passenger-traffic receipts, and somebody connected with that department writes courteously to the refunding person, thanking him or her for the consideration extended and politely closing the incident. All correspondence is kept in its special file.

A glance at the various letters displays various acute angles of the mystery termed human nature. Some of the communications are frankly hysterical, almost breathing of sleepless nights over the sin committed, which through long brooding has assumed distorted proportions in the minds of the sufferers.

Some are from stern parents who have taken upon their own shoulders loads of sinful responsibility that belonged to their children. Some are pathetic, the stories of humble and poverty-stricken people who slave and make heroic sacrifices to scrape together the few dollars needed to reimburse the railroad.

And still others are couched in terms of levity, treating the matter as a joke on the railroad that is literally too good to keep. So the correspondent sends the corporation its money with a slap between the shoulder blades and a jovial grin.

* * * * *

... The rule ... is rigid covering items of interest on the conscience fund. Many persons, in sending remittances, include interest, in some cases covering many years. The railroad people invariably deduct the interest and return it to the sender in the form of a draft. ... In some instances ... where the attacks of conscience were particularly acute,

---

From "Railways' Quaint Conscience Fund," by Theodore Benton, *The Railroad Man's Magazine,* Vol. XXXIV (October, 1917), No. 2, pp. 257–261. Copyright, 1917, by the Frank A. Munsey Co. New York.

a long correspondence has been necessary before the "guilty" person could be dissuaded from his determination to make the railroad company accept that interest.

* * * * *

Surprisingly few of the letters are from persons of the ignorant and illiterate type. The great majority of them are grammatical, well punctuated, and admirably constructed. Many are neatly typewritten and quite a few are dictated to stenographers.

* * * * *

. . . Little oversights on the part of conductors are frequently played up in these conscience letters. Some of the guilty, in their zeal to atone for wrongdoing, even go to the trouble of digging up the names of the conductors who accidentally passed them by. Whether these persons even think of the possible embarrassment to the man of the brass buttons is debatable, to say the least.

"They don't, not these extremists," declares a veteran of the passenger department. "The hysterical portion of these refunders think of nobody but themselves. There is no thought of shielding the busy conductor who, through an honest mistake, passed them by.

"The extremist, a term I use to indicate the more morbid of these persons, suffers from an inflated ego, self-consciousness gone mad. There is a deadly selfishness in unrestrained remorse; it fairly exudes injustice toward every other person in sight.

"When you analyze it, one of these extremists deludes himself. He honestly thinks that he is doing a noble act, and it's nothing of the kind. It's the last word in self-seeking. He's not thinking of justice toward the railroad; he's thinking of his own soul. It's concern over his own salvation. Take it from me, your real extremist in conscience has a yellow streak."

* * * * *

"We always notice an excess of these letters and remittances from certain sections after large religious revivals," says John Duffy, chief of the [Lehigh Valley] railroad's advertising department. "Billy Sunday's work is proved potent here. When he's traveling through Lehigh territory, the railroad always finds that it has debtors hitherto unsuspected."

The most curious letter of this type that one of the big Eastern roads ever received was from the pastor of a sect calling itself "The Church of the Burning Bush" out in the Middle West. The minister wrote that a young man who had recently been converted was "sore beset" because he had, some years previously, stolen a ride of seventy-five miles on a freight-train belonging to the company.

The young man desired that the railroad be given his name, but the minister added that he had then no money to pay the debt. He added that the young man was perfectly willing to work out the debt, and said that if the railroad people would arrange for his transportation east, and maintain him while there, he would be glad to come on and work out that seventy-five miles' worth.

As the expense of thus importing unskilled labor would far exceed the original debt, the system's powers did not figure long on the proposition.

In a postscript the minister desired the railroad people to write whether they would forgive the debt, thereby lifting a great burden from the mind of the young man. The road's general passenger agent passed on the correspondence to the vice-president with the penciled memorandum: "May we lift this burden?"

The vice-president deliberated for a time, and then shunted the problem upon the Legal Department to settle. The Legal Department took a month to consider it, and then sent formal word to the Middle West that it found it had due authority, so extended to the young man the formal forgiveness of the road.

Stormy's Million-Dollar Cap

Railroad men are tireless inventors. They've cooked up stokers and chair cushions, collar buttons and perpetual motion machines, always hoping to clean up a million dollars. Cases where they got the million are so few that you could ignore them if it were not for "Stormy" Kromer who invented the cloth cap now widely used in engine cabs: a peaked cap that pulls down over the ears.

One autumn day in 1905 the wind was howling through the cab of a Chicago & North Western locomotive switching near Kaukauna, Wisconsin. George J. Kromer was fireman. Engineer, fireman, and head brakeman were hanging on to their caps which were just bandannas wrapped around their heads. The brakeman let go of his—and cracked into profanity as a wind squall whipped it thirty feet down the track.

"Boys," said Kromer, "I got an idea."

The same evening he told the idea to his wife, Ida.

"I figure that by shaping some cloth and putting a sunshade on it, you could make a good strong cap not so likely to blow off."

"Well, now, maybe I could," she said, going to work with some heavy material, possibly mattress ticking, and evolving a trig headgear which George proudly wore on the job next day.

From "Stormy's Million-Dollar Cap," by Leslie E. Arndt, *Railroad Magazine,* Vol. XXVI (October, 1939), No. 5, pp. 48–49. Copyright, 1939, by the Frank A. Munsey Company. New York.

The all-cloth cap had a springy sweatband, a great comfort feature which helped to hold it on, and it was big enough so that the wearer could pull it down over his ears without being cut by the band.

"That's my idea of a cap," his engineer said with envy. "I wonder could you get Mrs. Kromer to make me one like that."

"Me, too," put in another fireman.

Stormy and Ida Kromer soon found themselves in the cap business, on a small scale, Mrs. Kromer doing most of the work. So many men wanted the caps that she never could catch up with the demand.

Stormy was the least likely man in Kaukauna to make a million out of anything. Genial son of a local hotel-keeper, lazy to a degree, he had been a baseball player for years before he drifted into railroading.

"If anybody but Stormy Kromer had that cap he'd make a million," said the men at the roundhouse.

When Stormy heard this remark, he got another idea. During one of the many layoffs, he shuttled over to Milwaukee where he knew there was a cap factory. The manufacturer looked over his cap dubiously, and finally said: "I don't see how you can sell more than a few dozen. I can make them if you want to put up the money, but as an investment for me—no."

"Fine—make a hundred dozen," said Stormy, and the manufacturer looked rather startled as he took down the order.

Kromer chuckles as he tells how he made the first sale. He just walked into the railroad lunchroom one day wearing the cap. One of the engineers, Charlie Clark, took a good look at the cap, snatched it from Stormy's head, threw fifty cents on the counter, and left in great haste.

Other men bought caps, but a hundred dozen is a lot of caps. Stormy ran small ads in some of the enginemen's magazines, which disposed of quite a number of the caps. But the money did not come fast enough to please the Milwaukee cap factory, so Stormy paid his account with them and set up as a manufacturer at Kaukauna. The slight matter of capital was solved by donations from friends; and the factory was an abandoned shack, where Ida took charge of three girls. When the work got too heavy, they persuaded housewives nearby to run in for a few hours and sew caps. Orders at last became so plentiful that the Kromers moved to Milwaukee and a bigger plant.

Sales climbed for a while to dizzy, rarefied heights. Thirty thousand dozen! After a few years Stormy was surprised to find that he had taken in a million dollars.

Then the inevitable happened; other manufacturers turned out similar caps, helped themselves to Stormy's sweatband, ear space, and what not, till he was driven to patenting every feature he could. Business reverses took most of the money; but [by 1937] things began to pick up. [In 1938] the plant made 14,000 dozen caps and . . . they are now selling caps to farmers also. These and a few other items for railroad men mean an annual business of something like $200,000. . . .

How the Underground Railroad Got Its Name

The name by which it is known to history was not given it at first. The story is that a discomfited Kentucky planter, having followed a warm trail into Ohio, was baffled by the complete disappearance of his quarry. "He must have gone down an underground road." When railroads became more common, it became known as the Underground Railroad, with a whole set of terms taken over from this new method of transportation. The places where slaves were cared for and hidden were "stations"; the owners, "agents"; the men who escorted the fugitives from one station to another, "conductors"; and the slaves, "passengers," though "freight" would have been more accurate, as they were actually shipped, sometimes in crates or cases. The railroad offered a new means of transportation, and companies of Negroes were sent through in freight cars, which eased the burden of the agents, and made pursuit even more difficult.

How the Shortest Station Name Happened

Uz, Ky., on the Eastern Kentucky Division of the Louisville & Nashville, takes its name from the Bible. W. S. Morton, division engineer of construction during the building of that extension in 1911–12, tells the story. From the very beginning, the railroad encountered tough sledding in and around what is now Uz. Property owners forbade surveying parties to cross their land; then the right of way could not be bought at a reasonable price; ground for a depot was hard to obtain; the contractor was always behind with his work; bootleggers kept the construction camps in an uproar, and the contractor and the resident engineer were always squabbling. Finally one day, Chief Engineer Willoughby, after listening to a "recap" of Morton's troubles, said:

"Morton, did you ever hear of a man named Job?"

Morton replied that he had, and he doubted if Job had had half the trouble he had, but he was willing to give him the benefit of the

---

From *They Broke the Prairie*, by Earnest Elmo Calkins, p. 228. Copyright, 1937, by Earnest Elmo Calkins. New York: Charles Scribner's Sons.

From "Our Station Names—their Family Trees," in *The Louisville & Nashville Employes' Magazine*, Vol. 25 (October, 1949), No. 10, pp. 14–15. Louisville, Ky.

doubt. However, he would like to name this station in honor of Job's homeland, and thus, according to Mr. Morton, "Uz wuz." Uz, incidentally, is pronounced "U-Zee" by neighborhood folks.

"Who Is This J. B. King"

Recently a desperate management at the Henry Kaiser shipyards in Oregon and Washington issued flat orders that any one caught writing on a freshly painted surface would be fired. The order was aimed at the insidious and ubiquitous signature of J.B. King, Esq., which had broken out like a rash in the yards. War workers were writing it up on the whirly cranes and down in the double bottoms, and every new ship that went to sea had "J.B.King, Esq.," scrawled on it somewhere.

Railroad men had a good laugh over the front-office order to suppress the signature in the shipyards, because railroad brass hats have been fighting it for forty or fifty years. You can still see "J.B.King, Esq.," on box cars all the way from the B&O to the Santa Fe.

The old brakeman explained it. "The name," he said, "was old when I first started railroading in 1896. I guess I've wrote it myself a thousand times. Used to be a poem about it:

Who is this fellow J. B. King,
Who writes his name on everything?
'J. B. King' on every wall,
On flat cars low and box cars tall.
Whether he does it for money or fun,
He sure is a scribbling son of a gun.

"I've heard plenty of theories about the original J.B.King. I've heard he was yardmaster for the Kansas City belt line in 1900, and I've heard he was an ex-con from Sing Sing. I've heard he was a

---

By Jean Muir. From *The Saturday Evening Post,* Vol. 217 (May 19, 1945), No. 47, p. 6. Copyright, 1945, by the Curtis Publishing Company. Philadelphia.

"J. B. King" is obviously a rival of "Kilroy," for which see *A Treasury of New England Folklore* (New York, 1947), pp. 831–832.

A variant reads:

Who in the hell is J. B. King?
You see his name on everything!
On boxcars high and [flatcars] low,
You see his name wherever you go.

Who in the hell is J. B. King,
Who writes his name on everything?
He may be poor, he may be rich.
Who in the hell is the sonofabitch?
—*Railroad Magazine,* Vol. 38 (November, 1945), No. 6, p. 6.

boomer come out of the Southwest around 1910, and with my own eyes I've seen that name in a passbook of the old International Great Northern. They're still arguing about him in yard offices. Some say he was only a myth—that there never was such a person and that 'J.B.King' is just a doodle you write on box cars. But ask any old railroad man who remembers back to wood-burner days. Or get to talking to the 'boes when they're squatting over a five-gallon oil can of mulligan in the jungles. They'll tell you a history that goes way back to the early Eighties.

"You heard of the millionaire hobo? Well, they'll tell you that was J.B.King. Instead of the cushions he'd ride the rods and the blinds. Never bought a ticket in his life and went wherever he wanted to go. Looked like the rest of the hoboes, they say; could walk the top of box cars going 50 miles an hour like a cat. Had cat eyes, too, that could see in the dark. Probably kept his regular boil up day like the rest of them. Sure. You know, peel everything off and boil it up."

But there was a difference about J.B. King, according to railroad lore. He had one burning ambition—to write his name on every box car and water tank in the country. Sometimes he'd even say "in the whole world."

J.B.King never got around to every box car. "What happens to hoboes, anyway?" the brakeman said. "Just a heap of bones and rags along the tracks some morning maybe. Or stretched out stiff by a jungle fire." But it begins to look as if his dreams were coming true all the same. The King signature is a tricky and challenging one. It is written in one stroke, without lifting the chalk from the box car side or ship hull and the *J* is the last letter made. Railroad men who saw the signature found out how to do it and began writing it themselves, just for the fun of it.

There used to be a saying around railroad yards: "You can't be a good switchman till you can write 'J.B.King,Esq.,' without lifting your chalk from the box car; dot the *i*, too—and all in one flourish." They tell about the callboy at Umatilla for the old Oregon-Washington Railroad & Navigation Company in 1902, who called a crew for an important run—a Harriman special. After all five men had signed his call book, he noticed that every man Jack of them had written, "J.B.King, Esq."

Box cars went into construction camps, and construction men caught the knack and began writing it, too. When war broke out, construction men moved into the shipyards and brought the signature with them. Before long, shipbuilders were doing it. Now railroad men are betting that when the ships pull into foreign ports with the name plastered over them, people in Australia and Russia and Egypt will begin writing it.

"It'll be all over the world, just like the hobo dreamed," the brakeman said. "All over Tokyo and Berlin before we're through. First thing I expect to see when I get to heaven is 'J.B.King, Esq.,' scrawled across the pearly gates."

The Story of Phoebe Snow

The name "Phoebe Snow" and "The Road of Anthracite" are synonymous because in the early days coal was closely identified with the origin of the Lackawanna Railroad and anthracite was burned exclusively in all of its passenger locomotives. So general was the appreciation by the traveling public of the importance of this feature that Phoebe Snow, the Lackawanna's impersonation of this idea, became in the public's mind the synonym of cleanliness in travel. . . . While the advertising character of Phoebe Snow, as shown in the car cards and newspapers some forty years ago, was the creation of an artist's fancy, to the traveling public she [became] almost a living personage. . . .

The idea of a series of advertising jingles, exploiting the adventures of a girl dressed in white typifying such cleanliness, was originated by the Advertising Department of the Lackawanna Railroad about 1900, and was continued up to World War I, when the railroads of the country were placed under Federal control, and bituminous coal was substituted for hard coal, or anthracite, in Lackawanna passenger locomotives.

At the start of the Phoebe Snow campaign of advertising, the verses were parodies on the familiar nursery jingles:

> Here is the maiden all forlorn,
> Who milked the cow with crumpled horn.

The first one of the series [was] as follows:

> Here is the maiden all in lawn
> Who boarded the train one early morn
> That runs on Road of Anthracite,
> And when she left the train that night
> She found to her surprised delight
> Hard coal had kept her dress still bright.

From *The Story of Phoebe Snow and Reprints of Original Phoebe Snow Jingles.* Lackawanna Railroad, Passenger Service, Traffic Department. New York. [N.d., n.p.]

Owing to the limited number of characters in this nursery epic, this meter was abandoned and a new form of verse adopted. For the sake of euphony and because of its obvious rhyming possibilities, the "maiden" was given the name of Phoebe Snow.

Years of publicity have resulted in giving "Phoebe" a foremost place among the characters in America's advertising hall of fame. Phoebe still lingers in the minds of Lackawanna travelers and shippers, and recently the Lackawanna revived the name "Phoebe Snow" by painting on the side of box cars the inscription "Lackawanna–The route of Phoebe Snow."

[A selection from fifty-nine "Phoebe Snow" jingles follows. The first of these is printed in the original seven-line form; the others have been rearranged for space reasons.]

Says Phoebe Snow
About to go
Upon a trip
To Buffalo,
"My gown stays white
From morn till night
Upon the Road of Anthracite."

The man in blue now helps her through
And tells her when her train is due.
"He's so polite. They do things right
Upon the Road of Anthracite."

Now Phoebe Snow direct can go
From Thirty-third to Buffalo.
From Broadway bright the "Tubes" run right
Into the Road of Anthracite.

Now Phoebe may by night or day
Enjoy her book upon the way–
Electric light dispels the night
Upon the Road of Anthracite.

The evening flies till Phoebe's eyes
Grow sleepy under mountain skies.
Sweet dreams all night are hers till light
Dawns on the Road of Anthracite.

No trip is far where comforts are.
An observation Lounging Car
Adds new delight to Phoebe's flight
Along the Road to Anthracite.

This scene reveals a chef on wheels
With care preparing Phoebe's meals.
He, too, wears white from morn till night
Upon the Road of Anthracite.

On railroad trips no other lips
Have touched the cup that Phoebe sips.
Each cup of white makes drinking quite
A treat on Road of Anthracite.

Miss Snow draws near the cab to cheer
The level-headed engineer,
Whose watchful sight makes safe her flight
Upon the Road of Anthracite.

Miss Snow, you see, was sure to be
The object of much courtesy,
For day or night they're all polite
Upon the Road of Anthracite.

The stars now peep at her asleep,
While trackmen keen their night watch keep,
For Phoebe's flight must be all right
Upon the Road of Anthracite.

Chessie, the Sleepy Cat

"Chessie," the cat, the well-known trade symbol of the Chesapeake and Ohio Railway Company, is straying into other fields. Its likeness is appearing or will soon appear on such articles as neckties, scarves, lamps, and slippers under a licensing arrangement by C&O with manufacturers in those fields. . . . Behind this move is an interesting story of how the railroad happened to pick the cat for use in its advertising.

Back in 1933, the late L. C. (Dick) Probert, then vice president of C&O, with general supervision over advertising, among other things, noticed the reproduction of an etching entitled "The Sleepy Cat" in a Sunday magazine section. As an animal lover he was intrigued and clipped the picture with the thought of obtaining the original, done

From "News of the Advertising and Marketing Fields," by James J. Nagle, *The New York Times*, Sunday, October 12, 1952. Copyright, 1952, by the New York Times Company.

by a Viennese, G. Gruenwald. About that time the company had introduced a new train, the George Washington, featuring as an innovation air-conditioned sleeping cars. It was looking for some way to characterize the sleep-inducing qualities of such a vehicle. Dick and Walter S. Jackson, advertising manager of C&O, agreed that "Sleeping like a Kitten" was a better phrase than "Sleeping like a Top" and decided to use the etching of the cat in an advertisement.

It was a "hit," judging from the nearly 300 letters that were received asking for copies of the picture within two days of publication. Dick and Walter thereupon secured commercial rights on the etching and featured it on the company's 1934 calendar. Then the cat was christened "Chessie." In 1935 some one dreamed up the idea of having "Chessie" present twin kittens, and a picture of all three was used. This went on three years before it was decided she had better have a "husband" of record. Thus, a handsome tom known as "Peake" was introduced.

More than 3,000,000 calendars containing likenesses of "Chessie" and her family have been distributed since 1933. Her fan-mail has reached movie-star proportions and requests for pictures have been received from nearly all over the globe. She has helped brighten the ward rooms of battle fleets, and the rooms of children and hospital shut-ins.

Owney, the Rail Dog

. . . Owney, the famous traveling dog, of the R.P.O's, attached himself to the Albany, New York, post office in 1888, and the clerks made a collar identifying him therewith. Taken out for one trip in a mail car, he became an inveterate traveler. To his collar were attached checks, medals, verses, and postmarks by men in most states of the Union, plus a dollar from Old Mexico. Postmaster General Wanamaker made him a harness to carry the tags and medals, with memo book attached, but the accumulation became too heavy and it was sent to Albany for display.

Owney was shut up in Montreal for nonpayment of board, which the Albany clerks had to foot; and seapost clerks later took him across the ocean—even to Japan, for a tag bestowed by the Emperor, and thence around the world (in 132 days). He was exhibited with his medals in halls and dog shows as "The greatest dog traveler in the world," and was right in his element at postal clerks' conventions. He stole the show at the 1897 National Association of Railway Postal

From *Mail by Rail,* The Story of the Postal Transportation Service, by Bryant Alden Long and William Jefferson Dennis, pp. 93–94. Copyright, 1951, by Simmons-Boardman Publishing Corporation. New York.

Clerks (now N.P.T.A.) Convention by wagging his stumpy tail in a run down the aisle, to thunderous cheers, to mount the stage. He looked all around in glee, and it was fifteen minutes before order was restored.

It was Owney's last triumph. He was a very ordinary-looking dog, almost ugly; and when he was in Toledo that August the postmaster did not know who he was and ordered him shot. The body was eventually mounted and sent to the old Post Office Department Museum in Washington, thence to several World's Fairs, ending with the Chicago Century of Progress (1933), always attracting great attention. Today, resting in storage at the Washington City Post Office, is all that remains of the faithful "clerks' best friend" who had traveled 143,000 miles and received 1,017 medals.

And as a final sequel, it seems that Owney has an inanimate successor of today which is traveling in R.P.O. pouches all over the United States and Canada—an old gray hat from California named "Dapper Dan!" Plastered with postmarks and tags inside and out, an album was finally attached to hold photos and data, and it was last heard of near Quebec about 1948.

Rails and Robins

Superstitious sailors are afraid that bad luck will come from shooting an albatross, and, by the same token, railroad men refuse to annoy a robin redbreast. . . . In the busy freight yard of the Milwaukee Road at Tacoma, Washington, a robin had built her nest under a sill step of an air-dump car. C. A. Norwood, a yard clerk, found the nest and announced his discovery to the office force. Whereupon Superintendent F. E. Devlin issued the following order:

> Under no circumstances is that car to be moved. Air dump No. X9–5,055 must stay. If possible, don't even move the other cars on the same track. But first and last, keep that car stationary until the eggs are not only hatched but until the robins fly.

On the Pere Marquette, a train of empty freight cars was rumbling out of the yards at Benton Harbor, Michigan. Back in No. A616, Conductor Roy Blodgett called over to his rear brakeman, Charlie Webster: "A bird is chasing us." When the train stopped, the trainmen discovered that a mother robin had built her nest on the under side of the crummy. In it were three blue eggs. Ward Salsbury, head brake-

---

From "Stranger than Fiction," by E. J. Burns, *Railroad Stories*, Vol. 12 (November, 1933), No. 4, pp. 82–83. Copyright, 1933, by the Frank A. Munsey Company. New York.

man, saw the men peering under the caboose and he yelled: "Whatsa matter; got a hot box down there?"

"No," the conductor shouted back. "A robin's nest. Go easy, will you?"

So Engineer Charlie Wilcox did his darnedest to make the starts and stops as joltless as possible all the way to Hartford, Michigan. The fireman was Howard Peck. On the return trip to Benton Harbor, the caboose was placed exactly in the same spot on the storage track from which it had been taken, in the hope that Mrs. Redbreast would go back to her eggs. Sure enough, she did.

The story spread, arousing sympathetic interest. C. A. Wilkins, general agent and former train dispatcher, decided that something should be done about it. He telegraphed J. G. Grigware, superintendent of the Chicago-Petoskey Division at Grand Rapids, explaining the situation. Back came the order:

> Use extra caboose until robin is done with car.
> Mr. Grigware sent an extra crummy to Benton Harbor. . . .

Railroad Superstitions

I. Turning an Engine "Agin the Sun"

Harry Davidson knocked a boss hostler into the turntable pit, and injured him so badly that he was laid up for more than a month, because the man refused to allow the wipers to run Harry's engine "with the sun." It had been noticed that for some mysterious reason Davidson was always present when his engine was turned, and insisted upon having her turned in the same direction every time. He would sit up for hours, after a long hard run, to see this done. Interest became aroused, and then curiosity. Finally, to see what would happen, the hostler told his crew to turn her the other way, regardless of anything Harry might say. Davidson remonstrated, and there was a clash of authority, the hostler claiming to be in charge. He argued that it would expedite his work to turn her the shorter way. Harry showed him that he was turning her the longer way. The hostler laughed in his face, and made a sneering remark.

Those who saw the fracas said that Davidson seemed to become insane. He jumped at the hostler and beat him savagely, ending by knocking the man into the turntable pit, where he lay unconscious until picked up. The frightened wipers then turned the engine according to Harry's instructions.

From "Railroad Superstitions," by Herbert E. Hambler, *Munsey's Magazine,* Vol. 27 (July, 1902), No. 4, pp. 598–600. Copyright, 1902, by the Frank A. Munsey Company. New York.

Davidson apologized to the hostler, and paid his doctor's bill and expenses until he was able to return to work; but such a serious disturbance could not be overlooked. In the investigation it came out that Davidson's father and two brothers, who had always had their engines turned "agin the sun," had all been killed in accidents.

The engineer's seat is on the right hand side of the cab, and his natural route to the ground is by the right hand gangway; yet I have known several engineers—and now that I come to think of it, they were all Pennsylvanians, of the variety known in railroad parlance as "lop-eared Dutch"—who, when going to oil, would never get down on their own side. I never heard any reason given for it, though I have often heard it laughingly commented on by others.

I now come to the second question—are there well defined popular superstitions pertaining to the railroad? I know of none, unless the unsavory reputations of certain "unlucky engines" be so considered; but when the evidence is so overwhelmingly against these insensate machines, what is one to think?

While many of these superstitions may have their apparent justification traced to rational causes—and usually preventable ones—there are others which do not appear to be susceptible of such an explanation.

II. The Deadly Number Nine

Many engineers are prejudiced against certain engine numbers. Consequently, everything that happens to an engine with the hoodoo number is noticed and remembered. While I have never known thirteen to be particularly conspicuous in this way, I do know that number nine and its multiples are commonly regarded with disfavor; though doubtless many a man is running an engine without observing the fact that her number is a multiple of that unpopular digit.

On the road where I worked for some years, No. 9 comported herself as any self-respecting engine should, until the opening of a new division gave her an opportunity to take the center of the stage. She improved it with a vengeance, and thereafter remained true to the character which she then assumed.

It was to be a ceremonious affair, as we were competing with an old established road, and our officers wished to impress the traveling public. Our west bound train started simultaneously with our competitor's flier, but the running time had been considerably shortened over the new division—which ran parallel with the rival road—in order to furnish an object lesson to the other company's passengers. Engine No. 9, thoroughly overhauled and broken in, was coupled to the head of our train. Of course every precaution had been taken to prevent mishaps. Time tables had been perfected and scrutinized, meeting points adjusted to a nicety, and everybody cautioned to be on the alert, that nothing might mar the grand opening.

As there were no freights on the division yet, the proposition was so simple that a fool could hardly have jumbled it. On a long, straight stretch of track, visible for a couple of miles from both directions, was the meeting point for the west bound flier and a fast east bound train. The time had been so arranged that the east bound train would get to the siding a few minutes before the other was due, so as not to delay her. *But this did not give the west bound train the right to pass that siding, if the opposing train had not arrived, without an order from the dispatcher.*

The crews of both the engines and trains were selected for their known abilities and proven trustworthiness. Harry J. Daly, the man on the right hand side of No. 9, had run locomotives for nearly twenty years. He was well known to the higher officials of many roads, and was one of those fortunate few of whom it is customary to say, "He can get a job anywhere."

True, some of the old hardshells muttered about the roundhouse that it was rather tempting Providence to start out two opposing fast trains with engines numbered respectively nine and thirty-six, and the opening of the division on Friday met with general disfavor; but as this took place in the last quarter of the nineteenth century, such remarks were only quiet asides.

The east bound train was delayed by a hot box on a car, and Daly went whooping by a red flag at a telegraph office—put out to stop him for orders—passed the vacant siding, and collided with engine No. 36 in a deep cut. It was estimated that both trains were running at the rate of fifty-five miles an hour when they met. Both engine crews were killed, so the cause of Daly's insane action has never been discovered.

Like a tiger who has once tasted human blood, No. 9 became thereafter a veritable hoodoo. She was forever in trouble. The men became shy of her, several of them taking terms of suspension in preference to going out on her, while many more were "jacked up" for the accidents they had with her. She took to running away when left alone, and was barely saved from dashing into a night express by the operator getting word of her approach in the nick of time. He pulled his semaphore up just as the express was pulling out from his station, and it was only because the engineer was a punctilious, crabbed old fellow that he stopped—the engine cab not having quite passed the semaphore pole when he heard the rattle of the chain as the operator pulled the blade up.

Of course there were the most commonplace reasons for the hoodoo's antics, but it was impossible to forestall them; no man could say where she would break out next. Ned Haley ran her into an open draw and was discharged. For several years she seemed to have sated her appetite for blood, but it returned, as everybody knew it would. Some six or eight years ago she left the track while running at high speed, and plunged into a sixty foot hole in the river, drowning her crew. It was at a curve on the main line, where nothing ever happened before or since. When they fished her out, it was found that a broken flange on the leading wheel of the engine truck had caused her to mount the rail.

The most prized watch charms on the road to-day are diminutive nines cut from the scrap of her bell, after the collision with No. 36.

The Maco Ghost

The presidential train bearing Grover Cleveland, President of the United States, paused near Maco Station, fourteen miles west of Wilmington, North Carolina, on the Wilmington, Manchester & Augusta (now the Atlantic Coast Line) Railroad, to let the engine, a woodburner, take on fuel and water. It was 1889. The day was balmy, so President Cleveland alighted from his coach to take a stroll along the tracks. While walking along, he saw the train brakeman with two signal lanterns in his hand—one green, one white. "Tell me," said the President, "what is the purpose of the signal lanterns?" Before the presidential train began rolling toward Wilmington again, President Cleveland had the full story of "Joe Baldwin's Ghost Light." He also learned that the two lanterns were used on the Maco district so that engineers would not be deceived by the ghostly weaving of the Joe Baldwin light.

A late employee of the auditing department of the ACL [named Jones] was there when the presidential train stopped. He was a small, barefooted boy, but he well remembered being hoisted up by his father so President Cleveland could shake his hand. He also remembered the Baldwin light. "One night I was in a group of boys who were walking along the track," Jones said, "when we saw the light. It seemed to be weaving along, directly over the tracks at a height of about five feet. Then the light described an arc and landed in a swamp beside the track."

The legend of the Joe Baldwin ghost light was born in 1867. During that primitive era of railroading, cars were joined by links and pins and trainmen had to stand between the cars to make a connection. Joe Baldwin, legend has it, was conductor on a train that came uncoupled near the old station of Farmer's Turnout (now Maco, North Carolina). He was killed with a lantern in his hand as he tried to recouple the cars. Shortly after the fatal accident, the mysterious light appeared for the first time. Scores of witnesses say it still appears. The popular explanation is that Conductor Baldwin, decapitated in the accident, is taking the nocturnal walks in search of his head. Some people say they have been close enough to the light to observe the

---

From *Railroadiana,* leaflet issued by the Atlantic Coast Line, pp. iv–v.

guards around the lantern. In 1873, a second light appeared and the two, shining with the brightness of a 25-watt electric light bulb, would meet one another going in opposite directions. It took an earthquake to halt temporarily Joe Baldwin's nightly jaunt. For a short while after the quake of 1886, the two lights disappeared. Soon after, however, weaving silently along the tracks near the trestle which bridges Hood's Creek, they reappeared. Folks knew then that Joe was again in search of his head; maybe, they speculated, the other light was Joe's head in search of his body.

The ghost light story gained credence enough to cause a Washington, D. C., investigator to visit Maco to try to explain the thing scientifically. But Joe was too fast for him. The investigator saw enough to convince him, he said, the lights were not "jack-o-lanterns," or, as he called it, "ignis fatuus." A machine-gun detachment from Fort Bragg, North Carolina, encamped briefly in Maco to try to solve the mystery, or at least perforate it. They did neither. An ACL operations official, veteran of forty years of railroading, has actually seen the light from the cab of a locomotive. He knows of instances when the trains stopped on account of it. On at least one occasion he and the engineer with whom he was riding began to stop for the light when it disappeared.

An old Negro states that when he was a boy, working with the section force in this area and living in a shanty near the tracks, he has known trains to stop for the light, the engineer appearing to be under the impression he was meeting another train. The engineer slowed down his engine and he and the fireman jumped, the latter suffering injury which necessitated another member of the train crew firing his engine to the terminal.

Unbelievers explain the phenomenon as reflecting auto lights from a nearby highway. However, there were no autos at the time the light was first noticed and for years thereafter. Then, too, the road has been rerouted several times with no apparent effect on the light. The weather and the seasons have no connection with the light's visibility. Sometimes it vanishes for a month at a time, only to reappear several nights in rapid succession. It seems to be a matter of Joe's discretion.

The Phantom "Lincoln's Funeral Train"

On the right-of-way of the New York Central Railroad, track-walkers, sand-house men, "shacks," and section-hands used to tell this ghost story of Lincoln's funeral train. So said the Albany *Evening Times:*

X

Regularly in the month of April, about midnight the air on the tracks becomes very keen and cutting. On either side of the tracks it is warm and

---

From *Myths after Lincoln,* by Lloyd Lewis, pp 344–345. Copyright, 1929, by Harcourt, Brace and Company. New York.

still. Every watchman, when he feels the air, slips off the track and sits down to watch. Soon the pilot engine of Lincoln's funeral train passes with long, black streamers and with a band of black instruments playing dirges, grinning skeletons sitting all about.

It passes noiselessly. If it is moonlight, clouds come over the moon as the phantom train goes by. After the pilot engine passes, the funeral train itself with flags and streamers rushes past. The track seems covered with black carpet, and the coffin is seen in the center of the car, while all about it in the air and on the train behind are vast numbers of blue-coated men, some with coffins on their backs, others leaning upon them.

If a real train were passing its noise would be hushed as if the phantom train rode over it. Clocks and watches always stop as the phantom train goes by and when looked at are five to eight minutes behind.

Everywhere on the road about April 27 watches and clocks are suddenly found to be behind.

Daddy Joe

. . . The most terrific Pullman porter who ever made down a berth . . . was Daddy Joe. No living porter claims ever to have seen him, but a few of the older veterans vow they once knew somebody who had seen Daddy Joe in the flesh. He was so tall, this dusky Daddy Joe, and so strong, that he commonly stood in the car aisle, on the floor, and let down an upper berth with each hand; then he made down both uppers and lowers simultaneously. And when Daddy Joe was really in a hurry, the thud and clatter of uppers sounded like a giant walking downstairs.

Once, on the Yazoo & Mississippi Valley Railroad, Daddy Joe's sleeping car and all the train were surrounded by the rising waters of the river. There was panic in the Pullman, with passengers screaming and trying to get out the doors in order to drown in the open rather than in the car. Daddy Joe rose nobly to the emergency. He stood up tall on his long legs and delivered such a powerful oration that the passengers were soothed. They took their seats again. The waters fell and the train proceeded to Memphis, arriving four hours and thirty minutes late, which was the exact time consumed by Daddy Joe's sermon.

Once, on the Central Pacific, it was just as tough. Hostile Indians attacked the train at a water tank. Daddy Joe climbed on top of his car—a notable infringement of Pullman regulations—and there harangued the redskins in their own tongue, dazing them into inaction by the sonorous periods of his great voice, which was like thunder. Then Daddy Joe came down. He tossed a pretty brown Pullman blan-

---

From *The Story of American Railroads,* by Stewart H. Holbrook, pp. 337–338. Copyright, 1947, by Crown Publishers. New York.

ket to each of the seven chiefs and subchiefs in the attacking party, gave them his blessing, and the train rolled on in safety to Salt Lake City.

The boys don't talk about him much any more, but they used to, and Daddy Joe came down through the years and on every railroad in the country performed his wondrous feats. Sometimes, it appears, he was known as Daddy Henry, but Joe or Henry, he was always master of the situation and never failed to bring his charges unscathed through fire, hurricane, high water, Indians, and robbers. "We don't get no tips till the end of the run," Daddy Joe always said. . . .

Porter Daniels

Pullman porters have proven their mettle many times, but the most outstanding Pullman hero was O. J. Daniels, who died in a Lackawanna Road wreck near Rockport, N. J., on June 16, 1925, and for whom a Pullman car was later named.

The entire train crew of the special train carrying German tourists was killed in the wreck, and this put the rescue work up to the Pullman conductor and his porters. Porter Daniels was sitting in the smoking room at the forward end of the first sleeper on the train. His car, curiously enough, was named "Sirocco," meaning a hot wind from the Sahara. A recent storm had washed sand and gravel on the track. The locomotive jumped the rail and went into the ditch. One day coach fell across the locomotive; another went into the embankment alongside the right of way. The "Sirocco" was derailed and almost paralleled the engine that was now emitting scalding blasts of steam. The second Pullman was on its side. The other three Pullmans in the train kept the rails.

Simultaneously with the derailment of the "Sirocco" the forward end door flew open and the burning steam rushed into the car. Getting to his feet, Daniels braved the deadly blast and closed the door; then, his task accomplished, fell unconscious at his post. Daniels was carried from the car and laid with other injured awaiting first aid treatment. He regained consciousness, and when doctors started to alleviate his suffering, he refused their efforts.

"Attend to that little girl first," he said, indicating a seven-year-old child near him.

The doctors obeyed, and when they returned to Daniels he was dead. In memory of Porter Daniels' heroic deed, the car "Sirocco" in which he received his death wounds was named the "Daniels" when it left the repair shops for further service.

From "Heroes of the High Iron," by Ted O'Meara, *Railway Progress,* Vol. VI (February, 1953), No. 12, pp. 12–13. Copyright, 1953, by Federation for Railway Progress. Washington, D.C.

John Henry

When John Henry was a little boy,
He was sitting on his papa's knee;
He was looking down on a piece of steel,
Says, "A steel-driving man I will be, Lord, Lord,
A steel-driving man I will be."

When John Henry was a little boy,
He was sitting on his mamma's knee;
Says, "The Big Bend Tunnel on the C and O Road
Is going to be the death of me, Lord, Lord,
Is going to be the death of me."

A steel driver . . . is about as obscure an employee as one could imagine. He's the man who strikes a steel drill with a heavy hammer to sink it into rock to make holes for explosives. . . . The mile and a quarter of Big Bend Tunnel, cut through green West Virginia hills near Hilldale, is just a minute or so of lost reading time when you flash through it on a train today. Big Bend Tunnel, a-building, was a different story. Have a look inside in those days. The light faded just within the entrance. Beyond, the hot, murky, foul-smelling blackness smothered the lungs. The high ring of steel on steel driving into rock reverberated throughout the cave above the heavy chants of hundreds of Negroes singing work songs as they toiled. Their bodies gleamed in the smoky flare of burning lard oil and blackstrap.

Hardly the spot one would expect to stumble on a mythical hero. But when the machine age reared its mechanical head and a steam drill appeared in the tunnel, one of these workers in the dark, John Henry, refused to accept this threat to his time-honored profession. As a human being, he stood up and challenged the steam drill to a duel. You can imagine the event—Henry, a powerful Negro with his two ten-pound hammers or his twenty-pound sledges. . . . The steam drill braced and ready. The crowds of Negro laborers craning to see a brown David in a pitched fight against an industrial Goliath.

The steam drill set on the right-hand side,
John Henry was on the left.
He said, "I will beat that steam drill down
Or hammer my fool self to death!"

From "Tracking down a Ghost," by Marion Cooke, *Tracks,* Chesapeake & Ohio, Nickel Plate, Pere Marquette, Vol. 29 (February, 1944), No. 2, pp. 24–27. Copyright, 1944, by the Chesapeake & Ohio Railway Company. New York.

For the song and the story of John Henry, see *A Treasury of American Folklore* (New York, 1944), pp. 179, 230–240; also *A Treasury of Southern Folklore* (New York, 1949), pp. 748–749.

The men that made that steam drill
  Thought it was mighty fine.
John Henry sunk a fourteen-foot hole
  And the steam drill only made nine.

This battle between man and the machine probably looked unimportant at the time, just a sporting event of the day. . . . But something in what Henry did appealed to the human soul. The effort is supposed to have killed him, but he did not die unsung. An unknown poet put the story in a song and look what happened. Today you can hear the song in hundreds of different versions in all corners of the United States. The Negroes in Jamaica sing it. It has been translated into French and German. . . .

Legends immediately raced up around Henry's name. He was white. He was black. He was yellow. He was a murderer and an outlaw. He was a family man. He was a steel driver. He was a watermelon catcher. Every state in the South claimed him. His songs were analyzed by Freudians and misquoted by governors. Even George Lyman Kittredge of Harvard thought he was two other fellows. He was positively identified as a one-armed Negro with a thumb like a man's wrist on the Tennessee Central Railroad. He was a Tallega, Kentucky, boy who could carry three railroad ties at once. A play on Broadway killed him off loading cotton in competition with a steam crane. Dinner tables seethed with the discussion. Bibliophiles stopped fighting about who wrote Shakespeare's plays, Bacon or Shakespeare, looked around to see what was happening, and started shaking their eyeglasses over John Henry.

At this point university detectives appeared to the rescue. One of them, Louis W. Chappell, an associate professor of English at West Virginia University, took up Henry's cause. He personally tracked down every rumor about Henry, from the Great Lakes to the West Indies. He came back from long search in the Henry country with the mystery solved for all time and compiled the findings in a painstaking volume, entitled *John Henry, A Folklore Study.*[1] In a day which debunks all heroes, John Henry came through exhaustive investigation with his halo on straight and his hammer in his hand.

He undoubtedly lived, worked on the Big Bend Tunnel, drove steel, challenged the steam drill, and beat it down. He may even have survived the duel. His reputation as a murderer and outlaw is cleared, and now he can go comfortably down in legend for the paragon he was: a man who sang at his work, played cards only occasionally, and even sent letters home.

Tracking down the life story of a ghost is as elusive a business as

---

[1] Published by Frommannsche Verlag, Walter Biedermann. Jena, 1933. See also Guy B. Johnson, *John Henry: Tracking Down a Negro Legend,* University of North Carolina Press, Chapel Hill, 1929.

anything the FBI attempts. The first clues came from the ballad itself. The steam drill loomed up instantly as an important piece of evidence. Next, the fact that Henry must have been a steel driver in a tunnel. The detailed description of his relation to the personnel of a tunnel—to his captain, boss, foreman, turner, and shaker, eliminated any other possibility. . . .

Some of the ballads mentioned Henry as a murderer and an outlaw. This shady evidence was disproved on the grounds of mistaken identity. Verses from the ballads about John Hardy, an out-and-out murderer, early began to seep into the songs about Henry. . . . John Hardy became confused with a white man, Benjamin Franklin Hardin. In no time these mix-ups had Henry white and a murderer. From all this we can safely deduce that John Henry, an upright Negro steel driver, must have flourished sometime in the early 1870's, when the steam drill was first introduced.

Now towns and tunnels from Lake Michigan to Jamaica have sworn up and down that John Henry was their own local boy who made good. One half the John Henry ballads testify to this. With the above information, however, a myth expert has no trouble testing and eliminating claims. King's Mountain Tunnel in Kentucky, which was sure it was haunted, happened to be built too late. So were all the tunnels in Jamaica. Alabama, when pressed, could not offer a likely spot for the scene of the competition. One by one, the various states' rights to John Henry were disproved. The other half of the John Henry ballads link him to the Big Bend Tunnel. Interestingly enough, Big Bend, built between 1870 and 1873, fits in with the first use of the steam drill.

But, most startling of all, old-timers living in the vicinity—sober, reputable men who worked on the tunnel in the Seventies—when questioned, gave eye-witnesss accounts of John Henry. Here, then, is the truth about him.

About 1870, John Henry was a black, raw-boned Negro from North Carolina, about 30 or 35, six feet tall, and weighing about 200 pounds. He was the "singingest man" on the gang. When he was driving steel, he sang, "Can't you drive her, huh?" and when he was thirsty he sang, "I am getting dry," as a signal for the waterboy to bring him a drink. He was keen, full of jokes, a banjo and a card player. One day a steam drill was brought to Big Bend Tunnel as an experiment. Evidently one of the five crews working on the tunnel used the steam drill, the others, man power. When the steam drill appeared, Henry, the best driver on the C&O, rejecting the invention and everything it was apt to stand for, rose up in his integrity and announced that he could sink more steel than the drill. The contest was arranged.

The event took place at the east portal of the Big Bend Tunnel. The marks of John Henry's hammer are said to have remained until the tunnel was double tracked, many years later. The foreman bought two twenty-pound hammers for Henry. The steam drill was set on the right, and John Henry on the left. Laborers on the work gang crowded around man and machine, in a grunting, cheering throng. For thirty-five minutes the great Negro, with a twenty-pound hammer in each hand, slung them down, one after the other, on the steel, driving it into the rock. In the midst of the excitement, the steam drill got hung in the seam of the rock and lost time. When the contest was over, Henry had drilled two holes, each seven feet deep, a total of fourteen feet. The steam drill, one hole, nine feet deep.

Eye-witness accounts differ as to what happened to Henry afterward. The majority agreed that he did not die that night from a burst blood-vessel in the head, but drove in the heading for some time afterward. Some of the old-timers insist Henry just drifted away from the tunnel. Others, that he was killed in a blast of rock and buried under the big fill at the east end of the tunnel.

III. TOLD IN THE ROUNDHOUSE

The President's Daughter

It was at a railroad mechanical men's convention in Chicago some years back; a paper was presented and read by an official of a Middle-Western railroad. The subject matter was the proper method of drifting locomotives at high speeds. A locomotive is said to drift when steam is shut off and the momentum already attained carries the train forward. The reading of the paper and the technical adjuncts thereto

From "Comin' Down the Railroad," by A. W. Somerville, *The Saturday Evening Post,* Vol. 201 (September 15, 1928), No. 11, pp. 18–19. Copyright, 1928, by the Curtis Publishing Company. Philadelphia.

occupied the afternoon, and an informal discussion of the matter was scheduled for the following day.

That night some fifteen or twenty of the conventionites met in a large room at one of the hotels; the room belonged to a representative of a railway supply house. Railway supply men are great entertainers. The mechanical men sat around and swapped lies and chewed the fat; many were acquainted, many others were not. Introductions were hard to keep up with, and the common bond of the locomotive was all that was necessary.

The talk centered on the paper that had been presented during the afternoon. . . .

* * * * *

"You boys wanta know somethin' about speed?" observed a railroad supply man. "I can tell you one that'll curl your hair. I was a hogger on the Iron Mountain when it happened. We hadn't had air very long an' somethin' was always goin' wrong. I had seven cars behind an old ten-wheeler an' it was downhill through most of Arkansas. I made a running test when I pulled out an' everything seemed O.K., but when I went to hold her back I didn't have nothin'. We was slidin' down a hill about fifty per when I found I didn't have no air, so I whistled for brakes to beat hell. The skipper an' the shacks musta been asleep; they didn't pay me no mind, an' we kept goin' faster an' faster. We'd go downhill like a bat an' then up a little hill, an' mathematically speakin', we kept a-goin' faster an' faster. I kept a-whistlin' an' a-whistlin'. I like to whistled all the steam outta that old pot, but they wouldn't give me no brakes behind. If I was to tell you how fast I know we was goin', you boys might not believe me."

"I could believe pretty near anything tonight," declared the B. & O. man dreamily.

"We was goin' so fast," declared the speaker, "that one of the reasons why the train crew didn't put on the brakes was because the noise the whistle made went past them before they could hear it."

"Wait a minute," said the B. & O. man. "I've got some figgerin' to do."

"Don't stop him," advised the Burlington man; "he's pretty near got 'em strung out."

"Well, gentlemen," continued the speaker, "you may gather from that statement that we were certainly moving right along. Yes, sir, we certainly were. I called the fireman over to my side and I said to him: 'Jim'—that was his name, Jim—a fine boy, too, was Jim—'Jim,' I says, 'we're certainly in one hell of a pickle. Them boomers back behind us are either dead or asleep, an' maybe both, an' if anybody is goin' to stop this train, it's gonna be you an' me, Jim.' Jim, he looked me square in the eye, he did, an' he says, says he—I never will forget it—

Jim, he says, 'You an' me, brother!' Just like that. An' do you know what we did?"

"Dropped an anchor?" asked the Santa Fe man.

"We didn't have no anchor," declared the speaker gravely, "but I'll tell you what we did do. We got a-hold of that old reverse, me an' good old Jim, an' though it took all the strength we had between us, we set her in the back corner."

There was dead silence in the room.

"And then?" questioned the B. & O. man cautiously.

"Well, sir," said the speaker, "you may not believe it, but it's a fact. That old train run backwards till it caught up with the sound of the whistle, an' the train crew heard it, an' tied her down with hand brakes, an' we stopped twenty feet from the worst washout in the history of the railroad. Yes, sir, it took some quick thinkin' on the part of Jim an' me. Did I mention the president's daughter?"

"You forgot that part," some one said.

"How careless of me!" said the speaker. "You see, she was a passenger, an' when she heard how we'd saved all their lives, she wanted to marry us both. But I was too old an' Jim, he was too young, so she had to be content with a middle-aged brakeman."

"Well," remarked the B. & O. man after some of the clamor had died down, "that may not be the best lie I ever heard, but I'll be hanged if it isn't the biggest. Who ever heard of a brakeman gettin' married?"

"It's God's truth," declared the speaker.

Wild Hoggers on the "Hook and Eye" Division's Loop

. . . An alternate crossing of the Blue Ridge forking from the high iron [or main line of the Louisville & Nashville] at Etowah, Tennessee, . . . is the famous "Hook and Eye" Division, first pike in that region to tackle the mighty Appalachian barrier (known successively as the Marietta & North Georgia, the Knoxville & Atlanta, and the Atlanta, Knoxville & Northern). Built in a day when hairpin turns and switchbacks were the only answers to mountain grades, it takes its name from two of the engineering feats incorporated in its mileage.

One of these [the "Hook"] is the 15-degree double reverse-curve buried deep in the shadow of Tate Mountain, in northern Georgia, where it is said that when a hogger wants a light, the conductor reaches out of a crummy window and hands him his cigar. The other feature [the "Eye"] is even more remarkable, taking the form of a

From *"Hook and Eye* Division," by H. G. Monroe, *Railroad Magazine,* Vol. XXVIII (June, 1940), No. 1, pp. 6–7, 12–13, 15. Copyright, 1940, by the Frank A. Munsey Company. New York.

spiral loop that crosses under itself, lowering northbound traffic with a scream of flanges into the canyon of the Hiwassee River. . . .

* * * * *

. . . Seven-eighths of a mile long, the spiral, as finally completed, came very close to crossing itself twice. . . . Many stories are told of this loop—one of the very few such features on a U.S. railroad.

A favorite among the yard shacks is the one about Bud King. King was a wild hogger, back in 1905. One day he was heading north towards the loop with 700 tons of freight. As the wheels gained speed, skipper John Beeler, back in the crummy, began to bite his nails.

Air brakes were far from dependable in those days, with the little single pump, and if a man didn't start braking in time on heavy grades, it generally resulted in a neat job for the wrecker.

John got up, finally.

"That wooden axle must have made his peace with the devil," he growled, as he staggered through the reeling hack and pulled the air on Bud. But instead of slowing down, the hogger pumped off the brakes and roared across the three-span trestle which formed the lead-in for the loop. At that, the outraged conductor really went into action.

Now every one knows that a fusee is a signal flare, shaped like a Roman candle with a nail-like end, which may be dropped from a moving train to protect its rear. It has a burning time of about ten minutes, and when a hogger runs onto one, he must stop and wait until its red flame fizzles out.

All unmindful of what was going on in the caboose, Bud let his little kettle squeal through the long curve of the loop, and presently it teetered drunkenly to meet the tangent under the trestle.

At that moment the tallowpot turned positively white.

"Look out!" he yelled. "A fusee on the track!"

For the next few minutes Bud was a mighty busy hogger, trying to halt his 700 tons of freight. By the time he did, the fusee was burning cheerfully beneath the trestle, halfway up the train. Bud glared at the crimson blurb until the fireman's guffaws attracted his attention.

"What's so damned funny, Fireboy?" he wanted to know.

"You dumb cluck," jeered the other, "you've been flagged by your own skipper." And he pointed up to where John Beeler had dropped the fusee through the center span.

But King was not, however, the only throttle-jerker with a reputation for fast running. A happy-go-lucky knight of the rails named John Finn at about the same time tarnished his escutcheon by repeated violations of Rule G. Run off the road, he rented a wornout farm beside the track of the Murphy Branch. He knew that Bolling Glover —the brass-hat who had fired him—must inevitably pass this spot some day, on an inspection trip. He therefore made a point of getting out and plowing with an old, broken-down bull every time a passenger train was due.

Glover saw him one day. The unwilling farmer was sweating as he struggled mightily to drive a furrow through the rocky ground. Pity welled in the official breast and believing that John had learned his lesson, Glover put him back to work.

Shortly thereafter the hogger was wheeling a passenger train towards Knoxville, with Glover and other brass-hats aboard. In spite of his probationary standing, John could not resist an urge to pick up an empty whisky bottle at Blue Ridge, together with an old throttle swiped from the engine house.

Then, as the train dropped through the loop and entered a succession of reverse curves beyond, things began to happen. The engine gathered speed while the cars behind swayed crazily. Leaning out of an open vestibule, Glover caught a glimpse of John, with a bottle to his mouth, each time the locomotive lashed to the right.

Suddenly the hogger gave a mighty war whoop and heaved the empty glassware far out into space. On the next turn, a throttle scaled through the casement, hung for a moment gleaming on thin air, then broke the satiny sheen of the Hiwassee, far below, where its waters leveled out beyond a riffle.

They say pandemonium reigned in the official car, before John brought the train to an easy stop at Appalachia. Bolling Glover was the first man into the cab. He meant mayhem, but John Finn's grin disarmed him. Glover never forgot that wild ride, however.

Plugging Leaky Flues

Boney Young was a boomer; he had the itching feet, always moving on to somewhere new, looking for better times. As we roared through Pooleville, where a small lake, as blue and clear as mother's rinse-water on washing day, came up and lapped at the track, he told me tales of the high iron—especially of the Pacific Coast, where he had pulled a string of sleepers the year before. He was firing a Mallet, and, like all of these powerful drivers, she leaked at the flues; so they were always running in a cloud of steam. The eagle-eye kept a bag of flour and made Boney put a little of it in the tank to plug the leaks. When the engine hit a grade and the draft was strong, the oil

---

From *Clear the Tracks!* The Story of an Old-Time Locomotive Engineer, by Joseph Bromley, as told to Page Cooper, pp. 72–73. Copyright, 1943, by Joseph Bromley. New York and London: Whittlesey House, McGraw-Hill Book Company, Inc.

from the cylinder mixed with the flour, and gobs of it flew out of the stack, baked as hard as bread from an oven.

"And they were cooked so well," Boney said, looking me straight in the eye, "that when the chef ran short of bread, he hung off the diner steps, caught the hunks of dough in a skillet, and served them for biscuits."

In the Fog

You may hear tall stories among the railroad men, if you only know how to get at them. I have whiled away many a long journey listening to them. I can assure you only the other night I occupied the top of a trunk in a baggage car at the rear of a way train from Philadelphia, on the Pennsylvania Railroad, and every one of the train hands spun a yarn before we reached Jersey City.

. . . The conductor had the story which captured the bakery. As we passed Tullytown, he pointed out of the door and asked: "Do you see those telegraph poles?"

We couldn't well help seeing them, for they were ordinary poles, perhaps twenty-three feet high.

"Well," he continued, "a good part of a train was lifted as high as the tops of those poles, and one or two cars were thrown clear over the wires into that field yonder. That little stream we passed a minute ago was covered by a thick fog one morning—a dense belt of fog twenty feet wide and as long as the stream, although elsewhere the air was reasonably clear. One of our freights, a long train pulled by a whopping big six-driver engine, was nosing along close behind a slow passenger train. They both started from Tullytown together, and weren't many feet apart at the brook. The engineer of the freight was keeping a close watch on the tail of the passenger, when he suddenly found himself in a dense fog, unable to see three feet ahead. He is usually a clear-headed, cool man, but he lost his head at that moment, and he slammed on the steam brake so hard that it ground fire from the tires of the drivers and brought the train to all standing. The funny thing was that the train was made up of empties except the last two or three cars, and they were loaded with very heavy stuff. Now, what I tell you I'll swear to, and so can many men along the road. When that big fifty-five-ton engine stopped dead, those heavy box cars on the further end of the train pushed the empties so that the middle ones left the track and went up and up until the train was arched

---

From *The Fast Men of America;* or, Racing with Time from Cradle to Grave, The Romance and Reality of Life on the Railroad, Illustrated with Pen and Pencil, by an Old Railroader, [Alfred Trumble], pp. 42–45. New York: Published by Richard K. Fox, Proprietor, *Police Gazette.* [1882.]

like a bow, and more than one car at the top of the arch was higher than the tops of the telegraph poles. The conductor—he lived in that house by the depot, and his father stood on the platform as we passed—the conductor, I say, was braking in the middle of the train. He was squeezed to death and his body and one of the cars were thrown over a telegraph pole into that field alongside of his house."

The only man in the baggage car beside myself who had not told a story was a Western railroad man, who had exhibited as a card of introduction an annual pass over the railroad. When he cleared his throat, no one spoke. One could see by the expression of his face that he had something to say. And he had.

Grasping the conductor's hand, he shook it with much fervor and remarked in expressive accents: "Thank you, pardner. Thank you."

"What for?" demanded the conductor in no little amazement.

"For making me solid. I've told that story till I'm sick of it, but nobody would believe it till now."

"And how did you get to know it?"

"Why, pardner, between you and me, I was that conductor."

Mosquito Story

[It was during] the plague of mosquitoes I ran into twenty-five years ago when I was firing in the Gulf Coast country, "the mosquito belt of the world." One night on a hotshot run I had shoveled about fifteen tons of coal into the locomotive firebox. I fainted from exhaustion and staggered to my seatbox, leaving the firedoor wide open. Regaining consciousness, I noticed a steady stream of mosquitoes being drawn into the firedoor by the draft of the engine.

I thought the steam pressure would go down, but I was too tired to look at the steam gauge or warn the hogger. Imagine my surprise when the steam pressure went up so high that the safety pop valve opened and started blowing off steam!

You see, the skeeters were so big, oily, and fat that they made more steam than we could use. But I overcame this easily by opening the firedoor just wide enough to let in enough mosquitoes to keep the boiler hot and not burn them up any faster than they could breed in the swamps beside the track.

After learning this, I had an easy job, and was later appointed traveling fireman of the entire system. . . .

By "Bozo Texino (MoPac hoghead)," Laredo, Texas, *Railroad Stories,* Vol. XXI (May, 1937), No. 6, p. 93. Copyright, 1937, by the Frank A. Munsey Company. New York.

Smart Dog

I [1]

"In my younger days I was a telegraph operator and station agent at a small station in Missouri," said John E. Izzard. "One night a number of toughs entered the station and bound me hand and foot and tied me to a chair some distance from the instruments. They then went through the building and carried off everything that they could find, and went away leaving me tied to the chair. Carlo had just gone with a note over to my house stating that I would be back at the usual time. The toughs were gone before he got back, so he could be of no assistance to me. When he returned he took his key and opened the back door and came in. Seeing me tied, he howled as loud as he could until I made him stop. He was wet all over and kept pointing up toward the bridge. I was at first at a loss to know what it meant. Finally it all came to me like a flash. The recent rain had flooded the river and washed away the bridge. He had to swim across and this was why he was wet. He was trying to let me know that the bridge was out. I turned pale and could hardly move, but I looked first at the dog and then at the instrument. He seemed to know what I wanted. He knew that a train would be along in two hours and that unless there was some warning it would tumble headlong into the river. But he prevented this catastrophe. He went to the table where the instruments were and sent this message which I easily read as he sent it:

> Master is tied to a chair. The bridge is washed away.
> Carlo

This he sent up the line beyond the bridge in the direction of the coming train. Then he sent this down the line:

> Master is tied to a chair. The bridge is washed away. Send some help quick.
> Carlo

He then came over and began to gnaw the ropes that bound me, but he knew it was an all night's job, so he had sent a message first. After he had gnawed for over half an hour four men came in and untied me. They had come up from the next station on a hand car in response to Carlo's appeal for help."

---

[1] By Waldo P. Warren. From the records of the Munchausen Club of Omaha, Fifteenth Meeting, *Omaha World-Herald,* 1895. Contributed by Glen R. Miller, Manuscripts of the Federal Writers' Project of the Works Progress Administration for the State of Nebraska. 1937.

II [2]

. . . When [Conductor] John [Mullen] was running on the local from Marquette to Council Grove, he says he had a collie dog that was the smartest animal you ever saw. Said the dog went with him every trip, and when they'd come into a station, the dog would run over to the head end and duck into the station, look at the switch list, then hike off up town. He'd always come back just as we were getting through with the switching and ready to leave town. That dog was so smart he could look at a switch list and tell just how long the local would be in town. He got left one Saturday, though. John was headed east and when they stopped at Salina, the dog ran up to Agent Coffee, looked at the switch list and figured they had about two hours' work to do, and beat it up town. After awhile Coffee came out and said that on account of it being Saturday, they'd cut out some of the switching. The boys looked around for the dog and he couldn't be found. After they had been gone about an hour, the dog came back and saw the local was gone. He hiked over to the UP, rode up to Junction City, caught the Katy into Council Grove and was standing on the platform waiting for Mullen when the local got in.

Budd McKillips' Cal Bunyan Railroad

Almost every one knows how Paul Bunyan, with the aid of Babe, the Blue Ox, who measured seven ax handles and three plugs of chewing tobacco between the eyes, cut down the immense forests which once covered every inch of North Dakota, Iowa, South Dakota, Kansas, and Ohio and then dug dozens of rivers on which to float the logs to the mills. But it is not generally known that Paul had a brother—Cal S. Bunyan—who built the largest and most wondrous railroad in the world.

I first heard about Cal from "Springheels" Conley, an old boomer who, in talking about some of the railroads where he had worked, mentioned the IJA&SI.

---

[2] From *Boomer Bill, His Book,* by I. M. Brown, p. 108. Copyright, 1930, by I. M. Brown. [No publisher or place.]

By Budd I. McKillips. From *Tracks,* Chesapeake & Ohio, Nickel Plate, and Pere Marquette, Vol. 31 (January, 1946), No. 1, pp. 52–54. Copyright, 1946, by the Chesapeake and Ohio Railway Company. New York. Reprinted from *The Signalman's Journal.*

This was one of Budd McKillips' most popular stories. When it was first printed in December, 1936, many readers wrote in about it. Budd McKillips died six years ago, and for the good he did on earth he deserves a comfortable seat on that fast train of the IJA&SI, which is still rushing through space.—*The Signalman's Journal.*

"What?" demanded Conley, when I told him I couldn't remember any railroad with those initials. "Do you mean that you've never heard of the Ireland, Jerusalem, Australia & Southern Indiana Railroad?"

I confessed that I never had, and "Springheels," after pouring himself another malted milk from the shaker the soda fountain clerk had set on the counter in front of us, told me all about Cal Bunyan and his railroad.

"You see, it was this way," said "Springheels," as he helped himself to my cigarettes. "Cal got the idea about starting the IJA&SI after Jim Hill finished building the Great Northern. I guess Cal was a little jealous of all the nice things the newspapers were saying about Hill. Anyway, Cal decided to build a road bigger than any that Jim Hill or any of those other guys could build.

"So he started laying the track of the IJA&SI. Ordinary ballast, such as cinders and gravel, wouldn't do for the tracks, so Cal used boulders which he brought from the Rocky Mountains. Each boulder weighed six tons and Cal used millions of them.

"Present-day section men think that big rails are now being used. They should have seen the kind on the IJA&SI. It took the largest steel mill in the United States, operating on a thirty-six-hour-day and nine-day-week schedule, two years to produce one rail for Cal.

"Each tie was made from an entire giant redwood tree. And the section men had to use pile-drivers to spike down the rails. One day a section foreman slipped and fell to the ground from the top of a rail. It was a 500-foot sheer drop and he was killed instantly.

"After the track was built, the next job was to get an engine and cars. They had to be made to order and it was a hard task finding machinery large enough to turn out the parts. Cal finally solved the problem by taking the two largest Ferris wheels he could find and setting them in line about a block apart to use for lathes in which to turn the axles for the new locomotive. He bought a merry-go-round and used it for a journal box boring mill. The Eiffel Tower in Paris was rigged up for a drill press.

"The rivets and staybolts used for the engine's boiler and firebox were 24 feet in diameter. A volcano was used to heat the rivets, and then the boiler-makers drove them in place by firing cannon balls at them.

"Building the coaches was some job, too. Each nail was driven by two husky carmen wielding fence post mauls. Long-stroke air hammers were used for tacking the upholstery on coach seats.

"Finally, an engine and 700 cars were ready for the first train. Before the engine was fired up, however, the 3,600 members of the road's board of directors held a banquet in the locomotive's firebox.

"There was only one tragedy to mark the day of the train's first run. When the engineer started the air pump, the first stroke sucked all of the air out of four neighboring States and hundreds of people suffocated to death.

"A roll of paper, like is used on newspaper printing presses, was used to write out orders for the engineer and conductor. The telegraphers who sent these orders were all clog dancers. They pounded out the dots and dashes by dancing jigs on the keys of their instruments.

"All of the clerks on the IJA&SI used fountain pens which, like Johnny Inkslinger's, took a barrel of ink at each filling.

"The engineer and fireman had to use a balloon to get up to the engine cab. If they had tried to climb up the gangway the 16-hour law would have caught them long before they got near the top.

"No man was strong enough to pull the throttle on this locomotive, so a stationary engine was installed on the right side to do the job.

"Mules and mine cars were used to haul coal from the tender and dump it on the deck in front of the firebox door. The fireman's scoop shovel held two tons.

"The train was so long that the conductor rode on a motorcycle to take up the tickets. He punched each ticket by shooting holes through it with a .45-caliber automatic pistol.

"On the dining car, a whole beef was used for each steak. Two cement mixers were required to stir the gravy, and potatoes were lifted out of the frying pans by steam shovels. A tank car was coupled in the front of each diner to carry the cream for the passengers' coffee.

"Just as the train started out, the engineer blew the whistle. When the steam condensed, it made a cloudburst which flooded the whole country.

"The train started to pick up speed and the engineer had to put on a pair of goggles that had lenses 18 inches thick. By and by he got going so fast that the suction from the train picked all of the leaves off the trees and pulled the farmers' corn out of the ground for eight miles each side of the right-of-way.

"No train ever went at the speed this one did. It went so fast that after it was brought to a dead stop it was still making 65 miles an hour. Two months later the schedule was speeded up so that the train arrived at its destination an hour before it left its starting point.

"At first there was a lot of trouble on the night runs—over the headlight. It was so powerful that it lighted up an area of 50,000 acres on each side of the track and kept it lighted for twelve hours after the train had passed. The farmers raised an awful rumpus about this—all of their chickens were dying from the loss of sleep. Also, the heat from the headlight was burning up wheat fields and drying up rivers. So the engineer tried to cover the headlight with a shield of six-inch armor plate, but the light shone through just the same. Finally, he took out the reflector, cut all the wires, and smashed the dynamo with a sledge hammer. This cut down the range of the light to a mile and a half, and half of the farmers stopped kicking.

"After that everything went along fine until one day when it was decided to double the speed of the train. It was no trick to do this, because at no time had the engineer ever had the throttle open more than three notches.

" 'Give her all she's got,' Cal Bunyan told the engineer when they started out on the new test run.

"The engineer opened her wide up. And did she make speed! But that was the end of the IJA&SI. The train went so fast that the friction melted all the rails and burned all the ties to ashes. And on the last half mile of the line, where the track went up a steep grade, the train was going at such a speed that when it reached the top the engine took off like an airplane and carried itself and its 700 cars so far into the stratosphere that the law of gravitation quit working. That was years ago, but the train is still rushing through space up there."

That was all of the story. "Springheels" tried to add a few more words, but his voice broke and he began sobbing. I got up quietly and slipped out a side door. The next day when I passed there, I glanced in. "Springheels" was still standing at the soda counter, crying into his malted milk over the sad fate of the IJA&SI.

IV. THE PASSENGER IS ALWAYS RIGHT

The Passengers Were Hysterical

New Year's, 1953, we had the usual passengers over the holidays. One young lady was put on the train the evening of December 31st.

As told by a conductor on the New York Central's Hudson Division, Harmon, New York, July 13, 1953. Recorded and transcribed by B. A. Botkin.

She had a beautiful bun on—the cops put her on the train and seated her. On the way up the Hudson I asked her how she was going home. She happened to live in Tarrytown Gardens. She said she was going to drive, of course. "Well," I said, "I don't doubt it because you're in no condition to walk. But what *are* you going to do?" "I don't know," she said. Well, I asked one of the other commuters to drive her home—he had a car at the station, too. "There's only one thing to do," I told him, "drive her home." He was a good samaritan, this commuter. "There's only one thing I want of you," I said to him. "What's that?" he asked. "When you get her up there in the house, ring the bell and run like heck," I said, "because if her husband—a six-footer—comes out and sees you, he'll think you got her drunk!" And the passengers around her were all hysterical.

Well, we had another one with a bun on. This was about four days after the first of January. He had a beautiful load on. He held on to the seats coming up the aisle to get off at Glenwood. One of the passengers remarked, "Look, he's got another load on." "No," I said, "that's the same one he's had on since New Year's."

We get them on quite regularly. I try to help them off, otherwise they only get to be a pain in the neck by going past their stop and then having to explain to their wives or husbands why they were late.

You know, of course, that we load a Hudson Division train, 5:52 P.M., and a Harlem Division train alongside of us—the 5:47—off the same island platform. And it never fails but we get Harlem Division passengers on the Hudson train. A Harlem Division commutation ticket, you know, is good on the Hudson Division, for the same mileage. Well, this particular night I saw this fellow there had a commutation ticket for the Harlem Division, and it had got to the stage where I was getting six or seven every night. Well, this particular night the fellow flashed his ticket and I kept going on. And leaving Dobbs Ferry, I yelled, "Ardsley-on-Hudson, next!" And this fellow stands up in the car and yells out, "What am I doing on this train?" "Well," I said, "you're obviously riding it." "But," he said, "I want to go to Mt. Vernon." "Well," I said, "as good a time as any to find out that you're going to Mt. Vernon." "Well," he says, "what am I going to do?" "Well," I says, "we'll get you off at Irvington station. I'll give you a check to get back to Yonkers." "Then what?" he says. "Then take a bus," I says, "a No. 7 bus from Yonkers to Mt. Vernon—very easy."

With that I went into the next car. I was working the next car, and I happened to look back and noticed that he was walking up and down the aisle, approaching different passengers, as if he were annoying them. I walked back in the car and I said to him, "Listen, mister, what's going on here? What's the trouble with you? What are you asking the different passengers?" "Oh," he said, "I'm trying to find out what to tell my wife when I get home." "Well," I said, "there's only one thing to do." "What's that?" he said. "Well," I said, "you go to Tarrytown and stay in a hotel over night, and then you'll really have something to tell her the next day."

Gee, the passengers were hysterical!

It goes on every night! I had one here only last Friday. A nice old lady came on there at 125th Street. I said, "Ludlow, next." I walked in and she handed me a Harlem Division Crestwood 26-tripper. I said, "You're going to Crestwood?" "Why, of course," she said. "It really is a nice town," I said. "We go right by it on this train, don't we?" she said. "Unfortunately," I said, "today's Friday. We go up the Hudson on Friday. You better get off at Yonkers."

We had a train that didn't stop at Yonkers. We used to go from 125th Street right to Hastings-on-Hudson. And I had a guy with an awful bun on. He came down and sat in the first seat in the car. I had to give him a little shake in order to wake him and find out where he was going. He said, "Yonkers." "Let me see your ticket." And he showed me his commutation ticket. And I said, "Get off at 125th Street. Take the next train to Yonkers." "All right." With that he conks off and goes right to sleep. At 125th Street I looked in and saw he was not making any effort. As you probably know, the 125th Street station has the double platform similar to Yonkers. I walked in there and I give him a shake—I was holding the train up—I give him a shake, and said, "Hey, buddy, you got to get off here." He looked up and saw the platform—it looked so similar to Yonkers. "Gee," he said, "that was a fast trip to Yonkers!"

One of those things!

I'll never forget Yonkers. You probably know the train crews have a habit of putting their clothes up right above the rack of the first seat, so they can keep an eye on it. There are no lockers on these locals. And it's easy to get it if they need any paraphernalia out of their bags, or their clothes. This particular day we had a tough time. This fellow was going to Yonkers, and every station he wanted to get off, except Yonkers. Well, finally we got him off at Yonkers. I was working the second car. And the conductor said to the brakeman, who was up on the platform—he says, "Give him two, so we can proceed with the train. We've got him off here. This is his station." Well, the brakeman reached up and started to give him two, and then he remembered this fellow didn't have a hat on his head. And above where he was sitting was a hat. And he put two and two together, rushed in and grabbed the hat and ran out and yelled, "Here!" and threw it out to him. And as the train started to move out, the conductor jumped on. The train was about near Glenwood station when finally the brakeman looked up and said, "Gosh darn it," he said, "I just made a bull." I said, "What was that?" "I threw my own hat after the passenger."

A number of years ago I was working the 9:32 A.M. local out of New York, and we had these two women on the train. One was going to Hastings and one was going to Dobbs Ferry. Now Dobbs Ferry comes after Hastings. And in leaving Greystone, which is the station before Hastings, we announced, "Hastings-on-Hudson next!" At that point the woman from Dobbs Ferry had to go to the ladies' room, which was just opposite where she was sitting. The woman behind her was going to Hastings. The woman from Dobbs Ferry left her umbrella on the seat. And then as we were coming to Hastings the fellow working the car behind me saw that the woman from Hastings had got off, but looking back in the car, he noticed the umbrella, not associating it with the woman that was getting off at Dobbs Ferry and that was in the ladies' room. The train started moving. He grabbed the umbrella and he saw the lady from Hastings walking along the platform. "Lady, lady, you forgot your umbrella, you forgot your umbrella!" With that she grabbed it. That was during the war years and that was like giving some one a five-dollar bill. The lady in the ladies' room couldn't get out fast enough. And when she came out she laced it into him, with the most profane language I have ever heard. She called him everything under the sun. "You gave her my umbrella! I heard you give that lady my umbrella!" He said, "Oh, I'll get it back for you. I know the lady that I gave it to." "See that you do." Well, that was about ten years ago, and to this day I don't think she ever got her umbrella back.

Working the 12:35 P.M. Saturday local out of New York, I checked the passengers and noticed one fellow asleep. I shook him and I noticed his commutation ticket to Dobbs Ferry, and I checked him to Dobbs Ferry. Further up the river, as we were leaving Hastings-on-Hudson, I announced "Dobbs Ferry next!" Noticing my sleeper still asleep, I shook him gently and woke him. I said, "Dobbs Ferry next." With that he became very belligerent and bawled me out for not waking him up at Hastings. "Hastings?" I said. "Why? You have a Dobbs Ferry commutation ticket." "I know that," he said, "but I left my car at Hastings this morning."

I always find the best way to wake up a sleeping commuter is to shake him a little and ask him: "Where you going, young man?" (No matter how old they are, I always call them "young man.") "Tuckahoe or Crestwood?" (stations on the Harlem Division). That always brings the passenger to his feet, yelling, "No, Yonkers," or whatever his station is.

I try to be humble and not smart alecky. I just try to get passengers to their destination as quickly as possible. I found out that the Westchesterite can never be wrong. You'll always find a passenger who states he has been riding the train for 30 years and this is the first time he ever got on the wrong train. But there's always a first time. I don't like to tell them that I'm on the right train, because I don't want to be smart alecky.

Battle of Jokes

Seated around a luncheon-table in a down-town New York restaurant were several men whose outburst of laughter made the diners at the tables close by regret that they had not been privileged to hear the quip that had caused the merriment.

The luncheon-party in question was made up of F. D. Underwood, president of the Erie Railroad, and two of his close friends. The latter gentlemen were regular commuters over the road of which Mr. Underwood is the chief executive, and the conversation had turned to the jokes that were being told all over the country at the expense of the rural service of the Erie.

"If it were not for the Erie," said one of the men to Mr. Underwood, "half of the vaudeville performers in this country would be looking for jobs. A vaudeville act without a funny remark about your railroad would be like home without mother."

"Yes," put in the second diner laughingly, "half the pleasure we commuters get out of life consists in springing jokes on the service of the road during our trips to and from the city."

Mr. Underwood thought a moment, and slapped the table with his hand. "Right!" he exclaimed. "And now my plan is made. I am going to make the joke-bread you have cast upon the waters come back to you. I am going to get even with the commuters."

"How in the world are you going to do that?" asked the others.

"Wait, look, and listen," replied the chief executive.

How Mr. Underwood, aided by his associates, succeeded in turning the multitudinous array of Erie jokes on the commuters, and how, by turning the tables on the latter, he succeeded in putting almost a full stop to the ubiquitous puns and sarcastic funnyisms through making the commuters realize that the joke was on them, has been well appreciated ere this by the suburban travelers.

Mr. Underwood's plan, in brief, was this: He collected every good joke that had been told at the expense of the Erie's suburban service. These jokes were inserted in the time-tables of the railroad, and in such positions that the commuter who was looking up the trains could not fail to see them.

New jokes were to be inserted as new batches of time-tables were issued, and not a joke was to be allowed to go unnoticed. For more than a year and a half this order was put into execution, and only recently, after several thousand commuters had written to the Erie company that the laugh was on them, was the great joke campaign called off.

From "Railroad and Commuters in Battle of Jokes," by George Jean Nathan, *The Railroad Man's Magazine*, Vol. 10 (January, 1910), No. 4, pp. 743–748.

To demonstrate the extent to which the "campaign" was carried, and to give an idea of the huge variety of jokes that were turned against the commuters by making the latter read them regularly in the time schedules, the following collection of the best of these jests was made.

Man Falling Might Beat Erie

Recently an old man *en route* to Binghamton, while passing from one coach to another, fell from the train and rolled down a steep embankment, but was not seriously hurt. One of the train crew asked him what he thought of as he was falling.

"Well," he said, "Oi don't want to hurrt yer feelings, sor; but whin I was rolling down the bank, thinks Oi, 'Begorry, if Oi kin kape up this gait a thrifle longer, I'll be in Binghamton ahead of the train.' "

To Discontinue Return Tickets

Nelson.—"It is intimated that the Erie is going to discontinue the sale of return tickets from New York to stations on the New Jersey and New York Railroad."

MacDougal.—"Why?"

Nelson.—"Because their lease of that line will expire in ninety-nine years."

Worth the Fare

It was during a very tedious ride on the "Erie," and the passengers, tired, dirty, and thirsty, all berated the company with the exception of one man. His fellow passengers commented on this, and asked him why he did not denounce the company, too.

"It would be hardly fair," he replied, "as I am traveling on a pass; but, if they don't do better pretty soon, blame me if I don't go out and buy a ticket and join you."

Put the Cowcatcher Behind

During the floods a few years ago, many bad washouts occurred on the Erie, and the trains were run at a low rate of speed. When the conductor was punching the ticket of a passenger he remarked:

"Does this railroad company allow passengers to give it advice, if they do so in a respectful manner?"

The conductor replied that he guessed so.

"Well, then, it occurred to me that it would be well to detach the cowcatcher from the front of the engine and hitch it to the rear of the train; for, you see, we are not liable to overtake a cow, and what's to prevent a cow from strolling into this car and biting a passenger?"

It is an old joke. It originated with Mark Twain back in the '80's, but even the conductor laughed.

Time-Tables

At all the shows ridicule is the big hit. The minstrel middleman asks the endman, "Where do you get your funny jokes?"

Endman replies: "Comparing the running time with the time-tables of the Erie Railroad."

Boy Running Beats Erie Train

An Upper Montclair newsboy beat an Erie passenger-train from Pompton to Pompton Junction.

Returning from an excursion, he got off the train at Pompton to purchase some peanuts, and the train started before he had completed his purchase. Nothing daunted, he started after the train, crossing lots and bridges, and when the train stopped for about a minute at Pompton Junction, the swift-footed newsboy, out of breath, swung aboard and rejoined his astonished companions, who believed that he had been left behind for the night.

Heard at the Post-Office

"Well, spring is here at last. I noticed this morning that the Erie has replaced the snow-plows on the cowcatchers with mowing-machines."

A Sad Case

"This is a sad case," said the attendant at an insane asylum, pausing before a padded cell. "There is no hope for the patient whatever."

"What's his trouble?" asked the visitor.

"He thinks he understands an Erie time-table."

Half Fare

A patriarch, who presented a half ticket for a ride between Suffern and Jersey City, was informed that he must pay full fare. He replied: "When I purchased that ticket before boarding this train I was entitled to the half-fare rate."

Together with these jeers and jokes and verses, hundreds of others of a like character were printed in the time-tables, which, in a few months after the joke campaign was begun, became known as the Erie Joke Books. The extent to which this characterization went is made known in the following quotation from one of the schedules:

> While looking for information recently in connection with the running of trains for certain shipments, a patron was referred to the superintendent of transportation for a set of working tables. When making application for them in writing, he requested that "Erie Joke Book No. 2" be sent to him.

Many of the letters that were received at the Erie offices from commuters, after the joke campaign was well under way, were quite as amusing as were the jokes that had been turned on them.

One commuter wrote: "The jokes are worse than the train service. Please discontinue one or the other."

Another wrote: "I will never say another mean thing about the Erie if you will only stop those awful jokes. I can bear rough travel better than be compelled to hear, or read, the same funny story twice."

Still another wrote: "I will agree to quit kicking if you will agree to stop printing and reprinting that weird array of old jokes."

But the favorable outcome of the joke campaign—favorable to the railroad—was best illustrated by a letter from a commuter in Tenafly, New Jersey.

"Your time-tables," read the letter, "have had the effect of a sort of Keeley cure on us Tenaflyers. If you will stop dosing us with our own jokes, we promise you to henceforth abstain from all forms of alcoholic Erie jests."

Corn by the Carload

The drummers in the smoker were telling 'em fast and funny, with scarcely a wait for the rewarding guffaws. They were more interested in telling than in listening, but whenever the sample and satchel boys got together there was one pair of eager ears in the crowd. They belonged to Thomas W. Jackson, member of the crew.

When his duties as brakeman permitted, Jackson sat in on this humor exchange while his train crawled back and forth across the face of Arkansas. And thus Tom Jackson came to know intimately of the latest misadventures of the farmer's daughter and her city cousin, as well as the endless variations of stock humor that was currently laying 'em in the aisles from Broadway to Pumpkin Center.

In time Jackson's memory became surcharged with the stuff of which laughs are made and, although his own skill as a raconteur kept a lot of jokes in circulation, he was hearing them faster than he could tell them. At this point some latent commercial instinct took over, for Tom Jackson added paper and pencil to his equipment and he began writing down the best jokes he heard during his visits to the smoker. It was a blue pencil, naturally, for the man who was later to found "The House That Jokes Built" knew that the picturesque phrases used in the smoker would have to be edited for reading in the parlor car.

Jackson's world was one of trains and passengers and when he published a joke book it was inevitably written about, and sold to, travelers. So it was that *On a Slow Train through Arkansaw* came to life in cold type and established Thomas W. Jackson as the American Joe Miller on Wheels.

Success was something less than instantaneous. Indeed, before Jackson managed to peddle his first 1,000 books, he vowed that if he ever got rid of them he would never touch another. But just as he was deciding that joke books were neither funny nor profitable, repeat orders began to come in. Jackson risked another 2,000 copies.

By David Brittle. From *Tracks,* Chesapeake & Ohio, Nickel Plate, Pere Marquette, Vol. 35 (August, 1950), No. 8, pp. 12–16. Copyright, 1950, by the Chesapeake & Ohio Railway Company. New York.

Today, those repeat orders are still coming in and since *On a Slow Train Through Arkansaw* first came off the press in 1903, seven million copies have been sold. And that is less than half of the Jackson success story. Twelve other Jackson books, all cut from the same pattern, have swelled the grand total to fifteen million copies.

Each book is pocket size, has ninety-six pages and is paper backed. Stacked together they would fill thirty standard box cars from floor to roof—thirty cars of good old American corn. Or chestnuts, if age is to be respected. Still, they are largely the same imperishable chestnuts being displayed today in the fancier showcases of radio and television.

Through all of Jackson's books runs a theme that calls up memories of Mr. Bones and Mr. Interlocutor, Weber & Fields, and Cohen on the Telephone, all woven into a fabric of travel and travelers. As proclaimed on the cover of *Slow Train,* it is a collection of "Funny Railroad Stories, Sayings of the Southern Darkies, All the Latest and Best Minstrel Jokes of the Day." Other books of the series make differing cover claims as to content but all of it attacks the funny bone with the same feather. Rated on radio's applause meter, Jackson's broad brand of humor would give the needle mild conniptions at the haw-haw level. And all of it could be read aloud at a Sunday School picnic, with no hysteria over occasional use of the double-entendre.

By the time Jackson got around to writing *Slow Train* he had moved from Arkansas to Washington where he had a passenger run between Spokane and Pendleton on the Oregon Railroad and Navigation Company. Jokes continued to pile up and Jackson continued to screen and refine them until only the golden kernels remained. Then he would corner his conductor, C. J. "Mickey" Carr, and hold an audition. If Carr laughed, the joke went into the book. It was Carr, too, who helped Jackson untie the first bundle of books received from the printer.

After its faltering start, *Slow Train* moved right along and Jackson was soon reordering at a 5,000 clip, for the news butchers were doing bonanza business in day coaches up and down the West Coast. Paper supply suddenly became a problem and Jackson moved to Chicago, resolved to shoot the works with an order of 10,000 books. He tied a string to his job with the O. R. & N. by taking a sixty-day leave, then resigned by mail when midwesterners in large numbers began tucking *Slow Train* in their coat pockets.

The year was 1904 and millions of Americans were riding the cushions to St. Louis to see the Louisiana Purchase Centennial Exposition. *Slow Train* headed the best seller list on all trains, and anyone could get a laugh by saying, "Then the brakeman come in and hollered, 'Take your partners for the tunnel.' " That was the opening crack of *Slow Train* which then proceeds thus:

"You are not the only pebble on the beach for there is a little rock in Arkansaw. It was down in the state of Arkansaw I rode on the slowest train I ever saw. It stopped at every house. When it came to a double house it stopped twice. They made so many stops I said, 'Conductor, what have we stopped for now?' He said, 'There are some cattle on the track.' We ran a little ways further and stopped again. I said, 'What is the matter now?' He said, 'We have caught up with those cattle again.' "

And so it goes for ninety-six solid pages of puns, gags, monologs and spoofing of everything dear to the heart of a jokesmith. Climb aboard the *Slow Train* for a short run with Jackson down page 54—and don't be surprised if you meet some characters you've known for years.

* * * * *

As might be expected, Arkansas, its railroads, people, and cities take quite a ribbing in *Slow Train,* and for a time the name of Jackson was mud in Arkansas. It seems that the sovereign dignity of Arkansas had been badly riddled by some earlier literary sharpshooters and some folks mistakenly blamed Jackson for all of it. But all is set right in the final gag in *Slow Train.* It says, "When you read this book you will like Arkansaw so well you will keep a heater under your bed so as to have Hot Springs."

While the traveling public was still grabbing at his first book, Jackson published his second, in 1904. It was *Through Missouri on a Mule,* and that fixed the title pattern for several others which followed. Among them are *I'm From Texas, You Can't Steer Me; From Rhode Island to Texas; O U Auto C the U. S. with Jackson;* and *See America First.*

So well was the pattern established that when Jackson's son, Harry G., took over the business upon his father's death, he wrote the thirteenth book of the series and called it *On a Fast Streamliner, Fun from New York to Frisco.*

Tom Jackson originated all of his titles and much of his material, but he never claimed to be the father of all he published. A good yarn spinner himself, it was nevertheless his idea that the original jokes of one man would make a pretty flat book. And so he traveled far and wide, over the rails, to catch the latest in national and local humor.

Business was so good for the elder Jackson that he set up his own printing establishment and took Harry in with him. Before long their joke books were being sold on nearly every railroad and in every depot of the country. Millions more went round the globe in the pockets of American soldiers in two world wars. Now, the joke book game isn't what it used to be. For one thing, the news butch is a vanishing American, along with the day coach which was his bazaar. For another, according to Harry, too many people are listening to radio and looking at movies and television instead of reading joke books.

Harry isn't complaining, although his ulcer kicks up now and then when he hears of the fabulous fees paid to radio comedians who sometimes seem to have clipped their scripts from his father's books. But Harry is now at that age where he "takes things as they are, not as they should be."

Gone is the day of big joke book sales, such as the 1,000 per day once taken by Union News Company alone, but the colored covers of the Jackson joke books still draw the eye on the station newsstands and in the news butcher's basket. Many a one still peeks from a traveler's pocket. With *On a Slow Train through Arkansaw* approaching its half-century milestone, Jacksonian humor still is abroad in the land and will no doubt remain so long as people laugh.

Slow Train

I [1]

On some of the Western roads they attach a passenger car to a freight train and call it "mixed." It isn't in the order of things that such trains should run very rapidly, and sometimes there is considerable growling along the "traffic."

"Are we most there, conductor?" asked a nervous man for the hundredth time. "Remember my wife is sick, and I'm anxious."

"We'll get there on time," replied the conductor, stolidly.

Half an hour later the nervous man approached him again.

"I guess she's dead now," said he, mournfully, "but I'd give you something extra if you could manage to catch up with the funeral. Maybe she wouldn't be so decomposed but what I would recognize her!"

---

[1] From *Brother Jonathan's Jokes, Funny Stories, and Laughable Sketches. . .*, pp. 38–39. Copyright, 1885, by Excelsior Publishing House. New York.

The slow or late train, like the Ford joke, is one of the hardy perennials of the humor that crystallizes popular distrust of new-fangled inventions. In earlier days the speed of trains was the subject of jests and tall tales: "Now I kin git from Bosting to Filadelphy in one day, and I've been cal'latin' that if the power of steam increases for the *next* ten years as it has been doin' for the *last* ten years, I'd be in Filadelphy just two days before I started from Bosting" (*A Treasury of New England Folklore*, New York, 1944, p. 232). Then, as people became accustomed to speed and were irked by the lack of it, it was the slow train that, like other old-fashioned things, appeared funny. Of late, however, the wheel has turned full circle; and with the cult of the short line, the slow train is regarded with nostalgic affection and passionately defended by its fans, while the fast train has again become the subject of jest. "I lit my cigar leaving New York, knocked the ashes out the window, and they fell on a man's head standing on the platform at Syracuse, three hundred miles away" (Harry G. Jackson, *On a Fast Streamliner*, 1938).

James R. Masterson (*Tall Tales of Arkansaw*, 1942, p. 269) traces the first slow train joke (including the cows that climb aboard the rear car and disturb the passengers) to Mark Twain's *The Gilded Age* (1873) and the first slow-train-in-

The conductor growled at him, and the man subsided.

"Conductor," said he, after an hour's silence—"conductor, if the wind isn't dead ahead, I wish you would put on some steam. I'd like to see where my wife is buried before the tombstone crumbles to pieces! Put yourself in my place for a moment!"

The conductor shook him off, and the man relapsed into profound melancholy.

"I say, conductor," said he, after a long pause. "I've got a note coming due in three months. Can't you fix it so as to rattle along a little?"

"If you come near me again I'll knock you down," snorted the conductor, savagely.

The nervous man regarded him sadly, and went to his seat. Two hours later the conductor saw him chatting gayly and laughing heartily with a brother victim, and approached him.

"Don't feel so badly about your wife's death?"

"Time heals all wounds," sighed the nervous man.

"And you are not so particular about that note?" sneered the conductor.

"Not now. That's all right. Don't worry. I've been figuring it up, and I find that the note has been outlawed since I spoke to you last."

II [2]

Scrub Race. We saw a North Amherst man the other day fairly run down the A&B [Amherst & Belchertown Railroad] cars. The train had

---

Arkansas joke to Opie Read's periodical, *The Arkansaw Traveler,* in 1882. The real vogue of Arkansas slow train humor dates from the appearance in 1903 of *On a Slow Train through Arkansaw,* the first of the twelve paper-backed jokebooks by Thomas W. Jackson (1867–1934). On the first page is a variant of the Mark Twain cow story: "One old cow got her tail caught in the cow-catcher and she ran off down the track with the train. The cattle bothered us so much they had to take the cow-catcher off the engine and put it on the hind end of the train to keep the cattle from jumping up into the sleeper."

Other states have their slow trains. Indiana: "You may think I'm overdrawing it, but I'm not when I tell you that a fellow took down with typhoid fever on the thing just after I got on, and when I got off at the end of my journey, he was sound and well, and he had a long siege of it too" (George D. Beason, *I Blew in from Arkansaw,* 1908, p. 49). Idaho: "It's so slow that farmers who load hay at Kamiah discover that the cars are empty by the time they reach Lewiston, because cows along the way have eaten it" (*Idaho Lore,* 1939, p. 119).

Closely related to slow train humor are the late train [IV, p. 428], the rough train, and the crooked line ("Whenever the conductor wanted the engineer to stop," writes Harry G. Jackson, "he would just swing out going around a curve and slap the engineer on the back").—B. A. B., *Standard Dictionary of Folklore, Mythology, and Legend* (New York, 1950), Vol. II, pp. 1028–1029.

[2] From *The Hampshire and Franklin* (Amherst, Massachusetts) *Express,* Vol. 13 (July 3, 1857), No. 45, Whole No. 494, p. 2. col. 3. In the Jones Library, Amherst.

a start of a minute or two and he was left behind, his wife being aboard, but he overtook them in the "deep cut" in Judge Dickinson's pasture. The fortunate winner of this race has been somewhat noted for speed from his youth up; has *run* admirably as candidate for divers high offices in the gift of the town, and never yet lost a race. Perhaps it is proper to state in this instance that the engine at the head of the train was not the best one of the company. If the "Vermont" had been on instead of the "Bates," the result with the same start might have been different.

III [3]

On a dilapidated narrow gauge railroad in a certain state, a traveler was struck with the general air of hopelessness of the entire country. Rundown farms, fences falling to pieces, and houses unpainted and dismal were seen as mile after mile was reeled off. Finally a countryman got on and the two fell into conversation.

"Country around here looks fearfully dilapidated," remarked the traveler.

"Yeah, but jist wait, and ye'll see somep'n wuss," replied the countryman.

The train stopped. They looked out and saw a rail missing ahead. The train crew clambered out, crowbars in hand, proceeded leisurely to the rear of the train, loosened a rail, and carried it forward. It was spiked into position and the train proceeded.

"Somebody stole a rail?" asked the traveler.

"Yeah, about twenty year ago, I reckon. Ever since, they hain't nobody bought a new one. When the train comes back, they've got to stop and tear up that rail agin."

IV [4]

Down in Arkansas in the old days there was a jerk-water railroad with a reputation. The reputation was that it never adhered to its schedule. Operating crews, and patrons as well, came to regard the timecard as the work of a practical joker.

There was a certain traveling man who rode over the line at frequent intervals. One afternoon when he disembarked from a smelly daycoach at his destination he hailed the conductor.

"Old man," he said, extending a large cigar, "accept this with my compliments as a slight token of gratitude."

"What's the notion?" inquired the other.

"Because I've been traveling on this road for twelve years and this is the first occasion when the train ever got in exactly on time."

---

[3] From the *Express Gazette,* May, 1916, quoted from "an Iowa exchange."

[4] From *Many Laughs for Many Days,* by Irvin S. Cobb, p. 25. Copyright, 1925, by George H. Doran Company. New York.

"Mister," said the conductor, "that looks to me like a mighty good cigar and I'm fond of smokin'. But I can't take nothin' on false pretenses. I've got to tell you the truth. This ain't today's train. This is yesterday's train."

Whistle Stop

A millionaire . . . bought a large estate near a tiny whistle-stop station on a neglected branch line [of the Chesapeake & Ohio Railroad]. From Sears Roebuck he ordered a prefabricated chicken coop and, when he received word that it had arrived, set out in a truck with his butler to bring it home. No one was about when he spied the coop along the right of way, and he soon had it loaded on the truck. Half a mile up the road they passed a little man in blue who had "Station Master" written on his cap. He took one look and shouted, "Stop that car. What do you think you got on that truck?" "My new chicken coop," explained the millionaire. "Chicken coop, my eye," cried the station master, "that's Grigsby Junction."

Snoring on a Sleeper

I once asked a conductor on a Chicago and Northwestern sleeper whether he didn't often have trouble with snoring passengers. He replied, with fervor:

"Don't I? Oh, no! never, by no means! Why, there's one man, a drummer for a Chicago house, who crosses regularly with me every week, who'd drive a deaf corpse crazy. He's a little bit of a man, and don't weigh much more than a hundred, but he can snore for twenty. He lays himself out and falls asleep the minute he gets the covers over him. Then the fun begins. I've known him to have the whole car awake and yelling for me and the porter, and he snoring away as calm and peaceful as a baby. The last trip he made we had a minister with us, a big jolly gentleman, who had the berth next to him. He snored for half an hour at a stretch, and the poor preacher didn't get a wink of sleep. But he didn't say anything till the others had given up yelling in despair. Then the drummer rolled over on his side and, giving

---

From *Shake Well before Using*, by Bennett Cerf, p. 181. Copyright, 1948, by Bennett Cerf. New York: Simon and Schuster.

From *The Fast Men of America;* or, Racing with Time from Cradle to Grave, The Romance and Reality of Life on the Railroad, Illustrated with Pen and Pencil, by an Old Railroader, [Alfred Trumble], p. 60. New York: Published by Richard K. Fox, Proprietor, *Police Gazette.* [1882.]

a kind of choking snort, like a man having his throat cut, he stopped snoring. For about half a second there was dead silence in the car. Then we heard the minister say: 'Thank God! The scoundrel is dead!' "

Public Relations

While Stewart was president of the Hannibal & St. Joe, his policy was to make the new means of transportation as popular as possible with Missourians. One night the president was traveling over the road—it was before the era of the sleeping car—when a baby set up an outcry which disturbed the whole coach. The mother tried in vain to quiet the little one. Stewart rose from his seat, went to the mother and said:

"Madam, my name is Stewart. I am president of this road and it is my duty to look after the comfort of the patrons. Hand that baby to me."

He took the baby in his arms and walked up and down the aisle until he put it to sleep.

The Upper Is Lower

"Let me have sleeping accommodations on the train to Ottawa," I said to the man at the window, who didn't seem at all concerned whether I took the trip or stayed at home.

"For a single passenger?" he finally said.

"No," I replied. "I'm married; but I'm not taking anybody with me. A single berth will answer."

"Upper or lower?" he asked.

"What is the difference?" I inquired.

"A difference of 50 cents," came the answer. "Our prices to Ottawa are 1.50 and 2. You understand of course," explained the agent, "the lower is higher than the upper. The higher price is for the lower berth. If you want a lower, you'll have to go higher. We sell the upper lower than the lower. It didn't used to be so, but we found everybody wanted the lower. In other words, the higher, the fewer."

"Why do they all prefer the lower?" I broke in.

"On account of its convenience," he replied. "Most persons don't

---

From *Centennial History of Missouri*, by Walter B. Stevens, Vol. I, p. 401. Copyright, 1921, by S. J. Clarke Publishing Co. St. Louis and Chicago.

From *The Chesapeake & Ohio Railway Employes' Magazine*, Vol. VI (February, 1921), No. 1, p. 42. Cleveland, Ohio.

like the upper, although it's lower, on account of its being higher and because when you occupy an upper you have to get up to go to bed and then get down when you get up. I would advise you to take the lower, although it's higher than the upper, for the reason I have stated, that the upper is lower than the lower because it is higher. You can have the lower if you pay higher, but if you are willing to go higher, it will be lower."

A Variant of "Put Me Off at Buffalo"

Fellow got on train at Buffalo and instructed the porter: "I must be sworn in tomorrow morning as a Legislator, in Albany. It is very important that I get off there. Even if I'm asleep and in my pajamas, don't fail to put me off when we arrive in Albany."

The porter promised he'd see to it that it would be done.

The next thing the Legislator knew is that he found himself in Grand Central Station in New York City. He was burning; he rushed up and down Grand Central Station in his pajamas, yelling and swearing at the top of his voice. The porter saw him and hid behind a post. Another porter walked over to the hiding porter and asked: "What's the matter with that man running in his pajamas—boy, is he mad!"

"Yeh, but nothing compared to the man I put off at Albany."

Where He Got the Ice

There was a party of gentlemen the other day on a train on one of the roads coming into Nashville, and none of the party being strictly temperance men, one of the crowd suggested a drink. Another wanted to know where to get it. All seemed willing, but the day was warm, very warm. At last the fourth man in the party said he had a bottle of fine "cock-tail," which he would furnish if anybody could get ice. A fellow passenger remarked that he would do that if they would share with him. He left the car and came back with plenty, which was duly used. As a matter of course, in a short time another drink was proposed and the ice man kindly requested to furnish that necessary article to a cocktail, but with his mouth watering for a drink and every look one of longing, he said: "Gentlemen, I want the drink, and I could furnish the ice, but I am afraid if I take any more off the corpse it will spoil."

By Bill Hardey. From *Variety*, Forty-Seventh Anniversary Number, Vol. 189 (January 7, 1953), No. 5, p. 99. Copyright, 1953, by Variety, Inc. New York.

From *The Railroad Gazette*, September 8, 1882, p. 555. New York.

Commuter Tricks

I [1]

Rackets pulled on the railroads by penny-pinching passengers are numerous. There are a few which have just about made Long Island conductors tear their hair. Although the business men who spend their summers at such resorts as Rockaway Beach, Far Rockaway, and Long Beach, New York, are above the average in means, some of them aren't above cheating the railroad now and then by lending their commutation tickets. Here's how it works: The commuter uses his ticket to leave busy, crowded, noisy Manhattan on a Friday afternoon, then promptly mails the ticket to a friend whom he has invited to visit his vacation home over the week-end. The friend receives the ducat Saturday morning. He utilizes it that day to join the lawful owner at the beach, and again on Sunday to return to the city. He then posts it by special delivery to the owner, who receives it in time to go to work Monday.

* * * * *

Another trick which has been pulled on many pikes is the one where a strip-ticket holder catches the disk of cardboard or paper which the conductor has punched out of his ticket and puts it back again. [One has to pound the disk in with a rubber mallet so that there are no visible defects around it. If, as sometimes happens, unbeknownst to him, the conductor's punch isn't sharp enough to cut through the ticket, the passenger rides free.] An owner of one of the Long Island's 50-trip tickets admits he usually gets 60 or 70 rides out of it.

II [2]

A commuter lends his commutation ticket to a friend and tells the conductor he has left it at home. Whereupon he pays a cash fare, gets a receipt, and redeems it. In this way two persons ride on one ticket. To discourage the practice, the Long Island permits only two redemptions a month.

The people at Peekskill used to have a good dodge. One person, with a New York commutation ticket, gets on at Peekskill. His friend drives to Harmon and parks. They add extra cars at Harmon. Then the first party gets off a rear car with his seat check and walks for-

[1] From "On the Spot," *Railroad Magazine*, Vol. 36 (November, 1944), No. 6, pp. 113, 115. Copyright, 1944, by Popular Publications, Inc. New York.

[2] As told by a conductor on the New York Central's Hudson Division to B. A. Botkin, Harmon, New York, October 12, 1953.

ward on the platform. He meets his friend and gives him his ticket. So one passenger has the seat check and the other has the commutation ticket. This is good for week-end guests. To call their bluff, the conductor doesn't pick up their transportation until after he gets to Harmon. Sometimes the two might sit together inadvertently in the head car and the conductor asks them both for their transportation!

In the old days they would rig up a string under the seats. To work this trick you have to have a group of four or six occupying two or three whole seats, one behind the other. A person in the front seat shows his commutation ticket, concealing the string attached to it. Or the string may be tied to the case that holds the ticket. Then the person in the rear seat pulls the string and the ticket back to him. This has to be worked by the persons on the inside so that the passengers across the aisle can't see them.

Then there is the guy who is dead asleep, and you can't wake him, come heck or high water. He usually has a 26 rider buried in his pocket. Now the commutation tickets are marked F for Female. And when a woman uses her husband's ticket, she flashes it with her finger over the end of it where it is usually stamped F.

The toilets are supposed to be locked leaving the Grand Central Terminal. Sometimes the toilet might be overlooked, and the passenger hides in it, locking himself in, until the transportation has been lifted. Of course, once a passenger is known as a dead beat (not a *deadhead,* who carries a pass), he is marked by the men via the grapevine, and they are always on the alert for him.

Senator Sherman and the Beans

Senator Sherman was going to some remote point in the West. He dined at the station restaurant, not noticing that there was a table d'hote dinner served for one dollar. He selected a cup of coffiee and a plate of baked beans from the menu, and was indignant at being charged one dollar for the same by the attendant, who blandly told him that he could have anything on the bill of fare he cared to for the charge. The extortionate price, as he considered it, rankled in the senatorial breast, and he telegraphed C.O.D. to the manager of the restaurant from Omaha: "I think the charge of one dollar for a plate of baked beans and a cup of coffee altogether too high." The C.O.D. cost the restaurant man more than the price paid for his frugal meal. Arrived in San Francisco, the Senator sent another C.O.D. telegram: "I still think the price of your baked beans too high, but shall say nothing more on the subject."

From *The Depew Story Book,* edited by Will M. Clemens, pp. 65-66. Copyright, 1898, by Will M. Clemens. New York and London: F. Tennyson Neely.

PART FIVE

Blues, Ballads, and Work Songs

"Lonesome Whistles"

Lord, I hate to hear that lonesome whistle blow,
Lord, I hate to hear that lonesome whistle blow.
It blows so lonesome and it blows so low,
It blows like it never blowed before.

All through the strip of country that runs from Maryland, south and west to Oklahoma, which is the land of fiddlers, guitar players, banjo pickers, and harp blowers, you can hear them making lonesome whistle tunes on their instruments. A fiddler will pull his bow in a long, minor moan across his top string and then start jerking it in quick, raspy strokes until you can close your eyes and hear a heavy freight train running down a steep grade. A harmonica player will blow out the high, hollering notes of a fast passenger engine, while the guitar player will make a rhythm on his bass strings like a train crossing a trestle. Together they'll play in the rhythm of car wheels clicking over sleepers; as counter-rhythm, they'll whip out the rattling bounce of a caboose as it shakes and jounces along a rough roadbed. Then they'll throw back their heads and holler—

Lord, Lord, I hate to hear that lonesome whistle blow.

These folk musicians and the people they're playing for listen to railroad whistles the way fisherfolk listen to bellbuoys and foghorns. Out in the country they tell time by the whistles of the trains that fly past their fields. The railroad whistles bring them good news and bad news. The whistles talk to them about the places they have never been, the women they've never seen, the fine clothes they have never worn.

Lord, I'm goin' where the water tastes like wine,
'Cause the water round here tastes like turpentine.

From *Folk-Song: U.S.A.*, the 111 Best American Ballads, collected, adapted, and arranged by John A. Lomax and Alan Lomax; Alan Lomax, editor; Charles Seeger and Ruth Crawford Seeger, music editors, pp. 244–245. Copyright, 1947, by John A. and Alan Lomax. New York: Duell, Sloan and Pearce.

The prize instrument for train whistle imitations, according to Pete Seeger, is the harmonica. The player cups it tightly with his hands, sucks it in on one or two of the lower notes, pressing his tongue against the instrument so that it takes great force to pull any air in at all. This lowers the pitch of the note, approximating the locomotive whistle sound. When this is combined with the hands flaring outwards to give a *wah-wah* effect, a highly musical imitation of the train whistle results. Sanders ("Blind Sonny") Terry and Woody Guthrie, among others, are known for their virtuoso performances. Cf. "The Train," played on the harmonica by Chub Parham, *Folk Music of the United States,* Issued from the Collections of the Archive of American Folk Song, Library of Congress, Washington, D.C., 1942, Record No. AAFS 10.

The whistles talk to them about the folks who have gone down that long, lonesome road and won't be back again.

Every time a freight train makes up in the yard,
Some po' woman got an achin' heart.

The whistles talk to them about the great big raw country they live in. The whistles remind them that every man is a traveler on a lonesome road.

I'm goin' lay my head on that lonesome railroad line.
Let the 219 ease my troubled mind.

Mostly the whistles talk to them about freedom. Before the railroads knit the whole country together in their shining web of steel, these folks were pinned down and forced to inch along across the big sea of the land in wagons. When the railroad whistles began to blow, these people found they could almost fly across their country any time they paid their fare or caught a free ride on a freight.

Listen to the jingle, the jumble and the roar,
As she glides along the woodland, through the hills, and by the shore.
Hear the mighty rush of the engine and the merry hobo's squawl,
As he rides the rods and brake-beams of the Wabash Cannonball.

Restless by instinct, travelers by tradition, they began to move around more and more, taking in the new towns, new jobs, and new sweethearts. Then, sometimes, when they were off somewhere in a new town, broke and hungry and out of a job, they'd hear that railroad whistle blow and then it meant "home" and all they'd left behind.

If that wheeler runs me right,
I'll be home tomorrow night,
'Cause I'm nine hundred miles from my home,
And I hate to hear that lonesome whistle blow.

The railroad has been for these people both villain and hero. Sometimes it was—

There's many a man been murdered by the railroad, railroad, railroad,
There's many a man been murdered by the railroad,
And laid in his lonesome grave.

And sometimes it was—

Here she comes, look at her roll,
Ridin' those rails, eatin' that coal,
Like a hound waggin' its tail,
Dallas bound, bound, bound,
It's the fireball mail.

They made scores of ballads about wrecks and heroic engineers who stuck to their throttles till the end, just as their ancestors had heroized the gallant captains who stayed with their ships until they went down. The hoboes who rode the rods beneath the cars and the blinds between the cars made a whole literature of ballads and poems about their wandering lives. The blues blowers and the hillbilly yodelers have laid down a line of railroad ballads, which, strung together, would cover as much territory as the Santa Fe.

It is in the texture of our popular music, however, that the railroads have left their deepest impression. Listen to the blues, the stomps, the hot music of the last fifty years, since most Americans have come to live within the sound of the railroad. Listen to this music and you'll hear all the smashing, rattling, syncopated rhythms and counter-rhythms of trains of every size and speed. Listen to boogie-woogie with its various kinds of rolling basses. Listen to hot jazz with its steady beat. Listen to the blues with those hundreds of silvery breaks in the treble clef. What you hear back of the notes is the drive and thrust and moan of a locomotive. Of course, there's the African influence, the French influence in New Orleans, the Spanish influence from Cuba to account for the character of our hot music. These cultural elements have left their mark in our music, as they have elsewhere in this hemisphere, but, in our estimation, the distinctive feeling of American hot music comes from the railroad. In the minds and hearts of the people it is the surge and thunder of the steam engine, the ripple of the wheels along the tracks, and the shrill minor-keyed whistles that have colored this new American folk music.

The railroad has also left its mark on American religious music—spirituals and gospel songs—e.g., *This Train, The Little Black Train Am A-Coming, Git on Board, Gospel Train, Life Is Like a Mountain Railroad.* Perhaps the most famous of all anti-slavery songs is *Get Off the Track,* introduced in 1844 by the Hutchinsons who wrote the words and set them to an old slave melody. *The Hell Bound Train* is a classic of moralizing; *In the Baggage Coach Ahead* and *The Engineer's Child* are standard tear-jerkers. For lists of railroad songs, see Frank P. Donovan, Jr., *The Railroad in Literature* (Boston, July, 1940), pp. 59–76; the *Grosvenor Library* (Buffalo) *Bulletin,* Vol. 27 (June, 1945), No. 3, pp. 77–91. For further discussion and examples, see Stewart H. Holbrook, *The Story of American Railroads* (New York, 1944), pp. 429–442; Archie Robertson, *Slow Train to Yesterday* (Boston, 1945), pp. 89–98.—B.A.B.

I. IRISH IMMIGRANTS AND WESTERN EMIGRANTS

Paddy Works on the Erie

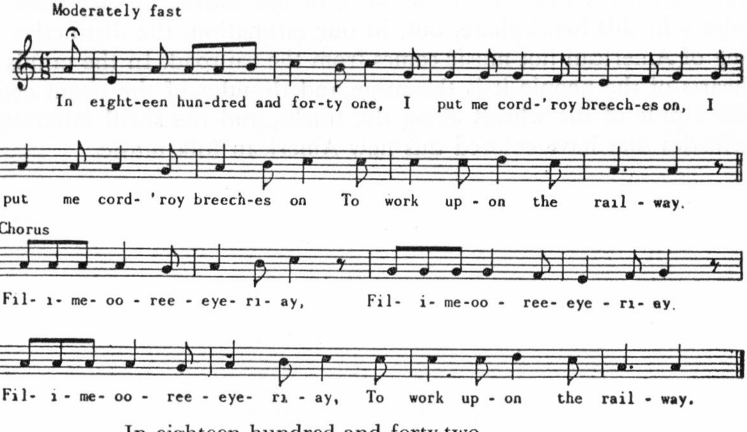

In eighteen hundred and forty-two
I left the ould world for the new.
Bad cess to the luck that brought me through
To work upon the railway.

When we left Ireland to come here,
And spend our latter days in cheer,
Our bosses, they did drink strong beer,
And Pat worked on the railway.

Ibid., pp. 270–271.

For "The Irish Immigrant" and his songs, see John Greenway, *American Songs of Protest* (Philadelphia, 1953), pp. 39–44.

Our boss's name, it was Tom King,
He kept a store to rob the men,
A Yankee clerk with ink and pen,
To cheat Pat on the railway.

It's "Pat, do this" and "Pat, do that,"
Without a stocking or cravat,
And nothing but an old straw hat
While Pat works on the railway.

One Monday morning to our surprise,
Just a half an hour before sunrise,
The dirty divil went to the skies,
And Pat worked on the railway.

And when Pat lays him down to sleep,
The wiry bugs around him creep,
And divil a bit can poor Pat sleep,
While he works on the railway.

In eighteen hundred and forty-three
'Twas then I met Miss Biddy Magee,
And an illygant wife she's been to me,
While workin' on the railway.[1]

In eighteen hundred and forty-seven,
Sweet Biddy Magee, she went to heaven.
If she left one child, she left eleven,
To work upon the railway.

In eighteen hundred and forty-eight,
I learned to take my whisky straight.
'Tis an illygant drink and can't be bate
For workin' on the railway.

[1] For additional stanzas see Carl Sandburg, *The American Songvag* (New York, 1927), p. 357.

Way Out in Idaho

I was roaming around in Denver one luckless rainy day
When Kilpatrick's man, Catcher, stepped up to me and did say,
"I'll lay you down five dollars as quickly as I can
And you'll hurry up and catch the train, she's starting for Cheyenne."

He laid me down five dollars, like many another man,
And I started for the depot as happy as a clam;
When I got to Pocatello, my troubles began to grow,
A-wading through the sagebrush in frost and rain and snow.

From *Our Singing Country,* A Second Volume of American Ballads and Folk Songs, collected and compiled by John A. Lomax and Alan Lomax; Ruth Crawford Seeger, music editor, pp. 269–270. Copyright, 1941, by John A. Lomax. New York: The Macmillan Company.

Sung with guitar by Blaine Stubblefield, Washington, D.C., 1938. Recorded by Alan Lomax. Archive of American Folk Song, Library of Congress, Washington, D.C. Record No. 1634 B1.

The tune is that of "Sam Bass." Cf. "The State of Arkansas," *A Treasury of American Folklore* (New York, 1944), pp. 316–317; also *Railroad Stories,* Vol. XIX (April, 1936), No. 5, p. 113, where the closing stanza reads:

> I am sick and tired of railroading and I think I'll give it o'er.
> I'll lay the pick and shovel down and I'll railroad no more.
> I'll go out in the Indian nation and I'll marry me there a squaw,
> And I'll bid adieu to railroading and the State of Arkansaw.

James R. Masterson discusses this and related versions in *Tall Tales of Arkansaw* (Boston, 1942), pp. 255–268.

When I go to American Falls, it was there I met Fat Jack.
He said he kept a hotel in a dirty canvas shack.
"We hear you are a stranger and perhaps your funds are low.
Well, yonder stands my hotel tent, the best in Idaho."

I followed my conductor into his hotel tent,
And for one square and hearty meal I paid him my last cent;
But Jack's a jolly fellow, and you'll always find him so,
A-workin' on the narrow-gauge way out in Idaho.

They put me to work next morning with a cranky cuss called Bill,
And they gave me a ten-pound hammer to strike upon a drill.
They said if I didn't like it I could take my shirt and go,
And they'd keep my blanket for my board way out in Idaho.

It filled my heart with pity as I walked along the track
To see so many old bummers with their turkeys on their backs.
They said the work was heavy and the grub they couldn't go,
Around Kilpatrick's tables way out in Idaho.

But now I'm well and happy, down in the harvest camps,
And there I will continue till I make a few more stamps.
I'll go down to New Mexico and I'll marry the girl I know,
And I'll buy me a horse and buggy and go back to Idaho.

Jerry, Go and Ile That Car

Tune from *The American Songbag,* by Carl Sandburg, pp. 360–361. Copyright, 1927, by Harcourt, Brace and Company, Inc., New York. Text from *The Railroad Man's Magazine,* Vol. IV (February, 1931), No. 3, pp. 478–479. Copyright, 1931, by the Frank A. Munsey Company. New York.

For twenty years a section boss, he worked upon the track,
And be it to his credit, he never had a wreck.
For he kept every joint right up to the point with the tap of a tamping bar,
And while the boys would be shimming up the ties, it was "Jerry, go and ile that car."

God bless you, Larry Sullivan, to me you were kind and good,
You always made the section men go out and split me wood,
And fetch me water from the well, and split me kindling fine.
And any man who wouldn't lend a hand, 'twas Larry give him his time.

And every Sunday morning unto the gang he'd say,
"Me boys, prepare ye, be aware, the old lady goes to church today.
Now I want every man to pump the best he can, for the distance it is far,
And we have to get in ahead of No. 10, so, Jerry, go and ile that car."

'Twas in November, in the winter time, and the ground all covered with snow.
"Come, put the hand car on the track and over the section go."
With his big soldier coat buttoned up to his throat, all weather he would dare,
And it's "Paddy Mac, would you walk the track?" and "Jerry, go and ile that car."

"Give my respects to the roadmaster," poor Larry he did cry,
And lay me up that I may see the old hand car before I die.
Then lay the spike maul on me chest, the gauge and the old claw bar,
And while the boys would be filling up the grave, oh, Jerry, would you ile that car?"

Drill, Ye Tarriers, Drill

Now our new foreman was Jean McCann,
By God, he was a blame mean man.
Past week, a premature blast went off
And a mile in the air went big Jim Goff,
And drill, ye tarriers, drill!

From *The People's Song Book*, edited by Waldemar Hille, pp. 36–37. Copyright, 1948, by Boni and Gaer. New York.

This is a composed song, so folklike in character that it slips easily and naturally into the folk category. Published in 1888, the melody is by Charles Connolly, the words by Thomas Casey, who sang the song extensively. The song is generally accepted as the theme song of those sturdy Irish-Americans who worked on the railroads in the East during the latter part of the last century.—*American Songs for*

Now the next time payday comes around,
Jim Goff a dollar short was found.
When asked, "What for?" came this reply,
"You're docked for the time you was up in the sky."
And drill, ye tarriers, drill!

Now the boss was a fine man, down to the ground,
And he married a lady, six feet round.
She baked good bread and she baked it well,
But she baked it hard as the holes of hell.
And drill, ye tarriers, drill!

American Children, Presented by the Music Educators' National Conference at the 1944 Biennial Meeting, St. Louis, Missouri, March 1–8, p. 2.

Beatrice Landeck notes ("Git on Board," New York, 1944, p. 59): "The workers' beards gave them the nickname of *terriers,* pronounced *tarriers.*" More likely the word refers to the burrowing habits of dog and rock driller alike.

Zack, the Mormon Engineer

(Sung to the tune of Stanza 1)

4. Now listen, everybody, because this story 's true.
Old Zack, he had a wife in every town that he passed through.
They tried to make him transfer on to the old UP,
But Zack said "No," because his wives were on the D&RG.

From *Mormon Folk Songs,* recorded and notes by Willard Rhodes. Folkways Records, Album No. FP 36 A6. New York: Folkways Records & Service Corp. 1952. Sung by L. M. Hilton.

II. NEGRO GANG WORK SONGS

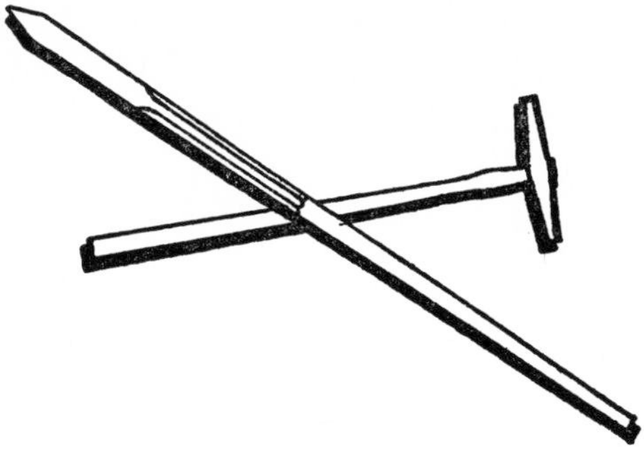

Tamping Ties

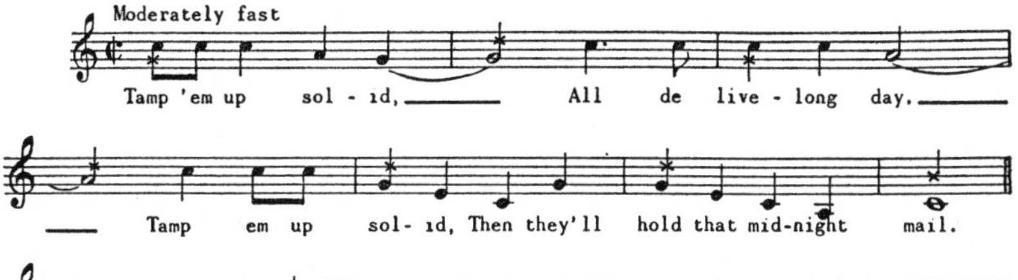

Called by Henry Truvillion at Wiergate, Texas, 1940. Recorded by John A. and Ruby T. Lomax.

From *Folk Music of the United States,* Issued from the Collections of the Archive of American Folk Song, Library of Congress, Washington, D.C., Album 8, "Negro Work Songs and Calls," edited by B. A. Botkin, Record No. 36 A2.

Track Lining Song

From *Folk Music of the United States,* Issued from the Collections of the Archive of American Folk Song, Library of Congress, Washington, D.C. Album 8, "Negro Work Songs and Calls," edited by B. A. Botkin, Record No. 40 B2.

Sung by Allen Prothero at State Penitentiary, Nashville, Tennessee, 1933. Recorded by John A. and Alan Lomax.

There is a special kind of song for every job in the South, and on the railroad there is a special kind of song for every job on the railroad. In the railroad songs one finds a sort of tenderness not to be found in other work songs, because these songs are all led by a tender-voiced tenor who is hired to do nothing else but sing, to soothe the men's feelings and keep them all working together so they won't get hurt on the job. . . . [This is the order of work.] About four o'clock in the morning the camp cook goes around the bunk car, banging on a dishpan, and he wakes the men up with a song . . . "Raise up, boys, raise up!" . . . When the men reach the stretch of roadbed they are going to lay track on, they first have to unload the steel rails from the flat cars, and the foreman tells them just how this must be done.

Foreman

Now look here, men, we got a carload of steel to unload here now and this is a ninety-pound steel rail and it's thirty foot long. We don't want to lose nary a finger. 'Course there's plenty more in the market down yonder where them come from, but they don't fit like these. Now, this here's a good way to get a leg broke. It's a good way to get somebody killed, an' every man lifting that rail got to lift it together an' any man lift before I say, "Lift," we're gonna run him away from here. Now git around here, boys, and grab that rail like a cat grabbing a hot hoecake.

Leader

Come on now, boys, gather round.
Bow down, put your glad hands on it.
Raise up! Throw it away!
That's good iron, I heard it ring.

Come on now, boys, come on back now, boys,
Get another one,
Etc.

If I could, I surely would
Stand on the rock where Moses stood,
Oh, boys in the morning,
Hi, hi, a'ternoon,
Hi, boys, in the evening
I'd be standing there all the time.

Oh, boys, want to tell you something now.
Oh, way down yonder in the harvest field,
Angels working at the chariot wheel.
Oh, boys, won't you line 'em, (*Three times*)
See Eloise go lining track.

Oh, if I'd known my cap'n was blind,
Wouldn't went to work till the clock struck nine.
Ho, boys, he can see.
Hi, hi, he ain't blind.
Hi, hi, got a Waterbury.
Hi, hi, he can tell time. . . .

After the rails have been placed on the ties, the next job of the gang is to spike the rails down with their spike-driving hammers, and for this they have their own special song, "O Lulu":

Leader

O Lulu! O gal!
Want to see you so bad.

Group

Gonna see my long-haired babe,
Gonna see my long-haired babe,
O Lawd, I'm going 'cross the water,
See my long-haired babe.

[Zora Neale Hurston, *Mules and Men,* Philadelphia, 1935, pp. 319–321]

After the rails have been spiked down temporarily, the next job is to line the track up, to straighten it so the work train can move on down the line. The song sung with this work is the most widespread of all railroad work songs. The foreman straddles the rail, sights down it to find out where the crooked part is:

Foreman

Look here, fellows, this rail is as crooked as a slavery time fence rail. Now I want you to get this track lined up right now, so get your crow bars on your shoulders and run down about the fourth joint ahead and touch it just a little bit north.

[Here follows "Track Lining Song."]

As the train passes over the new track, gravel is dumped out of the cars and some of the men stay behind to tamp the gravel between the ties—that is, to pack it in tight around the ties so the railroad will not go crooked again—and the foreman hollers to his men to give him the tie-tamping song about "TP and the Morgan":

Foreman

Give us some gravel here, old man, and let's get to tamping those old loose ties down. All right, boys, gather round and get them tampers ready. Don't be afraid to bend your back. We'se railroad men! All right, caller, sing about the TP and the Morgan, [which run through Louisiana, where some verses of this song were recorded].

Leader

TP and the Morgan
Standin' side by side.
TP throwed the water,
Water in the Morgan's eye. . . .

—Alan Lomax, "Reels and Work Songs," The Festival of Music, Friday evening, December 20, 1940, Coolidge Auditorium, Library of Congress, Washington, D.C., in *75 Years of Freedom,* Commemoration of the 75th Anniversary of the Proclamation of the 13th Amendment to the Constitution of the United States, pp. 32–35. Washington: U.S. Government Printing Office. 1940.

For other railroad work songs and comment, see the Lomax collections, *American Ballads and Folk Songs* (New York, 1934), pp. 3–23; *Our Singing Country* (New York, 1941), pp. 258–267; also, John A. Lomax, *Adventures of a Ballad Hunter* (New York, 1947), pp. 253–262; *Folk Music of the United States,* Issued from the Collections of the Library of Congress, 1943–1944, Records No. AAFS 36, 39, 40; *A Treasury of Southern Folklore* (New York, 1949), pp. 746, 749–750.

III. BRAVE ENGINEERS

The Wreck of the Old 97

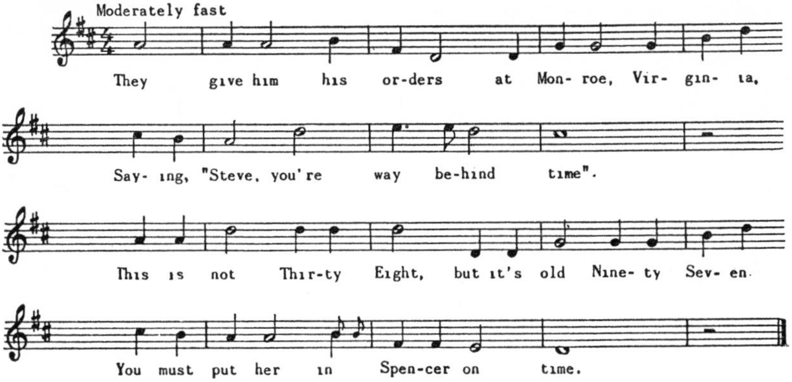

Sung by Vernon Dalhart. Victor Record No. 19427.

Published as "The Wreck of the Old 97 (The Wreck on the Southern Old 97)," by Henry Whitter, Charles W. Noell, and Fred J. Lewey. Copyright, 1924 and 1940, by F. Wallace Rega; 1939, by R.C.A. Manufacturing Co., Inc.; assigned to and copyright, 1944, by Shapiro, Bernstein & Co., Inc. The song and the drawing on p. 434 (from the song-sheet cover) used by permission of Shapiro, Bernstein & Co., Inc., New York.

In the Dalhart version, "Steve" is corrupted to "Pete."

A convention of railroad men would probably rate *The Wreck of the Old 97* second only to *Casey Jones* as a classic. This ballad has had a curious history. I don't believe anybody knows just when it was written, although it was inspired by a wreck that occurred on September 27, 1903, to the *Fast Mail* of the Southern Railway on its run between Monroe and Spencer, Virginia. Ninety Seven was an hour late when Engineer Joseph A. ["Steve"] Broady, and a fresh crew climbed aboard at Monroe. Broady was instructed, so the song has it, to "put her into Spencer on time." Spencer was 166 miles from Monroe and the *Fast Mail's* normal running time between those points was about 4 hours, 15 minutes.

Broady was given two firemen in order that the steam pressure should hold high, and the challenge of a timecard was all else he needed. He opened her up "rugged like," nor did he cut off power as he approached Stillhouse Trestle, a high structure over Cherrystone Creek, just out of Danville. The combination of a curve and descending grade made Stillhouse Trestle a danger spot, and on both sides of the track at this point were signs: "Slow up, Trestle!" Joe Broady had an hour to make up, and perhaps he didn't believe in signs, anyway. He paid no heed to the signs or to Stillhouse Trestle, and just as Old 97 hit the curve, everything sort of let go at once and an instant later the locomotive had leaped the rails and plowed a hundred feet to bury her nose in the muddy bank of a stream. All five cars followed her. Both firemen were mangled beyond recognition. Conductor Blair died, so did Flagman Moody, and eight others, mostly postal clerks. As for Engineer Broady, much of the United States must know by now that he was "found in the wreck with his hand on the throttle, a-scalded to death with steam."

Such was the wreck that was to put all other wrecks but Casey's into the shadows of memory. The immortalizing agent in this instance was David Graves George,

He looked round and said to his black greasy fireman,
"Just shovel in a little more coal,
And when we cross that White Oak Mountain,
You can watch old 97 roll."

It's a mighty rough road from Lynchburg to Danville,
And a line on a three-mile grade.
It was on that grade that he lost his average [air brakes],
And you see what a jump he made.

He was going down grade, making 90 miles an hour
When his whistle broke into a scream. [*Wooo! Wooo!*]
He was found in the wreck with his hand on the throttle,
And a-scalded to death with the steam.

Now, ladies, you must take warning.
From this time now and on [learn]:
Never speak harsh words to your true loving husband,
He may leave you and never return.

---

a hillbilly of the region who had worked at braking on the railroad, at farming, and even as a boxer and a revenue agent. He was present at the scene of the wreck while it was still smoking and went away impressed with the tragedy. When a real hillbilly is impressed with a tragedy, a ballad is likely to be the result. Sure enough, David G. George sat down and composed *The Wreck of the Old 97,* then and there. A good melody was handy. This was *The Ship That Never Returned* [by Henry C. Work, 1865], already an old favorite in the mountain country. George fitted his words to the tune and first sang the number in, appropriately enough, a barber shop [a livery stable, according to his son] at Franklin Junction, Virginia.

Well, Old Ninety Seven rolled away from Dave George. It wafted out of the Virginia hills and into the cities. It went across the plains, over the mountains, it permeated all of the United States, in sheet music, phonograph records, finally on the radio. Dave George did not know how far his song had gone until one day in 1927, when he had driven a mule team into some crossroads village in Virginia and heard a phonograph bleating out a familiar song. Yes, it was his song. He was amazed to hear it coming forth from a talking machine, and he went in to ask the man who was playing it how come they had his, Dave George's piece, on a record. Not long afterward he read in a Richmond newspaper that the Victor Talking Machine Company was trying to find the composer of the song. Dave filed a claim, and so did a score of, perhaps a thousand, others, both hillbillies and lowlanders.

The case meandered through the courts and at last reached the United States Supreme Court, which upheld George's authorship but subsequently refused to rule on the matter of compensation. The Victor people said they had already paid for rights to Old Ninety Seven to three different claimants. In any case, Dave George never got any of the gravy. The song goes on, year after year, with no sign of abating popularity.—Stewart H. Holbrook, *The Story of American Railroads* (New York, 1947), pp. 430–432.

The Wreck on the C&O

From *Folk-Songs of the South,* Collected under the Auspices of the West Virginia Folk-Lore Society and edited by John Harrington Cox, pp. 226–227, 525–526. Copyright, 1925, by Harvard University Press. Cambridge.

Reprinted in *A Treasury of Southern Folklore* (New York, 1949), pp. 725–727.

And when she blew for Hinton, her engineer was there.
George Alley was his name, with bright and wavery hair;
His fireman, Jack Dixon, was standing by his side,
Awaiting for strict orders and in the cab to ride.

George Alley's mother came to him with a basket on her arm.
She handed him a letter, saying, "Be careful how you run;
And if you run your engine right, you'll get there just on time,
For many a man has lost his life in trying to make lost time."

Original title: "George Alley." Communicated by Professor Walter Barnes, Fairmont, Marion County, May, 1916; obtained from George W. Gregg, Durbin, Pocahontas County, who learned it from Addison Collins.

. . . The facts out of which the song grew were obtained from Miss Margaret Alley and Mr. Ernest N. Alley, Alderson, West Virginia, sister and brother of George Alley, the man killed in the wreck, and from Mr. R. E. Noel, Hinton, formerly an engineer on the Chesapeake & Ohio Railroad.

George Alley was born in Richmond, Virginia, July 10, 1860, was married November 10, 1881, and had four children. The wreck on the C. & O. in which he was killed occurred at 5:40 A.M., October 23, 1890. He was running train No. 4, the F. F. V. (Fast Flying Vestibule), engine No. 134. He lived five hours after being hurt. The wreck occurred three miles east of Hinton, and was caused by a landslide. Lewis Withrow, the regular fireman, was firing the engine. He had been "laying off," but, on the morning of the wreck, took his run back at Hinton. Jack Dickinson was not on the engine, but Robert Foster was. He had been working in Withrow's place, and his run being out of Clifton Forge, he was deadheading back home that morning. Neither he nor Withrow jumped into the New River: he went out of the window on the left side of the engine, that being the side away from the river, and Withrow went out of the gangway on the same side. The engine turned over on the opposite side from which they jumped, that is, toward the river. Withrow was badly hurt, and for a long time it was thought he would not live. Hinton is an important town on the C. & O. in Summers County. Sewell is forty miles west of Hinton; the Big Bend Tunnel is eight miles east of Hinton; Stock Yards, then, is now Pence's Spring, fourteen miles east of Hinton; and Clifton Forge, a terminal, or division point, where train crews change, is eighty miles east of Hinton.

George Alley was six feet tall, weighed about one hundred seventy pounds, had a dark complexion, black eyes, and straight black hair. At the time of the wreck, his home was at Clifton Forge. His father and his stepmother lived at Alderson, West Virginia, his own mother having died many years before, when the family was living at White Sulphur Springs, in the same state. Mr. Ernest N. Alley thinks the ballad was first started on its way by a Negro engine-wiper, who worked in the roundhouse at Hinton. Mr. H. S. Walker, a former student in West Virginia University told the Editor that the ballad was composed by a Negro who worked in the roundhouse at Hinton.

George Alley said, "Dear mother, your letter I'll take heed.
I know my engine is all right and I know that she will speed;
So o'er this road I mean to run with a speed unknown to all,
And when I blow for Clifton Forge, they'll surely hear my call."

George Alley said to his fireman, "Jack, a little extra steam;
I intend to run old No. 4 the fastest ever seen;
So o'er this road I mean to fly like angels' wings unfold,
And when I blow for the Big Bend Tunnel, they'll surely hear my call."

George Alley said to his fireman, "Jack, a rock ahead I see,
And I know that death is lurking there for to grab both you and me;
So from this cab, dear Jack, you leap, your darling life to save,
For I want you to be an engineer while I'm sleeping in my grave."

"Oh no, dear George! that will not do, I want to die with you."
"Oh no, no dear Jack! that will not be, I'll die for you and me."
So from the cab dear Jack did leap, old New River was running high,
And he kissed the hand of darling George as No. 4 flew by.

So in the cab dear George did leap, the throttle he did pull;
Old No. 4 just started off, like a mad and angry bull.

. . . .

. . . .

The ballad and the facts agree as follows: (1) The F. F. V., train No. 4, running east on the C. & O. Railroad, was wrecked near Hinton by a landslide. (2) The regular engineer, George Alley, was killed. (3) The fireman saved his life by jumping from the engine. As in "John Hardy" ["John Henry"], certain fundamental facts are retained in an atmosphere of verisimilitude, but the details are entirely untrustworthy.—J. H. C., *ibid.*, p. 221.

The Wreck on the C&O is the father of a long line of railroad wreck songs that have sprung out of or entered into hillbilly tradition, including *The Wreck of the C&O Number 5, The Altoona Freight Wreck, The Wreck of the Number 9,* and *The Wreck of the 1256,* all included in *Vernon Dalhart and Carson Robison's Album of Songs* (New York, 1928). For other songs of the troubles and trials of the railroad man, see also *Railroad Songs of Yesterday,* by Sterling Sherwin and Harry K. McClintock (New York, Shapiro, Bernstein & Co., Inc., 1943).

To prove that railroad ballads can still be written, in 1950 L. Parker ("Pick") Temple, of Washington, D.C., and WTOP-TV, turned out *The Runaway Logging Train,* based on the following incident: Wesley Clark, conductor on the Apache Railway, was on a logging train that ran away on a mountain grade between Maverick and McNary, Arizona, December 7, 1949. He stayed with the train after the engineer and fireman had jumped and succeeded in stopping it and preventing a bad smashup in McNary at the foot of the mountain. The song also proves that a heroic railroader sometimes can stay with his train and also stay alive.—B.A.B.

So up the road she dashed; against the rock she crashed;
The engine turning over and the coaches they came last;
George Alley's head in the firebox lay, while the burning flames rolled o'er:
"I'm glad I was born an engineer, to die on the C. & O. Road."

George Alley's mother came to him and in sorrow she did sigh,
When she looked upon her darling boy and saw that he must die.
"Too late, too late, dear mother! my doom is almost o'er,
And I know that God will let me in when I reach that golden shore."

The doctor said, "Dear George, O darling boy, keep still;
Your life may yet be spared, if it be God's precious will."
"O no, dear Doc, that can not be, I want to die so free,
I want to die on the engine I love, 143."

The people came from miles around this engineer to see.
George Alley said, "God bless you, friends, I am sure you will find me here."
His head and face all covered with blood, his eyes you could not see,
And as he died he cried aloud, "O near, my God, to Thee!"

The Little Red Caboose behind the Train

Sung by L. Parker (Pick) Temple, Silver Spring, Maryland, August 15, 1953. Recorded by Bill Randolph and B. A. Botkin.

Words and music by Bob Miller. Copyright, 1932, by Bob Miller, Inc. New York: Bob Miller, Inc., Music Publisher. Also recorded by Bob Ferguson (Bob Miller) and His Scalaywaggers, Columbia Record No. 15616-D.

Cf. Horace Reynolds, "On the Trail of *The Little Red Caboose behind the Train*," *Trains,* Vol. 31 (August, 1946), No. 8, pp. 8–10, for a discussion of this song; a second song, *Little Old Caboose behind the Train,* about bums riding on a freight, wishing, "If only we were in the caboose behind the train"; and a third, which seems to be the original, beginning "We are jolly American railroad boys, and braking is our trade"—all sung to the tune of Will S. Hays' *The Little Old Log Cabin in the Lane* (1871). "The angels all are sober" is a corruption of "The angels, they will watch o'er them," in the third song. Reynolds concludes: "Somebody's addition of the descriptive adjective *red* to *caboose* was a stroke of genius. It placed the little red caboose beside the little white church and the little red schoolhouse to form a trinity of America's most lovable institutions."

He met her in September, she was so fair and sweet.
  Oftimes together they'd walk lovers' lane.
Never was a girl more fair, no sweeter ever rode
  In that little red caboose behind the train.
'Twas on a frosty morn, the cold north wind did blow.
  The cold had frozen up the window pane.
They were riding to the city, it was on their honeymoon,
  In that little red caboose behind the train.

The engineer had ridden that line for many years.
  He said the cold was driving him insane.
But he held on to that throttle, his pal was in the rear,
  In that little red caboose behind the train.
The fast express came roaring at ninety miles an hour.
  The brakie tried to see, but it was in vain,
For his fingers all were frozen. He said a silent prayer
  For that little red caboose behind the train.

'Twas after that collision, among the wreckage there,
  They found her body crushed amid blood stain.
Many were the tears and heartaches, and many were the prayers,
  For that little red caboose behind the train.
They laid her in the graveyard beside the railroad track.
  He still works in the sunshine and the rain.
And the angels all are sober, as he rides all alone
  In that little red caboose behind the train.

Been on the Cholly So Long

From *Folk-Song: U.S.A.*, the 111 Best American Ballads, collected, adapted, and arranged by John A. Lomax and Alan Lomax; Alan Lomax, editor; Charles Seeger and Ruth Crawford Seeger, music editors, pp. 264-265. Copyright, 1947, by John A. and Alan Lomax. New York: Duell, Sloan and Pearce.

Casey Jones was a good engineer,
Tol' his fireman not to have no fear.
"All I want's a li'l water an' coal.
Peep out de cab and see de drivers roll,
See de drivers roll, see de drivers roll"—
Kaze he's been on the Cholly so long.

When we got within a mile of the place,
Old Number Four stared us right in the face.
Conductor pulled his watch, mumbled, and said,

John A. and Alan Lomax (*American Ballads and Folk Songs,* New York, 1934, pp. 36–39) trace this song to *Jimmie Jones,* one of the prototypes of *Casey Jones.* In 1933 the Lomaxes went to Canton, Mississippi, to find Wallis Sanders (Wallace Saunders), Casey Jones's engine wiper, to whom in 1910 O. L. Miller, Mayor of Canton, erroneously attributed the authorship of *Casey Jones.* Wallis Sanders, write the Lomaxes, "was dead. . . . But [the late Mayor O. L. Miller's] married daughter took us to see an old Negro whom she had known in the roundhouse ever since she was a little girl—Wallis Sanders' close friend, Cornelius Steen. Cornelius Steen, seventy years old, retired after nearly forty years of coal-heaving in the old roundhouse at Canton, told us this story about the origin of *Casey Jones.* While visiting in Kansas City many years ago, he had heard the song *Jimmie Jones* (of which the only verse he could remember is quoted below) sung by a strolling street guitarist. He brought the tune and some of the verses back with him to Canton and to the roundhouse where he worked. 'Wash' Sanders, who also worked as a coal-heaver, heard the song, liked it, and made it his own by adding verses that described the wreck in which poor old Jimmie Jones was killed. When sufficiently in his cups, he could sing on for a long time and never repeat a stanza. Some time after, Casey Jones, who had a regular run as an engineer between Memphis and Canton, and whom Steen said he knew well and saw often, was killed in the now famous wreck. Sanders then changed the words 'Jimmie Jones' to 'Casey Jones.' . . . The following is the only verse of *Jimmie Jones* that Cornelius Steen could remember:

On a Sunday mornin' it begins to rain,
Round de curve spied a passenger train,
On de pilot lay po' Jimmie Jones,
He's a good ol' porter, but he's dead an' gone,
Dead an' gone, dead an' gone,
Kaze he's been on de Cholly so long."

. . . "On de Cholly" is equivalent to "out on the hog" or "on the bum."

For Elliott Shapiro's account of the origin of *Casey Jones* as we know it today (copyright, 1909, by Newton & Seibert; assigned to and copyright, 1937, by Shapiro, Bernstein & Co., Inc.), see John A. and Alan Lomax, *Folk Song U.S.A.* (New York, 1947), p. 250.

A variant of the stanza beginning "When Casey's wife heard dat Casey was dead" appears in *Mama, Have You Heard the News?* in Carl Sandburg's *The American Songbag* (New York, 1927), p. 369. Sandburg also gives (pp. 364–365) *Jay Gould's Daughter* to the same tune as *On the Charlie So Long,* while *Jay Gould's Daughter* appears under the title *Hobo John* in George Milburn's *The Hobo's Hornbook* (New York, 1930), pp. 250–251. Sandburg (*op. cit.,* p. 366) also mentions a song *Vanderbilt's Daughter* as among the prototypes of *Casey Jones.*

"We may make it, but we'll all be dead,
All be dead, all be dead"—
Kaze he's been on the Cholly so long.

Oh, ain't it a pity and ain't it a shame?
A six-wheel driver had to bear the blame.
Some were crippled and some were lame,
And a six-wheel driver had to bear the blame,
Bear the blame, bear the blame—
Kaze he's been on the Cholly so long.

When Casey's wife heard dat Casey was dead,
She was in de kitchen, makin' up bread.
She says, "Go to bed, chillun, and hol' yo' breath,
You all get a pension at yo' daddy's death,
At yo' daddy's death, at yo' daddy's death"—
Kaze he's been on the Cholly so long.

Jay Gould's daughter said before she died,
"Father, fix the blinds so the bums can't ride.
If ride they must, let 'em ride the rods,
Let them put their trust in the hands of God,
Hands of God, hands of God"—
Kaze he's been on the Cholly so long.

Hurry up, engine, and hurry up, train,
Missie gwine ride over the road again,
Swift as lightnin' and smooth as glass.
[Buddy], take yo' hat off when the train goes past,
When the train goes past, when the train goes past,
Kaze he's been on the Cholly so long.

IV. HOBO SONGS

The Gambler

"It's nine-sixteen and two-forty-four,
Twenty-five minutes till five.
Thank you Mr. Railroad man,
I want to watch your trains roll by."

Sung with guitar by Cisco Houston. From *900 Miles and Other R.R. Songs.* Folkways Records Album No. FP 13 B2. New York: Folkways Records & Service Corp. 1953.

For other hobo and Wobbly songs, see *Hallelujah, Bum Again, The Big Rock Candy Mountain, Pie in the Sky* in *A Treasury of American Folklore* (New York, 1944), pp. 882–887; *The Dying Hobo, The Portland County Jail* in *A Treasury of Western Folklore* (New York, 1951), pp. 773, 777–778.

For a discussion and selection of hobo, tramp, and Wobbly songs, see George Milburn, *The Hobo's Hornbook* (New York, 1930).

Standing on a platform,
Smoking a cheap cigar,
Waiting for an old freight-train
That carries an empty car.

Well, I pulled my hat down over my eyes,
And I walked across the track,
And I caught me the end of an old freight-train,
And I never did come back.

I sat down in a gambling game,
And I could not play my hand,
Just thinking about that woman that I love
Run away with another man.

Run away with another man, poor boy,
Run away with another man.
I was thinking about that woman that I love,
Run away with another man.

You Wonder Why I'm a Hobo

Now I could ride the pullman, but there it is again,
The plush they put on the pullman seats, it tickles my sensitive skin.
Now I could be a conductor and never have a wreck,
But any kind of a railroad man to me is a pain in the neck.

Now I could be a banker, if ever I wanted to be,
But the very thought of an iron cage is too suggestive to me.
Now I could be a broker, without the slightest excuse,
But look at 1929, and tell me what's the use.

Now I could be a doctor, my duty I never would shirk;
But if I doctored a railroad bull, he'd never go back to work.
Now you wonder why I'm a hobo, and why I sleep in the ditch.
Well, it ain't because I'm lazy; NO, I just don't want to be rich.

Sung with guitar by L. Parker (Pick) Temple, Silver Spring, Maryland, August 15, 1953. Recorded by Bill Randolph and B. A. Botkin.

This song, by Carson J. Robison, is originally entitled "Naw, I Don't Want to be Rich," and is used by special permission of Peer International Corporation, New York, by whom it was copyright in 1930.

The Wabash Cannonball

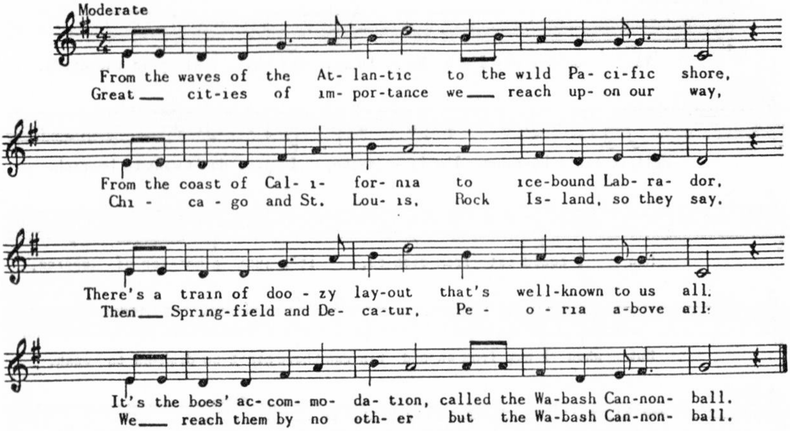

This train she runs to Quincy, Monroe, and Mexico,
She runs to Kansas City, and she's never running slow;
She runs right into Denver, and she makes an awfull squall.
They all know by that whistle it's the Wabash Cannonball.
There are other cities, pardner, that you can go to see—
St. Paul and Minneapolis, Ashtabula, Kankakee.
The lakes of Minnehaha, where the laughing waters fall—
We reach them by no other but the Wabash Cannonball.

Now listen to her rumble, now listen to her roar,
As she echoes down the valley and tears along the shore.
Now hear the engine's whistle and her mighty hoboes' call
As we ride the rods and brakebeams on the Wabash Cannonball.
Now here's to Long Slim Perkins, may his name forever stand.
He'll be honored and respected by the 'boes throughout the land.
And when his days are over and the curtains round him fall,
We'll ship him off to hell and on the Wabash Cannonball.

Text from *The Hobo's Hornbook,* A Repertory for a Gutter Jongleur, collected and annotated by George Milburn, pp. 188-191. Copyright, 1930, by George Milburn. New York: Ives Washburn.

Tune (by William Kindt) from *The Wabash Cannonball,* sung by the Galli Sisters, MGM Record No. 10411, 1949.

The Wabash Cannonball is for the hobo what the spectral "Flying Dutchman" is for the sailor. It is a mythical train that runs everywhere, and the ballad about it consists largely of stanzas enumerating its stops. *Doozy:* grand, gorgeous.—G. M.

V. BLUES AND LOVE SONGS

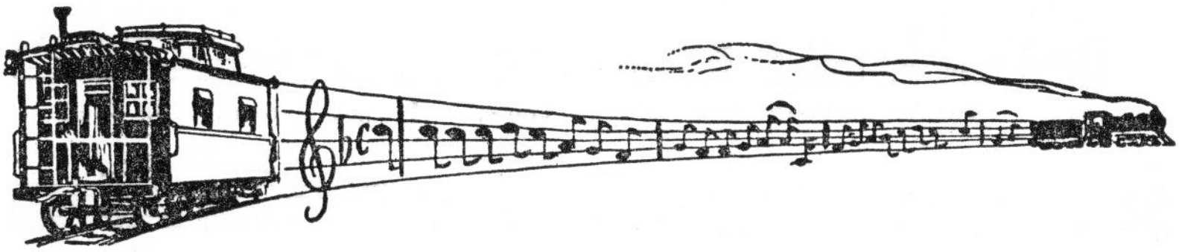

Cannonball Blues

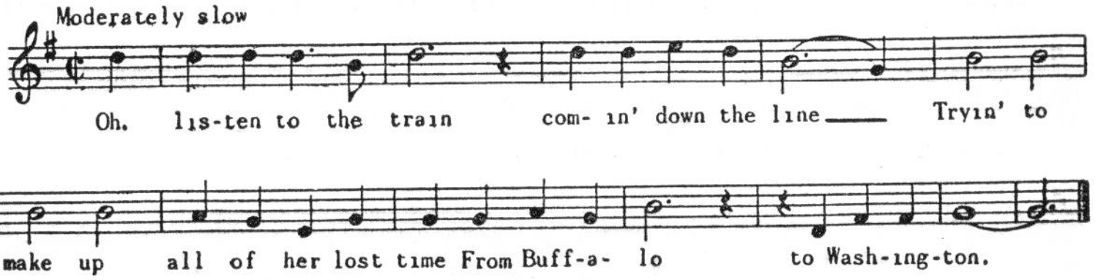

You can wash my jumper, starch my overhalls [*sic*],
Catch a train they call the Cannonball
  From Buffalo to Washington.

My baby's left me, she even took my shoes.
Enough to give a man these doggone worried blues.
  She's gone—she's—started—gone.

Yonder comes the train, coming down the track.
Carry me away but ain't gonna carry me back,
  My honey babe, my blue-eyed babe.

I'm going up North, I'm going to start this fall.
If luck don't change, I won't be back at all.
  My honey babe, I'm leaving you.

Sung with guitar and autoharp by the Carter Family, Perfect Record No. 7-05-55. The tune is related to that of the ballad of McKinley and Roosevelt, known as "The White House Blues" (see John A. and Alan Lomax and Ruth Crawford Seeger, *Our Singing Country,* New York, 1949, pp. 256-258).

900 Miles

From *Folk-Song: U.S.A.*, the 111 Best American Ballads, collected, adapted, and arranged by John A. Lomax and Alan Lomax; Alan Lomax, editor; Charles Seeger and Ruth Crawford Seeger, music editors, pp. 254-257. Copyright, 1947, by John A. and Alan Lomax. New York: Duell, Sloan and Pearce.

This song is related to "Old Reuben," a mountain banjo song dealing with "Reuben's fondness for liquor and his consequent difficulties as a railroad man." See R.W. Gordon, *New York Times Magazine,* January 1, 1928; also Henry M. Belden and Arthur Palmer Hudson, *The Frank C. Brown Collection of North Carolina Folklore,* (Durham, 1952), Vol. III, pp. 264–265.

The train I ride on
Is a hundred coaches long.
You can hear the whistle blow a hundred miles.
  If that train runs right,
  I'll be home tomorrow night,
  'Cause I'm nine hundred miles from my home,
  An' I hate to hear that lonesome whistle blow.

If my woman says so,
I'll railroad no more,
But I'll sidetrack my train and go home.
  If that wheeler runs me right,
  I'll be home tomorrow night,
  'Cause I'm nine hundred miles from my home,
  An' I hate to hear that lonesome whistle blow.

A Railroader for Me

From *Folk Music of the United States,* Issued from the Collections of the Archive of American Folk Song, Album XX, "Anglo-American Songs and Ballads," edited by Duncan B. M. Emrich. Record No. 96 B2.

Sung with guitar by Russ Pike, Visalia, California, 1941. Recorded by Charles Todd and Robert Sonkin.

Now I would not marry a blacksmith,
He's always in the black.
I'd rather marry an engineer
That throws the throttle back.

I would not marry a farmer,
He's always in the dirt.
I'd rather marry an engineer
That wears a stripéd shirt.

Appendix

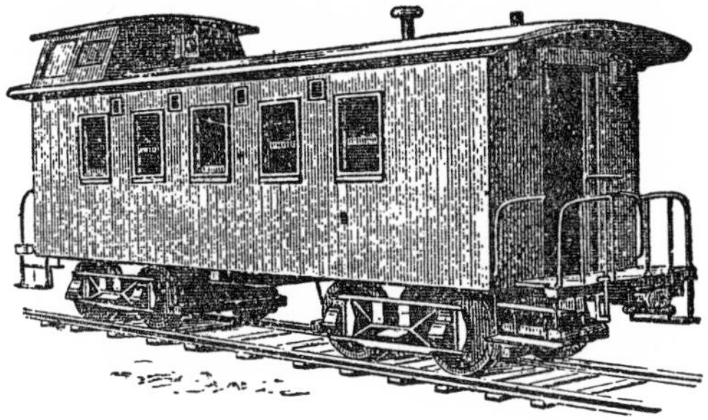

RAILROADIANA

A Century of American Locomotives and Their Builders

[A NOTE ON THE WHYTE SYSTEM—In 1901 F. M. Whyte, the Mechanical Engineer of the New York Central, devised the system of locomotive notation which bears his name. It was almost immediately accepted for general use in this country and England. Prior to that time, engines were known by type names. Back in the 1840s, Baldwin introduced a system of locomotion classification based on the types then made, but although it was expanded to include every locomotive built by the company, it never found general application. In the year that the Whyte system came out, the Brooks Locomotive Works designated Baldwin's "Atlantic" and "Prairie" as "Chautauqua" and "Lake Shore."

The Whyte system provides a numerical notation for lead trucks, drivers or sets of drivers, and trailing wheels. When one of these groups is missing, "0" is the common notation. Thus the eight wheeler or American, with a wheel arrangement of oo 00, is a 4-4-0; and a Prairie type, with a wheel arrangement of o 000 o, is a 2-6-2. Unlike the systems evolved later in France and Germany, the Whyte system counts the wheels, not the axles.]

By now, nearly every one has some idea of the earliest American locomotives. A few have been preserved, and others have been re-created in the form of full size working reproductions. Few people, however, realize the amount and diversity of early locomotive building. In 1829 there were four locomotives in the United States: the famous *Stourbridge Lion,* and its less well known sisters, the *America,* the *Delaware,* and the *Hudson,* which never ran on the railroad which ordered them. All were English locomotives, of a type which had already justified its utility on English mine railroads, but they were too heavy for American track. At the time the Delaware and Hudson Canal Company imported these engines, John Stevens had previously built an experimental model of a steam locomotive which he operated on his estate at Castle Point, Hoboken.

By George Zabriskie, Washington, D.C., 1953.

Only ten years after the *Stourbridge Lion* made its adventurous trip, railroads were well established in the United States. In 1838 the Treasury Department made a survey of all steam boilers in the country, and found 345 of them on locomotives. Research by later historians has shown that the errors of the Treasury Department list were generally those of omission, since whole railroads were left out. At the time the Treasury Department statistics were being compiled, Franz Anton Ritter von Gerstner, a German engineer, was engaged in visiting every steam railroad he could find in the United States. While his findings generally agree with those of the Treasury Department list, a comparison of the two sources, published by Charles E. Fisher, shows how many railroads the Government agents missed. Since von Gerstner, for all his thoroughness, must have neglected a few railroads too, we can probably guess that at the middle of 1839 there were over 400 locomotives in the United States.

What were they like? At least 25 different American builders, including railroads, and 8 different English manufacturers constructed them. They ranged from the *Monster* of the Camden and Amboy, with its 8 drivers, and the 2-2-2-2 double end locomotives on the South Carolina Railroad down to the tiny *York* of the B&O. Every one of the builders had a different pattern of engine, and most of them had experimented with more than one type. Furthermore, the operating conditions of the time were so widely varied that many designs which were highly successful, such as the B&O grasshoppers, with their vertical boilers and cylinders, which worked through an intermediate axle and gearing, were really temporary expedients. So, too, were the Norris 4-2-0 engines with the axle placed in front of the firebox. One of these, the *George Washington,* ascended an inclined plane of the Philadelphia and Columbia Railroad and startled American railway managers. By now, we know that the little Norris engine was carrying much more steam pressure than her builders said she carried. For years afterwards, Norris safety valves were calibrated to show a lower pressure than the one at which they operated.

At this late date, the actual appearance of the *George Washington* is a mystery. There is good reason to believe that she was an inside connected engine, with a cranked driving axle. Most of the contemporary engineers who witnessed the hill climbing trial said as much. However, a few months later, *The Washington County Farmer,* another Norris engine, ascended the same inclined plane to demonstrate the ability of a changed design. A more or less contemporary drawing which shows a locomotive named "*Washington*" is probably not the *George Washington* but another locomotive of the changed outside connected design as represented by *The Washington County Farmer.*

In the standard 4-2-0 Baldwin of the day the driving axle was placed behind the firebox, and the wheels were driven by half-cranks, an arrangement patented by Baldwin for inside connected engines. In this arrangement the cylinders were placed outside the smokebox rather than under it, which was customary with the usual inside connections. The inside faces of the drivers made one arm of the crank, the other being forged from the axle.

However, of all the types of locomotives in service in 1839, only one, the 4-4-0, represented the line of future development. In 1836, Henry R. Campbell patented a 4-4-0 design which was inside connected. When the Campbell engine was put to work on the Philadelphia and Germantown Railroad, it rode unevenly and was destructive to the track because the drivers were sprung independently. The same year the firm of Garret and Eastwick brought out another 4-4-0 with a "vibrating frame" which, although it remedied some of the defects of Campbell's engine, had the drawback of distorting the main frame of the engine on very rough track. Only two years later, Joseph Harrison, who became a partner of Garret and Eastwick, invented the equalizer, an iron beam connecting both sets of springs, which enabled them to adjust to irregular track independently while keeping a uniform load distribution. Harrison's original patent covered nearly every type of equalizer now in use, including that of the car truck. This simple invention was one of the most important in railroading, and today we see it embodied in some form in every locomotive, steam or diesel, every passenger car truck, and a few freight car trucks built for high speed service.

The 1840's showed continued improvement in locomotive design, with the introduction of 0-8-0's of more functional types than the *Monster,* and the appearance of the first wagon top boilers instead of the old Bury "Haystack" design. Yet the great decade of locomotive design came just 100 years ago. The 1850's saw the development of the steam locomotive from a gawky and undependable machine to the forms it took for the rest of the nineteenth century.

It is a commonplace fallacy, even among people who know something about locomotives, to suppose that wood burning locomotives came first, and coal burners were a later improvement. Actually, the first English locomotives burned coal or coke, and the *Stourbridge Lion* was meant to be a coal burner. The earliest engines on the Baltimore and Ohio, the grasshoppers, burned coal, as did their successors, the crabs. Wood came to be used as a locomotive fuel for two excellent reasons: outside of the Pennsylvania and Maryland coal fields, it was cheaper than coal, and in passenger service it was much cleaner. The early coal burners were so dirty that Parliament passed an act compelling English railroads to build smoke-consuming engines, and using coke for a fuel was for a time the only way out. In America, the B&O, the Pennsylvania, and the Lackawanna all used wood burning engines for passenger service and coal for freight. New England, Southern, and Western roads almost invariably began using wood as a fuel for economic reasons. Unless you can see what was in the tender, you can't tell too easily which fuel an engine of a century ago used. The Pennsylvania used the French and Baird patent stack, designed for wood, on some coal burners; other wood and coal burners had a straight stack; the diamond stack, invented by George S. Griggs for the Boston and Providence Railroad, was meant for coal, not wood burners. At about the same time Griggs invented the brick arch, the first step towards modern efficiency in burning soft coal.

The anthracite roads had their own problems. So, too, had the B&O, with rich Maryland coal fields on its route west, and heavy grades to overcome. In 1848 the B&O took a great interest in the 0-8-0 type of locomotive, following the success of the "mud diggers" designed by Ross Winans. The "mud diggers" were geared engines, enlarged crabs with horizontal boilers, and the B&O wanted direct connected engines. The first of the newer type were built by Baldwin and the Newcastle Manufacturing Company, but these were quickly followed by a batch of the most remarkable locomotives of the time: the Winans camels. The camels must not be confused with the later "camelbacks" or "Mother Hubbard" engines, which had their cabs astride, and not on top of the boiler.

The first camel, which gave its name to the type, had a short firebox, but by the 1850's, the "long furnace" engines were perfected. These were the first really standardized locomotives, and were built in quantities; not only for the B&O, but for the Reading, Pennsylvania, Cleveland and Pittsburgh, Cumberland and Pennsylvania, Northern Central, and others. When the Marietta and Cincinnati Railroad tried to order some Winans camels, the waiting period was too long to suit the managers and they settled for some Baldwin 10-wheelers instead.

The standard long furnace camel had 19″ x 22″ cylinders, 43″ diameter drivers, a long narrow firebox with sloping roof sheets and interior dimensions very close to the Pennsylvania Class I (New Class H-1) locomotives built twenty years later. They had a very large dome, with the same diameter as the boiler barrel, in the cab, and were fired through double doors at the back of the firebox and two chutes on top. (The very last camels built had only one chute.) The valve gear was unique in being, when new, the most efficient built in its time, and when old, the noisiest ever built. The main axle was equipped with six cams, working in square boxes, to drive the drop hook motion of the period. One cam worked forward motion, one back, and the third worked a half stroke cut off on each side. As all the builders of the 1850's were trying to work toward a good valve motion, Winans did not completely adhere to his original pattern, and some of the contemporary drawings seem to contradict each other. Yet the rattle of the worn cams and the weaving gait of these locomotives was noted by so many nineteenth century writers that they must have been as impressive as their pulling power.

One mystery of the camels is the hook attached to the main rod, just behind the crosshead. This hook was supposed to be used to drive the feed water pump, which was located at the side of the firebox, but in the drawings, it connects with the valve rod. If this connection were used to drive the valve motion, it might be an anticipation of the Joy valve gear, but it would be good for one motion only, and therefore totally useless. If the valve rod was driven by a rocker shaft, as two otherwise conflicting authorities, C. H. Carothers and Angus Sinclair, seem to agree, where did the rocker shaft connect? Mr. W. R. Hicks once published a photograph of a wrecked camel, in which the main rod hook shows clearly. From the photograph, one can only guess that the valve rod had an extension, the front end of the feed water pump rod was in the shape of a tube, and they telescoped. From the drawings, one might guess that both rods were in the same plane, but one behind the other, with the rocker shaft hidden by the hook, but the photograph disproves any such theory. It would, of course, have been possible to drive the feed pump directly from the valve motion, but then the hook would not have appeared.

All the Winans locomotives, short furnace and long furnace alike, seem to have lacked boiler lagging when they left the works. Later photographs suggest that the operating railroads added this necessity at some time or other. Probably Winans provided a wooden grate of some sort for the engineer to stand on, but it does not appear in existing drawings. The fireman had a much more unpleasant spot in these engines. Since the firebox was below the normal line of draft, the tender was coupled by a V-hook riveted to the ashpan and the front end of the firebox. The firing deck was lower than the tender floor. This arrangement not only limited the capacity of the locomotive, but it also made the fireman, who worked from this lowered platform in the front of the tender, particularly vulnerable. The fireman's shelter was grimly called "the kitchen" because of the number of men roasted alive there in collisions. When the fireman was not in the kitchen he was on the roof of it, furiously shoveling coal into the top firing chutes.

The 1850's saw James Millholland appointed Master of Machinery on the Philadelphia and Reading. At the time of his appointment, Millholland inherited an odd assortment of machines the best of which were the Winans camels and some Baldwin 0-8-0's. His first group of locomotives, called the Pawnee Class, although the first engine was the *Wyomissing* and the second the *Pawnee,* show at once the ability of Millholland and the difficulties which locomotive designers of the period faced. The Pawnees were far superior to any of the Winans engines in workmanship, and they used a form of link motion instead of the odd Winans reversing gear. Their defects came from Millholland's superior knowledge of the scientific theories then current, since they had intermediate flues and a combustion chamber in the middle of the boiler, where the firebox and flue temperatures of that time made such features worthless. The most interesting departure from the contemporary practice was that they were 2-6-0's—not Moguls in the modern sense, but engines with the cylinders forward of all the wheels, then with a pair of "grinding" wheels, as they were called, followed by six coupled drivers. It is debatable, but the idea has been suggested, back in the first decade of this century, that "pony" wheels, for a lead truck, came from "Pawnee wheels." On the Pawnees, only the "grinding" and the last pair of drivers were flanged, giving the locomotives approximately the same rigid wheelbase as the Winans engines. For some reason, this design became very popular, and Smith & Perkins of Alexandria, Va., Baldwin, and Norris, repeated it in locomotives for the Pennsylvania Railroad, while Danforth, Cooke and Co. built a six foot gauge replica of the Pawnees for the Lackawanna Railroad.

The Lackawanna, which was built to transport anthracite, was skeptical about using it for fuel. Locomotives which burned soft coal were one thing: the success of the B&O and the Reading with anthracite was regarded with incredulity. The failure of the first anthracite coal burner, patterned after the Millholland design, was not reassuring, neither were the special Winans camels, built for the six foot gauge. The Winans engines, the largest he ever built, burned anthracite, as guaranteed, but on a road used to Paterson engines, the cam reversing gear was not popular. Neither was the weak single riveted boiler, and in 1859 all but one of the camels were scrapped. Yet they left a legacy to the Lackawanna: as long as center cab engines with wide fireboxes were used, the fireman's shelter continued to be known as the "kitchen."

Zerah Colburn, the engineering genius of the time, and perhaps the most brilliant and unhappy man who ever had to do with the steam locomotive, had an answer. He designed a six coupled locomotive with a firebox wider than the six foot track gauge—but he left the employment of the builders before the locomotive was finished. They cut down his grate area, and produced a locomotive which was inferior until the railroad restored the firebox to the dimensions of the original drawings. Colburn, alcoholic and unstable, went on to Europe, where he produced the most beautiful treatise on railroads ever published, and finally committed suicide.

Charles Graham, master mechanic of the Lackawanna and Bloomsburg, a short line, was quick to perceive the virtues of the Colburn firebox, and equally quick to realize the deficiencies of the coupling arrangement, which Colburn took over from the Winans camels. Eventually, he produced a wide firebox locomotive with a modified Colburn firebox and a center cab: one of the early camelbacks. The Wooten boiler, which was a successor to Millholland's work, was evolved, it seems, independently of these Lackawanna engines. Yet the peculiar deficiencies of the original Wooten design led to the "improved" Wooten boiler of the Baldwin Locomotive Works, which very closely resembled the firebox and boiler design of Charles Graham.

While the middle Atlantic states were working on problems of combustion, New England was working on problems of design. In the 1850's, most New England builders favored inside connected engines, after the English pattern. They ran more smoothly, damaged the track less, and looked better than engines with inclined cylinders and drop hook or V hook valve motion scrabbling on the sides of the boiler. Even William Swinburne, in Paterson, N. J., succumbed to the lure of inside connections, and built some ten wheelers for the Erie on that plan. To this day, England and the continent have never given up the inside connected engine completely. Unfortunately, the New England builders applied the design to 4-4-0's, where its advantages showed up less than in the 0-6-0 goods engine so popular in Britain.

Among the New England builders—Seth Wilmarth, Hinkley, Taunton, Manchester and others—William Mason stands out. While he claimed for himself "improvements" which were made before he started building locomotives, it does not detract from his greatness to say that the first of these—the spread truck and cylinders in line with the center line of the drivers—were in road service on the engines of other builders before his first engine, the *James Guthrie,* rolled out of his shop. Mason claimed that he "cleaned up" American locomotive design, and no one can dispute his claim, for like Colburn, Millholland, and a few others, he paid attention to continental design. English locomotives of the 1850's were clean and uncomplicated in appearance; most of the American productions were the sign painter's delight and the mechanic's despair. The Mason engines were neat and straightforward.

Twenty years after the decade we are discussing, William Mason brought out his "bogie" type. These engines were based on the design of Robert Fairlie, an Englishman, but they were improved by Mason's addition of the Walschaerts valve gear. Mason's bogies must not be confused with the Forney type, which had rigid drivers and a swivel truck. The Mason engines had the drivers swiveling, with steam supplied to the cylinders through a flexible joint. These engines enjoyed a limited popularity; the objections to a small coal and water space, which hampered all tank engines, hampered them as well, and the master mechanics of the time did not like the Walschaerts valve gear. It was not until the first decade of the 20th century, when the link motion on the larger engines began to weigh 1745 lbs. more than Walschaerts gear applied to the same class of engine that Mason's foresight was realized.

The Boston, Revere Beach and Lynn, a narrow gauge railroad which connected the cities of its name, liked the Mason bogies so much that when William Mason died of pneumonia and the works shut down, it ordered locomotives after Mason's designs from the Manchester Locomotive Works. After Manchester was closed, the last group was built by Alco at Schenectady.

After the experiments of the middle of the century, locomotive progress was slow and orderly until the 1890's. In 1862, John P. Laird, the master mechanic at Altoona, rebuilt a Winans camel, the *Seneca,* into a true mogul. The success of the design was so great that all the camels were rebuilt, and the New Jersey Railroad and Transportation Company, now part of the Pennsylvania, ordered a 2-6-0 built new the following year. The Sixties, too, saw the appearance of the Consolidation, with Alexander Mitchell's engine of that name followed by his introduction of the decapod, inappropriately named the *Ant* and the *Bee.* These last two locomotives, although modern in appearance, were not as successful as Millholland's 0-10-0 *Kentucky* class pushers on the Reading, the last of which survived into the present century.

As the locomotive evolved between 1860 and 1900, names and bright colors generally disappeared. All the early locomotives were named, and some roads used a combination of names and numbers. In England, locomotives named after characters in classical mythology were common: in America, they were infrequent. The *Camel* on the B&O gave its name to an engine type, but the second camel was named *Iris* and the third, *Mars.* By 1853 the B&O had generally given up names—one of the first roads in the country to do so.

On the Reading, there was some attempt to make name groups correspond to locomotive types. 4-4-0's were generally named after cities, 4-6-0's after nationalities, 0-6-0's after mythological characters, 0-8-0's and larger engines after states. Happiest in the choice of names were the little 0-4-0's used for dock work. What else could suit them better than *Wharf Rat, Mole,* and *Otter* as they shunted cars around Philadelphia?

If the most pleasing names came from Indian place names, mythology, and a sense of humor, the most common names came from human vanity and political appeasement. Nearly every railroad president and director had one or more locomotives named after him, nor was a re-naming out of order if the sponsor left the company under hostile circumstances. It was always useful to name a locomotive after the governor, or members of the state legislature who might do favors, and congressmen were similarly honored. But locomotives named for Presidents of the U. S. were christened in sheer patriotism, and from the monotony of the *George Washingtons* on down, we gather that many railroad officials were more patriotic than original.

Named locomotives were doomed, not by the crassness of railroad officials (after all, Pullman cars are still named, not numbered) but by the exigencies of American train dispatching. Even with numbered locomotives, a meet order can take a page or two, but with names alone the situation would be a nightmare. Named locomotives lingered in England, because written train orders there are rarities, and since the earliest days some sort of permissive block signal system has been used.

While named locomotives were disappearing, so, too, were the bright colors of a century ago. Economic considerations and the increasing use of coal for fuel doomed the tenders with colorful landscapes, the decorated headlight sides, and the ornate cabs. It was relatively easy to keep $2000 worth of decoration clean on a wood burner, but on a coal burner, particularly with the straight stack and short front end favored by many of the Eastern roads, it was almost impossible. Freight engines were the first to receive somber black, and passenger engines followed. To a generation used to synthetic lacquer finishes of the Duco type, it is difficult to realize how little durability the early oil paints possessed, and how often the equipment had to be refinished. True, on wooden passenger cars, the pigments ground in oil would last a lifetime, but on the metal sides of a tender or headlight, alternately blistering hot and ice cold, bonding was precarious and flaking a real problem. The popularity of "Russia Iron," which had a finish resembling the modern stovepipe, for locomotive jackets came from the fact that it could be kept handsome by rubbing it with oil, which firemen dutifully pilfered from the company whenever possible.

Just before the beginning of the twentieth century began the relatively short era of the compound locomotive —a fascinating period which has been largely neglected by railroad historians and others. The compound was the delight of its builders, the pride of railway master mechanics, and too often the despair of its engineers.

The idea of compounding, using steam expansively more than once, was not new. It had been common in marine practice for many years, and without it the large steamship, driven by a reciprocating engine, would have been impossible.

In American railroad work there were four principal types for locomotives with a rigid wheelbase: the cross compound, with the high pressure cylinder on one side of the locomotive and the low pressure on the other; the Vauclain, with a high and low pressure cylinder on each side, one located above the other, and with piston rods working on a common crosshead; the tandem, in which the high pressure cylinder was placed ahead of the low pressure cylinder and in line with it; and the balanced, a four cylinder type with the low pressure outside the frames and the high pressure inside, driving a cranked axle, with the cranks set at 180 degrees from the corresponding outside crankpin. With this design the inside and outside pistons on each side always moved in opposite directions, one reaching the front end of the stroke at the same time the other reached the back.

Although experimental American compounds of the Sixties and Seventies had been successful, they failed to start a new trend. Suddenly, in 1889, Baldwin produced the first Vauclain compound, and Schenectady its first cross compound from Albert J. Pitkin's patents, and the race was on. By the middle of the 1890's, every manufacturer had at least one type of compound to offer; even Baldwin was producing cross compounds as well as the Vauclain type, which, because of its symmetry and simplicity, was far more adaptable. By 1906, Baldwin was the only works which had built all of the popular types of compound, with Schenectady, by then Alco, a runner up, since it had built every type except the Vauclain.

The cross compounds, whatever their type or maker, invariably performed well when just out of the shops, but their good behavior was not of long duration. They required constant maintenance, which they rarely received, and a sympathetic nursemaid for an engineer. Since pooling of locomotives nearly coincided with the introduction of compounds, engineers who had lost their pet engines were resentful and took out their resentment on whatever engine they received, including compounds.

Probably the most publicized of the cross compounds was the Richmond Tramp, built by the Richmond Locomotive Works as a demonstrator. A ten wheeler, proportioned for dual traffic work, she came as close to being handsome as a cross compound possibly could. If she had been a simple engine, or even a Vauclain compound, her grace might have been as conspicuous as her performance. As it was, she sold Richmond cross compounds, on the basis of her trial runs, from the South to Canada, and from Virginia to the Far West. Other makers tried to imitate the Richmond Tramp with other traveling locomotives, and they, too, convinced many railway managers that cross compounds were just the thing for slow heavy freight service. Some roads, such as the Chicago and Eastern Illinois, tried cross compounds for passenger service too.

If the cross compound made a good record for itself in demonstration runs, its performance in actual service was less spectacular. Since every cross compound had to be started as a simple engine, with the steam passing through a reducing valve, starting was less rapid than with a simple engine, and a number of flaws could give the low pressure cylinder, almost three times as large as the high pressure, a sudden increase of steam which racked the frame. Under other conditions, the high pressure cylinder did an unequal amount of work with the same results. Unless delicately handled, cross compounds were always in the shops for frame repairs. And while all compounds had a reputation for front end leaks, because the packing of the day was not up to the demands put upon it, the cross compounds seemed to be perpetually wreathed in steam on cold days. The relatively greater success of cross compounds in Europe makes us think that the haphazard working conditions in America exaggerated the fundamental weaknesses of the design.

The Vauclain compound, with an even distribution of high and low pressure cylinders, had no more tendency to uneven cross strains than a simple locomotive. It demonstrated itself in flamboyant high speed running on the Atlantic City Railroad and handling slow heavy tonnage in the West, but the last Vauclain compounds to be scrapped were on the Pike's Peak and Manitou, the famous mountain cogwheel road. While it never managed the spectacular low speed tonnage ratings of the cross compounds, it kept its frame square, and was less prone to front end leaks. Its defects were the use of a piston valve, then difficult to lubricate but later common practice in locomotive design, and a tendency of some of the engines to break the front rails of the frame, or bend the crossheads when starting. Certainly its drawbacks could be eliminated by modern design, and next to the balanced compounds, the Vauclain presented a possible pattern for an improved steam locomotive of the future.

The tandems were nearly all freight machines, and none of them were very attractive. John Player, the famous designer of the Brooks Works, revived the tandem, first used by Perry and Lay in 1867, and it was soon taken up by Schenectady, Pittsburgh and Baldwin. The first Santa Fe types, built for that road by Baldwin in 1903, were tandem compounds, as were the decapods which preceded them in the same service. These locomotives had a small crane hung on the side of the smokebox for convenience in servicing the cylinders.

But the most graceful, the quietest and smoothest running of all the compounds were the four cylinder balanced compounds built by Baldwin and Schenectady, by that time Alco. The first Baldwin engine was built for the Plant System, but went to the Chicago Short Line instead. Pictures of it as originally built show Plant System lettering and a Vanderbilt type tender, which the final purchasers replaced by a rectangular type.

The Santa Fe was so impressed by the design that it became the largest purchaser of the type. The first lot were some unusual front coupled Atlantics, and perhaps the most handsome were the 1871 series of Prairies built for fast freight service. The last balanced compounds built were heavy superheated Pacific types which the Santa Fe purchased in 1913. A simple locomotive, with its valves properly set, has a sharp, staccato exhaust, but the balanced compounds in their prime had a heavy gentle breath which became a blurred panting as they reached speed, for, like all four cylinder locomotives, they had twice as many exhausts as two cylinder ones.

While the compound fever was on, the Pennsylvania imported two European locomotives to test them in American service. The first of these was a Webb three cylinder compound of the design used on the North Western. When it arrived in 1889, the men nicknamed it "The John Bullgine." The English engineer, sent over to instruct Americans in its operation, viewed the Pennsylvania's rolling stock gloomily. "Hit was sent over 'ere to pull cars, not 'ouses," he commented.

The Webb was actually a 2-2-2-0, the first pair of drivers driven by the low pressure cylinder and the second set by two outside high pressure cylinders. Webb was so impressed by the performance of the English "singles" of the day that he was determined to make his engines "double singles." Unlike American compounds, they had no intercepting valves, so in starting, the rear drivers slipped until enough steam had been exhausted to start the front pair.

The next imported experiment of the Pennsylvania was more successful, but again, the engine was too light. This was the famous De Glehn Atlantic, which arrived from France in 1904, just in time for the Saint Louis Exposition. The De Glehn was the model on which the Baldwin and Cole (Alco) balanced compound designs were based, but unlike them had its low pressure cylinders inside the frames, and two separate sets of Walschaerts valve gear.

At the Saint Louis Exposition, in the same hall as the light and graceful De Glehn, stood a very different type of compound. It was the largest locomotive built up to that time, but the principle of design it used had originally been worked out for the tiny twisting narrow gauge roads of France. James E. Muhlfeld of the Baltimore and Ohio designed the 2400 following the system of compounding and articulation used by Anatole Mallet. The 2400 was an 0-6-6-0, looking very trim and modern. Its subsequent performance in road service justified Muhlfeld's faith in Mallet's system, but before long it was too small for the work it had to do, and after an appearance at The Fair of the Iron Horse in 1927 it was stored until 1938, when it was scrapped. The Mallet type has been the last of the compounds to survive, for the Norfolk and Western has continued to build them—gigantic machines which would dwarf "Old Maud," as the 2400 was known, much as she dwarfed all the engines in St. Louis.

If Muhlfeld did not immediately go overboard for his own design and build innumerable duplicates of the 2400, other roads saw in the Mallets a quick solution to innumerable problems. The Erie quickly followed Muhlfeld's lead with a series of three gigantic center cab, wide firebox 0-8-8-0's known then as the "Angus" type. Since the stoker had not yet proven itself a success, the Erie articulated camelbacks were stoked by two sweating firemen, sometimes three, as they pushed trainloads of steel coal hoppers up Gulf Grade.

The mechanical department of the Santa Fe had always been fond of compounds, and in 1909 it embarked on a career of building the most spectacular Mallets of the day. A 2-8-8-2, the "largest locomotive in the world," was built, along with the first high wheeled articulated engines—some 4-4-6-2's for passenger service. The 2-8-8-2's seemed such a good idea that some of the Santa Fe types were converted from tandem compounds to 2-10-10-2's by the addition of a new front section. Before too long, these locomotives were back at work in the form of simple 2-10-2's.

In 1910 the Santa Fe outdid itself with some 2-6-6-2's for fast freight service. These were high wheeled locomotives with a general design well in advance of their time. But no longer was Mallet's original pattern of an articulated front frame, swinging under the boiler, apparent. Instead, the boiler itself was articulated, the fire tubes terminating at the pleated boiler joint, and the barrel of the first section being filled with a superheater and reheater. Samuel Vauclain originated the idea, and said happily in 1908: "The excellence of this design has yet to be appreciated, but what little mechanical or engineering reputation I may enjoy is cheerfully placed in jeopardy by its recommendation. No fear may be had as to the life of the flexible connection. There is no more opportunity for cinders to invade its minor recesses than has water to get under the scales of a fish."

Despite the conspicuous failure of his flexible boilers, Sam Vauclain continued to enjoy the respect of the engineering world for his other achievements. Cinders did get under the skin of his accordion pleats, and the joints burst, sending clouds of steam skyward. Furthermore, the front ends showed deterioration from electrolysis, little understood at that time, and very soon the whole batch of engines were cut down to conventional types.

With the 2-8-8-8-2 triplexes built for the Erie and the 2-8-8-8-4 engine of a similar design built for the Virginian, the steam locomotive reached its maximum size. These locomotives appeared in 1914 and 1919, and had their boiler design been as much in advance as their wheel arrangement, they might have been successful. As it was, they were constantly short of breath, and by 1920 the Virginian converted its monster into a 2-8-8-0 and a Mikado. The Erie persisted with the Matt Shay type until the 1930's when the last of them were scrapped, although they had been withdrawn from road service in 1927.

While all the compound excitement was going on, a little ten wheeler on the Canadian Pacific carried a contraption which would settle the hash of all the compounds. Number 548 was built in 1891, and when she was rebuilt in 1901, a Schmidt smokebox superheater was added. The modern superheater, of course, has many improvements over the original design, but the principle is the same. Steam, taken directly from the boiler at common locomotive pressures, is still saturated steam; that is, the water is not completely vaporized. The function of the superheater is to make the steam hotter than it would normally be for the same pressure and convert all the water into gas. For example, a theoretical boiler pressure of 1000 lbs. per square inch has a steam temperature of 640° Fahrenheit, but steam taken from an actual boiler pressure of 200 lbs. per square inch can be superheated and given the same temperature of 640°, drying it and increasing its efficiency.

The superheater brought about the modern locomotive, and the developments between the first big superheated locomotives built in the 1915–20 era and the present are fairly well known. Since superheat made it possible for a simple locomotive to show the same efficiency as a saturated compound, the compounds were doomed, either to be rebuilt as simple locomotives with superheat, or scrapped.

At this late date, with the diesel taking over, one can only wonder at what might have happened had James E. Muhlfeld's experiments with high pressure compounds succeeded. Built in the Twenties and early Thirties, for drag freight, which was already becoming an obsolete concept, they might have made a more impressive performance had they been styled as 4-8-4's instead of low wheeled 2-8-0's and 4-8-0's.

Today, only two major coal roads persist in trying to improve steam motive power. The Norfolk and Western continues to build new steam locomotives at its Roanoke Shops, and the Virginian uses steam exclusively. How long they will last in defying the diesel, no one knows. The diesel is an anomaly in an industry where the four cylinder locomotive was generally rejected on the grounds of complexity. To have efficient railroads, the engine of the future will have to be complex, beyond the wildest complexity ever added to the reciprocating steam engine. But there are many people who still do not consider the diesel a final answer.

Locomotive Naming

The very first locomotive created to draw a public conveyance had a name —*Locomotion,* of course. Stephenson followed this with his famous *Rocket,* while a rival concern was turning out its *Novelty*. Thereafter, for many years, all or nearly all locomotives—in America, at least—were named. There were definite reasons for the naming of the very earliest ones in America. The *Stourbridge Lion* of the Delaware & Hudson, the first to run on rails in this country, was made in England and christened there. The Mohawk & Hudson's first machine was named, with unconscious irony, in honor of DeWitt Clinton, builder of the Erie Canal, which the railroad was destined largely to supersede. The Camden & Amboy, an early unit of the Pennsylvania, permitted its first engine—imported, of course—to trundle around under the name of *John Bull,* a person who was by no means popular in the brash young republic of those days; but apparently there was no serious complaint of it. Matthias Baldwin's first essay at a locomotive was christened *Old Ironsides*. Peter Cooper pieced from scrap a locomotive for the infant Baltimore & Ohio, which he called *Tom Thumb* because it was so small.

Charleston, South Carolina, was in a state of worry because of fear for the loss of her commercial eminence and prosperity. Other seaports were gaining at her expense, the great Mississippi River system was drawing the commerce of the interior to New Orleans, and Charleston felt herself slipping. Her only salvation, as she saw it, was a railroad to the interior—hence the 136-mile Charleston & Hamburg (later the South Carolina Railroad), then the largest railroad in the Nation, and, in fact, the longest in the world. Before it had begun to be built, a locomotive was ordered from an iron works in New York, and when it came, it was given a name which expressed what Charleston believed or hoped it would be—the *Best Friend of Charleston*. That the railroad didn't quite fulfil Charleston's hopes is another matter.

At first the locomotive builders named most of the machines, but as might be expected, it wasn't long before the railroad officials decided that they preferred to do the naming themselves. To some extent, they carried on trends which had been started by the builders. One was a desire to indicate high speed. The Boston & Worcester

By Alvin F. Harlow. A compilation based largely on articles and rosters appearing in The Railway & Locomotive Historical Society's Bulletins from 1921 to 1953. Charles E. Fisher, President of the Society, and an eminent authority on locomotives, has not only granted permission for their use, but has related some interesting anecdotes as sidelights on the subject.

quickly acquired a *Meteor* and a *Comet,* and these were soon followed in New England and elsewhere by *Rocket, Mercury, Arrow, Lightning, Racer, Swiftsure, Express, Despatch, Speedwell, Velocity, Pegasus, Torrent, Tornado, Dart, Cyclone, Antelope, Post Boy, Phaeton* and *Arabian*—referring to the Arabian horse. The Boston & Lowell's *Stampede* might be a boast of high velocity, too, but she had another one named *Ambler,* which certainly was not. Some of these engines were really swift, too. No one knew just how fast the *Lightning,* built by Norris for the Utica & Schenectady Railroad, could run, for they didn't dare extend her to the limit.

Tremendous power was another property which the early builders and owners sought to prove by such names as *Hercules, Goliath* (with *Goliah* as a variant), *Samson* (sometimes spelled *Sampson*), *Milo, Giant, Atlas, Titan,* and *Ajax,* which were used over and over again. Another favorite name, remindful of the glowing forge and the brawny, smoke-blackened giant who wrought at it, was *Vulcan.* There were many *Vulcans;* and others of a fiery tendency, such as *Spitfire, Firebrand, Firefly.* By the same token, volcanoes were favorites—*Volcano, Vesuvius, Aetna, Hecla.* And there was vague groping towards the as yet little known power of electricity in *Spark, Electric, Magnet.*

The names of states, towns, and counties through which the railroad passed and rivers which it crossed were drawn upon and having exhausted these, they began using more distant states anywhere and everywhere, and great all-embracing names, such as *United States, Union, National, Constitution, Independence, Liberty, President, Commonwealth.*

The historic notabilities of New England—*Governor Bradford, Governor Carver, John Eliot, Roger Williams, Miles Standish, Paul Revere, General Warren, General Putnam, James Bowdoin, John Winthrop,* and many more, on down through *John* and *John Quincy Adams* and *Daniel Webster,* to mention only a few, were all honored, some of them repeatedly. The Founding Fathers and national heroes were all enlisted, including the Presidents as far as they went. The Father of his Country was named on engine flanks variously as *Washington, George Washington, Gen'l Washington* and *President Washington.* The coming of the Civil War brought other Generals on both sides.

Some railroad officials early saw opportunities for glory in those panels under the cab windows or metal plates displayed farther forward. When the little New Albany & Salem—which eventually grew into the Monon—was first operating in 1850, it had just two locomotives, named *James Brooks* and *Phoebe Brooks,* for its president and his wife.

Every railroad president's name in history was seen at one time and another on an engine cab; and not only they, but general managers, superintendents and an occasional master mechanic—yes, down to humble *Myron Dow,* yardman of the Cleveland & Columbus in its beginning days, who did the switching of the little four-wheel freight cars with a horse, and in later years was honored by having a yard engine named for him.

Somebody placed the name and portrait of *George S. Griggs,* master mechanic of the Boston & Providence, on a locomotive in early days, but it exploded and when it was reconditioned, Griggs wouldn't let his name continue on it—either because he feared to lose face thereby, or because he thought the men might be superstitious about it. So he ordered the name changed to *King Philip,* for a 17th century Indian Chief.

There was a New York Central superintendent named Zenas Priest for whom a locomotive was named, and his portrait, painted on the headlight, was said to have been the best likeness ever made of him. Another under-official in the early 1870s who got his name on a locomotive, and a stylish one at that, was Cephas Manning of the New York Central, whose namesake is said to have been a beauty—red drivers and so on, and some small parts gold-plated—at least, it looked like gold. It was too beautiful to remain *Cephas Manning,* so it was ordered to exchange names with the *William H. Vanderbilt.* But when Reuben Allen, the regular engineer of the *Vanderbilt,* heard of the order, he was so indignant that he refused to operate the engine under its new and commonplace name; and the story is that to placate him, for some time no name was painted on his engine.

Of course there were a *George W. Whistler* and a *William G. McNeill,* honoring two of our earliest great railroad engineer-builders. Prominent industrialists—and, inevitably, heavy shippers—such as *J. C. Ayer* (medicine man) and *Pepperell* were honored, too. And even as a rich uncle who has come down handsomely with the cash or, it is hoped, will do so in the future, is flattered by having a baby named for him, so locomotive builders were sometimes cajoled by struggling rail corporations, which had to ask for time, and almost invariably pressed the builder to take stock in the company in at least part payment for engines. Walter Lucas has found fully half a dozen, mostly in the South, named *Thomas Rogers,* in honor of the Paterson, N. J., locomotive builder, at one time the largest producer in the country. For similar reasons, a *Nicholas Biddle* (Philadelphia banker) is encountered here and there in that area.

No one has yet fathomed the reason why so many locomotives were given Indian names—not only well-known ones like *Taconic, Housatonic, Katahdin* and *Narragansett,* but many rugged, polysyllabic words which most people never heard of otherwise. On Maine railroads were *Kenduskeag, Ammonoosuc, Nulhegan, Mattapoisett, Massawippi, Wannalancet, Machigonne, Memecho, Ogiochock,* and *Washacum.* The Old Colony offered *Pokanocket,* the Somerset Railway had *Carratuck, Norridgewock, Carrabasset, Bombazine* (did they think that an Indian word?) and *Moxie!*

But the Lackawanna topped them all with a list including *Analomink, Tobyhanna, Kittatinny, Mehoopany, Aquashicola, Meenesink, Pohatacong, Nay Aug, Monocanock, Hackensack, Senecawanna, Pequannock, Musconetcong, Watsessing, Wawayanda, Papakating* and *Succasunna.* We have no record of what some of the engine crews thought of those names. The Galena & Chicago Union, ancestor of the Northwestern, had one which must have been a translation of an Indian word—*Whirling Thunder.* And the Aurora Branch Railroad in the 1850s had *Big Indian* and *Little Indian, Big Rock* and *Little Rock.*

Even in the earliest days, when the builders were still naming engines, there were ventures into mythology; first of all, the planets and stars—*Jupiter, Mars, Mercury, Saturn, Uranus, Orion,* the New Haven & Northampton's *Altair, Arcturus, Sirius, Polaris* and *Leo;* or just *Star;* but it is noticeable that they shied away from Venus. To begin with, feminine names were not favored for locomotives; and Venus's reputation was not quite—well, there was that ribald poem of Shakespeare's, you know. We find a couple of instances of the name, but their crews no doubt blushed for them.

Mythology supplied many more names—*Ariel, Adonis, Cupid, Minerve, Vesta, Atalanta, Agamenticus, Perseus, Andromeda, Ceres, Aeolus, Jason, Memnon, Hector, Achilles, Ajax, Menelaus, Diomedes, Priam, Ulysses.* The

North Carolina Railroad, most classical of all in the 1850s, had all these plus *Astron, Helios, Cyclops, Sisyphus* (another criminal), *Kratos, Apollo, Pactolus, Cybele, Midas,* and finally, *Traho,* the first person singular form of a Latin verb, meaning "I draw," and *Pello,* "I push."

Ancient history supplied some names —*Alaric, Attila, Trajan, Hannibal, Archimedes* and few others, but it is noticeable that the early Roman emperors were touched very lightly, perhaps because of a suspicion that they were in general bad eggs.

The infrequency of feminine names (noted above) has been much dwelt upon and somewhat overdrawn. It is true that feminine names were infrequent, but not as infrequent as alleged. Mention such classical femmes as *Atalanta, Andromeda, Minerva, Vesta, Cybele, Ceres, Juno,* and *Hecate* (Queen of Hades, by the way), and objectors will say, "Oh, those don't count; they're ancient—and in most cases, the fellows who named them probably didn't know the names were feminine." But one may retort with the Philadelphia, Wilmington & Baltimore's (now Pennsylvania) *Princess Anne* and *Lady Washington,* the *Empress* built by Mason for the Jersey Central in '69, while Taunton's second job was the *Witch,* and the Boston & Maine had two *Camillas,* years apart.

The Morris & Essex, an early larval form of the Lackawanna, had four switch engines in the Hoboken yards in the latter '60s named *Ida, Eva, Ella* and *May,* said to be the names of the Superintendent's four daughters; but we do not know who *Jennie* and *Grace,* who soon followed, were, nor *Edith,* who came along in 1875. The Old Colony had a *Susan Nipper,* named by some Dickens fan.

The Northern Railroad in 1873 had a locomotive primly named *Mrs. Dustan* (also spelled Dustin and Duston), honoring one of New England's noted heroines, a two-fisted lady who was snatched from her home by a band of Indians in 1699, but who, with the assistance of a 14-year-old boy, killed ten of her captors, and brought back their scalps as proof of her story.

The odd thing is that notwithstanding the seemingly predominant reluctance to give locomotives feminine names, to an engineer and fireman, their machine is always "she." Its name might be *Hercules* or *Andrew Jackson* or *General Grant* or *Davy Crockett,* but to its crew it was nevertheless "she."

Mr. Fisher tells an amusing story anent the occasional feminine name for a locomotive. A joker rushed into the parsonage of one of the prominent churches of Salem, Massachusetts, one evening in the long ago and told the clergyman, "There's a sailor boy and a factory girl together over in the round-house." The preacher, a worthy successor to Cotton Mather, clapped on his hat and cloak and rushed to the round-house to correct this unseemly situation, but suffered a painful shock and loss of face when all he found was two locomotives named *Sailor Boy* and *Factory Girl* standing meekly side by side; the latter named in honor of those remarkable feminine textile workers in the mills at Lowell who discussed literature, wrote poetry, and pasted it on the walls of the mills; Dickens went to see and marvel at it and them.

The living honorees weren't always political or military or railroad high brass, or heroes or heroines. There was an engine on the Fall River Railroad in an early day named *Job Terry,* for a retired sea captain. Mr. Fisher doesn't know whether he purchased the honor with pelf, but it is significant that he was expected to give the railroad operatives a clambake every year. This steadily grew to be such a large and well attended affair that Cap'n Terry wished he had never seen the engine, and was mightily relieved when it was taken into the U. S. military service in wartime.

Commonplace town names were applied, with the idea that no village of any importance along the line must feel snubbed—such as the Lackawanna's *Factoryville, Spragueville* and *Bridgeville* and the New York and Harlem's *Yorkville* and *Manhattanville.* These "villes" were particularly numerous in the middle West, where one might see an item like this in a Cleveland paper in 1853, "Locomotive Salineville collided with Locomotive Wellsville on the pier last evening, cutting off an arm and a leg of the engineer of the latter."

The animals favored in locomotive naming were as a rule noted either for speed or ferocity—*Antelope, Reindeer, Gazelle, Elk, Stag, Roebuck, Moose, Greyhound, Lion, Lioness, Tiger, Tigress, Panther, Jaguar, Python, Rhinoceros, Leopard,* and milder ones, such as *Zebra, Elephant, Buffalo* and *Bison. Pony* and *Boy* or *The Boy* were favorite names for small machines or yard engines, as were *Mule, Utility* and *Useful.* On the Norwich & Worcester there was even a *Pup.*

Landscape features were favorite names. The Boston, Concord & Montreal had an *Old Man of the Mountains,* and the Atlantic, Mississippi & Ohio (now Norfolk & Western) had *Peaks of Otter* for those lovely pinnacles between Lynchburg and Roanoke. If you wonder at an early Philadelphia, Wilmington & Baltimore name *Gunpowder,* it is that of a tidal river crossed by the railroad in Maryland. One of the queerest was *Horse Heads,* owned by the Utica, Ithaca & Elmira Railroad, and named for a small town on its line. On its tender were the letters "U.I.," followed by a circle, in which were painted three horse-heads, two black and one white, and this was followed by the letters "& E. R.R." The Old Colony went in for place names, too—*Plymouth Rock, Brant Rock, South Boston, South Shore, Highland Light.*

Some names had a contemporary significance which must be searched for now. Master Mechanic Griggs named one of the Boston & Providence machines *Viaduct,* in justifiable pride over the great Canton viaduct, and over which heavy New Haven locomotives and trains still thunder, more than a century later. The *St. James* was named for a hotel in Boston. The Old Colony's *Extension* signified the triumph of the directoral faction that wanted to extend the railroad out on Cape Cod, and *Right Arm* is the old Massachusetts nickname for the Cape Cod peninsula itself, from its resemblance to a man's right arm, clenched in the manner of the trademark of a well-known brand of baking soda. After the South Carolina Railroad had had two locomotives built in New York, it erected one in its own shop and pridefully christened it *Native.*

The *Pilgrim,* turned out by Amoskeag in 1853, had on each side of the tender, almost covering it, what is said to have been a good reproduction of a famous painting of The Landing of the Pilgrims. Taunton outshopped the *Narragansett* in 1869 to pull the Fall River Steamboat Express, with large paintings of two of the big Fall River boats, *Bristol* and *Providence,* one on each side of the tender. Rogers produced the *Cataract City,* with a view of Niagara Falls. Such paintings frequently cost a thousand dollars each. There were other scenes and portraits, as we have indicated, on the headlights. There was so much polished metal that a crew of rag-wielders was kept busy between trips shining it up, to say nothing of the additional labor of love on it by the engineer and fireman.

The Denver & Rio Grande must have been a gorgeous pageant in the 1870s and '80s. Its locomotives were for the most part christened for topographical and scenic features of the system, such as *Spanish Peaks, Old Baldy, Silver Cliff, Royal Gorge, Elk Mountain, Grand Canyon, Las Animas, Copper Gulch, Texas Creek, Gold Town, Mt. Holy Cross, Frying Pan, Sera la Sal* and some forty others; and we are told that paintings of the scenes represented by the names are on many of the tenders.

Commodore Vanderbilt put a curb on this in the East in the 1870s when he ordered that locomotives on the New York Central be all black, with a minimum of brass and gold striping. That marked the end of an era which had already begun to fade a little. Rapidly the gorgeous creations disappeared. The Southern was the last to go somber, its rich green locomotives, with a modest but attractive brightening of brass trimming, being for years a pleasant note in the Southern landscape.

But the old itch for locomotive coloring is hard to down. The East Tennessee & Western North Carolina's beloved little "Tweetsie," had red and brass capped stacks and red cab window frames on its dainty little narrowgage engines. In even later days we hear of the Frisco having engines glistering in the manner of long ago, with blue paint and red-and-gold trim, and brass mountings.

The Philadelphia & Columbia in the 1830s had among its county and place names an engine called *Washington County Farmer,* and on its connections to westward were a *Flying Dutchman,* a *Mountaineer* and a *Backwoodsman.* In the 1850s there was evidently some whimsical, fun-loving, literate fellow among the Philadelphia & Columbia's officials, and for him Shakespeare supplied *Falstaff, Bardolph* and *Yorick,* Dickens *Tony Weller* and *My Son Samivel,* Sterne *Uncle Toby* and *Corporal Trim,* Prof. Longfellow's latest poem *Hiawatha,* while from other sources came *John Gilpin, Old Fogy, Fingall's Baby, Tam o'Shanter* and *Young America.* The Boston & Lowell became quite literary, with *Hamlet, Coriolanus, Hotspur, King Lear, Othello* and *Minotaur.* Elsewhere were *Lochinvar, Ivanhoe* and *Uncle Tom.* There was a Dickensian in the Old Colony organization in the '70s, to name engines *Mark Tapley, Micawber, Sam Weller, Jack Bunsby* and *Pancks* —a yard engine, of course. *Susan Nipper* came along later, in 1888.

Oddities in locomotive naming intrigue us. Some, such as *Rover, Traveller, Wanderer,* some gently boastful —*Leader, Conqueror, Eclipse, Vanguard, Resolute, Onward, Brilliant, Sans Pareil, Nonpareil*—are understandable; but *Perseverance* is a little queer and *Rescue* puzzles us. The New York, Providence & Boston had a *Little Rest* in 1836, which few people today recognize as the Kingston Village of "Shepherd Tom" Hazard's *Jonny-Cake Papers.* The West Feliciana Railroad in Louisiana had an *Escape* during the Civil War, a consummation difficult to realize on a 27-mile pike in 1863 with the woods thereabouts swarming with Yankees.

The Lackawanna very aptly named its first locomotive to burn anthracite coal *Investigator;* later they had an *Anthracite* and a *Carbon.* Their *Frugality, Decision, Dynamics* and *Economy* may have been reminders or admonitions to their men. But how shall we account for *Stranger* (Vermont Central), *Red Clover, Dictator, Regulator, Manager,* and most amazing of all, the Boston, Hartford & Erie's *Plumber* and *Trustee;* or the Boston & Lowell's *Dabster* in 1879? The Boston & Providence named an engine *Iron Horse,* which was a very early use of a now common term. There was a *Chipso* built for the Panama Railroad in 1854, which sounds like a present-day packaged soap flake; but the climax—to our ears—of bizarre names south of the border was that on one of the Mexican railroads, *Jesus Cristus.*

There was some rapid renaming of locomotives around Civil War times. Of course the South after 1860 couldn't use an engine named *United States* or *Winfield Scott* (a Virginian who chose the Northern side) or one named for a Northern State, so they were rechristened, usually for Southern leaders. But when Federal troops captured a locomotive named *Gen. Beauregard* or *Robert E. Lee,* the name had to be painted out. Then perhaps it would change hands again and again be renamed.

Of all railroads, the old Michigan Central had perhaps the most colorful list of locomotive names. They were mostly in series or categories. Among them in 1858 were *Ranger, Rover, Rambler, Rattler, Racer* and *Rusher; Bald Eagle, White Eagle* (four more eagles); *White Cloud, Flying Cloud; North Wind, East Wind* (four more winds); *Greyhound, Staghound Foxhound, Wolfhound; Grizzly Bear, Brown Bear, Black Bear, White Bear; Circassian, Arab, Mameluke, Corsair, Egyptian, Persian, Saxon, Stranger, Foreigner; Storm, Torrent, Hurricane, Cataract; Atlantic, Pacific, Arctic, Baltic; North, South, Red, Caspian, Black* and *White Sea,* and many classical names.

Locomotives underwent name-changes elsewise than in war. The famous old *Pioneer,* the Galena & Chicago Union's first machine, which is still cherished by the North Western, did not begin life under that name. Baldwin built it in 1836 for the Utica & Schenectady, where it seemingly went nameless, but was soon sold to the Michigan Central, which christened it *Alert.* In turn, the MC sold it to the Galena & Chicago Union, which renamed it *Pioneer.*

Mr. Fisher spins some interesting yarns of the vicissitudes and name-changing of new locomotives. William Mason, at Taunton, built the *Tomales* for the North Pacific Coast Railroad in California, a narrow gage, in 1876. Shipped in knocked-down condition, it got as far as Framingham, about 20 miles from Taunton, when it was stopped and returned to the builder at his request. George Haggerty, a Mason erector, who had started with it, was now sent to Ithaca, N. Y., to bring back an engine, the *Leviathan,* which was to be rebuilt. In the meantime, the *Tomales* was remodelled to standard gage, renamed *Mankato,* and again Haggerty started with her, this time for the Central Railroad of Minnesota. On this occasion he got only as far as the factory-yard gate when a man from the office intercepted him with a hold order. He was next sent with a locomotive to the little Peach Bottom Railroad in Pennsylvania. Returning, he found that the *Tomales,* alias *Mankato,* had been done over again and was now the *Dixie Crosby* for the Galveston, Harrisburg & San Antonio; and this time he completed delivery. Remaining there under orders, presently along came the former *Leviathan,* now the *Commodore Garrison,* and Haggerty tuned that up and some others that followed.

The naming of engines had apparently died out when the Baltimore & Ohio, always a devotee of history, christened twenty-five handsome new Pacific locomotives for the first twenty-six Presidents of the United States, omitting John Quincy Adams because his name was too nearly like his father's. They were finished in dark green, striped in red and gold, and were always known as the Presidential engines.

The urge to name locomotives continues to bob up every little while. In 1937 the Boston & Maine conducted a contest among New England school children for the naming of a group of passenger engines, and the winning entries included some novelties—*Bumble Bee, Camel's Hump* (a Vermont mountain), *Rogers' Ranger, Bee and Emma* (a play on "B&M-er"), *Ye Salem Witch, Old North Bridge, Oliver Wendell Holmes* (the first author so honored), *Hannah Dustin,* and to add a chic modern touch, the selection of Soprano Lily Pons as one of the godmothers. There was a celebration in Boston on the day when the prizes were awarded to the children, with Miss Pons present. She was photographed in the cab of "her" engine, sitting in the engineer's lap and blowing the whistle. It was quite a day.

And now we hear that the sturdy old Frisco is naming its Diesel passenger locomotives for noted racehorses—and other horses. We hear of *Dan Patch, Whirlaway, Seabiscuit, Gallant Fox, Twenty Grand, Winchester,* and *Traveler;* "the last two the mounts of Civil War Generals Sheridan and Lee," so runs the story. Well, General Sheridan's horse was originally named Rienzi; "Winchester" was an afterthought—but let that pass.

Passenger Train Naming

Time was when trains had no names except—for people along the line—the "Mail Train" and the "Accommodation." Or if it was a line which had only one train a day each way, one which did all the chores, they were apt to be known as the "Up Train" and the "Down Train" respectively. This oldest of designations is still quaintly preserved by the Boston & Maine in its *Up Portsmouth* and *Down Portsmouth,* two trains which shuttle between Boston and Portsmouth, N. H.

Then, as faster trains became more numerous, there was an occasional one known as the Express or the Fast Mail. Those old-fashioned folk out in the middle Northwest still have three *Fast Mails,* one each on the Burlington, Great Northern and Milwaukee. And when the railroads began putting on what was regarded as a terrifically fast train, one which actually passed more than half of the stations along its course without stopping, it began to be called, more or less informally, the Cannonball—though the name was not printed on the time table. There are still four *Cannonballs* left, too—Wabash, Norfolk & Western, Boston & Maine and Long Island.

The longest-lived train in America to date was the Fall River Line *Steamboat Express,* on the Old Colony Railroad and its successor, the New Haven. This train began operating coincidentally with the famous Fall River Line of overnight boats between New York and Fall River. The *Boat Train,* as it was popularly known, left Boston at 5 P.M. and dashed down to Fall River in an hour, stopping right alongside the boat. In 1853 its leaving time was changed to 5:30 and in 1875 to 6 P.M., at which time it left ever afterward, save for some variations during the Spanish-American and First World Wars. When the Fall River Line of boats ceased operation in 1937, the *Boat Train* also halted forever, after ninety years of uninterrupted service.

The Old Colony launched another famous train in 1884, a three- or four-car private affair for subscribers only —extra fare, of course,—which left Bos-

By Alvin F. Harlow. A compilation from *Named Passenger Trains,* pp. 1–24. Washington, D.C.: Association of American Railroads. February, 1952. With additions from other sources.

ton on summer afternoons at three o'clock and skittered over the 72 miles to Woods Hole in an hour and a half, so that bankers and other Predatory Plutocrats, closing their roll-top desks a little early, might eat supper at the Sea View Hotel on Martha's Vineyard as early as six o'clock, if they wished. It was promptly nicknamed by railroaders the *Dude Train,* and so it continued to be known, quite matter-of-factly, until the National Railroad Administration of the First World War abolished it in 1918.

The stories are several and conflicting as to the first "name train." The Central of Georgia for a time claimed precedence for a *Nancy Hanks,* back in the 1890's, "named for the famous trotting horse," foaled in the latter 1880's. The Nancy Hanks train (the fastest train in the South at the time) ran briefly in 1890–91, then faded away; but the Central of Georgia revived the name in recent years as the *Nancy Hanks II;* nice train, too. The peppery little Central even has a *Little Nancy* between Savannah and Augusta, and (someone down there must be a racing fan) a *Man o' War* for the 117-mile Columbus-Atlanta run, rare combination of a Diesel-drawn, air-conditioned *local,* with observation-club car serving food and beverages, maid and porter service.

A train which may be destined to outdo the Boat Train in longevity is the one between Boston and Washington, originally known as the *Washington Night Express,* launched by the New Haven in 1876, principally because of the Centennial Exposition at Philadelphia. It bypassed New York, being carried by a big car-ferry nine miles between the New Haven tracks in what is now the Borough of the Bronx and Jersey City. For thirty years this train—whose name was changed in 1892 to the *Federal Express*—was ferried thus, and then it became all-rail, going from New Haven via Danbury, the Poughkeepsie bridge, and Trenton to Philadelphia, but continuing to do a good business despite this long detour. When the Hell Gate Bridge across East River was opened in 1913, the train began taking a direct course through the Pennsylvania station in New York. Now known merely as the *Federal,* it won notoriety in 1952 by crashing into the Washington Union Terminal and causing a terrific mess.

In 1881 the Pennsylvania launched what is said to have been the first extra-fare train in history. It was then called the *New York-Chicago Limited,* but in 1891 was rechristened the *Pennsylvania Limited,* and as such, still operates. At the start, it was all-Pullman, an innovation, including some "hotel cars," was gas-lighted, and you still had to use a hand-pump to draw water for the lavatory. Dining cars were added a year later, electric lights in 1887 and an observation car in 1889.

Speaking of name-trains, the Chicago & Alton started one known as the *Hummer*—Chicago to Kansas City —in 1880, and ran it for half a century before its passing; and in 1889 the grand old Alton put on its *Alton Limited*—Chicago-St. Louis—which it frankly admitted was the handsomest train in the world, and maybe it was. It is still around, though others have long since challenged its magnificence. The spring of '89 saw the birth of another famous train, when the Chesapeake & Ohio deftly seized upon the initials of the First Families of Virginia and named its new golden yellow speedster the *Fast Flying Virginian,* or in common usage, the *F.F.V.*

Meanwhile the New York Central had launched its *Chicago Limited,* and in 1891 its shrewd passenger agent, Daniels, created the *Empire State Express,* to ply between New York and Buffalo, and built it into world-wide fame. In 1902 he scored another hit with the flashiest and most famous greyhound of them all, the *Twentieth Century Limited,* which literally had everything, and whose first trip in each direction carried more reporters than paying passengers. In that same year the Pennsylvania started the *Pennsylvania Special,* which ten years later began challenging the *Century* as the *Broadway Limited.* Attempting schedules practically impossible to maintain, they reduced them by mutual agreement for a few years after 1912 until their improved equipment made greater speeds practicable.

The 1890's spawned some other famous trains, as the vogue for naming them grew apace—the Lehigh Valley's *Black Diamond Express* in 1896, named of course for the anthracite coal which was that road's life-blood; the Pennsylvania's *Congressional Limited,* the Union Pacific's *Overland Limited,* the Southern Pacific's *Sunset Limited,* the Santa Fe's *California Limited,* the Alton's *Midnight Special,* "a real hotel on wheels," the B&O's *Royal Blue Flyer,* and the Big Four-New York Central's *Knickerbocker,* to name a few which are still running. Many trains that used to be are, alas, no more—the Alton's *Hummer* and *Nighthawk,* the Chicago Great Western's *Red Bird* and *Blue Bird,* and the Northwestern's *Nightingale*—Omaha to St. Paul and Minneapolis, where no name train runs now—to mention only a few.

The idea of a "limited" train was that of a sort of wager between railroad and passenger. The latter paid extra fare to ride on the train, against the railroad's bet that it would deliver him at destination on scheduled time or very nearly so, and if not, it would refund a part of his fare. But the word "Limited," like "Express" and "Special," came to be used very loosely. (Many people still think it means a limited number of stops.) "Flyer" was another rash boast. At least one "Flyer" could be named, which, in its 285-mile run, averaged little more than 25 miles an hour, even when it was on time.

The "Limited" custom ended long ago, but there are still "Limiteds" all over the country, as well as "Specials" and "Expresses." There were some 65 Expresses operating at last report (including a *Pony Express* on the Union Pacific), about 57 Limiteds (some of which never were Limiteds in the original meaning of the word), and more than 40 Specials.

The Nation's Capital has supplied some roads, notably the Baltimore & Ohio and the Pennsylvania, with train names smacking of Government and the armed forces—the B&O's *Ambassador* (the Boston & Maine-Canadian National also have one), the B&O's *Capitol Limited, Diplomat, National Limited* and *Washington,* (which it sends via the Pittsburgh & Lake Erie and Erie to Cleveland). The Pennsy has a *Washingtonian,* too, which it sends via the New Haven, Boston & Maine and Canadian National to Montreal. Other Pennsylvania trains include *The Congressional, The Constitution, The Executive, The President, The Federal* (already mentioned), *The Judiciary, The Embassy, The Legislator, The Senator* (the Southern Pacific also has one, Sacramento to San Francisco). *The Representative, The Statesman* (also a Southern Pacific name), *The Speaker, The Admiral, The Commander,* and perhaps the *Mount Vernon, Arlington,* and *Potomac* might be included. And on a State level, there is *The Governor,* Philadelphia to Harrisburg.

The Chesapeake & Ohio, which claims close kinship with the Father of his Country, is the only road that has ventured to name a train *George Washington.* The same road also honors *Pere Marquette.* The New York Central and the Boston & Maine each have a *Paul Revere,* while the New

Haven remembers *Nathan Hale.* The Alton, now taken into the Gulf, Mobile & Ohio, has long had an *Abraham Lincoln* and an *Ann Rutledge.* The Pennsylvania naturally has a *William Penn.* And there must be a *Ponce de Leon,* running from the Middle West to Florida, via the New York Central and Southern. The *Dixie Flagler* (C&EI-L&N-NC&StL-ACL-FEC) recalls Florida's great rail and resort promoter. As for Indians, the most famous is the Milwaukee's fleet of *Hiawathas;* the Northwestern has a *Mondamin,* the Norfolk & Western *Pocahontas* and *Powhatan Arrow,* and the Burlington a *Black Hawk.*

As for the tribes, the Missouri Pacific sends the *Aztec Eagle* into Mexico, the Rock Island the *Cherokee Imperial* to Los Angeles and *Choctaw Rocket* to Oklahoma; the Milwaukee has a *Chippewa Hiawatha* and the *Sioux;* the Illinois Central the *Chickasaw,* and with the Georgia Central-ACL-FEC the *Seminole;* the NYC the *Iroquois* and *Tuscarora,* and the Southern Pacific of Mexico *El Yaqui.* New England rails still have many of the old, well-known names like *Narragansett, Kennebec, Penobscot,* and *Katahdin;* and the New Haven, with that deep-seated liking for jaw-wringers, has lately added *Umpechanee, Mahkeenac,* and *Mahawie.*

The Pennsylvania's New York-Washington *Edison* notices the fact that it passes through Menlo Park, where the Wizard's famous early workshop was located. The Frisco has named a St. Louis-Oklahoma City train *Will Rogers.* The Pennsylvania must be about the only one that remembers *Nellie Bly,* once-famous globe-trotter. The Burlington named its early Diesel speeders *Zephyrs;* and among them there is a *Mark Twain Zephyr.* The Fort Worth & Denver has a *Sam Houston Zephyr,* a combination which would have puzzled the craggy old fighter of San Jacinto no end. The Illinois Central, one of whose ports is Paducah, has an *Irvin S. Cobb,* and the New York Central, a *James Whitcomb Riley,* a Cincinnati-Chicago daylight mile-a-minuter, touching Indianapolis, of course.

As you would expect, the New York Central has a *Commodore Vanderbilt* (as fast as the *Century*), as well as a *Commodore II,* and an *Advance Commodore Vanderbilt.* Several of the big flyers have an *Advance* So-and-so, as well as being in several sections themselves. The Lehigh Valley honors *James Wilkes,* pioneer of Wilkes-Barre, and its own chief builder, *Asa Packer.*

In imitation of the former practice of naming big river steamboats, there are so-called streamliners named the *City of Denver,* of *Kansas City, Los Angeles, Miami, Mliwaukee, New Orleans, Portland, St. Louis* and *San Francisco.*

Trains are citizens of many places—*Akronite* (Pa.), *Bostonian* (NH), *Chicagoan* (SFe and NYC), *Cincinnatian* (B&O), *Clevelander* (Pa.), *Detroiter* (NYC), *Houstonian* (MoPac), *Miamian* (Pa-RF&P-ACL-FEC), *Nashuan* (B&M), three *New Yorkers* (DL&W; NH and Sou-Pa), and *Orleanean* (MoPac), *Patersonian* (NYS&W), *Pittsburgher* (Pa.), *San Diegan* (SFe), *Scrantonian* (DL&W), *Shreveporter* (L&A-KCS), *Trojan* (B&M, Boston to Troy), *Tulsan* (SFe) and two *Washingtonians,* taken out of that city by the Pennsy and the B&O respectively. And there is an *Easterner,* a *Westerner* and a *Southerner,* a *New Englander* and several State citizens—a *Coloradoan,* a *Dakotan,* a *Georgian,* a *Kansan,* an *Idahoan,* a *Kentuckian,* a *Marylander,* a *Texan* and several more, even an *Ozarker.* College towns are spotted by the *Dartmouth* (B&M) and two *Varsitys*—CM&StP through Madison, Wis. and CI&L through Bloomington, Ind.

The sidewalks of New York yield several names—*Broadway Limited* (Pa.), the NYC's *Fifth Avenue Special,* the New Haven's *Forty-Second Street, Murray Hill,* and *Pershing Square,* and the Reading-Jersey Central's *Wall Street.* For Pittsburgh there is the *Golden Triangle* (Pa.) and for Chicago the *La Salle Street Limited* (Rock Island).

The time of day plays a part in the naming of many trains. There are both *Day* and *Night Cape Codders* (NH) and a *Day White Mountain* (B&M); several *Daylights,* a few *Morning* and *Afternoon* This and Thats, even a *Morning Daylight* (SP); the New Haven's *Sundown,* the SP's *Sunset Limited,* two *Twilights* (DL&W and NYC), several *Midnights,* and an *Overnighter* (NH-B&M-CV); even a *Night Cap* (NH).

Many train names indicate the area in or to which they operate; as the Southern Pacific's *Acadian, Alamo, Gila, Tomahawk, Argonaut, Cascade,* and *El Dorado,* the Sante Fe's *Chief* and *Super-Chief, Grand Canyon, Golden Gate,* and *El Capitan,* the Great Northern's *Cascadian,* and the Rio Grande's *Prospector.* Wherever there are mountains, there is a *Mountaineer*—four of them. Products give their names to the Reading's *King Coal,* the Frisco's *Black Gold* (Oklahoma oil), the Bangor & Aroostook's *Potatoland Special,* the Pennsy-Southern's *Peach Queen,* the RF&P-SAL's *Cotton Blossom.* In the Mid-West there are the IC's *Hawkeye* and *Land o' Corn* and the CRI&P's *Corn Belt Rocket.* Indiana gets much notice in train-naming, with the CI&L's *Hoosier* and *Tippecanoe* and the NYC's *Sycamore* ("Banks of the Wabash"). The Lehigh Valley's *Maple Leaf* means that it continues on into Canada.

To southward, there are the FEC's *Gulf Stream* and L&N-SAL's *Gulf Wind.* The Columbus & Greenville once had a *Deltan* (Yazoo Delta, of course), but now, sad to say, operates nothing but freight trains. The Gulf, Mobile & Ohio's rash naming of a train *The Rebel* proved highly controversial. The management feebly tried to deny that it referred to one of those gray-coated soldiers of the "Wah" Between the States, but, as might be expected, convinced nobody.

To northward, three official State animals are honored by the *Badger Express* and *Gopher* (both GN) and the *Wolverine* (NYC). In New England there are the Boston & Maine's *Flying Yankee, Skipper,* and *Beachcomber,* the New Haven's *Yankee Clipper, Nutmeg* and *Puritan* and its two Cape Cod trains, *Cranberry* and *Sand Dune.* But how many people know that *Dirigo* (B&M) is the motto of the State of Maine—"I lead," possibly the original version of "As Maine goes, so goes the Nation?" How many know that a *Sooner* (MKT) was one who jumped the gun in the Oklahoma land rush? But few more are aware that Southern Illinois, with its Cairo and Thebes, is nicknamed "Egypt" and thus gives its name to the NYC's *Egyptian.*

Finally, there are the birds—*Blue Bird* (Wabash), *Flamingo* (L&N-CofGa-ACL-FEC), *Flying Crow* (KCS-L&A., because of its directness), *Gull* (B&M-MeCen. into Canada), *Humming Bird* (C&EI-L&N), *Kentucky Cardinal* (IC), *Lark* and *Oakland Lark* (SP), *Meadow Lark* (C&EI), *Nightingale* (C&NW), *Pelican* (Pa-N&W-Sou). Then there are the flock of *Eagles* on the MoPac and its subsidiary, the Texas & Pacific—*Aztec, Colorado, Delta, Missouri River, Valley, Louisiana,* and *Texas Eagles.* Three roads—Southern Pacific, New Haven, and Lackawanna—have *Owls,* and the Boston & Maine paints the lily with a *Night Owl.*

Scores of others must go unnoticed, as well as the nicknames, mostly opprobrious, which many of the less glamorous trains acquired, especially the ones on little draggletail branches of larger roads, where "Dog" with or without adjectives is a favorite epithet for crawlers made up of cast-off equipment of the parent road, and covering only a few miles daily, there and back.

"Short Dog," "Hound Dog," "Bulldog," "Runt," the insults mostly have a certain similarity. Here and there one finds a variation, as in the case of an Illinois Central train which used to, in local option days, run from dry Kentucky to wet Cairo, Illinois, carrying citizens intent on replenishing their stocks of liquor. The train's very apt nickname was "Whiskey Dick," after one of Bret Harte's most comically solemn tosspots. That name nowadays has been transferred to an Illinois Central freight train running out of Louisville, in delicate allusion to the quantities of bourbon produced in that city.

Sleeping and Parlor Car Naming

Pullman cars were not quite the first cars in the railroad world to be named, just like ships. Before or about the same time when Pullman began naming sleepers, Daniel Torrance, one of the several sons-in-law of Commodore Vanderbilt and superintendent of the New York Central for several years, had one of the earliest private cars ever seen in America. It was painted a dark brown with its name, *Shoo Fly,* in a scroll on its side, the "Shoo" in gilt letters, followed by a picture of a fly in red. The Commodore himself announced his presence in the hinterland by the name *Vanderbilt* on his private car. And Adolphus Busch, chief builder of the great St. Louis brewery, rode around in a gorgeous chateau on wheels modestly named *Adolphus.*

George M. Pullman had plenty of competition at the start. He was not the first in the business, though he seems to have been the one who introduced the naming of cars. John Webster Wagner, a former New York Central station agent, remodelled a baggage car into his first sleeper in the late '50s. Commodore Vanderbilt took him up, and for years thereafter he supplied some formidable opposition for Pullman. There were several concerns in the business; Knight sleepers were being used on the Camden & Amboy before the Civil War. Then there were the Gates Company (absorbed by Wagner in 1869), Woodruff, Joy and Flowers.

When Pullman remodelled a Chicago & Alton coach into his first sleeping car in 1859, he gave no thought to the matter of how his cars were to be designated, and just let that one remain under its old Alton number, 9. When he built the first one from rail to roof in 1865, he thought of it as Car A, but called it informally the *Pioneer.* Greatly underestimating the growth of his business, he began lettering his cars, A, B, C, but found that he would soon be down to Z, with nowhere else to go, and so turned to numbers. But this interfered with the railroads' coach numbers, so he was driven to using names.

A committee of officials of his company was given the task, and with the exception of a few classical and literary words, the early sleepers nearly all bore geographical names, drawn mostly from the area in which the cars on each large system operated. When five sleepers were completed in 1866 for what was soon to be the Chicago, Burlington & Quincy, they went far afield and chose *Atlantic, Pacific, Aurora,*

By Alvin F. Harlow. A compilation from the Pullman Company's lists and other sources.

Omaha and *City of Chicago*. The influence of steamboat naming is seen in that "City of."

It was firmly believed in America during the first half century of sleeping cars—and some people believe it yet—that Mr. Pullman's daughter Florence—later Mrs. Frank O. Lowden—named all the cars; that she began as a small girl, receiving a dollar per name from her father, which rose in popular report to $100, $500, $1,000, the climax of the legend being reached when she was placed on a flat salary of $20,000 a year. The truth of the matter is that she never named a car.

It was decided at the very start that no name should ever appear on more than one car—another example of underestimation of the magnitude of the task in the future. This was faithfully carried out for decades and has resulted in some weird car-naming, but in recent years, the rule has on a few occasions been relaxed.

It was not long before the Woodruff Company was absorbed, but there remained two other important ones, Wagner and Mann. Wagner introduced the first two parlor cars, *Catskill* and *Highlander*—each including three bedrooms, too—on the New York Central in 1868, and Pullman quickly took it up. He was early seized with the idea of building cars that would both sleep and feed their passengers; hotel cars, he called them. His first one, the *President,* put in service between Detroit and Buffalo in 1866, was a section sleeper 75-feet long with a small kitchen in one end, from which a chef and two porter-waiters dispensed hot meals on folding tables set in the section after the berths had been stowed for the day. The clashes that might have been expected between persons in the same section who wanted early breakfast and those who preferred to sleep late did not seem great deterrents to their popularity, for Pullman promptly built two more, *Western World* and *Viceroy*. When the *Western World* made its first trip eastward through Buffalo and Albany to New York, an observer at Albany said it had a wine-cellar, which might have been true. Following these, the *City of Boston* and *City of New York* were built, surpassing all others in elegance, costing, it was reported, more than $30,000 apiece.

Two more hotel cars, *Arlington* and *Revere,* were built for the Boston Board of Trade's excursion from Boston to San Francisco in 1870, and thereafter the production of such vehicles slowed a bit. The first dining car—Pullman built—appeared on the Chicago & Alton in 1868, and of course was named *Delmonico,* that being the *ne plus ultra* in restaurants in the American mind of those days.

Europe was introduced to luxury cars by Americans. Pullman had begun operating sleeping and parlor cars in England by 1873, and in that same year the Mann Boudoir Palace Car Company—the creation of Col. W. D. Mann, publisher of the Mobile (Ala.) *Register,* a curious ambidexterity—introduced the European continent to sleepers with a line between Vienna and Munich, and elsewhere soon thereafter. The Mann cars were divided transversely into "boudoirs," each entered directly from the sides, and connected by private doors to which only the porter carried the key. Supposed to be the ultimate in silken elegance, those in America had names such as *Adelina Patti, Marie Antoinette* and *Fontainebleau.*

A British tourist of 1872 was greatly impressed by our parlor cars. Said he, "By paying an extra dollar for about every 200 miles, you can have a seat in a luxurious saloon, with sofas, armchairs, mirrors and washing rooms—and the inevitable spittoons." [1]

---

[1] Julius George Medley, *An Autumn Tour in the United States and Canada* (London, 1873), pp. 70–71.

It is noticeable that Indian names predominated in the early sleeper naming, even more so than in locomotive names, though more musical and attractive ones were usually chosen. John Buchan, Lord Tweedsmuir, found "names like symphonies" among our American Indian place names. An old-timer remembers that in the 1880s, fully four-fifths of the sleepers patrolling the Louisville & Nashville between Cincinnati, Louisville, Memphis and New Orleans bore Southern Indian names, though they were not all from the L&N system; some were in neighboring States—*Tullahoma, Tallapoosa, Tallahassee, Tuscumbia, Tuscaloosa, Tuskegee, Etowah, Muscogee, Watauga, Wetumpka, Pontotoc, Oconee, Altamaha, Congaree, Aucilla.* There were very few Caucasian names.

When the Pennsylvania Limited (New York-Chicago) became the first all-Pullman train in 1887, it strove for global implications with its specially-built sleepers named *Germany, England, France, Italy, China, Spain,* etc. As early as the late '80s a drift away from geography was seen in certain quarters in such names as *Morning Star, Evening Star, Lone Star, Twilight, Olive Branch, Wild Rose* and *Monte Cristo.* The Pennsylvania stuck to place names until its supply began to run low, as proven when it christened a sleeper *Gap,* for a little town on its main line. Of course Pullman supplied and owned the cars, but let the railroads where they ran have a voice in the naming.

The Union Pacific-Central Pacific combination led all others in 1888 with its all-Pullman vestibuled *Golden Gate Special* to the West Coast, which boasted such luxuries as a library, barber-shop and bath. The first vestibules were narrower than those of today, only slightly wider than the end doors of the cars.

Hotel cars, though fewer, continued into the '90s, when they were apt to be named for famous hostelries, such as *St. Nicholas* and *Gilsey.* Some dining cars were named for noted chefs—*Savarin, Aberlin, Valentin.* In the latter decades of the century, private cars, intended to serve as rolling homes for twelve to eighteen vacationing Fortunati or perhaps a famous stage star with his or her select company, or maybe just one eminentissimo traveling in lonely, undisturbed state, with a colored staff to gratify every wish, were proffered by both Pullman and Wagner. Their names hinted at carefree roaming in fields of asphodel—*Arcadia, Utopia, Riviera* in earlier years, and later on *Wanderer, Traveler, Idler, Idlewild, Newport,* and French and English light opera names—*Mascotte* (which introduced a word into the English language), *Olivette,* and *Iolanthe.* Pullman also had cars, *Izaak Walton* and *Davy Crockett,* for hunting and fishing parties, with kennels for dogs and racks for guns and chefs especially skilled in broiling fish and game.

The Mann Boudoir Car Company was taken over by Pullman in 1889, but its territory was limited, and there were not a great many duplicates of Pullman names on its cars. But when the Wagner Company was absorbed in 1899, no less than 300 of its car names, mostly geographical, were duplications of those on Pullman cars. Something had to be done, and done quickly. Richmond Dean, then a vice-president in charge of nomenclature, had a friend in the person of the City Librarian of Chicago, and to him Mr. Dean turned for first aid. The librarian consented to admit a squad of researchers from the Pullman offices to the library at night; and so into the small hours they dug deep into ancient history and the classics, coming up with words, some of which twisted the tongues of travelers and porters for long afterward—*Theocritus, Hyperion, Demosthenes, Diogenes, Circe, Archimedes, Beli-*

sarius, Hesiod, Antiphon, Berosus, Hippocrates, Simonides are a few samples.

Then, towards the end of the century, changes began to appear in the picture. The sections, upper and lower, began to be rearranged, with a drawing room or two at the end of the car, and later, a little lounge. New types of sleeping quarters began to be devised—bedrooms, roomettes, compartments—and steadily they began mixing these with sections in every way imaginable, often with bars and buffets thrown in. Some cars are predominantly lounge or parlor cars, but with one, two or three sleeping rooms ingeniously shoe-horned in somewhere, perhaps an eating and drinking place, too.

These different varieties of cars, it seemed to the authorities, called for categorical names, so that the type of car might be identified at a glance by the name. "Park" and "Star" were two of the earliest lists, 25 or 30 of each—*Park Lane, Park Glade, Park Vista, Park Valley, Star Beam, Star Island, Star Cluster, Star View,* and for some unknown reason, *Star Grass* and *Star Finch* (both New York Central). These were the old-fashioned 14-section sleepers. Then came "Red" for 12 sections and a drawing room; *Red Bay, Red Bird, Red Jacket, Red Maple,* and so on until the supply ran low, when they came down to *Red Gravel.* Some fifty more of the same design were put under "New," where the field is boundless between *New Acton* and *New York University.*

There are but few 16-section sleepers left, but one class particularly interests us, in view of the tenacity with which both Pullman and the railroads since they began specifying car design hold to the theory that practically nobody is six feet tall or over. There are just twelve of the section-sleepers of which the Pullman list informs us, "Berths on sections 1 and 2 are 6 feet, 8 inches long"; only a dozen in all the land—all in the West, where men tend to grow taller, we suppose; *Silver Aspen, Silver Skate, Silver Maple, Silver Poplar,* etc., all on the Rio Grande, Burlington and Western Pacific.

The largest class of all has 12 sections and one drawing room. And this includes the "Mcs"—247 of them from *McAdam* to *McZena,* if there ever was such a word. They are all here, even the rugged *McElligott, McGlashens, McJunkin, McSpadden* and *McCorkle,* and some you never heard of—*McClammy, McAra, McLoon, McSwynes, McTwiggan.* The "Easts," from *East Akron* to *East Youngstown,* supply 73 more of the same diagram. The "Lakes," from *Lake Ainslie,* to *Lake Zurich,* have a slightly different plan and number nearly 250. The "Glens" are another list of 130, and there is even a series of 58 "Littles," the 14-section kind, from *Little Bear* to *Little Vine.* But it is under "Villa" that one encounters some of the most precious names. Here among the *Villas* are *Artistic, Beautiful, Charming, Cheer, Comfort, Enchanting, Ideal, Palatial, Peerless, Real, Regal,* and *Superb.* The 60 or more "Imperials" gave the godfathers quite a tussle, too. *Imperial Crown* and *Imperial Domain* weren't bad, but *Imperial Brink, Imperial Carriage, Imperial Chamber* and *Imperial Empire* make one wonder whether the strain hadn't proven too much for the official brains.

There are yet other groups—the "Regals" for example—all Santa Fe; the 52 "Points," from *Point Abbage* to *Point Vincente;* the 50 "Pacifics", every one owned by Union Pacific; the "Oaks," the "Firs," the "Pines," the "Oranges," the 56 "Forts" (mostly 8 sections and lounge); the 95 "Clovers" (8 sections, 5 double bedrooms), including such gems as *Clover Gloss* and *Clover Gully;* the 85 "Cascades," where one finds *Cascade Elf, Cascade Faun, Cascade Den, Cascade Roar, Cascade*

Spirit and *Cascade Whisper;* the "Camps," the "Capes," the "Capitols" and several other groups.

And here it is time to explain that in 1941, fifty-seven major railroads took over all the newer, lightweight cars being manufactured by Pullman, leaving the older type (still a very respectable minority) remaining in Pullman ownership. The roads since then have done more naming of their own, though almost always consulting Pullman, and leaving the cars to Pullman for operation and service. Until July 1, 1947, the Pullman Company continued both to build and to operate cars. On that date, after years of hammering by the Government in an anti-trust suit, a separation of functions was forced, and since then, cars have been built by one Pullman company and operated by another.

The International-Great Northern, touching the Rio Grande and being in effect a continuation of a Mexican railroad, has a Mexican touch with its *Rio Grijalva, Rio Panuco, Rio Guayalejo,* and *Rio Papaloapan;* not only these but add that Mexican mountain *Ixtaccihuatl,* which probably no passenger from the States ever tries to pronounce. For that matter, the I-GN's mother company, MoPac, has a *Popocatepetl,* and probably never warns passengers that it should be accented on the fourth syllable.

The Pennsylvania was early in seizing upon the names of Revolutionary patriots and Signers of the Declaration for parlor cars on its *Congressional Limited—Gouverneur Morris, Benjamin Franklin, Thomas Jefferson, Caesar Rodney, Charles Carroll, Richard Henry Lee, Roger Sherman,* and *John Hancock* were some of them. The *Alexander Hamilton* has a distinctive design—12 parlor seats, 16 lounge seats, 8 *sun room* seats, one drawing room and buffet.

Hundreds of cars of all types have been named for notables and near-notables in every department of political, military, social, professional, industrial, railroad and other type of business life in America—and a few in the cultural. Some of the honorees are still living. Here you may find *Roger Williams, Thomas Paine, Thomas Hart Benton, Daniel Boone, Salmon P. Chase, John Hunt Morgan, Joel Chandler Harris, George Westinghouse, Walter Reed, James D. Eads, Roger B. Taney, Admiral Dewey, Samuel Morse* (Pa.), minus the initials, for the Pennsy doesn't like initials, though it yielded slightly in the cases of *Cyrus H. K. Curtis* and *Cyrus H. McCormick.* Down South, initials don't bother folk at all; there's *L. L. Shreve* (L&N), *P. G. T. Beauregard* (Frisco), and *L. Q. C. Lamar* (Southern) for examples: whereas the Pennsylvania spreads the names of its past presidents, *William Chamberlain Patterson, Alexander Johnston Cassatt,* and *William Wallace Atterbury,* along the sides of its cars in full without even condensing the lettering. There is a pleasantly old-South, small-town touch in the Gulf, Mobile & Ohio's *Judge Milton Brown.* Foreigners are not barred; there are *Marco Polo, Christopher Columbus, George Stephenson, Henry Bessemer, Alfred Nobel, Roentgen,* and several authors and composers.

The Chesapeake & Ohio, claiming descent from George Washington's canal project by which he hoped to connect Virginia with the Ohio Valley, has gone in delightfully for early American history, laying stress on anything connected with Washington—*American Revolution* (there are more than 60 "Americans," most of them owned by UP) *Spirit of '76, Valley Forge, First Citizen, Commander-in-Chief, Pohick Church* (attended by the First President), *Tobias Lear* (his secretary), *Lord Fairfax* (his early employer), some of his comrades-in-arms, *Marquis Lafayette, Count de Rochambeau, Baron von Steuben,* even a gallant enemy, *Lord Cornwallis. Brother Jonathan* is here, too, and *Pierre l'Enfant,* who designed the city of Washington, and *Jack Jouett,* who made that hell-for-leather ride to warn Thomas Jefferson that Tarleton and his cavalry were coming with intent to capture him. They have paid much attention to pioneer Kentucky, too; *Isaac Shelby, Simon Kenton, James Harrod, Kentucky Home, Anne Bailey,* who, when her husband was killed in the Point Pleasant battle with the Indians (1774), donned male attire and became a valued scout and messenger; and most humble of all, *Ann McGinty,* who brought the first spinning wheel into the Kentucky wilderness, and spun and wove (on a loom built by her husband) the first linen in Kentucky, from the lint of nettles, and the first linsey-woolsey cloth, from this nettle-lint and buffalo wool.

The C&O's restaurant cars are named for famous old taverns in the Washington country—*Michie's Tavern,* built by Patrick Henry's father; *Gadsby's Tavern* in Washington and *Union Tavern* in Georgetown—whose guest lists included all the early Presidents, statesmen and diplomats, and half a dozen others.

The L&N, in 1937 took a literary turn, and sponsored cars named *James Lane Allen, John James Audubon, Stephen Collins Foster, Sidney Lanier, Theodore O'Hara* (author of "The Bivouac of the Dead"), and *Sam Davis* (the Confederate Nathan Hale).

Counties of their traversed States are honored by ACL, Southern, N&W, Pennsylvania, and others. The Illinois Central, in addition to local place names, honored its territory with *King Coal, King Cotton, Sugarland, Timberland, Pelican State* and finally went chichi with *Land o' Strawberries.* The NYC's room-lounge-observation cars on streamliners are named for streams or islands—*Bedloe's Island, Bonnie Brook, Singing Brook, Rippling Stream, Crystal Stream, Manhattan Island, Thousand Islands.* The Pennsylvania's room-lounge, observation types run to "Views"—*Skyline View, Metropolitan View, Federal View, Washington View.* For room-bar-lounge facilities, it has 17 "Colonials."

The Great Northern, publicizing the little-known fact that we have glaciers in this country, has chosen most of its names from the rugged geography of its territory, stressing glaciers, rivers and mountain passes—*Big Horn Pass, Bad Axe River, Blackfoot Glacier, Bois de Sioux River, Chumstick River, Firebrand Pass, Gunsight Pass, Hanging Glacier, Kintla Glacier, Lewis and Clark Pass,* and a few dozen more. The Santa Fe has an almost interminable list of those weird southwestern Indian names—*Betahtakin, Biltabito, Seboyeta, Hualpai, Jadito, Otowi, Kaibito, Moencopi, Nankoweap, Puye, Salahkai, Saydatoh, Tsankawi, Chimayo*—and with these we have scarcely made a start on the list. The Rock Island notices its mountain area with *Grand Mesa* and *Garden of the Gods.* The Southern Pacific collaborates with the UP and Northwestern in those great Chicago-to-Coast streamliners, on some of which—an unusual feature—are pairs of cars, articulated units—*Fisherman's Wharf* and *Golden Gate Park, Seal Rocks* and *Union Square, Arroyo Seco* and *Beverly Hills, Santa Monica* and *San Fernando, Cache la Poudre* and *Ogalalla* and others. Pullman has *Bear Flag* and *California Republic* in a unit. CB&Q has *Silver Arrow* and *Silver Sides, Silver Screen* and *Silver Skates,* etc.

Oddities are numerous. *Temperance* (Pullman) and *Courageous* (Penna) startle us only slightly, but we are floored by the New Haven's *Game Cock,* the IC's *Petroleum,* Pullman's *Tie Binders* and *Wastrel,* UP's *Cinema* and Seaboard's *Weeper's Tower*—one of several "Towers" on that road. GM&O's *Show Me* is of course a reference to that road's trackage in Missouri. But we cannot guess whether B&O's *Commoner* is a wistful backward glance at William J. Bryan or a reminder that anyone may ride on a Pullman—if he has the price, of course. The New Haven, on the other hand, comes right out frankly and names a car *Wall Street*. Supposing, on a broiling hot day, you looked forward to a cool seat in a parlor car, would you be daunted at discovering that the car is the *Sally Ann Furnace*? Yet that is the name the Pennsylvania has given to one.

Who is the *Sovereign of the Seas* (NH)—a nation or a ship? The word "Rose" seems to drive car-christeners into a species of ecstasy. *Sunburst Rose* (SP), *Sunstar Rose* (N&W), and *Crusader Rose* (GN) are somewhat wild-eyed, but Pullman goes off the deep end with *Radiance Rose* and *Gorgeous Rose*.

On the positive side, it is pleasant to find the Pennsylvania spelling that graceful old Welsh feminine name *Gwladys* correctly, though it may excite the wonder of some passengers.

And could there be a prettier, more fitting name for a sleeping car than the New Haven's *Nightfall*—with the same road's *Nightvale* and the Pennsylvania's *Nocturne* closely following—and the B&O's *Night Watch* and the NYC's *Night Sky*? There is magic in the word "night."

Freight Train Names and Nicknames

It is difficult to discover when the first formal naming of freight trains took place, but the nicknaming of them by employes began long before. It is often difficult to distinguish official names from nicknames—both taken from the vernacular. Two Pennsylvania trains consisting of empties returning to Chicago and St. Louis used to be the Home Run and the Refiller. Man o' War and Thoroughbred carried live stock.

The Pennsy has grown more humorous in its old age. In midsummer, 1953, it announced a freight train serving the Southwest, to be known as the Texas-Oklahoma-Missouri-Kansas-Arkansas-Traveler, or to boil it down to the initials, the TOMKAT. (The Norfolk & Western has a Tom Cat, too, properly spelled, as well as a Catbird.)

Speed is promised by many train names; Rockets, Clippers, Cannon Balls and Bullets are numerous, as well as Hot Shots and Red Balls, both in railroad lingo promising velocity. These names are variously modified; as Hoosier Hotshot (NYC), Silver Bullet (L&N), Chicago-Colorado Redball (Rock Island), etc. And the CRI&P-SP have some presumably super-fast Gold Balls; maybe they even run on gold ball-bearings. And there is a Speed Witch on the New Haven. Of course in times like these, there would have to be a couple of Flying Saucers (Erie and Wabash), probably not named in the front office.

The nicknames bestowed by crews and yardmen are almost invariably breezy. Sometimes a nickname such as Whammy just springs from some chap's brain for no particular reason,

---

By Alvin F. Harlow. A compilation from *Names and Nicknames of Freight Trains, Operated on the Railroads of the United States and Canada*, pp. 1–22. Washington, D.C.: Association of American Railroads, February, 1952. With additions from other sources.

and sticks. Some others sound just as nonsensical but have a real background. The Central of New Jersey has two which go far back into the past when freight schedules were very uncertain, indeed. "Maybe" was christened when the crews used to muse, "Maybe we'll get there in time to start back on schedule, and maybe we won't." Grab, running from Allentown to Philipsburg, meant that it grabbed any business it could from rivals by hook or crook. It is related that once a prominent Boston undertaker gave a rush order to "Hatter's Town," Danbury, for a whole new outfit of plug hats for himself and his staff, and when they came in good time, he gave the discarded ones to the crew of the New Haven fast freight which made the delivery. Some old-timers swear that the crew wore those toppers for long afterwards, though we cannot imagine a brakeman on top of a train in full cry wearing one with any degree of success. Anyhow, that train was called The Silk Hat for a long time, though the name has now passed away.

Sometimes it is next to impossible to learn just how a nickname began. The Baltimore & Ohio has two freights nicknamed Dirty Shirt, and one would expect to find the origin of such a colorful tag on the tip of somebody's tongue. But both go back a long way into the past, and the reason for neither joking name is quite clear now. The train in Ohio-Indiana so named is believed to have been christened by two assistant trainmasters who had to ride it frequently, to the detriment of their linen. The one which ambles down the main line below Cumberland has the job of picking up and taking care of cars set out by other trains because of hot boxes or other defects, and also does some odds and ends of local business. In other words, says an official theorist, it does a lot of dirty work, and so was called Dirty Shirt.

What the train carries is frequently indicated by its name or nickname. Banana Specials come out of the ports of Baltimore and Weehawken, through which much of our upper Eastern supply of that fruit comes; The Apple (IC) out of an orchard country around Albert Lea, Minn.; two Blue Gooses from down Florida way (GA and G&F); two Packers (C&EI out of Chicago and C&NW out of Council Bluffs); Coal Digger (B&O); several Paper Trains on Canadian roads bringing newsprint to the U. S.; Pork Chops (IC meat train out of Council Bluffs); The Textiler (SAL); Camel Special (we need not further identify the product which this N&W train takes out of Winston-Salem); Bean Train (Southern) and Bean Extra (ACL) seem to mean Florida vegetables; Spark Plug (Southern, carrying motor parts, Cincinnati to Atlanta); Cabbage Cutter and Fruit Block (Western Pacific out of the central California valley); Gas Wagon (PRR out of Detroit). The Northwestern has a cereal train out of Cedar Rapids known to the personnel as Mush. When the Southern announced its Textile Special from Southern cotton mills to New York, the operatives promptly renamed it Boll Weevil.

Short runs are almost invariably nicknamed by the men, frequently Dog, Short Dog, Bull Dog, etc. Some others are Peanut Run (B&O, Akron-Norwalk, O.), Peanut Pusher (Elgin, Joliet & Eastern, Chicago-Gary), Pea Vine (ACL, Palatka-Rochelle, Fla.), Rabbit Run (B&O, Flora-Shattuc, Ill.), Bogey (SAL, Jesup-Folkston, Ga.), and Waukegan Turn-around (C&NW, Waukegan, Ill.-Butler, Wis.). Several which operate in big-city environs are frivolously entitled Candy Run (B&O, Pittsburgh), two Ping Pongs (D&RGW, Salt Lake City and NYNH&H, Boston), Silk Train and Dive Bomber (B&O, Baltimore). The Mule on the IC between Jackson and Canton, Miss., does only 23 miles, but with much switching, and so is likened to the slow-moving but hard-working Southern farm indispensable.

Fanciful names intrigue us—the N&W's Nomad and Zipper, the C&NW's Rob Roy, Pennsylvania's Cock o' the Walk, ACL's Hobo, the Rutland's Whippet. There are a Tarheel (SAL), a Jackpot (Southern), an Alaga (SAL, Alabama-Georgia), three Orioles, two Gophers (in and out of Minnesota, of course), a Badger (in Wisconsin), two Hawkeyes (Iowa), three Westerners—one of them, believe it or not, on the Boston & Maine. The Toledo, Peoria & Western, which ends at the Mississippi River, emphasizes its far Westernness with The Plainsman and The Prairie Marksman. The C&NW also likes "North" in its train names—North Shore, Northerner, Northland, Northwest. There are a North Star (B&M), North Wind (BAR), two Northwest Specials (CRI&P and SP), and two North Coasts (SP, Los Angeles to Portland, and AT&SF-WP-GN, Los Angeles to Seattle).

When the New York Central decided to put on a mile-a-minute freight called The Pacemaker, mounted on passenger car trucks for smoother riding, between New York and Buffalo, the cars were specially manufactured for it, but in the meantime a preliminary Pacemaker was assembled out of all the old baggage cars that could be scraped together. All blackened with soot, it was promptly christened Blackbird by the crews. But when the new train was assembled, 75 to 80 cars all exactly alike, the upper half painted a delicate rose, the lower half gray, it was too beautiful to be nicknamed.

Few freight trains are named for persons, but for notable exceptions, we have to go to the CI&L. For a road that is not top-ranking in mileage, the Monon is remarkable for its number of formally named trains, all rigidly Indianan. They include James Brooks, founder and first president of the road, and the only railroad official in history so honored; Ben Harrison, the only National President on the Nation-wide list, John Purdue, George Ade, Lew Wallace and his most famous novel, Ben Hur, Ike Elston, Abe Martin, the beloved backwoods epigrammatist, and finally, a Mononeer and a Mononette. Mae West and Sally Rand on the Illinois Central are supposed to have been so named because their runs are full of curves. The Milwaukee's Stump Dodger, which traverses a Wisconsin byway, was so named for the same reason. It is alleged that the track practically encircles one house, all four sides of which can be seen from a train at one time and another.

The men on two systems, the New York Central and Illinois Central, have gone in more enthusiastically for nicknames than any others. Freight trains are known at headquarters by numbers or symbols, the latter being some mysterious combination of letters and figures, such as CC2, TN6, BFNY4 or CPSS. Sometimes the symbols are evolved from the name of the train, such as the St. Louis Southwestern's IV for its Imperial Valley Block, and the Western Pacific's NCX for its Northern California Express; but more frequently, waggish nicknames are concocted around the switch shanties and railroad YMCAs from the train symbols. On the NYC, LS6 has been interpreted as Lamb Special, LS5 as Long Suffering, BH2 as Big Horse, DZV4 as Dizzy, while DG19 has become The Dagger. On the Illinois Central CN1 stands for Cousin Nelly, SJ1 is either Smoky Joe or Son John, BC4 is Bear Cat, and SM3 becomes Smoky Mountain, though its East St. Louis-Memphis run is nowhere near the mountains. Finally, the initials of the Milwaukee's South Omaha Stock Express are loosely translated as Socks.

On the other hand, the initials of termini may on occasion become the

name of a train; as the Lehigh Valley-Reading's Buffalo-Philadelphia speeder known as Bee Pee Two.

The list goes on and on—Whiskey Dick for an IC train out of Louisville, where so much bourbon is made; Bull Run (IC) so named by a colored brakeman when it was assigned the chore of gathering up livestock at way points; the St. Louis Blues (NYC), headed from central New York to St. Louis. The New Deal (IC) named in 1937 at the height of the Roosevelt era has long since lost its distinction, and is now known as mere humdrum MS1. The C&NW's Manifest Express, a name too stiff and colorless for the boys who ran it, was soon retabbed Madame X, though how they became acquainted with that old French play one doesn't know.

For more than forty years there has been a local train on the IC in Mississippi called The Ripper. They tell of a conductor, Gaerig, who was running between Gwin, Miss., and Memphis. The through freight made the run several hours quicker than the local, though the crews' pay at that time was the same for both. Gaerig had somehow drawn the local job several times in succession when he came into the dispatcher's office at Gwin one day and said, sarcastically, "I'm ready for that Rip Track Special." This was an allusion to the fact that cars headed for the "rip" or repair track had to be moved slowly because of their mechanical defects. The quip was abbreviated to The Ripper, and so the train has been called for nearly half a century.

Another name equally as old for a train on the IC down there in the Faulkner country is High Brown. An old-timer tells how train 172 from Grenada to Memphis came to be so called:

"Mississippi highways were in their infancy in 1916–17 and automobiles were few. Consequently, the Mississippi Negro depended upon rail transportation to carry him to Memphis and the glamorous Beale Street.

"[Engineer] Sid Law was the hero of the Negro cotton pickers, and they came from miles around to ride his train. He had his own assigned engine and whistle, and they all knew the way he blew that whistle. There is many a 30-year-old Negro in Mississippi today named Sid in honor of Sid Law. There would always be a large number of non-paying passengers on No. 172 when it arrived in Memphis, ranging in age from 14 or 15 to 60 or 70. They never disturbed anything on the train. They just went for the ride.

"Due to the regularity of these unpaid passengers, who on Saturday would almost cover the top of the train, I started to call No. 172 the 'High Brown.' Yardmaster Spencer liked the name, and then others started using it. When the merchandise run came off, the name was transferred to the local freight in the same district. To this day it has kept the name, although it lost its passenger load many years ago." [1]

Another of those Mississippi freight train nicknames dates back to the somewhat legendary time when there is said to have been a little railroad, mostly for logging, down there named the Yazoo Delta. It had yellow cars, and one version even has it that the locomotives were yellow, too. One story is that an IC yardmaster, making up a train one day, had to take over some cars from that road, and said, "All right, now let's get this Yellow Dog moving," and unintentionally so named his own train. But the favorite version is that of the Negro lounging on a baggage truck who was asked by a stranger what the initials, "Y.D.,"

---

[1] E. M. Carr, *Illinois Central Magazine* (December, 1947), pp. 2, 3.

painted on one of the little line's cars near by meant.

"I don't know, boss," was the reply, "unless it means Yellow Dog. It sure does take its time goin' places." The name stuck and was inherited by the IC local running today from Tutwiler to Yazoo City.

Railroad Names and Nicknames

In the beginning days, railroads were short, and their names were correspondingly modest or realistic—Boston & Lowell, Boston & Worcester, Boston & Providence, Mohawk & Hudson, Philadelphia & Columbia, Camden & Amboy, South Carolina—just the cities or areas actually reached by them. The sole example of bombast, as the level heads regarded it, was that of those reckless Baltimoreans who spoke of their little pair of rails as the Baltimore & Ohio. Ohio, indeed! said the wise ones. Well, don't let's hold our breaths until they get there!

When a group of daring Yankees planned a railroad from Worcester to Albany, actually traversing the Berkshire Hills into an alien land of Dutchmen and Erie canalers, they themselves regarded it as such a far-flung, antipodean venture that they named it the Western Railroad. Sober-minded Bostonians shook their heads over the idea, and Captain Basil Hall, a British tourist, considered it "madness." As every one knows, it, with the Boston & Worcester, is now the Boston & Albany line of the New York Central.

But with another decade of population movement westward, ambitions and imaginations expanded. Railroad projects began to swagger a bit, and the words "and Western" began to be tacked onto their names; New York, Lake Erie & Western, Delaware, Lackawanna & Western, New York, Ontario & Western, Norfolk & Western, and as the rails surged into the middle West, a smaller Lake Erie & Western, a Toledo, Peoria & Western, Indiana, Bloomington & Western, Indianapolis, Decatur & Western and others followed. "Northwestern" became a good word, too—Chicago & Northwestern, St. Louis, Keokuk & Northwestern, Minnesota & Northwestern, etc. But imaginations had already leaped far beyond, even to the surf booming on the California and Oregon coasts, and the word "Pacific" became almost a must. The east-west line which did not call itself Something-or-other Pacific was regarded as over-modest.

The names "Missouri Pacific" and "Northern Pacific" were being bandied about, and the latter even began to be built in the 1850s; as did the Memphis, El Paso & Pacific, mentioned elsewhere, which accomplished only the 42-mile stretch between Marshall, Texas and Shreveport, hundreds of miles distant from anything mentioned in its name, though it might very justly blame war for its failure to do more. But jostling each other in rapid succession came the Kansas Pacific, Union Pacific, Central Pacific, Southern Pacific, Atlantic & Pacific, Northern Pacific (completed), Vicksburg, Shreveport & Pacific, Chicago, Rock Island & Pacific, Wabash, St. Louis & Pacific, Georgia Pacific, Iowa Pacific, Wisconsin, Minnesota & Pacific, Texas & Pacific, and that string of five railroads connecting Cincinnati with New Orleans and Shreveport and operating under one overall corporation with the incredibly clumsy title of Cincin-

---

By Alvin F. Harlow. A compilation from various sources.

nati, New Orleans & Texas Pacific. (Its main line is under lease to the Southern now, while its Meridian-Vicksburg-Shreveport section has passed to the Illinois Central.) Of those named, only one-quarter ever saw the Pacific shore.

And then, in the 20th Century, came the Western Pacific and the Northwestern Pacific; while the Chicago, Milwaukee & St. Paul, when it thrust a line out to Seattle, thought it necessary to add "Pacific" to its name. Meanwhile, small fry which obviously never expected to reach the Pacific used the magic word—Denver, South Park & Pacific, Butte, Anaconda & Pacific, Quanah, Acme & Pacific. And there is at least one whose name trends in the opposite direction—the Oregon Pacific & Eastern, with general offices at an Oregon town with the pleasant, sylvan name of Cottage Grove and extending twenty miles eastward from there.

"Gulf" was another goal really or professedly aimed at but seldom reached. There were and are dozens of roads, mostly little ones with names ending in "and Gulf," but which never saw the Gulf of Mexico. And there are little "Westerns," "Northerns" and "Southerns" by the dozen. It sounds much better to call one's road "Carolina Western" than to name the two little towns, 4½ miles apart, which are its termini—and who can blame them?

"Great" was another word which promoted importance—Alabama Great Southern, International & Great Northern, Chicago Great Western, and finally, James J. Hill's Great Northern, which really lived up to the adjective. There is still a Great Western in Colorado, with a total trackage of 55 miles. There used to be some comic examples of little roads which resembled Aesop's frog in the expansiveness of their names—a finger-length Mobile & Alabama Grand Trunk, for example, and the New York, Texas & Mexico which was hard to find on the map of Texas. There are still a Midland Continental (31.4 miles) in North Dakota and a Philadelphia, Bethlehem & New England, which, so the Book says, runs from Bethlehem to Didier, Pa., 3⅛ miles; in fact, it is just an intra-mural road of the Bethlehem Steel Company.

The public and railroad employes have cooperated in creating nicknames and even in reshaping the corporate names of several roads. As the pace of life in these United States reached higher tension, as people became busier and busier, they found railroad names of three and four words too long and cumbersome to deal with in conversation, and selected in many cases just one word to designate the line. The noticeable tendency was to pick the most colorful, even though sometimes least important word. It was enevitable that the Chicago, Rock Island & Pacific should become just the Rock Island. Chicago is in too many railroad names to be chosen as the significant one, while Rock Island has the color. By the same token, the Chicago & Northwestern became popularly the Northwestern, and the Chicago & Alton just the Alton.

This sort of thing began a century and more ago, when the New Orleans, Opelousas & Great Western was being built westward from New Orleans in the 1850s (it later became Morgan's Louisiana & Texas Railroad and finally the east end of the Southern Pacific). Its clumsy name was presently shortened in public conversation to Opelousas. As that was rather a mushy mouthful, it was eventually turned into "Applesauce."

The New York, Lake Erie & Western was soon being mentioned as the Erie, and is one of the examples of the popular abbreviation which finally became the legal name of the road. Most people of today never heard the older name. The Philadelphia & Reading is another example—informally shortened to Reading for so long that the corporation at length made it just the Reading Company. The Wabash, St. Louis & Pacific, now simply the Wabash, is another. And as a minor example, the Toledo, Ann Arbor & North Michigan, with its key trademark ("the key to North Michigan") became corporately the Ann Arbor. Of course the Carolina, Clinchfield & Ohio was soon whittled down to Clinchfield, and now there is a supervising Clinchfield corporation which operates the C. C. & O. Railroad.

New Haven is not the least important factor in the name of the New York, New Haven & Hartford Railroad; but there is a lilt to it which perhaps touched the popular ear and caused it to be adopted as the common designation of the road.

The St. Louis & San Francisco, which, in the 1870s, really intended to reach San Francisco, but bogged down at Sapulpa, in the Indian Territory, for many years before accumulating a considerable system in the Mississippi valley, was immediately and inevitably tagged with that telescoped nickname "Frisco"—which San Franciscans so fervently wish the rest of the country would forget—and has for decades used it as a trademark.

The Atchison, Topeka & Santa Fe Railroad is known to almost everybody as the Santa Fe; in fact, many people don't know that it has any other name. But the Stock Exchange still prefers to call it Atchison. The Chicago, Milwaukee & St. Paul was for many years popularly the St. Paul; and though in comparatively recent days custom has veered to "Milwaukee," one notices that many of its own people still call it St. Paul. Some still like to call the Chicago, Burlington & Quincy the "Q," though for the generality, it is the Burlington. It was a foregone conclusion that an overwhelming name like Minneapolis, St. Paul & Sault Ste. Marie would have to be shortened, and so it has become the "Soo" Line, the near-French pronunciation of "Sault." Likewise the Central Railroad of New Jersey was bound to be condensed to Jersey Central.

The Chicago & Alton, which was added to the Mobile & Ohio to make up its system, for a long time waved a familiar pennant. In September, 1899, a fine dramatization of Dicken's *Tale of Two Cities* was launched under the name of *The Only Way,* and was a great success throughout the country. The story goes that two officials of the Alton—then at the peak of its glory with its double track and its gorgeous *Alton Limited*—saw the play in Chicago one evening, and as they were leaving the theatre, one said to the other with a smile, "Our road is The Only Way between Chicago and St. Louis."

"That's it!" exclaimed the other, smacking his fist into his hand. "There's our slogan!" And so the Chicago & Alton was The Only Way that day forward.

Other trademarks with more or less significance are the Boston & Maine's Minute Man (French's statue "by the rude bridge that arched the flood" at Concord), the Jersey Central's bust and uplifted arm of the Statue of Liberty, and the Union Pacific's shield, with field and stripes in palpable suggestion of the National flag—all effective, all readily paintable on freight cars, which is essential. The Southern used to have just the letters SR pierced by an arrow; but not satisfied with this, an official during a waiting quarter-hour (probably in an ICC anteroom), is said to have absently doodled the present one—a heavy, angular SR in a circle, with the legend on the surrounding belt, "The Southern Serves the South."

When you hear among some veteran railroaders in Michigan fleering allusions to the New York Central's oval trademark, as "the Goose Egg," you begin to learn that Michigan has never become quite reconciled to the New York Central's taking over of the Michigan Central. In that State, it is still the Michigan Central. Buses and taxis in Detroit take you, not to the New York Central station, but to the Michigan Central. The loyalty is deep-rooted and fervent.

The Chicago & Northwestern trademark displays a circle crossed diagonally by a broad band upon which is the word "North Western," whose fatal flaw is that it rises from the lower left-hand corner to the upper right-hand corner, thus making it, according to the cardinal principle of cartography, trend north*east*ward instead of north*west*ward. But the Northwestern was always a little queer, anyhow—sometimes called "Southpaw," because it is the only major railroad in the country which operates left-handed; on double track, its trains keep to the left instead of to the right. That this is an aping of the English fashion is vigorously and no doubt truly denied; it seems to have begun as an emergency measure on the old Galena and Chicago Union, the germ of the Northwestern.

The initials of some roads spelled out an acrostic nickname. Those of the New York, Pennsylvania & Ohio, the early southwestern arm of the Erie, extending from Salamanca, N. Y., diagonally across Ohio to Cincinnati, were quickly seen to spell Nypan'o—pronounced Nipanó—and so it was popularly known until the Erie made it a real marriage. It took the MK&T much longer to become known as the Katy, and the Kansas City Southern as Casey.

The perfect example of an acrostic nickname is the 92-mile Tennessee, Alabama & Georgia, which became the "Tag," the moment its name was changed from Chattanooga Southern, three or four decades ago.

The initials have played a part in other nicknames, too—the Louisville & Nashville, for example, playfully known as Ellen N., though its publicity myrmidons insist that everybody thinks of it as Old Reliable; and the New York, Susquehanna & Western, from being called the Susquehanna, is now, by the Jersey commuters who give it the major part of its business, called—when they aren't calling it something worse—Susie Q. Then there are some amusing telescopings. The Missouri Pacific, aside from being jokingly referred to as Misery Pacific, is condensed in print to Mopac, while the Southern Pacific (Sunset Route to itself, "Soup" to some of the jesters) is Espee. The Bangor & Aroostook is BAR.

The Pennsylvania, New York Central, Baltimore & Ohio, Southern, Union Pacific and some others have never acquired any real nicknames or diminutives, though some who find Pennsylvania rather a mouthful call it the "Pennsy." Its old Pittsburgh, Cincinnati & St. Louis area was known long ago as the Panhandle, from that slender northern extension of West Virginia which it crossed, and for a time, that name threatened to spread to the entire system, but it never quite did.

There have been some famous nicknames or trade names, often used by the road itself, but now passed away. Once there was a busy system in Ohio and Indiana known as the Bee Line. Among the little neighborhood rails being built here and there in earlier days was one called the Bellefontaine & Indiana, which name was presently shortened to Bellefontaine. But railroad men found that word too long, and so shortened it to B. Line. Quite naturally "B" suggested "Bee" and so Bee Line became an advertising boast of the road's directness. When the Bellefontaine combined in 1868 with others as the Cleveland, Columbus, Cincinnati & Indianapolis, the system was known as the Bee Line for 21 years thereafter, until merged with the Big Four.

The name Big Four was first applied to the Cincinnati, Indianapolis, St. Louis & Chicago Railroad in the early 1880s, though it came nowhere near one of the four, St. Louis. But Melville E. Ingalls, its great promoter, saw to that. He combined it with the Bee Line and half a dozen others in 1889 to form a new, giant Big Four, the Cleveland, Cincinnati, Chicago & St. Louis, which lived up to its name and more. However, it steadily came under the influence of the New York Central, which in 1930 finally took it over. But at a recent date, the bulletin boards at way stations along its lines were still headed C. C. C. & St. L., and in the Indianapolis office building where its offices are located, you might look in vain on the lobby directly for New York Central; but look for Cleveland, Cincinnati, Chicago & St. Louis, and there it was. To the mid-West, it's still the Big Four.

The Cincinnati, New Orleans & Texas Pacific, by virtue of its termini, Cincinnati—"Queen City of the West," and New Orleans, "the Crescent City," was known for many years by the particularly catchy name, Queen and Crescent—which of course disappeared when it passed under Southern Railroad hegemony. Its operatives had another name for it, or rather, for its Cincinnati-Chattanooga section — the Rathole, because of its fifteen tunnels; one of them, under King's Mountain in Kentucky, so long that engine crews were almost suffocated by its supersulphurous coal smoke, while red-hot cinders burned their gauntlets to lace. Eleven of the tunnels have now been eliminated.

Monon, Indiana, is a curious example of an undistinguished little town whose name has long been written prominently in railroad annals. The courageous and vociferous little railroad long known as the Louisville, New Albany & Chicago and in recent years as the Chicago, Indianapolis & Louisville crosses its two lines at that town in a long diagonal, like a pair of scissors, and almost as far back as the memory of man runneth, it has been known, and lustily heard of as the Monon Route.

The Union Pacific still casually uses the term, Overland Route, but doesn't stress it greatly. The St. Louis Southwestern (formerly St. Louis, Arkansas & Texas) once cherished the name Cotton Belt, but has dropped that term in recent years, and uses just a formalized trademark design. The Minneapolis & St. Louis ("Peoria Gateway" in its own mind) once had the head, feet and hands of a little running man almost hidden behind a circle, but he too is gone. The Chicago, St. Paul & Kansas City (now Chicago Great Western) once decided to call itself the Maple Leaf, and placed its three prongs, uniting the three cities named, on the three lobes of such a leaf in advertising; but later on, when it acquired more territory, the design was discarded. The Toledo, St. Louis & Kansas City, whose single line used to amble precariously from Toledo to St. Louis called itself the Clover Leaf, for no discernible reason.

There are many nicknames for lesser roads, often founded on the initials, as noted elsewhere, but some on other reasons or no valid reason—such as "Mud Hen" for the 42-mile Central Indiana. The Trinity and Brazos Valley was nicknamed Boll Weevil for no other reason than that it was built just at the time when that foreign pest began to be all too noticeable in Texas. The Detroit, Toledo & Ironton, when Henry Ford owned it, was quite naturally christened Model T, after the early car which made him wealthy and famous. The Bangor & Aroostook, Maine's noted potato carrier, is the Spud Drag. The Sumpter Valley Railroad in Oregon, built to work out a great timber area, was built by capital predominantly Mormon, and the lumberjacks called it Polygamy Central.

There are many today who wonder why the Pere Marquette Railroad is so named. Its first appellation just after the Civil War, was Flint & Pere Marquette and it connected two small towns thus named, one in eastern Michigan, the other on the shore of Lake Michigan. But presently along came a hustling promoter named Ludington, who practically took over the western terminus, the little hamlet named for Father Marquette, the 17th century Jesuit missionary-explorer, eliminated Marquette's name and substituted his own. The railroad mantained its name, increased its trackage, and when in 1900 it combined with two other lines in a 1700-mile system, as if in defiance of Mr. Ludington, it took the single name, Pere Marquette.

Fun with Initials

Railroad employes and travelers have long enjoyed concocting humorous and often scathing nicknames by misinterpreting the initials of the company. Some are purely whimsical, like the following. (Most of these roads have been welded into larger systems).

Baltimore & Ohio—Beefsteak & Onions

Chicago, Bluffton & Cincinnati—Corned Beef & Cabbage

Cincinnati, Portsmouth & Virginia (Cincinnati extension of Norfolk & Western)—Coat, Pants & Vest

Colorado & Southern—Cough & Snort

Colorado & Wyoming—Carpenter & Walrus

International-Great Northern (Missouri Pacific)—Irishman Going North

Jeffersonville, Madison & Indianapolis (Pennsylvania)—Jerusalem, Mexico & Ireland

Louisville & Nashville—Long & Narrow

Maryland & Pennsylvania—Ma & Pa

New Orleans & Northeastern (Southern)—No Omelettes, No Eggs

Pennsylvania, Poughkeepsie & Boston—Pickles, Pork & Beans L.N.E.

Pittsburgh, Fort Wayne & Chicago (line of Pennsylvania west of Pittsburgh)—Pigs' Feet, Whisky & Cigars.

Toronto, Hamilton & Buffalo—To Hell & Back

West Virginia Central & Pittsburgh—Watch Very Carefully & Proceed

Zanesville & Western—Zealous & Willing

In a few cases the names have apt local significance.

Atchison, Topeka & Santa Fe—Ate Tamales & Spit Fire; also, All Tramps Sent Free

East Tennessee, Virginia & Georgia—Eat Turnips, Vinegar & Greens (applied after the Civil War, when times were hard and food was scarce)

Georgia, Florida & Alabama—Gophers, Frogs & Alligators

Pierre, Rapid City & Northwestern—Plenty Rough Country & No Water

Richmond, Fredericksburg & Potomac—Rich Folks & Pedigrees

Several of the following were palpably cooked up by employes in early days, and some by disgruntled investors.

By Alvin F. Harlow. A compilation from various sources.

Bellaire, Zanesville & Cincinnati—Bent, Zigzag & Crooked

Boston & Maine—Busted & Mined

Cincinnati, Hamilton & Dayton—Cold, Hungry & Dirty

Detroit & Mackinac—Defeated & Maltreated

Dubuque & Dakota—Damned Doubtful

Duluth, South Shore & Atlantic—Damned Small Salaries & Abuse

Georgia & Florida—God-Forgotten

Georgia Southern & Florida—Go Slow & Flag

Houston & Texas Central—Hoboes & Tin Cans; also, Hell on Texas Contractors (meaning that its builders had difficulty in collecting their money)

Lake Shore & Michigan Southern—Large Stations & Miserable Salaries; also, Less Sleep & More Speed

Minneapolis & St. Louis—Midnight & Still Later; also, Maimed & Still Limping

Morris & Essex (Lackawanna)—Methodist & Episcopal (a jeer at the fact that the road had no Sunday operation until 1899)

Nevada-California-Oregon—Narrow, Crooked & Ornery

Travelers and hoboes may have had a hand in devising the last mentioned, and they were certainly responsible for the following.

Buffalo, Rochester & Pittsburgh—Bumpy, Rocky & Peculiar

Carolina & Northwestern—Can't & Never Will

Cincinnati, New Orleans & Texas Pacific (Southern)—Connections No Object, Tickets Please

Delaware & Hudson—Delay & Hesitate

Delaware, Lackawanna & Western—Delay, Linger & Wait

Hoosac Tunnel & Wilmington—Hoot, Toot & Whistle; Hot Tea & Whisky; Hog Tied & Weary (rail fans have had much fun with these)

Houston, East & West Texas—Hell Either Way You Take It

Jamestown, Westfield & Northwestern—Jesus Wept & No Wonder (said to have sprung from the brain of a traveling salesman after one trip over the road)

Lake Erie & Western (Nickel Plate)—Leave Early & Walk

Leavenworth, Kansas & Western—Leave Kansas & Walk

Lehigh & Hudson River—Late & Hungry

Live Oak, Perry & Gulf—Lean Over, Push & Grunt

Missouri & North Arkansas—May Never Arrive

Nevada County Narrow Gauge—Never Come, Never Go

Newburgh, Dutchess & Connecticut—Never Did & Couldn't

New York, Ontario & Western (popularly shortened to Ontario & Western)—Old & Weary

New York, Susquehanna & Western—Now You Sit & Wait

St. Johnsbury & Lake Champlain—St. Jesus & Late Comin'

Stockton Terminal & Eastern—Slow, Tired & Easy

Terre Haute & Peoria—Take Hold & Push

Texas Pacific & Western—Take Your Parcels & Walk

Waco, Beaumont, Trinity & Sabine—Wobblety, Bobblety, Turnover & Stop

And this one must have been dreamed up by the publicity department of the company:

Chicago, Burlington & Quincy—Cheapest, Best & Quickest

Railway Post Office Route Nicknames

. . . The colorful or paradoxical titles and unusual nicknames for [railway post office routes] are amazing in themselves. Actually used officially are such romantic or weird titles as the "George. & Grace." (L&N) in Alabama, with its closed-pouch extension to Graceville, Florida; and the "Pad. & Hick." (NC&StL), from Paducah to Hickman, Kentucky. But the prize one of all was doubtless the officially titled "Thief. & Crook." from Thief River Falls to Crookston, Minnesota (GN), now discontinued. The Cincinnati & St. Louis (B&O) is, of course, dubbed the "Sin & Saint" and the N. Y. & Mauch Chunk (CNJ) "The Chunk" or "The Much Junk." There was a Welch & Jenkinjones (N&W) in West Virginia.

* * * * *

. . . Who but postal clerks could ever have conjured up "The Dreamliner" (Detroit & Grand Rapids), "The Galloping Goose" (Spokane & Coulee City), "The Horny Toad" (Albuquerque & El Paso), "The Leaky Roof" (Kansas City & Memphis), "The Little Windy" (Little Rock & Forth Worth), "The Macaroni" (Houston & Corpus Christi), "The Monkey Wrench" (Pulaski & Mt. Airy, Va-N. C.), "The Old Man's Darling" (Akron & Delaware), and "The Ox Cart" (Knoxville, Cartersville & Atlanta)? Or, "The Pow Wow" (Eugene & Coos Bay), "The Preacher" (St. Louis & Parsons, Kan.), "The Puddle Jumper" (Portland [Ore.] & Seaside), "The Pumpkinvine" (Roanoke & Winston-Salem), "The Poor Boy" (Jacksonville & Tampa), "The Raging Sioux" (Chicago & Sioux City), "The Rickety Bang" (Grand Jct. & Ogden, Utah), "The Scissorbill" (St. Louis & Memphis), "The Pickle Vat" (Texarkana, Arkansas Terminal), "The Mountain Goat" or "Belvidere" (Phillipsburg & Trenton), "The Pedro" (Ogden & Los Angeles), and to cap it all, "The Wooden Axle" (Harriman & Nashville). . . .

. . . The MoPac's Kansas City & Pueblo is called "The Doghouse" (and so are the Philadelphia and Harrisburg, Pennsylvania Terminals). . . .

But utterly fantastic were some nicknames of discontinued lines! . . . We recall Idaho's Ketchum & Shoshone (UP)—"The Ketch & Show," of course; the one-time Elkton & Bridgewater (N&W), formerly CWRy, Va., and thus "Crooked & Weedy"—now a C.P.; the horrifying "Fish & Dirty Feet" (the G&P's old Salmon and Blackfoot, Ida.); the "Tin Can" (Waco & Stamford, Texas—MKT); the "Underbrush Limited" in Michigan (Frankfort & Toledo, AARy), and "The Two Brothers" (Harry & Frank—the Pennsylvania's Harrington, Del., & Franklin City, Va., just discontinued). Then there were "The Sowbelly," an old Kansas City routing; and "The Kite," a loop-like, kite-shaped former local run on the Albuquerque & Los Angeles (Santa Fe)—the name still clings to the remaining part. At least nine lines out of New York, St. Louis, Council Bluffs, San Francisco, and elsewhere are called "The Valley." . . .

From *Mail by Rail*, The Story of the Postal Transportation Service, by Bryant Alden Long, with William Jefferson Dennis, pp. 181, 183–184. Copyright, 1951, by Simmons-Boardman Publishing Corporation. New York.

The Tangle of Gages

The very first little railroads created in Massachusetts bought their locomotives from the Stephensons in England; and they, having no orders to the contrary, built them of the same width as their own gage, 4 feet 8½ inches, and thereby unfortunately set the pattern of all the railroads on our continent to this day. The legend that this was the exact width of the Roman Imperial chariot wheel-tread will probably persist to the end of time, like that other belief that General Forrest said, "Git thar fustest with the mostest."

There was no premonition in those days that the whole country would eventually be interlaced, tied together by a network of rail lines, which ought all to be of the same width. Transportation thinking was political, provincial, even parochial. By way of demonstrating that Americans were freemen, not bound by anybody else's gage or rule, nearly everybody chose his own width of track; in fact, it was even thought to be advantageous to differ from neighboring railroads in gage, for then the other fellow couldn't sneak over into your territory and steal some of your business.

Just why the Mohawk & Hudson chose to make its gage 4′ 9″, only half an inch wider than the Massachusetts roads, we cannot understand now, but it thereby led astray a couple of other little roads in the vicinity. When the Western came in from Boston with its "standard," as we now call it, width of 4′ 8½″, that was considered to be practically the same thing. But when the Delaware & Hudson came tooling up from Pennsylvania with what it mystifyingly called "Standard gauge; 6 foot and 4 foot, 3 inches" (the latter on its gravity lines around Scranton and Honesdale, the former a copy of its connection, the Erie), there was a pretty *impasse* at Albany. Fortunately, that city did not react as Erie, Pa., did [see Erie Gage War], and it was not many years before the matter was adjusted, everybody in the vicinity taking to the standard gage.

But to southward there was a worse mixup. Peter Cooper built his B. & O. locomotive Tom Thumb 4′ 6″ wide. The Philadelphia & Columbia, the germ of the Pennsylvania, chose 4′ 9″ while directly across the Delaware River the Camden & Amboy built to 4′ 9¾″. The Baltimore & Susquehanna was 4′ 9¼″. Pennsylvania was studded with three-foot railroads, though in the west end of the State there were several of 4′ 3″, and the Susquehanna & Eagles Mere was 3′ 8″. The New Brunswick & Canada, a Canadian promotion which crossed Maine from Quebec to New Brunswick in 1871, was 3′ 6″. Eight years later it was standardized and became an important part of the Canadian Pacific. The Philadelphia & Atlantic City, built in 1877, was also 3′ 6″. There were many of this width. An oddity was the ten-mile Hecla & Torch Lake, in the Calumet copper country of Michigan, which was 4′ 1″. The Arcata & Mad River, an early-day promotion in California, pondered the matter of its gage very seriously, and finally decided that the most comfort-

---

By Alvin F. Harlow. A compilation from "The Muddle of the Gauges," by Linwood W. Moody, *Bulletin No. 47,* The Railway & Locomotive Historical Society, Inc., September, 1938, pp. 59–66, and "Gauges—Standard and Otherwise," by Robert R. Brown, *Bulletin No. 88,* the same, May, 1953, pp. 77–85. Copyright, 1938, 1953, by The Railway & Locomotive Historical Society, Inc. Boston: Baker Library, Harvard Business School. With additions from other sources.

able width for its motive power, which was a single horse, was either 3′ 9½″ or 3′ 9¼″.

John A. Poor and fellow-enthusiasts succeeded in throwing that State into a hurly-burly of gages and conflicting interests which was epochal. Poor vociferously boosted Maine, and specifically Portland, as the natural sea-outlet for Canada. His ideas crystallized as a railroad from Montreal to Portland and he won the Canadian government over to chartering the St. Lawrence & Atlantic Railway, connecting those cities. It is uncertain who specified the Scotch gage—5′ 6″—for this road. Some say it was Poor, some a Canadian engineer. One favorite legend was that the British Government —Canada then being still a mere colonial possession—not only favored Portland over Boston as a terminus, but specified the broad gage, differing from all United States widths, in order to make troop and munition movements into Maine difficult for our Government in case of war—which may or may not have a factual foundation. Anyhow, it planted the 5′ 6″ gage firmly in Canada, and caused several small railroads in Maine to be built of that width. The St. Lawrence & Atlantic eventually became a part of the Grand Trunk Railroad, a predecessor of the Canadian National.

A half-dozen shorter roads connecting Augusta, Bangor, Waterville, Gardiner, Lewiston and other towns in Maine were in a dither over the matter of gage, the southerly ones wanting a connection with Boston, and therefore leaning towards the standard gage, while Poor and his cohorts fought against it. There were angry allusions to "the railroad power which controls the Legislature," meaning the broad gage group, while Poor sneeringly referred to the standard width as "the narrow gage." When the promoters of the Somerset & Kennebec Railroad entered the Legislature in 1852 with a petition for a standard gage charter, there was a terrific battle on the floors of the Legislature, one prominent attorney for the broads threatening in his excitement to plant cannon at a certain point and "blow the Somerset road to hell" if it was chartered. Which of course he didn't when the Somerset won and was built.

Several years later, when a little road, the Androscoggin, which was in the broad-gage network, wanted to reduce to standard so that it might tie in with the Boston-bound rails, the broad-gagers procured an injunction against it; but the Androscoggin officials, getting wind of the move, ducked out of sight and dodged the process servers until night. This was on a Saturday; and on the following day, when the Law was off the job, a force of men changed the gage to standard. Three years of "lawing and sueing" over this incident followed, the Androscoggin at length being sustained.

In upper New Jersey, 4′ 10″ was the favorite gage, and from there it was introduced into Ohio. President James of the Mad River and Lake Erie, a pioneer concern just organized in the Ohio woods, went east in 1837, shopping for equipment. At the Paterson, N. J., factory of Rogers, Ketchum & Grosvenor, he saw an engine of that gage, built and tried out on the little New Jersey Railroad, but for some reason not taken over by that line. Mr. James bought the machine, had it shipped to Ohio via the Hudson River, Erie Canal and Lake Erie, and as not a foot of track had yet been laid on his road, the engine established the gage, not only for the Mad River & Lake Erie, but for most of the railroads of Ohio as well. In fact, the Legislature passed a law, making it the legal gage for all railroads, though this was persistently violated.

The 4′ 8½″ gage, or something approximating it, was spreading pretty well all over the North with the exception of Ohio. In New England (outside of Maine) and on the chain of little roads linking Albany with Buffalo, where this gage prevailed, loaded freight cars had begun to wander over other lines than their own by 1850, as they do now, necessitating the employment of car tracers. The importance of this through transportation, avoiding unloading and reloading, began to be understood. The Pennsylvania and its connecting lines in New Jersey settled on a 4′ 9″ gage and used that for years before yielding to the general pattern. Standard gage rolling stock could be used on it, though it ran a bit loosely. The Missouri Pacific and some other major roads continued at 4′ 9″ almost until the end of the century. But the South, with a typical liking for elbow room, firmly decided upon a 5-foot gage, and stuck to it—except in Louisiana, where they chose 5′ 6″; and there were a few three-footers down there, too.

But the Erie—there was the bull in the china-shop! With the evident intention of doing the biggest thing ever, it fixed its gage at 6 feet, and it managed its curves up along the upper Delaware River very well at that width, too, despite the objections of protagonists of standard gage that it can't be done. But having reached Lake Erie, it decided to thrust a line diagonally across Ohio to Cincinnati, under the name of Atlantic and Great Western (later changed to New York, Pennsylvania & Ohio, or "Nypano"). It created consternation among the other Ohio roads, though it graciously offered to stop at Galion, if the other lines between there and Cincinnati would widen to 6 feet. They couldn't see that as feasible, so the big boy forged right on.

The Ohio roads were milling confusedly about in a welter of four or five gages. There was even one seven-mile pike that was 5′ 9″ wide! The roads along the lake shore were using 4′ 9½″, and the Cleveland, Columbus & Cincinnati, which was on 4′ 10″, decided to reduce its width by one-half inch, "it being found," said the management, "that locomotives and cars of either 4′ 8½″ or 4′ 10″ gage can run on a 4′ 9½″ track." (It is significant that they reduced the speed of their trains within a year after making the change.) There had already been incidents proving that such makeshifts were unsafe. The Indianapolis *Sentinel* reported in October, 1853 that "the Bellefontaine train, due in at 11:45 A.M., did not arrive until 4:16 P.M. Near Farmland, the driving wheels of the engine were thrown off the track and then on again. By this sudden jar, the last car, occupied principally by ladies, was thrown off the track sideways into the ditch. The car, while yet in motion, fell upon a stump which raked it from one end to the other. The car is a complete wreck. The wounded are eight in number. . . ."

The weekly *Locomotive* of Indianapolis, added, "We are informed the accident was caused by running the narrow gauge cars on the wide gauge track at rate of eighty miles an hour." By "narrow gauge" the editor means 4′ 8½″ and "wide gauge" 4′ 10″.

The Erie succeeded in influencing the Ohio & Mississippi (now a part of the B. & O.), completed from Cincinnati to St. Louis in 1857, to make its track 6 feet also; so now there was a 6-foot line all the way from New York to St. Louis. The Indianapolis *Journal,* much annoyed, said on February 5, 1853, "The time was when the ordinary gauge was entirely satisfactory—but in these modern times the wide 6-foot track is all the rage, and the public are ready to catch at the idea as of the utmost importance."

But the broad gage went no farther. The Indianapolis & Cincinnati, a new project with its own peculiar gage of 4′ 8¾″, was disconcerted when the Ohio & Mississippi announced a 6-foot gage, for it had hoped to use the latter's track for some 20 miles along the Ohio River as an entrance to Cincinnati. The O. & M., however, amiably contracted to lay a third rail of the I. & C.'s gage, on that stretch. The same thing was done by the Great Western Railway of Canada to permit Michigan Central trains to run between Detroit and Buffalo. And in 1868 Jay Gould, then in control of the Erie, planned a branch from his Atlantic & Great Western to Toledo, and suggested to the Michigan Southern that it lay a third rail to 6-foot gage from Toledo to Chicago, to give the Erie an entry into the midwestern metropolis. The idea was rejected, and when the Erie, under Gould's mismanagement, became badly run down, he proposed laying a third rail to standard gage from Buffalo to New York, so that midwestern trains might operate over it, but had no encouragement.

When the Union Pacific was planned under United States auspices, President Lincoln was asked to fix the width of the track. The few little railroads that had been built in California were of 5-foot gage, like those in the South, and after much thought, Mr. Lincoln suggested that figure. If this had been adopted, the whole railroad system of the North might have conformed to it. But the main roads of the North and East, nearly all standard gage, were appalled by the thought of the expense of such a change, and they exerted so much pressure on Congress that it overruled the President. It is a great pity that the 5-foot gage (5′ 6″ would have been even better) was not adopted. That additional 3½ inches of track width would have meant even more inches of car width, hence roomier seats, wider aisles—making it possible for two fat people to pass each other in the aisle without danger of throwing the train off the track—less roll and sway, and for freight cars, greater carrying space.

A strange anomaly was the road which began life as the Madison & Indianapolis, State-owned and the first railroad in the State. Under the direction of a Legislature composed of novices in every subject, including lawmaking, the road was built to a 4-foot gage, and when an extension was made to a point opposite Louisville and it became the Jeffersonville, Madison & Indianapolis, it continued in that width. But in the 1880s it began to come under Pennsylvania influence, its cars turned red and it was widened to standard gage.

In 1871 there were no fewer than twenty-three gages, ranging from 3 feet up to 6 feet on the railroads of the United States. Less than fifteen years later there were twenty-five; a considerable group of roads in Maine had been born only two feet wide, whilst a logging company in Oregon had built one that sprawled over 8 feet of ground. Cincinnati was one of the worst imbroglios in the country, with half a dozen gages, from 3-footers up through the several half-inch Ohio variations to the 6-foot Nypano and O. & M. The little Cincinnati, Georgetown & Portsmouth—it never got any farther than Georgetown—was an example of variety. Beginning as a 3-footer, it was later standardized, except that it had a branch of "street-car gage"—5′ 2½″, then was electrified, and finally gave up the ghost in the 1920s.

A remarkably large mileage of narrow gage had been built for economy's sake, most of it 3 feet. The Cotton Belt was narrow gage in the beginning, the Denver & Rio Grande entirely so, as was a large percentage of the Oregon Short Line, now the Union Pacific's line through Idaho & Oregon. Many trunk lines had narrow-gage appendages to their systems—Union Pacific, Colorado & Southern, Northwestern, Milwaukee, Southern Pacific, Atlantic Coast Line were a few; and some of the narrow-gage mileage, such as the SP's remnant of the Carson & Colorado, was still in existence at a recent date.

As years went on, it became evident that the South must reduce its tracks to standard width. At many junction points between the two sections, passenger trains were delayed from 15 to 30 minutes, while cars were lifted by steam hoist or jacks, their trucks rolled out from under and trucks of another gage rolled in. The Illinois Central, now operating from Chicago to New Orleans, had to change at Cairo, and cars from the Cincinnati division of the L&N—which had been built as a separate line—at Louisville. The Grand Trunk had cars with adjustable wheels, which could be unlocked and moved on the axles to suit another gage, but this was troublesome and expensive, and it did not include the locomotives. No, the South must change, but the railroads delayed action, dreading the expense. There were 13,000 miles of main track, 1,500 miles of sidings, 1,800 locomotives and 40,000 cars to be converted. It was a staggering task.

The Illinois Central showed the way. After the last broad gage train had passed on the evening of August 1, 1881, it threw a big force into action by torchlight, and changed the 600 miles of track south of Cairo by noon of the next day. Nearly four years passed before another move, and then the Mobile & Ohio, spurred by the example of its neighbor and parallel, assembled an extra force and altered its 472 miles of track between Mobile and Columbus, Ky., on July 8, 1885. That brought a convention of Southern railroad presidents together at Atlanta on February 2, 1886, and they agreed to make the change on June 1, or on the week-end beginning May 29th.

Such cars and locomotives as could be spared from daily operation were brought into the shops and changed in advance, as were some unimportant branches, thus releasing forces of men for work on the day of the big push. Tie plates were not in general use then, and all over the South, roads prepared for the change by drawing every other spike from the inside of the rails on one side and resetting it in place for the rail's new position. Of course, on bridges and in tunnels, both rails had to be moved, thus making a very slight kink in the track at each end, but as time went on, these were gradually smoothed out.

The most difficult task was the remodelling of the rolling stock. From all over the system, locomotives and cars were rushed into the shops. Some effort was made to return cars to their home lines, but this was not entirely feasible, and cars were converted where they were. An augmented force worked around the clock, resetting the locomotive truck wheels, removing the tires from the driving wheels and moving them inward 1½ inches, or whatever was needed, on each side. Some of the older engines had fireboxes too wide to permit the narrowing, and these were disposed of in any way possible, some being sold to logging railroads which still retained the 5-foot gage.

It is interesting to notice that some roads such as the Louisville & Nashville couldn't bring themselves to adopt the Yankee gage outright; they compromised, showed a last ripple of independence by changing only to 4′ 9″, blandly rejecting the other half-inch. Inter-operation thus, even if a little loose, was possible. A few years later —it took the Ellen N ten years to come around—everybody became standard.

Many extra men were employed for the final effort. As a rule, the roads were divided into eight-mile sections, with a gang of 24 men assigned to each—6 spike-pullers, 4 rail-movers, 12 spike-drivers, and usually a couple of men to push handcars and carry water. Two gangs would start together, working in opposite directions, so that the work of each was completed when it met the gang approaching it.

Many railroads made the change in one day. Others took from Saturday to Monday or Tuesday to do it. The L&N, then the South's largest system, with more than 2,000 miles of track, had 8,763 men poised to tackle the task early Sunday morning, May 30th. Prizes were offered to sections doing the quickest work. Some sections had their job completed by noon. One section changed 11 miles of track in 4½ hours. All were done by nightfall. One shop changed 19 locomotives, 18 passenger coaches, 11 cabooses, 1,710 freight cars and a lot of non-revenue equipment "between sunup and sundown." That evening, barbecues were staged by the company along the line, and there was a noisy celebration. Next morning the railroad was operating smoothly in its new size.[1]

By this time the Erie had, at long last, dropped back to standard size, but a new gage had appeared in the far Northeast. There were a few 3-footers scattered about New England, but in 1876 the Billerica & Bedford, 8⅓ miles long and 2 feet wide, was incorporated in northeastern Massachusetts. It folded up within two years, but meanwhile some country folk up in western Maine had felt the need of a railroad. They bought the B. & B. equipment in 1879 and organized the Sandy River Railroad, which was followed by three others, all connecting with it, forming a perky little network, which for several years showed signs of near-prosperity. The Sandy River even had a "saloon" or parlor car—with only one row of chairs, of course, but it was a tissue of amusing contrasts. In time of deep snows, its trains sometimes took two or three days to cover the 18 miles from Farmington to Phillips, the passengers camping at night in the cars or at houses along the way. Game was plentiful in the woods, and all train crews carried guns. Once an engineer and fireman leaped from opposite sides of the cab to get a shot at a flock of deer they ran through, leaving the engine trundling along untended, until a brakeman crawled over the tender to shut it off. Another time a Phillips & Rangeley train was skirting a millpond when the track dropped from under it; it was discovered that a colony of beavers had undermined the piles supporting it.[2]

Then came the motor age, and reduced to one rail bus and occasional freight train, the S. R. & R. L. struggled along until 1935, when it gave up. There were four other 2-footers in Maine, all dismantled long ago and some of their metal sold to Japan, to be dumped upon our ships at Pearl Harbor. But happily, some of their bunty little engines and cars were saved by a rail fan who owned big cranberry bogs in Massachusetts, and became the rail fans' joy as trains of the Edaville Railroad.

The East Broad Top Railroad, which leaves the Pennsylvania's main line at Mount Union and runs 33 miles to Alvan, is the only remaining narrow gage to operate passenger trains—three a day each way by a recent report. Its notice in the Official Guide says that "Standard gauge freight cars are handled over the entire line by transferring bodies to specially designed 3-ft gauge trucks, with no extra charge for this service." Its officials' business car is said to once have been President Cleveland's favorite car for his fishing jaunts.

X

---

1 Kincaid A. Herr, "The Louisville & Nashville Railroad, 1850–1942," *Louisville & Nashville Employes' Magazine* (Louisville, 1943), pp. 45–48.

2 H. T. Crittenden, "Sandy River & Rangeley Lakes R.R." *Bulletin No. 37*, The Railway & Locomotive Historical Society, Inc. (Boston, May, 1935), pp. 15–25.

The Coming of Standard Time

There are many persons now living who recall the period when railway operations were in a state of confusion due to the lack of a uniform time standard. Prior to the adoption of Standard Time on November 18, 1883, the only "time" that existed in this country was local time, commonly called "sun time," which was based upon the transit of the sun across the meridian, and which varied in the latitude of Boston, Chicago, and Salt Lake City approximately one minute for every thirteen miles, or one second for every 1,140 feet of longitude. In Washington, D. C., there is a difference of 7 seconds between sun-time at the Capitol Dome and sun-time at the Lincoln Memorial. Sun-time at the eastern and western extremes of Chicago differs by about 67 seconds. It differs about 30 seconds between the two ends of the San Francisco-Oakland Bridge.

So, of course, such a thing as true local or sun-time was never observed at all points in the country. This would have led to unending confusion, because the longitudinal variation is constant. Moreover, owing to the eccentricity of the earth's orbit, there is a seasonal variation of several minutes, so that exact sun-time at a given point on the earth's surface in January will not correspond to exact sun-time at the same location in April or August or November. But each of numerous cities or towns adopted a time standard which was based upon mean local sun-time at the city hall or some other designated location. Many another city or town adopted the time standard of one of its railroads or of the principal city in its area. Each railroad adopted the time standard of its home city or of some other important city on its lines.

For instance, the Pennsylvania Railroad in the East used Philadelphia time, which was 5 minutes slower than New York time and 5 minutes faster than Baltimore time. The Baltimore & Ohio used Baltimore time for trains running out of Baltimore, Columbus time for trains in Ohio, Vincennes time for trains running west of Cincinnati, and it scheduled some of its trains under New York time, Philadelphia time, and Chicago time. The Michigan Central Railroad operated its trains on Detroit time. In the Chicago district the New York Central and the Pennsylvania used Columbus time which was 6 minutes faster than Cincinnati time and 19 minutes faster than Chicago time. Generally speaking, the railroads running westward and southward from Chicago used Chicago time; those running westward from St. Louis used St. Louis time. When it was noon in Chicago it was 12:31 in Pittsburgh; 12:24 in Cleveland; 12:17 in Toledo; 12:13 in Cincinnati; 12:09 in Louisville; 12:07 in Indianapolis; 11:50 in St. Louis; 11:48 in Dubuque; 11:39 in St. Paul; and 11:27 in Omaha.

The Union Pacific Railroad operated its trains by at least six different time standards—based on sun-time at Omaha, Jefferson City, St. Joseph, Denver, Laramie, and Salt Lake City.

The *Chicago Tribune* listed 27 local times in Michigan, 38 in Wisconsin, 27 in Illinois and 23 in Indiana. There is no telling how many different "local times" there were in the United States prior to the adoption of Standard

---

Abridged from *The Day of Two Noons,* by Carlton J. Corliss, pp. 1–14. Washington, D.C.: Association of American Railroads. February, 1952. With notes from other sources.

Time, but we do know that there were at least 68 different times used by the railroads, and according to one authority, there were, a few years prior to 1883, something like 100 different times in use by the railroads of this country. A traveler going from Maine to California, if anxious to have correct railroad time, was obliged to change his watch some twenty times during the journey!

In the railroad station in Buffalo, there were three clocks—one set to New York time, by which the New York Central Railroad operated; one set to Columbus time, by which the Lake Shore and Michigan Southern and other railroads were operated; and the other set to local Buffalo time. The situation was even worse in Pittsburgh, where there were six different time standards for the arrival and departure of trains.

In Kansas City each of the leading jewelers furnished his own "standard time," and no two of these standards agreed. Sometimes the range was as much as twenty minutes. Each jeweler took his own readings. He had his own customers who set their watches by his regulator and were willing to wager on the correctness of his time.[1] According to one account, "the people of Kansas City never did have accurate information on the arrival and departure of trains, except such as was gained by going to the edge of the hill and looking down on the railway station." The situation became so notorious that Professor H. S. Pritchett, an astronomer of note then connected with Washington University in St. Louis, was called upon to untangle the mess. On his recommendation, the problem was solved by the city adoption of a *time ball* system.

These time balls, now almost forgotten, were great institutions in their time. Each day at official noon at a particular location, a large ball, sometimes three or four feet in diameter, so as to be visible for several miles, was dropped from a lofty mast. As the ball fell, the people—watching from many vantage points—adjusted their timepieces to noon, and thus everyone in the city was provided with uniform time. In the large cities, thousands of persons watched the time balls daily. Scientists wrote learned papers about them, argued about the best diameter or weight and height of the mast, and whether the ball should start falling at noon, or reach the bottom at noon.

Of course, with such multiplicity of time standards throughout the country, passengers and shippers, and railway officers and employees who were responsible for the operation of trains, the sale of tickets and the making of schedules were confused and bewildered. Mistakes and errors were frequent and sometimes disastrous.

Proposals for a uniform time system were not new. As early as 1828, Sir John Herschel was urging the standardization of time in England. Later, its advocates appeared in the United States. Nothing ever came of these proposals until the railroads took the matter in hand. The railroad movement may be said to have had its beginning in May, 1872, when an association of railway officers, a forerunner of the Association of American Railroads, held its first meeting at the old South-

---

[1] The Rock Island ad appearing in the *Chicago Tribune,* March 1, 1853, during the building of La Salle Street station, carried this note: "The clock in Sherwood and Waiteley's store, at the corner of Lake and Dearborn streets, is at present the adopted standard time, and the traveling public are reminded that the trains will arrive and depart promptly at the time stated, and as indicated by that clock."

Southern Pacific Rules and Regulations for 1868 specified that "The clock of G. M. Parker, 34 K Street [Sacramento] is the time by which trains are to be run. Conductor and Enginemen will compare their watches with it daily, when practicable."

ern Hotel in St. Louis. This was a meeting of railroad superintendents called for the purpose of arranging summer passenger train schedules. At the St. Louis meeting a permanent organization was formed which became successively the Time-Table Convention, the General Time Convention, the American Railway Association, and finally, the Association of American Railroads. The General Time Convention of October 11, 1883, at the Grand Pacific Hotel in Chicago definitely adopted Standard Time. Having voted overwhelmingly for the plan, the convention issued a notice, directing that all railway clocks governing the operation of trains throughout the United States be set to the new standard at exactly 12 o'clock noon, Sunday, November 18, 1883.

Detailed instructions and recommendations were issued, giving the exact changes which were necessary for the many railroad companies to adjust their clocks and watches to the new standard, and similar information was furnished public officials of cities throughout the country. It was realized that the success of the plan would depend largely upon the cooperation of cities and towns in adopting the new time locally. Newspapers and local public officials enthusiastically approved the change, and only here and there was opposition.

There were those who felt that, by the adoption of Standard Time, they were being robbed of some of their daylight, or that they were being compelled to reckon time "contrary to nature."

Newspaper accounts and editorial comments reveal that the public attitude toward the change ranged from enthusiastic approval to belligerent opposition. Some editors discussed it humorously; others accepted it without criticism.

A dispatch from Rockford, Ill., two days before the time set for the change, said: "The time here is taken from the Rockford Watch Company, and they are opposed to the change, as are the majority of their customers." Yet there were persons who felt that the railroads or the watch-makers were trying to put something over on them for selfish reasons.

An officer of the United States Coast Survey, writing in *Science Magazine,* said, "All ordinary business everywhere must be forever conducted on *local mean solar time,* and we may rightly ask the railroad companies to give in their timetables for public use the *mean local time* for the departure and arrival of trains."

Webb C. Ball, of the Ball Railway Time Service said, "In one place I visited, a venerable inhabitant—a local literary character—flourished his hickory cane over my head, saying, 'Damn old Vanderbilt's time! We want God's time! The Vanderbilts cannot run me if they run the rest of the country, by Jehosaphat!' "

Five days before Standard Time was to go into effect, the United States Attorney General issued an edict that government departments had no right to adopt railroad time until authorized to do so by Congress. However, this did not prevent the railroads from putting Standard Time into effect. But apparently the Attorney General did not believe they would do so, for a few hours after Standard Time went into effect, he went to the railway station to take the train for Philadelphia and was astonished to find that he was 8 minutes too late.

November 18, 1883, was called *"the day of two noons"* by reason of the fact that in the eastern part of each zone there was a noon based upon sun-time; then clocks and watches were set back from one to thirty minutes to the new Standard Time, so that there was another noon when Standard Time in the community reached 12:00 o'clock. If the community used railroad time, the difference in many instances was more than 29 minutes. In eastern Georgia where Savannah time was used, there was a 44-minute gap between the old and new time.

In a nationwide time change such as this, the railroads had no previous experience. The adjustment called for careful planning and preparation and the greatest of care and watchfulness by railroad men. Specific orders were issued on every division, instructing every officer and every employee as to what should be done in making the change. Train crews on line were instructed in every instance as to what change to make in their watches. Members of each crew were also instructed to check their watches with the telegraph operator upon arrival at the next scheduled stop.

A graphic account of what was probably a typical scene in railroad offices throughout the country at the zero hour is contained in the *Chicago Tribune* on the day following the change to Standard Time. It says in part:

> Shortly before the new time was to be put into effect, a Tribune representative called at the office of the Train Dispatchers of the Pennsylvania, Burlington, Panhandle, and Alton railroads at the West Side Union Depot. The Division Superintendents, Train Dispatchers, Depot-master and Telegraph Operators were all at their desks. All looked unusually solemn, and their faces showed that something of an extraordinary nature was about to happen. At about a quarter of 12 o'clock, Chicago time, the conductors, engineers and other trainmen dropped in one by one, each having his time-piece in his hand and watching closely the hands of the dials. Depot Master Cropsey had his chronometer under a powerful magnifying glass to be sure that he had made no mistake. When the clock on the wall in the office, by which the running of the trains in the depot is regulated, stood at 12, it was stopped. The telegraph instruments were then connected with the pendulum of the clock in the observatory at Allegheny, Pa. . . . Each move was faithfully repeated on the telegraph instruments, and at precisely 9 minutes 32 seconds after 12, Chicago time, the movement of the pendulum stopped, indicating that it was exactly noon by 90th meridian time.
>
> The fact successfully accomplished, a general murmur of satisfaction ran through the room. . . .

Sunday was selected because there were fewer trains in operation at that time and the change could be made with the minimum of inconvenience and the maximum of safety.

Many cities and towns located on the borderline between two time zones found it difficult to decide which time to adopt. Pittsburgh and Erie, Pennsylvania, were on the borderline between the Eastern and Central time zones, and public opinion in those cities were divided as to which time should be used by business establishments, schools, churches, theatres, and citizens generally.

There were many amusing incidents and a few slight hitches in changing from local to Standard Time. The mayor of Bangor, Maine, refused to recognize the new time on the ground that it was unconstitutional. He even threatened to have the police prevent the churches from ringing their bells on the new time, but popular feeling ran against him and he did not carry out his threat. However, he continued to display the courage of his convictions, and Standard vs. Sun-Time became a first rate political issue in Bangor. The City Council voted for Standard Time; the mayor promptly vetoed the order, declaring that no one had power "to change one of the immutable laws of God."

There were many persons who favored some sort of standard time, but could not agree that the system adopted was the best. Some wanted time throughout the United States to be uniform, without any time zones. There were others who were convinced that a mistake was made in not adopting 24-hour time, thus abolishing the necessity of using A.M. and P.M. The

Detroit Evening Journal actually did adopt 24-hour time and published its paper with headings reading 14 o'clock edition, 16 o'clock edition, etc., proclaiming itself ahead of the times. The Cleveland, Mt. Vernon & Delaware Railroad, now a part of the Pennsylvania Railroad between Cleveland and Columbus, Ohio, published timetables on a 24-hour schedule. For instance, Train No. 4 left Cleveland at 14:00 o'clock, arriving in Columbus at 21:10 o'clock. Train No. 3 left Columbus at 11:40 arriving in Cleveland at 21:04 o'clock. But a few months after Standard Time was adopted this railroad fell in line with other roads and published its schedules in the conventional style.

The American people soon came to accept Standard Time without question, and it has since spread to other lands until today it is in almost universal use.

It is an interesting fact that the method of reckoning time instituted by the railroads in 1883, although adopted and used by the Federal Government and States, cities and towns through the country, was put into effect without federal legislation of any sort. It was not until thirty-five years later—on March 19, 1918, during the first World War—that Congress passed what is known as the Standard Time Act. But this does not mean that government officials did not coöperate in making the Standard Time system a success. The contrary is true. All branches of the government coöperated whole-heartedly in the movement, and, of course, regulated their own clocks by Standard Time.

The Official Guide

If some sampler of public opinion should poll railway ticket agents for the name of the one book above all others which they would prefer to have at their elbows, it is almost certain that the majority of them would name the Official Guide of the Railways. The Guide packs between its covers more useful information than can be found in any other single volume concerning railway routes, trains and train schedules on the North American continent.

But ticket agents are by no means the only group of railroaders who make use of the Official Guide. Nor is the use of the Guide confined to railroaders alone. Indeed, nearly one-half of its circulation is outside the railway field.

As far back as the oldest railroad man can remember, the Official Guide has been a familiar object and a handy working tool in railway offices from coast to coast. Now commencing its eighty-sixth year of continuous service, this 1500-page reference volume is not only the oldest periodical of its type in the American transportation field, but in point of contents, it is the largest monthly publication in the world.

Here in one volume is found a complete arrangement of up-to-date passenger train schedules and parlor and sleeping-car routes. It shows the equipment operated on each named train, as well as railway-system maps, junction points, connecting railways, station-to-station mileage, a station index listing the railroads which directly serve each town and city, names and addresses of railroad officers, railway

---

Abridged from *A Book That Gathers No Dust,* by Harold H. Baetjer, pp. 1–12. New York: National Railway Publication Company. 1950.

associations and their officers, and the personnel of federal agencies and commissions connected with transportation. It also lists steamship companies and airlines with their terminals and schedules, as well as the location of military posts, national parks and government hospitals.

The Guide is widely used by tourist agencies, hotels, and shippers of freight. Nearly every chamber of commerce and many banks, investment houses and newspapers have been on its subscription list for many years. Telephone and telegraph companies use the mileage figures in the Guide as their basis for charges in extending lines into new territory. The many offices of the Railway Express Agency use it for checking mileage and accounts. It is used in libraries, where teachers, students and others come to obtain vacation travel data or perchance to brush up on their geography. Railroad "fans" collect back numbers of the Guide as philatelists collect postage stamps.

The latest copy of the Guide is always kept in the White House. In fact, it has been a ready reference volume in the office of every President since Andrew Johnson. The railway ticket office maintained in the Capitol for Senators, Representatives and members of their staffs, as well as newspapermen, keeps one or more copies of the Guide in daily use. Army, Navy, and Air officials in the Pentagon Building and elsewhere are also frequent users, as are also the Post Office Department, the Interstate Commerce Commission and other boards, as well as Congressional committees.

The successive issues of the Guide, extending back more than three-quarters of a century, form a fascinating and graphic histroy of American railway development. They record the extension of railway lines and the establishment of stations which often grew into towns and cities. They record the development of sleeping cars, dining cars, observation cars, parlor cars, club cars, buffet cars, tavern cars, and so on down to the latest observation-dome and all-electric dining cars. They show when and where vestibules, steam heat, gas lighting, electric lighting, fluorescent lighting, air conditioning, all-steel cars, and diesel streamlined trains came into use. They record such great forward steps as the adoption of Standard Time and the conversion of the "medley of gauges" in the '70's and '80's to the standard gauge. They record the extension of through-train service over long distances and the gradual but constant increase in passenger train speeds.

Before the Guide put in its appearance in 1868, several railway guides had been in common use in the United States, in some of which the information was notoriously inaccurate. The first issue of the Official Guide (then called the Travellers' Official Guide) appeared in June, 1868. It contained 140 pages, less than one-tenth the number in recent editions. The book proved so superior to other railway guides in information and accuracy that it was promptly accepted as the official organ of the National General Ticket Agents' Association.

The 1,021st issue rolled off the press in June, 1953. With each issue averaging about two inches in thickness, a complete file of the Guide would fill a four-shelf bookcase forty-three feet in length. The immense space required to store it is probably one reason why so few of the early numbers are in existence. If there exists in the world today a complete file of the Official Guide from its first number in June, 1868, the publishers would like to know about it. Probably the most extensive file extant is in the New York Public Library, which lacks only five numbers from being complete. This set includes the only copy of the first number known to exist. The earliest number in the files of the publishers, the National Railway Publication Company, is for April, 1869. The file of the Library of Congress begins with the January, 1878, issue; of the Association of American Railroads with January, 1880.

Consider what a tremendous amount of work is involved in revising, printing and distributing this 1500-page volume each month. The schedules of the trains of more than 700 railways listed in the Guide must be checked, and in a great many instances, numerous revisions in the schedules must be made. Because of the nature and complexity of the work, all typesetting is done by hand, and in many instances three full days are required by one man to set or reset a single page. About eight days are required to print each monthly edition, and when the presses finally roll to a stop, more than thirty tons of paper and nearly 800 pounds of ink have been consumed. By a carefully planned and executed system of shipping and mailing, copies of the Guide, containing up-to-the-minute train schedules, are in the hands of subscribers throughout the country in from one to three days.

Editors of the Guide strive meticulously to maintain the publication's well-deserved reputation for accuracy. However, it would be a miracle if some error did not creep into a compilation that runs into several millions of figures each month. But even an occasional error does not shake a railroader's faith in the Guide. It is related that the Guide once showed a stop for a through train at a station where it was not scheduled to stop on the road's official timetable. When the error was called to the attention of the railroad's passenger traffic manager, he exclaimed, "Well, if the Official Guide says the train stops there, then dammit, have it stop there!"

A Century of Passenger Train Coloring

When passenger cars began to assume something of the shape of modern coaches, a larger compartment with an aisle through the middle and seats on each side, the favorite color for their exteriors, at least for all roads running out of Boston, as well as the Hartford & New Haven, New York & New Haven, Norwich & Worcester and others, was yellow. A rail veteran years later spoke of it as "straw color." European tourists who hadn't seen quite everything thought American cars were all yellow. But this wasn't quite true, even in New England, which those tourists frequented most. The Housatonic's cars were red, and for several years around 1850, the Northern Railroad of New Hampshire painted entire trains, locomotive and all, from cow-catcher to car-tail, sky blue. The difficulty of keeping such a train clean and the tendency of the blue paint to fade eventually taught the inevitable lesson.

But the BC&M went a step farther. In strenuous competition with other lines for White Mountain summer business, it planned a train which would be irresistible, which would fairly knock the vacationers' eye out. It was called the White Mountain Ex-

---

By Alvin F. Harlow. A compilation from "Famous Color Trains of America," by Charles E. Fisher, *Bulletin No. 4,* The Railway & Locomotive Historical Society, Inc., pp. 24–30. Copyright, 1923, by The Railway & Locomotive Historical Society, Inc. Boston: Baker Library, Harvard Business School. With additions from other sources.

press, and it left Boston daily at 1 P.M. by the Boston & Lowell, transferring to the BC&M when it entered New Hampshire, and continuing to that famous old White Mountain hostelry, Fabyan's. It also carried through equipment for Montreal via the Vermont Central Railway. The cars that ran to Fabyan's—and this included everything, coaches, parlor cars, even baggage cars—had a chocolate brown roof, red letterboard above the windows, very light yellow, almost cream-colored panels between the windows, blue body below the windows, and red-and-green trucks and running gear. The interiors were gorgeous, too. There were two trains of these cars, one running each way daily. The "One o'clock" continued to run through to Montreal the year round, but these bird-of-paradise cars which ran to Fabyan's were too precious to be allowed out of doors in winter. They ran only during the summer season, and at the end of that season, they were taken to the BC&M shops at Lakeport, N. H., renovated, retouched, and stored under roof until the following June 1st.[1]

Passenger trains on the small roads which eventually made up the New York Central were, on the whole, rather an unattractive lot, from what we hear. The New York & Harlaem cars seemed to waver between a dull, dark blue, and pea green. The eight or nine little railroads which, laid end to end, reached waveringly from Albany to Buffalo, were of varied hues, with yellow predominating. President Gibson of the Auburn & Rochester made some suggestions to his neighbors in 1842, one of which was that they run a through second-class train, "a daily line of cars of a plain but substantial character," slower and cheaper than the better ones, to run from Albany to Rochester, and eventually to Buffalo. As if to emphasize its ignominy, this train was painted a semi-dark, nondescript color—dun is as near as we can come to it—and carried travelers over the 78 miles from Auburn to Rochester for 87½ cents, whereas on the first class cars the fare was $3. The public promptly nicknamed it the "Hyena Train," but rode on it in droves. In fact, the officials were so shocked to discover that so many well-to-do folk, who could afford better accommodations if they chose, were using this cheap-jack train that it was discontinued, although a through agreement for it had been made with the other railroads. This is the only known instance of a train's being made unnecessarily ugly to emphasize that it was intended for *canaille* only.

When the string of little roads was welded into the New York Central in 1853, yellow seems to have been the prevailing color for the passenger cars. Then Commodore Vanderbilt, having taken over both the New York Central and the Hudson River Railroads, bridged the Hudson River for the first time at Albany, and launched a series of Red Trains between New York and Buffalo, the cars being painted a rich crimson. Gossip had it that they had cost from $18,000 to $24,000 apiece! News writers gazed with rapt admiration at their ceilings, "highly finished in green and gold and fresco," and noted that "at each end are convenient saloons and costly mirrors." (Of course they did not mean liquor saloons.) John Webster Wagner's sleeping cars ran on these trains and became very popular when he replaced the old flat-topped, poorly ventilated cars with his clerestory roof, a superimposed roof with ventilators along the sides. The New York Central's trains soon became all crimson, with the car-ends striped with gold, and so remained for three decades thereafter.

---

[1] Information from the files of Charles E. Fisher, President, The Railway & Locomotive Historical Society, Waban, Mass.

In the latter '90's, its passenger cars were changed to the dark olive green which—with a few notable exceptions—was becoming the prevalent color for trains, until smoke and soot changed it to black. It is the predominant color yet, though the diesel age has brought an explosion of brilliant hues on the major lines.

In 1875 William H. Vanderbilt launched the "Fast Mail" from New York to Chicago, with white postal cars—or cream color, very nearly white—with gold striping and lettering, a fashion which spread to other parts of the country. The NYC cars were all named for current or past Governors of the States they traversed. The four on the first train that ran were named for New York executives—*Governor Dix, Governor Morgan, Governor Tod,* and *Governor Tilden.* At various times a sleeper and a coach or two were added to the train. The Post Office Department also went slightly zany, and dyed the mail bags used on this train red. One car, which reached the unusual length of 60 feet, was given over entirely to newspapers.

Other roads adopted the white mail cars; we hear of the *Fast White Mail* which began running on the CB&Q from Chicago to Omaha on March 10, 1884. The Vandalia (now the Pennsylvania main line from Indianapolis to St. Louis) had a *White Mail*—cream white, with gold lettering edged with black—whose clerks, so legend says, became decidedly autocratic. When the engineer ran so fast that he threw the clerks around, making it difficult for them to hit a pigeon-hole with a letter at five feet distance, they sometimes pulled the bell cord on him, admonishing him to slow up, or even applied the brakes themselves. Even in the Twentieth Century the Great Northern operated a train between St. Paul and Seattle known as the "White Fleet." It had three through mail cars, one railway postoffice, and three express cars, all white with brown trimmings.

When the New York & New England, a flashy promotion of the late 1870's, attempting competition with the New Haven, found the going tough, it tried a new publicity stunt—a train painted all white with gilt lettering from stem to stern, with the exception of the locomotive, and known as the *White Train;* a name that lingers in the memories of some who have forgotten all else about the NY&NE—all else, perhaps, save another nickname which presently attached to that train; for as its pale, sinuous length streaked across the Connecticut countryside through the dusk, it had so eerie an effect that it came to be popularly known as the Ghost Train. Its running time was presently reduced from six hours to five hours and forty minutes. Rudyard Kipling, then sojourning in Vermont, was intrigued by it and found in it the idea for a short story entitled "007."

The Pennsylvania's early adoption of Tuscan red for its passenger cars has made it distinctive, unmistakable. As rapidly as other lines came under its influence, their cars were painted in the characteristic hue; and the time came when even the Pullmans operating on the system were also painted red. Only once, so far as we can discover, did the Pennsylvania lapse from the established color. In 1891 Frank Thompson, then its vice-president, visited Mexico, saw President Porfirio Diaz's private train, and became so enamored of its color scheme that he imitated it on the *Pennsylvania Limited,* their New York-Chicago speedster. The trucks and car sides were a rich, not too dark green, the spaces between the windows were cream color. This same decor was adopted on the *Congressional Limited,* the fast day train between New York and Washington, save that a stripe above the windows was red. After three or four years this innovation was abandoned, and the trains went back to the old Tuscan red. It was then that Pullmans operating on the system began to be red, too.

In 1898 the Baltimore & Ohio inaugurated its *Royal Blue Limited,* a rich, dark blue train, at first operating only between New York and Washington, but later extending to the mid-West; in fact, the color was extended to the entire system. In the present century, another road, the Wabash, has adopted blue for some of its streamliners—a deep, distinctive blue which it calls Wabash blue. Some of its other trains are stainless steel in the modern manner, with Wabash blue trimmings.

In 1899 the *Alton Limited* began flashing over the Chicago & Alton's double track between Chicago and St. Louis, and was regarded by many observers of the day as the handsomest train in the world. It had passenger cars whose exterior glistened in graduated shades of red, from rose color below to a velvety wine color at the top, and all trimmed and lettered in gold. It had the largest and most palatial cars yet built, and a dining car cuisine, both à la carte and table d'hote, which was spoken of with rapture by those who had sampled it.

The Indianapolis & Bellefontaine, organized in the 1850s, chose crimson for its cars, and therefrom, as the big Cleveland, Columbus, Cincinnati & Indianapolis—the "Bee Line"—system was put together, piece by piece, from the I&B and other roads, its trains were all red. Some railroads in the Midwest clung to the old yellow long after it had been generally abandoned by the Eastern lines; in fact, some have it yet. The Cincinnati, Indianapolis, St. Louis & Chicago, the first Big Four, had orange cars with a brownish-maroon name-strip above the windows. The orange became a deeper, richer color as years went on, and it may or may not be significant that Melville E. Ingalls, the creative genius of the Big Four, was also president of the Chesapeake & Ohio in 1889 when its crack train, the *Fast Flying Virginian,* was launched and took on the same orange-and-maroon color combination. But in that same year the Big Four and Bee line were consolidated in a new and greater Big Four, the Cleveland, Cincinnati, Chicago & St. Louis, taking in three other more or less important lines within a year or two. With that, it was decided that the Bee Line red and the Big Four orange must disappear; neither must displace the other. So the sprightly and individualistic colorings vanished before a rule of uniformity; all cars became the conventional dark olive-green. A legend pervaded the midwestern air that a master painter, the only one who had the formula for mixing that wonderful orange color, had died and taken the secret with him. The truth was that it was individuality which had been stunned momentarily.

The Chicago, Milwaukee, St. Paul & Pacific is the remaining road which clings to the orange cars with the maroon name-strip. The Chicago & North Western has bodies of a lighter yellow, with the upper parts forest-green. During the presidency of A. B. Stickney (1892–1908), the Chicago Great Western had a touch of color, in that the locomotives flaunted red stacks. His successor, S. M. Felton, went a step further. In 1923 he put on a train known as the *Red Bird* between St. Paul-Minneapolis and Rochester, the Mayo city. It had red cars, and other parts of the locomotive than the stack red, especially the drivers, though their spokes were picked out with gold. Six years later, when the automobile was cutting into passenger business, Felton installed a three-car, gasoline-electric train between the Twin Cities and Rochester, called the *Blue Bird;* blue with gold trimmings without; blue, old rose and gray within. Unfortunately, the crash of '29 shortened its life.

Numerous smaller lines have from time to time chosen car-colorings of their own. The Columbus & Greenville in Mississippi, what's left of the old Georgia Pacific, is vested in brown. The Denver, South Park & Pacific, now gone, used dark brown with red trimmings and gold lettering. The Sumpter Valley Railroad in Oregon, a thin-gager which has long since ceased carrying passengers, went in for salmon-colored cars with round-arching, half-circle ceilings and roofs. And these are but a few of many.

With the coming of the diesel locomotive, the so-called streamliner, and the increased competition of the automobile, a wild burst of color, gaudier than a rocket star-shower, began to dazzle the eyes of travelers. The stainless steel car was another epochal discovery, and "silver" trains, such as the *Empire State Express* and others, became eye-filling features of the landscape. Some of the steel bodies are now painted all over, some have just one gorgeous stripe, preferably of red, at top or bottom from end to end of the train; for there is one seldom-violated stipulation—in the streamliners all cars must be uniform; just one long, gracefully curving integrity, on most roads as brilliant in color as a king snake, and with joints no more perceptible.

The New York Central, apparently with the stern eye of Commodore Vanderbilt still upon it, paints its diesel engines black, with modest gold striping. The Pennsylvania's electric "juice jacks" are also black, with gold lettering. But diesels elsewhere exhibit all the colors of the spectrum and more, too—old rose, mauve, cerise, lilac, orchid, wine, taupe, sepia and elephant's breath. Sometimes the engine's coloring is carried all through the train, sometimes the train has a color-scheme of its own. The crack Chicago-San Francisco streamliners have gone back to the original pioneer yellow. Here is one diesel whose three broad bands of color cover it completely; the topmost one, seemingly a wine color or deep red, extending over the roof, the central one a bright sulphur yellow, the lower one vermilion. All of them dip jauntily down and up on the rounded nose of the locomotive. Back of the three diesel units comes a long, silver-steel train whose only color is a fairly broad band of red over its windows. Railway travel of today is a livelier, more vivid experience than it used to be.

Index

Authors, Characters, Railroads, Subjects, Songs